Ecopsychology

Ecopsychology
Advances from the Intersection of Psychology and Environmental Protection

VOLUME 2: INTERVENTION AND POLICY

Darlyne G. Nemeth, Set Editor

Judy Kuriansky,
Volume Editor

Practical and Applied Psychology
Judy Kuriansky, Series Editor

 PRAEGER ™

An Imprint of ABC-CLIO, LLC
Santa Barbara, California • Denver, Colorado

Library of Congress Cataloging-in-Publication Data

Ecopsychology : advances from the intersection of psychology and environmental protection / Darlyne G. Nemeth, set editor.
  volumes cm. — (Practical and applied psychology)
  Includes bibliographical references and index.
  Contents: volume 1. Science and theory — volume 2. Intervention and policy.
ISBN 978–1–4408–3172–0 (hard copy : alk. paper) — ISBN 978–1–4408–3173–7 (ebook)
1. Environmental psychology. I. Nemeth, Darlyne Gaynor.
BF353.E29 2015
155.9′1—dc23   2015001807

ISBN: 978–1–4408–3172–0
EISBN: 978–1–4408–3173–7

19 18 17 16 15   1 2 3 4 5

This book is also available on the World Wide Web as an eBook.
Visit www.abc-clio.com for details.

Praeger
An Imprint of ABC-CLIO, LLC

ABC-CLIO, LLC
130 Cremona Drive, P.O. Box 1911
Santa Barbara, California 93116-1911

This book is printed on acid-free paper ∞

Manufactured in the United States of America

Be Gentle My Friends

Be gentle my friends
saddened while we watch
ice to water,
water to drought,
rivers run dry,
eroding shores,
yellow air,
dying fish
and birds soaked in oil.

Be gentle my friends
with Earth's fragile beauty
Be gentle my friends
and
protect it,
treasure it,
save it,
save it.

—Susan Melman

Contents

Preface: Intervention and Policy

We humans have been advancing civilization, improving the standard of living, and exponentially increasing population by using earth resources and destroying the environment at an unprecedented scale and speed. We should be aware that when humankind destroys the earth environment, the environment in turn devastates humankind. The protection of the earth environment and our well-being are intricately intertwined. The value of such protection is vast: with a clean and beautiful environment, we become more human. For example, we experience optimal mental health, inner peace, compassion, trust, and full aliveness. Basically, we become happier. This anthology presents a powerful picture of our relationship to the earth and our interrelationship with the environment in current times, as well as looking ahead to the future. Volume 1 discusses environmental science and theory. This present Volume 2 deals with how we can achieve harmony with the earth environment by developing and implementing successful interventions and policy. The chapters in this volume, by a diverse group of experts from many fields, all raise our awareness and incentive to take action, in that the authors present interesting, unique, and inspirational programs and efforts being made on local and international levels.

Over my extensive work on environmental issues, I have noted how severely the damaged environment affects people. This is clearly demonstrated by the 1986 Chernobyl nuclear accident. A study by the United Nations about the Chernobyl accident states that about 4,000 people would die from the Chernobyl radiation exposure, but it also shows that the greatest impact of this tragic event is on psychological functioning—for example, leading to people suffering from depression, despair, hopelessness, and lack of the will to live. Similar to the Chernobyl case, the environmental remediation of the areas contaminated by the 2011 Fukushima nuclear plant accident in Japan faces difficulties being accepted by the locals from lack of trust in the authorities by the affected local public. I know this well, since I have been closely involved in the remediation of the Fukushima environment. These two cases—of Chernobyl and Fukushima—clearly show that environmental protection and remediation are not only technical, but also psychological. Thus, the theme of these two volumes becomes so very useful and appropriate for our times and survival: We need to combine science and psychology to protect the earth and ourselves.

As a scientist, I am naturally inclined to think of evidence and facts when considering what is needed to protect our environment and to recover from disasters. But after all my experiences regarding such natural and man-made environmental onslaughts, I am convinced that there are actually three legs to recovery: (1) environmental clean-up; (2) economic recovery; and (3) mental health support. The suffering of so many people after these events has become so evident to me; hence I believe that psychological attention and services are critical to help people regain their strength and their hope to carry on in life. It is significant that I say this as not only a scientist but as a native Japanese, since I acknowledge that my own native culture has traditionally been stoic and private when it comes to expressing emotions; however, suppression of severe emotion is causing a serious problem to regain resiliency to overcome the difficulties in the face of disasters like the nuclear plant explosion in Fukushima and the natural disaster of the tsunami/earthquake in Japan. In fact, the greatest problem for the people is becoming recognized as being psychological, in dealing with the shock and sadness given the extent of losses and the distress of the situation. In fact, I have become an advocate for this issue, for example, when I speak at working groups of Japanese representatives that I have been invited to, as an official adviser. As we explore the ways of cooperating with Americans in the recovery of the Fukushima area, I raise the importance of also helping the people recover emotionally. The three legs I mentioned above, I emphasize, are all crucial for any effective recovery to stand upon. This is why I think this book is so very important and interesting.

The chapters in this volume present valuable and creative solutions to the challenges we face to support the health of our earth environment. I completely agree with this goal. I have been working on the issues of environmental protection and remediation for over 40 years. My daughter told me that she wants to save the earth by becoming an environmental engineer/scientist like me. I told her that what I was doing was to repair environmental damages caused by actions taken by governments and companies in the previous era. I mistakenly thought that we humans would soon learn that it is much better and more economical to manufacture goods and produce energy without damaging the environment. So I suggested to her that she become a chemical engineer, who would be in a forefront profession to transform industrial activities so they do not assault and damage the earth environment in the first place. How wrong I was to think that we have learned the lesson to preserve our environment! In fact, we are damaging the earth much more now than before. So it is even more imperative that we act now. The contributors of these chapters present this point convincingly.

This volume provides scholarly guidance from the fields of environmental psychology and many other disciplines, describing programs from diverse cultures and recommendations for policy. Perspectives and solutions are presented in these chapters from a wide variety of stakeholders, ranging from government agencies to the private sector and civil society, including representatives of grassroots organizations, NGOs, academia, the law, and volunteers. The contributors are all expert in their field and articulate in their presentations, offering informed, insightful, and enlightening views from their extensive professional as well as personal experience. Lessons and solutions from environmental disasters are offered that involve communities in countries around the world. The examples and case studies are vast and illuminating, including about healing from natural disasters like Hurricane Katrina that hit the Louisiana and Mississippi Gulf Coast in the United States, and earthquakes in Haiti and China, as well as about new models and projects that honor people, communities, biodiversity, and the environment that are being done in the United States as well as in other countries around the world from Azerbaijan to Belize and Ecuador. New approaches and advances in ecopsychological research, clinical techniques, educational initiatives, and policy are also elucidated, including those being proposed at the United Nations. All these offer hope for the future.

We have a responsibility to protect the environment for us, as well as for all other living beings. This anthology is a must-read, to save us from ourselves, and to have a just, spiritually fulfilling, responsible, and sustainable society and world for adults and all generations to come.

Yasuo Onishi, PhD
President, Yasuo Onishi Consulting, LLC
Adjunct Professor, Department of Civil and Environmental Engineering,
Washington State University

Acknowledgments

DARLYNE G. NEMETH

For the second time, I have been so blessed to have Dr. Bob Hamilton and Dr. Judy Kuriansky as coeditors on this amazing anthology. Our first joint endeavor, *Living in an Environmentally Traumatized World: Healing Ourselves and Our Planet*, was published in 2012 by ABC-CLIO/Praeger. To my knowledge, it was the first book of its kind to combine the science and practice of ecopsychology and to offer guidelines for intervention at all levels. Dr. Hamilton, an inveterate scientist and philosopher, addressed the importance of a holistic approach to environmental management. Dr. Kuriansky, an amazing interventionist, championed the need for post-environmental trauma psychological intervention to assist in recovery.

Once again, the team of Nemeth, Hamilton, and Kuriansky has joined forces to produce this current anthology, *Ecopsychology: Advances from the Intersection of Psychology and Environmental Protection*. With the very skilled and supportive guidance of Debbie Carvalko, senior acquisitions editor, we were able to offer an in-depth understanding of the field of ecopsychology. We brought together individuals from many fields to share their very meaningful contributions to this emerging field. Some were scientists. Some were interventionists. Some were activists. Some were lawyers. Others were psychologists. Some represented governments; others represented business entities. All expressed their love and longing for their oikophilia—their home-place. I am very grateful to all our chapter authors for their dedication and final work product. For all of us, it was truly a labor of love.

To Bob Hamilton, I will always remember our many weekend discussions. Listening to his brilliant and free-flowing ideas was truly inspiring. I often found myself documenting Bob's "stream of consciousness." I could hardly keep up. Bob has such an active mind and is able to process information in a very holistic way. His efforts to seek truth and dispel propaganda were deeply appreciated. Bob, the primary editor of Volume 1, kept the scientists, practitioners, and contributors to this volume on track. All deadlines were met. Furthermore, his editorial skills were truly representative of all the many dissertations he guided while a member of the faculty at Louisiana State University.

Now to "Dr. Judy." Words cannot adequately express my appreciation for her robustness, her resilience, and her leadership in her many academic, professional, and nongovernmental activities and for her friendship. Judy is a whirlwind of energy; she appears everywhere she is needed, just when she is needed. As the primary editor of Volume 2, Judy's contributions were inspiring. She was able to invite individuals to share their valuable ideas, work, and experience from many corners of the world, from Azerbaijan to China, and Bolivia. And they did! No one can turn down an invitation from this multitalented woman. Dr. Judy was also a superb editor, picking up large or small problems that had escaped me.

Chelsie Songy, as project contributor coordinator, has been a godsend. I could not have carried out my job as lead editor without her diligent assistance. Chelsie is a very calm, careful manager who is always a part of the solution and never a part of the problem. I know that she will be an amazing doctoral student and future psychologist. She also made many excellent contributions to our chapters on neurocognition and leadership and prepared our anthology for publication.

And then there was the vibrant Traci Wimberly Olivier, whose contributions to our chapters on perception and neurocognition were truly remarkable. Mrs. Olivier, who is a doctoral student in clinical and neuropsychology at Nova Southeastern University, is now serving an elective practicum here at the Neuropsychology Center of Louisiana (NCLA). She is and will be a credit to psychology.

Furthermore, I am deeply grateful to Yasuo Onishi for his thoughtful Prefaces, and to Susan Melman for setting the tone for our anthology with her inspiring poem.

Lastly, without the love and support of my husband, Donald (who authored our chapter on understanding our environment); and my brother, Richard Gaynor, who is an internist; and my former psychology mentor, who is now my sister-in-law, Sue Jensen, this anthology would not have been possible.

ROBERT B. HAMILTON

I want to especially thank Darlyne Nemeth for continuing her efforts to promote ecopsychology as a discipline to combine the physical and biological aspects of ecology with the psychological aspects. She especially understands how our environments affect people and how we should deal with both the positive and negative aspects of this dynamic. She understands how our attitudes and perceptions affect our environmental decisions and the importance of basing them on good science. As a non-psychologist, I have learned how our combined disciplines benefit us all in our responsibility as ultimate controllers of the earth environment. Her guidance, as lead editor, coordinated a rather complicated task, and made my job easier.

Despite her busy schedule, Dr. Judy is always enthusiastic. Her enthusiasm is contagious and has kept all of us inspired. I believe it will inspire our readers as much as it has inspired me.

My interactions with our authors have been overwhelmingly positive; I hope they feel the same.

My wife, Jean, seems to have dedicated herself to the set as much as I have. She has adjusted schedules and plans to accommodate my time needs in preparation for this effort. I do not know what I would do without her.

Lastly, I am grateful to the media that supplies continuous information about what is happening in our confusing and changing world. This information either confirmed or denied many of my ideas in real time. That has been invaluable to me.

JUDY KURIANSKY

My appreciation is on many levels, to many people, and for many influences and collaborations, that have led to my heightened awareness, intense commitment, and rewarding work in the important intersection of ecopsychology and environmental protection addressed in these volumes. I greatly honor and cherish my colleague and friend Darlyne Nemeth, PhD, MP, for her prescience about the importance of integrating the fields of science and psychology and for her vision that led to our previous volume, *Living in an Environmentally Traumatized World: Healing Ourselves and Our Planet*, as well as a special issue of the journal *Ecopsychology*, and these two volumes on this important topic. She is truly a pioneer and a visionary, in the forefront of merging science and psychology, and always on the cusp of what matters in the world. We have shared many wonderful and growth-inspiring times together, personally and also professionally, imprinting wonderful memories, like being together at the World Congress for Psychotherapy in Buenos Aires, when we stayed up all night working at a desk in a hotel lobby drafting a policy statement; presenting so many symposia over so many years at conferences worldwide from Argentina to China; and supporting her in the valuable trainings she organized brilliantly after Hurricane Katrina in her beloved state of Louisiana. Darlyne is creative, caring, devoted, supportive, and loving of her friends, family, interns, and colleagues; her big heart and bright mind are a dynamic and unique combination that I—and all who know her—are blessed to share this life path with.

My appreciation also goes to Bob Hamilton, coeditor of our first book, whose consistently strong voice from his insightful scientific mind always makes me keenly aware of the importance of our biosphere; his combination of sensitivity with a strong ethic of dedication is impressive. Also part of the team for these volumes, production assistants Chelsie Songy and Traci Olivier have been invaluable. As Darlyne's protégés in neuropsychology, it is comforting to know the future is in the hands and minds of young professionals like them, with their dedication, kind hearts, and responsible work ethic.

These volumes are possible because of the vision and brilliance of Debbie Carvalko, our editor at the publishing company, ABC-CLIO/Praeger, who also supervises my series on Practical and Applied Psychology, of which this anthology is a part. Over the many years I have worked with Debbie, I am continually inspired by her and impressed with the breadth of her creativity, incisive thinking and superb judgment. Besides all this, I am proud that she is a good friend, and marveled at how she has balanced being a consummate and hard-working professional with being such a good friend and so devoted to her family. The world is a better place because of people like Debbie being in it.

The hard-working and good-natured efforts of our book's project manager Magendra Varman, of Lumina Datamatics Ltd., are much appreciated, including his impressive attention to detail, with similar recognition of our dutiful copyeditor. Thank you, too, to production editor Nicole Azze of ABC-CLIO in that process, and to Anthony Chiffolo, who in the midst of being an admirable publishing executive at ABC-CLIO—who has always been so supportive of my projects—is a published author of many books himself with multifaceted interests and talents and an appreciation for nature, a subject addressed in these volumes. Another thank you from us goes to the designer of these volume covers, Silvander, for their impressive artistic cover design for these volumes—with the image of a person crossing a bridge in a green environment, out of darkness into light, that captures the essence, intention, and vision of the content and message of the anthology.

I further acknowledge and honor all my colleagues and good friends who are contributors in this volume. They are wonderful human beings who care for others and the environment. They are also all outstanding in their respective fields. Seeing them here as a group representing so many important sectors—including academics, business, environmental activism, government and nongovernment organizations—they truly embody the model of the multi-stakeholder partnership that is essential for a sustainable planet and future. I reflect with great appreciation and pride about how their work covers so many important aspects of programs and policy being explored and advanced in so many parts of the world, from the United States to Haiti, Belize, Bolivia, China, Ecuador, Azerbaijan, and others. They create a very wonderful and touching tapestry of humankind, with their caring for the future of the "world we want," to use a phrase from the vision of the United Nations.

The United Nations plays such a major role in my life, as reflected in my chapters in this book. My perspective in this writing has been greatly influenced by my work there related to so many global issues and to the Post-2015 agenda. Regarding that, I extend intensive appreciation to delegates of member states at the United Nations, colleagues of the Psychology Coalition of NGOs at the UN, and particularly the UN ambassador of Palau and public health physician, Dr. Caleb Otto, who partnered with me in the successful campaign I led with him to include mental health and well-being in the new global goals, as well as to advocate for psychosocial resilience in the face of deleterious climate change. That all came about because of former president of the International Association of Applied Psychology Ray Fowler, PhD—a visionary and kind-hearted soul—to whom I am forever grateful for asking me to be a UN NGO representative so many years ago, out of the blue, as if he knew my childhood dream to make the world a better place. Reflecting about so many years I've spent in countries around the world doing trainings and workshops and providing psychosocial support after disasters, blessings go to my team and all my partners who have been such an important part of those ventures. That includes my dear friend and collaborator Father Wismick Jean-Charles for the strength and love he shows in helping his beloved Haiti heal, and for taking me to his country to share that mission, reflected in a chapter in this book; I smile every time I think of his big heart, bright spirit, quick mind, and deep love of people and God. Endless blessings go to my best friend, Russell Daisey, for his kind heart, wisdom, enthusiasm, caring, sweet soul, creativity, and unending devotion in codesigning and cofacilitating so many projects and presentations with me around the world, and providing brilliant and inspiring original music we have written and performed around the world. The topics, including "Every Woman, Every Child" (the title of the UN Secretary General's initiative), "Towers of Light" about healing from the 9/11 tragedy, "Rebati" about building back better in Haiti (described in Chapter 9 in this volume), and "Hope is Alive" inspiring healing from the West African Ebola epidemic, all make me feel such "Appreciation" (*kansha shimasho* in Japanese) that is actually another of our song titles.

So much love, encouragement, and appreciation is extended to so many trainees in workshops I've done after many disasters and in dire conditions, as well as to many students and interns who helped, and to many courageous survivors who offered their trust and shared their hearts, thoughts, and feelings.

As a psychologist who believes in how childhood shapes us, I honor my mother Sylvia as a model of unconditional love and support, and my father Abraham as an example of disciplined hard work and unending dedication to always doing the most you can—and your best—for the betterment of humankind. My own appreciation for nature is easily traceable to memories like routine Sunday family trips exploring and enjoying the beauty of parks, caverns, zoos, and all kinds of natural attractions. To see, do, and appreciate everything, was a lesson from my father, along with the encouragement to have multiple perspectives; it wasn't enough to look at Niagara Falls, you had to go through it, under it, behind it, and over it. That multidimensional view has served me in putting together this volume and this team of chapter contributors. I look upon these chapter authors with great appreciation and pride in my colleagues, students, and friends. Working on these volumes has served to intensify my love for people and my interest, awareness, and commitment to the preservation of our planet; I hope it does the same for readers.

1

Introduction

Darlyne G. Nemeth and Judy Kuriansky

In order to understand the policies of environmental protection, we must first understand the ecodynamics of ecopsychology. We must understand how humans affect nature and how nature affects humans. According to Lorenz, even before humans, there was an apparent "link between aperiodicity and unpredictability" (as cited in Gleick, 1987, p. 22). The world has always been in the process "of becoming, rather than being" (Gleick, 1987, p. 5). For example, ice ages have come and gone. Episodes of chaos (e.g., hurricanes, tornadoes, and other natural disasters) tend to emerge from periods of apparent calmness.

Since humans evolved, they have increasingly affected the environment. Their goals, at first, reflected basic needs for food, shelter, safety, etc. As explained by Maslow (1943), people eventually sought more. Some became pro-social and self-actualized. Others became antisocial and self-aggrandized. Some perceived themselves as caretakers of the land, whereas others took on the role of conquerors and exploiters. Historically, those who chose the roles of "caretakers" were no match for those who chose the roles of "conquerors." Caretakers, such as the world's indigenous peoples, found themselves subjugated, raped, and dehumanized. They often lost their homes, their cultures, and their families. For centuries, the world has endured "man's inhumanity to man," and it is still continuing. Chapters in Volume 1 describe the theory and science of the status of our environment today, and offer two examples of indigenous survival in spite of external forces; chapters in this volume present many examples of survival and resilience, and describe programs and policies that offer solutions to these problems regarding the predicament of our planet today. Many environmental traumas plague our people and planet today. All people can be affected by environmental trauma; yet, the elderly, the poor, and/or those who live closest to the water are most likely to suffer its direct effects and aftermath. The authors in these chapters offer hope in the face of these dire situations.

As Hurricane Katrina's brutal strike on Louisiana and the Gulf Coast region was one of the most formidable examples of recent environmental trauma, it is used for illustration and discussion. According to authors Speier and Pratts in Chapter 3 of this volume (2015), of the 1,459 confirmed Katrina-related deaths in Louisiana, almost 50% were over the age of 74. The elderly are least likely to survive environmental trauma. Next are the poor, who have the least available resources to evacuate. The 2005 Katrina trauma represented a combination of fatal factors. It was both an environmental and a human-induced disaster. It also represented a failure of leadership at all levels. Its aftermath was filled with examples of spin and fraud. Lessons were learned, at the federal, state, and individual levels. Many of these lessons are described in the chapters in Volume 2. Questions remain, however. What was really learned? How will the lessons of Katrina impact future preparedness? Will proactive environmental management prevail, or will the mentality of power, corruption, and greed prevail? Well-meaning environmental efforts, especially those on a local level, find the truth not to be a powerful partner in their efforts to succeed. Special interests often corrupt the process. Eventually, the courts, not the people's elected representatives, are left to decide.

But, when people do prevail, individual and/or community efforts do make a difference. Whether it is restoring communities through music or restoring hope via international children's projects, when people can be revitalized, the results are amazing. Then, once people are revitalized, the land can be protected for future generations. Lessons learned from environmental tragedies in various parts of the world, from America to Haiti and China, are presented in these chapters. Also, unique programs to protect the people and the environment, such as those in Belize, Ecuador, and Azerbaijan, are described in this volume, with benefits of vast experience and expertise of the authors. These all bring optimism as well as renewed hope about efforts to respect and protect our people and our environment.

Furthermore, public- and private-sector policies may indeed turn shareholders into stakeholders. Once we learn to invest in relationships and the land we love, once we learn to share and give rather than acquire and take, once we develop the goal of seeking what we need versus pursuing what we want, we will be able to set a brighter course for our future. Then, and only then, will we be able to rid the world of physical and emotional suffering. Hopefully, the chapters in Volume 2 will offer inspiration in this quest.

REFERENCES

Gleick, J. (1987). *Chaos: Making a new science*. New York, NY: Viking.

Maslow, A. H. (1943). A theory of human motivation. *Psychological Review, 50*, 370–396.

Speier, A. H., & Prats, R. (2015). Post Hurricane Katrina and the preparedness-response-recovery cycle: Integrating behavioral health into a state's disaster-response capabilities. In D. G. Nemeth & J. Kuriansky (Eds.), *Ecopsychology: Advances from the intersection of psychology and environmental protection*, Volume 2 (pp. 15–34). Santa Barbara, CA: ABC-CLIO.

2

From Chaos to Community: The Federal Response—an Account of Lieutenant General Russel Honoré's Leadership during Hurricane Katrina

Darlyne G. Nemeth

This chapter chronicles Lieutenant General Russel Honoré's journey from the First Army's leader of the Joint Task Force Katrina (JTF Katrina) to the citizen army's leader of the environment protection movement in Louisiana. Honoré, known as the "Hero of Katrina," learned of the extent of the devastation of Louisiana's coastline during his role in Katrina. Now, this founder of the Green Army has learned that reestablishing order post-Katrina was considerably easier than rebuilding Louisiana's coastline. Organizing citizens to understand what has happened and is happening, along with encouraging positive action, is a new frontier for this amazing man.

BACKGROUND

When Hurricane Katrina hit New Orleans on Monday, August 29, 2005, chaos abounded. It was the most destructive human-induced disaster in U.S. history. Eighteen hundred lives were lost across the U.S. Gulf Coast region, and more than 200,000 homes were destroyed or severely damaged. Over 800,000 people became homeless overnight (Nemeth, 2014). People were traumatized. Confusion and lawlessness reigned. Local, state, and individual citizen efforts, although well-meaning, were not up to the task of restoring order on such a grand scale.

On Wednesday, August 31, 2005, Honoré, the commanding general of the First U.S. Army, which is responsible for mobilizing and training National Guard and Reserve Troops, arrived. The federal response had finally begun.

The *Washington Post* dubbed Honoré the "Category 5 General" (Duke, 2005). And so he was. Perhaps it was his vast military training, or his "take charge" personality, or his Creole background, or all of the above, but Honoré just instinctively seemed to know what to do. In an instant, the hopeless began to feel hopeful. Someone was in charge. Someone knew what to do. As retired army general Dennis Reimer said, Honoré brought "that pointed, no-nonsense sensibility to an unprecedented humanitarian disaster that requires a tough leader" (Duke, 2005).

In 2005, Honoré was the Joint Task Force Katrina commander. He led the "Department of Defense response to Hurricanes Katrina and Rita in Alabama, Mississippi, and Louisiana, and directed the operations of over 22,000 Service members, 200 aircraft, and 20 ships" (Curriculum Vitae, n.d.). Lt. General Honoré also "collaborated with Federal, State, and local authorities to coordinate and conduct all response, recovery, and mitigation operations" (Curriculum Vitae, n.d.).

A HISTORICAL ACCOUNT

History professor and author Douglas Brinkley (2006), in his innovative book *The Great Deluge*, characterized Lieutenant General Honoré as having "the kind of cool strength for which New Orleans had been longing for days" (p. 525). Perhaps it was because of his heritage that New Orleanians trusted him. As described in Brinkley's book, the Honoré family was "a little bit of French, a little bit of Indian, a little bit of Creole, a little bit of black, a little bit of white—just like a gumbo" (2006, p. 525). So New Orleanians were able to relate to and respect this magnificent 6'2" commander when Lieutenant General Honoré barked, "Please put your weapon point down. This is not Iraq" (Brinkley, 2006, p. 525). Even New Orleans Mayor Ray Nagin knew that Honoré came to get things done (Brinkley, 2006, p. 531).

One of the major problems that Lieutenant General Honoré had to face "was that the city was still largely under water" (Brinkley, 2006, p. 616). Major General William Caldwell IV, of the 82nd Airborne Division, was called in "to oversee the Great Deluge operation personally" (Brinkley, 2006, p. 615), only to learn that boats, not helicopters, were needed. Only four boats were sent when 82 were needed. As Caldwell stated, "We eventually became the 82nd Waterborne Division" (Brinkley, 2006, p. 616). While his division was working timelessly to organize the evacuation process, Lieutenant General Honoré and his soldiers were working to keep the peace. According to Brinkley (2006), "by Saturday, New Orleans had been wrestled from the chaos of the preceding week. A kind of calm settled over the streets, not a calm of relaxation or relief, but a weary calm, resigned to the fact that the future was going to be painful but at least it would not be as ugly as the previous week" (pp. 616–617).

Although Lieutenant General Honoré was, unintended, the voice of moderation (Horne, 2006, p. 104), he was not averse to "dressing down reporters at his briefings" (p. 105), when they became too aggressively critical. In his unique way, Honoré was endeavoring to bring perspective to a very traumatic situation.

THE U.S. ARMY'S ACCOUNT

According to Dr. William Robertson's Foreword in James A. Wombwell's 2009 Occasional Paper, *Army Support during the Hurricane Katrina Disorder*, "The most severe loss of life and property damage occurred in New Orleans, Louisiana, where the levee system catastrophically failed, flooding the city and large tracts of neighboring parishes" (p. iii). Although accurately predicted by the National Weather Service (NWS), mobilizing a military force to act takes time. In fact, two days before Katrina hit New Orleans, the NWS issued the following statement: "Most of the area will be uninhabitable for weeks," even without a levee breech, "perhaps longer," and also predicted "human suffering incredible by modern standards" (Horne, 2006, p. 102). Although the U.S. Coast Guard was ready and took action immediately, the army was delayed (Horne, 2006, p. 102). Eventually, as Robertson stated, 22,000 active duty personnel and 50,000 National Guard personnel were assembled to assist with relief-and-recovery operations in Mississippi and Louisiana and to deal with the storm's aftermath. Camp Shelby, Mississippi, became the command center of the JTF Katrina (Wombwell, 2009, p. iii). The army was on standby awaiting orders. They were issued by President George W. Bush on Saturday, August 27, 2005, when he declared a state of emergency in response to Governor Kathleen Blanco's request. The Federal Emergency Management Agency (FEMA) then requested the use of the Meridian Naval Air Station in Mississippi, as a Federal Operational Staging Area (FOSA) on Sunday, August 28, 2005, with the Barksdale Air Force Base as a backup (Wombwell, 2009).

Lieutenant General Honoré was perceived as an "experienced general officer" who was "well versed in domestic disaster response procedures," having had "firsthand experience with hurricane relief operations after four hurricanes hit Florida over a 3-month period in 2004" (Wombwell, 2009, p. 148). Wombwell further stated that, "Because of his extensive disaster-related experience, he knew that saving lives would be the critical focus after the storm made landfall and that boats, helicopters, and communications gear would be in great demand to support the lifesaving mission" (Wombwell, 2009, p. 148). Although Honoré submitted appropriate capabilities requests to the Pentagon, on Sunday, August 28, 2005, the Joint Staff did not act on his request because they had not received any official requests from FEMA, which is the protocol. According to Wombwell (2009), "the Pentagon's failure to act proactively in the face of the impending crisis was a mistake" (p. 148). On the other hand, Honoré displayed proactive leadership: "He was always forward, in contact with Federal, State, and local leaders, so that he personally understood what they needed from him" (Wombwell, 2009, p. 150). Honoré personally drove from Atlanta to Camp Shelby on Tuesday, August 30, 2005, and expected his staff to be assembled by noon (Wombwell, 2009). By August 29, 2005, "Active Duty forces were much more prepared to meet the situation than during past emergencies" (Wombwell, 2009, p. 151). This was due, in large part, because of Honoré's leadership. He understood that preparedness was the key. Thus, it was not surprising that, on Tuesday, August 30, Honoré was selected as the commander of Joint Task Force Katrina and that the U.S. Fifth Army was designated as a supporting command. Initial Work priorities were established as follows:

- Account for people
- Set up communications
- Develop situational awareness
- Develop a contact roster
- Identify future requirements
- Build a situation map
- Prepare to take control of all Title 10 forces in the JOA (Wombwell, 2009)

Then, "Lieutenant General Honoré drove to Gulfport (Mississippi) where he met with Governor Haley Barbour and Major General Harold Cross to coordinate efforts with 'key leaders' " (Wombwell, 2009, p. 153). There, Honoré learned that over 100,000 Gulf Coast survivors were in need of food, water, and ice. Problems abounded, including food shortages, electricity outages, and impassable roads, to name a few. On Tuesday, August 30, 2005, Honoré then traveled to Louisiana to meet with Governor Blanco, Major General Bennett Landreneau, and other key leaders, with whom he maintained close contact throughout the crisis (Wombwell, 2009). On Wednesday, August 31, 2005, Governor Blanco asked Honoré, a fellow Louisianan, to take over the evacuation mission. After agreeing to her request, Honoré directed Brigadier General Mark Graham to do so. Then, Honoré's staff conducted a "bottom-up" assessment of what was needed to improve inter-agency coordination (Wombwell, 2009, p. 154). Relief efforts were assessed. Civilian and military communication systems were linked. Basically, Honoré was on the front lines working "with state leaders, FEMA officials, and his subordinate Active component commanders to identify and solve problems" (Wombwell, 2009, p. 155).

By September 16, 2005, the 498th Medical Company, via their helicopter teams, conducted more than 200 rescue missions, performed 65 resupply missions, and rescued 917 people (Wombwell, 2009). Due to FEMA's lack of ability to track shipments, commodities often ended up at the wrong locations (Wombwell, 2009). But the Corps of Engineers managed to deliver "considerable quantities of water and ice" to the right locations in Mississippi and Louisiana. Then, the Corps had the levee breeches to address (Wombwell, 2009, p. 161).

By the time President Bush called out the U.S. Army's active component, on Saturday, September 3, 2005, order had been restored, and things were starting to improve. Therefore, it was time for reflection. As Lieutenant General Honoré stated of the nation's emergency response plan, "We've got a plan, but don't confuse the plan with execution" (Wombwell, 2009, p. 164). In the final analysis, using a sports analogy, Honoré admitted that although we "lost the first quarter to Hurricane Katrina," he was confident that "under his leadership, the home team" would prevail (Wombwell, 2009, pp. 164–165). And it did. Under his leadership, lives were saved, the New Orleans airport was restored to operational status, humanitarian assistance was provided, and priority needs and problems were addressed and resolved (Wombwell, 2009). As Wombwell (2009) stated, "Lieutenant General Honoré's proactive leadership style facilitated unity of purpose ... He knew what the states needed and pushed his staff to provide it" (p. 184).

Two years after Hurricane Katrina, Honoré was interviewed on National Public Radio's program *Wisdom Watch*. It has been well established that an "anniversary reaction, which occurs on or around the date of a past traumatic event, involves reactions to an emotionally charged episode which hold tremendous significance for an individual or group" (Borstein & Clayton, 1972). As Borstein and Clayton (1972) stated, "When the initial event is experienced as traumatic, individuals may tend to become sensitized to re-experience the symptoms under reminiscent circumstances" (pp. 470–472). Anniversary reactions, and methods to ameliorate them, have also been described by this chapter author and colleagues, specifically after Hurricane Katrina (Kuriansky & Nemeth, 2013; Nemeth et al., 2012). *Wisdom Watch* host Michael Martin wondered what memories Honoré held about his experiences during the aftermath of Hurricane Katrina. Honoré responded that his focus during Katrina was on getting things done. When asked what he learned from the experience, Honoré stated, "Homeland Security starts at home" (Martin, 2007). He emphasized how ill-prepared people, at all levels, were to deal with, let alone survive, Hurricane Katrina. Evacuees had not even gathered their medical records, other key documents, and a reasonable amount of cash money. As Honoré stated, "Preparation in the home and in the family is key" (Martin, 2007). When asked what he learned about leadership, Honoré responded, "The key premises in leadership is understanding your role ... If you say you're going to do something, you need to do it. Always tell the truth to people. They can handle it. It's best to tell the truth, because if you don't, it will come back and have some negative effects on you" (Martin, 2007). Honoré described these principles as key when "operating in a crisis" (Martin, 2007). When asked to address his emotions regarding Hurricane Katrina, Honoré responded, "It's emotional from looking back on the people who were waiting to be evacuated ... it reminds us the power of such things as hurricanes and earthquakes and how fragile life could be" (Martin, 2007). He then added, "But I do still see those faces standing on the street, on the bridges, and at the Super Dome and at the Convention Center, waiting to be moved out"

(Martin, 2007). His emotions were quite apparent when this man of action reflected on his superior's commands, "Do routine things well. Don't fear the impossible. Act in the face of criticism" (Honoré, 2012, p. 25). There will always be criticism of a leader who is making a difference, but, as Honoré wrote, "People are a lot more understanding when they see the leader as an action figure rather than a figurehead" (Honoré, 2012, p. 89).

But, what is leading? According to Honoré (2012), it's about "getting people to willingly do what must be done to complete the mission" (p. 92). Getting people to "do what they ought to do, even with they don't want to" is the responsibility of an effective leader (Honoré, 2012, p. 97). According to Honoré (2012), "Leadership fails to do this when its confidence exceeds its competence" (p. 97). Both must be equal.

HONORÉ'S ACCOUNT

Leaders encourage preparedness. As Lieutenant General Honoré stated, "Bad things will always happen, and it costs a lot more to fix them than to prevent them" (Honoré, 2012, p. 112). At times, issues of politics, budgets, and entitlements interfere with doing the right thing. As Honoré reflected, "People who do the right thing rarely are recognized and rewarded, and people who do the wrong thing rarely get punished" (Honoré, 2012, p. 113). Regardless, it is all about resiliency. According to Walker and Heffner (2010), "Resilience is the positive capacity of people to withstand stressors and to cope with trauma" (para. 1). Nemeth and Whittington (2012) point out that resilience involves the ability to be focused on today, to learn from yesterday, and to imagine oneself in tomorrow; it requires adaptability and flexibility (p. 116). According to Honoré (2012), "resiliency is the ability to come back and be effective after a change— the ability to re-form a staff, to re-open a business, and to adjust" (p. 127). Honoré, who retired from the U.S. Army on February 29, 2008, after 37 years of active service, expressed his strong belief that New Orleans has a "unique opportunity to reinvent itself and to divest itself strictly from the tourist industry and be able to build a better and stronger New Orleans for our future" (Martin, 2007).

Since his retirement from the army, Honoré has been asked to comment on many domestic issues. Furthermore, he has authored two books, *Survival: How Being Prepared Can Keep You and Your Family Safe* (2009) and *Leadership in the New Normal* (2012). In a November 26, 2012, article in the *Advocate*, Catherine Threlkeld quoted Honoré as saying, "People can't take risks and not be prepared for potential disasters because they think the government is going to come take care of them" (Section D). In reference to Superstorm Sandy, Honoré commented, "By and large, people learned from Katrina" (Threlkeld, 2012). Whereas of the 1,800 Katrina deaths, of mostly the elderly, disabled, and poor, only 100 deaths were attributed to Superstorm Sandy. What was the difference?

According to Honoré, "The people that could evacuate did evacuate" (Threlkeld, 2012). People taking responsibility for their future; people being prepared to deal with their present; and people who are willing to learn from their past will propel us forward. Leading others to move forward is, and has always been, Lieutenant General Honoré's mission.

A NEW MISSION

Currently, that mission has evolved into "The Green Army," which is doing its best to protect and preserve Louisiana's delicate environment. According to newsman Mark Ballard's editorial in the *Advocate* (2014a), the Southeast Louisiana Flood Protection Authority–East's lawsuit contended that "the energy industry cut canals through marshes in pursuit of oil and natural gas. In the permits, the 97 companies said they agreed to repair the damage, but they didn't, which allowed salt water to intrude and kill off vegetation needed to slow hurricane storm surges" (p. 9B). Lieutenant General Honoré agreed that "having a strong regulatory system would set the boundaries in advance. Corporations invest in stable environments where they know the rules going in and know that the rules won't change down the road" is all about preparedness (Ballard, 2014a, p. 9B). According to Ballard (2014a), "Honoré says he became an environmentalist while flying into New Orleans after Katrina and mistook abandoned oilfield equipment as hurricane damage," but was immediately corrected by the helicopter pilot (p. 9B). Unfortunately, Governor Bobby Jindal, big oil, and their lobbyists won out, and the bills to crush the lawsuit advanced in the Louisiana legislature and politics, as usual, prevailed. Not accustomed to defeat, Honoré conceded, "The people are going to have to act. This will not change unless the people tell them to change it" (Ballard, 2014a, p. 9B).

As the leader of Louisiana's Green Army, Lieutenant General Honoré organized rallies at the state capital, gave numerous interviews, called for action at Baton Rouge's April 27, 2014, Earth Day celebration, and authored paid public service announcements. In his September 9, 2013 public service announcement, Honoré stated, "Growing up in Pointe Coupee Parish, I never thought I'd see my home state battered as it was during Hurricane Katrina. I never imagined I'd have the privilege of serving as commander of Joint Task Force Katrina, the operation that spearheaded the government's relief efforts after the storm. And I never thought I'd see the day when we would allow the oil companies to kill our wetlands, destroy our fisheries, and threaten our water supplies and livelihoods" (p. 5A). He went on to say that, "The wetlands serve as our buffer against storms and hurricanes. The more wetlands between you and the water, the less impact a storm is going to have on you. But when you destroy these wetlands, you destroy your protection" (Honoré, 2013). Honoré concluded, "I'm writing to enlist your support in this battle to save Louisiana. Our coast, our water, our lifestyle, and our lives depend on it" (Honoré, 2013).

ADDRESSING THE PAST TO PREPARE FOR THE FUTURE

In his May 2014 address at the Louisiana State Capital, Lieutenant General Honoré decried, "Oil has captured our democracy." This speech was one of many examples of the Green Army's attempts to rally opinion to oppose "legislation that would sidetrack environmental damage lawsuits filed by a New Orleans-area levee board" (Ballard, 2014b, p. 3B). In spite of 74% of survey respondents in Baton Rouge and New Orleans citing opposition to this legislation against current legal action, the people's efforts failed, and big oil prevailed (Sentell, 2014). In fact, a bill was passed by the Louisiana legislature in May, 2014 to kill the levee board lawsuit. In spite of Louisiana attorney general Buddy Caldwell's recommendations for Governor Jindal to veto this bill because of "the potential for an unintended effect on the state's, or a local governmental entity's, claims against BP related to the Deepwater Horizon incident," Jindal was considering signing it into law over the attorney general's recommendations (Ballard, 2014d). Even without his signature, the bill could eventually have become law (Ballard, 2014c, p. 5A); however, Jindal signed it into law on June 6, 2014. His actions have now paved the way for court challenges, at the expense of Louisiana citizens (Adelson & Ballard, 2014).

As Lieutenant General Honoré well understands, losing one battle does not preclude winning the war. Perhaps, however, it is time to reflect, regroup, repackage, and reposition the Green Army for the future and for the court challenges that will certainly lie ahead.

REFERENCES

Adelson, J., & Ballard, M. (2014, June 7). Jindal signs bill that could kill levee suit. *The Advocate*, pp. 1A, 5A.

Ballard, M. (2014a, April 20). Honoré wants public involved on environment. *The Advocate*, p. 9B.

Ballard, M. (2014b, May 6). Honoré: Oil "has captured our democracy." *The Advocate*, p. 3B.

Ballard, M. (2014c, May 31). Bill seeking to kill levee board lawsuit approved. *The Advocate*, p. 5A.

Ballard, M. (2014d, June 5). AG recommends veto for levee board lawsuits bill. *The Advocate*. Retrieved April 2, 2015, from http://theadvocate.com/home/9365200-125/attorney-general-recommends-veto-levee

Borstein, P. E., & Clayton, P. (1972). The anniversary reaction. *Diseases of the Nervous System, 33*, 470–472.

Brinkley, D. (2006). *The great deluge: Hurricane Katrina, New Orleans, and the Mississippi Gulf Coast*. New York, NY: Morrow.

Curriculum Vitae. (n.d.). *About General Honoré*. Retrieved April 2, 2015, from http://www.generalhonore.com/Documents/Russel_L%20_Honore_Curriculum_Vitae_2010.pdf

Duke, L. (2005, September 12). The category 5 general. *The Washington Post*.

Honoré, R. L. (2009). *Survival: How being prepared can keep you and your family safe*. New York, NY: Atria Books.

Honoré, R. L. (2012). *Leadership in the new normal: a short course*. Lafayette, LA: Acadian House Publishing.

Honoré, R. L. (2013, September 9). Public service announcement. *The Advocate*, p. 5A.

Horne, J. (2006). *Breach of faith: Hurricane Katrina and the near death of a great American city*. New York, NY: Random House.

Kuriansky, J., & Nemeth, D. G. (2013). A model for post-environmental disaster wellness workshops: Preparing individuals and communities for hurricane anniversary reactions. *Ecopsychology*, 5(Suppl. 1), S38–S45.

Martin, M. (2007, August 29). *Wisdom watch: Lt. Gen. Russel Honore* [Interview]. Retrieved April 2, 2015, from http://www.npr.org/templates/story/story.php?storyId=14018130

Nemeth, D. G. (2014, April). *The roles of psychology and medical psychology in environmental trauma and environmental protection*. Presented at the Louisiana Academy of Medical Psychologists CME/CE Conference, Baton Rouge, LA.

Nemeth, D. G., Kuriansky, J., Reeder, K. P., Lewis, A., Marceaux, K., Whittington, T., ... Safier, J. A. (2012). Addressing anniversary reactions of trauma through group process: The Hurricane Katrina anniversary wellness workshops. *International Journal of Group Psychotherapy*, 62(1), 129–142.

Nemeth, D. G., & Whittington, L. T. (2012). Our robust people: Resilience in the face of environmental trauma. In D. G. Nemeth, R. B. Hamilton, & J. Kuriansky (Eds.), *Living in an environmentally traumatized world: Healing ourselves and our planet* (pp. 113–140). Santa Barbara, CA: ABC-CLIO/Praeger.

Sentell, W. (2014, March 4). Barry decries efforts to shelve oil lawsuit. *The Advocate*, p. 4B.

Threlkeld, C. (2012, November 26). Honoré praises officials handling of Sandy aftermath. *The Advocate*.

Walker, J., & Heffner, F. (2010, Summer). Resilience is a critical factor in the workplace. *New Worker*. Retrieved April 2, 2015, from http://cecassoc.com/download/i/mark_dl/u/1389501/5180391/Summer%202010.pdf

Wombwell, J. A. (2009). *The long war series: Army support during the Hurricane Katrina disaster*. (Occasional Paper No. 29). Fort Leavenworth, KS: Combat Studies Institute Press. Retrieved April 2, 2015, from http://usacac.army.mil/cac2/cgsc/carl/download/csipubs/wombwell.pdf

3

Post Hurricane Katrina and the Preparedness-Response-Recovery Cycle: Integrating Behavioral Health into a State's Disaster-Response Capabilities

Anthony H. Speier and Rosanne Prats

Severe weather incidents, with devastation of the catastrophic proportions of Hurricane Katrina, are historic events. As such, they require careful review and analysis so that, if at all possible, history does not repeat itself. In this chapter, we examine the strengths, innovations, and gaps in the planning, response, and recovery phases of one state's behavioral health response within the context of the overall disaster environment. Given current weather patterns, storms of greater intensity are increasingly threatening our coastal areas, and thus threatening the safety of communities and their residents. Lessons learned from the Hurricane Katrina experience continue to inform contemporary emergency preparedness, response, and recovery cycles. Behavioral health interventions delivered during the acute, intermediate, and long-term phases of recovery are examined, and implications for further development and implementation are discussed.

BACKGROUND

Severe weather events are taken very seriously in Louisiana and throughout the Gulf Coast. Exposure to horrific storms and their consequences is well-engrained in the culture of coastal communities, and how individuals and families structure their living situations and future plans. For many, the hurricane season of June 1 to November 30 is known and respected as the fifth season of the year. From 1992 to 2014, 14 hurricanes threatened the Louisiana coast. Of those 14, Louisiana endured the impact of 10 named hurricanes. Of historic significance are hurricanes Andrew (1992), Katrina (2005), Rita (2005) and Gustav (2008). In 2005, the state experienced three hurricanes, and in 2008, two hurricanes, with an average of one hurricane every 1.6 years over the 22-year period. During this time period, hurricane preparedness and response strategies at both the national and state level, consistently improved in their operational response capabilities. Preparedness training and practice scenarios occur throughout all 12 months of the year. The major emphasis of these efforts involve activities that help people get out of harm's way, prevent loss of lives, and protect critical public and private infrastructure. In Louisiana, the Governor's Office of Homeland Security maintains a strong partnership with the federal Department of Homeland Security and specifically with its subentity, the Federal Emergency Management Agency (FEMA). Planning and response activities at both the state and national levels are based on the National Response Framework and its functional components. A detailed description of federal response planning strategies is available at http://www.fema.gov/national-response-framework.

The tipping point marking a significant rethinking of national- and state-level hurricane response strategies was the 2005 hurricane season. When Hurricane Katrina made landfall on August 29, 2005, on the southernmost point of the Louisiana coast, not just Louisiana, but the entire nation, was dramatically and forever changed in how hurricane response would be conceptualized and managed. Prior to Katrina, most hurricanes had traditionally been managed as 7- to 10-day events involving several days of emergency response preparation, limited evacuation of areas most at risk to storm surge, sheltering at-risk populations, enduring the day of the storm's path over land, and then rapidly initiating post-landfall response strategies necessary to restore basic infrastructure (utilities and debris removal) so evacuees and shelter-in-place residents who did not evacuate could begin to rebuild and recover from losses incurred. Usually, within a year post incident, the majority of communities and individuals were well past the major consequences of the event and were moving forward with their lives.

The impact of Katrina was in a different class, a catastrophic event not previously experienced in the United States (Brinkley, 2006). Coupled with Hurricane Rita striking the southwestern Louisiana coast three weeks later, on September 24, 2005, the entire coastal area and five of the eight major metropolitan statistical areas in Louisiana were directly impacted. These population areas included the greater population centers of New Orleans, Baton Rouge, Terrebonne/Lafourche, Lafayette, and Lake Charles. The remaining areas of the state were impacted by tornadoes in the central part of the state, and evacuees sheltering in towns and communities overwhelmed resources throughout the remaining parishes. The summary of factual data below (Hietman, 2011; Plyer, 2013), provides a brief glimpse of the devastation so striking that numbers alone fail to capture its significance for the people and communities who experienced its impact.

- 1,469 confirmed storm-related deaths (almost 50% over age 74)
- 1.8 million evacuees from the greater New Orleans area
- 100,000 remained in the area and did not evacuate

- Three major canals breached (London Avenue, 17th Street, and the Industrial Canal), putting 80% of the city underwater
- Destruction to virtually all buildings in lower Plaquemines Parish
- 95% of St. Bernard parish underwater
- 40,000 homes destroyed in St. Tammany Parish
- 1.1 million homes and buildings without power
- Eight oil refineries inoperable (8% of U.S. production capacity)
- 26,000 remaining New Orleans residents sought sheltering of last resort at the New Orleans Superdome, and another 25,000 at the Ernest J. Moriel Convention Center
- 4,000 residents stranded on highways and bridges within New Orleans
- 3,000 evacuated by air from medical treatment sites at the Louis Armstrong New Orleans International Airport
- 13,000 National Guard troops deployed
- Estimated property damage between $75 billion and $100 billion
- Widespread looting and a barely operational New Orleans Police Department
- 1.1 million volunteers provided assistance throughout the United States
- One month post impact, 600,000 households still displaced
- 273,000 persons housed in hurricane shelters
- 110,000 households living in FEMA trailers
- Population decrease of the city of New Orleans by greater than 50%; by 2012, the population was 75% of pre-storm levels.
- Total damage in 2005 dollars: $150 billion ($135 billion Katrina-related, and $15 billion Rita-related)

While these statistics are staggering, more detailed and comprehensive accounts of damage to the environment and individuals are widely available from a variety of news-reporting agencies, public policy, and scholarly reports.

THE PUBLIC HEALTH RESPONSE TO HURRICANE KATRINA

The Louisiana Department of Health and Hospitals (DHH) is the designated primary agency responsible for public health emergency response operations as described in the state's emergency response plan (Governor's Office of Homeland Security and Emergency Preparedness, 2009). The State Emergency Preparedness Plan is consistent with planning documents nomenclature and functions similarly outlined at the federal and local governmental levels. Emergency Support Function Eight (ESF-8) is the response component responsible for addressing public health and medical activities. In Louisiana, ESF-8's scope of operations include public health and sanitation, emergency medical and hospital services, crisis counseling and mental health services to disaster victims and workers, supplement and support to disrupted or overburdened local medical personnel and facilities, and relief of personal suffering and trauma. In addition, ESF-8 provides coordination of the state's Catastrophic Mass Fatality Plan, which may be activated during a state declaration. In addition to DHH's role as the primary ESF-8 agency, numerous university systems, health organizations, and state agencies support the delivery of services and related operational responsibilities tasked through DHH as the primary agency.

DHH response capabilities have continued to evolve from basic response duties associated with Hurricane Andrew (1992) to what at the time of Katrina were considered highly evolved response capabilities. The department's response plans are consistently rated highly by FEMA and draw upon the vast resources within the offices of public health, behavioral health, citizens with developmental disabilities, and adult and aging services as well as related support services within the office of the secretary. Most notably, prior to Hurricane Katrina, DHH relied on its workforce of almost 12,000 employees to staff state and department level emergency operations centers, mobilize 24-hour facilities for sheltering of special populations, and staff Medical Special Needs Shelters (MSNS) for up to 2,000 evacuees in need of medical support not available in American Red Cross shelters for general populations. On August 23–24, 2005, the DHH staff was deeply involved in the FEMA-sponsored Hurricane Pam exercise, which was based on a scenario of a major storm flooding New Orleans. The Hurricane Pam exercise simulated the mass evacuation of the city. The models practiced were made operational just five days later as the major response strategy for rescuing thousands of stranded residents as the city flooded.

The operational mission practiced in the Hurricane Pam exercise focused on the evacuation of New Orleans, the immediate provision of emergency health care, and the sheltering of evacuees. A detailed account of behavioral health interventions (Speier, Osofsky, & Osofsky, 2009) highlights aspects of the Hurricane Pam model activated during the Katrina immediate response phase. Of particular note, planning exercises occurring pre-Katrina viewed behavioral health as a supportive function with a limited role of counseling of evacuees and staff in shelter settings. The unanticipated range of acute behavioral health interventions that became essential during the immediate response phase of Hurricane Katrina have vastly altered how behavioral health services are utilized during all phases of disaster preparedness, including the acute response, and long-term recovery operations. Behavioral health interventions and locations for intervention included stress management support to staff at various state-operated emergency operations centers, establishment of a behavioral health unit during the immediate phase of implementation of the Temporary Medical Operations and Staging Area (TMOSA) in Baton Rouge, ongoing support to first-responder units including the New Orleans Police and Fire Department, and Wildlife and Fisheries officers who were boating evacuees out of New Orleans. Other support sites included the Search and Rescue Base of Operations (SARBO) located on Interstate 10 and Causeway Boulevard, the medical operations unit at the Louis Armstrong New Orleans International Airport, the mass casualty operations at designated mortuary sites, and the Family Assistance

Center (FAC). The FAC was established as a call center and a central location for families to assist in the identification process of deceased family members. Behavioral health teams supported and supervised spiritual counselors staffing the call center and provided operational debriefing and stress management support to FAC staff. As the response phase transitioned from acute response to an intermediate response phase (several weeks post-incident), behavioral health teams assisted local parishes with direct support to school personnel, administrators, and public officials. Throughout the response phase, behavioral health teams continued providing assistance to first responders at temporary firehouse and police district/unit locations.

In testimony provided by DHH state officials to the U.S. Senate Committee on Homeland Security and Governmental Affairs regarding evacuation of New Orleans and related acute response phase activities, the following lessons learned were identified as areas needing improvement: (1) functional inter-operational communications systems; (2) accuracy of information being communicated; (3) risk of medical facilities sheltering patients in-place instead of evacuating; (4) policy issues such as air transport of hospital patients; (5) integration of federal, state, and regional response plans; (6) federal grants for emergency response equipment, especially generator capacity for health care facilities; (7) building code requirements; and (8) transportation strategies.

An analysis of the Katrina response released on September 21, 2005, by the Government Accountability Office (GAO) provides a perspective as to the scope and complexity of the immediate response during the acute phase of the incident. The GAO report characterizes the impact of Katrina as catastrophic based on: the massive evacuation of victims; failure of communication networks; lack of surge capacity of the health care workforce; the absence of an adequate health care information technology; the extremely hazardous environmental, health, and social conditions faced by victims and responders; and this being a mass fatality event with numerous deaths, injuries, and chronic health conditions requiring treatment.

Federal resources deployed and response efforts are discussed elsewhere in this volume (see Chapter 2 [Nemeth, 2015]). From a state perspective, local and state resources were quickly overwhelmed and further complicated by a delayed federal response for National Disaster Medical System (NDMS) resources and teams. However it is important to note the issues highlighted by the GAO report are acknowledged as situational features never previously encountered in a major domestic disaster incident. These include:

- Lack of access to health care facilities for victims
- Extensive damage to health care facilities
- Failure of hospital and nursing home facilities, which chose not to evacuate, to be able to maintain conventional standards of care, forcing closure and evacuation of medically compromised patients

- Limited field level access to essential medicines and treatments such as oxygen, insulin, and kidney dialysis for evacuees
- Loss of contact with family members for victims transported out of state to one of nine host receiving states
- Deployment of 87 NDMS teams, including 50 Disaster Medical Assistance Teams (DMAT), 4 Veterinary Medical Assistance Teams (VMAT) and 4 Disaster Mortuary Assistance Teams (DMORT)
- Over one million people evacuated without access to medical records

Section Summary

A final report by the Bipartisan Committee of the U.S. Congress, established to investigate the preparation for and response to Hurricane Katrina (U.S. Congress, 2006), provides multiple perspectives on what transpired and its immediate impact on the people and communities affected. This congressional report and many related reports to this historic disaster are a synthesis of many factors. The general consensus of most reports is that the response was limited in its effectiveness and that future response efforts to similar events should address the limitations associated with the Katrina response. A perspective based on the historical context for hurricane preparedness and response accounts for many aspects of the incident. Residents and organizations such as health care facilities have a mixed experience regarding the need to evacuate and their relative ability to successfully evacuate. With the experience of Katrina, that attitude has changed. Hurricanes are unpredictable forces of nature, not to be taken lightly. Evacuation and preparedness are now essential components of Louisiana culture.

BEHAVIORAL HEALTH CHALLENGES

The focus for the remainder of this chapter is on the role of the Louisiana Office of Mental Health (OMH) (now called the Office of Behavioral Health [OBH]) in establishing a recovery initiative consistent with the incredible range of events and experiences endured by the people of Louisiana as a result of the destructive impact of Hurricane Katrina. As discussed above, the primary mission of any disaster-related response effort is to protect the people exposed to the event. Thus the vast majority of resources were expended extracting people out of harm's way and caring for them. The immediate behavioral health response functions related to the primary mission draw upon the skills of state behavioral health employees who, during non-disaster times, administer and staff hospital and community mental health programs throughout the state.

Routine duties of behavioral health staff in non-disaster times involve the provision of direct clinical services to persons who are suffering from serious emotional/behavioral disorders or severe and persistent mental illness.

Services include crisis counseling and stabilization, acute and intermediate-level hospital treatment, therapeutic counseling, and medical treatment necessary to assist persons in maintaining their ability to successfully function in their day-to-day lives in the community. During a typical major disaster incident, routine clinical services are suspended and staff is deployed as necessary to various sheltering sites, mobile crisis teams, emergency operations centers, and first-responder operations. Once the storm passes through the state, behavioral health staff return to their routine job functions, reopening clinics and reestablishing daily clinical operations. The aftermath of Katrina presented an entirely different set of circumstances and challenges. The reality in the days and weeks post-Katrina were more akin to the surreal surroundings and extraordinary circumstances often experienced by characters in episodes of Rod Serling's classic television drama *Twilight Zone*. Within this context, administrators were confronted with building response strategies sufficient to assist survivors, communities, and responders, and facilitating a return from the surreal into a "new" normal where healing and recovering could begin.

In the immediate aftermath of a disaster, recommended interventions are not standardized clinical models, but a range of empathic stress-reducing techniques. The intent is to help people impacted by the event maintain or reestablish adaptive functioning. As noted by the authors of the *Field Guide for Psychological First Aid* (PFA), disaster-related experiences (physical, psychological, behavioral, and spiritual) may disrupt normal coping abilities and recovery (Brymer et al., 2006). Our experience over many disaster response operations confirms from an experiential perspective that assisting disaster survivors in focusing on an orientation to the present and addressing immediate needs in a compassionate and calming manner constitute a realistic intervention strategy for the majority of survivors.

The assumption in most disaster instances is that once the major threat has passed, what lies ahead for survivors are the challenges associated with recovery. However, consider the circumstances immediately following Katrina's passage over land. Many survivors' disaster experiences had not stabilized; they endured an involuntary dislocation from their homes and communities, in the worst case anticipating a few days away from home; instead, they were faced with not having a home at all, and ill-equipped to move forward. Tens of thousands had to seek refuge in shelters or other temporary locations, virtually without warning, and without their personal belongings and resources, including items for addressing basic needs such as clothes, food, and essential medications. Survivors in many cases were separated from family members and pets with no means of locating them. Most were housed in unfamiliar locations, and for a significant number of New Orleans residents, it was the first time in their lives being away from their home neighborhoods (CDC, 2006; Henry J. Kaiser Family Foundation, 2007). Even after several days turned into weeks, their experience continued to be a dynamic and often chaotic sequence of ongoing events, which were not readily reconciled. The city of New Orleans and Plaquemines and St. Bernard Parishes remained flooded for three weeks after Katrina. As the area became "un-watered," it became obvious that continued search-and-recovery operations for body removal, as well as biohazards and infrastructure issues, would continue to keep residents from returning for a protracted period of time.

Within this environment, providing the very basic objectives/core actions of PFA became the behavioral health mission. This included: (1) establishing a human connection; (2) providing safety and comfort; (3) assisting in stabilization; (4) helping with information gathering; (5) providing practical assistance; (6) connecting with social supports; (7) providing basic coping information; and (8) linking to survivor resources. How to provide these objectives became the challenge for the state's behavioral health system.

RESOURCE DEVELOPMENT

Utilizing training strategies and models available through federal resources (U.S. Department of Health and Human Services, 2003) and learning from experiences of previous hurricane seasons, the Louisiana Office of Mental Health implemented a number of disaster response training initiatives in 2004–2005. State hospital staff participated in hazard analysis, evacuation, and shelter-in-place emergency preparedness plans. Local community mental health center staff in collaboration with Office of Public Health staff practiced emergency scenarios for maintaining continuity of operations and staffing special needs shelters. Ninety-nine percent of the OMH staff completed the four basic National Incident Management System (NIMS) courses. All staff had personal readiness plans and were available for emergency response duties via a statewide call-tree program for activating staff. Additionally, in partnership with the Louisiana State University Health Sciences Center, in late May 2005, the state provided three days of operational training for 350–400 public- and private-sector behavioral health professionals who, in exchange for no-cost continuing education credits received for their training, agreed to be available for deployment in a disaster incident. Including the behavioral health Hurricane Pam exercise, through the summer of 2005, OMH and later OBH trained over 4,000 behavioral health staff in emergency operations prior to Hurricane Katrina (Speier, 2006).

On August 26, 2005, OMH (1) activated hurricane pre-incident plans that included deployments to emergency operations centers, placing clinical and administrative staff on alert for deployment throughout the state; (2) began evacuation procedures of two state psychiatric hospitals in the greater New Orleans area to other locations in the state; and (3) designated staff for deployment to MSNS locations in New Orleans, Baton Rouge, Lafayette, Lake Charles, Alexandria, and Monroe. Staff resources were compromised from the beginning of operations as staff from the southeastern areas of the state were under mandatory evacuations and not available for deployment, thus reducing available behavioral health resources throughout the state.

During the immediate incident response phase, OMH staff were deployed for extended service in the various operations and command centers, SARBO and TMOSA sites, and MSNS locations. As it became evident that the active phase of this event was not ending, but instead devolving into an extended crisis event requiring an evolving and more comprehensive behavioral health response, OMH and OAD established a Behavioral Health Command Center and initiated expanded response services. Basic clinical services were reduced in scope throughout the state as a substantial number of state staff remained deployed in a disaster response status. OBH extended operations to include PFA and other interventions for survivors and staff in major general population shelters in Baton Rouge, Lafayette, Alexandria, and Monroe. As tensions and stress were escalating in a number of shelter sites, seven mobile crisis teams were activated on a 24-hour basis through October 19, 2005. These teams provided 4,992 hours of professional staff time dedicated to crisis response services for survivors housed in shelters statewide. OMH continued to seek assistance from our federal partners, finally securing additional clinical staff from the Uniformed Public Health Service (UPHS) and the Substance Abuse and Mental Health Services Administration (SAMHSA) "federalized" volunteers from across the nation, who were deployed on two-week rotations. Using a hastily submitted SERG grant to SAMHSA, OMH and OAD established 24-hour telephone access to substance abuse and mental health counseling services as well as additional substance use and counseling resources (SAMHSA, 2005). Stress management and post-deployment counseling was made available for first responders and others involved in search and rescue/recovery operations. Debriefing sessions/retreats were implemented for administrative staff and senior administrators. These strategies were all directed at keeping limited emergency response and public health staff mission ready, even as the demands of extended deployment were taking its toll on staff and families.

BUILDING A LONG-TERM RESPONSE STRATEGY

The Robert T. Stafford Disaster Relief and Emergency Assistance Act is the legislative authority for federal crisis response. Within the Stafford Act is language authorizing the federal government to provide short-term behavioral health support when disaster support needs exceed a state's internal capabilities. The Crisis Counseling Program (CCP), administered by SAMHSA and funded through FEMA, is the administrative program tasked with providing behavioral health disaster assistance (FEMA, 2015). The CCP is organized into two phases: the Immediate CCP program, lasting for 60 days after a presidential disaster declaration is issued; followed by a nine-month Regular CCP for extended recovery.

The federal program assumption is that the surge in behavioral health needs related to the disaster incident will have been adequately addressed during this period and any remaining needs for behavioral health will be addressed within the state's capacity to deliver the necessary services. While this may be accurate for small-scale disaster incidents, this was obviously not the case following Hurricane Katrina. The basic service components of the CCP are: (1) supportive counseling, coping strategies; (2) outreach and education regarding stress reactions, individual coping, and resource availability; (3) group counseling; (4) public education and community networking; (5) assessment and referral for clinical and other services; (6) development of self-help materials; and (7) media and public service announcements.

Prior to Hurricane Katrina, the largest mass fatality disaster in the United States, and hence the largest CCP program, was associated with the New York State response to the 9/11 terrorist attack. Staff associated with New York State's CCP program, Project Liberty, provided technical assistance to the Louisiana Office of Mental Health in developing a comprehensive and expanded program design for the CCP response to Hurricane Katrina. The expanded concepts successfully used in Project Liberty included an emphasis on a greatly expanded media design, broad-based community education materials in multiple languages, stratified outreach and crisis counseling by distinct high-risk population groups, culturally competent intervention strategies, emergency crisis response staff, stress management staff, and detailed evaluation and quality assurance plans to assure the project stayed on track with the program objectives. In addition, a comprehensive fiscal management and business plan was developed. Essentially, Louisiana was building a separate behavioral health workforce and intervention model specifically designed and dedicated as a response to the vast demands and scope of the Katrina catastrophe (Norris & Bellamy, 2009).

The CCP plan required an easily recognized "branding" that reflected the natural resilience of survivors and minimized public resistance to the stigma associated with needing mental health services. A strategy for normalizing recovery through strength-based supports was critical for the program to be effective and trusted by survivors and the general population. After much feedback from community stakeholders and advisors, the CCP was labeled "Louisiana Spirit." Its familiar tagline, "Hope is the Enemy of Despair ... if you think you have lost yours, call to just talk and be heard," was well accepted, and it continues after nine years as the recognized theme for behavioral health assistance following disaster incidents within Louisiana.

The Louisiana Spirit program had to be carefully crafted and implemented so it would be perceived as a legitimate resource, and not just another federally funded, ineffective, and nonresponsive recovery effort. It was clear from the disaster behavioral health literature that a program must be trauma informed, with developmentally appropriate interventions, and a culturally competent approach

(Norris et al., 2002; Norris, Friedman, & Watson, 2002; Norris & Stevens, 2007). Interventions must be sensitive to the known risk factors for adverse recovery outcomes, including the degree of exposure to the disaster, female gender, middle age, minority status, additional stressors secondary to exposure, a history of psychiatric issues, and a lack of psychosocial supports. Additionally, the emphasis on family, personal resilience, and building healthy, developmentally appropriate social support systems would be crucial for long-term recovery (Masten & Obradovic, 2008; Norris, Stevens, Pfefferbaum, Wyche, & Pfefferbaum, 2008; Pfefferbaum, Pfefferbaum, & Norris, 2010). The Immediate CCP was designed to provide survivors with broad access to services and conduct additional needs assessment to further refine the long-term Regular CCP program to meet community and survivor needs. It was anticipated that the Louisiana Spirit program would provide services for several years as the recovery trajectory was poorly understood at the time.

The goals for the OMH operational response delivered through the Immediate and Regular CCP Louisiana Spirit programs were the following:

- Deliver services to large numbers of survivors who are diverse in age, ethnicity, and needs.
- Utilize a multifaceted program design reflecting the culture, traditions, needs, and values across the spectrum of Louisiana residents.
- Design services to promote recovery among individuals and communities throughout the state.
- Implement evaluation and quality improvement programs to provide a continuous flow of feedback in order to inform and evolve service delivery.
- Solicit feedback from survivors as to services and supports desired.
- Utilize a sustainable recovery model through community engagement and systematic monitoring of the health and recovery of the population.

The core program model was conceptualized as community-based, not office-based, and would employ as many survivors to be program staff as feasible and appropriate. Interventions were practical and designed to assist providers in reestablishing the adaptive functioning necessary to move forward in recovery and renew their spirit and that of their communities. Particular emphasis was focused on developing unique service models for the special populations of children/families, persons with preexisting health and behavioral health vulnerabilities, older adults, first responders, and priority populations, which emerged as needing tailored services as a result of the storm's impact and their unique recovery challenges. Service components included individual and group counseling, stress management, education and outreach, and trauma-informed grief and loss counseling, utilizing cultural and community liaison staff and staff specific to the FAC. The state management team, comprised of executive leadership and functional coordinators for each population group, provided the necessary program oversight to assure compliance with federal and state requirements. Team members, with input from the community and regional providers, worked as a management unit to ensure that appropriate implementation and monitoring of services occurred. This was accomplished through a combination of training, on-site evaluation and coaching, conference calls, videoconferences, written management protocols, and state/provider partnerships developed along functional lines of program services.

PARTNERSHIP DEVELOPMENT

Implicit in the overall Louisiana Spirit program was the emphasis on building collaborative partnerships and integrating behavioral health services into the broader Hurricane Katrina recovery operations. The complexity of the recovery response involved the temporary resettlement of persons without housing into alternative living arrangements. For some survivors, the temporary arrangements would last from weeks to months, and for a large number of survivors, the temporary living conditions would last for several years. The housing accommodations ranged from short-term shelters to longer-stay hotel rooms, and for over 100,000 households, FEMA provided travel trailers. These trailers were located throughout the state in large settlements referred to as Transitional Living Communities (TLCs), or in the front yards of their destroyed homes in New Orleans and the surrounding parishes throughout southeastern Louisiana. One of the biggest recovery challenges for the Louisiana Spirit staff was assisting survivors to establish a sense of community at these locations, which included establishing a healthy and psychologically nourishing environment for children and families.

In successful collaboration with the state and federal agencies responsible for managing the housing programs, the Louisiana Road Home Program was charged with bringing dislocated Louisiana residents back so they could reestablish their lives in Louisiana, preferably to return to their homes, or at least to their general residential areas. Louisiana Spirit staff worked closely with the Louisiana Family Recovery Corps, public and private schools, state agencies at the regional and district level, faith-based organizations, crisis line programs, first-responder agencies, and various community advocacy groups. Maintaining local, regional, and state-level collaboration with recovery agencies allowed Louisiana Spirit staff to be responsive to counseling and educational needs immediately. Examples of the diversity among the various agencies assisted by Louisiana Spirit include the Louisiana Supreme Court, foster care agencies, Louisiana's Department of Workforce Development, agencies providing domestic violence assistance, school boards and schoolteachers, local governmental units, and hundreds of faith-based organizations and churches.

In order to accomplish such a broad agenda, a workforce of over 600 counselors and outreach workers were recruited and hired through five core community-based agencies geographically divided throughout the state. A key to the success of this approach was to assure the staff hired reflected the cultural and demographic diversity of the survivor communities being served. Consequently, the Louisiana Spirit program became known as a people-helping-people approach, providing jobs and skills, which would further improve long-term recovery options for many survivors.

A key aspect of crisis counseling programs is to establish high visibility in communities. Besides providing direct services, the CCP model also uses educational and media strategies to establish the CCP as a resource available to everyone whenever they may need it. The result is that disaster survivors trust that help is available, thus developing a non-ambiguous perception of the availability of concrete support if needed for themselves or family members. Community outreach via brief educational/informational contacts and wide spread media public service announcements were modeled on the Project Liberty approach post 9/11.

The media plan for Louisiana Spirit was designed as a three-part initiative, which would parallel the three phases of recovery. The initial phase focused on recovery from Katrina's initial impact and reconciling loss. The initial theme, "You're Not Crazy," emphasized that it was normal to be overwhelmed with feelings and to have a difficult time accepting what had occurred; it was okay to be sad, and it was okay to talk about it. The intermediate phase, "Rebuilding Lives," transitioned away from acknowledging feelings of overwhelming loss to a message of rebuilding, using more uplifting messages and imagery. The final phase, "Neighbors Helping Neighbors," continued to reinforce hope and recovery and focused directly on individuals rebuilding communities by helping each other in their recovery. By urging survivors to reach out to each other, the implicit message was that not all people recover at the same rate, and some may need more time and assistance than others. The media project within Louisiana Spirit was unique to CCP models and demonstrated the importance of using well-designed media messaging to provide services and support to the general population.

CULTURAL AND LINGUISTIC COMPETENCY

Another innovative design feature of Louisiana Spirit was the overarching role of respecting and appreciating the cultural diversity among survivors, emphasizing the value of each person, their individual beliefs, and expectations. By focusing on the value of the individual, personal resilience was reinforced as a recovery strategy. Louisiana Spirit staff used cultural brokering communication methods for helping survivors and their new host communities learn about each other's culture, experiences, and expectations. Simple things like understanding importance of personal distance, language idioms, culturally specific foods, and spices being available in local grocery stores opened the doors of cultural awareness and facilitated the recovery process. A strategy for showcasing cultural differences and acts of valor during the hurricane was the publication of *Unsung Heroes*, a collection of stories describing individual acts of kindness from all areas of Louisiana during and immediately following the storm. The *Unsung Heroes* collection was distributed to libraries in all 64 parishes in Louisiana and the National Library of Congress as an unofficial anthology of community pride, resilience, and hope reflecting Louisiana's finest hour within its most challenging time.

SCOPE OF SERVICES

The Louisiana Spirit Immediate and Regular Services Program operations began September 1, 2005, and extended through December 31, 2008. During that time, 509,351 individual counseling contacts were made, 494,839 group counseling sessions were conducted, and 159,341 networking meetings were held in communities. Additionally, 2,822,179 brief contacts of less than 15 minutes were made with survivors, where outreach workers distributed 21,252,949 pieces of educational and informational materials. As discussed above, the major goals of the project were to reach out to survivors and to provide support and assistance in helping persons and communities recover from the catastrophic impact of Hurricane Katrina. The multifaceted strategy provided individually tailored services to special population groups with elevated risk factors for successful recovery, as well as general outreach and support to thousands of Louisiana residents. Over the last few months of the Hurricane Katrina response, Louisiana was struck by Hurricane Gustav on September 1, 2008, resulting in damage to areas of the state just recovering from the 2005 hurricanes Katrina and Rita. Fortunately, the Louisiana Spirit teams had not completely stopped services, and the program was refunded as a CCP activated in response to Hurricane Gustav.

SPECIALIZED CRISIS COUNSELING SERVICES

Through the outreach and counseling activities of the Louisiana Spirit program, it became apparent that a substantial number of survivors would need more intensive and structured services in order to move forward in their recovery process. These were individuals who reported intense storm experiences including fear for their lives, who had witnessed the death and injury of others, and/or who had family members who were still missing or were deceased as a result of the storm. For many survivors, recovery from these traumatic experiences were further complicated by the stress of their own recovery experience, extending for a period exceeding 12 months after the storm. Stressful recovery issues included their housing conditions, unemployment, and financial hardship. Many survivors continued to report experiencing depression, sleeplessness, poor concentration, and irritability. Survivors were frustrated with the day-to-day life challenges they were experiencing and needed more formal intervention in order to move forward. Referral to public behavioral health services was a limited option as Louisiana had lost many of its professional providers after the storm and had limited access to mental health providers in rural and storm-ravaged areas, as many of these professionals were also survivors were now displaced. In collaboration with the Center for Mental Health Services and FEMA, OMH developed an enhanced counseling model in the summer of 2007. The model developed was labeled Specialized Crisis Counseling Services (SCCS) and was loosely based on the enhanced treatment models developed as a part of the Project Liberty program, enhanced services in Florida after the historic storm season in 2004, and in Mississippi following Hurricane Katrina (Bassilios, Reifels, & Pirkis, 2012; Donahue, Jackson, Shear, Felton, & Essox, 2006; Jones, Allen, Norris, & Miller, 2009; Norris & Rosen, 2009).

The SCCS model in Louisiana was developed within a highly structured program design framework. In order to assure consistency with evidence-informed practice and successful organizational management, the Louisiana Spirit Compliance and Practice Directorate (PD) was formed. The PD provided expert consultation, and ongoing assessment of program needs, development of policy and procedures, training, data collection, and evaluation. The PD was comprised of Louisiana Spirit senior staff, Louisiana State University Health Sciences Center, Department of Psychiatry faculty, and faculty from the National Child Traumatic Stress Network and the National Center for PTSD. The SCCS (Riise et al., 2009) was based on the following operational principles as an enhancement of the existing CCP model:

- Provide services by team dyads of a master's-level counselor and a resource linkage coordinator.
- Use a solution-focused intervention model within a single session design construct.
- Deliver services within a culturally respectful context.
- Focus interventions on immediate practical needs and priorities of survivors.
- Integrate ongoing training and supervision into the intervention strategies.
- Emphasize the survivor being in charge of his/her recovery.

Referrals for SCCS services were accepted through Louisiana Spirit outreach teams. The model assumed a strengths-based strategy, primarily using the recently developed Skills for Psychological Recovery (SPR) intervention (Berkowitz et al., 2010). Cognitive-behavioral-focused traumatic stress interventions included the core skills of (1) gathering information and prioritizing assistance; (2) building problem-solving skills; (3) promoting positive activities; (4) managing reactions; (5) promoting helpful thinking; and (6) rebuilding healthy connections.

While an informal approach to service delivery was emphasized, the actual delivery of services followed a well-structured 10-step model. The 10 steps were (1) discuss availability of SCCS; (2) review privacy rights; (3) conduct an interview with the survivor; (4) obtain a release of information authorization from the survivor; (5) hold a team meeting; (6) provide SCCS services; (7) provide follow-up support as requested by the survivor; (8 & 9) direct and indirect resource linkage coordination; and (10) end SCCS services.

SCCS staff participated in weekly group consultation and training sessions with practice directorate members who provided didactic sessions on the delivery of specific core skills of SPR. Additionally, individual staff supervision was provided to clinical staff regarding service delivery by appropriately credentialed Louisiana Spirit staff. Fourteen *Fact-Sheets* were provided as quick reference guides for a range of child and adult interventions. The topics covered included social skills training, positive activity scheduling, enhancing social support, developmental progression for children, parenting skills, promoting leisure/recreational activities, motivational interviewing, problem-solving, grief and loss, cognitive reframing, emotional regulation, promotion of self-care, supportive strategies, and self-care. Each *Fact-Sheet* provided suggestions for when the intervention was appropriate, the skill sets necessary to use the intervention, the basic steps for using the intervention, and the measures of its effectiveness.

A unique feature of the SCCS was the use of a two-person team meeting with survivors. This established the interpersonal dynamic of one person focused on psychological support and skill acquisition, and the other focused on assisting with the practical access to needed recovery resources. Staff also received training on assessment and interviewing techniques, motivational interviewing, suicide assessment and prevention, substance abuse and referral, anger management, trauma reactions, vicarious traumatization, and terminating SCCS services. Feedback regarding the SCCS model and its utility was routinely solicited, and appropriate changes were continuously integrated into the program. Formal evaluation of staff trainings indicated that the strengths of the approach were the highly skilled and knowledgeable trainers, the specific skills taught, and feedback regarding actual case experiences. Counselors also strongly indicated that having a well-articulated and structured format for assisting survivors strengthened their ability to deliver more effective services and provided greater professional satisfaction in their work (Hansel et al., 2011).

Consistent with the overall philosophy of Louisiana Spirit, services were provided in settings of the survivor's choice and were flexible in design. However, as a more intense service model, the approach was structured around three basic objectives: engagement, empowerment, and recovery. The intervention began with discussions reinforcing the present reality, the importance of choice and decision-making, and the acknowledgement that making choices and decisions result in outcomes that can have positive or negative results. This approach helped survivors begin to take an active role in moving forward in their recovery by experiencing the value of choice and through making choices, experiencing empowerment and, through empowerment, personal recovery. The SCCS program provided initial assessments to 4,090 adults, with the majority of persons reporting being severely affected by the hurricane and their post-disaster conditions. Many reported being more stressed by the aftermath of the recovery process than the storm. Common issues were damage/loss of one's home, displacement, prolonged separation from family, being overwhelmed by multiple stressors, and health conditions. SCCS assessments were provided to 818 children. Many witnessed the destruction of their neighborhoods and homes, were evacuated and displaced, were transferred to unfamiliar schools, and lost their personal belongings. Over 70% of adults and children assessed for SCCS services chose to proceed with services. Reassessment after three and six visits indicated a significant reduction in severity of emotional/behavioral reactions to disaster-related events.

CONCLUSION

Hurricane Katrina shocked the nation with its destructive force and devastation to so many people and communities. The Louisiana response to the threat of Hurricane Katrina, its impact and aftermath, was complicated and lacking in relation to the catastrophic impact experienced by the state and its residents. In the nine years since Katrina, Louisiana has experienced Hurricanes Humberto (2007), Gustav (2008), Ida (2009), and Isaac (2010). With each passing storm season, the efficiency of enhanced planning and preparedness activities is evident. Sheltering capacity has evolved over the last few storms. For example, general shelters operated by ARC are capable of accommodating to the functional support needs of many residents who otherwise would be required to find a MSNS. Pet identification and sheltering has advanced, as have strategies for registering evacuees and keeping families together during the evacuation and sheltering process. Medical support resources and improved collaboration between federal and state operations have become more streamlined. Emergency response plans for hospitals and other health facilities are more realistic. Most importantly, the entire hurricane response culture has evolved within the state. Storms and pre-incident preparedness are addressed proactively across the vast majority of public- and private-sector entities, and by the general public.

From a behavioral health perspective, response strategies have improved, and an early and widespread behavioral health presence throughout all phases of disaster planning, preparedness, response and recovery is now in place. However, the trauma experienced by so many people after Hurricane Katrina remains a vivid memory for most, and a painful and terrifying unresolved traumatic memory for many in our state. The scientific literature on disaster behavioral health since Katrina has grown exponentially and provides helpful guidance to communities and individuals regarding preparation for disasters with disaster preparedness kits and plans.

A broad range of resources, in their early stages of implementation following Katrina have continued to evolve. For example, the American Red Cross (2014) offers excellent and interesting preparedness materials and activities that engage the whole family in planning for hurricane and other disasters. Psychological First Aid is an informed best practice with a growing evidence base regarding its utility (Allen et al., 2010). Cognitive-behavioral interventions are known to be effective with persons who have experienced multiple trauma exposures. Models such as Skills for Psychological Recovery have provided an evidence-informed structured approach that is effective in helping people temporarily overwhelmed by the recovery process.

Since Hurricane Katrina, the state of Louisiana has implemented revised models of the CCP program for Hurricanes Gustav (2008) and Isaac (2012). In both instances, the core design of the Louisiana Spirit outreach model and the SCCS model have been tailored to the unique recovery demands of persons and communities affected by these incidents. Today, an essential feature of any CCP in Louisiana is the professional Practice Directorate (PD) as a method for maintaining access to best practice models and guidance to CCP staff. The Center for Mental Health Services, Disaster Relief Branch has recognized this approach as most effective after Hurricane Isaac. Taken together, the practices for emergency preparedness planning and response are more nimble than they were nine years ago. Communication and clarity of roles and available resources enhances the likelihood of building successful immediate and long-term response to major disaster incidents.

REFERENCES

Allen, B., Brymer, M., Steinberg, A., Vernberg, E., Jacobs, A., Speier, A., & Pynoos, R. (2010). Perceptions of Psychological First Aid among providers responding to Hurricanes Gustav and Ike. *Journal of Traumatic Stress, 23,* 509–513.

American Red Cross. (2014). *Tools and resources: Disaster and safety library.* Retrieved April 14, 2015, from http://www.redcross.org/prepare/disaster-safety-library

Bassilios, B., Reifels, L., & Pirkis, J. (2012). Enhanced primary mental health services in response to disaster. *Psychiatric Services, 63,* 868–874.

Berkowitz, S., Bryant, R., Brymer, M., Hamblin, J., Jacobs, A., Layne, C., ... Watson, P. (2010). The National Center for PTSD and the National Child Traumatic Stress Network. In *Skills for psychological recovery: Field operations guide.*

Brinkley, D. (2006). *The great deluge: Hurricane Katrina and the Mississippi Gulf Coast.* New York, NY: Morrow/HarperCollins.

Brymer, M., Jacobs, A., Layne, C., Pynoos, R., Ruzek, J., Steinberg, A., ... Watson, P. (National Child Traumatic Stress Network and National Center for PTSD).

(2006, July). *Psychological first aid: Field operations guide* (2nd ed.). Retrieved April 14, 2015, from http://www.nctsn.org/content/psychological-first-aid

Centers for Disease Control (CDC). (2006). Assessment of health-related needs after Hurricanes Katrina and Rita: Orleans and Jefferson Parishes, New Orleans area, LA, October 17–22, 2005. *Morbidity and Mortality Weekly, 55*, 38–41. Retrieved April 14, 2015, from http://www.cdc.gov/mmwr/preview/mmwrhtml/mm5502a5.htm

Donahue, S. A., Jackson, C. T., Shear, K. M., Felton, C. J., & Essox, S. M. (2006). Outcomes of enhanced crisis counseling services provided to adults through project liberty. *Psychiatric Services, 57*, 1298–1303.

Federal Emergency Management Agency (FEMA). (2015). *Crisis Counseling Assistance and Training Program, FEMA.* Retrieved April 14, 2015, from https://www.fema.gov/recovery-directorate/crisis-counseling-assistance-training-program

Governor's Office of Homeland Security and Emergency Preparedness. (2009). *State of Louisiana emergency operations plan.* Retrieved April 14, 2015, from http://www.gohsep.la.gov/plans/EOP200961509.pdf

Hansel, T. C., Osofsky, H. J., Steinberg, A. M., Brymer, M. J., Landis, R., Riise, K. S., ... Speier, A. (2011). Louisiana Spirit Specialized Crisis Counseling: Counselor perceptions of training and services. *Psychological Trauma: Theory, Research, Practice and Policy, 3*(3), 276–282.

Henry J. Kaiser Family Foundation. (2007). *Major house-to-house survey finds New Orleans area residents hit hard by Katrina and struggling with serious life challenges.* Retrieved April 14, 2015, from http://kff.org/other/poll-finding/major-house-to-house-survey-finds-new/

Hietman, D. (2011). Hurricane Katrina. In KnowLA (Ed.), *Encyclopedia of Louisiana.* Retrieved April 14, 2015, from http://www.knowla.org/entry/539/&ref=author&refID=139

Jones, K., Allen, M., Norris, F. H., & Miller, C. (2009, April). Piloting a new model of crisis counseling: Specialized crisis counseling services in Mississippi after Hurricane Katrina. *Administration and Policy in Mental Health and Mental Health Services Research, 36*(3), 195–205. Retrieved April 14, 2015, from http://www.springerlink.com/content/bk721l75528133t7/fulltext.pdf

Masten, A., S., & Obradovic, J. (2008). Disaster preparation and recovery: Lessons from research on resilience in human development. *Ecology and Society, 13*(1), 9. Retrieved April 14, 2015, from http://www.ecologyandsociety.org/vol13/iss1/art9/

Nemeth, D. G. (2015). From chaos to community: The federal response—an account of Lieutenant General Russel Honoré's leadership during Hurricane Katrina. In D. G. Nemeth & J. Kuriansky (Eds.), *Ecopsychology: Advances from the intersection of psychology and environmental protection,* Volume 2 (pp. 5–13). Santa Barbara, CA: ABC-CLIO.

Norris, F. H., & Bellamy, N. D. (2009, April). Evaluation of a national effort to reach Hurricane Katrina survivors and evacuees: The Crisis Counseling Assistance and Training Program. *Administration and Policy in Mental Health and Mental Health Services Research, 36*(3), 165–175. Retrieved April 14, 2015, from http://www.springerlink.com/content/b01m07140151v537/fulltext.pdf

Norris, F. H., Friedman, M. J., & Watson, P. J. (2002). 60,000 disaster victims speak: Part II. Summary and implications of the disaster mental health research. *Psychiatry, 65*(3), 240–260.

Norris, F. H., Friedman, M. J., Watson, P. J., Byrne, C. M., Diaz, E., & Kaniasty, K. (2002). 60,000 disaster victims speak: Part I. An empirical review of the empirical literature, 1981–2001. *Psychiatry, 65*(3), 207–239.

Norris, F. H., & Rosen, C. (2009). Innovations in disaster mental health services and evaluation: national, state, and local responses to Hurricane Katrina. *Administration and Policy in Mental Health and Mental Health Services Research, 36*(3), 159–164.

Norris, F. H., & Stevens. S. P. (2007, January). Community resilience and the principles of mass trauma intervention. *Psychiatry: Interpersonal and Biological Processes,* 320–328.

Norris, F. H., Stevens, S. P., Pfefferbaum, B., Wyche, K. F., & Pfefferbaum, R. L. (2008). Community resilience as a metaphor, theory, set of capacities, and strategy for disaster readiness. *American Journal of Community Psychology, 41*(1), 127–150.

Pfefferbaum, B., Pfefferbaum, R., & Norris. F. (2010). Community resilience and wellness for children exposed to Hurricane Katrina. In R. P. Kilmer, V. Gil-Rivas, R. G. Tedeschi, & L. G. Calhoun (Eds.), *Helping families and communities recover from disaster: Lessons learned from Hurricane Katrina and its aftermath.* Washington, DC: American Psychological Association.

Plyer, A. (2013). *Facts for features: Hurricane Katrina impact.* Greater New Orleans Data Center. Retrieved April 14, 2015, from http://www.datacenterresearch.org/data-resources/katrina/facts-for-features-katrina-recovery/

Riise, K. S., Hansel, T. C, Steinberg, A. M., Landis, R. W., Gilkey, S., Brymer, M., ... Speier, A. H. (2009). *Specialized Crisis Counseling Services (SCCS) Final Program Evaluation* (Unpublished report). Office of Mental Health, Department of Health and Hospitals, Baton Rouge, LA.

SAMHSA (2005, November–December). *SAMHSA News.* Retrieved April 14, 2015, from http://www.samhsa.gov/SAMHSA_News

Speier, A. (2006). Panel presentation III at the Symposium on Mental Health in the Wake of Hurricane Katrina. In *The Twenty-second Annual Rosalynn Carter Symposium on Mental Health Policy* (pp. 66–68). Atlanta, GA: The Carter Center.

Speier, A. H., Osofsky, J. D., & Osofsky, H. J. (2009). Building a disaster mental health response to a catastrophic event: Louisiana and Hurricane Katrina. In K. Cherry (Ed.), *Life span perspectives on natural disasters* (pp. 241–259). New York, NY: Springer.

U.S. Congress. (2006). *A Failure of Initiative: Final report of the Select Bipartisan Committee to investigate the preparation for and response to Hurricane Katrina.* Retrieved April 14, 2015, from http://katrina.house.gov/full_katrina_report.htm

U.S. Department of Health and Human Services. (2003). *Mental health all-hazards disaster planning guidance.* DHHS Pub. No. SMA 3829. Rockville, MD: Center for Mental Health Services, Substance Abuse and Mental Health Services Administration.

4

Grassroots Leadership and Involvement: Experiences and Guidelines

Nara Crowley and Fernando Pastrana Jr.

One of the best definitions for delineating a true grassroots environmentalist is Roger Scruton's *oikophilia*—the love of one's home (Scruton, 2012). Oikophilia is the stimulus, but the word heard most often—tenacity—is the heartbeat of a grassroots environmentalist. Scruton (2012) analyzes and theorizes about the effects and interactions of governmental and nongovernmental organizations (NGOs) worldwide, and supports local initiatives as having the most successful outcomes.

A review of the literature that focuses on ecopsychology and environmental protection, shows that much thought has been dedicated to the future design of communities and their support systems. This chapter is devoted to understanding the mind-set, efforts, and challenges that small-scale environmentalists face while doing what they do because of the love they have for their home communities. It includes stories and accounts that inspired them to act. Also discussed are the roles of NGOs in social change, opposition that NGOs may face, and basic guidelines for organizing a grassroots movement, as well as the roles of the media, state bureaucracy, politics, and funding. The special case is presented of the efforts exerted to save Lake Peigneur, located in Louisiana near the northernmost tip of Vermillion Bay. The first author of this chapter is the president of this effort, called Save Lake Peigneur, Inc. (SLP).

LOCAL CITIZENS WHO BECAME GRASSROOTS ACTIVISTS

Grassroots activities are often initiated and led by local citizens who want to effect social change. The following stories of such activists—some in their own words—describe their commitment, inspirations, and challenges.

The Case of Mike Schaff and Nick Romero of Bayou Corne, Louisiana

Mike and Nick were living happy, comfortable lives working, fishing, and traveling until the day the earth literally swallowed their lives away. Nick had recently completed his new retirement home at Bayou Corne, a community 77 miles west of New Orleans, Louisiana.

Mike, Nick, and their families lived 2,500 feet away from the edge of the Napoleonville Salt Dome, the host for approximately 50 salt caverns that store a variety of hydrocarbon and brine mining materials. The outer wall of the brine cavern nearest to their homes was breached, collapsed, and began leaking. This resulted in the creation of a sinkhole that had grown to 29 acres and continued to grow as of this writing. Natural gas also began bubbling to the surface, both in the bayous and in the community. Over 300 residents have been permanently evacuated from their homes.

Some members of SLP and Wilma Subra, a chemist, president of Subra Associates, and founder of LEAN (Louisiana Environmental Action Network), who is renowned for her environmental work internationally, met with Mike, Nick, and several other residents shortly after the sinkhole first appeared. Although several residents were actively involved, Mike and Nick were the primary organizers to connect with officials, media, and other grassroots groups.

As families tried to get compensation from the company that forever changed their lives, they discovered that recovery and movement toward a new and different future would be challenging. This begged the question, how long can authorities keep citizens under an evacuation order before providing support for relocation and compensation? Also, as lives must be completely rearranged due to relocation, how can those affected be expected to cope with the intense stress and chaos for an undetermined time?

All the residents of Bayou Corne suddenly had to give up what everyone appreciates in life, including their space, daily routines, and family traditions. Residents evacuated to camping trailers, to the homes of friends and family members, and to hotels. Children had to deal with missing the joys of having their own rooms and backyards while having to simultaneously adapt to a new environment. These changes lingered for nearly two years.

Mike and Nick became active environmentalists by uniting the residents and organizing meetings. Retired lieutenant general Russel Honoré, who led Task Force Katrina in the aftermath of the devastating hurricanes of 2005, was at one of the earliest community meetings, which included SLP. This meeting became the impetus for the development of the Green Army, headed by Honoré.

Mike and Nick, as well as many other residents and local officials, were assured that weekly meetings would be held at which entities such as the

Louisiana Office of Conservation, the Department of Natural Resources, and Texas Brine (the company responsible for the storage caverns), would be invited in order to discuss the progress for finding a solution to the growing sinkhole and compensating the evacuated families.

One of the most selfless acts completed by Mike and Nick was to work on creating legislation assuring that, if a similar disaster occurred in the state of Louisiana, victims would not have to wait longer than six months to be compensated. This piece of legislation passed unanimously.

One might ask, what prompted Mike and Nick to take this type of action while still in the midst of their own personal crises? They indicated it was due to the anger they felt toward the incompetence and negligence demonstrated by the state and the company. They further reported a sense of satisfaction associated with the legislative action that was passed, knowing that it would positively affect the course of action for any future crises.

Mike, Nick, and many other residents had begun to move forward with their lives. At the time of this writing, both were involved with the Green Army and hope to continue to help make needed legislative changes that will be fair to both the citizens of Louisiana and the companies who bring economic growth to the state.

The Personal Account of Gloria W. Conlin of Abbeville, Louisiana

My husband was a football coach, thus our family moved a lot. We fell in love with the community of Abbeville, Louisiana. Over the years, I volunteered for different things because there was a need. The local library tax did not pass and there was going to be another chance to vote for a renewal tax. In one community, the tax did not pass and some libraries were closed. I thought we could not let that happen here. A meeting was organized to discuss the possibility of library closure. People realized that the libraries would not be able to operate without the tax passing. The tax passed. Our parish (in Louisiana, counties are referred to as parishes) Police Jury voted to develop a burn site less than two miles from a grammar school near my home. Again, community involvement was needed and we stopped the burn site.

My husband and his three brothers were coaches and teachers and I knew how hard they worked. When the state started bashing teachers, someone was needed to e-mail information around the state to keep school board members and teachers informed about various policies of the Department of Education. By this time, I was getting angry.

In 2011, I read what a company man said about the expansion and addition of two natural gas storage caverns under Lake Peigneur in the Jefferson Island Salt Dome. He was rather misleading. There was a need for more people to get the facts out. I e-mailed so much that a local TV station interviewed me and another lady who lived on Lake Peigneur. The TV station was planning to run the story for one week, but the company's public relations man went to the station and stopped the story. Of course, this made me very angry. So, I started e-mailing more and have not stopped trying to fight this expansion and addition.

Later, I began to learn about all the other problems throughout the state with pollution and how people are treated in the various communities. Lieutenant General Russel Honoré's involvement and development of the Green Army has given these people a chance to connect with other advocates for the environment and get their message out.

[When asked about what motivated her to become involved in helping her community, Gloria indicated it had to do with a combination of love, need, frustration, and anger.]

The Personal Account of Charlene Jannise of Gueydan, Louisiana

In 2010, I saw a public notice in the *Abbeville Meridional* that stated a saltwater injection well would be erected approximately one mile from my home and much closer to the homes of some of my neighbors. Despite never having been too concerned with the environment in the past, this raised a red flag for me.

The first person I was advised to call was environmentalist Mrs. Wilma Subra. She worked closely with me, advising me every step of the way. I called the Department of Natural Resources (DNR) and spoke to Mr. Joe Ball, who informed me that the only thing that could slow or stop the process was to start a petition, which I did. I went house to house in a seven-mile square area and began hearing horror stories of oil companies dumping waste into ditches near their homes and about loved ones that had died from rare cancers that were all linked to the environment. I also learned that this was not the first injection well near my home, but was in fact the fourth.

After having our public meeting, which was standing room only, I knew I needed some kind of counsel and contacted the Tulane Environmental Law Clinic, whose members introduced me to a superior aspiring lawyer. Our court date was set in November 2010 with the Nineteenth Judicial Court in Baton Rouge with Judge Timothy Kelly. After hearing the evidence, he ruled in our favor on the grounds that the DNR was rubber-stamping every permit coming through without considering the people of Louisiana. It was the first case won in our state and I am so proud to have been a part of it. We have now formed a group called Concerned Citizens of Louisiana.

The Personal Account of Hays Town of Baton Rouge, Louisiana

How and why I became an advocate to save the fresh drinking water aquifer beneath Baton Rouge.

While taking a hydrology course at Louisiana State University (LSU), I did a term paper on the Southern Hills aquifer system and the rumored saltwater intrusion into the fresh drinking water. I started this project by gathering information, first from the United States Geological Survey (USGS) in Baton Rouge. The managers at the USGS office were very helpful in furnishing numerous reports and studies of saltwater intrusion under Baton Rouge. Together, we discussed the challenges to the aquifer. Before leaving their office, it was evident to me that the aquifer was possibly not being managed in a sustainable manner.

That evening, after digesting the reports and studies, there was no doubt in my mind that the fresh water aquifer was in danger and that something needed to be done. After talking to all involved in this issue, including the Department of Natural Resources, the Commissioner of Conservation, and the Capitol Area Ground Water Conservation Commission (all of which are state agencies responsible for the management of these valuable natural resources), I concluded that all were unconcerned with the problem.

It was inconceivable to me that these governing bodies, responsible for the preservation of this wonderful natural resource, had known of the intrusion for many years and had done nothing to date. Furthermore, they had no plans to slow down or stop the salt-water intrusion.

To me, taking no action to save this natural resource for future generations was immoral. As a result, I began working to save this natural resource for the people of Louisiana.

THE ROLE OF NONGOVERNMENT ORGANIZATIONS (NGOS)

The previous section introduced a variety of homegrown grassroots organizers. Some simply organized as the need arose, others formed longstanding organizations, and still others were professionally driven from the onset. Additionally, the techniques used to achieve goals varied. Some organizations preferred quiet, methodical strategies, while others preferred drawing attention through various actions. From a personal perspective, I, Nara Crowley, prefer the slow methodical approach, as I have not observed rapid positive results via the use of demonstrative actions to publicize issues/concerns.

Over the years, technologies such as the Internet have allowed for more effective and efficient communication over long distances. As a result, I have been able to be in contact with numerous organizations worldwide. One such example is in the Finger Lakes region of New York, where small groups have united to fight the development of natural gas storage caverns at Seneca Lake. Another example includes the homegrown NGO in Connecticut that has been successful in preventing the dredging of the Connecticut River, which would permit barges to carry liquid natural gas upriver to Fall River, Massachusetts. An NGO in Germany prevented the development of additional natural gas cavern storage through diligent research. They were able to illustrate to government officials the potential environmental disaster related to cavern failure.

Fracking, a modernized version of drilling into shale for natural gas, has created a multitude of grassroots groups and has also inspired Hollywood films. *Gasland* (Fox, 2010), one such film and the first of two documentaries by Josh Fox, earned him an Oscar nomination.

Wilma Subra (the environmentalist introduced earlier) learned a lesson as a young chemist while working for the company that brought notoriety to upstate New York's Love Canal in the 1970s. The discovery of contamination by dumping 21,000 pounds of toxic waste into the canal in a community in Niagara Falls resulted in innumerable health issues including cancer, birth deformities, and miscarriages. Public outcry from the horror of the catastrophe resulted in a major movement toward environmental protection.

From that point on, Subra vowed to work toward establishing safe health measures in industry. One of her earliest actions toward protecting her home state was the establishment of the Louisiana Environmental Action Network (LEAN), now administrated by the very devoted Marylee Orr. LEAN is an example of a homegrown, one-person effort that has evolved to become a small but funded NGO and is one of Louisiana's leading NGOs, working with communities throughout the state. There are numerous NGOs that provide employment for many through contributions and grants.

Scruton (2012) discusses the effectiveness of large versus small NGOs. According to Scruton (2012), large NGOs tend to look at the big picture, or worldview. This is in contrast to small NGOs that tend to focus on local issues. He theorizes that the foundation for true change begins at the bottom, not the top.

FACING THE OPPOSITION: THE CHALLENGE OF GRASSROOTS ORGANIZERS

Understanding the opposition is a difficult task for small NGOs. Overall, the perception by small NGOs is that the opposition is an inhuman entity. The reason for this is reflected by the opposition's lack of interaction with the NGO. There appears to be a script that the opposition follows instead of open communication with NGOs. Typical opposition behavior includes bypassing NGOs and working directly with public officials as if NGOs do not exist. Large donations to the state, local government, or schools and terminology such as "good neighbor" are some examples that are typically found in opposition behavior.

Following the tragedy at Bayou Corne, the company involved gave out nylon bags to those affected, labeled with the company's name and containing miscellaneous promotional items commonly given out at conferences, such as writing utensils, manicure items, and tape measures. This fueled the perception of complete disregard for the residents' crisis. A more appropriate response would have been to assist residents with relocating their belongings and their lives. Yes, the residents received weekly compensation for their evacuation, but the money had to cover things such as hotel expenses and the relocation of personal items, which they had to manage on their own.

The question as to why the opposition bypasses the NGO likely stems from the fact that citizens have inherently turned to the state for protection against environmental harm and have not confronted the opposition directly. Unfortunately, in recent years, the local and federal governments have done less to protect citizens and the environment, which has led to a change of citizens' actions.

Bayou Corne's sinkhole disaster resulted in quick action by residents and local government. The state Office of Conservation, the Department of Natural Resources (DNR), and the company in charge became involved, but the governor remained incognito until nine months after the disaster. This event changed the lives of over 300 citizens.

As in all relationships, the bottom line is communication. Without communication, misunderstandings ensue and complications develop. Third-party mediators should be a last resort.

SLP (discussed in greater detail later) had requested numerous times over a seven-year period to meet and discuss the issues with the opposition. The dispute pertained to the development of natural gas storage caverns in the Jefferson Island Salt Dome under Lake Peigneur. The drilling company touted the economic benefits and offered information about how the caverns were safe. At the onset, SLP determined that safety was a primary criterion, but in the years that ensued, major issues such as drinking water quality for 15 parishes and the integrity of the salt dome became paramount.

The company sponsored meetings that were basically dog-and-pony shows and would talk to people only on an individual basis. Public discussion was out of the question. As a result, SLP sponsored numerous public meetings, including offering open forum discussions with opportunities for questions and answers. The company refused to attend. The company did, however, sponsor a very controlled public meeting with a local TV station anchor as moderator. Attendees were asked to sign in and give permission to be photographed—which we did not do, as photographs are often used to illustrate positive communication with the community and foster a positive image for the company's investors.

During the meeting, a microphone controlled by the company public relations person was delivered to select members of the audience. When an SLP member managed to intercept the microphone and ask a question, it was then passed to other SLP members. This created a problem for the company since we asked real questions regarding the major issues. The microphone was then promptly taken away from SLP members and the security forces that were hired to ensure civil obedience made their presence known. It should be known that several SLP members in attendance were senior citizens.

On one occasion, a local talk radio show invited both the company and SLP to an open discussion. The company refused to attend. The company did sponsor a dinner, but again information was provided and open discussion was limited. Questions that could not be answered, such as insurance questions, were sometimes answered via e-mail, if at all. Communications essentially stopped after the first few years, and most information was relayed through the Department of Natural Resources. In more recent years, the company became more courteous by informing SLP that maintenance or dredging would be taking place in the lake, but most communication involved verbal debates at various legislative hearings.

The company's position was clear; their efforts were to bypass citizens and convince politicians to work against their cause. In fact, they accomplished that goal with the one individual who actually represented the Lake Peigneur district. While outwardly supporting the citizens and their endeavors, this elected representative undermined them by voting against their bills and by directly lobbying for the company.

In 2014, a renaissance occurred. SLP and the company met in an unofficial, neutral location, which was a restaurant. Three SLP board members and two company officials ate at the same table, discussed their opposing issues, and attempted to come to a resolution. Compromise was necessary from both parties. A deep sense of distrust permeated, but both parties made sacrifices in an effort to move forward.

The resulting agreement, which was implemented via a legislative bill by a very supportive state senator, consisted of a two-year moratorium on permits that would create storage caverns. Also, the company would fund scientific studies selected by the company and SLP to determine the cause of the unknown bubbling occurring in Lake Peigneur as well as a study of the structural integrity of the salt dome. SLPs involvement in the selection process alleviated some fear that the company's funding would influence the outcome of the study. In 2016, we would know if our efforts to discuss and compromise was a step others should follow.

THE STORY OF EIGHT YEARS OF SAVING LAKE PEIGNEUR: THE FIRST AUTHOR'S PERSONAL ACCOUNT

In 2001, my husband and I found the home of our dreams a quarter of a mile, as the crow flies, from Lake Peigneur. Life was good until 2005, when I read an article in the local paper relating that nearby neighbors were fighting a company to stop the development of injection wells to create natural gas storage in the salt dome under the lake.

I only knew a few neighbors in my immediate area, so I contacted the president of Iberia Parish, who gave me the names of neighbors involved with the dispute. These neighbors lived on the side of the lake near the compressor plant. To my horror, I discovered that two natural gas storage caverns the size of the former Twin Towers in New York City already existed under the lake.

I attended a meeting that was organized and hosted by residents who lived on the side of the lake closest to the plant. No one living on my side of the lake seemed to take notice. In addition to the two aforementioned caverns created in 1994 that held billions of cubic feet of natural gas, there were plans to create caverns for millions more cubic feet of storage.

What I also discovered at my first meeting was the major catastrophe that occurred at Lake Peigneur in 1980. This event was big enough to make the *Modern Marvels: Engineering Disasters* show on the History Channel (2008). Before then, I was unaware of the magnitude of the damage to the Jefferson Island Salt Dome that occurred due to a miscalculation while drilling for oil. This event caused the once freshwater lake to be drained, creating the one and only over 100-foot waterfall in Louisiana, and drew in waters from the Gulf of Mexico forming the new brackish Lake Peigneur. Hundreds of people who worked for the Diamond Crystal Salt Mine at the time were left unemployed. Many years passed before the wildlife returned to the lake.

The community from the opposite side of the lake educated me regarding the caverns created in 1994. At a personal cost to residents, the Twin Parish Port Council in the town of Delcambre, located at the foot of Lake Peigneur, filed a lawsuit to stop the development of the caverns. The lawsuit was thrown out by a ruling that the suit was unconstitutional. Apparently, only the company's constitutional rights were violated.

Once again, wildlife was destroyed and the environment disrupted due to the dredging and creation of two natural gas storage caverns. More than four years passed before nature reclaimed its home. I decided to go door to door. I went to every neighbor on each street on the north side of Lake Peigneur, which was at least 50 homes. No one I spoke to knew that there were two natural gas storage caverns beneath our homes. Once informed, most became concerned.

The next step was to continue to attend the meetings already organized on the opposite side of the lake. My motivation to act quickly did not concur with the plan of the president of the community group. I volunteered to coordinate a public meeting and did so; however, the president of the group became angry that I had proceeded without further consent, which created a new problem. We had a very successful public meeting that included local officials and media, but I had overstepped my boundaries, and the group began to dissolve. Several of us remained connected and a new group was formed. The new president was the former vice president from the previous group, and I was elected vice president. Thus, the development of SLP began.

A few months earlier, members from the original group attended a public meeting sponsored by the company where they announced the potential for

23 caverns under Lake Peigneur. The company mistakenly thought this announcement would bring great pleasure to the community. This is one example of a complete misconception by the company of the residential community.

Approximately 4,000 residents within a one-mile radius of Lake Peigneur did not want the development of natural gas storage caverns under the lake. Following the gradual recuperation of Lake Peigneur from the 1980 disaster and the development of the 1994 caverns, which damaged flora and fauna, the lake had returned to an environmentally beautiful lake used for fishing and water sports. The possibility of the development of new caverns under the lake once again brought great fear to the residents.

The company's plant is located in the town of Erath in Vermilion Parish. The caverns are located in nearby Iberia Parish. As a result, two parishes and three towns are involved in the jurisdiction of the company's project, as well as the state of Louisiana, which has jurisdiction of all navigable waters in Louisiana. The company desired to make the state, Vermilion Parish, and Erath happy, and they did so initially by creating Palmetto State Park in Vermilion Parish. They also provided new fire trucks and school equipment to the town of Erath. The town of Delcambre was not included in compensation until many years later.

The community surrounding Lake Peigneur was disregarded, and most of all, the answers the residents sought regarding safety were not adequately addressed. For example, the community was told that, if an explosion were to occur, we would likely hear a small "poof" and a small flame would rise and dissipate into the sky without any repercussions. When the community asked why residents within a three-mile radius were evacuated following a Moss Bluff Salt Dome explosion or why flames could be seen 20 miles away, however, we did not receive an answer.

As SLP continued to develop, years were spent doing research. We spent months at the DNR office obtaining records. We quickly came to realize that record keeping was not a priority of the DNR. The documents were kept haphazardly in cartons requiring each and every document to be scanned and filed in its appropriate location. We currently have at least 40 boxes of research material should they be necessary for future litigation.

During our years of research, our scientific experts discovered a significant risk of salt-water intrusion into the Chicot Aquifer that could occur if the project to create new storage caverns at the Jefferson Island Salt Dome under Lake Peigneur were to move forward. This aquifer is the primary source of drinking water for 17 parishes. We also learned from USGS records that a 10-foot drop in the aquifer water level occurred within the four years of creating the two new caverns (the same amount that had previously taken 50 years).

In addition to our concerns for drinking water and safety, a new problem developed. In 2006, unusual bubbling began occurring in Lake Peigneur.

Long zigzag lines of bubbling ran across the lake in various locations. The lines could be anywhere from 20 feet long and a few feet wide to 3,000 feet long and 15 feet wide. The bubbling lasted from 20 minutes to over 24 hours. No one knew the cause. Normal lake methane bubbling appeared differently.

At personal cost, we hired a geologist who worked at a very low pay rate. This geologist, Dr. George Losonsky, provided additional expert testimony to Steven Langlinais, one of our hydrology engineer members of SLP. They concluded that the Chicot Aquifer was at risk for saltwater intrusion and that the Jefferson Island Salt Dome's structural integrity to hold natural gas cavern storage was in jeopardy.

Legislatively, we persistently worked to stop the development of new storage caverns. Following a meeting with then-Governor Kathleen Blanco in 2006, the company's lease with the state was terminated for nonpayment of rent and a lack of salt mining. Governor Blanco also stated she wanted a federal standard Environmental Impact Statement (EIS) before any permit was issued. Subsequently, Iberia Parish state representatives and senators filed several legislative bills. Iberia and Vermilion Parishes provided resolution after resolution to stop the development of storage caverns, but the state continued to process the application. The previous rubber-stamp process now had a few obstacles.

We vigorously sought support from other citizens, parishes, municipalities, congressmen, senators, and media. Convincing the media and citizens deeply committed to the oil and gas industry were our roadblocks. We contacted the media for every event dedicated to our cause. When bubbling appeared, we called, and they televised stories and wrote articles, and we wrote innumerable editorials.

The company received equal media time, bought space in local papers, and wrote articles that appeared to be written by a local reporter. Ultimately, we received over 4,000 letters from concerned citizens that were submitted to the DNR. Additionally, 52 parishes, municipalities, and state and federal officials submitted letters of support. As we appeared for various hearings for the Mineral Board and various House and Senate committees as well as the House and Senate, we had to request new letters from officials for each event.

In 2007, Representative Sydney Mae Durand attempted to pass a bill to stop the creation of natural gas storage caverns under Lake Peigneur. The following year, in 2008, Senator Troy Hebert passed a bill to protect our drinking water, which was signed and put into law by Governor Bobby Jindal. At the same time that our bill was moving through the legislature, the company had a bill written by two representatives from North Louisiana to create an agreement between the state and companies that developed natural gas storage caverns. Senator Hebert attempted to add an amendment exempting the Jefferson Island Salt Dome. His amendment was voted down. Our new local representative voted against the amendment. She pretended to be on our side but then worked against us.

The company sued the state for passing our bill, the judge ruled in favor of the company stating there were legislative technicalities that deemed the bill unconstitutional. The company's bill then passed. Subsequently, the state and the company entered into an agreement and the permit application moved forward.

Our next step involved attempting to stop the Operational Agreement from being approved. Once again, we had to pull together our letters and records and appear before the Mineral Board. We could not afford an attorney because we had already expended thousands of dollars on copying, scanning, and printing information for our records as well as providing informational materials wherever there was a need to inform others of our issue (including but not limited to hearings, public meetings, government officials, the U.S. Army Corps of Engineers, the USGS, and the media).

A wonderful young woman by the name of Judy Rosenzweig came forth and offered her services pro bono to represent us at the Mineral Board hearing. Our attorney, 4,000 letters, the officials' letters, and the data that supported our research proved not to be enough to stop the Mineral Board from approving the Operational Agreement. The Operational Agreement moved forward and an Environmental Impact Study (EIS) was required by the state.

A play on terminology by the state and company would convey to the media and public that they were satisfying SLP's desires for an EIS, but the state's EIS (Environmental Impact Study) differs considerably from the federal EIS (Environmental Impact Statement) in that the federal statement requires new data. SLP wanted up-to-date information and answers regarding the state of saltwater intrusion into the aquifer, the unexplained bubbling, and the integrity of the salt dome. This required new research, not old data.

SLP met with the USGS, and attempts were made to collect samples of the bubbling/foaming occurring in Lake Peigneur. The company did their own sampling and testing. USGS collected one sample that provided no answers for the source of the bubbling. The USGS laid a platform with testing vials in the bottom of the lake to obtain additional samples; however, the lines were cut and the platform disappeared. The Louisiana Department of Environmental Quality (LDEQ) provided the community with sample bottles and a boat. The boat was chained to the historic Rip Van Gardens pier. The boat was stolen.

The core group of SLP worked diligently together. Everyone had expertise and experience to offer. We could not have succeeded without complete team dedication. We all had busy lives with our professions and personal commitments; however, we all worked and pulled together as each need arose. We also encouraged teenagers to become involved in SLP. A granddaughter of a Board of Directors member became the first teenage Board member. She attended and spoke at hearings and started a youth group dedicated to SLP.

August 1, 2014, marked a success for our grassroots efforts in that Senator Fred Mills's bill, SB585, officially became Act 766 (described below) as signed by Governor Jindal. As of this writing, our next step was to work with the company to obtain the answers to the questions we asked before the moratorium.

Earlier, the development of the Green Army was mentioned during the Bayou Corn crisis. Lieutenant General Russel Honoré's leadership has led to unification of citizens throughout Louisiana who have been damaged by vast contamination and pollution in an effort to restore the state's natural health and beauty. Although many of us were in contact with one another prior to the Green Army, uniting under one umbrella required two facets: a notable figure, and the time to lead under one authority. Lieutenant General Honoré has been able to do this for the citizens of Louisiana.

The Details of Act 766 of 2014 (SB 585—Senator Fred Mills)

Act 766 (2014) reads as follows:

The legislation relative to enact R.S.30: 4 (N), relative to solution-mined cavern permits addresses the following: to require public notice for certain solution-mined cavern permits in Iberia Parish; to require a public hearing for permits to drill, expand, operate, or convert certain solution-mined caverns; to provide terms, conditions, and requirements; and to provide for related matters. Notice of intention to introduce this Act has been published.

[Section 1 R.S. 30:4 (N)] is hereby enacted by the Legislature of Louisiana, to read as follows: §4. Jurisdiction, duties, and powers of the assistant secretary; rules and regulations:

N. *(1) No permit to drill or operate a new solution-mined cavern, or expand or convert an existing solution-mined cavern in Iberia Parish may be issued until after a public hearing is held no earlier than August 15, 2015, on the application for the permit. The commissioner shall promulgate rules and regulations to provide for such public hearings and shall fix the date, time, and place therefor. The operator or owner, prior to such a public hearing, shall give public notice on three separate days within a period of thirty days prior to the public hearing, with at least five days between each publication notice, both in the official state journal and in the official journal of the parish in which the well is to be located.*

(2) At least thirty days prior to such a public hearing on a permit to expand or convert an existing solution–mined cavern or to drill and operate s new solution-mined cavern in Iberia Parish, the permit applicant shall submit a report to the commissioner of conservation, to Save Lake Peigneur, Inc. and to the governing authority of Iberia Parish. The report shall provide a baseline analysis of groundwater levels and salt content in the nearby groundwater wells that can be accessed for such analysis; a plan to monitor groundwater levels and salt water content for the duration of the activity for the creation of cavern storage should a permit be granted; a geologic analysis by a qualified third party geologist that examines the integrity of the salt dome; and the results of an analysis of testing that attempts to determine the source and composition of intermittent foaming or bubbling appearing in Lake Peigneur.

(3) No permit to expand or convert an existing solution-mined cavern or to drill and operate a new solution-mined cavern in Iberia Parish shall be issued prior to January 31, 2016.

(4) The provisions of this Subsection shall not apply to any activity or operation related to safety, maintenance, inspection, testing or regulatory compliance, when necessary, or when required by regulators.

A BASIC PLAN FOR BECOMING A GRASSROOTS ORGANIZER

The foundation of each grassroots organizer has been the ability to define a problem that is being disregarded by authorities. Subsequently, the question arises: Is there commitment to follow through on the plan to effect change? What is essential is "tenacity," a word introduced at the start of this chapter and that has been exemplified throughout in these examples. By definition, being tenacious denotes being very determined to do something ("Tenacious," n.d.). Relating to grassroots, tenacity also means making personal sacrifice. Grassroots leaders must also have support from their family and a team to work toward achieving the goal.

As each organizer has stated earlier in this chapter, the next major steps are informing and organizing a team. Most people are unaware of the issues surrounding them because they are busy working, taking care of their children, and living their lives. Most people do not have the time to commit, and generally, if their lives are overly busy as most people's lives are today, they prefer to ignore the problem. Most people will not act or support until a tragedy or near tragedy occurs.

Once the organizer has brought together other interested citizens, the team members must understand that they are all spokes of a wheel. The wheel cannot be supported without the spokes, and no one has more or less value. Each person is equal, including the leader. Every individual has a specialty. Sometimes that specialty will not be immediately apparent. The most important contribution, however, is attendance at meetings and hearings, and being present in general.

Once the group is organized, in-depth research of the issue is essential. This means researching any and all documents related to the issue. SLP spent thousands of person-hours and dollars copying, scanning, organizing, and compiling.

The following sections are devoted to discussing some of the challenges commonly faced by grassroots organizers as well as suggestions for meeting those challenges.

ADVICE ABOUT DEALING WITH THE MEDIA

Your local media must be your friend. Establishing a positive rapport is essential. There might be times when favorable reporting for your opposition will sting, but this is all part of the function of the press. Be prepared to write Letters to the Editor for publication.

The opposition may buy space and write articles that appear to be written by reporters. Counteract the opposition by writing letters to the Opinion page.

There will be incorrect information written or voiced on radio and TV stations. A nice thank-you note for the interview or story with a polite statement correcting the error will go a long way in establishing a working relationship.

Visit station managers and editors and provide them with background information on your issue and thank them for any story they might cover. Also meet with reporters and include them on your contact list.

Get the word out! A public meeting starts the ball rolling. Invite local politicians, media, and the general public. Have a sign-in table for those who would like to be on an e-mail list. Be prepared that whatever you e-mail will also go to your opposition, who will likely attend your public meetings.

ADVICE ABOUT DEALING WITH STATE BUREAUCRACY

The state may not be your friend. Most localized NGOs are ordinary citizens who have the hope that our federal government and states work for the benefit of the people. This may not be true. As Hays Town noted in his personal account above, none of the agencies were protecting the Southern Hills Aquifer. Although the potential for further contamination of saltwater into the Southern Hills Aquifer was a growing threat, none of the federal or state agencies made steps to protect the drinking water.

An NGO must first understand that laws have been written to protect industry. Therefore, the state agencies only follow the laws—sometimes. Part of the research is to determine if the agency is following or ignoring the law. If the agency is enacting a law that does not protect the citizens or environment, the NGO must work toward changing the law. If the law does protect citizens and the environment and the agency is not diligent in carrying out this responsibility, this negligence must be brought to the attention of the public.

ADVICE ABOUT POLITICS

As noted earlier, finding a politician who will truly work toward making changes that will protect citizens and the environment can be a difficult task. Citizens may give votes, but your organization must have strong influence for voting to go against companies that give huge donations to campaigns. Companies often give money to their employees, who in turn give it to the politicians, to avoid making public the actual figures that are donated.

A person within the NGO must be dedicated to knowing the laws as best as possible. After years, we still do not know the many tricks of legislation. Many companies have a bottomless pocketbook for lawyers and lobbyists.

ADVICE ABOUT FUNDING

Money is an essential component for winning an issue. As mentioned above, the opposition usually has limitless funding. NGOs should seek supporters, have fund-raisers, utilize the Internet, and find larger NGOs that can offer assistance. There are numerous methods for getting assistance, whether it is in the form of money or other resources. For example, some universities can assist with research, and perhaps young students will become involved.

The Louisiana Environmental Action Network (LEAN) became one of our greatest supporters and opened a door for us with Tulane University Environmental Law Clinic by joining us in a legal suit. We could not afford to retain lawyers for any suit and were fortunate to have a pro bono attorney in our early years to speak at the Mineral Board hearing.

In our final endeavor in 2014 as organizers, Green Army members stood by our side prior to our meeting with the company as we began our effort to bring forth our legislative bill.

ADDITIONAL ADVICE

Do not despair if the plan does not fall into place immediately. As of this writing, we had been working on our Save Lake Peigneur efforts for eight years. Supporters that become resources will come forward, but tenacity and patience are essential. In an interview conducted by the lead editor on Earth Day, 2014, William A. Fontenot, a member of the East Baton Rouge Parish Historic Preservation Commission, offered the following words of wisdom: "A lot of people get involved in these kinds of issues and they get just totally focused on it . . . remember that you need to stay healthy and you need to keep yourself in connection with your family and your friends and your neighbors . . . if you do it correctly, you can solve a lot of problems" (Fontenot, personal communication, April 22, 2014).

A FINAL NOTE ABOUT GRASSROOTS ORGANIZING

A grassroots organizer must be prepared for a small following. Understanding that one can be an oikophiliac without grassroots participation may be difficult. The reality is, most people who have worked hard to create the special living space they call home, generally love their communities. They also do care if their drinking water or air is clean, but not all people have the time or capability to become a leader or a member of an NGO.

Scruton's concept that small NGOs are not politically motivated is evident by the stories included in this chapter. In each example, the individuals became grassroots organizers because their concerns fell on deaf ears, so to speak.

Working within the various systems did not yield the desired results. These citizens were ignored, repelled, and often told half-truths. Their elected representatives were typically more interested in the companies in their districts than in the people who lived there. Therefore, they essentially decided to create a collective voice and take action on their own.

No matter how much passion you have in your issue, money still talks. Raising money to conduct activities is a challenge that must be faced and mastered. Most of all, however, people must present a strong, vocal, and united front in order to be heard. This requires holistic thinking and planning. Even if an individual does not wish to be a grassroots organizer, there is always a way to make a contribution. Ideally, environmental issues should not be politically motivated, but rather prosocially driven to protect the health and well-being of nature and humanity.

REFERENCES

Act 766 of 2014, 2014 Regular Session of the Louisiana Legislature (2014). Retrieved April 14, 2015, from http://www.legis.la.gov/legis/ViewDocument.aspx?d=9103 03&n=SB585%20Enrolled

Fox, J. (Director). (2010). *Gasland* [Motion picture]. USA: Independent.

History Channel (Director). (2008). *Modern marvels: Engineering disasters* [DVD]. USA: A&E Home Video.

Scruton, R. (2012). *How to think seriously about the planet: The case for an environmental conservatism*. New York, NY: Oxford University Press.

Tenacious. (n.d.). *Merriam-Webster.com*. Retrieved April 14, 2015, from http://www.merriam -webster.com/dictionary/tenacious

5

The Effects of Environmental Trauma on Our Thinking: Research on Cognition and Implications for Public Policy

Robin K. Gay, Darlyne G. Nemeth, Judy Kuriansky, Traci W. Olivier, and Chelsie Songy

The devastation caused by environmental trauma is pervasive and persistent, with long-lasting effects upon individuals, communities, and countries. On an individual basis, people's personal lives are disrupted on many levels. They may find themselves physically and medically compromised, emotionally traumatized, and separated from loved ones. As a result of trauma, lives are often lost, and livelihoods disrupted or demolished. Changes at the level of communities are also common, whereby entire groups of people are forced to evacuate and/or relocate prior to or following a disaster. More widespread, countrywide impacts also result, especially in the case of large-scale environmental traumas, where areas of an entire nation can be affected.

Despite numerous physical impacts, environmental trauma inevitably leaves a trail of untold psychological consequences. As Charles Cameron, senior analyst at the Arlington Institute, stated, "Tragedy or crisis is never purely economic, political, or military. It is always preeminently psychological" (Nemeth, Cameron, Creveling, Draeger, & Schexnayder, 2000). The psychological sequelae following a disaster impact individuals who are immediately affected, as well as the larger interwoven local and global communities of which they are a part. Acute and chronic prolonged psychosocial stress often accompanies physical and property damages. This can result in negative psychosocial changes. For example, people's day-to-day functioning becomes disrupted. Posttraumatic distress can result, expressed in several forms. Physical and medical problems can result. Occupational performance can be impacted. Interpersonal relationships may suffer distress. Financial stress is also common, with money problems adding further stress to other aspects of life. Overall, individuals' psychosocial functioning declines. These effects of trauma, however, as we are learning, are not the only ones. What recent research has discovered is that trauma also impacts one's ability to think.

The psychological consequences of such trauma are well-documented, albeit still not fully understood; what is less well understood, however, are the short- and long-lasting effects of trauma on cognition and the way that individuals process information. Although the primary focus during difficult times is on restoring the physical safety of those involved, the emotional safety of survivors must also be secured. Physical and psychological triage must occur concurrently to mitigate long-lasting effects not only for people's mental health and physical well-being, but also for their cognitive functioning.

BACKGROUND

One of the most recently devastating environmental disasters in the United States was Superstorm Sandy, which wreaked havoc along the East Coast. This storm impacted the lives of thousands close to the shoreline and resulted in unprecedented damage, especially in Staten Island, the southernmost borough of New York City, as well as in Rockaway Beach in the borough of Brooklyn, and in the shorelines of New Jersey. Besides extreme floods in these and other areas, blackouts and electrical outages were pervasive throughout New York City and the surrounding areas of New York and New Jersey. The effects of this overwhelming storm were felt by the residents in these and surrounding areas long after the storm subsided. Shoreline communities that had remained unchanged for decades were completely transfigured. Although assessment of the physical damage caused by the storm was important, there remained a strong need for mental health professionals to provide services to those affected.

Reestablishing psychological stability is often not given the same level of priority as is ensuring physical safety. In this chapter, we propose that physical stability and ensuring the emotional stability of those involved must be given equal priority. The effects of emotional states on overall health as well as the health of children have been well-documented, starting in the late 1950s by the many Kaiser Permanente studies (as cited in Cummings & Cummings, 2013). This awareness, however, has not seemed to affect changes in public policy for those affected by trauma.

Much attention has been focused on the psychological sequelae of major disasters. Post-traumatic stress disorder (PTSD), depression, anxiety, and sleep disturbances are all common among natural disaster survivors (Canino, Bravo, Rubio-Stipec, & Woodbury, 1990; Freedy, Saladin, Kilpatrick, Resnick, & Saunders, 1994; Green, Lindy, Grace, & Leonard, 1992; Kaiser, Sattler, Bellack, & Dersin, 1996). Fewer studies, however, have focused on the neuropsychological sequelae, for example, the effects on cognition, of environmental trauma.

More recently, research has begun to focus on the negative effects of trauma and prolonged stress on cognition. Exposure to trauma impacts the ability to problem-solve, the ability to process information, and attentional capacity

(Helton & Head, 2012). Therefore, one of the more unseen, subtle effects of trauma is the impact on thinking. These neurocognitive impacts have been highlighted by research examining the effects of PTSD (Eren-Kocak, Kilic, Aydin, & Hizli, 2009).

It has been pointed out that the long-lasting cognitive effects of such environmental traumas deserve more comprehensive examination and study (Brandes et al., 2002; Helton & Head, 2012; Liu et al., 2012; Nemeth, Hamilton, & Kuriansky, 2012). More varied and additional assistance from mental health professionals for those affected by environmental trauma is warranted, as few of the types of assistance that have been offered address the many cognitive issues that survivors face. This chapter addresses this issue and provides a brief review of currently available literature regarding the neurocognitive effects of trauma, as well as suggestions for how public policy may change in order to better address the needs of individuals who have experienced trauma.

CURRENT RESEARCH REGARDING THE NEUROCOGNITIVE SEQUELAE OF ENVIRONMENTAL TRAUMA

Findings from currently available research on the neurocognitive sequelae of environmental trauma reveal changes in memory, executive functioning, and attention. For example, Eren-Kocak et al. (2009) compared memory and verbal fluency in three groups of earthquake survivors. The three groups included earthquake survivors with current earthquake-related PTSD, a past earthquake-related PTSD group, and those who did not develop PTSD. They found that survivors with current PTSD had poorer memory and verbal fluency as compared to the other two groups.

Another group of researchers studied the effects of trauma on attention, before and after a 7.1-magnitude earthquake, and concluded that natural disasters negatively impacted cognitive performance (Helton & Head, 2012). Furthermore, attention span was found to be affected as much as one year later (Cassels, 2009). Additionally, other studies suggest that *duration* of PTSD was highly correlative with attentional differentiations (Sachinvala et al., 2000). Thus, the research shows that the neurocognitive effects of trauma are lasting, often continue long after the physical damage has been cleared away, and may extend past the expected period of grieving.

Studies suggest that cognitive issues resulting after a natural disaster must be addressed early in the recovery process. While chronic PTSD had been long associated with deficits in memory and attention, the association between acute PTSD symptoms and cognitive impairment was less clear. This led researchers to study the relationship between cognitive disorders and the time lapse after disaster. As an example, Brandes et al. (2002) proposed that cognitive symptoms associated with early PTSD symptoms may lead to poorer outcomes.

Their results showed that PTSD symptoms impacted cognition among survivors very soon after the disaster (i.e., no more than 10 days post-trauma). Additionally, these researchers found that cognitive symptoms were likely to lead to decreased ability to process the traumatic memories, which could be a contributing factor for the development of PTSD. Specifically, they found reductions in performance on measures of cognition that may have contributed to the development of PTSD. Furthermore, individuals with the greatest number of PTSD symptoms showed the largest decreases in performance on measures of attention and immediate figure recall. Yet, verbal recall and verbal learning were unaffected.

This research on cognition and PTSD suggests that the retelling of traumatic events and how they are etched upon memory is affected by cognitive performance. Additionally, in the Brandes et al. study, when depression was controlled for, meaning when they partialed out the effects of trauma on cognition that may have been a result of depression, this association was no longer present. These results suggest that depression may contribute to the development of cognitive symptoms and psychological disorders, such as PTSD. As decreases in attentional functioning were found to be associated with both early PTSD and depressive symptoms, the authors suggested that decreased attention may impact and shape traumatic memories. They hypothesized that, when individuals cannot attend to and process trauma, they are unable to create a narrative that can lead to healing.

The Long-Lasting Effects of Trauma

The neurocognitive sequelae of trauma may persist for years, long past the actual event. In another study, researchers followed the neurocognitive effects of trauma on soldiers who were on deployment (Vasterling et al., 2006). In this study, 268 men and women were followed from the year 2002 on for several years. Results revealed that increased PTSD was associated with decreased attention one year later. Interestingly, the study revealed that duration of PTSD, not severity, correlated with the greatest cognitive effects. Individuals with long-lasting PTSD, even if less severe, showed the greatest decreases in attentional functioning. In other words, the lasting effects of continued hypervigilance as a result of trauma took a significant toll on cognition, resulting in diminished attentional performance years later.

Stress, Cognition, and Human Performance

Research has demonstrated the clear link between trauma and subsequent stress as well as the presence of cognitive intrusions. As noted in research by Helton, Head, and Kemp (2011), however, past studies do not examine in detail the effect of trauma-induced stress on human performance. To address this, these researchers assessed the impact of a 7.1-magnitude earthquake in New Zealand on self-reports of cognitive impairment as well as the relationship of these reports to observed performance. They asked individuals who had experienced the earthquake to perform a cognitive test (measuring reaction time) and to provide a self-report of their performance. Individuals performed more poorly after experiencing the earthquake, although they thought they had performed better than they actually did. The results showed that cognitive self-regulation was affected beyond the level of conscious control. Here again, the effects of trauma on the ability to think clearly and on attention are evident. This type of research is important because it shows that individuals suffering from the cognitive effects of trauma may be more likely to react in ways that lead to more trauma as well as to an increase in accidents.

Increases in Accidents Following Environmental Trauma

Increases in accidents following trauma have been shown in research. For example, while Helton and Head (2012) were investigating the effects of trauma caused by tornadoes, their research team happened to be present during an earthquake that occurred in the area of the tornado. Thus, they were able to take measures of cognitive performance of survivors before and after the event. As they had already gathered a sample of cognitive performance after the earthquake, including changes in reaction time, they were able to use this data to compare to data on reaction times they collected after the tornado. The results showed that several types of cognitive errors, including errors of commission and reaction time correlated to the level of stress response the individual had experienced. Specifically, individuals who were anxious appeared to be less careful and made more errors. Conversely, people who responded to the natural disaster predominantly with depression had slower reaction times. This study demonstrates how emotions related to a trauma, whether depression or anxiety, affect cognition.

Of note were the types of errors varied by levels of experienced anxiety or depression due to increased cognitive load. To explain this, cognitive capacity can be conceptualized as a finite resource, such that too many demands placed on the system result in an overload and decrease in performance. These findings can be easily compared to the well-documented increase in accidents when people drive and talk on their cell phones, which similarly creates an increased cognitive load. For example, a few years ago, the second author was involved in a serious motor vehicle accident wherein the car she was driving was hit broadside. This caused her car to spin around multiple times before coming to a stop. Although this process prevented serious injury to the driver, her car was totaled. The young driver, who was held responsible and ticketed, had run a red light as a result of allegedly being distracted by his cell phone.

In a similar way, people may be cognitively processing information and emotionally preoccupied with the aftereffects of natural disaster while they are attempting to perform other tasks. This could also lead to an increased cognitive load and increased error potential. This potential error rate can have serious consequences and can sometimes even be deadly. Supporting this point, research by Helton and Head (2012) found evidence that people make more errors after a trauma, including dangerous ones. The researchers found that the number of car accidents rise for some period after an environmental trauma has occurred. They hypothesized that this happens because people may be "zoning out" while driving. Thus, as people attempt to return to activities of daily living and their previous work positions, serious unintended consequence of impaired cognitive performance may ensue.

These results are also important with regard to the functioning of first responders in a disaster. First responders are not immune to errors in cognitive performance, as they themselves are affected by the stress caused by the trauma and may be preoccupied with their own emotional response. As a result, the likelihood of mistakes can increase, which impairs their ability to perform their important and lifesaving duties. Helton and Head (2012) suggest that communities focus on these risks and develop measures to circumvent the negative consequences of distraction caused after natural disasters. Identifying those individuals most at risk, as well as developing methods to insulate them against such risks, is essential.

Cognitive Effects of Trauma in Children

Identifying those most at risk is even more important when considering the effects of trauma on children. Research shows the need to better understand the unique effects trauma can have on children. Since their brains are still in the process of developing, children exposed to trauma are especially vulnerable (Enlow, Egeland, Blood, Wright, & Wright, 2012). The particular risk for children is that exposure to trauma impacts their developing brains and hence their later ability to perform cognitive tasks as efficiently as they would have otherwise. Although it is clear that childhood exposure to trauma can result in lasting cognitive effects and impairments in functioning, what is less well-understood is the timing of the trauma on the developing brain and the effects at different stages of brain development (Enlow et al., 2012). Research is needed to clarify the effects of trauma on children at different ages, and how to reduce this stress.

According to linguists Chomsky (1957), Lenneberg (1964), and other developmental psychologists (Grimshaw, Adelstein, Bryden, & MacKinnon, 1998; Hurford, 1991), there are certain critical periods in infant brain development. For example, if the infant is not exposed to specific stimuli, like spoken language or visual field depth cues, these abilities will either not develop or be severely impaired. Likewise, children's ability to perform cognitive tasks occurs on a more or less specific timeline. Some cognitive processes develop first, while others occur later on in the child's development. For example, executive functioning (e.g., problem-solving) does not emerge in a fully developed manner until early adulthood, as certain areas of the brain responsible for executive functioning—the frontal lobes—are the last area of the brain to compete the process of myelination. Myelination serves as the protective sheath surrounding the nerve axons that allow neurons to communicate. In this way, the sheath acts similarly to the plastic surrounding electric cables.

The full effects of trauma on the developing brain and how trauma may impact brain development at different ages are not fully known. Therefore, policies that are developed in the hopes of effectively ameliorating the negative effects of trauma on children need to incorporate specific interventions that are age-appropriate for the developing child's brain. Some research has attempted to understand this process. For example, Enlow et al. (2012) sought to understand the specific effects of trauma on brain development in the early years of life. These researchers performed a study to examine the impact of interpersonal trauma exposure on cognitive development and functioning.

Interpersonal trauma specifically relates to abuse, witnessing abuse, or maternal partner abuse. Witnessing abuse or trauma has an effect on children's developing brains even when they are not directly affected by the trauma. What is relevant to understanding the effects of environmental trauma is that the impact of natural disasters often creates a stressor that allows for already-dysfunctional relationships to experience more volatility. Witnessing this volatility has the potential of negatively impacting the developing child's brain. Children of parents who have lost their homes or livelihoods, or who have even experienced the loss of a loved one, are also witnessing or experiencing trauma that may affect their cognition.

Enlow et al. (2012) studied over 200 children exposed to interpersonal trauma and followed them over a period of 96 months and tracked their IQ scores. The children's IQs were assessed with age-appropriate forms of IQ tests at several discrete time periods, namely, at 24, 64, and 96 months of age. The results showed that, at each assessment period, those children who had been exposed to trauma revealed decreased scores on the administered cognitive tests. The researchers had statistically controlled for other factors, such as cognitive stimulation at home and birth complications, which may have impacted the results. The conclusions were startling; namely, that exposure to interpersonal trauma was especially detrimental within the first two years of life. This research also has implications for children exposed to environmental trauma, as witnessing this type of trauma also likely affects cognitive development.

The study revealed that the IQs for children exposed to trauma within the first two years of life was significantly lower when compared to children who had not been exposed to trauma. In fact, there was a full half standard deviation —7.5 standard score points—of difference between the two groups of children. This amount of difference was large enough to place children exposed to trauma in the below-average range of intellectual functioning compared to children not exposed to trauma. As the period before the age of 2 is especially crucial for later cognitive development, public policy should specifically focus on interventions that mitigate the negative effect of trauma on children.

Effect of Children Witnessing Trauma

Additionally, if interventions are not targeted toward these children, they run the risk of being perpetually left behind in intellectual and academic performance. Children who are at such an early disadvantage will likely have a more difficult time "catching up" if the effect of the trauma is not appropriately attended to and mitigated. If not addressed, these traumatic effects have the potential of leaving a lifelong impact on those exposed. As such, this research has major public policy implications.

EFFECTS OF ENVIRONMENTAL TRAUMA ACROSS THE LIFESPAN

Epigenetic Research

Understanding the effects of environmental trauma is especially important in light of new evidence that the experience of our ancestors may impact both the cognitive and genetic expression of future generations (Rudenko & Tsai, 2014). Thus, the epigenetic effect that trauma can pose is real. Epigenetics refers to alterations in gene expression based on the lived and felt experience of one's direct ancestors. Transition of material from one generation to the next that is not in our DNA is called transgenerational epigenetics, an emerging area of interest and research (Kollias, 2014). This new understanding suggests that what individuals experience and do to their bodies may cause changes in the access and expression of genetic material of their offspring. According to this theory, damage to an individual's body, by excessive use of alcohol or smoking, not only damages the individual's body and health, but also changes the expression of genes and, potentially, the expression of the genes in one's offspring. Therefore, if the causes and impacts of stress are not addressed by the present generation, this can impact generations to follow. Whereas it was previously believed that individuals could abuse their body with alcohol or excess food and still produce offspring who are genetically healthy, it is now known that permanent changes in the gene expression in one's offspring can result from the treatment and care of the body in one's life. In this way, stress not only affects our own health, but the health of our offspring as well.

A striking example of this theory involves people conceived during the Dutch famine in 1944. The children of those people who lived during the famine had greater rates of glucose intolerance, obesity, and cardiovascular health problems when compared to people who were not born from parents who lived during the famine. This was discovered in a longitudinal research study by Lumey et al. (2007), where researchers compared the health of those whose ancestors lived through the famine to that of a group who did not. The findings showed that the bodies of parents who lived during the famine, on a cellular level, learned to use glucose more efficiently in order to survive. The bodies of the children born to them, and their children's children, however, also used glucose more "efficiently" on a cellular level, even though they had never experienced a famine firsthand. As such, generations later, people whose direct relatives lived through the famine were prone to higher rates of diabetes, obesity, and heart problems (Lumey et al., 2007).

Other epigenetic research demonstrates that the early experience of parental caregiving can impact the caregiving style and expression of intelligence in subsequent generations of mice (Masterpasqua, 2009; Szyf, McGowan, & Meaney, 2008). What is important about these studies is that abuse and neglect in mice models have been shown to result in cognitive and emotional changes, revealing how genes are expressed in generations to follow. This research has important implications for human modeling and parenting, which, for obvious ethical reasons, cannot be experimentally researched. As such, if parents are victims of prolonged stress, the effects can transfer to the generations that follow (Masterpasqua, 2009; Szyf et al., 2008). Thus, the effects of environmental trauma may impact not only the present generation, but generations born after the trauma.

As newer research confirms these findings, and the importance of understanding the cognitive as well as emotional and physical effects of environmental trauma, and its intergenerational sequelae, it may be possible to mitigate more long-lasting negative effects of such traumas.

Prenatal Maternal Stress and Cognition

Studies have shown that prenatal maternal stress has negative consequences on the development of offspring (King & Laplante, 2005). These effects include negative impacts on physical development as well as decreased cognitive capacity and subsequent problems in behavior. Yet, what has not been studied is the effect of stress from natural disasters on prenatal infant development independent of maternal, possibly genetic, styles of reacting to trauma. To explore this, researchers followed 150 children in a project entitled "Ice Storm" (King & Laplante, 2005). This study examined mothers who were inadvertently exposed to environmental trauma while carrying offspring in utero. This type of study illuminates the impact of trauma on future generations and reveals unforeseen consequences. Such research is important as it points to long-lasting effects of trauma that span generations to come and serves to further highlight the need to develop measures and interventions that can help to ameliorate the effects of environmental trauma. Knowing that implementing public policy that aims to ameliorate the long-term effects of trauma will affect our children and children's children, highlights the importance of these measures. As such, public policy needs to address the long-term effects of stress and trauma.

Cognitive Functioning in Adults Following Childhood Trauma

Majer, Nater, Lin, Capuron, and Reeves (2010) investigated the long-term impact on adulthood of exposure to childhood trauma. They hypothesized that cognitive deficits resulting from childhood trauma may leave people at greater risk for developing psychological problems later in life, especially depression and PTSD, which are both disorders known for having corresponding changes in cognition. This area of investigation has received very little attention in the field of ecopsychology. Studies of this nature are especially important as they highlight the long-range and far-reaching consequences of trauma on the lives of those affected.

Specifically, individuals who were exposed to trauma early in life may have increased risk of poor cognitive performance later in life. Arguably, these individuals are more at risk for developing severe negative consequences as a result of natural disasters. Majer et al. (2010) examined cognitive performance in a group of adults who were administered trauma questionnaires and measures of cognitive performance. The results showed that the specific type of trauma experienced was related to specific types of impairments on cognitive tasks. For example, emotional abuse was correlated with poorer performance on spatial working memory tasks, while physical neglect was associated with decreased spatial working memory functioning as well as decreased pattern recognition memory.

These findings suggest that emotional abuse as well as physical neglect may lead to decreased memory into adulthood. Further, Majer et al. (2010) postulate that these deficits in memory may pose particular susceptibility to the development of mental illness in adulthood. If exposure to abuse in childhood leads to increased vulnerability for mental illness later in life, then, in a similar fashion, exposure to environmental trauma in childhood may make such individuals more prone to mental illness. Public policy needs to more carefully consider the consequences of natural disasters and environmental traumas that affect thousands of individuals and children. As research has begun to show, trauma experienced in childhood may lead to populations being at greater risk for the development of psychological disorders. Thus, public policy can benefit greatly from intensive and timely longitudinal studies of the effects of such environmental trauma.

WHAT NOW, WHAT CAN WE LEARN, AND HOW CAN WE HEAL?

A Step toward Physiological Healing

Now that the possible long-term consequences of trauma on cognition for the present and future generations are recognized, it is important to consider what can be done to prevent such damage. Research by Liu et al. (2012) sheds light on this issue, in their findings that chronic stress has a negative effect on brain anatomy and function. Research has begun to show that stress may affect the brain at the neuronal level, thereby influencing the development of psychiatric disorders such as PTSD. As PTSD has a known cognitive component, in that it affects individuals' memory, attempting to understand the brain mechanism by which this happens may shed light on treatment for this disorder. These researchers found that chronic stress may lead to the development of PTSD by interrupting type 2 ryanodine receptors in the hippocampus, which is the area of the brain most often associated with memory functioning. These receptors control the flow of calcium into the cell, which is a fundamental process involved in the synapse and neuronal survival. Reversing this flow of calcium, which is disrupted as a result of PTSD, may be a way to help individuals recover from PTSD.

A Step toward Psychological Healing—Healing through Storytelling

As research has begun to show the negative consequences of trauma on our thinking and ability to process information, more attention will need to focus on what individuals and communities can do to ameliorate these negative effects. Two important aspects of healing relate to the stories people create as well as to their connection to their community. Stories of strength and survival, as opposed to those that focus on victimhood, strongly contribute to the healing process. The stories people create are strengthened if they can be formed into a group narrative. Thus, one way to heal in the event of trauma is to have a strong connection to other people who have just had similar experiences. The narrative stories told by people, individually and collectively, greatly affect our thinking and ability to recover from trauma. Telling these stories can be facilitated by techniques such as drawing, music, group interaction, and dance.

E. O. Wilson, a leading contemporary biologist, said during a 2013 National Public Radio (NPR) interview, "We're all storytellers, you know, all of us, from the novelist, to the artist trying to say something new and take us in a new direction on canvas, to scientists who have discovered something." He said that humans have an instinct for storytelling. "Everything in the mind is a story" (Wilson, 2012).

The healing impact of the combination of group sharing and activities, relaxation exercises, and artistic expression of drawings and music has been shown in wellness workshops conducted after Hurricane Katrina (Kuriansky & Nemeth, 2013; Nemeth, Kuriansky, Reeder, et al., 2012). These workshops were held for survivors on the one-year anniversary of the trauma. The authors stated:

> Participants shared the tragedies that they and their families had witnessed and/or endured during and since Hurricane Katrina. Being heard by others in a group setting was an extremely important part of the healing process. Almost all participants had lost loved ones, and many had been stranded in New Orleans for several days, if not weeks, with no food or clean drinking water, prior to their rescue. Most participants reported not having had their suffering validated by anyone. Utilizing the container-contained model of intersubjective thinking . . . was very helpful. This created group process allowed feeling, thinking, relating, and skill building to flourish. Via a tripartite group format—group-as-a-whole, fishbowl, and small groups—participants were able to spend equal amounts of time learning, doing, and relating. The exercises allowed both a cognitive container (i.e., structure) and an affective freedom of expression in a contained (i.e., safe) environment to emerge. Participants were able to express their anxieties and frustrations. Via group process, participants began to understand how their thoughts and emotions were interrelated. They also learned specific stress-relieving techniques for coping, including deep breathing and relaxation strategies, and ways to combat negative thoughts and feelings. Overall, by the end of the workshop, participants expressed appreciation and enthusiasm for their group experiences. Several participants vowed to become proactive in order to deal with the problems of their life situations. The obvious reductions in anxiety and the increased community attachments displayed by participants were clear markers of the value of the anniversary reaction group intervention process (Nemeth, Kuriansky, Reeder, et al., 2012, pp. 137–138).

Nemeth, Songy, and Olivier (2014) adapted the Hurricane Katrina Anniversary Wellness Workshops to address healing among a group of post-trauma, neurocognitively impaired individuals. The authors purported:

> Group therapy can help patients to restore hope, allowing hopelessness to fade. Group therapy also provides members with an opportunity to relate to, share with, and care about one another when facing similar issues . . . group therapy can increase self-esteem, hope, and well-being . . . Realistic hope allows patients to see alternatives and solve problems . . . and is inextricably linked to one's sense of self-esteem (i.e., self-worth). Supportive group therapy can provide neurocognitively challenged individuals with the opportunity to reframe their sense of self. Feelings of hope can be sabotaged by trauma . . . yet hope must be rekindled to maximize neurocognitive recovery (Nemeth, Songy, & Olivier, 2014, pp. 3, 4).

Facilitation Rather Than Direction

Studies by Nemeth, Kuriansky, Reeder, et al. (2012) and Nemeth, Songy, & Olivier (2014) suggest that using healing narratives (e.g., storytelling) in a group wellness workshop format can be effective in ameliorating both the psychological and neurocognitive effects of environmental trauma. The researchers caution, however, that facilitators should inquire only about what the experience meant for the individuals and let them entirely construct their own narratives. This form of storytelling is a part of the healing process and helps avoid the possibility of revictimizing individuals and communities affected. Instead of stories of victimization and powerlessness, some individuals are able to construct narratives of helping and healing others, which gives them a feeling of control and purpose.

Care needs to be taken so that, instead of asking questions that lead to the individuals' identifying with the facilitator's expectations of how they should feel, questions are open-ended and serve only to elicit the individuals' subjective experiences of the trauma. In other words, survivors of trauma must be allowed to tell their stories. For example, the second author (Nemeth) was attending a meeting of the World Council for Psychotherapy (WCP) in Buenos Aires, Argentina, when Hurricane Katrina hit the Gulf Coast of the United States in August 2005. She watched in horror the devastation on Argentinean television. In a personal recounting of the situation, she stated:

> I felt so guilty for being away and for being safe. Then I was asked by the WCP Executive Council to attend a Non-Governmental Organization (NGO) meeting at the United Nations in New York City wherein Hurricane Katrina would be discussed. WCP was in the process of introducing a resolution, at the U.N, on Emotional Suffering. When I arrived at the Baton Rouge Metropolitan Airport, it had become the busiest airport in the United States. Helicopters. First Responders. Confusion. Elderly blind women in wheelchairs separated from their seeing eye dogs. Complaints. Chaos. Complaints. Hysteria, and more complaints. No solutions were forth coming. Some of the female first responders had congregated in the women's restroom to regain their composure. I entered unknowingly. Without identifying myself as a psychologist and without making any attempt to offer psychological first aid, I merely said, "Thanks for all you are doing." The flood gate opened and several hours later, having born witness to their pain, I left the restroom.

Use of the Arts in Healing Cognitions

Performance and arts therapy activities, including music, drawing, and dance, have been shown to be very useful in trauma recovery, especially with youth (Kuriansky & Jean-Charles, 2012; Kuriansky, 2013a; Nemeth, Kuriansky, Reeder, et al., 2012). Research has found that alterations of brain activity add to the healing response, not only by creating relaxation but by altering neurotransmitter pathways in the brain (Salimpoor, Benovoy, Larcher, Dagher, & Zatorre, 2011). The anticipation of listening to music releases dopamine from the caudate part of the striatal system of the brain, which is involved in emotional integration, learning, and memory. Changes may be observed in the autonomic nervous system during "peak emotional response," as demonstrated by chills or changes in heart rate. This releases increased dopamine in the nucleus accumbens, an anatomical area of the brain associated with stress release, pleasure, and reward (Salimpoor et al., 2011). While research on brain functioning shows that just as brain injury can cause cognitive symptoms as headache, dizziness, vertigo (i.e., a sensation of *spinning* around), confusion, and decreased concentration and attention, selected physical activities can stimulate brain function and chemical reactions in the body. These activities can restore brain function, e.g., by the release of adrenalin and endorphins that can result in a sensation of pleasure in the brain and body. The activity of drawing further triggers creativity and concentration that leads to new connections in the brain, and occupies the mind, that in turn lessens dysfunctional cognitive symptoms. This principle, the third author (Kuriansky) believes, helps explain the effectiveness of the workshops she has been conducting with youth around the world after disaster. The exercises in those workshops, described in Chapter 9 of this volume about the Global Kids Connect Project (Kuriansky et al., 2015), and in other articles, are intended to engage the physical body and mental state, through a combination of mental occupations and physical movements intended for distraction and focusing on positive thoughts as well as experiencing enjoyment. Stress reduction from both natural and man-made disasters results from learning specific psychological exercises and also through engaging in activities like singing, music-making, and dance movements. One particular activity for children involves creating an object that is sent to other youth suffering from similarly difficult circumstances. Such activities reduce personal distress and also facilitate feelings of connectedness, and that others care, and promote healing. These have been shown to be applicable in a variety of settings with varied populations worldwide (Kuriansky, 2006a, 2007, 2008, 2010, 2012c, 2012d, 2013a; Kuriansky & Jean-Charles, 2012).

Treatment through Cognitive Structuring—Additional Ways to Heal

If one of the main ways we can heal from trauma is by being cognitively ready to process the emotional experience and create a narrative for it, then it is paramount that this process is not circumvented by trauma survivors' inability to cognitively perform these tasks. Few studies have been done on the use of cognitive structuring as a method of treating the effects of trauma. Most prior research focuses on treating the cognitive correlates of mental illness, such as the cognitive changes resulting from schizophrenia, depression, obsessive compulsive disorder, or eating disorders (Sibel & Cummings, 2002). If cognitive changes may, in fact, underlie and be risk factors for the future development of mental illness, then one way of treating the effects of trauma may be to provide early interventions that target cognitive functioning. When cognitive functioning is intact, people are more resilient and better equipped to deal with the prolonged stress that results from environmental trauma.

Cognition and Sleep

Cognition can be negatively affected by poor sleeping patterns, and sleep is often disrupted after environmental trauma. People are usually unable to sleep in their own beds with their usual sleep patterns. Superstorm Sandy, Hurricane Katrina, tornadoes, and earthquakes typically result in dislocation whereby personal safety and security are at risk. In the presence of acute fear, sleep is usually not an option unless, of course, people fall asleep due to pure exhaustion.

Charles Czeisler, PhD, MD, FRCP, chief of the Division of Sleep Medicine at Brigham and Women's Hospital and director of the Division of Sleep Medicine at Harvard Medical School, has studied sleep hygiene for many years. He and his colleagues have found that "four major sleep-related factors affect cognitive performance ... The first has to do with the homeostatic drive for sleep at night ... the second major factor that determines our ability to sustain attention and maintain peak cognitive performance has to do with the total amount of sleep you manage to get over several days ... The third factor has to do with circadian phase—the time of day in the human body that says 'it's midnight' or 'it's dawn' ... and the fourth factor affecting performance has to do with what's called 'sleep inertia,' the grogginess most people experience when they first wake up" (quoted in Fryer, 2006). Czeisler also stated that, when these functions are not in alignment because of lack of sleep, individuals function at a "far lower level of performance than they would if they were well-rested" (quoted in Fryer, 2006). "We now know that 24 hours without sleep, or a week of sleeping four or five hours a night, induces an impairment equivalent to a blood alcohol level of 0.1%. We would never say, 'This person is a great worker! He's drunk all the time!' yet we continue to celebrate people who sacrifice sleep for work" (quoted in Fryer, 2006). At the time of this writing, Czeisler was considering a research project evaluating the effects of sleep on PTSD and developing methods of preventing this disorder (Czeisler, personal communication, 2014).

In a recent continuing education program at the Louisiana Psychological Association, Pears and Drew (2011) reported that the use of Prazosin HCl significantly reduced the intensity of nightmares of soldiers suffering from PTSD. In regard to a recent industrial explosion (see Chapter 6 in this volume [Tramontara, 2015]), many injured workers who developed PTSD were treated with Prazosin HCl by the second author, a medical neuropsychologist with prescriptive authority. The results, which were positive for the reduction of PTSD nightmares, enhanced the psychological interventions provided.

Trauma Recovery and Circadian Rhythms

Further, the possibility exists that the time of day can be related to the degree of adjustment to trauma. While not proven by scientific research, extensive clinical experience providing psychological first aid after disasters by the third author of this chapter (Kuriansky) suggests that nighttime is a unique time to provide support to survivors—when other resources may not be offered, when darkness is often associated with increased intimacy and can provide a sense of privacy, and when isolation and fears may be at their height—leaving people more fragile both emotionally and cognitively and thus more open to sharing deeper emotions. These impressions are based on extensive experience giving support to first responders immediately after terrorism attacks, specifically the 9/11 attacks on the World Trade Center, after which the third author assisted first responders in the "pit" (the central place where the buildings collapsed) as well as families in a Family Assistance Center (Kuriansky, 2003). Similar observations emerged when working with people after natural disaster. For example, in the immediate aftermath of Superstorm Sandy, Kuriansky (2013d) interviewed couples in the streets during the blackouts caused by the storm. The conditions imposed by the darkness (e.g., restricted activities and isolation from distractions), led to couples reporting more time spent together, more appreciation for taking care of each other, and more intimacy in spending imposed time together.

Research correlating cognitive and emotional symptoms to interventions and interactions during nighttime compared to those conducted in daytime would be useful to establish potential differential value of such interventions. Further, Kuriansky's clinical experience also suggests that the intensity of the cognitive association to a particular event can affect the intensity of the experience of a trauma. For example, several traumatic events have happened around the time of the Christmas and New Year's holiday, namely, the Asian tsunami of 2004, which occurred on December 26, Boxing Day; the 2010 Haiti earthquake, which occurred on January 11; and the December 14, 2013, shooting rampage at Sandy Hook Elementary School. The cluster of well-known traumas like these, around a specific time that is normally associated with joy and celebration, can create exaggerated mental stress (i.e., "cognitive dissonance") derived from the contrast and contradiction between two very divergent and contradictory experiences, namely the joy of the holiday and the trauma of the disaster (Kuriansky, 2012b).

New Research on Restructuring Cognition in the Aftermath of Trauma

Studies treating the cognitive correlates of trauma, as a means to heal emotional effects, are scarce. A few studies were underway at the time of this writing, funded by the National Institutes of Health (NIH). For example, in one study by the Veteran's Affairs in Connecticut, in collaboration with Yale University in New Haven, researchers explored if impairments in attention and memory commonly found in individuals suffering from PTSD can be lessened by cognitive restructuring, similar to the effects of storytelling mentioned above. Another study, which recruited participants at the Veteran's Healthcare System in San Diego, California, looked at whether a form of cognitive therapy may be enhanced by simultaneously providing cognitive restructuring aimed at compensatory skills. The researchers hoped to find that this may lead to fewer PTSD symptoms and improved quality of life. A further study, at the Bronx VA Medical Center, aimed to find an intervention to help people recover both emotionally and cognitively from PTSD.

These studies intended to find ways of identifying subgroups of people "at risk" and offering meaningful interventions as early as possible post-trauma. Avoiding the long-term psychological effects of environmental trauma is an important goal. These interventions can prevent a dangerous cycle whereby people who may appear to have returned to their normal lives may still be at risk. These programs can then be supported by public policy that focuses on reducing the onset of symptoms through early identification and intervention.

FUTURE IMPLICATIONS

Healing through Community and Connection

The importance of support systems in facilitating healing has been established (Kuriansky, 2012c, 2013a, 2013b, 2013c, 2013d). Through strong community identification, people can adapt a narrative of strength and empowerment to the point where they no longer see themselves as passive victims of nature's potential for destruction, but rather as active agents of change and healing. Communities that come together after a trauma can even be stronger than before, as their collective identity becomes more tightly woven together. As noted above, workshops that promote group activities, with drawing, music, and dance, are excellent vehicles for rebuilding individuals and communities.

Creating connections also heals man-made trauma in situations of conflict. In these conditions, cognition plays a significant role in either decreasing or escalating trauma; in the latter, this may occur by alienating one from the "other" by ascribing negative characteristics to individuals or groups.

Changing perceptions and belief systems can decrease both personal stress and interpersonal tension. The third author of this chapter has documented how interactions and cooperative activities with the "other" perceived as the cause of man-made trauma, for example, in the Middle East conflict, is possible (Kuriansky & Elisha, 2007; Kuriansky, Traubman, & Traubman, 2007).

Screening Methods

In order to allow communities to heal and develop narratives of strength and cohesion, however, the impact of environmental trauma on cognition must be mitigated and treated early after a trauma. Without fully being able to emotionally process and attend to the collective narratives a community will share, healing will be thwarted. It is therefore essential to utilize appropriate and targeted screening measures to identify those individuals who are most likely "at risk" and who will need and benefit most from interventions focused on cognitive and affective strategies. Ideally, such screening measures would also include an indication of which cognitive and affective domains are likely to be affected, and which types of cognitive and affective strategies might work best.

A more immediate way to do this is to use the formula that was developed to identify the psychological damages resulting from the Livingston Parish Train Derailment disaster of September 28, 1982 (Lemoine, Rostow, Nemeth, & Ellis, 1984). The lives of nearly 3,000 community residents were disrupted, and many individuals were forced to evacuate after a derailed train caused chemical spills and explosions. As the researchers explained, "Over the months that followed, the residents were subjected to additional stressors as they attempted to adjust to altered social and economic conditions, performed clean-up and other activities associated with restoring the affected areas, and experienced the threat of exposure to possibly hazardous residues in the air, water, and soil" (p. 1). Using a Static Group Comparison, individuals who experienced the stressful event were compared to a control group, and the groups were compared on several measures. Results of the study indicated that, "the closer the subject's residence to the derailment site, the higher the degree of both global and specific psychological distress, particularly the resident's level of anxiety" (p. 30). Residents experienced personality disturbances, evidencing patterns of avoidance, negativity, and withdrawal. Cognitive patterns of the residents were also distorted. Notably, the symptoms were evident nine months following the derailment and appeared to "represent a chronic stress reaction to the disaster event" (p. 38). A class action legal suit was launched, with a settlement that used a formula based on concentric rings, meaning that those survivors closest to the damage received the greatest compensation, and those further from the damage received the least compensation. The concentric rings formula, based on this psychological research, can be generalized to other experiences of environmental disaster, wherein the greatest effort to relieve emotional suffering should first be offered to those who were most severely affected. This formula can also be applied to the neurocognitive effects of trauma. Measurement and research take time—time that is often at the expense of healing. As interventions need to be proactive and occur soon after the disaster, this concentric rings formula can also be applied to the neurocognitive effects of trauma. Such a model can assist with the rapid, effective delivery and implementation of post-environmental trauma interventions.

IMPLICATIONS FOR PUBLIC POLICY

The findings and issues highlighted above in this chapter have implications for public policy. Research studies and interventions cited in this chapter demonstrate the importance of early interventions to address psychological and cognitive impacts of disaster, both immediately after a trauma as well as over time, to avert long-term consequences, including PTSD and anniversary reactions. As such, public policy needs to consider these findings when determining ways that victims of trauma are treated and resources that are provided. For example, it is not nearly enough to house people in makeshift temporary tents and provide food and water. The emotional needs of survivors must be attended to in a manner that allows them to create healing narratives.

Advocacy is also an important aspect in regard to research funding for disaster recovery, particularly that which focuses on the impact on cognitive functioning, and potential therapeutic interventions. Data from measurements of function and dysfunction is essential in order to build a scientific foundation for this emerging field of inquiry. The particular focus on cognition can come under the umbrella of promotion of well-being that is now a health goal agreed upon by governments as part of the Sustainable Development Goals. An increasing number of psychologists are developing skills in advocacy in order to accomplish these goals (Kuriansky, 2006b, 2011, 2012a, 2012e).

THE ROLE OF MEDIA

An important factor affecting public approaches to disaster management is the role of the media. Trauma that is repeatedly broadcast into people's living rooms, via television, Internet, and other communications, may lead to continued traumatization and prolonged stress and feelings of powerlessness, even for those who are removed from the location of the trauma. It is necessary to find ways to counteract this outcome. For example, the second author had to hospitalize several Louisiana patients who were mesmerized by the 9/11 television coverage, and others had to be limited to no more than 20 minutes of viewing a day. Therefore, journalists must be held to a higher standard. Instead of reporting endlessly on the horrific impact of trauma and the constant stream of repeated images of people in distress (which may boost ratings), the public may be better served by a focus on reporting details in a manner that empowers resiliency, rather than catastrophic hopelessness. Of course, it must be recognized that the media can also be used in a very positive way, to offer the public who remotely witness the trauma ways to constructively help.

Experts in the psychological and public policy communities need to find ways to provide support to individuals, institutions, and agencies that have an instrumental role in designing and implementing public policy that addresses the immediate neurocognitive and emotional interventions post disaster, whether due to natural or man-made causes. As more becomes known about the effects of environmental trauma on cognition and emotion, and ways to facilitate healing, we will be in a better position to assess and target individuals and groups who are "at risk" and to provide interventions specific to the areas of cognitive and emotional vulnerability that are most in danger of becoming disrupted. This is important, given that a well-functioning brain is instrumental for the healing process and the reintegration of self. Thus, it is paramount that survivors engage in healthy interactions, including narratives/storytelling, drawings, music, and/ or sharing experiences, in a timely fashion after experiencing environmental disasters. Through these processes, survivors can once again view themselves and their communities in the light of strength, health, recovery, and resilience.

REFERENCES

Brandes, D., Ben-Shachar, G., Gilboa, A., Bonne, O., Freedman, S., & Shalev, A. Y. (2002). PTSD symptoms and cognitive performance in recent trauma survivors. *Psychiatry Research, 110,* 231–238.

Canino, G., Bravo, M., Rubio-Stipec, M., & Woodbury, M. (1990). The impact of disaster on mental health: Prospective and retrospective analyses. *International Journal of Mental Health, 19,* 51–69.

Cassels, C. (2009, April 23). Brains of veterans with and without PTSD differ, imaging study shows. *Medscape.* Retrieved April 15, 2015, from http://www.medscape.com/viewarticle/701855

Chomsky, N. (1957). *Syntactic structures.* Berlin: Mouton de Gruyter.

Cummings, N., & Cummings, J. (2013). *Refocused psychotherapy as the first line intervention in behavioral health.* New York, NY: Routledge.

Enlow, M. B., Egeland, B., Blood, E. A., Wright, R. O., & Wright, R. J. (2012). Interpersonal trauma exposure and cognitive development in children to age 8 years: A longitudinal study. *Journal of Epidemiology and Community Health, 66*(11), 1005–1010. doi:10.1136/jech-2011-200727

Eren-Kocak, E., Kilic, C., Aydin, I., & Hizli, F. (2009). Memory and prefrontal functions in earthquake survivors: Differences between current and past post-traumatic stress disorder patients. *Acta Psychiatrica Scandinavica, 119*(1), 35–44.

Freedy, J. R., Saladin, M. E., Kilpatrick, D. G., Resnick, H. S., & Saunders, B. E. (1994). Understanding acute psychological distress following natural disaster. *Journal of Traumatic Stress, 7*(2), 257–273.

Fryer, B. (2006, October). Sleep deficit: The performance killer. [A conversation with Harvard Medical School Professor Charles A. Czeisler.] *Harvard Business Review, 84* (10), 53–59. Retrieved April 15, 2015, from http://hbr.org/2006/10/sleep-deficit-the-performance-killer

Green, B. L., Lindy, J. D., Grace, M. C., & Leonard, A. C. (1992). Chronic posttraumatic stress disorder and diagnostic comorbidity in a disaster sample. *Journal of Nervous and Mental Disease, 180*(12), 760–766.

Grimshaw, G. M., Adelstein, A., Bryden, M. P., & MacKinnon, G. E. (1998). First-language acquisition in adolescence: Evidence for a critical period for verbal language development. *Brain and Language, 63*(2), 237–255. Retrieved April 15, 2015, from http://search.proquest.com.ezproxylocal.library.nova.edu/docview/619344892?accountid=6579

Helton, W. S., & Head, J. (2012). Earthquakes on the mind: Implications of disasters for human performance. *Journal of Human Factors, 54*(2), 189–194. doi:10.1177/0018720811430503

Helton, W. S., Head, J., & Kemp, S. (2011). Natural disaster induced cognitive disruption: Impacts on action slips. *Journal of Consciousness and Cognition, 20*(4), 1732–1737. doi:10.1016/j.concog.2011.02.011.

Hurford, J. R. (1991). The evolution of the critical period for language acquisition. *Cognition, 40*(3), 159–201. Retrieved April 15, 2015, from http://search.proquest.com.ezproxylocal.library.nova.edu/docview/618115420?accountid=6579

Kaiser, C. F., Sattler, D. N., Bellack, D. R., & Dersin, J. (1996). A conservation of resources approach to a natural disaster: Sense of coherence and psychological distress. *Journal of Social Behavior and Personality, 11*(3), 459–476.

King, S., & Laplante, D. P. (2005). The effects of prenatal maternal stress on children's cognitive development: Project Ice Storm. *Stress, 8*(1), 35–45.

Kollias, H. (2014). Research review: Epigenetics. *Precision Nutrition.* Retrieved April 15, 2015, from http://www.precisionnutrition.com/epigenetics-feast-famine-and-fatness

Kuriansky, J. (2003). The 9/11 terrorist attack on the World Trade Center: A New York psychologist's personal experiences and professional perspective. *Psychotherapie-Forum, 11*(1) [special edition on terrorism and psychology], 36–47. Blackwell Publishers.

Kuriansky, J. (2006a). Making paper flowers bloom: Coping strategies to survive the Israeli-Palestinian conflict. In J. Kuriansky (Ed.), *Terror in the Holy Land: Inside the anguish of the Israeli-Palestinian conflict* (pp. 239–247). Westport, CT: Praeger.

Kuriansky, J. (2006b). Your voice counts: Public policy advocacy for psychologists. *Amplifier,* newsletter of Division 46 Media Psychology of the American Psychological Association.

Kuriansky, J. (2007). Healing after a terror event on campus in Israel: Unique workshops and allied techniques for international Jewish and Arab students, staff and extended community. In J. Kuriansky (Ed.), *Beyond bullets and bombs: Grassroots peacebuilding between Israelis and Palestinians* (pp. 315–325). Westport, CT: Praeger.

Kuriansky, J. (2008). A clinical toolbox for cross-cultural counseling and training. In U. P. Gielen, J. G. Draguns, & J. M. Fish (Eds.), *Principles of multicultural counseling and therapy* (pp. 295–330). New York: Taylor and Francis/Routledge.

Kuriansky J. (2010, July 28). *Techniques for helping students recover from natural disaster and other stress.* Plenary at the International Forum for Post-disaster Health Aid. Qinghai, China.

Kuriansky, J. (2011, January–March). Guidelines for mental health and psychosocial support in response to emergencies: Experience and encouragement for advocacy. *The IAAP Bulletin of the International Association of Applied Psychology, 23*(1–2), 30–32. Retrieved April 18, 2015, from: http://www.iaapsy.org/Portals/1/Bulletin/apnl_v23_i1-2.pdf

Kuriansky, J. (2012a, Summer). Advocacy about psychological contributions to the global agenda at the United Nations: Preliminary experiences, case studies and lessons learned about principles, procedures and process. *International Psychology Bulletin, 16*(3), 46–60. Retrieved April 15, 2015, from http://internationalpsychology.files .wordpress.com/2013/01/ipb_summer_2012-07-14-8_final.pdf

Kuriansky, J. (2012b). Christmas curse or celebration: From Superstorm Sandy to Sandy Hook to the Financial Cliff, seven questions in crisis. *Huffington Post.* Retrieved April 15, 2015, from http://www.huffingtonpost.com/judy-kuriansky-phd/sandy-hook-elementary-shooting_b_2357207.html

Kuriansky, J. (2012c). Our communities: Healing after environmental disasters. In D. G. Nemeth, R. B. Hamilton, & J. Kuriansky (Eds.), *Living in an environmentally traumatized world: Healing ourselves and our planet* (pp. 141–167). Santa Barbara, CA: ABC-CLIO/Praeger.

Kuriansky, J. (2012d, July–October). Recovery efforts for Japan after the 3/11 devastating tsunami/earthquake. *Bulletin of the International Association of Applied Psychology, 24*(2–3), Part 22. Retrieved April 15, 2015, from http://www.iaapsy.org/Portals/1/ Archive/Publications/newsletters/July2012.pdf

Kuriansky, J. (2012e, July–October). Well-being: An important issue at the United Nations and for the International Association of Applied Psychology. *Bulletin of the International Association of Applied Psychology, 24*(2–3), 64–70. Retrieved April 16, 2015, from http://www.iaapsy.org/Portals/1/Archive/Publications/newsletters/ July2012.pdf

Kuriansky, J. (2013a). Helping kids cope with the Oklahoma tornado and other traumas: 7 techniques. *Huffington Post.* Retrieved April 15, 2015, from http://www.huffington post.com/judy-kuriansky-phd/helping-kids-cope-with-the-oklahoma-tornado_b_3322 238.html

Kuriansky, J. (2013b). Katrina vs. Sandy: Essays on nature-induced, human-induced, and nature + human-induced environmental trauma. *Ecopsychology, 5*(S1), S2–S3. doi:10.1089/eco.2013.5502

Kuriansky, J. (2013c). Superstorm Sandy 2012: A psychologist first responder's personal account and lessons learned about the impact on emotions and ecology. *Ecopsychology, 5*(S1), S30–S37. doi:10.1089/eco.2013.0010

Kuriansky, J. (2013d). *The aftermath of Superstorm Sandy* [Video]. Retrieved April 15, 2015, from http://www.youtube.com/watch?v=2W1OUHH8IPA

Kuriansky, J., & Elisha, T. (2007). Cooking, climbing, camping and other creative cooperations between Palestinians and Jews: Successes and challenges. In J. Kuriansky (Ed.), *Beyond bullets and bombs: Grassroots peacebuilding between Israelis and Palestinians* (pp. 227–242). Westport, CT: Praeger.

Kuriansky, J., & Jean-Charles, W. (2012, July–October). Haiti rebati: Update on activities rebuilding Haiti through the Global Kids Connect Project. *Bulletin of the International Association of Applied Psychology, 24*(2–3), Part 21, 116–124.

Kuriansky, J., & Nemeth, D. G. (2013). A model for post-environmental disaster wellness workshops: Preparing individuals and communities for hurricane anniversary reactions. *Ecopsychology*, 5(Suppl. 1), S38–S45. doi:10.1089/eco.2013.0006

Kuriansky, J., Traubman, L., & Traubman, E. (2007). Food for thoughts of peace: Jews and Palestinians sharing dinner and dialogue. In J. Kuriansky (Ed.), *Beyond bullets and bombs: Grassroots peacebuilding between Israelis and Palestinians* (pp. 349–353). Westport, CT: Praeger.

Kuriansky, J., Zinsou, J., Arunagiri, V., Douyon, C., Chiu, A., Jean-Charles, W., ... Midy, T. (2015). The effects of helping in a train-the-trainers program for youth in the Global Kids Connect Project Providing Psychosocial Support after the 2010 Haiti earthquake: A paradigm shift to sustainable development. In D. G. Nemeth & J. Kuriansky (Eds.), *Ecopsychology: Advances from the intersection of psychology and environmental protection*, Volume 2 (pp. 135–169). Santa Barbara, CA: ABC-CLIO.

Lemoine, R. L., Rostow, C. D., Nemeth, D. G., & Ellis, J. S. (1984). *The Livingston train derailment accident: An evaluation of the psychological impact on community residents— an evaluation report prepared for the plaintiff's steering committee by Baton Rouge Psychological Associates*.

Lenneberg, E. (1964). The capacity for language acquisition. In J. A. Fodor & J. J. Katz (Eds.), *The structure of language* (pp. 579–603). Englewood Cliffs, NJ: Prentice Hall.

Liu, X., Betzenhauser, M. J., Reiken, S., Meli, A. C., Xie, W., Chen, B., ... Marks, A. R. (2012). Role of leaky neuronal ryanodine receptors in stress-induced cognitive dysfunction. *Cell*, 150(5), 1055–1067. doi:10.1016/j.cell.2012.06.052

Lumey, L. H., Stein, A. D., Kahn, H. S., van der Pal-de Bruin, K. M., Blauw, G. J., Zybert, P. A., & Susser, E. S. (2007). Cohort profile: The Dutch Hunger Winter families study. *International Journal of Epidemiology*, 36(6), 1196–1204. doi:10.1093/ije/dym126

Majer, M., Nater, U. M., Lin, J. S., Capuron, L., & Reeves, W. C. (2010). Association of childhood trauma with cognitive function in healthy adults: A pilot study. *BMC Neurology*, 10, 61. doi:10.1186/1471-2377-10-61

Masterpasqua, F. (2009). Psychology and epigenetics. *Review of General Psychology*, 13(3), 194–201. doi:10.1037/a0016301

Nemeth, D. G., Cameron, C., Creveling, C., Draeger, R., & Schexnayder, R. (2000). *Outcome of Millennium 2000: Historical, technical, psychological, and research-based perspectives*. Presented at the 108th Annual Convention of the American Psychological Association, Washington, DC.

Nemeth, D. G., Hamilton, R. B., & Kuriansky, J. (Eds.). (2012). *Living in an environmentally traumatized world: Healing ourselves and our planet*. Santa Barbara, CA: ABC-CLIO/Praeger.

Nemeth, D. G., Kuriansky, J., Reeder, K. P., Lewis, A., Marceaux, K., Whittington, T., ... Safier, J. A. (2012). Addressing anniversary reactions of trauma through group process: The Hurricane Katrina anniversary wellness workshops. *International Journal of Group Psychotherapy*, 62(1), 129–142.

Nemeth, D. G., Songy, C. S., & Olivier, T. W. (2014). Increasing success in neurocognitively impaired patients via group therapy. Manuscript accepted by the *International Journal of Group Psychotherapy*.

Pears, K., & Drew, L. R. (2011). *PTSD and evidence based treatment*. Presented at the 63rd Annual Convention of the Louisiana Psychological Association, Baton Rouge, LA.

Rudenko, A., & Tsai, L. H. (2014). Epigenetic regulation in memory and cognitive disorders. *Journal of Neuroscience, 264*, 51–63.

Sachinvala, N., von Scotti, H. McGuire, M., Fairbanks, L., Bakst, K., McGuire, M., & Brown, N. (2000). Memory, attention, function and mood among patients with chronic posttraumatic stress disorder. (2000). *Journal of Nervous and Mental Disease, 188*(12), 818–823.

Salimpoor, V., Benovoy, M., Larcher, K., Dagher, A., & Zatorre, R. J. (2011, February). Anatomically distinct dopamine release during anticipation and experience of peak emotion to music. *Natural Neuroscience, 14*(2), 257–262.

Sibel, T., & Cummings, J. L. (2002, August). Frontal-subcortical neuronal circuits and clinical neuropsychiatry: An update. *Journal of Psychosomatic Research, 53*(2), 647–654.

Szyf, M., McGowan, P., & Meaney, M. J. (2008). The social environment and the epigenome. *Environmental and Molecular Mutagenesis, 49*(1), 46–60. doi:10.1002/em.20357

Tramontara, J. (2015). Psychological sequelae and treatment of survivors of man-made disasters: Overview and a clinician's experience. In D. G. Nemeth & J. Kuriansky (Eds.), *Ecopsychology: Advances from the intersection of psychology and environmental protection*, Volume 2 (pp. 77–88). Santa Barbara, CA: ABC-CLIO.

Vasterling, J. J., Proctor, S. P., Amoroso, P., Kane, R., Gackstetter, G., Ryan, M. A., & Friedman, M. J. (2006). The neurocognition deployment health study: A prospective cohort study of army soldiers. *Military Medicine, 171*(3), 253–260.

Wilson, E. O. (2012, January 1). On the origins of the arts. *Harvard Magazine*, 32–37.

Wilson, E. O. (2013, June 21). E. O. Wilson's advice for future scientists [Interview]. Retrieved April 15, 2015, from http://www.npr.org/2013/06/21/194230822/e-o-wilsons-advice-for-future-scientists

6

Psychological Sequelae and Treatment of Survivors of Man-Made Disasters: Overview and a Clinician's Experience

Joseph Tramontana

The critical importance of environmental protection emerges from the unfortunate experience of environmental traumas. These can be the result of natural causes or man-made actions. Both types lead to similar residual effects. Since the Industrial Revolution, many environmental accidents caused by human error have occurred that result in death and suffering on both physical and emotional levels. Such man-made disasters that wreak havoc on the environment include those that involve hazardous materials; power service disruptions and blackouts; nuclear power plant accidents and nuclear blasts; radiological emergencies; chemical threats; cyber attacks; explosions; building collapses and civil unrest. This chapter refers to such events, analyzing the interaction of the environmental and psychological factors, and includes my own personal experience in one such event.

A recent Internet article (Dimdam, 2013), entitled "25 Biggest Man Made Environmental Disasters in History," includes an account of a recent occurrence referred to as "The Deep Water Horizon (BP) oil spill" ("Gulf Oil Spill Now Largest Offshore Spill," 2010), which affected my own habitat on the Mississippi Gulf Coast and claimed 11 lives in addition to drastic effects on the environment.

There have been, of course, many disasters related to the defense industry, including accidental explosions of munitions or chemicals to be used in manufacturing munitions. These incidents have led to loss of life and injury. Additionally, there have been many accidents in the energy industry, which is described as the totality of all of the industries involved in the production and sale of energy (including fuel extraction, manufacturing, refining, and distribution). These include incidents such as the Three Mile Island partial nuclear meltdown (Walker, 2004), and the Chernobyl nuclear meltdown with ensuing steam explosion and fire that killed 50 people with estimates that between

4,000 and several hundred thousand additional cancer deaths have resulted over time (U.S. Nuclear Regulatory Commission, 2014).

In 1988, another incident (close to the homes of the authors in these book volumes living in the state of Louisiana) occurred at the Shell Oil refinery in Norco; Louisiana state police evacuated 2,800 residents from nearby neighborhoods. Seven workers were killed and 42 injured. Another example is the *Exxon Valdez* oil spill in Prince William Sound, Alaska.

The food industry has had its own share of disasters. A large molasses tank burst and a wave of molasses rushed through the streets of Boston in 1919 at an estimated speed of 35 mph, killing 21 and injuring 150 (Puleo, 2003). The event reportedly entered local folklore, as residents claim that on a hot summer day, the area still smells of molasses. More recently, a Georgia sugar refinery exploded in 2008, killing 13 and injuring 42 workers (Dewan, 2009).

Disasters in the manufacturing industry predate some of the other industries. For example, as far back as 1860, a large factory in Lawrence, Massachusetts, collapsed, killing 145 workers and injuring 166 more. In 1905, a boiler explosion occurred in a shoe factory in Brockton, Massachusetts, causing the building to collapse and a fire that killed 58 people and injured 150 others. More recently, in 2012, a seven-story factory in Bangladesh caught fire and killed at least 112 people, 12 of whom jumped out of windows to escape the blaze (Manik, 2012). There were reports of gross negligence. Nine midlevel managers and supervisors were said to have prevented employees from leaving sewing machines after the fire started.

Likewise, there have been many recorded disasters in the mining industry worldwide, such as the Benxihu Collier disaster in China in 1942 and the Coalbrook mine disaster in South Africa in 1960 ("The World's Worst Coal Mining Disasters," 2014). Other industrial disasters include the 1947 Texas City Disaster, in which an explosion occurred aboard a docked cargo ship—a disaster that was called the worst industrial disaster in the United States (Stephens, 1997). This negative distinction was based on the number of fatalities and injuries. At least 578 people lost their lives, another 3,500 were injured, and the blast was said to have shattered windows from as far as 25 miles away. This fertilizer ship was supposed to aid the struggling farmers in Europe recovering from World War II. More recently, in 2014, an explosion occurred in a fertilizer plant in West, Texas, which killed at least 14 people and injured more than 160. It was reported that 150 buildings were damaged or destroyed (Seba, 2014). Such events have also occurred close to home to the authors in these two volumes— myself, and the coeditors of this book who live in the state of Louisiana, including Darlyne Nemeth and Robert Hamilton. The impact of this event is explored in this chapter.

On June 13, 2013, the Williams Olefins chemical plant in Geismer, Louisiana, tragically exploded. The first reports were that two workers were killed and 77 more workers were injured. A later report indicated that more than 100 workers were injured. The plant produces both ethylene and propylene, two highly flammable gases utilized in the petrochemical industry.

One of the workers of this plant did research on the Internet regarding legal firms that were experienced in handling cases involving industrial explosions and found a Houston firm whose website identifies itself as "explosion attorneys" or "plant explosion lawyers." This employee referred many of his coworkers to this firm. Subsequently, the firm contracted with a psychological group practice in Kenner, Louisiana, to do comprehensive psychological evaluations of victims. Most victims were found to have either physical or psychological (PTSD) sequelae of the accident. Many had both.

Those victims with psychological difficulties from the traumatic experience were recommended for psychological treatment. The legal firm then contracted with three different psychology groups in Louisiana, to whom they made referrals based on the proximity of the therapists' offices to the clients' homes. I was given as a referral to 18 victims who live in Baton Rouge or the surrounding area. Since many of these patients were found to need psychotropic medications, I subsequently had the legal firm refer them to an associate, Dr. Darlyne Nemeth, a neuropsychologist with prescription privileges and special expertise with such patients who could provide management of their psychotropic medications in consult with their surgeon, primary care, or other medical providers. This treatment is further described below.

SURVIVORS OF WILLIAMS-OLEFINS EXPLOSION

Posttraumatic stress disorder (PTSD) has been defined as a psychological disorder characterized by a preoccupation with a traumatic event beyond "normal" human experience, such as rape or assault, combat, violence, natural disasters, accidents, and torture (Barabasz, Barabasz, & Watkins, 2011). In general, traumatic experiences can result in a variety of long-lasting psychological symptoms, including intense terror, fear, and paralyzing feelings of helplessness (Frankel, 1994). Traumatized individuals may experience such symptoms on a daily basis.

Victims of trauma often have a significant decline in their overall functioning, thereby eroding their ego capacities (van der Kolk, 2001). This erosion deteriorates one's self-view (safe, worthwhile, loved) to a very poor self-concept (danger, worthless, and hated). Further investigation into the aftereffects of trauma suggest that sensory input stimulates hormonal secretions and influences activation of brain regions that effect attention and memory, resulting in the fact that conscious control over one's actions may be limited (van der Kolk, 2007). Reminders of past trauma can activate certain neurobiological responses, thus making survivors of trauma even more vulnerable physically and psychologically. This vulnerability may lead to irrational and subcortically initiated responses that are irrelevant or harmful, such as substance abuse, binge eating, self-injury, clinging to potentially dangerous partners, and extreme over- and/or underarousal (van der Kolk, 2007).

Of the 18 victims from this Louisiana chemical plant explosion referred to me, all have symptoms of PTSD, and many of them have physical injuries including burns, back or neck pain, leg or shoulder injuries, and other symptoms. Many have had surgeries or at least procedures such as epidural steroidal injections or radio frequency ablation (RFA). These two procedures are a frequent part of the "toolkit" of physicians who specialize in pain control. The injections are typically cortisol injected, under fluoroscopy, into the problem area. RFA is a process in which needles with electric currents are used to dull nerve sensations. In fact, patients often describe the process to me as "having my nerves burned." Their PTSD symptoms vary in frequency and intensity, usually as dependent on the nature of the patient's experience. For example, all feared for their life or well-being, but some were closer in proximity to the explosion than others. Some were friends with and/or observed the two workers who were burned and died. Some felt the heat on the back of their necks or fell from scaffolding. There is evidence to support a linear relationship between proximity to the trauma and intensity of symptoms (Blanchard, Rowell, Kuhn, Rogers, & Wittrock, 2005).

Most of the survivors, except for a few who have returned to work (including two who returned to that plant), are experiencing significant financial distress. One of the employees who returned to work did so at a different type of plant and made it clear that she was working in a coal-fueled plant, not a chemical-fueled one. Making this distinction was important in her adjustment. Two of the employees who returned to work went back to the same plant. Both have made it abundantly clear that they are working there temporarily, while the plant is not operational. Neither intends to stay there once the plant is "up and running." Both present this distinction as important because they feel safer when it is not fully functional. Although they describe that just being at that site brings back bad memories, the fact that no chemicals were actively running through the pipes makes it less frightening. Another survivor is working in a job much different from plant work (at a company that installs glass mirrors and shower stalls), even though he is making much less money than he had been in the past at the plant. One survivor, a welder, is not physically cleared to return to work, but makes it clear that he would only weld on new construction or on structures that do not involve chemicals.

At first, the legal firm was giving monthly stipends to the employees who had no salaries. After that fund was depleted, the attorneys arranged for loans through a third party, at an interest rate of 33 1/3%. All of these advances will, of course, come out of any eventual settlements. Only one of the victims being treated by me is receiving workers' compensation benefits at the time of this writing (one year after the explosion). That one seems to have "lucked out" (in her words), because when she was in the hospital emergency room on the day of the explosion to be treated for her burns, there was a workers' comp adjuster there to see another patient (who was not in the explosion), and he vowed to help her get benefits. The others all talk frequently about their financial difficulties, fear of losing their homes and vehicles, their workers' comp lawyer (different from the "explosion attorneys"), and not getting results. All of these financial issues compound their overall psychological dysfunction of anxiety, depression, and PTSD symptoms.

CLINICAL INTERVENTIONS: TECHNIQUES USEFUL IN ENVIRONMENTAL DISASTERS

In this section, I discuss my clinical considerations in working with these survivors of the chemical plant explosion.

Reassurance and Normalization Are Key

Many individuals with non-military-related PTSD mistakenly believe PTSD is a condition experienced only by war veterans. Consequently, one of the first considerations in treating these patients is to reassure them that their symptoms are "normal," in light of their experiences.

Evaluations Are Helpful

Interestingly, two of the patients who were referred to me had previous PTSD conditions. One, a Vietnam War veteran who also suffers from alcoholism, especially has had difficulties. In our first session, not only was he intoxicated, but also he spent most of the session talking about his Vietnam-related PTSD. The other patient had prior PTSD symptoms from being a survivor of Hurricane Katrina, the severe natural disaster that hit Louisiana in 2005 (Russell, 2005). In sessions with me, he referred to "dead bodies floating around like a bunch of magnolia tree leaves." This man made a point that while Hurricane Katrina was a natural disaster, the flooding of the city was the result of a man-made disaster (the Corps of Engineers has been blamed for the inadequacy and subsequent breach of the levee system). This is consistent with the fact that patients with prior PTSD experiences are pre-sensitized to fears of death/impending doom (University of Maryland Medical Center, 2014).

Because all of the survivors referred to me were psychologically evaluated prior to their referral for psychotherapy, all had been administered a PTSD Civilian Checklist.

Reframing Is Another Good Technique

Following the aforementioned supportive therapy and psycho-education regarding PTSD, a good beginning point for me as the clinician to address early in the therapeutic program with clients who experienced physical injury is to use reframing techniques. I often administer the Tampa Scale of Kinesiophobia, a pain/fear avoidance behavior scale (Lundberg, Styf, & Carlsson, 2004). This is a scale I frequently utilize with pain patients in other settings—i.e., the pain clinic at which I work part time. Reframing involves ideas/verbalizations such as "discomfort" versus "pain" or "mildly distressing" versus "excruciating pain." The goal is to lessen their fears of movement/physical activity. The concept that "movement is your friend" is reinforced. Pain patients are instructed about the importance of "external focus," referring to focus on people, things, and activities outside of themselves. I explain that internal focus is not good because "it hurts inside!"

The First Approach: Narratives

All of the above approaches follow a considerable amount of therapy time that is given to listening to the stories of the patients. As pointed out by Nemeth while I was being trained, along with other local mental health providers, to assist in her First Anniversary Wellness Workshop for Hurricane Katrina survivors: "If the victims still needs to discuss their traumatic experience, they haven't completely achieved closure" (Darlyne G. Nemeth, personal communication, 2006). More information on this topic is available in the excellent articles by Kuriansky and Nemeth (2013) and Nemeth et al. (2012) regarding preparing individuals and communities for anniversary reactions that occur after a natural disaster.

Self-Hypnosis Training

After considerable time is spent listening to survivors' stories, and after discussion of the efficacy of clinical hypnosis and self-hypnosis training, and if they give informed consent (which is important since some individuals are afraid of the idea of hypnosis or for some religious reason think it is a bad thing or a "possession trance"), victims/patients are taught hypnosis/self-hypnosis techniques for both decreasing stress/anxiety reactions as well as decreasing subjective pain for those with physical injuries. I often refer to therapy that includes hypnotic work as "hypnotically enhanced psychotherapy" (Tramontana, 2005, 2009). The idea is that hypnosis is not the treatment; rather, it sets the stage for other forms of psychotherapeutic treatment to be more effective. These include cognitive behavioral therapy (CBT), behavior modification, regression therapy, hypnoanalysis, and others. Reframing techniques also seem to have more impact when presented hypnotically versus just conversationally.

While I have published two books on hypnosis (Tramontana, 2009; Tramontana, 2011), the clients are informed that while one of these two books deals with hypnosis for addictions and the other with performance enhancement in sports, I have utilized hypnotic techniques for decreasing anxiety and for reduction of subjective pain more than for the applications described in the books. The latter symptoms were not the targeted topic of the books, because there was already a great deal of literature regarding the efficacy of hypnosis for pain reduction and anxiety reduction.

With anxiety, for example, the concept is that, if the patient can be taught to relax via self-hypnosis training, in situations that previously caused anxiety, then the anxiety is diminished. The patient is told that relaxation and anxiety are incompatible or mutually exclusive behaviors. He/she is told: "You can't be relaxed if you're anxious, nor anxious if you're relaxed. So rather than try to un-learn a negative behavior, the goal is to learn a new behavior that is incompatible with the old negative behavior."

Likewise, with pain patients, the focus is on teaching the patient relaxation techniques to reduce subjective pain. If a patient enters the office on a particular day and says their pain level is an "8" on a 10-point scale of intensity, with 10 being the most extreme, and after hypnosis it is a "5," or they start with a "5" and reduce it to a "3," this reduction is considered significant improvement by the therapist. The difference-decline in intensity also demonstrates feedback about improvement to the client that there are techniques they can utilize to lower their subjective pain on their own. I have never had a client report that the pain level was higher after hypnosis, and only rarely do patients report no improvement. When there is no positive change, this finding suggests the need for investigative techniques to determine if there are psychological reasons for holding on to the pain. One such technique involves "age regression" (see Tramontana, 2009). Hypnotic age regression involves taking the patients back to some significant experience in their past, which are related to the problems in the present. I tell the patients to imagine sitting in a safe room in which there is a movie screen or giant television screen, and there is a film all about their lives. The patients are told that the film is a symbolic representation of their subconscious minds, and that all of their experiences are stored there. I tell the patients that, in just a moment, I will count backwards from 5 to 1; and as I count, I want them to imagine the film rewinding, so that at once a picture will come into focus, that will tell us the salient information that the subconscious believes to be important. Often, the patients will recount some past experience, often a traumatic one, that perhaps was dormant but exacerbated by this new trauma. Another is a version of hypnoanalysis, a technique referred to as "rapid hypnoanalysis using ideomotor signaling" that I learned in workshops and books by Dr. Dabney Ewin, a preventive medicine physician in New Orleans (Ewin, 2014; Ewin & Eimer, 2006). The patients are told: "Even in hypnosis, people often respond to questions with their left-brain functioning (i.e., what they think is the logical answer). But I want you to answer from a feeling, or right-brain, level. So when I ask a question, I want you to respond with your fingers." They are then taught signals for "yes," "no," "I don't know," or "I'm not ready to deal with that." They are told there are seven possible causes for symptoms that we want to investigate. These are: conflict (when you want to do one thing but you believe you should do another), organ language (for example, "I feel like I've been stabbed in the back" might lead to back pain), motivation (secondary gain), past experience, identification (with someone with the same or similar condition), self-punishment (for real or imagined guilt), and suggestion (by some authoritative person).

The above hypnotic techniques for anxiety reduction and for pain reduction are presented to the clients as "coping skills." They are instructed to practice the self-hypnotic techniques at home, as a homework assignment, thus giving clients "tools" that they can utilize to improve their daily functioning.

Mindfulness Training

Mindfulness meditation also fits well into the hypnosis/relaxation approach. Much interest and research has recently focused on this topic (Greeson, 2009; Holroyd, 2003). At a recent presentation on this topic (Quang, 2014), the speaker, a Buddhist monk, spoke about how mindfulness meditation helps decrease ruminative thinking that contributes to the high levels of stress prevalent in our society. Rumination about the trauma is certainly an important symptom to consider in dealing with trauma victims. One aspect of "mindfulness" is to get across to the client that "that was then, this is now—it is not happening now—you are safe here (e.g., in my office, or in your own living room, or anywhere other than that chemical plant)." I must confess that in no cases have I suggested to the victims that they return to their previous place of employment. I tell them that I will support them in whatever decision they make, but the decision is theirs and only theirs.

Psychotropic Medication

As noted above, a number of these individuals have been referred to a neuropsychologist (Dr. Darlyne Nemeth) for management of their psychotropic medication regimen. One frequently prescribed medication, Prazosin HCl, is intended to help with sleep disturbances and to decrease nightmares. Some of these clients are already seeing psychiatric providers who manage their medications. Others, however, had no psychiatric provider and either seemed much too depressed and anxious, or appeared to have too many intense symptoms of PTSD for psychotherapy alone to work. For these individuals, I determined, with agreement of the clients, that they needed referral for medication.

All of the above is a very slow, arduous process, with frequent setbacks. The aforementioned patient, the Vietnam War veteran who is also an alcoholic, was admitted to an inpatient psychiatric facility due to his suicidal ideation. Now released, he has been sporadic in keeping appointments for outpatient psychotherapy. As of this writing, another patient was in the hospital with a physical condition (i.e., a heart condition). Of course, the fact that he was addicted to crystal meth certainly affected his physical health. While there was a reported history of use of this substance prior to the explosion, he reported increased usage after the trauma. Another patient is in jail for driving under the influence of alcohol. Others have had various surgeries, each time setting them back a bit physically and further insulting their psychological well-being. The aforementioned financial stressors have led to marital or relational conflicts, thus further disturbing their psychological integrity and stability.

Involving the Spouse

At times the spouses/mates have been invited to the therapy sessions in an attempt to smooth out the conflict through psycho-education regarding PTSD. This approach is incorporated when the patient indicates marital conflict subsequent to the trauma that was not identified prior to the explosion. Most of the spouses I have seen relate significant behavioral changes in their partners since the explosion. They have been described by mates as grumpy, having a short temper with their spouse or children, isolative, fearful, angry, and disinterested, among other symptoms.

Anniversary Reactions

Particularly vulnerable times for patients experiencing trauma following environmental disasters occur on the anniversary of the event (Kuriansky & Nemeth, 2013; Nemeth et al., 2012). One of my patients from the explosion discussed a setback, common for such survivors, that she had on the anniversary of the explosion, saying that when local media showed pictures of it on the TV news, she felt like it was happening all over again and had a nightmare that night. Another talked about how he just had his "nerves burned" (meaning a radio frequency ablation procedure) and was hurting, and how every time he has such a procedure, it reminds him of the trauma. He had surgery on his shoulder a couple of months earlier and may need it on the other shoulder, and felt that the physical setbacks (or at least the lack of progress), only further affected his already shaky psychological adjustment. This same client reported how he was sent a great deal of documents by his attorney, with paperwork that involved written descriptions of what happened to him, pinpointing on a map of the facility where he was at the time of the explosion. Completing the paperwork took him four days, efforts that only further reminded him of the trauma.

Legal Complications

The above phenomena are not very different from that experienced by individuals who have experienced traumatic accidents. For example, a female client of mine was working as a security guard at a prison when she was assaulted by an inmate. While workers' compensation is paying for her treatment and part of her salary, she filed suit against the prison. After almost a year in which her attorney did very little—finally admitting that he was preoccupied with running for a judgeship, so he did not have time to focus on her case—she decided it was time to change attorneys. She consulted with one of his associates, and then another attorney with whom she contracted. This experience of recounting her story to several attorneys repeatedly brings up painful memories for her of the trauma.

Another client of mine was working in a parking garage, and the device that takes the drivers up to higher floors collapsed, causing serious physical injury. This resulted in an extensive legal case. Like the patient described above, he reports how the legal dealings remind him of his fear of impending doom at the time of the accident.

In summary, the legal procedures in man-made disasters, which often involve interrogatories, depositions, preparation for trial, and workers' compensation proceedings, do not allow the client to go through a healthy processing and adjustment to deal with the hand they are dealt. Rather, the legal efforts are constant reminders of the traumatic events.

Successes in Adjustment

Other victims of the chemical plant explosion, however, have progressed nicely. Some are working at jobs and have "graduated" from psychotherapy. Some are seen monthly, whereas at first it was weekly, then biweekly, and now they show less need regarding frequency of contact.

CONCLUSIONS

Much is written about PTSD in combat veterans and victims of natural disasters. Man-made disasters seem to bring a multitude of other considerations. As described in the section on legal considerations, the victims must deal with the lawyers/courts and workers' compensation adjusters to obtain fair compensation for their loss of income and their physical and psychological injuries. At least when all of the financial and legal stressors are completed, the victims can more completely focus on getting well physically and mentally. For some, however, psychological recovery is also impeded or limited by physical recovery. I have seen patients for whom recovery from serious physical injury had to occur, or at least be in the process of occurring, before any attempts at psychological recovery could be implemented. Even in these cases, when the patient is ready, psychotherapy proves to be a valuable part of recovery.

More research is needed on issues such as the relationship between proximity to the traumatic event, relationships with those who have lost their lives, and personal physical injury. Additionally, greater exchange of treatment strategies and techniques would benefit all providers in working with survivors of disaster.

REFERENCES

Barabasz, A. F., Barabasz, M., & Watkins, J. G. (2011). Single-session manualized ego state therapy (EST) for combat stress injury, PTSD, and ASD, Part 1: The theory. *International Journal of Clinical and Experimental Hypnosis, 59*(4), 379–391.

Blanchard, E. B., Rowell, D., Kuhn, E., Rogers, R., & Wittrock, D. (2005). Posttraumatic stress and depressive symptoms in a college population one year after the September 11 attacks: The effect of proximity. *Behaviour Research and Therapy, 43*(1), 143–150.

Dewan, S. (2009, September 24). Report cites lack of precautions in 2008 sugar plant fire. *USA Today.*

Dimdam, E. (2013). Twenty-five biggest man made environmental disasters in history. *List25.* Retrieved April 15, 2015, from http://list25.com/25-biggest-man-made -environmental-disasters-in-history/

Ewin, D. M. (2014). *Easy to read body language: Ideomotor techniques.* Workshop presented at the New Orleans Society of Clinical Hypnosis, New Orleans, LA.

Ewin, D. M., & Eimer, B. N. (2006). *Ideomotor signals for rapid hypnoanalysis: A how-to manual.* Springfield, IL: Charles Thomas.

Frankel, F. (1994). The concept of flashbacks in historical perspective. *International Journal of Clinical and Experimental Hypnosis, 42*(4), 321–336.

Greeson, J. M. (2009). Mindfulness research update: 2008. *Complementary Health Practice Review.*

Gulf oil spill now largest offshore spill in U.S. history as BP continues plug effort. (2010, May 27). *USA Today.*

Holroyd, J. (2003). The science of meditation and the state of hypnosis. *American Journal of Clinical Hypnosis, 46*(2), 109–128.

Kuriansky, J., & Nemeth, D. G. (2013). A model for post-environmental disaster wellness workshops: Preparing individuals and communities for hurricane anniversary reactions. *Ecopsychology, 5*(Suppl. 1), S38–S45. Retrieved April 15, 2015, from http:// online.liebertpub.com/doi/pdf/10.1089/eco.2013.0006

Lundberg, M. K., Styf, J., & Carlsson, S. G. (2004). A psychometric evaluation of the Tampa Scale for Kinesiophobia—from a physiotherapeutic perspective. *Physiotherapy Theory and Practice, 20*(2), 121–133.

Manik, J. A. (2012, December 17). Bangladesh finds gross negligence in factory fire. *The New York Times.*

Nemeth, D. G., Kuriansky, J., Reeder, K. P., Lewis, A., Marceaux, K., Whittington, T., Olivier, T., . . . Safier, J. A. (2012). Addressing anniversary reactions of trauma through group process: The Hurricane Katrina Anniversary Wellness Workshops. *International Journal of Group Psychotherapy, 62*(1), 129–141.

Puleo, S. (2003). *Dark tide: The Great Boston Molasses Flood of 1919.* Boston, MA: Beacon Press.

Quang, T. D. (2014). *Mindfulness meditation.* Workshop presented at the Louisiana Psychological Association, June 13, Metairie, LA.

Russell, G. (2005, August 29). Ground Zero: Superdome becomes last resort for thousands unable to leave. *The Times-Picayune* (New Orleans, LA).

Seba, E. (2014, April 22). West, Texas fertilizer warehouse explosion was preventable, investigators find. *Reuters.*

Stephens, H. W. (1997). *The Texas City Disaster, 1947.* Austin, TX: University of Texas Press.

Tramontana, J. (2005). *Hypnotherapy and hypnosis as an adjunctive technique in psychotherapy.* Continuing education unit seminar presented at the Veterans Administration Hospital, Gulfport, MS.

Tramontana, J. (2009). *Hypnotically enhanced treatment for addictions: Alcohol abuse, drug abuse, gambling, weight control, and smoking cessation.* Carmarthen, UK: Crown House Publishing.

Tramontana, J. (2011). *Sports hypnosis in practice: Scripts, strategies and case examples.* Carmarthen, UK: Crown House Publishing.

University of Maryland Medical Center. (2014). *Post-traumatic stress disorder.* Retrieved April 15, 2015, from http://umm.edu/health/medical/altmed/condition/post traumatic-stress-disorder

U.S. Nuclear Regulatory Commission. (2014). *Backgrounder on Chernobyl nuclear power plant accident.* Retrieved April 15, 2015, from http://www.nrc.gov/reading-rm/doc-collections/fact-sheets/chernobyl-bg.html

van der Kolk, B. (2001). The assessment and treatment of complex PTSD. In R. Yehuda (Ed.), *Traumatic stress.* American Psychiatric Press.

van der Kolk, B. (2007). *New frontiers in trauma treatment.* Institution for the Advancement of Human Behavior. Presented by Bessel A. van der Kolk, Seattle, WA.

Walker, J. S. (2004). *Three Mile Island: A nuclear crisis in historical perspective.* Berkeley: University of California Press.

The world's worst coal mining disasters. (2014, May 16). Mining-technology.com.

7

Robust Leadership and Problem-Solving in the Face of Environmental Trauma

Darlyne G. Nemeth and Chelsie Songy

This chapter addresses the need for effective leadership, problem-solving, and coping skills in the aftermath of environmental trauma. Robust leaders must be able to make effective decisions in the here and now under the pressure of time. Coping is a five-part process that must be encouraged at all levels. Coping involves effective problem-solving. Lastly, the six universal stages of recovery from environmental trauma are outlined.

PROACTIVE DECISION-MAKING AND PREPAREDNESS

Every generation has had to face unique circumstances. Environmental trauma is one of this generation's greatest challenges. Whether nature-induced, human-induced, or a combination of both, preparedness is key. Preparedness is a three-level process involving government, media, and people. Each has an important role.

Making proactive decisions and developing and implementing comprehensive plans are the primary roles of government in dealing with environmental trauma. The media must offer factual, timely information and ongoing updates. People must heed the warnings/advice of government officials and media updates and act responsibly. Both physical and emotional preparedness are required for responsible action.

Physical preparedness involves an understanding of how to deal with an impending environmental event. If government officials mandate evacuation, people must evacuate! That means securing the needed clothing, fuel, money, food, and/or other supplies, and leaving in a timely manner. For a comprehensive physical preparedness plan, the reader is referred to http://www.disaster consulting.biz.

A comprehensive emotional preparedness plan requires robust resilience. With such an attitude, regardless of the circumstances, people can cope.

COPING

Coping is a five-part process according to a model postulated by the first author (Nemeth & Whittington, 2012, p. 113). First, people must *face their feelings* and process their experiences. This typically involves communication both verbally as well as nonverbally, since many emotions are shared nonverbally. Everyone's experience with environmental trauma is unique. The second step is for another person to *acknowledge and affirm* those experiences. Thus, coping is both an inter- and an intrapersonal process. Understanding one's own dynamics and having affirmation for one's experiences allows for the third step, *effective problem-solving*, to begin.

One method used to facilitate problem-solving is the "Getting to Yes" model as developed by Fisher, Ury, and Patton (1991). This includes the following four steps: (1) identify the problem and understand the history, (2) aftermath analysis, (3) effective approaches to resolution, and (4) nongovernmental organizations' ideas and actions (Nemeth, 2007). This four-step process, when followed in sequence, offers a way to take one good idea and build upon it in order to produce more good ideas (Fisher, Ury, & Patton, 1991, p. 67).

This process allows people to shift to the fourth stage, namely *reassessing and reprioritizing needs*. An example of this process, which was coordinated by the first author of this chapter, was used to facilitate a midday nongovernmental organization (NGO) workshop at the United Nations (UN) conference of the Department of Public Information (DPI) on September 6, 2007 (Nemeth et al., 2007). The workshop, moderated by Guillermo Garrido, MD, secretary general of the World Council for Psychotherapy (WCP), included the following speakers: Yasuo Onishi, PhD, adjunct professor of civil and environmental engineering at Washington State University and owner of Yasuo Onishi Consulting, LLC; Robert Hamilton, PhD, ornithologist, associate professor of wildlife management (retired) at Louisiana State University, and vice president, Envirosphere Consulting, LLC; Donald Nemeth, PhD, geologist and president, Envirosphere Consulting, LLC; and Joao Albuquerque, PhD, executive director of the Mata Atlantic Biosphere Reserve Council, United Nations Educational, Scientific and Cultural Organization (UNESCO) Man and Biosphere Program. During the workshop, participants were given a handout on how to use the "Getting to Yes" strategy (see Figure 7.1). Then, a blank copy was provided for each participant to include his/her ideas (see Figure 7.2). Ideas were then offered for Step I (see Figure 7.3), Step II (see Figure 7.4), Step III (see Figure 7.5), and Step IV (see Figure 7.6). This very effective form of problem-solving was of assistance to facilitate participants' understanding of what NGOs can do to address the need for biosphere management and lifestyle change. Frequently, this process involves reassessing and reprioritizing one's needs and expectations.

Figure 7.1.
How to use the "Getting to Yes" strategy

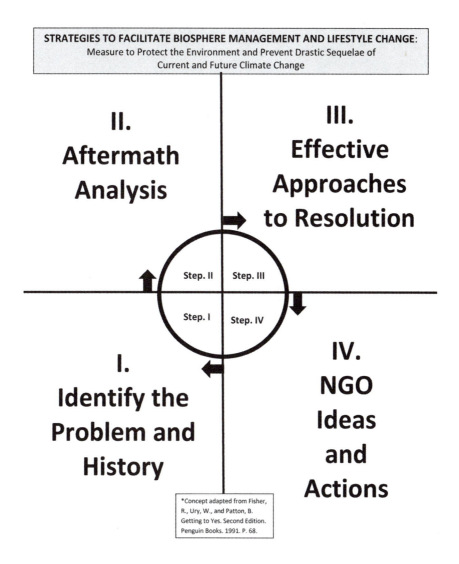

STRATEGIES TO FACILITATE BIOSPHERE MANAGEMENT AND LIFESTYLE CHANGE: Measure to Protect the Environment and Prevent Drastic Sequelae of Current and Future Climate Change

II.
Aftermath
Analysis

III.
Effective
Approaches
to Resolution

Step. II   Step. III

Step. I   Step. IV

I.
Identify the
Problem and
History

IV.
NGO
Ideas
and
Actions

*Concept adapted from Fisher, R., Ury, W., and Patton, B. Getting to Yes. Second Edition. Penguin Books. 1991. P. 68.

Figure 7.2.
Include your own ideas.

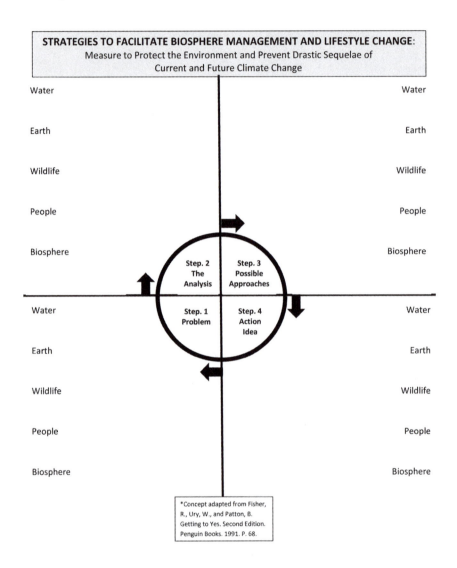

STRATEGIES TO FACILITATE BIOSPHERE MANAGEMENT AND LIFESTYLE CHANGE:
Measure to Protect the Environment and Prevent Drastic Sequelae of
Current and Future Climate Change

Water

Earth

Wildlife

People

Biosphere

Water

Earth

Wildlife

People

Biosphere

Water

Earth

Wildlife

People

Biosphere

Water

Earth

Wildlife

People

Biosphere

Step. 2
The
Analysis

Step. 3
Possible
Approaches

Step. 1
Problem

Step. 4
Action
Idea

*Concept adapted from Fisher,
R., Ury, W., and Patton, B.
Getting to Yes. Second Edition.
Penguin Books. 1991. P. 68.

Figure 7.3.
Step I: The Problems

Water:
- The quality and availability at appropriate times do not meet the needs of municipal/industrial water supplies, hydroelectric power generation, agriculture/irrigation, fisheries and recreation.
- Availability of stored water is decreasing, primarily through human use.
- Competition for water resources is increasing as supply is decreasing.

Earth:
- Mining and drilling cause many environmental problems.
  - Energy production causes increases in atmospheric CO_2.
  - Accidental fires in coal deposits and oil production areas release huge quantities of CO_2.
  - Climactic changes cause physical changes; these in turn, cause biological changes.

Wildlife:
- Man's appearance on earth has had a major effect on the environment.
  - Natural habitats have been destroyed or replaced by man-managed habitats.
  - Climax habitats have been selectively removed.
    - Remaining habitat is fragmented and disjointed.
      - Corresponding decrease in biodiversity.
      - Corresponding increase in extinction, endangered species, and threatened species.

People:
- Natural and man-induced disasters are increasing.
  - Effects are more severe because number of people is increasing and they congregate more in urban areas.
    - Increased damage and panic results.
    - Availability of secure areas is decreasing.
- Historical
  - Infrastructure neglect, bureaucratic inertia, and increasing physical and mental illness are occurring.
  - Biosphere abuse has resulted in many problems.
  - Increasing cultural negation, political corruption, and social complacency.

Biosphere:
- Global warming is increasing natural conservation challenges.
- Burning trees produces large amounts of CO_2 especially in the tropics.

- Deforestation negatively affects runoff, water retention, carbon sequestering, and biodiversity.
  - It also affects weather patterns and climate by changing patterns of atmospheric warming.
- Man, in general, does not understand the benefit and/or importance of natural systems or the costs of many of his over-consumptive/abusive activities.

Concept adapted from Fisher, Ury, and Patton (1991, p. 68).

Figure 7.4.
Step II: Aftermath Analysis

Water:

- High temperatures, more rain, and less snow affect availability of H_2O.
- Water temperature changes affect aquatic systems.
- Runoff and pollution increase with deforestation.
- Stored water is decreasing because of increased human usage.
- Amount of water required by man is increasing because of increasing number of people and resulting energy and material needs.

Earth:

- Global warming, whether natural or man-induced, is evident in regional changes.
  - Arctic lakes in Siberia are becoming larger.
  - On the Bering Sea, winter ice development forms later and melts earlier.
  - Glaciers and glacial ice caps are retreating.
  - A gradual rise in sea level is occurring.
- Landscapes are affected by global warming. This affects locations of cities as well as other human and non-human habitats.
  - Species are differentially affected by qualitative and quantitative changes in biota.

Wildlife:

- Atmospheric temperature and related changes can affect timing and availability of needed resources.
- Changes in locations and availability of remaining habitat could lead to mass extinctions.
- Competition for habitat is increasing because of increases of human numbers and their perceived needs.

People:

- Psychological chaos will increase.
  - Examples are denial, disbelief, shock, blame, misdirected focus, and inaction/reaction.
- There will be systems failures.
  - Examples are lack of effective leadership, no clear chain of command, lack of timely response or consensus on priorities, and no foresight.
- There will be social victimization.
  - This will be demonstrated by minimalization, dehumanization, labelization, criminalization, and separation.

Biosphere:

- It is important to focus actions in implementing conservation and sustainable development.
  - Despite many signs of devastation, society does not yet recognize the importance of the conservation of nature.
  - Carbon credits are generated by replicating the forest. The "standing forest" is a reservoir of sequestered carbon.

Concept adapted from Fisher, Ury, and Patton (1991, p. 68).

Figure 7.5.
Step III: Effective Approaches to Restoration

Water:

- Develop a global program for sustainable use.
  - Especially difficult if climate is warming, human population is increasing, and energy needs are rising.
- All planning should take into account highly probable and less probable future changes.

Earth:

- Environmental management plans must be based on geologic principles.
  - Plans must consider how natural processes operate with time and likely occurrences.
    - We should stop constructing cities on faults or bases of volcanoes.
    - We should not place dwellings in flood plains or reimburse for floods occurring there.

Wildlife:

- We should determine and rank wildlife needs.
- We should preserve remaining climax stands and encourage establishment of additional climax.

- We should anticipate and prepare for future habitat changes.
- We should establish corridors to connect habitat patches to facilitate movement between patches and increase effective block size.
- We should maximize block size as much as possible.
- We should prevent and/or minimize further habitat destruction.

People:

- We should develop institutions and infrastructure to aid affected people.
- We should develop programs for biosphere management.
- We should help develop a sense of cultural appreciation of nature and ecosystems.
- We should establish political responsibility for environment and viability of life on earth.
- We should become socially aware of our environment and consequences of our actions.
  - We must learn to "look, listen, and learn."
  - When disasters occur, we must seize the opportunity to initiate appropriate changes.
- We should be proactive in disaster and trauma preparation.
- We should develop a plan to address basic needs.
  - Some of these include medical, psychological, and social needs.
    - Others include food, shelter and safety.
- We must encourage individuals and communities to find a way to help themselves.

Biosphere:

- We must find and implement strategies to minimize impacts of global warming.
  - This requires the integration and cooperation of those who have other interests than conservation.
- People must understand the consequences of how they use the earth's resources.
- We must determine the consequences of increasing human numbers.
- We should encourage development of additional Biosphere Reserves and the restoration of more forested habitat.
- We must maintain as much biodiversity as possible.
- We should utilize plantings for carbon sequestering to help restore appropriate habitats.
- We should encourage the evaluation of the earth's ability to support humans and the education of how to use them responsibly.

Concept adapted from Fisher, Ury, and Patton (1991, p. 68).

Figure 7.6.
Step IV: NGO Ideas and Actions

Water:

- NGOs should encourage additional studies to objectively relate climate changes to water resource planning.
- NGOs should help to establish plans and guidelines to improve reservoir management.
- NGOs should encourage stakeholders to find ways to conserve water and objectively allocate resources.
- NGOs should help to find ways to conserve energy and to develop alternative energy sources for additional efficiency and environmental benefits.
- Ways to increase flexibility and efficiency, and diversity of water and electric systems, should be sought.

Earth:

- Rational development that is consistent with climatic and geologic realities must be encouraged.
- Ways to minimize climate and geologic changes on the environment should be sought.
- NGOs should aid in repairing damages of geologic events.
- NGOs should help establish realistic priorities for preservation, repair, and development.
  - With geologic risk factors, prudent plans at times may be to abandon and retreat.

Wildlife:

- Help create more Biosphere Reserves.
- NGOs should help promulgate landscape ecology principles where appropriate.
- NGOs should encourage the development of global habitat goals and plans to attain them.
- Encourage the formulation of global consensus on human use of the environment.
- Developing increased geopolitical cooperation is desirable.

People:

- NGOs should be the agents of change by encouraging grassroots efforts and supporting local experts, initiatives, and interventions.
- NGOs should challenge false beliefs.
- NGOs should encourage the preservation of local history and culture and help rebuild communities as well as preserve self-reliance and problem solving.
- NGOs should promote psychological wellness initiatives.

- NGOs should invest in rebuilding people who will in turn rebuild their societies.
- NGOs should avoid becoming part of the problem.

Biosphere:
- NGOs should help in developing methods to reduce harmful emissions.
- NGOs should help protect biodiversity in a changing world.
- NGOs should encourage conservation and global development.
- NGOs should help reforestation to maintain the biosphere.
- NGOs should encourage corporate participation to promote innovation and conservation.
- NGOs should help promulgate the concept that forest existence positively affects water quality and quantity and benefits us all.

Concept adapted from Fisher, Ury, and Patton (1991, p. 68).

Once a consensus regarding "Ideas and/or Actions" has been achieved, then the fifth stage, *implementation*, can commence. This is the hardest of all of the coping strategies because it involves changing behavior. People typically desire to return to the familiar; for example, to rebuild a home on the beach after a natural disaster like a hurricane. But, is this wise? Implementing change after an environmental trauma requires effective coping.

Being able to cope effectively and to withstand significant stressors is the mark of a resilient individual (Walker & Heffner, 2010). Environmental trauma is one of the most significant stressors of our time. Resilience in the aftermath of environmental trauma requires the ability to be focused on today, to learn from yesterday, and to imagine oneself in tomorrow (Nemeth & Whittington, 2012). Resilient people are adaptable and flexible.

ROBUST LEADERSHIPS

Lieutenant General Russel L. Honoré, who led the U.S. Department of Defense response to Hurricanes Katrina and Rita in Louisiana in 2005, was a robust, resilient leader who ameliorated chaos and restored order. He was an effective problem-solver who commanded respect. In his book *Leadership in the New Normal* (Honoré, 2012), he stated, "We were born free by good fortune. To live free is a privilege. To die free is an obligation. Each generation has the obligation to keep America free for the next generation" (pp. 16–17). Adapting Honoré's words to our environment, this restatement is now offered by this chapter's authors: "We inherited a beautiful world. To live in it is a privilege. To care for it is an obligation. Each generation has the obligation to keep our environment safe for the next generation."

According to Honoré (2012), "Good leaders need not always be at the front of the formation, but they always figure out where they are needed most. Being at the right place at the right time is what a leader does" (p. 22). Good, robust leaders possess a sense of mastery, authority, and purpose and inspire hope in others. Hope fuels our ability to persevere and to pursue a better life (Lopez, Rose, Robinson, Marques, & Pais-Ribeiro, 2009). Robust leaders know how (1) to do routine things well, (2) to not fear the impossible, and (3) to act in the face of criticism (Honoré, 2012, p. 25).

Protecting our environment requires robust leaders who can rise to the challenge. Leadership requires the ability to collaborate with others from many different backgrounds. As noted in our book *Living in an Environmentally Traumatized World: Healing Ourselves and Our Planet* (Nemeth, Hamilton, & Kuriansky, 2012), this process requires a holistic approach to problem-solving. Many different levels of expertise will be required to rise to the challenge. Collaboration, not competition, among scientists, professional politicians, and all stakeholders is the key.

PROACTIVE INCLUSION

To accomplish the goal of protecting our environment will require proactive inclusion. It will be important to understand what scientists, including geologists, hydrologists, climatologists, ecologists, and others, have learned and what interventionists such as Biosphere Reserve coordinators, psychologists, and others have accomplished. Individuals representing all levels and backgrounds, including politicians and stakeholders, must be included. Conferences sponsored by the United Nations, such as the Doha Climate-Change Conference held in Doha, Qatar, in November 2012, typically produce lofty goals. Oftentimes, many of these goals, such as the ones produced at the Kyoto conference on climate change held in Kyoto, Japan, in 1997 fail to be implemented. This conference led to the Kyoto Protocol, an international treaty, that committed state parties to reduce greenhouse gas emissions.

The first goal, or "mechanism" as the Kyoto Protocol states, is emissions trading, which is when "an Annex I Party may transfer Kyoto units to or acquire from another Annex I Party" (Boer, 2008, p. 16). This redistributes the allotted amount of units among the Annex I Party. The Annex I Party consists of the countries that pledged, as a group, to reduce their greenhouse gas emissions, by at least 5 percent, below the 1990 levels by the year 2012 (TFS Green, 2012). The second mechanism, "joint implementation" (JI), is when one Annex I Party "can invest in a project that reduces emission or enhances sequestration in another Annex I Party, and receive credit for the emission reductions or removals achieved through that project" (Boer, 2008, p. 17). The third mechanism of the Kyoto Protocol is the Clean Development Mechanism (CDM), in which "CDM credits may be generated from emission reduction projects or from afforestation and refor-estation projects in non-Annex I Parties" (Boer, 2008, p. 18).

According to Honoré (2012), "the U.S. has 5 percent of the world's popula-tion and consumes 25 percent of its resources" (p. 53). The U.S. leaderships rejected these Kyoto goals (United Nations Framework Convention on Climate Change, 2001). Why? Because it would require a change in behavior, at all lev-els, by American politicians, corporations, individuals, etc.

INFLUENCING CHANGE

Psychologists are trained in the art and science of behavioral change. Yet, most psychologists are not trained in leadership. According to Honoré (2012), leadership is defined as "the art and science of influencing others to willingly fol-low" (p. 133). Qualities of presence, character, credibility, integrity, and having a proactive sense of purpose are required. Psychologists are typically trained in doctoral programs that foster competitiveness, rather than collaboration. Fur-ther, they are not trained to lead. Yet, leadership is now required. Being able to influence government, corporations, stakeholders, and others, to adapt and implement important environmental goals is the challenge that lies ahead.

Nature-induced environmental trauma may not be preventable, but the human-induced contributions to it can be reduced, if not eliminated. For exam-ple, the BP oil spill was human-induced. It was preventable. In this case, both government and industry did not do their job (Onishi, 2012, p. 27). How can employees be inspired to do their job? The answer is straightforward. Robust leaders who command, rather than demand, loyalty, integrity, and accountabil-ity can set the tone through example, not rhetoric.

If not preventable, at least preparation for disasters can reduce the consequen-ces of environmental trauma. Lessons must be learned from the effectiveness of preparation; otherwise, these disastrous experiences will merely be repeated. For example, every major coastal city in the United States should have learned from Hurricane Katrina in 2005. Yet, the New York–New Jersey area seemed totally unprepared for Hurricane Sandy in 2012 (Anderson, 2012). Many people did not evacuate when ordered, and dealing with these people after the storm caused many unnecessary problems. Local utility crews were waiting for direc-tion, which frequently did not come; whereas utility crews from Louisiana who were called upon to help, did not wait for permission, they just started helping (Anonymous, personal communication, 2012). They knew what to do and they did it. They were robust leaders.

When trauma occurs, people cannot wait for permission to act. Frequently, as in post–Hurricane Katrina in New Orleans, no one was available to give permis-sion. People, even leaders, appeared frozen in a state of shock. This is a universal phenomenon. Without preparedness, shock, rather than action, is the norm.

THE SIX UNIVERSAL STAGES OF RECOVERY

According to Nemeth and Whittington (2012), a universal six-stage process follows environmental trauma. As stated above, *shock* is the first stage. Even when there are media warnings and government directions, many people do not or will not believe that the trauma will affect or even inconvenience them. Such questions as "Why don't I have electricity?" "When can I go back to work?" and "Why are the schools closed?" are frequently heard. This sense of entitlement, which is the "belief that one is deserving of or entitled to certain privileges" (Entitlement, 2013), occurs regardless of government and media warnings. It happened in the case of Hurricane Katrina and again in the case of Hurricane/Superstorm Sandy. There is often little sense of personal responsibility. People expect to live where they want to live and do what they want to do without interruption. They expect that the fact that they live in a city that is five feet below sea level (New Orleans), or that they live in a beach area (Gulf Coast or New York/New Jersey), should make no difference. Furthermore, as long as they can buy insurance to rebuild in the same area (Bellafante, 2012), people are unlikely to make a choice to relocate. According to Don Belt (2011; as cited in Nemeth, 2012, p. 66), "more than one-third of the world's population lives within 62 miles of current sea level."

Geologist Donald F. Nemeth (2012), states that "all U.S. coasts are vulnerable, but the most vulnerable are near sea level areas that are nearly flat and gently sloping" (p. 66). This certainly defines the New York–New Jersey area; yet there was a failure to learn from Hurricane Katrina, and shock prevailed.

Without light and heat and in the cold weather, people quickly moved into the second stage, *survival mode*. This can be ameliorated by effective intervention. With intervention, rather than becoming victims, people can then proceed to the third stage, *assessment of basic needs*. Giving up their desired "wants" and prioritizing their basic "needs" is a crucial step in the recovery process. In this stage, safety, food, and water become far more important than work, school, or entertainment. Reestablishing safety is usually the responsibility of government, whereas the responsibility of media is to offer factual information regarding shelter, food, and water availability. These functions are typically provided by community and religious organizations (Nemeth et al., 2012). For example, 42 students and eight adult volunteers from the Baptist Collegiate Ministry at Louisiana State University joined more than 500 students from organizations across the country to help in the Hurricane Sandy relief effort. The volunteers spent their time rebuilding homes. Tasks ranged from tearing up floorboards to spraying an antifungal chemical on exposed frames to help prevent mold growth. Some students helped clean out debris and belongings from survivors' homes (Hunter, 2013).

When safety has been reestablished, the people can then move into the fourth stage, *awareness of loss*. If evacuation occurred, it is at this point that individuals are usually allowed to return, if only briefly, to assess their losses—of people, pets, and/or property. Grieving can begin after loss has been determined, especially when a robust leader comes to acknowledge people's loss and their pain.

However, this fourth stage is frequently interrupted abruptly by unscrupulous individuals who arrive to offer easy solutions to complex problems. Thus, *susceptibility to spin and fraud* is the fifth stage. This was never more evident than in Hurricane Katrina. The Home Box Office (HBO) series *Treme* (Simon, 2010) frequently portrayed such examples. When people are overwhelmed emotionally, it is difficult for them to think logically and to engage in constructive problem-solving.

EFFECTIVE INTERVENTIONS

Effective interventions can best be accomplished in group settings, since when a trauma happens to a group (community), it must be addressed in a group (community) setting. This is where interventions, such as the Hurricane Wellness Workshops conducted by the first author (Nemeth et al., 2012) can be most helpful. People do not need in-depth psychotherapy at this point. Rather, they need to move away from isolation and decision reactivity and toward reconstruction and community responsibility. During these seven-hour, one-day wellness workshops, anxieties were reduced and empowerment was reborn (Nemeth et al., 2011). Anniversary wellness workshops are most successful when they are held on the first anniversary of an important environmental trauma, such as Hurricane Katrina.

RESILIENCE AND HOPE

Resolution is the sixth stage of the recovery process. It typically begins approximately one year after the trauma. Group process/community involvement usually facilitates resolution. In most cases, resolution can take as long as five years to achieve. It is usually more difficult when loved ones have been lost.

Property, pets, and people are frequently lost during environmental trauma. Yet, in order to recover, hope must be restored. Hope can be reinvigorated by robust leaders. According to Lopez (2010), "Hope can be enhanced and it is viral. Hope is goal-directed thinking in which people perceive that they can produce routes to desired goals and the requisite motivation to use those routes."

PSYCHOLOGISTS AS ROBUST LEADERS

According to Honoré (2012), "Whoever sees first, understands first, and acts first has decision superiority" (p. 100). Because robust leaders have decision superiority, they can make a real difference. They can inspire others to reach consensus and act responsibly. Psychologists are needed, at this time more than ever, to rise to the occasion and be robust leaders. But, do we have the courage and the training to step up?

ACKNOWLEDGMENTS

The authors wish to acknowledge all wellness workshop participants, facilitators, and supporters and all those who contributed to the journal articles and newspaper and media accounts regarding these experiences.

REFERENCES

Anderson, M. (2012, November 10). Power outages: New Jersey, New York slowly see lights back on after Hurricane Sandy. *Huffington Post.* Retrieved April 18, 2015, from http://www.huffingtonpost.com/2012/11/10/power-outages-new-jersey-york_n_2109654.html

Bellafante, G. (2012, November 16). Paying to rebuild, and rebuild again. *New York Times.* Retrieved April 18, 2015, from http://www.nytimes.com/2012/11/18/nyregion/paying-to-rebuild-after-the-storm-now-and-in-the-future.html

Boer, Y. D. (2008, November). *Kyoto protocol reference manual on accounting of emissions and assigned amount.* United Nations Framework Convention on Climate Change. Retrieved April 18, 2015, from http://unfccc.int/resource/docs/publications/08_unfccc_kp_ref_manual.pdf

Entitlement. (2013). *Merriam-Webster.com.* Retrieved April 18, 2015, from http://www.merriam-webster.com/dictionary/entitlement

Fisher, R., Ury, W., & Patton, B. (1991). *Getting to yes: Negotiating agreement without giving in* (2nd ed.). New York, NY: Penguin Books.

Honoré, R. L. (2012). *Leadership in the new normal* (pp. 16–133). Lafayette, LA: Acadian House Publishing.

Hunter, M. H. (2013, January 5). LSU students team with other Baptists in Sandy relief work. *The Advocate,* pp. 1D, 3D.

Lopez, S. J. (2010, April). *Hope: It's more than a feeling.* Paper presented at the 62nd Annual Convention of the Louisiana Psychological Association, Baton Rouge, LA.

Lopez, S. J., Rose, S., Robinson, C., Marques, S. C., & Pais-Ribeiro, J. (2009). Measuring and promoting hope in schoolchildren. In R. Gilman, E. S. Huebner, & M. Furlong (Eds.), *Promoting wellness in children and youth: Handbook of positive psychology in the schools* (pp. 37–51). Mahwah, NJ: Lawrence Erlbaum.

Nemeth, D. F. (2012). Our planet earth: Understanding the big picture. In D. G. Nemeth, R. B. Hamilton & J. Kuriansky (Eds.), *Living in an Environmentally Traumatized World: Healing Ourselves and Our Planet* (p. 66). Santa Barbara, CA: Praeger.

Nemeth, D. G. (2007, September 5–7). *The anatomy of a disaster: Streamlining the recovery process.* Presented at the 60th Annual UN DPI/NGO Conference, New York, NY.

Nemeth, D. G., Garrido, G., Onishi, Y., Hamilton, R., Nemeth, D. F., & Albuquerque, J. (2007, September). *Strategies to facilitate biosphere management and lifestyle change: Measures to protect the environment and prevent drastic sequelae of current and future climate changes.* Symposium presented at the 60th Annual United Nations DPI/NGO Conference Midday Workshops, New York, NY.

Nemeth, D. G., Kuriansky, J., Olivier, T. W., Whittington, L. T., May, N., Hamilton, J., & Steger, A. (2011). Group interventions for disaster/trauma anniversary reactions. *Global Horizons, 4*(1), 61.

Nemeth, D. G., Kuriansky, J., Reeder, K. P., Lewis, A., Marceaux, K., Whittington, T., ... Safier, J. A. (2012). Addressing anniversary reactions of trauma through group process: The Hurricane Katrina anniversary wellness workshops. *International Journal of Group Psychotherapy, 62*(1), 129–142.

Nemeth, D. G., & Whittington, L. T. (2012). Our robust people: Resilience in the face of environmental trauma. In D. G. Nemeth, R. B. Hamilton, & J. Kuriansky (Eds.), *Living in an environmentally traumatized world: Healing ourselves and our planet* (pp. 113–140). Santa Barbara, CA: ABC-CLIO/Praeger.

Onishi, Y. (2012). Our living waters: Polluting or cleansing. In D. G. Nemeth, R. B. Hamilton, & J. Kuriansky (Eds.), *Living in an environmentally traumatized world: Healing ourselves and our planet.* Santa Barbara, CA: ABC-CLIO/Praeger.

Simon, D. (Writer). (2010). In D. Simon (Executive Producer), *Treme* [TV series]. Home Box Office.

TFS Green. (2012). *Glossary.* Retrieved April 18, 2015, from http://tfsenergy.com/glossary.html

United Nations Framework Convention on Climate Change. (2001). Statement 8: United States of America. In *Implementation of the Buenos Aires Plan of Action: Statements Made in Connection with the Approval of the Bonn Agreements on the Implementation of the Buenos Aires Plan of Action (decision 5/CP.6).* Retrieved April 18, 2015, from http://unfccc.int/resource/docs/cop7/misc04.pdf

Walker, J., & Heffner, F. (2010, Summer). Resilience as a critical factor in the workplace. *New Worker.* Retrieved April 18, 2015, from http://cecassoc.com/download/i/mark_dl/u/1389501/5180391/Summer%202010.pdf

8

Empowerment in African Americans' Responses to Global Climate Change and Environmental Racism through an Integrative Bio-Interpersonal/Music-Based Approach

Tommy Davis III and J. Donald Dumpson

This chapter presents the thesis that climate change disproportionally impacts African Americans, provides a conceptualization for understanding this impact, and offers strategies for responding to resulting problems of this impact on the African American community.* An interpersonal and a bio-psychosocial perspective is offered to alert those who contribute to the impact on Black Americans of health disparities and to inform prevention and interventions about such disparities. Also, fundamental neuropsychological function influenced by cultural experience is presented as the foundation for developing unity, community, and motivation for social action in the Black community. Additionally, the authors draw on the theoretical formulations of Harry Stack Sullivan (1953), who has been deemed "America's Psychiatrist," for insights regarding attitudes that separate racial groups. Central to the thesis in this chapter are Sullivan's ideas about the common humanity that we all share and the importance of sociopolitcal factors and cultural predilections. In the case of African Americans, the authors highlight the role of music as one important form of cultural expression and agent for change.

The authors further specifically propose using music as an approach to mitigate this impact of climate change on African Americans. They argue that in the African American community, music unifies people, helping them adapt to changing physical and psychosocial environments. Hence, innovative programs based on music can be useful to target the deleterious psychological and physical effects and dangers of climate change on this population (as well as on the population in general). Historical observations support this assumption, as the role of music has been highly visible in the African American's survival story (Sullivan, 2001), examples of which are described below.

---

*The authors use the terms African Americans, Black Americans, and Americans of African descent interchangeably.

BACKGROUND

From the arrival in 1619 of the first documented Africans on American soil as indentured servants in Jamestown (Thornton, 1998) to the ongoing fight for social justice, music has been heard in the background of African Americans' freedom/civil rights journey from slavery toward liberty and justice. Along the way, music has held an important position in African Americans' experiences as well as in their fight for justice and, more broadly, in their social construction of reality (Reed, 2005; Smith, 1999). Negro spirituals, classical, gospel, jazz, rhythm and blues, blues, soul, and neo-soul music have motivated African Americans to fight oppression and to pursue justice. Examples of musical accompaniments in the struggles of Americans of African descent are extensive; they include: Negro spirituals that were sung in the cotton fields of American plantations; the famous contralto Marian Anderson's rendition of "My Country, Tis of Thee" sung on the steps of the Lincoln Memorial in 1930; Paul Robeson's placement of Negro spirituals into the center of America's mind; legendary gospel singer Mahalia Jackson's rendition of "How I Got Over," sung from the steps of the Washington Monument in 1963; James Brown's song "Black and Proud"; Coco Taylor's shout "I'm a Woman"; Public Enemy's rap song "Fight the Power"; and Aretha Franklin's soulful proclamation "Young, Gifted and Black" in 1972, and then her rendition of "My Country, Tis of Thee" at the inauguration of the nation's first African American president, Barack Obama. Most recently, neo-soul singer John Legend and hip-hop artist Common evoked a visible display of emotions among a diverse audience with their performance of "Glory" at the 2015 Grammy Awards. Each of these songs demonstrates the prominent role of music in response to oppression and injustice, and its ability to soothe emotions, stir action, instill pride and celebrate victories. With such an impressive record, music can play an important role in the pursuit of health and equality in the battle against what is called "environmental racism" in the twenty-first century.

Environmental Racism

Fundamental to the authors' thesis is the concept of environmental racism, which has been defined as the intentional and/or unintentional placement of low-income or minority communities in proximity of environmentally hazardous locales, such as near toxic waste, pollution, or urban decay (Holifield, 2001). This chapter elucidates environmental racism through the lens of an interpersonal perspective. Furthermore, the thesis presented in this chapter is that music may be one avenue to tackle the problem of environmental racism that is responsible for the disproportionate effects of global climate change on African Americans. Music can become a bridge between the probable toxic effects of climate change on African Americans and the African American community's pursuit of physical and emotional well-being as well as social and environmental justice. The authors believe that the road that divides a community's succumbing to global climate change versus a community successfully campaigning for environmental justice is essentially interpersonal in its nature.

Relevance of Sullivan's Interpersonal Theory

To provide support for this thesis, the authors have selected the interpersonal perspective of Harry Stack Sullivan (1953) as a foundation. The appeal of Sullivan's theories is inspired by the comprehensiveness of his work and particular personal dimensions of his life. As the child of Irish immigrants and Catholics, Sullivan grew up in an anti–Roman Catholic upstate New York community and learned early about discrimination and isolation, an experience that deeply influenced his life, and possibly his choice of profession and his sensibility to the situation of the disenfranchised (Chapman, 1976). Additionally, Sullivan stands among the most important historical figures in psychiatry and perhaps the single most influential figure in elevating the interpersonal perspective to prominence in psychoanalysis, psychiatry, and psychology (Perry, 1982).

Along with noted psychoanalysts Erick Fromm, Frieda Fromm-Reichmann, Clara Thompson and others, Sullivan founded the William Alanson White Institute in New York City and the Washington School of Psychiatry in Washington, D.C. The White Institute and Washington School became central to the application of interpersonal concepts to a wide range of social problems and included interdisciplinary collaborations with distinguished sociologists and anthropologists such as Harold Lasswell and Margaret Mead. Sullivan's collaboration with prominent Black sociologist Charles S. Johnson in 1937 studied the psychosocial problems of "Negro youth" as well as examined the perspectives of Black community leaders in Nashville, Tennessee. This was followed by a collaboration with another renowned African American sociologist, E. Franklin Frazier, examining the experience for Black youth in the "Border" States, primarily Washington, D.C., and Louisville, Kentucky. Noteworthy was Sullivan's influence on celebrated African American author Ralph Ellison, who worked as Sullivan's clerk/receptionist shortly after his arrival to New York City (Rampersad, 2007). Ellison later authored the book *The Invisible Man*, where he described the social and intellectual issues facing African Americans in the twentieth century. Rampersad stated that it was unheard of at that time for an eminent White professional to hire a Black receptionist and then to treat that worker with courtesy and respect as did Sullivan, asking Ellison to read excerpts from a book he was writing and to offer comments about the clarity of his writing. Gerald Early (2009), another biographer of Ellison, stated that Ellison's experiences with Sullivan inspired aspects of *The Invisible Man*, for example, citing the dream sequences that Ellison presented as being derived from his understanding of Sullivan's work.

Sullivan's concepts are relevant to understanding the struggles of African Americans in that his theory integrates sociocultural and sociopolitical influences and emphasizes the impact of discrimination and racism on emotional development, while also highlighting the similarity among different groups of people. Prominent historical African American scholars have been influenced by his approach, requesting his guidance in the 1930s and 1940s to understand concerns in the African American community through elucidating interpersonal characteristics. The interpersonal characteristics he described are similar characteristics that the authors of this chapter believe are basic to the creation and expression of music and the concerns presented here.

The Role of Music in Social Advocacy

Music, which is filled with interpersonal reverberations and images, is presented by the authors as the glue that can hold a social movement together. The interpersonal dimensions involved during the expression and reception of musical experiences can motivate people to action and maintain their attention while they manage the difficult task of social and political advocacy. Who can forget the images of Reverend Dr. Martin Luther King Jr. and other civil rights agents of change marching in Selma, Alabama, and other parts of the country, arms linked, singing "We Shall Overcome." To solicit music to help construct resilient communities is to solicit interpersonal interactions to give music an even deeper meaning and power.

The influence of music stems from its deeply embedded properties in people's minds and lives as evidenced by the similarity of neurological, cognitive, and emotional responses to musical experiences for all people (Levitin, 2007). Culture defines what experiences, musical and otherwise, and what forms of communication rank highest in value by a group (Benedict, 1934). Those high-ranking experiences may have a profound and lasting impact on psychological as well as physical composition, given mounting evidence that experiences may change brain structure and chemistry (Diamond, 1988). In addition to music's effects on the general public as agents of celebration, comfort, and organization, the authors argue, as have others (Reed, 2005; Sullivan, 2001), that music has played a unifying role, supporting efforts, particularly in the African American community, to adapt and/or change adverse conditions. Hence, if music plays such a prominent role in the culture, each effort that relies on music for coping allows the individual and/or group to become increasingly proficient in using music as an agent of comfort and change. A logical conclusion, then, is that African Americans in a broad sense may have developed a neurological predisposition to use music to manage environmental changes.

Whether or not such a neurological predisposition exists in African Americans, music can be used as a tool for social change. In particular, music can be combined with social media to heighten attention to a particular issue or concern. In this electronic age, social media is a valuable strategy to draw African Americans' attention to harmful environmental changes and to motivate proactive behaviors.

A strategy presented in this chapter is the development of music centers strategically located in socially and culturally relevant institutions such as churches, fraternity and sorority houses, schools, and community centers that can offer exposure to a variety of music forms from urban to classical music. Dumpson (2014), coauthor of this chapter, points out that classical music by composers of African descent, about whom many people may be uninformed, can be used to engage groups and instill further pride in the breadth of achievements in the African American community. These music-based undertakings can be directed toward supporting social advocacy.

When these music-based strategies are integrated into a comprehensive and multidimensional program, their potency may be amplified. The Talent Recovery for Resilient Living (TRRL) is a model for increasing resiliency and overall coping skills. Developed by Davis (2007b), the first author of this chapter, and proposed to the Philadelphia Department of Behavioral Health to address teen violence, this model takes a comprehensive approach encompassing many of the strategies and interventions presented in this chapter. The authors believe TRRL holds promise as a vehicle to awaken the talents and resilient acts of individuals and help mobilize people to fight environmental racism—an elaboration of which is presented later in this chapter.

With regard to mobilizing the fight against environmental racism and injustice, what better group to offer insights about resilience and social change than African Americans, given their history in this country? The authors emphasize that the role of music in African American culture and responses to oppression and racism can serve as a template for how music could be used to motivate positive change and resilience at personal and collective levels for other racial and ethnic groups. Hence, music-based strategies presented in this chapter are not limited to African Americans. Further, peoples' responses to music contain many similarities, regardless of race and ethnicity, and thus can be used to unite diverse groups toward a common purpose. Technological advances and social media make sharing experiences of diverse groups easier, helping to fill in the gap that separate people and promote receptivity in non-African Americans to acknowledging the unequal effects of climate change on Americans of African descent.

EFFECTS OF CLIMATE CHANGE ON AFRICAN AMERICANS

Why should global climate change have a disproportionate effect on African Americans? The answer lies in the concept introduced above called "environmental racism" that has been cited as a primary cause of this inequity

(Bullard & Wright, 2012). Environmental racism is evident in (1) the presence of a larger number of industrial sites near African American communities, and (2) the higher concentration of toxins in the vicinity of African American communities, which results in health problems like asthma and other respiratory diseases.

According to the *Environmental Justice and Climate Change Initiative* report (Hoerner & Robinson, 2008), over 72 percent of African Americans live in counties in violation of federal air pollutions standards compared to 58 percent of Whites. In every major U.S. city, Black Americans are more likely than White Americans to be exposed to higher air toxins concentrations. Asthma is expected to worsen, with Black Americans being about three times as likely to be hospitalized or die because of complications related to asthma than White Americans (Hoerner & Robinson, 2008). In addition, the concentration of African Americans in large urban centers such as New York City, Detroit, Chicago, and Philadelphia expose individuals to heat indexes that are expected to be lethal. African Americans suffer heat-related deaths at 150–200 percent the rate of non-Hispanic Whites. Further, the concentration of African Americans in southern cities and regions, which comprises approximately 55 percent of the African American population, may suffer severe blows due to dangerous storms, drought, and flooding (Hoerner & Robinson, 2008). Rising rates of infectious diseases that may be partially due to warmer climates and that may lead to greater mosquito infestations are expected. The recent threat to the Americas of the mosquito-borne chikungunya virus (Smith, 2013) is but one example. Given a history of well-documented health disparities between Black Americans and White Americans, the chasm is expected to widen, and these possible health concerns become more frightening.

A "fight for life and a livelihood," then, may be a suitable descriptor of African Americans' efforts to address the impact of environmental racism. The disproportionate impact may also be reflected in the larger percentage of African Americans who fall in lower income brackets and their limited access to ongoing preventive medical care. Future higher energy costs may be prohibitive for many African Americans. Hoerner and Robinson (2008) report that, "African Americans are more vulnerable to . . . unemployment, recessions caused by global energy price shocks, and a greater economic burden from military operations designed to protect the flow of oil to the U.S." (p. 1). Hence, climate change and severe weather conditions represent a significant public health problem, and as with other indictors like unemployment, housing deficits, and health disparities of impact suggest, the combined lethal impact of these factors is disproportionately greater for African Americans (Brulle & Pellow, 2006; Bullard & Wright, 1990; Morello-Frosch & Lopez, 2006; White-Newsome et al., 2009).

Hurricane Katrina awakened African Americans as well as other Americans to the vulnerability of Black communities to severe weather conditions.

Initial images of an almost submerged New Orleans and the destruction of many southern cities along the Gulf Coast by Hurricane Katrina forever carve a tragic American story of many African Americans into the minds of many. Scholars have warned of African Americans' vulnerability to weather disasters. Robert Bullard, Ph.D., who has been described as the "Father of Environmental Justice," argues that African Americans are more vulnerable to the effects of climate change despite having a smaller carbon footprint (Bullard & Wright, 2012). Bullard and Wright's *Race, Place, and Environmental Justice after Hurricane Katrina* (2009) and *The Wrong Complexion for Protection* (2012) document that racial disparities exist in disaster response, the cleanup operations, and rebuilding the communities. For example, African Americans spend more time in temporary housing, shelters, and hotels, and they are more often permanently displaced. Forman and Lewis (2006) explain Americans' shock response to the despair and utter terror engulfing New Orleans's "mostly brown people" through a conceptualization of racial apathy as the post–civil rights racism. The racial apathy has been described as a function of the individual's avoidance of racial issues and societal structures that systemically hinder the flow of knowledge to individuals regarding racial inequalities. Davis (2006), in his response to Hurricane Katrina's catastrophic impact, warns the public about potentially habituating to the images that traumatized many Americans hours and days after Katrina's landfall; he also appeals for sustained empathy for the long road of reconstruction for the affected people.

The impact of climate change on African Americans was clear from experiences of the first author and others who worked with Katrina survivors. As a first responder and member of a training team for volunteers at one of the largest religious congregations in the United States—Joel Osteen's Lakewood Church in Houston—the first author greeted Katrina evacuees upon their arrival at the Houston Astrodome and later fed information to the Philadelphia Department of Behavioral Health, which had plans to relocated nearly 2,000 people to Philadelphia. Katrina survivors told many tragic stories that revealed confusion and often delirium. For instance, one elderly lady, who was wondering around the Astrodome crying, described her last conversation with her sister before the phone lines dropped dead; while an African American man reported that he was offered refuge at a prison, which he refused for fear that he might never be released (Davis, Glass, Board, Williams, & Graves, 2006). Nemeth et al. (2012) described dramatic experiences by Katrina survivors that emerged on the anniversary of the tragedy, in this case one year post trauma, and that still reflected psychological distress. Kuriansky and Nemeth (2013) also described emotion-filled comments from Katrina survivors; one man identified as Charles stated that "his spirit was so broken that he now questions the existence of God." In contrast to this despair, one woman said that "her spirit was renewed when she was finally able to go to church, and felt safe enough to cry." Other survivors seemed to seek connection between the past and the future, perhaps to create a sense of continuity, reflected in their worries and regrets that they had not taken important items from their past, such as photos and other documents, when evacuating the city.

Although the disastrous effects of these weather patterns should be reason enough to deter a passive stance on climate change, there are other reasons for action that beckon political will and attention. On a positive note, sound policy to slow climate change may benefit African Americans disproportionately by protecting them from health risks (described above), enhancing the quality of life and providing economic benefits. On the other hand, if little is done to reduce the effects of severe weather changes, African Americans will likely endure heavy blows emotionally, physically, and economically. Clearly, the cost of inaction to all Americans is estimated to be far greater than the cost of taking action (Hoerner & Robinson, 2008). Further, it seems that shared needs among all segments of society recommend that we unite to promote a healthier environment and to confront hardships stemming from the earth's collapsing natural resources and perhaps a nation's collapsing social order.

RELEVANT INTERPERSONAL PRINCIPLES ACROSS RACIAL/ETHNIC GROUPS

H. S. Sullivan's One-Genus Postulate

In the 1930s, at a time when the accentuation of individual differences was the zeitgeist (Mullahy, 1970, 1973), the emphasis on commonality among racial and ethnic groups was championed by interpersonalists such as Harry Stack Sullivan. Sullivan's (1953) theory of interpersonal psychiatry puts forth the One-Genus Postulate, that "we are simply much more human than otherwise." The idea that we are more alike than we are different and that our communal proclivities are the defining quality of human existence stand among Sullivan's important contributions to psychological theory and social justice (Mullahy, 1973). These assumptions hold significant implications for community-building, public policy, and social movements as well as for soothing anxieties that perpetuate social division. This concept is just as relevant today, where division rests upon the idea of insurmountable differences that fuel environmental racism. The authors assert that Sullivan's theory offers common ground between the African American community and society at large, upon which to construct a meaningful response to current environmental and social threats. The concept of the common nature of people can serve as reminders of the commonality among diverse groups and help to promote unified responses to environmental threats.

The Role of Anxiety

Central to Sullivan's interpersonal approach is the role anxiety plays in determining the quality of relationships and an individual's receptiveness to others, including people of different racial and ethnic groups. Anxiety, Sullivan suggests, emerges in the other as a contagion, reflecting empathic connection to others. It is much like being swept up in the emotions of a crowd. Psychiatrist Arthur H. Chapman (1976) explains Sullivan's view of anxiety as follows:

> Anxiety (emotional discomfort) is caused by things that are going wrong, or have long gone wrong, in an individual's relationships with other people, and especially the emotionally close people, in his life. However, once anxiety appears it binds a person's capacity to improve his interpersonal relationships; he is less able to solve the problems that are producing, or have produced, his anxiety ... Anxiety has a tendency to bind a person in whatever unhealthy interpersonal patterns he has. (p. 84)

Sullivan (1953, 1956) asserts that each individual develops a self-system that consists of multiple security operations aimed at decreasing anxiety, enhancing security, and promoting emotional health. One such security operation, selective inattention, is fundamental to all other security mechanisms. Selective inattention occurs as people become selectively inattentive to processes that might produce emotional distress, cognitive dissonance, and/or interpersonal conflicts. Since Sullivan's formulations, selective inattention has found considerable empirical support in the study of implicit cognitions (Greenwald & Banaji, 1995; Mathews & Mackintosh, 1998; Mathews & MacLeod, 2005). Another security mechanism, "As if" operations, reflects an individual's proclivity to behave "as if" she or he is someone other than herself or himself in an interpersonal situation. The person adopts and acts out a role; the role is false, but it makes practical and comfortable an otherwise painful interpersonal situation. The problem with anxiety and the security operations, though, is that they may often contribute to distorted perceptions of interpersonal interactions. These distortions can be seen as the foundation for discrimination and racism. Hence, music- and non-music-related strategies that reduce anxiety help refocus distorted perceptions toward a clearer interpretation of social realities. Such strategies may serve as part of effective interventions for many social ills. However, toward such an end, it is important to have a theoretical framework to help identify different types of distortions and corrective experiences. This framework is described in the next section of this chapter.

Distorted Perceptions and Corrective Experiences

Parataxic distortions and consensual validation are two other Sullivanian concepts of relevance to understanding racism and community-building.

Parataxic distortions occur when an individual treats another person as if he were someone else, such as a significant other from the past. Consensual validation, on the other hand, corrects parataxic distortions and confirms the accuracy of a person's feelings, thoughts, and behaviors from others in his or her environment. It confirms that we are looking at the same world and perceive the world similarly enough so as to function in a communal fashion.

Multiple security operations, the self-system, and consensual validation play essential roles in determining healthy or unhealthy outlooks on the world. Even when these processes yield undesirable outcomes, Sullivan asserts that the original goal reflects a tendency toward obtaining healthy functioning (Sullivan, 1956). "The tendency toward health" manifests much like the body's antibodies fight invading viruses and bacteria in an effort to return the physical body to health. Similarly, these psychological mechanisms mobilize like little soldiers to defend the mind from dangers to mental health. The authors assert that this ubiquitous "tendency toward health," with its psychosocial and physiological mechanisms, is the cornerstone for hope and cooperation among different groups of people.

Although Sullivan may not have fully appreciated the degree to which behaviors can alter neurological functions, as recent research has suggested, he stands as a strong advocate for the commonality that exists among people biologically as well as psychologically. However, we know today that behaviors can create biological changes just as biology can create behaviors (Kolb, Gibbs, & Robinson, 2003). Since cultural experiences of African Americans may have given music a special role in individual and community life, musical expressions promote the development of neurological pathways that enhance the power of music in the individual's life. In this way, culture and neurology reinforce each other, and operate simultaneously to create a strong musical interest and foundation, perhaps based on African traditions and experiences found within a group's genotype.

NEUROLOGICAL CORRELATES IN MUSICAL EXPERIENCES ACROSS DIVERSE GROUPS

Human commonality is in few places as clear as it is in people's physical and mental characteristics. The effects of music in the brains of all people, for example, demonstrate that it is more pervasive than once believed. This means that instead of one music center in the brain, current thinking suggests that the whole brain is a music center. This is supported by the fact that the experience of music triggers several areas of brain function. Tempo seems to activate areas in the parietal, insular, frontal, and prefrontal cortex. Meter has been found to activate areas in the left hemisphere and in the basal ganglia and cerebellar areas of the brain. Melody involves the right and bilateral frontal, prefrontal, para-hippocampal, and cerebellar cortices. The auditory cortex, motor cortex, prefrontal cortex, sensory cortex, visual cortex, nucleus accumbens, amygdala, hippocampus, and cerebellum are all involved in music perception and processing. Janata et al. (2002) highlights the role of the prefrontal cortex as a site for "tonal mapping." Hence, music tends to stimulate and rely on multiple brain areas.

The brain areas that are activated during musical experiences can produce "goosebumps," sweat, and shifts in the heart rate and blood pressure (Levitin, 2007, 2008). It appears that listening to music releases neurochemicals such as dopamine, prolactin, and oxytocin—neurotransmitters related to feeling good, comfortable, and bonding with others. But the type of music makes a difference, maintains Mannes (2011), who cites cortisol studies conducted by Barry Bittman, MD, at the Mind-Body Wellness Center in Pennsylvania that indicate that music either lowers or increases cortisol levels, depending on its type.

Despite this, the potential benefits and uses of music to improve experiences of living seem available to everyone in a somewhat similar manner. For example, from a neurological perspective, there appears to be minimal difference in terms of gross neurological effects of music among musicians and nonmusicians.

The fact that music affects the same pleasure centers that are activated by sex and drug addiction (Levitin, 2007, 2008) speaks volumes to music's potential usefulness in promoting social change. In terms of social mores, the association of music with sex and drugs may seem troublesome. However, the authors assert that socialization processes and culture influence cognitions and imbue music with the power to "calm the savage beast."

COGNITIVE CORRELATES IN MUSICAL EXPERIENCES ACROSS RACIAL AND ETHNIC GROUPS

The cognitive processing of musical experiences is as complicated as the neural mechanisms in which such processing is grounded. The "illusion of the music" springs from these neural mechanisms, brain structures, and neurochemistry that, in turn, become the basis for constructing meaning and schemas (Chanda & Levitin, 2013). These schemas reflect the cultural experiences of the individual. The final products are sets of schemas upon which musical experiences are interpreted. In the lives of many Americans, music is used as a form of release and relief. However, unlike other Americans, African Americans as a group have used music as a direct and central response to oppression, economic discrimination, and the ongoing struggle with multiple forms of racism and trauma, and as an expression of jubilation and celebration of victories won on individual and collective levels. Music hence can fuel the engine against injustice, real and imagined, soothe the sting of illusive justice, and calm the tides of emotional storms.

In describing the power of music to soothe and calm emotions, as well as stimulate action, the codirector of the *Oxford Research Group Every Casualty Programme* and music psychologist Sloboda (2005) identifies the power of music as partially occurring when a musical piece defies the expectations and form that the listener has come to associate with that selection. Levitin (2007) offers multiple examples in popular music of this violation of expectations. For example, *Kamakiriad*, an album by Donald Fagan, has one song with blues and funk rhythms that lead the listener to expect the standard blues chord progressions, but it is initially played on only one chord. Another example is Aretha Franklin's "Chain of Fools" that is composed on one chord. As the brain functions to identify forms and patterns—hence facilitating the formation of cognitive schemas—musical selections are structured to engender a set of expectations in the listener. When the musician or songwriter deviates from the expectation established in the pattern of a song, listeners are intrigued and captivated.

Hence, Sloboda (2005) argues that the seductive power of music to arouse emotions in individuals stems from elements of surprise, when expectations are not fulfilled and something does not happen as planned. When listeners state that an aspect of music makes their "heart skip a beat," Sloboda states that they are referring to this experience of deviation from the expected, which stimulates neurological pathways and cognitive schemas. For instance, Sloboda identifies the appoggiatura, an embellishing note that is not a part of the harmony and that precedes the main melodic note, as a potential trigger for emotions, causing tears to swell in the eyes of many listeners. For some, surprise may be found in musical nuances, such as enharmonics where an A-sharp and B-flat, while sounding the same tone, may be experienced very differently. Likewise, rhythmic syncopation, which is a stress on a beat that is usually unstressed or a rest or silence where one would expect stress or sound, may stimulate an unexpected experience of surprise. These schemas can be viewed from the perspective of the developmental theory of Piaget (1952), whereby an individual must accommodate a pattern that differs from expectations; and this accommodation involves incorporating new information into an existing definition of an experience, thereby altering the definition or understanding of that experience. Other studies examining Western music indicate that fast tempi in major keys can induce happiness. In contrast, music in minor keys can invoke sadness and dissonance, while rapid tempo pieces can produce fear or anxiety. Following this principle, sounds that imitate war chants can trigger the chemical adrenaline to be released, which stimulates the "fight-or-flight" response activating the nervous system (Krumhansl, 1997).

The authors assert that there is a connection between these basic psychophysiological responses to music and the process of community-building to fight environmental racism. The effective use of music to mobilize people against racism may be enhanced considerably by understanding the role of music in the social consciousness of a particular group and the similar manner in which music can impact diverse groups, creating a bridge for collaborative efforts. Another connection between the neurological and cognitive foundation of music and community building is that community-building requires the organization of experiences around some well-defined purpose, the presence of physical move- ment and matching cognitions. Further, it engages multiple dimensions of indi- viduals. When all of these components are integrated, efforts can be directed to motivate people to take action against social injustice and racism.

ANXIETY, INTERPERSONAL MOTIVATION, AND RACISM

Just as Sullivan's concepts on human perceptions and emotions can be used to help unite peoples and reduce racism, they also reveal the degree of difficulty inherent in efforts to eliminate racism. This manifests from efforts to escape interpersonal anxiety, which threatens the individual's basic sense of security. Interpersonal situations influencing racist views can spring from the following three sources: (1) direct interactions with different racial ethnic groups; (2) indi- rect interactions via reports from others, the media, and social media; and (3) multiple imaginary interpersonal relationships simmering in the minds of people. The threat of being alone serves as another powerful psychological motivator to conform to "in group" behaviors that condone racism.

The City University of New York's Distinguished Professor of Clinical Psy- chology Paul Wachtel (1999, 2001, 2002) provides a number of insights into interpersonal dimensions of racism that includes recent research in social psy- chology and incorporates intrapsychic, interpersonal, and cognitive features. Wachtel applies his concept of *cyclical psychodynamics* to explain the delirious conditions that sustain racism as well as offering more clarity to the importance Sullivan placed on the communal nature of man and Sullivan's theorem of recip- rocal motivational patterns. This theorem states: "Integration in an interper- sonal situation is a reciprocal process in which (1) complementary needs are resolved or aggravated; (2) reciprocal patterns of activity are developed or disin- tegrated; and (3) foresight of satisfaction, or rebuff, of similar needs is facilitated" (Sullivan, 1953, p. 198). Anxiety appears to undergird this process as well, inter- fering with effective interpersonal communication and interactions and stifling community development. A multidimensional approach that includes music may operate to calm racial conflict and stimulate collaboration.

COMMUNITY-BUILDING IN A RACIAL SOCIETY

The choice for meaningful changes that protect African Americans and all Americans from the vicissitudes of the global climate, such as severe storms, droughts, flooding, and extreme heat, entails constructing resilient communities ready for action. Community development and preparation for positive social change rely on interpersonal relationships that foster group identity and co-operation toward accomplishment of designated goals (Minkler, Wallerstein, & Wilson, 1997). Positive social change involves the unbalancing of an unhealthy status quo toward a state that is unlike that which previously existed. The pro-verbial apple cart is upset, giving root to a more socially and politically fair social order. Oppressive conditions become intolerable, viewed as eventually disrup-tive to overall health and resiliency of the entire society. Several dimensions of interpersonal interactions offer insights into the barriers to community-building and social change. Once these barriers are identified and removed and effective strategies for community-building are applied, an unbalancing of the status quo can ensue.

The authors hypothesize the following types of drivers that maintain a status quo of racism: (1) thoughts and feelings of separateness; (2) high levels of anxi-ety, which disrupt cognitions and interpersonal relationships; (3) intense feelings of insecurity; and (4) unhealthy security operations. Drivers refer to the factors that contribute to a particular emotional, behavioral, social, or politi-cal status. Once the drivers are identified, the behaviors of a group make sense, as those behaviors fit in the context of the proposed drivers. To address the above drivers, interventions must follow the prioritization of the drivers' impact, with the most influential driver being specifically targeted first, then lesser-ranked drivers (Henggeler, 1999; Henggeler, Schoenwald, Borduin, Rowland, & Cunningham, 2002). For example, if thoughts and feelings of separation are hypothesized to be the number one driver, intervention might include psycho-education regarding similarities among groups along with careful attention to the degree of anxiety contaminating cognitions and interpersonal interactions and the use of anxiety reduction strategies.

In contrast to drivers for racism and division, the effective mobilization of a community includes the following drivers: (1) interpersonal interactions charac-terized by a strong sense of group identity; (2) relatively low levels of interper-sonal anxiety; (3) feelings of safety and security; (4) identification with a common purpose; and (5) the use of healthy security operations that promote connectedness to individuals or group. These conditions support multiple people uniting to create a sense of collective security. Building effective communities requires a comprehensive plan with target-specific strategies that focus on this positive psychology through efforts to enhance the group's interpersonal qual-ities and dynamics. Each such community plan and set of strategies must be tail-ored for the specific group and purpose that have been identified; hence, there is no one-size-fits-all-type plan.

The authors believe that Chapman's (1976) synthesis of Sullivan's principles for social change will aid in the development of interventions to address drivers. Sullivan's principles for social change involve the following processes: (1) taking the participant observation role; (2) identifying anxiety and security operations; (3) increasing awareness; (4) building consensual validation; (5) yielding to the tendency toward health; and (6) relying on the One-Genus Postulate. These processes then can be helpful in building a community of resilience among African Americans fighting against the problems of global climate change.

Among many African Americans who are living in urban environments, facing economic barriers, struggling with chaotic neighborhoods and social conditions, surviving ongoing trauma experiences, and/or managing past and present experiences with racism and discrimination are significant to their adaption to socio-economic, political, and physical environments (Duck, 2012; Franklin, Boyd-Franklin, & Kelly, 2006). A. J. Franklin, Boston University's David S. Nelson Chair and psychology professor, uses the literary work of Ralph Ellison upon which to build a conceptualization of the effects of racism on African American men. Franklin describes the invisibility of African American men in society (Franklin, 1993, 2004), a concept that escalates the impact of racism, including environmental racism. In Franklin's description of the Invisibility Syndrome, invisibility refers to the failure of African Americans to be featured by society, with the result that accomplishments and positive attributes remain invisible at individual and institutional levels, at the same time as individuals are subjected to multiple microaggressions from other individuals and institutions. These conditions contribute to the collective memories of many African Americans; thus, community activists and organizers need to form hypotheses about the manner in which collective memories influence the community's responses to issues such as climate change.

In community-building with African Americans, community activists must address these collective memories with specific interventions. For example, the collective memories of African Americans regarding slavery, racism, and discrimination may be acknowledged through open dialogue, focused groups or community meetings, and appropriate musical selections that demonstrate recognition of the impact of this history on current functioning (Ray, 2008). For some African Americans, collective memory manifests in intrusive thoughts and anxiety that interfere with current interpersonal connectedness on family and community levels, akin to forms of trauma reactions (Sanchez-Hucles, 1999). Various types of exposure through conversations and other means may be used to decrease the anxiety that would impair interpersonal interactions. For persons who perhaps have identified more strongly with "rugged individualism" in forms espoused by the economically and politically dominant group, their exhaustive efforts to discount the influence of race takes a toll on their psychosocial functioning. In both incidences, these sustained efforts require frequent psychological maneuvering, resulting in significant implications for physical, emotional, and interpersonal health (Sanchez-Hucles, 1999; Williams & Mohammed, 2009). In fact, mounting evidence indicates that the stress related to racism decreases life expectancy (Chae et al., 2014).

Successful strategies are needed for community-building that appreciate both perspectives and the overall impact of racism on health. Organizers must convey the message to people who hold either perspective that both views are authentic expressions of the African American experience. Emphasizing the strengths of both perspectives, instead of discounting or minimalizing one or the other, should characterize community campaigns. Consequently, a normal response of many African Americans to the macro- and micro-aggressions of institutionalized racism has been to develop a variety of psychosocial mechanisms against which to protect themselves (Davis, 1997b). In this way, Sullivan's security operations that arise to soften the blow of anxiety may be used to explain a variety of behaviors that have implications for building individual and community resiliency.

Community-building requires attention to multiple "resilient acts" (Davis, 2007a; Davis & Paster, 2000) of members of the community; "resilient acts" emerge out of Davis and Paster's efforts to focus on behavioral manifestations of resiliency. These resilient acts are hypothesized to compound over time, become habitual, and lead to a pattern of resilient living. When community organizers focus their attention on the resilient acts of any group and use those acts to propel the group's efforts toward desired change, they reinforce each separate "resilient act." The ability of a community of people to "turn lemons into lemonade" characterizes the positive psychology that has been the foundation for many achievements in the African American community. Nowhere is this more evident than in the arts and music, where African American music and styles have infiltrated American life (Baraka, 1963; Stoute, 2011).

Bridges to Resilient Communities

The authors of this chapter believe that the power of music to capture attention, passions, and dreams is unquestionable in any peoples' minds. The neural circuitry and cognitive and culture-based schemas that make for musical experiences provide the foundation for unity and community-building. Just as music has the power to promote healing in the individual (Mannes, 2011), the authors assert that it has the power to mobilize a community, offering the opportunity for healing. There are multiple examples in which the musical community has come together to mobilize a mass response to deal with trauma. Examples include the song "We Are the World," produced to aid in the fight against African famine; the song "We Are the World 25 for Haiti," produced following the 2010 earthquake in Haiti; and the Farm Aid concert that commenced as a musical event to help American farmers. Multiple celebrities joined these projects, resulting in a who's who of stars in the music industry, including Michael Jackson, Lionel Richie, Willie Nelson, John Mellencamp, Neil Young, Bob Dylan, and many others.

However, another type of "music community" consisting neither of stars nor of professional musicians, includes everyday people who, organized by their affinity to music, hold the potential to do extraordinary things. Specifically, this refers to African Americans who mobilize themselves to meet the challenge of a changing global environment. Black communities have often organized musical events in response to trauma experiences at local and national levels like events held in Philadelphia in response to the murder rate, and events around the country in response to the killing of the Florida teen Trayvon Martin. Music is solicited as an aid because of its power to hold people's attention and prime them for unity.

Although cognitive and cultural schemas imbue different meanings of a music selection for different individuals, these differences are not so enormous as to negate their ubiquitous effects. The power of the same musical selections to produce similar effects in communities of people creates perhaps, for that moment at least, a bonding at an emotional level and helps organize experiences into some coherent meaning. From stimulating the neurochemical release of oxytocin, the so-called "trust or bonding hormone," to the shared cultural experiences and language of a musical form, music can be used to promote feelings of unity and shared meaning. Individuals' similar responses to a musical selection also reflect another important psychological principle, which Sullivan (1953) has called "consensual validation."

As a prevention and/or intervention, the authors contend that building community via music promotes consensual validation. This process includes the often instinctual selection of musical pieces that fit the function and address several criteria: the overall mood of the group, the purpose for which the group has gathered or planned to gather, the wishes of the group's leadership, and a moment-by-moment assessment of the emotional climate among group members. This is a dynamic process that involves talented producers or musicians modifying program selections to match the needs of the people in the service of heightening or deepening interpersonal connectedness. As suggested, the use of music to build community is a multidimensional process, involving dyads and larger groups that can be based in community music centers as well as virtual communities. These different pathways to promoting resilience through community engagement have been conceptualized as features of the comprehensive Talent Recovery for Resilient Living (TRRL) program referred to earlier in this chapter.

Talent Recovery for Resilient Living Program

The TRRL program developed by the first author of this chapter can be based in such community music centers or other community settings as well as implemented through the adjunctive use of virtual communities. TRRL is presented here as a model that can be applied to mobilize a community to address the impact of global changes and hence promote resilient living. This program targets behavioral and emotional health, social skills development, and barriers to personal goal attainment (Davis, 2007b) by programming that helps individuals form a positive and strong connection to their talents and goals while increasing individual, family, school, and community bonds. The connection between talent recovery and the struggle against the harmful effects of global warming is threefold: (1) the multiple health and social problems stemming from climate change may stand as barriers to the recovery of talents and personal fulfillment, and, hence, they become targets for elimination; (2) music may be used to promote physical health by reducing destructive levels of stress and anxiety (Labbé, Schmidt, Babin, & Pharr, 2007); and (3) the organized activities in the service of promoting health offer opportunities for individuals to demonstrate and practice talent areas, consequently enhancing resilient living patterns.

TRRL addresses the lack of meaningful activities in the community by creating prosocial activities that are appropriate for youth, adults, and families. The program creates a foundation for lifelong development and achievement by increasing protective factors, including building skills needed to advocate for one's own health and well-being. As individuals engage in their talents, they strengthen their connections with supports in their natural ecology. The program is consistent with recent efforts in positive psychology and strength-based intervention (Smith, 2006). Unlike traditional behavioral health interventions, the goal is to promote talent development and expression while addressing emotional and physical concerns that may be barriers to the goal.

TRRL can be a potent strategy as it appeals to an individual's strengths, dreams, and proclivities toward positive behavioral health. The program focuses on psychosocial strengths, consistent with a humanistic and interpersonal philosophy of inherent healthiness. This model draws from the first author's experiences in two programs that targeted diametrically different populations. In one instance, the first author compiled approximately 15 years of observations followed by an empirical investigation while serving as director of the counseling division of a program aimed at promoting peak performance, group cohesion, and success-oriented behaviors in gifted and talented African American and Latino adolescents (Davis, 1997a; Davis & Paster, 2000). In the other instance, the first author served as codirector of the Philadelphia Multi-systemic Project, which applied Multisystemic Therapy (MST) (Henggeler et al., 2002), a U.S. Surgeon General–recommended evidence-based treatment for youth who exhibit conduct problems and behavioral health needs. MST engages youngsters in prosocial activities, as one therapeutic strategy. However, this engagement in prosocial activities often proves challenging due to limited community resources and local government budgets cuts to music, athletic, and academic enrichment programs. The most effective means to engage the youth appeared to be when the activities emphasized some talent area in which the youth showed interest or the recovery of a talent that had been abandoned, for some reason.

Talent Recovery Process (TRP)

"Talent recovery" (Davis, 2007a) includes the discovery or recovery of personal talents and gifts that imbue life with meaning, which promote adjustment and happiness, and that offer possibility for positive impact on the lives of others. The prospect of realizing a highly desired goal can motivate individuals and families to confront and overcome challenges on the path to recovery. The expression of talents is a source of resiliency in the midst of confusion and emotional distress. In the talent recovery process, people identify tangible goals to which they strive and for which they are willing to endure hardship to accomplish.

The uncovering of talents and prospect of achieving dreams provide the motivation and personal fortitude to remove physical, emotional, and social obstacles. TRP teaches individuals that the process of identifying special gifts and talents is as much a social or community process as it is a personal process; efforts to determine "intervention domains" inherently involve family and community.

TRRL: Intervention Domains

Intervention domains, as defined by the first author, refer to talent areas that become the focus of attention during prevention and interventions efforts. A domain is simultaneously a goal as well as a conduit for change. The domain represents the hope for a more meaningful life characterized by the practice of talents that are consistent with an individual's natural proclivity toward health and toward promoting community-wide health. Hence, participation in and development of a domain activity can lead to the realization of wishes and dreams, the enrichment of others' lives, and the removal of complacency that allow so many physical and emotional illnesses to gain a foothold in people's lives.

The development of intervention domains or core talent areas requires intensive study, exercise, and activities that aim at fortifying intrinsic motivations to excel. While there are multiple potential core talents, this chapter focuses on music. Children, adolescents, adults, and families can be organized according to the intensity of interest in a domain area. The intensity of interest can be determined through assessments of current types, frequency, and purposes of the use of music in individuals' lives. Where youngsters are concerned, activities are monitored by adults in order to be counted as acceptable prosocial and talent recovery activities.

The music programming of this model aims at engaging individuals who have identified musical aspirations as desired goals that they are willing to pursue wholeheartedly. Musical formats can be (1) vocal (e.g., a choir or small group); and/or (2) instrumental (e.g., playing the piano, drums, or guitar). The desired outcomes for music programming are the preparation of an individual to express her or his musical talent in a variety of professional, semiprofessional, and non-professional areas.

Hence, TRRL reflects in action the systemic characteristics it is designed to target. While talent recovery involves the individual acting in context with her or his environment, that environment in turn plays a role as recipient of talent expressions and as the interpersonal and social context through which those experiences receive consensual validation, forming meaningful cultural schemas. In this manner, the individual's experience of music is augmented, incorporating its social meaning and purpose in a process that may be further facilitated by the personal life coaching component of TRRL.

TRRL: In Action
Personal Life Coaching

Personal Life Coaching is a form of intervention that provides strategies and techniques to address many of the psychosocial barriers that individuals encounter. This level of intervention draws from evidence-based therapeutic approaches such as motivational interviewing, cognitive behavioral therapy, and brief interpersonal therapy, which address barriers such as substance abuse, depression, anxiety disorders, aggressive tendencies, and general motivation/ preparation to engage in treatments. Medical interventions target such conditions as asthma and other respiratory illnesses as well as any variety of physical ailments associated with climatic change. Individual-level intervention complements group prevention and intervention.

Group and Community Meetings

Group and community meetings are components of TRRL that can take place in community-based music centers described below.

Community-Based Music Centers for Resilient Living

The authors propose the use of community-based music centers to host TRRL's group interventions. Imagine music centers located throughout your community. On a hot summer's day, people can come in, have a glass of lemonade, and listen to music, whether live or recorded, that lifts their mood and refocuses their attention. These centers can be established in churches, neighborhood community buildings, medical offices, and schools, becoming essential partners in promoting health care and coping with environmental changes. Such music centers strategically placed throughout the community can become safe places for individuals to explore the various uses of music. Many individuals would eagerly receive the opportunity to showcase their talents, and others would want to enjoy the musical experience.

Additionally, music can be used to reduce stress by pairing the musical experiences, which have drawn the individuals to the center, with mindfulness exercises that can be taught at these centers. These centers can offer classes that emphasize nontraditional approaches to promote psychological and physical well-being and also collaborate with providers of traditional treatments. They can promote crucial connections to medical care for illnesses that may be associated with climate changes, as well as serve as places to provide support in the natural ecology when facing trauma events such as natural disasters. Moreover, these music centers can be locations for group meetings aimed at helping individuals navigate systems of information and services. Music can be integrated into all phases of prevention and interventions at these centers, providing a unique set of interactions that most people do not associate with formal health care, but at which many people may find great comfort. For example, at the Louis Armstrong Center for Music Therapy in New York City, music is used as a conjunctive treatment for a variety of respiratory illness, including asthma. The Mind-Body Wellness Center of Pennsylvania is another example of a program that provides various levels of holistic treatments that include music as a component.

Similar to these two treatment centers, the proposed music centers would serve an educational function. Adults can provide their children with a broad range of musical experiences that are culturally relevant, providing exposure to African American classical composers and drawing from a rich jazz heritage. Also, individuals can be exposed to diverse musical forms, possibly expanding their repertoire of music and exposing them to diverse musical forms that might aid in stress reduction and improved physiological states. For example, classical and jazz music have been associated with relaxation responses (Levitin, 2007); these can be available and taught in these centers.

The group and community meetings held in these music centers can occur on several levels:

1. *Participation in the intervention domain as a group member.* The group-based intervention will primarily involve practicing talents and skills development. A psychosocial component is an integral part of all domains with socio-psychological experts present at these groups and working along with the teacher-coach to apply psychological techniques for performance enhancement.
2. *Participation in socio-psychological groups on performance enhancement and removal of barriers.* This group is approximately 30 to 45 minutes in duration and is conducted like a traditional self-help group intended to encourage and inspire youth toward prosocial goals. The groups are composed of individuals who may have some emotional barriers, but whose dynamics and influence are conducive to promoting prosocial outcomes. To that end, the selection of group members represents a pivotal decision. The decision-making process is done by a variety of professionals who understand current empirical evidence regarding interpersonal group interactions and interpersonal processes related to a variety of barriers.

3. *Participation in large group meetings involving parents/guardians, other family members, siblings, and/or youth.* These meetings serve to increase connection by inspiring, encouraging and educating. In some instances, entertainment and information delivery occurs simultaneously. In other instances, there is a focus on teaching communication skills, and, yet, in other instances, youth and adults gather to create activities that support their goals for resilient and healthy living and learn to advocate for positive social and public policy changes. Musical engagement creates a fertile milieu for the aforementioned activities.

TRRL is characterized by an emphasis on community involvement and empowerment and by the manner in which communities of all types are used to advance resiliency. As community engagement is essential to TRRL, many of the interventions that have been described occur in physical locations but can be complemented by interactions in virtual communities.

Virtual Communities: Music App for Resilient Living

TRRL recognizes and integrates the technological advances today that have created situations whereby people can access many of their needs easily with information at their fingertips as they engage in their daily routines. The possibilities lead to the idea that a music-based website with a supporting app that provides information regarding the impact of global climate change could be accessed in a user-friendly manner and downloaded to the millions of smartphones used today. This website and app could specifically target the role of climate change in the lives of African Americans and offer strategies to cope with severe weather experiences, health information, and resources/places to receive care. The app could provide the nearest locations for resources, with the goal to decrease barriers to information and to care. Likewise, at a time when information is so copious, such a music-based app could help individuals gain clarity in a sea of information that may otherwise be overwhelming.

This idea is becoming a reality. BrighterDay.info, with supporting mobile apps, is being designed by the authors and is presently in early-to-middle stages of development. The website and apps provide information on the effects of climate change, with frequent updates on changes as they are occurring in a specific environment; describe stress-reduction exercises and strategies that involve music; and provide a directory of information sources and professionals in an individual's city who can provide various treatments and interventions. The music app can allow playing individualized music according to the musical preferences of an individual, determined by the individual's playlist contained in the smartphone that identifies the person's preferences in terms of the music genre and style they most frequently play. Additionally, the website and app can play a role in keeping individuals focused on talents that have been identified through the talent recovery process that guides people to engage in psychologically healthy activities (e.g., keeping a journal or rehearsing positive thoughts) and exercise that develop their talents. The website and app could also link to YouTube, Facebook, Twitter, Instagram, and other social media, expanding the individual's ability to connect with people all over the world.

Virtual Communities

TRRL acknowledges other electronic mediums that can connect people, whether people are in the same vicinity or divided by hundreds or thousands of miles. These mediums have quickly become the marketing tools for independent artists who want to disseminate their music or other art forms (Walker, 2008). They can also be harnessed to build resiliency and proactive responses to climate changes, since individuals of all ages have a cell phone; these devices can be a platform on which to have conversations about the impact of heat waves and concerns about medical issues or severe weather events. Real-time documentation of events can be shared, and a range of official and nonofficial responses to such events can be conveyed. Within the context of broader music-based strategies, people can share their experiences, frustrations, and apparent remedies and create a dynamic intercourse that can be used to propel social action and social change.

Although the interventions mentioned above may produce benefits when used alone, the authors feel that they hold greater promise as a component of a comprehensive program like TRRL because multiple dimensions of an individual's or group's concern are addressed. The implementation of such programs requires effective advocacy for funding and social policy that supports them. The advocacy for social change, though, is also a dimension of TRRL.

POSITIVE SOCIAL CHANGE AND PUBLIC POLICY

The process of positive social change involves: (1) information gathering and dissemination, (2) organization and preparation, (3) mobilization for political actions, and (4) actions that transform plans into real statements (Ren et al., 2012). Music provides a common language; stimulates relatively similar neurological pathways, thoughts, and emotions in people; and provides pleasant associations for the engagement with tasks. Every movement has its battle cry. In this way, songs are the glue that holds an organized movement together and provides or undergirds a rationale for change.

During musical presentations, individuals can be selected to gather information about the impact of climate change on the lives of African Americans. This information can be shared using music to set the tone or build expectations for the delivery of information. Although the musical selections may differ in tempo, form, structure, or even genre, the message is consistent. Either the music matches the tone of the group gathered, or it is intended to alter the tone in a certain direction. Music apps, music centers, and TRRL serve to provide either information, motivation, or skills needed to contribute to resilient living and community-building. Once communities have been constructed around the themes of talents, musical passions, resiliency, and change, these communities can spring into action in the service of an identified mission. African Americans who have been engaged in this manner can become a part of the movement to protect their health and the health of Mother Earth.

The activities associated with the Brighter Day website and mobile app discussed above can be used to organize themes, contribute to a sense of direction, and promote a sense of purpose and identity for participants. Masses of people can be drawn to such virtual activities if advertising campaigns promote awareness. Henderson (2013), a businesswoman and CEO of a Philadelphia-based mental health agency, notes that ordinary people can develop an entrepreneurial ministry; therefore, she makes an appeal for partnerships between businesses and religious communities to promote positive social change. Her efforts highlight the existence of a cohort of socially conscious individuals who are service-oriented instead of consumed by egocentric motivations. The drive toward positive social change may be as much a part of the human spirit as the drive toward self-preservation. There may be no shortage of people ready for social advocacy.

Future Direction for Public Policy

The authors propose that social advocacy should include lobbying government officials to view music as an instrument to promote public health. In this way, music would play a broader role in the education of African American children as well as children of other racial and ethnic groups. This would require an approach to music education that incorporates recent research in the neurobehavioral sciences. Children who receive this type of training would be primed to see their musical interactions as a part of self-care, as well as entertainment, and would learn to maximize the benefits of music in their lives.

Additionally, activists would need to advocate for funding to support primary and secondary schools, and music departments at institutes of higher education, to train musicians and teachers to deliver their craft with a greater understanding of the health implications of music. Recipients of such training would be more prepared to engage in music-based resiliency programs that mitigate against stresses in life in general as well as those emanating from climate change crises.

Educating older adolescents and adults regarding the benefits of music may be successful through public awareness campaigns. On one hand, such campaigns may be an easy sell given that the goal to convince people to listen to music is likely what they already enjoy. On the other hand, the task may prove challenging, since the idea that music has potential medical and behavioral health benefits is relatively new in the context of traditional health care practices.

The music-based website and mobile apps, virtual communities, and community-based music center described above would serve to reinforce that broad view as well as the value of music in the African American community.

SUMMARY

The thesis of this chapter asserts that music is, and can be, a powerful force in African Americans' efforts to build communities that are ready to respond to global climate change and environmental racism. The authors argue that the ubiquitous effects of music in people's lives offer evidence of music's potential power in the human experience. Furthermore, the neurological, cognitive, and social correlates of musical experiences demonstrate the similarities among people that support noted psychiatrist Harry Stack Sullivan's hypothesis that "we are simply much more human than otherwise." Sullivan's interpersonal theory is used as a foundation upon which to conceptualize basic personality and social characteristics that undergird environmental racism, which, in turn, exacerbates the impact of global climate change on the African American community. The interpersonal perspective is also used to describe processes for community-building specifically among African Americans that also apply to diverse groups. This is important given that the fight against the negative effects of global climate change requires all Americans to work together.

Although a commonality among people may be the basis for efforts to unify diverse groups, the role of music in African Americans' social construction of reality suggests that music can be a valuable instrument in educating and preparing African Americans to advocate for social change in environmental policy. Environmental policy has been touted to reflect a more recent form of discrimination that Bullard, the "Father of Environmental Justice," refers to as environmental racism. Just as music has taken center stage in past social movements and resilient acts from surviving slavery to fighting Jim Crow, the authors assert that music can play a prominent role in the fight for environmental justice, offering several interventions toward that end.

Several interventions for engaging African Americans in the battle against environmental racism and quest for justice can be integrated into one comprehensive program, the Talent Recovery for Resilient Living Program (TRRL). TRRL involves: (1) use of a music-based website with supporting apps for accessing information on climate change and the Black community, (2) development and/or use of virtual communities that emphasize environmental justice, and (3) development of community-based music centers. Although the components of TRRL offer value on their own, a comprehensive approach that integrates virtual communities, music-based resiliency websites with supporting apps, and community music centers, with TRRL would provide holistic and more effective education about the health effects of global climate change on African

Americans in the context of teaching or reinforcing "resilient acts" built upon the talents of a community. This integrative approach would provide strategies for altering the physical and emotional impact of environmental threats through stress reduction, cognitive strategies, strength-based interventions, and social advocacy techniques.

The appeal of music to African Americans, for its ability to provide comfort and as a catalyst for resilience and social change, has a record of success. Music has been used to change cognitions, to redefine painful situations, and to redefine society's portrayals of Americans of African descent. At nearly every front in the fight for social justice, African Americans have called on songs to soothe emotions and to stir action. Consequently, music is a logical choice for use as interventions to assist African Americans to cope with the dangers of global climate change and environmental racism.

REFERENCES

Baraka, A. (1963). *Blues people: Negro music in White America.* New York, NY: W. Morrow.

Benedict, R. (1934). *Patterns of culture.* Boston, MA: Houghton Mifflin Harcourt.

Brulle, R. J., & Pellow, D. N. (2006). Environmental justice: Human health and environmental inequalities. *Annual Review of Public Health, 27,* 103–124.

Bullard, R. D., & Wright, B. (2009). *Race, place, and environmental justice after Hurricane Katrina: Struggles to reclaim, rebuild, and revitalize New Orleans and the Gulf Coast.* Boulder, CO: Westview Press.

Bullard, R. D., & Wright, B. (2012). *The wrong complexion for protection: How the government response to disaster endangers African American communities.* New York, NY: New York University Press.

Bullard, R. D., & Wright, B. H. (1990). The quest for environmental equity: Mobilizing the African-American community for social change. *Society and Natural Resources, 3*(4), 301–311.

Chae, D. H., Nuru-Jeter, A. M., Adler, N. E., Brody, G. H., Lin, J., Blackbur, E. H., & Epel, E. S. (2014). Discrimination, racial bias, and telomere length in African-American men. *American Journal of Preventive Medicine, 46*(2), 103–111.

Chanda, M. L., & Levitin, D. J. (2013). The neurochemistry of music. *Trends in cognitive sciences, 17*(4), 179–193.

Chapman, A. H. (1976). *Harry Stack Sullivan: His life and his work.* New York, NY: G. P. Putnam's Sons.

Davis, T., III. (1997a). *Interpersonal correlates of success in gifted African American and Latino students* (Doctoral dissertation). City University of New York, New York, NY.

Davis, T., III. (1997b). Male engagement: Implications for practice. In J. R. Dumpson & A. Carten (Eds.), *Removing risk from children: Shifting the paradigm* (pp. 243–258). Silver Springs, MD: Beckham House.

Davis, T., III. (2006, March). Keep up empathy for Katrina victims. *Philadelphia Inquirer.* Retrieved April 18, 2015, from http://articles.philly.com/2006-03-14/news/25414963_1katrina-evacuees-poverty-racism

Davis, T., III. (2007a). The future of Black families in Philadelphia: Flipping the script. *The State of Black Philadelphia Report*. Philadelphia, PA: Urban League of Philadelphia.

Davis, T., III. (2007b). *Talent recovery for resilient living: A violence prevention program*. Proposal presented to the Philadelphia Department of Behavioral Health. Philadelphia, PA.

Davis, T., III, Glass, K., Board, S., Williams, M., & Graves, T. (2006). *Ethics amidst the storm: Welcoming Hurricane Katrina survivors to Pennsylvania*. Presented at the Pennsylvania Psychological Association Annual Conference, Harrisburg, PA.

Davis, T., III, & Paster, V. (2000). Nurturing resilience in early adolescence: A tool for future success. *Journal of College Student Psychotherapy, 15*(2), 17–33.

Diamond, M. C. (1988). *Enriching heredity*. New York, NY: The Free Press.

Duck, W. O. (2012). An ethnographic portrait of a precarious life getting by on even less. *The Annals of the American Academy of Political and Social Science, 642*(1), 124–138.

Dumpson, J. D. (2014). *Four scholars' engagement of works by classical composers of African descent: A collective case study* (Doctoral dissertation). Temple University, Philadelphia, PA. Retrieved April 15, 2015, from http://digital.library.temple.edu/cdm/ref/collection/p245801coll10/id/261236

Early, G. (2009). *Ralph Ellison: Invisible man*. Salt Lake City, UT: Benchmark Books.

Forman, T. A., & Lewis, A. E. (2006). Racial apathy and Hurricane Katrina: The social anatomy of prejudice in the post–civil rights era. *DuBois Review, 3*(1), 175–202.

Franklin, A. J. (1993). The invisibility syndrome. *Family Therapy Networker, 17*(4), 33–39.

Franklin, A. J. (2004). From brotherhood to manhood: How Black men rescue their relationships and dreams from the invisibility syndrome. Hoboken, NJ: John Wiley & Sons.

Franklin, A. J., Boyd-Franklin, N., & Kelly, S. (2006). Racism and invisibility: Race-related stress, emotional abuse and psychological trauma for people of color. *Journal of Emotional Abuse, 6*(2–3), 9–30.

Greenwald, A. G., & Banaji, M. R. (1995). Implicit social cognition: attitudes, self-esteem, and stereotypes. *Psychological Review, 102*(1), 4.

Henderson, J. B. (2013). *Entrepreneurial ministry: The catalyst to community social change*. Bloomington, IN: Trafford Publishing.

Henggeler, S. W. (1999). Multisystemic therapy: An overview of clinical procedures, outcomes, and policy implications. *Child and Adolescent Mental Health, 4*(1), 2–10.

Henggeler, S. W., Schoenwald, S. K., Borduin, C. M., Rowland, M. D., & Cunningham, P. B. (2002). *Serious emotional disturbance in children and adolescents: Multisystemic therapy*. New York, NY: Guilford Press.

Hoerner, J. A., & Robinson, N. (2008). A climate of change: African Americans, global warming, and a just climate policy for the US. *Environmental Justice and Climate Change Initiative, 1*, 1–59.

Holifield, R. (2001). Defining environmental justice and environmental racism. *Urban Geography, 22*(1), 78–90. doi:10.2747/0272-3638.33.1.178

Janata, P., Birk, J. L., Van Horn, J. D., Leman, M., Tillmann, B., & Bharucha, J. J. (2002). The cortical topography of tonal structures underlying Western music. *Science, 298* (5601), 2167–2170.

Kolb, B., Gibbs, R., & Robinson, T. E. (2003). Brain plasticity and behavior. *Current Direction in Psychological Science, 12*(1), 1–5.

Krumhansl, C. L. (1997). An exploratory study of musical emotions and psychophysiology. *Canadian Journal of Experimental Psychology, 51*(4), 336–352.

Kuriansky, J., & Nemeth, D. G. (2013). A model for post-environmental disaster wellness workshops: Preparing individuals and communities for hurricane anniversary reactions. *Ecopsychology*, *5*(Suppl. 1), 38–45.

Labbé, E., Schmidt, N., Babin, J., & Pharr, M. (2007). Coping with stress: The effectiveness of different types of music. *Applied Psychophysiological Biofeedback*, *32*(3–4), 163–168.

Levitin, D. J. (2007). *This is your brain on music: Understanding a human obsession*. New York, NY: Penguin Group.

Levitin, D. J. (2008). *The world in six songs: How the musical brain created human nature*. New York, NY: Penguin Group.

Mannes, E. (2011). *The power of music: Pioneering discoveries in the new science of song*. New York, NY: Bloomsbury Publishing USA.

Mathews, A., & Mackintosh, B. (1998). A cognitive model of selective processing in anxiety. *Cognitive Therapy and Research*, *22*(6), 539–560.

Mathews, A., & MacLeod, C. (2005). Cognitive vulnerability to emotional disorders. *Annual Review of Clinical Psychology*, *1*, 167–195.

Minkler, M., Wallerstein, N., & Wilson, N. (1997). Improving health through community organization and community building. *Health Behavior and Health Education: Theory, Research, and Practice*, *3*, 279–311.

Morello-Frosch, R., & Lopez, R. (2006). The riskscape and the color line: Examining the role of segregation in environmental health disparities. *Environmental Research*, *102*(2), 181–196.

Mullahy, P. (1970). *Psychoanalysis and interpersonal psychiatry: The contributions of Harry Stack Sullivan*. New York, NY: Science House.

Mullahy, P. (1973). *The beginnings of modern American psychiatry: The ideas of Harry Stack Sullivan*. Boston, MA: Houghton Mifflin.

Nemeth, D. G., Kuriansky, J., Reeder, K. P., Lewis, A., Marceaux, K., Whittington, T., & Safier, J. A. (2012). Addressing anniversary reactions of trauma through group process: The Hurricane Katrina anniversary wellness workshops. *International Journal of Group Psychotherapy*, *62*(1), 129–142.

Perry, H. S. (1982). *Psychiatrist of America: The life of Harry Stack Sullivan*. Cambridge, MA: Belknap Press.

Piaget, J. (1952). *Origins of intelligence in the child* (M. Cook, Trans.). New York, NY: International University Press. (Original work published 1936)

Rampersad, A. (2007). *Ralph Ellison: A biography*. New York, NY: Random House.

Ray, D. (2008). *A socio-historical examination of race, gender, and class in single-parent African American mothers of delinquent youth* (Doctoral dissertation). Drexel University, Philadelphia, PA.

Reed, T. V. (2005). *The art of protest: Culture and activism from the civil rights movement to the streets of Seattle*. Minneapolis, MN: University of Minnesota Press.

Ren, Y., Harper, F. M., Drenner, S., Terveen, L., Kiesler, S., Riedl, J., & Kraut, R. E. (2012). Building member attachment in online communities: Applying theories of group identity and interpersonal bonds. *Mis Quarterly*, *36*(3).

Sanchez-Hucles, J. V. (1999). Racism: Emotional abusiveness and psychological trauma for ethnic minorities. *Journal of Emotional Abuse*, *1*(2), 69–87.

Sloboda, J. (2005). *Exploring the musical mind: Cognition, emotion, ability, function*. New York, NY: Oxford University Press.

Smith, E. J. (2006). The strength-based counseling model. *Counseling Psychologist, 34*(13). doi:10.1177/0011000005277018. Retrieved April 18, 2015, from http://tcp.sagepub.com/content/34/1/13

Smith, M. (2013, December 26). CDC warns of new virus threat in the Caribbean. *MedPage Today*. Retrieved April 18, 2015, from http://www.medpagetoday.com/InfectiousDisease/GeneralInfectiousDisease/43583

Smith, S. E. (1999). *Dancing in the street: Motown and the cultural politics of Detroit*. Cambridge, MA: Harvard University Press.

Stoute, S. (2011). *The tanning of America: How hip-hop created a culture that rewrote the rules of the new economy*. New York, NY: Penguin Group.

Sullivan, H. S. (1953). *Interpersonal theory of psychiatry*. New York, NY: W. W. Norton & Company.

Sullivan, H. S. (1956). *Clinical studies in psychiatry*. New York, NY: W. W. Norton & Company.

Sullivan, M. (2001). African-American music as rebellion: From slavesong to hip-hop. *Discoveries, 3*, 21–39.

Thornton, J. (1998). The African experience of the "20 and odd Negroes" arriving in Virginia in 1619. *The William and Mary Quarterly, 55*(3), 421–434.

Wachtel, P. L. (1999). *Race in the mind of America: Breaking the vicious circle between Blacks and Whites*. New York, NY: Routledge Press.

Wachtel, P. L. (2001). Racism, vicious circles, and the psychoanalytic vision. *The Psychoanalytic Review, 88*(5), 653–672.

Wachtel, P. L. (2002). Psychoanalysis and the disenfranchised: From therapy to justice. *Psychoanalytic Psychology, 19*(1), 199.

Walker, J. L. (2008). *The business of urban music: A practical guide to achieving success in the industry, from gospel to funk to r&b to hip-hop*. New York, NY: Billboard Books.

White-Newsome, J., O'Neill, M. S., Gronlund, C., Sunbury, T. M., Brines, S. J., Parker, E., & Rivera, Z. (2009). Climate change, heat waves, and environmental justice: Advancing knowledge and action. *Environmental Justice, 2*(4), 197–205.

Williams, D. R., & Mohammed, S. A. (2009). Discrimination and racial disparities in health: Evidence and needed research. *Journal of Behavioral Medicine, 32*(1), 20–47.

9

The Effects of Helping in a Train-the-Trainers Program for Youth in the Global Kids Connect Project Providing Psychosocial Support after the 2010 Haiti Earthquake: A Paradigm Shift to Sustainable Development

*Judy Kuriansky, Joel C. Zinsou, Vinushini Arunagiri,
Christina Douyon, Adrian Chiu, Wismick Jean-Charles,
Russell Daisey, and Tarah Midy*

On January 12, 2010, a catastrophic earthquake with a magnitude of 7.0 on the Richter scale occurred in the country of Haiti. Millions of people were affected, with up to an estimated 320,000 people dead, 300,000 injured, and over 1 million displaced (BBC News, 2010). The damage to property from collapsed buildings and resulting destruction of livelihoods was extensive, and exceptionally devastating for a country that was already one of the poorest in the Western Hemisphere (U.S. Fund for UNICEF, n.d.). Many countries responded with humanitarian aid, pledging funds and dispatching rescue and medical teams, engineers, and support personnel. While basic supplies including food and water, medical assistance, and reconstruction are essential immediately following such events, psychological support is also critical, to address both immediate and long-term mental devastation and anguish after such a tragic event. Much research and practice has shown that despite general resilience of survivors after environmental disasters, the mental health and well-being of those at all levels of exposure, including children as well as adults, are impacted both immediately and long term, making effective intervention programs that support survivors and helpers alike essential (Alexander, 2005; Başlolu, Kiliç, Şalciolu, & Livanou, 2004; Kuriansky, 2012a, 2012b, 2012c, 2012d, 2012e, 2013a, 2013b, 2013c, 2013d, 2013e, 2014; Kuriansky & Nemeth, 2013; Liu et al., 2011; Nolen-Hoeksema & Morrow, 1991; Roussos et al., 2005; Satapathy & Subhasis, 2009; Save the Children, 2012; Thienkrua et al, 2006; Wang et al., 2009). The project described in this chapter was designed to address these needs.

This chapter focuses on the impact on groups of student volunteers of their participation in various workshops, including a model of a train-the-trainers program, giving them skills to support others in crisis after the 2010

Haiti earthquake. Specifically, the trainings consisted of elementary techniques of psychosocial support and stress reduction as well as creative arts activities to achieve recovery, resilience, and empowerment. Trainings were held both immediately and in intervals over a four-year period (until this writing) after the earthquake.

As will be discussed in this chapter, the results of evaluation of the helpers' status, and of the impact of the training, suggest the positive outcome of such trainings for helpers on several dimensions, including increased self-esteem and motivation to help and engage in further skills-building. Such trainings and mobilizations of volunteer resources are shown to be a valuable asset to build human capital especially in the context of developing countries after an environmental disaster. Efforts to evaluate such interventions are important, to validate their impact, support their replicability in other settings and with diverse populations, and indicate their applicability to the achievement of the global agenda, described in the next section.

CONTEXT

The project and evaluations presented here are relevant in the context of two important international agreements, similar to interventions after the earthquake in China, as discussed in Chapter 10 of this volume (Kuriansky et al., 2015). Both documents provide important support for this intervention, by emphasizing the importance of mental health and well-being for sustainable development, and of psychosocial support in the aftermath of disaster. The Sendai Framework for Disaster Risk Reduction, agreed to by governments of the world at the World Conference on Disaster Risk Reduction (WCDRR) held in Sendai, Japan during March 14–18, 2015 (attended by chapter coauthors Kuriansky, Zinsou, and Jean-Charles, who gave presentations, including at the Children and Youth Forum), includes an action priority to "enhance recovery schemes to provide psychosocial support and mental health services for all people in need" (UNISDR, 2015a, para. 30[o]). The Sustainable Development Goals (SDGs) that sets the global agenda, agreed to by member states (governments) of the United Nations to achieve over the period of the years 2015–2030, includes Goal 3, to "ensure healthy lives and promote well-being for all at all ages" and target 3.4, to "promote mental health and well-being" (United Nations Department of Economic and Social Affairs, n.d.). As such, the intervention described here can be a means of implementation, and monitoring, of the progress of these agreements. In order to achieve sustainable development, it is essential to ensure the psychosocial resilience and well-being of survivors, citizens and communities, and to build capacity to facilitate recovery and growth.

While it is increasingly recognized that psychological first aid is essential after a disaster, capacity to achieve this is often limited. The model of enlisting community volunteers described in this project offers a solution to this problem.

The first author of this chapter, Kuriansky, had already been collaborating with coauthor Wismick Jean-Charles in projects on the ground in Haiti related to community development, reconciliation between Dominican Republic and Haitian youth, and recovery from previous natural disasters. These efforts provided a valuable foundation for the present project. Additionally, Father Wismick, a native Haitian and Catholic priest, was already a leader in the local church and health communities, providing the infrastructure for this project. The urgency of this post-disaster intervention was escalated by the fact that 10 young priests whom Father Wismick had trained perished in the rubble of a school collapse as a result of the earthquake.

OVERVIEW OF THE TRAININGS AND THE GLOBAL KIDS CONNECT PROJECT

The Global Kids Connect Project (GKCP) is an international project developed by coauthors of this chapter (Kuriansky and Daisey), whereby youth from different countries who have been impacted by trauma are connected to each other (Kuriansky, 2010a, 2010c, 2010d, 2012b, 2012c, 2012d; UNISDR, 2015b). The project, based on a train-the-trainers model, is a resilience-building program of psychosocial and psycho-educational techniques and cultural arts experiences with two modules. One module is a workshop for children, with four components: psychosocial exercises for stress reduction; a geography lesson about the various impacted and participating countries; a cultural program of creative arts activities (e.g., song, dance, and art from the various cultures); and an exchange of an object crafted by the children (e.g., a pillow with their original drawings on material with colored pens) that is meant to offer contact comfort, provide play opportunities, and communicate caring across continents. The second module is a training workshop for volunteers, caretakers, psychosocial supporters, or others, to create sustainability whereby after being trained, they implement the workshop for children (e.g., in school, camps, church, or other community settings).

The training involves simple, easily learned techniques that follow established guidelines in several ways: involving local people to help; following a step model; being culturally sensitive; working in the local language; and being sustainable (IASC Working Group, 2007; Kuriansky, 2010a, 2010c, 2010d; Jean-Charles, 2011a, 2011b; Kuriansky & Jean-Charles, 2012; Kuriansky, Lytle, & Chiu, 2011).

The aim of the model is to provide support, rather than therapy. As such, trainees do not need extensive experience before becoming an on-the-ground helper. Trainees are given encouragement and reassurance of their ability to offer this support. The training involves information about trauma (recognizing symptoms on physical, psychological, behavioral, and spiritual levels and identifying steps in recovery) as well as learning to implement the workshop model for children consisting of the various psycho-educational techniques and exercises to encourage relaxation, safety, trust, connection, and fun. Techniques include those from a toolbox developed by the first author over many years, applied in workshops in various cultures under varied conditions, including post-disaster situations (Kuriansky, 2007, 2008; Kuriansky & Berry, 2011).

The GKCP team members include the cofounders, who are also authors of this chapter, and other professionals from the psychological and educational fields, as well as students and interns. The central partners are a clinical psychologist with decades of experience in trauma recovery worldwide (Kuriansky), a musician with vast international experience in music therapy and cultural arts (Daisey), and an educational psychologist who is also a Catholic priest and native Haitian (Jean-Charles). All are representatives of the International Association of Applied Psychology (http://www.iaapsy.org) at the United Nations, a nongovernmental organization accredited with the Economic and Social Council and associated with the Department of Public Information. Jean-Charles is also associated with the local church community and university in Haiti.

THE VALUE OF VOLUNTEERING AND HELPING

Given the impact of environmental disasters on a community and the general shortage of psychosocial personnel to help—especially in developing countries such as Haiti—an important solution is to enlist volunteers as helpers. Much research has shown the positive psychological and physical effects on individuals from volunteering and altruistic behavior (Morrow-Howell, Hinterlong, Rozario, & Tang, 2003; Schwartz, Keyl, Marcum, & Bode, 2009; Schwartz, Meisenhelder, Ma, & Reed, 2003; Smith, 1981; Willigen, 2000). Positive physical effects of volunteering for individuals have been shown to be direct, including lower mortality (Brown, Nesse, Vinokur, & Smith, 2003; Musick, Herzog, & House, 1999), as well as indirect, in terms of improving one's perception of health (Young & Glasgow, 1998). Psychological benefits include that helping others can lower one's own depressive symptoms, enhance self-worth, and induce greater calmness (Krause, Herzog, & Baker, 1992; Luks, 1988). For example, patients with multiple sclerosis benefited greatly from helping other patients with the same ailments, showing improvements in confidence, self-awareness, self-esteem, depression, and role functioning (Schwartz & Sendor, 1999). Youth who volunteer to help others are less likely to feel alienated, and more likely to experience self-acceptance, undergo moral development, and assume responsibility for their actions (Indiana Youth Institute, 2011; Moore & Allen, 1996). Further, giving help has even been shown to be associated with higher levels of mental health than receiving help (Schwartz et al., 2003).

THE MEANING OF VOLUNTEERING

A volunteer can be defined as "an individual engaging in behavior that is not bio-socially determined (e.g., eating, sleeping), nor economically necessitated (e.g., paid work, housework, home repair), nor sociopolitically compelled (e.g., paying one's taxes, clothing oneself before appearing in public), but rather that is essentially (primarily) motivated by the expectation of psychic benefits of some kind as a result of activities that have a market value greater than any remuneration received for such activities" (Smith, 1981). Incentives for volunteerism can be material or purposive, both of which lead to gains from engaging in the behavior, although the latter can be the most powerful; these purposive incentives are intrinsic, intangible satisfactions that result from feeling that one is contributing to some purpose, helping to achieve some valued goal, as a means to some valued end (Smith, 1981).

SPECIFICS OF THE TRAININGS IN HAITI

The extreme devastation in Haiti caused by the earthquake led several of the authors of this chapter to recognize the dire needs for psychosocial healing that would be required both immediately and also long term, and thus to initiate trainings for students of psychology and related fields as well as for community volunteers, to provide desperately needed support.

Immediately after the earthquake, authors of this chapter Kuriansky and Father Wismick traveled to Haiti, bringing with them suitcases of medical supplies collected in the short time before the trip. As air travel to Haiti was interdicted, they flew to the neighboring country of the Dominican Republic and took a bus across the island to Haiti. They immediately went to a major hospital in the capital city of Port-au-Prince to deliver the supplies, meet with the hospital administration and other staff, and assess the needs. With the help of the chief of social work (who fortunately survived the disaster while other staff perished), 30 volunteers were recruited to participate in the training program about how to help survivors of the earthquake (Jean-Charles, 2011b; Kuriansky, 2010a, 2010b, 2010c, 2010d; Luce, 2010). This group was comprised of students and a number of Boy Scouts, all of whom were known by the hospital staff and trainers, and who were contacted as best as possible through cell phones and referrals, given the breakdown of communication caused by the earthquake. The training was conducted over the course of two days after the trauma, led by Kuriansky with the assistance of Father Wismick, and primarily in French (locally spoken) with Father Wismick's assistance in the primary local language of Creole when necessary (Kuriansky, 2010a, 2010b, 2010d). The trainees then provided simple emotional support to the innumerable suffering patients at the hospital, lying injured in the grass, tents, and halls. Given these activities, the trainee/helpers have also been referred to as "comforters."

Assessments about the experience of these helpers, reported below, was collected when members of the team returned to Haiti to conduct further workshops six months later. At that time, the focus was on helping the children living in a local church and grammar school community in the capital city of Port-au-Prince (Church of Saint-Louis Roi de France, in the hillside Digicel Tower neighborhood) and piloting various aspects of the GKCP. An important part of the arts components of the intervention included teaching the children an original song in their local language, written by team members Daisey and Kuriansky with the input of native Creole musicians, poets, and a psychologist (Jean-Charles, 2011b; Kuriansky & Jean-Charles, 2012). The lyrics built on the theme of "Rebati" (meaning to "build back better") and included a familiar refrain sung in Creole, referencing empowerment, that "We are reeds in the wind, we bend but we don't break" (see Appendix). Cards were also distributed that were designed by children in a public school in New York City expressing greetings and support, a technique that has been a gold standard for children after many disaster situations. Such activities were deemed especially appropriate in this particular culture, which has such a rich music and artistic heritage.

Team members again returned to Haiti during the summer of 2011, to train a group of students following the GKCP model (Kuriansky & Daisey, 2011). The students then conducted the workshop with a group of over 100 children from the same church community. The ages of the children were purposefully selected to be about age 8, as that developmental stage matched well with the nature of the exercises, the intention of the workshop, receptivity of the children to the activities, and the children's ability to follow the instructions and maintain attention.

This same summer, a similar training was conducted with staff of a major hospital in New York City, to prepare children for any anniversary reactions and/or trauma associated with the 10th anniversary of the September 11 attacks on the World Trade Center; after which staff members conducted the workshop with children who attend the outpatient clinic. While these youth did not experience an environmental disaster as did the Haiti children, the model was shown to be applicable to this population, and the connection established between the children in the two countries as a result of the craft exchange was very well received. The children expressed considerable appreciation knowing that others in another country were thinking about them and cared about them, demonstrated by enthusiasm about the exchange of the object as well as the geography lesson (Kuriansky & Jean-Charles, 2012).

In keeping with the intention to continue capacity-building in Haiti, team members reconvened again, in the summer of 2014. A training and assessment were conducted with a group of volunteers (some of whom were in the original group), who then conducted a workshop with 60 children from the same church community. A description of this training and data from the assessment is described later in this chapter.

THE FIRST ASSESSMENT

Data was collected from 24 out of 30 helpers (Kuriansky, Lytle, & Chiu, 2011) who had been trained to be supporters immediately after the earthquake. All were Haitian from the local community; two-thirds were male and one-third were female, predominantly in their early 20s (with a range of 19 to 42 [$\mu = 27.04$ years, $SD = 5.23$ years]), and with a high level of education (96% of the comforters had obtained at least a high school education). The majority had a high degree of exposure to the event (i.e., half were within 0.25 km of Port-au-Prince, the capital city that suffered extensive destruction, even though the epicenter was in a city nearby). Three quarters of the group knew someone who died as a result of the earthquake.

The Assessment Protocol

The assessment protocol included self-report questionnaires, measuring symptoms during the earthquake (adapted from the Depression, Anxiety, and Stress Scale); the Immediate Impact of Earthquake (adapted from the Impact of Event Scale–Revised); Family and Friend Support (adapted from the Crisis Support Scale); the Impact of Helping (adapted from the Professional Quality of Life Scale); and Posttraumatic Growth (adapted from the Posttraumatic Growth Inventory).

Background Questionnaire

Adapted from the Screening Instrument for Traumatic Stress in Earthquake Survivors (SITSES-R) (Başloğlu et al., 2001), this 57-item questionnaire records demographic information as well as quantitative and qualitative data in response to the earthquake. Respondents are asked questions about their levels of preparedness, emotional trauma resulting from the earthquake, and levels of loss. These items responses are first rated on a Likert scale from "1" to "7" (when applicable) and then the respondents are asked to clarify their choice in rating.

Stress Symptoms at the Time of the Earthquake

Adapted from DASS—Depression, Anxiety, and Stress Scale (Australian Centre for Post-traumatic Mental Health, n.d.; Henry & Crawford, 2005; Lovibond & Lovibond, 1995; Psychology Foundation of Australia, 2010)—this 42-item scale measures distress along the axes of depression, anxiety and stress with questions as "I feel depressed and depressed" and "I had difficulty breathing," rated to refer to two points in time (in the past week and at the time of the earthquake). Each item is rated from "0" to "3," where "0" indicates that the item "does not apply to me at all" and "3" indicates that the item "fully applies to me, or the vast majority of the time," with a total score range of "0" to "126" divided according to gradated totals into categories of "normal," "mild," "moderate," "severe," and "extremely severe."

Immediate Impact of Earthquake

Adapted from the Impact of Event Scale–Revised (IES-R) (Christenson & Marren, 2013; Weiss & Marmar, 1997), this self-report questionnaire measures responses to the event in terms of intrusion (intrusive thoughts, nightmares), avoidance (numbing of responsiveness, avoidance of feelings, situations, and ideas) and hyperarousal (anger, irritability, hypervigilance). Twenty-two items are rated from "0" through "4" where a rating of "0" equals no symptom and "4" equals a high frequency of the symptom, with a resulting range from "0" to "88," and suggested cutoffs of "24" and "33" indicating respectively mild or moderate ranges. Sample items are "I felt irritable and angry" and "I stayed away from whatever reminded me about the event."

Family and Friend Support

Adapted from the Crisis Support Scale (Elklit, Schmidt Pedersen, & Jind, 2001; Joseph, Williams, & Yule, 1992), this 14-item self-report questionnaire assesses the availability of others, contact with other survivors, confiding in others, emotional support, practical support, negative responses and satisfaction with support. Items are rated on a 7-point scale, where "1" indicates "never" and "7" indicates "always," this higher scores indicate greater support.

Impact of Helping

Adapted from the Professional Quality of Life Scale–Version 5 (ProQOL) (Stamm, 2010), the 30 items in this scale measure the extent of being exposed to others' traumatic events as a result of one's work, leading to possible fear, difficulty sleeping, or avoiding things that trigger memories of the event. Items include effects of helping others who are suffering or experiencing trauma, effects that can be considered negative as well as positive (e.g., "through my work I feel satisfied"). These items are clustered into three dimensions: Compassion Satisfaction, Burnout, and Secondary Traumatic Stress (the latter two which are considered to reflect Compassion Fatigue). Self-report ratings are made on a scale from "never" to "repeatedly," with a range of scores from "0" to "150." These scores are converted into "high," "average," and "low."

Posttraumatic Growth

Adapted from the Posttraumatic Growth Inventory (PTGI) (Tedeschi & Calhoun, 2004), this 21-item questionnaire assesses positive outcomes that may result from experiencing a traumatic event, including positive reconstruction of perceptions of self, others, and the meaning of events. Subscales include personal strength, spiritual change, relating to others, and appreciation of life and new possibilities, with items like "I have a great appreciation about what is important in life" and "I have a greater sense of closeness with others." Supporters were asked to fill this out with regard to their role as a supporter. As a result, self-reports reflect the level of perceived change on a scale from "I did not experience this change at all as a result of my comforter help" to "I experienced this change to a very great degree as a result of my comforter help."

RESULTS AND DISCUSSION

Preliminary analysis of the comforters' self-reports after the earthquake reveal an overall mild degree of symptoms; their scores on the DASS depression and stress subscales were in the "normal" range (9.375 and 10.125, within the normative range of 0–9 and 0–14, respectively) and in the low moderate range on anxiety (10.75, within the normative range of 10–14). Further, the results on the Impact of Earthquake scale showed a mean score of 17.92, which reveals little to no impact according to the norm. However, scores were above average on the Secondary Traumatic Stress subscale on the Impact of Helping scale (i.e., a mean of 14.9 compared to the norm score of 13). This can be explained by the compounding of stress by being exposed to the same trauma as the children they were helping; nevertheless, this did not appear to distract from their motivation to help (Kuriansky, Lytle, & Chiu, 2011).

The hypothesis was posed that helping others would be a positive experience for the helpers, both in quantitative scores and qualitative responses. Scores on the Impact of Helping scale showed an average score on the Compassion Scale (37.04) consistent with the norm. Additionally, participants as a whole did not appear to be suffering from burnout, given that their scores on this subscale was low (i.e., 18.91), suggesting that individuals did not feel hopelessness or that their effort makes no difference. Half of participants rated "average" scores on Compassion Fatigue, with none rating "high" on this scale (high scores on this scale, especially if also reflected in scores by individuals on other ratings, would identify those who could especially benefit from clinical help).

The results revealed above-average scores (mean of 76.38) for participants on the Posttraumatic Growth Inventory. This finding is consistent with past research on posttraumatic growth (PTG) (Calhoun & Tedeschi, 1998, 2004; Linley & Joseph, 2004). The association between helping others and PTG is suggested by participants' spontaneous comments about helping, for example: "I believe that I was born to help everyone in need any way that I can"; "I have a new sense of solidarity and I am more hospitable"; and "The earthquake has affected my relationship with others because now I understand others better and I realize there is no such thing as superiority on this earth." The supporters' enthusiasm and dedication to helping others was evident to the trainers during the workshop and in supervising the comforters' behavior while they were implementing the techniques in helping the earthquake survivors. Their commitment was particularly commendable given the extensively difficult circumstances of poor or nonexistent transportation and financial constraints caused by the trauma, and especially being survivors themselves. This same commitment and satisfaction about helping was noted by the team facilitating the evaluation.

THE 2014 TRAINING

A train-the-trainers program was held in June 2014 in Port-au-Prince, Haiti, coincident with the fourth annual conference of the Center for Training in Mental Health and Spirituality, known as CESSA according to the French name standing for Centre de Spiritualité, d'Evangélisation et de Santé Mentale. This center was founded by the GKCP team member Father Wismick Jean-Charles in 2010, with help from many international professionals who came to Haiti from all over the world to provide short-term trauma services after the earthquake (Jean-Charles, 2011a, 2011b). The center creates multi-stakeholder partnerships and offers extensive opportunities for interdisciplinary training, to meet the long-term emotional and spiritual needs of Haitians. The first annual training conference was held in June 2011 at the University of Notre-Dame of Haiti, in Port-au-Prince, where the CESSA founder is also the vice president, whose responsibilities include organizing trainings for various cohorts. The 2014 training reported in this chapter was planned to coincide with the conference that year.

The trainees were students and practitioners in psychology and related fields recruited by team member Father Wismick, who was familiar with the volunteers and their motivation to participate. The purpose of the intervention was to further build capacity of human resources and the professional community in Haiti to offer psychosocial services, particularly for children, for the purposes of both long-term recovery from the trauma and resilience-building for the community in general. The workshop was again led by the first author of this chapter, Kuriansky, in the local French language, using a training manual she developed, and assisted by coauthor Daisey, who led the cultural exercises.

The training was held over a weekend, with sessions on Friday night (instructions and demonstrations), Saturday afternoon (continued training and participation with role play) and Sunday morning (review and practice) before the workshop with the children, which was conducted by the trainees on Sunday afternoon. The training manual that was prepared, with translation of the main instructions, was distributed. The training activities included the established psychosocial techniques of the GKCP and singing the original song about recovery ("Rebati") described above. Twenty trainees participated in the various sessions, with pre-post data available for 13 of these. This sample was about evenly divided by gender, with an average age of 27 and high school education level; 80% were single, and only one had a child. All were Christian (about evenly divided identifying as Catholic, Baptist, or Protestant), and gave a rating of above-average importance to religion (rating a "5" on a scale of "1" to "7"). All had been through the trauma of the earthquake, with a third describing stress also from economic insecurity and bereavement from loss of family and loved ones. Happy events reported included academic success, marriage, and helping others.

The assessment protocol consisted of several components, some of which were used in the previously reported evaluation. These included a background questionnaire of information about demographics, with self-report questions about previous experience in counseling, and various aspects of working with children (e.g., experience, comfort level, abilities), self-care activities, and locus of control (e.g., amount of self-control versus destiny); 10 questions on a scale of "1" to "10" designed by the researchers to reflect the psychological principles underlying the choice of the workshop material and exercises (e.g., to foster safety, self-esteem, strength, calm, renewed energy, and feeling caring and cared for by others), called the Global Kids Connect Project Scale (GKCPS); the Impact of Helping questionnaire (described above); and the WHO-5 Well-Being Index (Bech, 2004; Snoek, 2006). The latter self-administered questionnaire consists of five items: "I have felt cheerful and in good spirits"; "I have felt calm and relaxed"; "I have felt active and vigorous"; "I woke up feeling fresh and rested"; and "My daily life has been filled with things that interest me." These are rated according to self-report covering the past two weeks, on a 6-point Likert scale from "0" ("none of the time") to "5" ("all of the time") with the highest score being 25, and a score of "13" or lower indicating a need for further assessment.

The post-training questionnaire repeated relevant questions and included both quantitative and open-ended self-report questions about helpfulness of the training, what trainees particularly liked, further training/experiences they would like, and any other suggestions.

RESULTS AND DISCUSSION OF THE 2014 TRAINING

The results confirmed the hypothesis that the trainees were helped themselves by participating in the training; they felt better about themselves and more empowered. The positive impact of the experience was evident in their self-report ratings on the quantitative items on the questionnaire, and their qualitative answers to the open-ended questions. These all reflected high levels of motivation and satisfaction in helping others (especially children) recover from trauma as well as in contributing to their country. Examples of answers reflected the classic phrase that "helping others helps yourself," as well as related responses, e.g., "I feel good helping others with my heart," "I enjoy one of the three pillars of my university to do community service" and "[I feel] useful and helpful to my country."

Trainees rated high satisfaction, comfort, and motivation working with children even before the training (5.6 on a scale of 1 to 7). Ratings related to individual questions on these issues were high, both before and after the training (e.g., how much interest do you have in working with children). Responses included "Children are a gift from God," "I enjoy working with children," and "I need to give my all to bring them a little bit of smiling." Working with children specifically helped them, evident in answers like, "I want to learn to surpass my difficulties and see the good moments of life and help the young get over difficulties and discover the good moments of life," and "I relive my childhood when I help children." Given their interest in helping children, it is noted that some trainees had past experience working with children prior to this workshop; for example, some had been through a training about cognitive-behavioral techniques.

After the training, the participants' satisfaction in working with children was especially evident. This satisfaction from working with and helping children was consistent with the self-report ratings about motivation and enjoyment in working with children. Qualitative responses included that: "When I work with a child, I show him that he is in a safe place and that he can trust me," and "I like sharing the world of children." The experience of working with children in the workshop led to such responses as: "It makes me feel useful," "I'm doing something I love," "I feel divinely good in this experience," "I feel like a big family," "I was already used to working with children but the time I spent with the group, I feel even more capable," and "In helping the children through this workshop, I also gain energy and more comfort within myself and in my relationships with others." These responses reflect the self-efficacy and increased pleasure in the work intended by the workshop design. These results are further consistent with low ratings on fears or worries about doing such work.

Several trainees mentioned that children are the future, and in helping them, they feel they are helping their community and their country. Examples of such responses are, "I think I have to be useful to the community and with the children it will be important," and "I'm interested in helping the youth because it is important to participate in the transformation of the country and it will be achieved with the youth."

The intended purpose of the workshop—to connect children around the world—was also achieved, as confirmed by qualitative responses such as, "I learned how we can connect the kids of Haiti and the kids of the world." Knowledge and skills in working with children were also increased. Trainees specifically expressed feeling more prepared to work with children.

Ratings about self-esteem and feeling strong showed a trend toward improvement but were already at a high level. Ratings on the WHO-5 Well-being Index showed higher ratings than the cutoff score (i.e., of "13") and a trend toward an increase in the average total score for the group, from 17.7 to 20.5, suggesting an improvement in well-being, specifically feeling more calm and having more interesting things in their daily life.

Ratings on the Impact of Helping scale support the general findings about trainees' motivation for helping. Specifically, scores on the subscale of Compassion revealed that 80 percent of the trainees' scores rated in the "high" category before the training (i.e., that they had a high degree of compassion compared to the norm on the scale). This increased to 90 percent rated as "high" after the training, with no trainees' scores in the "low" category on the scale. On the Burnout subscale, all trainees' ratings were in the "low" category before the training (i.e., indicating low experience of burnout), except for one subject who rated "average." After the training, all trainees' ratings of burnout were "low." On the Secondary Trauma subscale, trainees' ratings were higher than on the Burnout scale (i.e., half the trainees rated "low" and half rated as "average"); however, there was no increase (i.e., no change) in this score after the training. Two trainees did specifically describe upset about others' suffering, saying, "To see them [children] suffer, traumatized, is traumatizing" and "I could not watch suffering."

Another hypothesis was that participation in the group experience of the training, given the focus on helping and the connection inherent in the exercises themselves, as well as the group experience as a whole, would increase the helpers' sense of connection with others and of feeling cared for and caring. Much research supports the value of social support in healing and of the group model in therapy (Yalom & Leszcz, 2005). Scores on the GKCPS revealed trends toward change in a positive direction, e.g., feeling caring about others and cared for by others, including how much they think others would help them.

Thus, the intentions of this training, reflected in the selected exercises, appeared to have been achieved (i.e., to build the confidence and empowerment of the trainees in themselves, to form supportive bonds, to support and inspire them to continue helping activities, and to implement the workshop in other contexts). Such qualitative responses reflect the psychological principles that formed the basis of the workshop exercises and design, which were to increase feelings of confidence, trust, comfort, and support.

An important finding was that the ratings and perceived sense of empowerment in helping children were linked to an increased sense of community and connection with others, both with their peers and fellow trainees and with the children they were serving. This was reflected in the trainees' answers on the questionnaire and also in their feedback and interviews. The importance of a strong social support system has notably been shown by much other research to be important in recovery, especially due to the trauma of environmental disaster (Kuriansky, 2012b).

It is noteworthy that these benefits are attained even after a single training. This finding has implications for environmental disaster planning, especially for efficient use and mobilization of resources in communities and clinics. Further, the techniques are simple and easily taught, such that trainees—who can be also called "supporters"—can provide valuable and immediate support service. The usefulness of simple interventions for a wide population in need has been evident to the first author in developing the "Reassure Model," and applying techniques worldwide involving psycho-education, reduction of stress and anxiety, and simple cognitive restructuring in the context of group support, to feel good about oneself and not feel alone (Kuriansky et al., 2009).

It was also hypothesized that the trainees would be motivated to continue this healing work, especially given its simplicity, effectiveness, helpfulness, and fun experienced by the children and the trainees themselves. This was overwhelmingly revealed in the qualitative answers and interviews, a crucial finding given the necessity of having sustainability in the training. This was shown in their answers on the questionnaire about interest in further training, and in their responses about how they would apply what they had learned. For example, trainees expressed interest in conducting workshops using this model in their church, school, and community settings, as well as with children in a foster home and in a research study about abused children. An important indication of the sustainability of this work is that the model is now being applied with groups of children in the parish school of Saint-Louis Roi de France Church (where the training took place in 2011), as well as in several primary schools in Port-au-Prince (Jean-Charles, 2015).

The intention of the workshop was to increase participants' feelings about having control over their lives and emotions, supported by answers to the questions that reflect locus of control. Initially, trainees reported feeling equally responsible for themselves (e.g., having free will), but believing that fate (or God) determines outcomes. After the training, however, there was a trend in reporting that fate and luck were less important determinants, and that personal effort counted in determining outcomes.

Before the training, several trainees reported needing help in handling their feelings (e.g., frustration, anger, impatience), and problems with money, family, and teachers. They anticipated both professional gains (e.g., learning more skills) and personal benefits (e.g., self-confidence).

Self-care is a crucial aspect of providing care to others, especially in emergency situations (Office of Emergency Preparedness and Response, 2013). The first author always includes this component in workshops after trauma (whether environmental or man-made, as in terrorism or school shootings). The trainees were asked what they did to take care of themselves. The responses included getting support from others (e.g., family), relaxation exercises, sports, study, and spiritual activities (e.g., prayer and meditation). After the training, many trainees mentioned that they would use the breathing exercises.

Participants gave both quantitative and qualitative responses about the value of the training. When asked to rate the benefits of the training to their professional and personal lives on a scale of "1" to "10" with "10" being the highest, the average scores rated were "9.5" and "9.4," respectively, indicating a very high perceived benefit of the experience on both aspects of their lives. When asked what they particularly liked in the workshop, a majority of the trainees answered "everything"; in addition, almost every exercise was mentioned as having a positive impact, including those targeted to self-esteem, personal strength, resiliency, energy, breathing and trust, as well as the games, songs, dances, and geography lesson. Examples of responses included: "The trust exercise really helped me especially in my personal life," and "I like everything, especially the therapeutic exercises."

REPORTS IN INTERVIEWS AFTER THE TRAINING

Open-ended, unstructured interviews conducted with the trainees after the workshop confirmed and reinforced the quantitative and qualitative results from the questionnaires reported above about the perceived and experienced benefits and value of the training to the trainees on many levels. With regard to what they learned, responses included: "I learned to better know children ... that you have to play with the children"; "I learned to better take care of children, and how to teach kids to recover from trauma, to help them rebuild their lives"; and "I learned how we can connect the kids of Haiti and the kids of the world." Increased self-efficacy was revealed in statements like, "I learned how we, the young professionals, can help the children to move forward"; and "I now have the capacity to help others and children." Many spontaneously mentioned wanting the program to continue, and also being further motivated to pursue further study in helping professions like the field of psychology.

Regarding which exercises they liked best, favorites included the finger lock (making a strong connection with the fingers of one hand, as if they are glued and cannot be broken apart) because "it shows how one can become strong despite the difficulties of life" and because it can be easily used at any time. Another favorite activity mentioned was the wind/reed and tree, where participants work in pairs, pretending to be wind blowing over reeds or a tree; the latter being difficult, with the lesson that you can be as solid as a tree in the face of challenges and that you can even tremble like reeds in the wind but still stay stable and survive difficulties. They also enjoyed the song, and playing games with the children, like pretending to be animals that taught a lesson about how to "accommodate to [others] in nature." Most trainees said they liked "all" the techniques, with one trainee elaborating, in an expansive view, that all the exercises and activities "had the lesson of solidarity, how to live together, share together and live in society together." Regarding the style of the training, they specifically mentioned appreciating how "animated" and "energetic" the experience was.

Personal growth was evident in statements like "I learned so much about how to be strong facing difficulties and surmounting sadness." One young couple who did the training together said the experience would even help their marriage; as the wife said, "It taught us how to connect better, to enjoy each other ... to have harmony ... and to help each other, as well as how to help others."

Trainees further expressed greatly enjoying the experience and feeling "love" for each other and for the trainers. This was reflected in comments like, "I found this experience magnificent and I was very happy"; "I had fun with the children, I learned a lot. I was able to understand that while they're having fun, they're learning"; "We learned a lot from your warmth, way of being with people, and to express our feelings, when we didn't have that habit before"; and "You gave us an interesting tools to help children and other people ... I feel there is something very profound in what we did." The words "magnifique," "formidable," and "experience extraordinaire" (in French) were mentioned often.

RESPONSES OF THE TEACHERS

The two schoolteachers who were present during the workshop, and observed the children from their classes who participated in the workshop, reported similarly positive appreciation and reflections about the experience as the trainees. Regarding the value of the experience for the children, teachers observed a positive impact, saying, "The students learned a lot. They had fun." And, "It was very amazing for the children. We need it. Security is very important. We live in a climate of stress and fear, without trust. But now, going through this experience, beginning at this age, the children can develop this climate of trust, and it will grow with them." The teachers particularly noted the exercises targeted at reducing stress (moving rapidly and then going into a meditative state) and the trust exercise (using blindfolds). The teachers further mentioned the positive impact for their own lives, saying, "We also liked it a lot as teachers. So we want to thank you." And, "We as well need to trust each other, because often we live in a climate of fear and stress. So we lack a lot of trust. But now we see that every day, we must trust and help others."

EXPERIENCE OF THE TRAINERS

It is interesting to note the reactions of the trainers, which greatly matched the appreciation, enjoyment, and educational value of the training and workshop expressed by the trainees, the children, and the teachers. Kuriansky and Daisey were exceptionally impressed with the trainees being such a quick study in learning and then applying the techniques of the workshop, as well as by their talent and creativity in how they implemented the exercises. The trainers were equally exceptionally moved by the trainees' warm-heartedness and enthusiasm, as well as their commitment and dedication to the healing of children and their country. Similar to the trainees' expressions toward the trainers, the trainers felt, and expressed, genuine affection, gratitude, and love, for the trainees, and for the children.

LIMITATIONS

The small sample size of these trainees can clearly limit generalizability of quantitative results; therefore, the results are best understood as trends, and interpreted in the context of the qualitative answers and open-ended interview responses. It should be noted that these were convenience samples, based on recruiting the volunteers, self-selection, and the realistic availability and accessibility of the helpers. In fact, the recruitment of 30 students immediately after the disaster was deemed impressive given the severity of the disaster, causing deaths of trained professionals and potential trainees as well as difficulties in transportation. Also, the number of helpers in the 2014 training was determined by the number of students available in psychology-related study at the local universities, who indicated interest in being trained.

Limitations in such studies as this one are commonly caused by constraints inherent in the logistics of a post-trauma crisis, which make empirical scientific methodology of data collection difficult, especially since research must take a back seat to clinical needs for survivors' healing, necessitating that some data may have to be collected retrospectively. In the 2014 training, time constraints for the trainees' participation was also an interfering factor. Language also presented challenges, since parts of the questionnaire were not in the Creole language, and only some trainees could be supervised while filling out the forms, given the multiple responsibilities of the team (e.g., attending to the child participants, conducting unstructured interviews). Where some items on a scale were not filled out, the data for that particular rating was eliminated; or, in some cases, the Creole French-speaking member of the team oversaw the completion of items with the individual participant. The present studies would have benefitted from a reliable and valid assessment package, in the local Creole language, which is more familiar than French, though the latter language is also understood and spoken.

Since the trainees were recruited, and also self-selected, the results showing their interest, commitment, and satisfaction in working with children can also be considered as skewed as they were already predisposed to working with, and helping, children. Also, the various populations, and assessment protocols at the intervals were not equivalent (e.g., only a few trainees overlapped in both trainings, and several factors including logistics required changes in the assessment package and procedures) and further analysis is warranted; however, preliminary pilot results still present a useful picture of the impact of helping that can be further explored in future studies using more scientific sample selection and methodology.

THEORIES OF HELPING BEHAVIOR

In light of these preliminary results and the observations made, several theories and explanations proposed to explain the positive physical and mental effects of volunteering are interesting to consider. The response shift theory (Schwartz & Sendor, 1999) proposes that altruistic behaviors have a positive impact on mental health because they facilitate adaptation via a response shift phenomena, referring to "a change in the meaning of one's self-evaluation of a target construct as a result of a change in internal standards of measurement, a change in the respondent's values, or a redefinition of the target construct." Having an outer-directed role allows an individual to disengage from previous patterns of self-reference and to engage in greater openness to changing internal standards and values. These shifts can lead to a new perspective on one's life circumstances, such as stressors and personal loss (Schwartz et al., 2003).

Role theory is based on one of the most popular concepts of social psychology, that people form behavior patterns consistent with their social positions and expectations (Biddle, 1986). Role theory has been used to explain helping behavior (Callero, Howard, & Piliavin, 1987) and an expanded concept, namely, the role theory of helping, is based on the proposition that roles alter how a person is treated, acts, behaves, and thereby thinks and feels (Bronfenbrenner, 1979, as cited in Moen, Dempster-McClain, & Williams, 1992). An aspect of role theory that has received much academic attention is that of prosocial behavior and its various levels, from provider-recipient dyads to larger organizations (Penner, Dovidio, Piliavin, & Schroeder, 2005). Similarly, according to Ecological Systems Theory, individuals have roles within four spheres, expanding from close interpersonal relationships and immediate surroundings to their social and cultural context, that affect their beliefs and behavior, all of which influence and feedback one another (Bronfenbrenner, 1979). The volunteers' experiences can be seen in this context, where their expressed benefits of helping expand from a connection to the inner self, to bonding with others, and then to a broader sense of connection to their social-cultural environment (e.g., their country). Interest has also focused on incentives or motivations for prosocial behavior, ranging from self-respect to altruism (Bénabou & Tirole, 2005). As has been shown in the current projects, engaging in a volunteer role increases a person's social network, power, prestige, resources, and emotional gratification, which result in healthier psychological well-being (Moen et al., 1992).

Helping others has been explained as regulating people's perceptions of internal and external realities that they are powerless to change, and empowering them to effect meaningful change (Schwartz et al., 2003). Volunteering has also been described as a form of social activity and participation that creates more social ties or relationships, which in turn yield positive mental health effects (Wilson & Musick, 1999). Further, providing help is a self-validating experience that fosters trust and intimacy and encourages the volunteer to anticipate that reciprocal help will be forthcoming when needed. These mechanisms help explain the appeal of volunteering to help others as a fundamental aspect of disaster relief work, for both survivors themselves and for others not directly affected. The present results are consistent with these theories.

The results of these trainings can be seen in the context of several disciplines of psychology. These include humanistic psychology, with its focus on human potential and growth (Schneider, Pierson, & Bugenthal, 2014), as well as transpersonal psychology, where identity extends beyond the personal self to wider aspects of life and humanity (Friedman & Hartelius, 2013).

The findings, observations, and experience of the present trainings support the general belief that doing good feels good; this in turn creates a feedback cycle, whereby high self-esteem and self-efficacy further encourages doing good. Such results are consistent with research about motivation for people to engage in pro-environmental behavior (Venhoeven, Bolderdijk, & Steg, 2014). The fact that people who behave in a more prosocial (or pro-environmental) way are actually more satisfied with their lives can be explained by both hedonistic aspects of behavior (meaning how pleasurable or comfortable the behavior is) and eudaimonic aspects (indicating how personally meaningful the behavior is), such that engaging in behavior deemed meaningful sends a positive self-signal that you are striving for a worthy cause, and thus, that you are a good person. Additional recent research about prosocial behavior is elaborated in Chapter 20 of this volume (Nemeth, Hamilton, & Kuriansky, 2015), in the section contributed by Kuriansky.

The benefits of the experience expressed by the trainees described here is consistent with research about the benefits of volunteering in helpful community activities. In one study, participants in a community beach cleanup reported personal benefits (Wyles, Pahl, & Thompson, 2014); also, citizens who volunteered to clean up after an oil spill reported a sense of satisfaction and renewed social ties and optimism after the community trauma (Sargisson, Smith, Hunt, & Hamerton, 2014). Volunteers' motivations were found to include the desire to: contribute to the community, connect with others, cope with their negative emotions, fulfill a sense of duty and responsibility, and ensure the heath of future generations—motivations similarly expressed by the trainees in this project. It would certainly be expected that benefits would accrue to volunteers when deeper emotional commitment and bonding were involved.

OVERALL DISCUSSION AND CONCLUSIONS

In the face of the ongoing struggle for Haiti's emotional and psychosocial recovery, the present study sheds a hopeful light, exemplified in the form of these groups of Haitian helpers, ready to devote their time and energy to helping others. Their values, commitment, enthusiasm, and personal strength—which were exceptionally evident during the training and workshop, and further revealed in their responses in the questionnaires and open-ended interviews— bodes well for Haiti's future as well as for Haitian "Rebati," meaning "to build back better." The trainees' devotion to helping the children of Haiti is especially inspiring and reassuring.

Despite the limitations of the present assessments, the results present valuable pilot experiences showing the positive impact of a training program on the well-being of a group of participant volunteers, as well as on the well-being of those they serve. These trainees, who had all been through the trauma of the earth-quake themselves, benefitted from helping children. This is consistent with research showing that givers see their ability to give support as evidence of their own recovery (Henderson, 1995). This dynamic reflects psychological principles of relationships, including symbiosis, identification, reciprocity, projection, and vicarious learning between helper and recipient, as well as the processes of (1) projecting outward and then reflecting inward, and (2) externalization of personal pain ultimately allowing for shared experience, personal processing, and renewed meaning, leading to healing.

The value placed on helping is consistent with religious principles practiced widely in this particular culture. The trainees in these workshops expressed considerable faith in God, which no doubt increased their commitment to, and benefits from, the act of helping. This is consistent with research showing that volunteering in a religious context has a positive impact on mental health (Wilson & Musick, 1999). The cultural context of the Haitian people deserves consideration. The commitment to helping others in these studies may be influenced by the communal nature of their culture and by the considerable religious beliefs rated by the trainees, which may increase their desire to "Do God's work" and may be greater when compared to comforters and trainees in more individualistic or less religious cultures. Despite these differences, the results of these explorations, when combined with other research, suggest that the positive effects and posttraumatic growth of helping may be a universal phenomenon.

The quantitative results from the questionnaires showing the positive impact of the training were supported by the qualitative responses, both in the questionnaires and in the open-ended interviews as well as in clinical observations of the project team. Clearly, a more scientific assessment with a more rigid methodology, built into the available time of the training and practicality of the logistics, with follow-up, would be valuable to be able to establish this model as a "best practice"; however, the present preliminary research suggests the value of this model, especially in light of the "face" validity yielded by the qualitative answers and positive feedback, regarding both the ease of the trainees' learning the workshop material in such a short period of time, their enthusiasm in doing the workshop with the children, and the positive reports of all involved (i.e., the trainees, children, and teachers).

It is worthwhile to note that the training was a holistic experience, creating a cycle of positivity for all involved. Similar to the beneficiaries of the training, the trainers and all the workshop team members also reported having an exceptionally positive and rewarding experience, one that was both professionally useful and personally satisfying. As described above, they spontaneously expressed feeling very bonded with everyone involved, being "touched" by everything that happened, and feeling "love," "caring," and great appreciation for the trainees, children, and each other. Similar to the trainees, they felt very satisfied and fulfilled from helping and committed to continuing to serve.

The experience appeared to effectively combine the aspects of what the trainers have learned is a useful model, built into the design and choice of the specific exercises—stress reduction, empowerment, and connection, to achieve the intended goals: (1) to be simple to administer by trainers and learn by trainees; (2) to result in psychosocial outcomes of recovery and resilience-building; (3) to be enjoyable for the trainees and the children; (4) to engender enthusiasm in trainees to repeat; and (5) to present potential for applicability by trainees in their varied settings. These aspects can valuably be considered when planning trainings and interventions, along with other models that have been shown to be useful in crises (Başloğlu & Şalcioğlu, 2011).

The results, both quantitatively and qualitatively, also underscore what has been shown repeatedly in other research as well as in the first author's work, particularly regarding recovery from trauma, crisis, or environmental disaster and the value of the group approach and the importance of community in healing (Clayton, Manning, & Hodge, 2014; Kuriansky, 2012b, 2013c; Kuriansky & Nemeth, 2013). Furthermore, they confirm the importance of measuring psychosocial resilience in the aftermath of natural disaster, in addition to structural resilience; a point emphasized by Kuriansky in her statement at the High level Multi-Stakeholder Partnership Dialogue during the WCDRR (Kuriansky, 2015), and in her extensive advocacy about disaster recovery.

Many scales were used in the present studies to give as broad a picture of the outcomes as possible and to test the appropriateness and applicability of various measures, given the lack of available appropriate and culturally relevant measures. Further exploration of the usefulness of each measure would be valuable, especially to select the most valuable measures for further study and to minimize the time required to complete the protocol. The development of a culturally appropriate and practical assessment package to measure the variables considered here (e.g., impact of helping, posttraumatic growth, commitment to helping) would be useful in further research of this nature, especially considering the increasing number of environmental disasters worldwide.

It should be pointed out that the helpers in this study were also survivors of the earthquake. It would be interesting to compare such a sample with volunteers who have not been affected at all, to determine whether helping others provides even more benefits when one is personally suffering, as the experience may provide an opportunity for vicarious healing. This would add to findings that already indicate that emotional involvement, in addition to physical proximity, to a trauma event is related to reported impact (Kuriansky, Bagenstose, Hirsch, et al., 2007).

The present results focus on assessing the impact of helping on the groups of helpers. In the 2014 training, a separate evaluation was piloted about the impact on the children who participated in the workshop. Results of this were not available at the time of this writing. Clinical observations revealed that the children greatly enjoyed the experience, and that parents and teachers on site reported a positive benefit for the children and for themselves.

It is likely that such trainings and support for children can be useful on an ongoing basis, over the long term after an environmental disaster, both for surviving children and for the subsequent generation, given that research shows the impact of intergenerational as well as transgenerational trauma (Connolly, 2011).

The present project and results of the evaluations underscore that the mobilization of volunteer helpers, as well as offering them fundamental training programs, can exponentially expand healing human resources, and therefore greatly aid in disaster situations where resources are strained. Students can certainly be a valuable resource for capacity-building; as shown in this project, they can provide invaluable psychosocial support even with elementary formal training in psychosocial support. This is consistent with the principle that investing in youth is highly useful in sustainable development. Clearly, a group of student volunteers can serve as extremely important comforters who can offer sustainable support. The participants reported ways in which they could apply the training, including in their school projects (e.g., for youth groups, orphans, and/or abused children), further maximizing value. Besides students, those who can be considered "ordinary" citizens can also be recruited as valuable helpers, as long as they are committed and caring. In the aftermath of the 2004 Asian tsunami, the first author found citizen volunteers (for example, a high school sports coach) invaluable as assistants in interventions for children, families, and adults in the emergency, even when initially recruited as translators (Kuriansky, 2005).

Overall, the present findings, though preliminary and pilot in nature, with convenience samples as opposed to rigorous sample selection and scientific methodology, provide highly useful indications about the value of volunteering and helping behavior for the helper. Comforters were able to aid children through grief, trauma, and loss, which also helped the comforters address their own suffering. The results show that such trainings are valuable for the helpers on both personal and professional levels. The present explorations support, and are supported by research that volunteering can have significant positive effects on people's physical and psychological health. The act of volunteering can help helpers cope and adapt, gain new perspectives on life, and increase social integration. In addition, volunteers can become "supporters" shortly after a disaster, offering emotional support with training in simple psychological first aid techniques. These outcomes are highly important in the aftermath of disasters, when resources, including human capital, are limited. Emphasizing the direct as well as indirect and vicarious benefits of such helping can encourage larger numbers of volunteers in such direct situations.

Explorations of human capital resources in response to environmental disasters adds to the growing awareness about the importance of addressing the issues related not only to such disasters, but also to climate change. The importance of considering the intersection of psychosocial aspects of environmental disaster with the science of these events has been pointed out in a previous book by the coauthors of this volume (Nemeth, Hamilton, & Kuriansky, 2012), especially given survivors' oft-repeated questions about why such events occur and when they might reoccur. The importance of education and knowledge, as well as action, about environmental disasters and climate change has come to the forefront of international concerns, and is addressed in Chapter 17 of this volume (Kuriansky, LeMay, & Kumar, 2015).

In summary, volunteers have a considerable impact on building civil society, especially in the case of rebuilding after a disaster. The psychological benefits of such service accrue to those helped and to the helpers, including stress inoculation, strengthening personal efficacy, and increasing social and community ties. When a developing (and developed) nation is hit by a devastating environmental disaster, training programs such as this one that mobilize the resources of local students studying psychology-related subjects, as well as teachers and community members interested in helping, can offer valuable support for rebuilding the community. This work can further strengthen the helpers' own resilience, especially when they have been similarly affected by the disaster. Training such helpers builds the human capacity of the community to serve survivors and pass along this learning to others. Such an approach holds great promise for the implementation of the new Sustainable Development Goals identified by the United Nations, which includes the promotion of people's mental health and well-being.

It is suggested that the present training and workshops could valuably be repeated with a more rigorous methodology, in order to establish the model as "best practices" and ultimately as a gold standard in such circumstances. The exercises have already been shown empirically to be useful in other post-disaster situations as in Japan (Kuriansky, 2012c, 2012d; Masangkay, 2015) as well as in situations of poverty in Tanzania (*Tanzania workshop DrJudy Kuriansky & Russell Daisey and children*, n.d.) and in the Ebola epidemic in Sierra Leone (Kuriansky, Polizer, & Milissen, 2015), to encourage children's empowerment and resiliency. Further, a group of youth interested in disaster recovery responded with enthusiasm to learning the techniques in a workshop given at the Children and Youth Forum as part of the World Conference on Disaster Risk Reduction (Kuriansky, Polizer, & Jean-Charles, 2015). Several youth were interested in applying the techniques in their particular country. It is suggested that the techniques and model of the training, with its specific methodology, modules, and exercises, can be usefully replicated in other settings, circumstances, conditions, cultures, and countries.

THE CLINTON GLOBAL INITIATIVE AND THE HAITI ACTION NETWORK

Ongoing attention is necessary for healing after such a natural disaster of such proportion as the 2010 Haiti earthquake. An organization providing such ongoing attention is the Clinton Global Initiative (CGI) (Jean-Charles, 2011b). In response to the hurricanes that hit Haiti in 2008, former U.S. president Bill Clinton shined special attention on this small suffering island. Clinton embarked on a tour around the world with fellow former U.S. president George H. W. Bush, appealing for financial support for the Clinton-Bush Haiti Fund. In another effort, Clinton mobilized the platform of his CGI—an annual summit of word leaders, businesspeople, and nonprofit organizations—to encourage partnerships to help. Over 30 commitments to action were made, valued at more than $100 million. The next year, in 2009, the Haiti Action Network (HAN) was set up, chaired by Irish billionaire Denis O'Brien, chairman of the telecom company Digicel that operates in Haiti and throughout the Caribbean and South Pacific. The HAN stepped up its efforts after the 2010 earthquake, at which time this chapter's first author was pleased to join the meetings and witnessed companies making commitments of money and projects, including by the Urban Zen Foundation founded by international fashion designer Donna Karan.

Kuriansky was again at the CGI annual meeting in 2011 when the newly elected president of the Republic of Haiti, Michel Martelly—a famous Haitian entertainer and hip-hop singer known as "Sweet Micky" turned politician—famously jumped to his feet onstage declaring, "Haiti is open for business!" touting the allure of the beautiful coasts, rich past—and voodoo. Also, the eight-member Haiti Adolescent Girls Network's program set up safe spaces (named "Espas Pa Mwen") for girls to gather and learn about reproductive health and rights, leadership, health practices, and financial literacy. At the CGI 2014 meetings, Kuriansky again attended the sessions on Haiti. By then, more than 60 commitments to action had been made by the CGI community since 2010, valued at $353 million, including building schools and supporting local artists and social entrepreneurs. The panelists emphasized that education was key to long-term recovery—since too few children go to, or finish, school—and that "investing in young people is the answer to sustainability." Noted medical health expert Paul Farmer, long dedicated to building Haiti's medical services, pointed to the model of Rwanda, where health care was linked to education, with a part of the government budget going to health care. One of his trainees noted the importance of mental health, integrated into primary health care.

RECOGNITION OF VOLUNTEERS AT THE UNITED NATIONS AND FOR SUSTAINABLE DEVELOPMENT

The value of volunteers to enhance human capital in the recovery from disasters, but also to advance sustainable development in general, is being brought to attention at the United Nations, especially in the context of the global agenda for 2015–2030. A report of UN Secretary-General Ban ki-Moon acknowledged the contributions of volunteerism to "help to expand and mobilize constituencies, and engage people in national planning and implementation for sustainable development goals" (United Nations Department of Economic and Social Affairs, 2015). An event at UN headquarters in New York on April 22, 2015, addressed "The Power of Volunteerism as a Cross-Cutting Means of Implementation" of the Sustainable Development Goals, impressively bringing together multi-stakeholders showing support. These included representatives of governments, i.e., from the UN Missions of Brazil, Japan (Deputy Permanent Representative Ambassador Hiroshi Minami), and Ireland (Deputy Permanent Representative Ambassador Tim Mawe); volunteers (a young volunteer for a girls' education program in Mozambique and another returned volunteer from Cuso International's Diasporas for Development program); the UN Volunteers Office (represented by its Chief Jordi Llopart); and civil society groups (including the International Federation of Red Cross and Red Crescent Societies represented by Shaun Hazeldine, head of Global Youth Action and Volunteering Development; VSO International represented by its CEO Philip Goodwin; and the World University Service of Canada, represented by Chris Eaton, also Chair of the International Forum for Volunteering in Development). Reports of the panelists pointed out the contributions of volunteers to community development as well as the benefits to the volunteers themselves, that has been well documented. Volunteerism strengthens trust, solidarity, and reciprocity amongst citizens (United Nations Volunteers, 2014), and especially extends services to poor and marginalized communities (VSO International and The Institute of Development Studies, 2014). Volunteers contribute overall to vibrant societies (Forum, 2014), such that "the act of contributing out of one's own free will, for broader societal benefit, is fundamental to our humanity and to the creation of an equitable and peaceful world" (Forum, n.d.).

RECOMMENDATIONS FOR DISASTER RELIEF POLICY AND PSYCHOSOCIAL CONSIDERATIONS

Based on the above interventions, results, and clinical observations, as well as documented reports of multinational organizations, the following recommendations are made regarding a paradigm shift for policies and programs in disaster situations:

1. Since emotional trauma is immediate and support needed, psychosocial relief and psychological first aid should be an integral part of immediate disaster relief operations and integrated into primary health care.
2. Children are particularly vulnerable and therefore would benefit from simple interventions to promote resilience and well-being; models for this are empirically effective.
3. All policies and programs should refer to "psychosocial" resilience as well as infrastructural resilience.
4. Community volunteers, and especially students in education and psychology-related fields (e.g., social work, sociology, family studies) should be recruited in the event of a disaster. A registry of these potential helpers should be kept, to be able to mobilize them in the event of an environmental disaster.
5. Training of such a potential pool of helpers/supporters should be made available in plans for disaster preparedness.
6. Funding should be appropriated to be able to cover expenses for such a community force (e.g., to cover their transportation to emergency sites, food, and basic supplies so they can do volunteer work).
7. Plans, programs, and policies need to take a long-term view, to ensure such psychosocial help continues years after a disaster.
8. A community-wide approach should be taken, integrating communication and services between local volunteers, schools, and hospitals, as sources for helpers and also sites for their work.
9. Education systems and public awareness programs should encourage values consistent with helping, given the positive outcomes on individuals involved as well as on communities and societies.
10. Research should be done to identify the best practices for intervention, including the identification of methodologies and assessment protocols that are adaptable and logistically practical in emergency disaster situations and for post-disaster follow-up. These should be culturally appropriate but also as cross-culturally applicable as possible, to allow for a template model that can then be adapted to a particular setting and population.

11. Intervention models for post-disaster recovery should take into account local culture and indigenous practices.
12. Programs can valuably include elements of basic psychosocial stress reduction techniques as well as culturally appropriate activities (e.g., music, dance, and art exercises respectful of (and indigenous to each culture) that have been shown to be universally helpful, especially with child populations, in programs like those offered by the GKCP and by large multinational organizations.

All the above recommendations should be considered in the context of the Sendai Framework for Disaster Risk Reduction and the Sustainable Development Goals, and targets, in promoting mental health and well-being, providing psychosocial support and mental health services when needed, and also taking urgent action to address climate change issues, specifically to strengthening resilience to environmental disasters. Mobilizations of volunteer resources, and trainings and workshops as in the Global Kids Connect Project presented here can be a valuable asset to human capacity–building, especially in the context of a developing country with limited resources after an environmental disaster. These types of programs can be considered as means of monitoring and implementation of the international agreements. Multi-stakeholder partnerships, as outlined in the SDGs, should be formed, including participation of governments. Practical programs, enlightened policies, and a paradigm shift will facilitate the development of sustainable psychosocial resilience and well-being, for both child and adult survivors of disaster who are being served, for a vast potential pool of community individuals who can serve as helpers, and for communities at large.

ACKNOWLEDGMENTS

The authors express deep appreciation to all the trainees who participated in the workshops, for their extremely touching dedication, courage, and love for children, each other, their community, and their country, helping others even when they, too, were suffering the aftermath of the disaster. We also greatly appreciate the children who were part of the workshops, being so cooperative and adorable as well as resilient, and their teachers who help them daily. We salute the entire staff of L'Hôpital de la Communauté Haïtienne and the Church of Saint-Louis Roi de France, the priests of the Montfort order, especially Bishop Quesnel Alphonse, and the nuns of the Congregation of the Daughters of Wisdom of the Haiti Province, particularly Sister Lamercie Estinfort, for their courage under crisis, and appreciate their support and collaboration both immediately after the earthquake and over time to maintain sustainability of the project. We also thank the Haiti Action Network youth and Boy Scouts, who stepped up to be part of the initial supporters. The assistance, talent, dedication, and valuable contributions of interns, students and assistants, including Youdelka John and Rebecca Houran, are also acknowledged, especially when also participating "on the ground."

APPENDIX: LYRICS TO REBATI SONG (Abbreviated; Order and repetitions adaptable)

"REBATI, NOU SE TANKOU ROZO NAN VAN"
(Lyrics by Dr. Judy Kuriansky & Russell Daisey; Music by Russell Daisey
© 2010)

Nap rebati, nap rebati, nap rebati peyia (repeated 6×)
Bon dye bon, dye bon (repeated 4×).

Nou se tankou rozo nan van, Nou pliye nou pa kase
Nou se tankou rozo nan van, Nou pliye nou pa kase

Ansamn, ansamn, Nap rebati peyi a, Nap rebati peyi nous
Men anpil chay pa lou, Anpil men, anpil men, Chay la vin leje

STANZAS
Se pi bel nan karayib la, Nesans ou fek komanse
Ayiti, louvri barye, Pa ghen tan pou w tann

L'union fait la force, Na tet ansamn, nou jwenn fos
Ayiti, louvri barye, Pa ghen tan pou w tann

Se yon zile ki make ak istwa, Ki chaje ak miste
Ayiti, louvri barye, Pa ghen tan pou w tann

Ou se pel de zanti, Petit ou yo viv au kreyol
Ayiti, louvri barye, Pa ghen tan pou w tann

ALTERNATIVE CHORUS IN FRENCH
Nous sommes roseaux dans le vent; nous plier, ne pas casser.
English translation: We're like reeds in the wind, we bend but we don't break.

REFERENCES

Alexander, D. (2005). Early mental health intervention after disasters. *Advances in Psychiatric Treatment, 11*(1), 12–18.

Australian Centre for Posttraumatic Mental Health. (n.d.). *Depression Anxiety and Stress Scale (DASS)*. Retrieved September 14, 2014, from http://www.acpmh.unimelb.edu.au/site_resources/TrainingInitiativeDocuments/follow-up/DASS.pdf

Başloğlu, M., Kiliç, C., Şalcioğlu, E., & Livanou, M. (2004). Prevalence of posttraumatic stress disorder in earthquake survivors in Turkey: An epidemiological study. *Journal of Traumatic Stress, 17*, 133–141.

Başloğlu, M., & Şalcioğlu, E. (2011). *A mental healthcare model for mass trauma survivors: Control-focused behavioral treatment of earthquake, war, and torture trauma.* Cambridge, UK: Cambridge University Press.

Başloğlu, M., Şalcioğlu, E., Livanou, M., Özeren, M., Aker, T., Kiliç, C., & Mestçioğlu, Ö. (2001). A study of the validity of a screening instrument for traumatic stress in earthquake survivors in Turkey. *Journal of Traumatic Stress, 14*(3), 491–509.

BBC News. (2010, February 12). Haiti will not die, President Rene Preval insists. *BBC News—Home*. Retrieved July 30, 2011, from http://news.bbc.co.uk/2/hi/americas/8511997.stm

Bech, P. (2004). Measuring the dimensions of psychological general well-being by the WHO-5. *QoL Newsletter, 32*, 15–16.

Bénabou, R., & Tirole, J. (2005). *Incentives and prosocial behavior* (No. w11535). National Bureau of Economic Research.

Biddle, B. J. (1986). Recent development in role theory. *Annual Review of Sociology*, 67–92.

Bronfenbrenner, U. (1979). *The ecology of human development*. Cambridge, MA: Harvard University Press.

Brown, S., Nesse, R., Vinokur, A., & Smith, D. (2003). Providing social support may be more beneficial than receiving it: Results from a prospective study of mortality. *Psychological Science, 14*(4), 320–327.

Calhoun, L. G., & Tedeschi, R. G. (1998). *Facilitating posttraumatic growth: A clinician's guide*. London, UK: Lawrence Erlbaum Associates.

Calhoun, L. G., & Tedeschi, R. G. (2004). The foundations of posttraumatic growth: New considerations. *Psychological Inquiry, 15*, 93–102.

Callero, P. L., Howard, J. A., & Piliavin, J. A. (1987). Helping behavior as role behavior: Disclosing social structure and history in the analysis of prosocial action. *Social Psychology Quarterly*, 247–256.

Christenson, S., & Marren, J. (2013). The Impact of Event Scale. *Try This: Best Practices to Nursing Care in Older Adults, 19*. Retrieved September 13, 2014, from http://consultgerirn.org/uploads/File/trythis/try_this_19.pdf

Connolly, A. (2011). Healing the wounds of our fathers: Intergenerational trauma, memory, symbolization and narrative. *Journal of Analytical Psychology, 56*, 607–626. doi:10.1111/j.1468-5922.2011.01936.x

Clayton, S., Manning, C., & Hodge, C. (2014). Beyond storms and droughts: The psychological impacts of climate change. Washington, DC: American Psychological Association and ecoAmerica. Retrieved April 10, 2015, from http://ecoamerica.org/wp-content/uploads/2014/06/eA_Beyond_Storms_and_Droughts_Psych_Impacts_of_Climate_Change.pdf

Elklit, A., Schmidt Pedersen, S., & Jind, L. (2001). The Crisis Support Scale: Psychometric qualities and further validation. *Personality and Individual Differences, 31*(8), 1291–1302.

Forum, International Forum for Volunteering in Development. (2014, April 5). *Key messages on the Role of Volunteerism in shaping and implementing an inclusive and sustainable development agenda for the future 2014*. Retrieved April 23, 2015, from http://forum-ids.org/2014/04/key-messages-on-the-role-of-volunteerism/

Forum, International Forum for Volunteering in Development. (n.d.). *The Lima Declaration*. Retrieved April 23, 2015, from http://forum-ids.org/conferences/ivco/ivco-2014/lima-declaration/

Friedman, H. L., & Hartelius, G. (Eds.). (2013). *The Wiley-Blackwell handbook of transpersonal psychology*. Hoboken, NJ: John Wiley & Sons.

Henderson, A. (1995). Abused women and peer-provided social support: The nature and dynamics of reciprocity in a crisis setting. *Issues in Mental Health Nursing, 16*, 117–128.

Henry, J. D., & Crawford, J. R. (2005). The short-form version of the Depression Anxiety Stress Scales (DASS-21): Construct validity and normative data in a large non-clinical sample. *British Journal of Clinical Psychology, 44*(2), 227–239.

Indiana Youth Institute. (2011, July). *Issue brief: Helping you—helping me: Why youth volunteering matters.* Retrieved September 24, 2014, from http://www.iyi.org/resources/doc/IYI-Issue-Brief-Youth-Volunteering-July2011.pdf

Inter-Agency Standing Committee (IASC) Working Group. (2007). *IASC guidelines on mental health and psychosocial support in emergency settings.* Geneva: IASC.

Jean-Charles, W. (2011a, Fall). First international conference on restoring life and maintaining hope in Port-au-Prince: Establishing a new "Center for Spirituality and Mental Health" in Haiti. *International Psychology Bulletin, 15*(4), 39–41. Retrieved September 12, 2014, from http://internationalpsychology.files.wordpress.com/2013/01/ipb_fall_2011-10-28-1_final.pdf

Jean-Charles, W. (2011b, January–March). Rebati: After the earthquake, the IAAP UN team continues to remember Haiti. *IAAP Bulletin of the International Association of Applied Psychology, 23*(1–2), 33–35.

Jean-Charles, W. (2015, March 16). The Global Kids Connect Project in Haiti: Overview and outcome. Panel presentation at the session on *Volunteering to Build Back Better,* Children and Youth Forum, World Conference on Disaster Risk Reduction, Tohoku University, Sendai, Japan.

Joseph, S., Williams, R., & Yule, W. (1992). Crisis support, attributional style, coping style and post-traumatic symptoms. *Personality and Individual Differences, 13*(11), 1249–1251.

Krause, N., Herzog, A. R., & Baker, E. (1992). Providing support to others and well-being in later life. *Journal of Gerontology: Psychological Sciences, 47,* 300–311.

Kuriansky, J. (Producer). (2005). Tsunami 2004 in Sri Lanka: Dr. Judy with Children. [Video]. Retrieved April 6, 2015, from https://www.youtube.com/watch?v=VQxwYLu1lwM&feature=youtu.be

Kuriansky, J. (2007). Healing after a terror event on campus in Israel: Unique workshops and allied techniques for international Jewish and Arab students, staff and extended community. In J. Kuriansky (Ed.), *Beyond bullets and bombs: Grassroots peacebuilding between Israelis and Palestinians* (pp. 315–325). Westport, CT: Praeger.

Kuriansky, J. (2008). A clinical toolbox for cross-cultural counseling and training. In U. P. Gielen, J. G. Draguns, & J. M. Fish (Eds.), *Principles of multicultural counseling and therapy* (pp. 295–330). New York, NY: Taylor and Francis/Routledge.

Kuriansky, J. (2010a). Bringing emotional first aid and hope to Haiti. *Beliefnet.* Retrieved April 6, 2015, from http://www.beliefnet.com/Inspiration/2010/02/Bringing-Emotional-First-Aid-and-Hope-to-Haiti.aspx

Kuriansky, J. (Producer). (2010b). *Haiti after 2010 Earthquake DrJudy mission.* [Video]. Retrieved April 7, 2015, from https://youtu.be/e7jLW4K0QWE

Kuriansky, J. (2010c). Haiti pre and post earthquake: Tracing professional and personal commitment past, present and future. *International Psychology Bulletin, 14*(2), 29–37. Retrieved April 6, 2015, from http://internationalpsychology.files.wordpress.com/2013/01/ipb_spring_2010_4_27_10.pdf

Kuriansky, J. (2010d). Stories of Haiti. Retrieved September 4, 2014, from, http://www.humnews.com/humnews/2010/4/13/stories-of-haitiapril-13-2010.html

Kuriansky, J. (2012a). Helping children recover from natural disasters: *Principles and practice from professional and personal experiences in the field in China, Sri Lanka, Haiti and Japan, skills building and psycho-educational techniques.* Presentation at the International Conference for Chinese Psychology and Health in Global & Fourth Congress of the IACMSP.

Kuriansky, J. (2012b). Our communities: Healing after environmental disasters. In D. G. Nemeth, R. B. Hamilton, & J. Kuriansky (Eds.), *Living in an environmentally traumatized world: Healing ourselves and our planet* (pp. 141–167). Santa Barbara, CA: ABC-CLIO/Praeger.

Kuriansky, J. (2012c). Recovery efforts for Japan after the 3/11 devastating tsunami/earthquake. *Bulletin of the International Association of Applied Psychology, 24*(2–3), Part 22. Retrieved March 30, 2015, from http://www.iaapsy.org/Portals/1/Archive/Publications/newsletters/July2012.pdf

Kuriansky, J. (2012d). Report: Soothing Sendai. Retrieved March 30, 2015, from http://www.humnews.com/the-view-from-here/2012/3/22/soothing-sendai-report.html

Kuriansky, J. (2012e). Train, retain, gain: Youth Volunteer Leadership for Intercultural Cooperation to Build Stronger Societies. Workshop presented at the DPI/NGO conference in Bonn, Germany. *Bulletin of the International Association of Applied Psychology, 24*(2–3): 23–26. Retrieved March 30, 2015, from, http://www.iaapsy.org/Portals/1/Archive/Publications/newsletters/July2012.pdf

Kuriansky, J. (2013a). Helping kids cope with the Oklahoma tornado and other traumas: 7 techniques. *Huffington Post*. Retrieved April 19, 2015, from http://www.huffingtonpost.com/judy-kuriansky-phd/helping-kids-cope-with-the-oklahoma-tornado_b_3322238.html

Kuriansky, J. (2013b). Superstorm Sandy: Coping with the one-year anniversary. *Citizens Magazine*. Retrieved March 30, 2015, from https://statenislandpolitics.wordpress.com/2013/10/26/drjudy/

Kuriansky, J. (2013c). Superstorm Sandy 2012: A psychologist first responder's personal account and lessons learned about the impact on emotions and ecology. *Ecopsychology, 5*(Suppl. 1), S30–S37. doi:10.1089/eco.2013.0010. Retrieved March 30, 2015, from http://online.liebertpub.com/doi/abs/10.1089/eco.2013.0010?src=recsys

Kuriansky, J. (2013d). Talking to kids about the anniversary of Superstorm Sandy. *Huffington Post*. Retrieved March 30, 2015, from http://www.huffingtonpost.com/judy-kuriansky-phd/talking-to-kids-about-the-anniversary-of-superstorm-sandy_b_4167294.html

Kuriansky, J. (2013e). Thoughts on Katrina vs. Sandy (Essays on nature-induced, human-induced, and nature + human-induced environmental trauma). *Ecopsychology, 5*(Suppl. 1), S20–S26. doi:10.1089/eco.2013.0039. Retrieved March 30, 2015, from http://online.liebertpub.com/doi/abs/10.1089/eco.2013.0039?src=recsys

Kuriansky, J. (2014). *Building resilience in children coping after disaster and living in crisis: Applied models in Haiti, Japan and Africa*. Presentation at the Louisiana Psychological Association, on "Resiliency, Mindfulness and Resolve: Coping with the Hand You're Dealt," New Orleans, Louisiana

Kuriansky, J. (2015, March 16). DrJudy Kuriansky: Statement at World Conference on Disaster Risk Reduction, Sendai, Japan, 2015 [Video]. Presented at the High level Multi-Stakeholder Partnership Dialogue, World Conference on Disaster Risk Reduction, Sendai, Japan, March 14–18. Retrieved April 10, 2015, from https://youtu.be/R72sDJ1xVZg

Kuriansky, J., Bagenstose, L., Hirsch, M., Burstein, A. A., & Tsaidi, Y. (2006). Terror at home and abroad: Israeli reactions to international incidents of violence. In J. Kuriansky (Ed.), *Terror in the Holy Land: Inside the anguish of the Israeli-Palestinian conflict* (pp. 85–95). Westport, CT: Praeger.

Kuriansky, J., & Berry, M. O. (2011, January–April). Advancing the UN MDGS by a model program for girls empowerment, HIV/AIDS prevention and entrepreneurship: IAAP project in Lesotho Africa. *IAAP Bulletin, 23*(1–2), 35–38. Retrieved April 7, 2015, from http://www.iaapsy.org/Portals/1/Bulletin/apnl_v23_i1-2.pdf

Kuriansky, J., & Daisey, R. (Producers). (2011). *Global Kids Connect Project.* [Video]. Retrieved April 7, 2015, from http://youtu.be/VUOOVjkK5-Q

Kuriansky, J., & Jean-Charles, W. (2012, July–October). Haiti Rebati: Update on activities rebuilding Haiti through the Global Kids Connect Project. *Bulletin of the International Association of Applied Psychology, 24*(2–3), Part 21, 116–124. Retrieved March 30, 2015, from, http://www.iaapsy.org/Portals/1/Archive/Publications/newsletters/July2012.pdf

Kuriansky, J., LeMay, M., & Kumar, A. (2015). Paradigm shifts in nature and well-being: Principles, programs, and policies about the environment and climate change with actions by the United Nations for a sustainable future. In D. G. Nemeth & J. Kuriansky (Eds.), *Ecopsychology: Advances from the intersection of psychology and environmental protection*, Volume 2 (pp. 307–358). Santa Barbara, CA: ABC-CLIO.

Kuriansky, J., Lytle, M., & Chiu, A. (2011, March 11). *Models addressing the UN MDGs (Millennium Development Goals): Outcome of projects in Africa and Haiti.* Paper presented at symposium at the Eastern Psychological Association, Cambridge, MA.

Kuriansky, J., & Nemeth, D. G. (2013, September). A model for post-environmental disaster wellness workshops: Preparing individuals and communities for hurricane anniversary reactions. *Ecopsychology, 5*(Suppl. 1): S38–S45. doi:10.1089/eco.2013.0006. Retrieved March 30, 2015, from http://online.liebertpub.com/doi/abs/10.1089/eco.2013.0039?src=recsys

Kuriansky, J., Nenova, M., Sottile, G., Telger, K. J., Tetty, N., Portis, C., . . . Kujac, H. (2009). The REASSURE model: A new approach for responding to sexuality and relationship-related questions. In E. Schroeder and J. Kuriansky (Eds.), *Sexuality education: Past, present and future* (Vol. 3, Chap. 8). Westport, CT: Praeger.

Kuriansky, J., Polizer, Y., & Jean-Charles, W. (2015, March 16). *Youth and mental health: Workshop of techniques.* Presentation at the Children and Youth Conference, World Conference on Disaster Risk Reduction, Tohoku University, Sendai, Japan.

Kuriansky, J., Polizer, Y., & Milissen, L. (2015). *Children coping with the Ebola epidemic: The Resilience and Empowerment Training and Workshop.* Unpublished paper.

Kuriansky, J., Wu, L.-Y., Bao, C., Chand, D., Kong, S., Spooner, N., & Mao, S. (2015). Interventions by national and international organizations for psychosocial support after the Sichuan earthquake in China: A review and implications for sustainable development. In D. G. Nemeth & J. Kuriansky (Eds.), *Ecopsychology: Advances from the intersection of psychology and environmental protection*, Volume 2 (pp. 171–231). Santa Barbara, CA: ABC-CLIO.

Linley, P. A., & Joseph, S. (2004). Positive change following trauma and adversity. *Journal of Traumatic Stress, 17*, 11–21.

Liu, M., Wang, L., Shi, Z., Zhang, Z., Zhang, K., & Shen, J. (2011). Mental health problems among children one-year after Sichuan earthquake in China: A follow-up study, *PLOS One, 6*(2), e14706.

Lovibond, S. H., & Lovibond, P. F. (1995). *Manual for the Depression Anxiety Stress Scales.* (2nd ed.). Sydney, Australia: Psychology Foundation of Australia.

Luce, J. (2010). Dr. Judy on the trauma of disasters—like Haitian earthquake. *Huffington Post*. Retrieved April 6, 2015, from http://www.huffingtonpost.com/jim-luce/dr-judy-on-the-trauma-of_b_461779.html

Luks, A. (1988, October). Helper's high. *Psychology Today*, 39–40.

Masangkay, M. (2015). Psychologist connects disaster-affected children around the world. *Japan Times*. Retrieved March 30, 2015, from http://www.japantimes.co.jp/news/2015/03/23/national/psychologist-connects-disaster-affected-children-around-the-world/#.VR4uT0tlQRw

Moen, P., Dempster-McClain, D., & Williams, R. (1992). Successful aging: A life-course perspective on women's multiple roles and health. *American Journal of Sociology, 97*, 1612–1638.

Moore, C., & Allen, J. (1996). The effects of volunteering on the young volunteer. *The Journal of Primary Prevention, 17*(2), 231–258.

Morrow-Howell, N., Hinterlong, J., Rozario, P., & Tang, F. (2003). Effects of volunteering on the well-being of older adults. *The Journals of Gerontology, 58B*, S137–S145.

Musick, M. A., Herzog, A. R., & House, J. S. (1999). Volunteering and mortality among older adults: Findings from a national sample. *Journal of Gerontology: Social Sciences, 54B*, S173–S180.

Nemeth, D. G., Hamilton, R. B., & Kuriansky, J. (Eds.). (2012). *Living in an environmentally traumatized world: Healing ourselves and our planet*. Santa Barbara, CA: ABC-CLIO/Praeger.

Nemeth, D. G., Hamilton, R. B., & Kuriansky, J. (Eds.). (2015). Reflections and recommendations: The need for leadership, holistic thinking, and community involvement. In D. G. Nemeth & J. Kuriansky (Eds.), *Ecopsychology: Advances from the intersection of psychology and environmental protection*, Volume 2 (pp. 413–428). Santa Barbara, CA: ABC-CLIO.

Nolen-Hoeksema, S., & Morrow, J. (1991). A prospective study of depression and post-traumatic stress symptoms after a natural disaster: The 1989 Loma Prieta earthquake. *Journal of Personality and Social Psychology, 61*(1), 115.

Office of Emergency Preparedness and Response (2013). Maintaining responder resilience through extreme disaster: Self care beyond lip service. *New York DMH Responder, 3*(4), 1–2. Retrieved April 19, 2015, from https://www.omh.ny.gov/omhweb/disaster_resources/health_responder/DMH_responder_fall2013.pdf

Penner, L. A., Dovidio, J. F., Piliavin, J. A., & Schroeder, D. A. (2005). Prosocial behavior: Multilevel perspectives. *Annual Review of Psychology, 56*, 365–392.

Psychology Foundation of Australia. (2010, March 30). Depression Anxiety Stress Scales—DASS. *The School of Psychology—UNSW*. Retrieved April 19, 2015, from http://www2.psy.unsw.edu.au/groups/dass/

Roussos, A., Goenjian, A., Steinberg, A., Sotiropoulou, C., Kakaki, M., & Kabakos, C. (2005). Posttraumatic stress and depressive reactions among children and adolescents after the 1999 earthquake in Ano Liosia, Greece. *American Journal of Psychiatry, 162*, 530–537. doi:10.1176/appi.ajp.162.3.530.

Sargisson, R., Smith, K., Hunt, S., & Hamerton, H. (2014, July 8–13). *Motivations to volunteer and effects of volunteering for oil-spill clean-up on citizen volunteers*. Presentation at the 28th International Congress of Applied Psychology (ICAP), Paris, France.

Satapathy, S., & Subhasis, B. (2009). Disaster psychosocial and mental health support in South and South-East Asian countries: A synthesis. *Journal of South Asian Disaster Studies, 2*(1), 21–45.

Save the Children. (2012, May). *Facilitator handbook 2: Workshop tracks*. Retrieved April 19, 2015, from http://pscentre.org/wp-content/uploads/Facilitator-handbook-2.pdf

Schneider, K., Pierson, J. F., & Bugental, J. F. T. (Eds.). (2014). *The handbook of humanistic psychology: Theory, research, and practice*. London, UK: Sage Publications.

Schwartz, C., Meisenhelder, J., Ma, Y., & Reed, G. (2003). Altruistic social interest behaviors are associated with better mental health. *Psychosomatic Medicine, 65*, 778–785.

Schwartz, C., & Sendor, R. M. (1999). Helping others helps oneself: Response shift effects in peer support. *Social Science and Medicine, 48*, 1563–1575.

Schwartz, C. E., Keyl, P. M., Marcum, J. P., & Bode, R. (2009). Helping others shows differential benefits on health and well-being for male and female teens. *Journal of Happiness Studies, 10*, 431–448.

Smith, D. (1981). Altruism, volunteers, and volunteerism. *Nonprofit and Voluntary Sector Quarterly, 10*, 21–36.

Snoek, F. (2006). *WHO-Five Well-Being Index*. Retrieved April 6, 2015, from http://www.dawnstudy.com/News_and_activities/Documents/WHO-5.pdf

Stamm, B. H. (2010). *The Concise ProQOL manual* (2nd ed.). Pocatello, ID: Proqol.org. Retrieved April 19, 2015, from http://www.proqol.org/uploads/ProQOL_Concise_2ndEd_12-2010.pdf

Tanzania workshop DrJudy Kuriansky & Russell Daisey and children [Video]. (n.d.). Retrieved April 7, 2015, from https://www.youtube.com/watch?v=3poxmUe6Nz8&feature=youtu.be

Tedeschi, R. G., & Calhoun, L. G. (2004). Posttraumatic growth: Conceptual foundations and empirical evidence. *Psychological Inquiry, 15*(1), 1–18.

Thienkrua, W., Cardozo, B. L., Chakkraband, M. L., Guadamuz, T. E., Pengjuntr, W., Tantipiwatanaskul, P., . . . Thailand Post-Tsunami Mental Health Study Group. (2006). Symptoms of posttraumatic stress disorder and depression among children in tsunami-affected areas in southern Thailand. *Journal of the American Medical Association, 296*(5), 549–559.

UNISDR. (2015a, March 18). Sendai Framework for Disaster Risk Reduction 2015–2030. Retrieved April 3, 2015, from http://www.wcdrr.org/uploads/Sendai_Framework_for_Disaster_Risk_Reduction_2015-2030.pdf

UNISDR. (Producer). (2015b). WCDRR: The Global Kids Connect Project: A model programme to promote resilience, Judy Kuriansky. Retrieved April 3, 2015, from https://www.youtube.com/watch?v=NM2DYaB4OYM&index=73&list=PLBDwPnveHho_fXUfFQaVkUGb1v4EcAcyO

United Nations, Department of Economic and Social Affairs. (n.d.). *Sustainable Development Knowledge Platform: Outcome document—Open Working Group on Sustainable Development Goals*. Retrieved September 30, 2014, from http://sustainabledevelopment.un.org/focussdgs.html

United Nations Department of Economic and Social Affairs (2015, January 7). *Synthesis Report of the Secretary-General on the Post-2015 Agenda*. Retrieved April 22, 2015, from http://www.un.org/en/development/desa/publications/synthesis-report.html

United Nations Volunteers. (2014). *Volunteering for the world we want: Annual Report 2013*. Retrieved April 23, 2015, from http://www.unv.org/fileadmin/docdb/pdf/2014/corporate/UNV-RA2013-web.pdf

U.S. Fund for UNICEF. (n.d.). UNICEF urgently appeals for aid for Haiti following devastating. Retrieved March 30, 2015, from http://www.abc3340.com/story/11812079/unicef-urgently-appeals-for-aid-to-haiti-following-devastating-earthquake

Venhoeven, L. A., Bolderdijk, J. W., & Steg, L. (2014, July 8–13). *Pro-environmental behavior as a self-signal: How seeing yourself as a "good" person may increase well-being.* Presentation at the 28th International Congress of Applied Psychology (ICAP), Paris, France.

VSO International and The Institute of Development Studies (IDS). (2014). *Valuing Volunteering: The Role of Volunteering in Sustainable Development.* Retrieved April 23, 2015, from http://www.vsointernational.org/sites/vso_international/files/the_role_of_volunteering_in_sustainable_development_2015_vso_ids.pdf

Wang, L., Zhang, Y., Wang, W., Shi, Z., Shen, J., Li, M., & Xin, Y. (2009). Symptoms of posttraumatic stress disorder among adult survivors three months after the Sichuan earthquake in China. *Journal of Traumatic Stress, 22*(5), 444–450.

Weiss, D. S., & Marmar, C. R. (1997). The Impact of Event Scale—Revised. In J. P. Wilson, & T. M. Keane (Eds.), *Assessing psychological trauma and PTSD: A practitioner's handbook* (pp. 399–411). New York, NY: Guilford Press.

Willigen, M. (2000). Differential benefit of volunteering across the life course. *The Journals of Gerontology, 55B*, S308–S318.

Wilson, J., & Musick, M. (1999). The effects of volunteering on the volunteer. *Law and Contemporary Problems, 62*, 141–168.

Wyles, K., Pahl, S. & Thompson, R. C. (2014, July 8–13). *What's in it for me? The psychological benefits of engaging in beach cleans compared to other coastal activities.* Presentation at the 28th International Congress of Applied Psychology (ICAP), Paris, France.

Yalom, I. D., & Leszcz, M. (2005). Theory and practice of group psychotherapy (5th ed.). New York, NY: Perseus Book Group.

Young, F., & Glasgow, N. (1998). Voluntary social participation and health. *Research on Aging, 20*, 339–362.

10

Interventions by National and International Organizations for Psychosocial Support after the Sichuan Earthquake in China: A Review and Implications for Sustainable Development

Judy Kuriansky, Li-Yen Wu, Chenlan Bao, Divya Chand, Shuyao Kong, Nia Dara Spooner, and Shiqian Mao

Disaster struck on May 12, 2008, at 2:26 p.m., in the southwestern Sichuan Province of China, when an earthquake measuring 8.0 on the Richter scale devastated that province and neighboring Gansu and Shaanxi Provinces. The quake, referred to by several names—512 (the date of the tragedy), the Great Sichuan Earthquake, and the Wenchuan earthquake (the county near the epicenter)—resulted in extreme loss of lives, homes, and livelihood. Over 45 million people were affected in what was considered one of the most severe natural disasters in China in decades (Wang, 2008). Since the quake struck in the early afternoon when students were in school, thousands of youngsters and teachers were among the dead (Liu et al., 2011). A series of aftershocks further challenged the recovery efforts.

Research and clinical practice has revealed the serious degree of psychological distress after such natural disasters and the importance of attention to psychosocial needs of both adult and child survivors of all ages immediately post disaster as well as in the long term (Alexander, 2005; Chan, Wang, Ho, et al., 2012; Chan, Wang, Qu, et al., 2011; Everly, Phillips, Kane, & Feldman, 2006; Kun et al., 2009; Kuriansky, 1990, 2010a, 2010b, 2010c, 2010d, 2010e, 2010f, 2012a, 2012b, 2012d, 2013b, 2013d, 2013e, 2013g; Kuriansky & Jean-Charles, 2012; U.S. Department of Education, 2008; Wang et al., 2009; Wang et al., 2011; Xu & Liao, 2008; Zhang, Shi & Wang, 2011; Zhang & Wang, 2008; Zhang, Kong, Wang, et al. 2010; Zhiling, 2008). However, resources for such care are not always available, as in the case of the Sichuan earthquake where many health care professionals in the earthquake-stricken area perished, making outside help from the region as well as from other countries important and useful (Satapathy & Bhadra, 2009). In many such disaster situations, local, national, and international relief organizations mobilize resources to provide immediate assistance, yet these efforts are often characterized by poor coordination and collaboration, and reports about interventions are either unavailable or hard to locate (Wong, 2012). Yet, collated reports of various interventions would be helpful, to monitor the psychosocial aid being offered and to guide future efforts in disaster risk reduction planning, especially given the proliferation of natural disasters worldwide of varied types, including floods, tsunamis, flash fires, and earthquakes (Than, 2005).

Such reports are further useful in the important process of monitoring the implementation of two important international agreements that determine the global agenda for the years 2015–2030. These are the Sendai Framework for Disaster Risk Reduction (UNISDR, 2015a) and the Sustainable Development Goals (United Nations Department of Economic and Social Affairs, n.d.). Both documents provide important support for these interventions, to promote mental health and well-being and to provide psychosocial support and mental health services for recovery. This will be discussed later in this chapter.

A comparison of psychosocial and mental health support after disaster has been presented across various countries in a region, i.e., South and Southeast Asian countries (Satapathy & Bhadra, 2009). The report presented here complements and expands this approach while focusing on projects that provided psychosocial support after one particular event in one country, namely, the Sichuan earthquake in China in 2008. This event was selected because of the first author's experience with the Chinese culture, giving trainings and workshops throughout the country, as well as her involvement specifically in providing psychological first aid and psychosocial support in China, as well as based on her trainings, workshops, and presentations related to psychosocial recovery after both man-made and natural disasters worldwide (Kalayjian, Moore, Kuriansky, & Aberson, 2010; Kuriansky, 1990, 2002, 2003a, 2003b, 2005, 2007a, 2007b, 2007c, 2007d, 2007e, 2007f, 2008a, 2008b, 2008c, 2008d, 2008e, 2011a, 2011c, 2012a, 2012b, 2012d, 2013b, 2013d, 2013e, 2013g, 2014a, 2014b; Luce, 2010). The documentation of projects presented in this chapter, while not covering every possible initiative, is still inclusive and can be a valuable foundation for recording efforts in similar situations, given that it reports efforts of local Chinese organizations as well as international aid organizations, some of which collaborated with local colleagues. The logistics of the projects, as well as psychosocial techniques applied in the efforts to support survivors, are summarized and recommendations are offered for future such reports.

EFFORTS BY INTERNATIONAL ORGANIZATIONS

In most cases described below, the international entities providing psychosocial aid after the Sichuan earthquake were humanitarian aid organizations with a long history of responding to natural disasters in various parts of the world. However, in several examples in this section, the intervention was initiated by individuals; in one case, a team comprised of a Chinese national and an American traveled from the United States to China, and in another case, two foreign-born professionals who were living in China carried out a project. In all cases, the interventions involved partnerships with local groups.

Médecins Sans Frontières (Doctors Without Borders)

Médecins Sans Frontières (MSF) mobilized to support survivors in the Sichuan disaster area soon after the earthquake occurred on May 12, 2008. A year later, by May 11, 2009, up to 40 international staff and 16 national staff of MSF were working in the affected regions to offer psychological support, relief materials and medical care (Médecins Sans Frontières, 2008; Médecins Sans Frontières Australia, 2008, 2009). The MSF teams assessed the mental health needs and provided psychological support to survivors in hospitals and camps for displaced persons; trained and provided consultation to medical staff on psychological first aid, patient management, and self-care; and conducted community outreach in the form of psycho-education about commonly expected reactions and self-help strategies for coping.

The work of MSF is identified in three stages: the emergency period, post-emergency period, and reconstruction period, providing mental health activities according to the needs and status of the affected people at different periods after the disaster.

Emergency Period

In their first phase, MSF counselors and psychologist volunteers provided psychological first aid in two hospitals (in Chengdu and Guanghan), which included psychological counseling, active listening, conveying compassion, encouraging social support, and screening for people with more severe mental health problems. Large-scale assessments by the MSF teams found that many survivors had lost family members and friends, seen others hurt or killed, witnessed devastating destruction, or been forced to flee homes. Many survivors were intensely afraid, in shock, and grieving over loss of loved ones, making the need for psychological support apparent. Specific groups identified as needing the most help were schoolchildren, whose school buildings collapsed and who lost schoolmates and parents; elderly, who were often ignored; and persons with disabilities, suffering from trauma injuries and for whom recovery and coping with the situation was difficult.

Post-Emergency Period

Two weeks after the earthquake, although reconstruction efforts were underway in Sichuan, many people were identified as still experiencing multiple stress-related psychosomatic symptoms, including feeling anxious and fearful of aftershocks. As a result, mental health support teams were deployed as of June 1, 2008, to several townships and cities to provide psycho-educational sessions and individual counseling when needed. Psycho-education included helping people express their traumatic experiences and feelings, and teaching survivors self-help strategies to normalize their reactions and manage their symptoms, including messages that fears and anxiety are normal reactions and that anyone can experience psychological issues. A total of 39 sessions of psychological education were conducted for 746 people, and 54 sessions of individual counseling were offered.

Reconstruction Period

Six months after the earthquake, while reconstruction work was still underway, many people were still living in temporary housing and found to be suffering from psychological symptoms such as insomnia, anxiety, fears, sadness, crying, difficulties with memory, concentration difficulties, and re-experiences of the trauma—symptoms that have been shown to require psychological help. In light of the limited number of trained psychologists available to provide the necessary professional help, by November 2008, MSF collaborated with the Chinese Academy of Science and Crisis Intervention Centre to provide clinical psychological services to people with psychological disorders. Ten Chinese counselors worked under the supervision of MSF psychologists to provide mental health counseling at consultation rooms established in five temporary housing sites and to make home visits to assess needs for psychological support (Médecins Sans Frontières Australia, 2009). By March 2009, MSF teams assessed more than 650 people, followed 300 patients, and conducted about 1,500 consultations. MSF also provided ongoing training and supervision to the Chinese counselors to ensure service quality.

Asia Australia Mental Health (AAMH) and AusAID

Less than one month after the 512 earthquake, AusAID sponsored Asia Australia Mental Health (AAMH) to form an expert team in disaster mental health to offer a national training program for psychiatrists, psychologists, counselors, and volunteers to provide psychosocial first aid to earthquake survivors in collaboration with Peking University Institute of Mental Health and other Chinese and Australian partners (e.g., Hope China, the Sichuan Health Bureau, University of Western Sydney, and the Australian Red Cross). The AAMH team developed a multidisciplinary training program in disaster mental health conducted July 10–13, 2008, in Chengdu, China, for 280 professional and volunteer leaders from all over China (Asia Australia Mental Health, n.d.; Parker, Ng, Coghlan, Fraser, & Raphael, 2009). The training program contributed significantly to the building of national and local capacity to deliver psychological first aid and psychosocial response management to assist the affected populations (Ng et al., 2009).

A $250,000 contribution from the Australian government to address the acute psychological crisis of affected communities supported a joint China Centre for Disease Control and AAMH facility. At the China Centre, Australian mental health experts trained over 1,000 mental health service providers to administer simple effective psychological first aid measures for children and adult survivors (Asia Australia Mental Health, n.d.). This project fostered a long-standing collaboration between Chinese and Australian mental health experts in developing community intervention strategies to deal with the psychological issues of disasters. For example, AAMH facilitated placements for two to three Chinese mental health professionals to be trained in disaster mental health in Australia at the Royal Australian and New Zealand College of Psychiatrists.

Hong Kong Committee for UNICEF and the National Working Committee on Children and Women

After the 512 earthquake, UNICEF (the United Nations Children's Fund), which intervenes on behalf of children's needs after disasters, found that children affected by the disaster were in urgent need of professional psychosocial support and community-based protection services as a result of being at high risk of danger, neglect, and abuse due to displacement and limited supervision (UNICEF, 2009). This finding was consistent with previous UNICEF field missions that found that while basic physical needs such as food, water, shelter, and health care were being provided, services for psychosocial needs, crucial to prevent long-term consequences of survivors' capacity to recover, were sporadic and uncoordinated, and often provided by less experienced and unqualified people. Given that previous relief efforts in China had revealed that 90–95% of children and women were able to recover with help from psychosocial services, UNICEF collaborated with the National Working Committee on Children and Women to establish professionally led "Child Friendly Spaces" (CFS) in camps and temporary shelters to offer children protection services and integrated psychosocial support in a secure and healing environment. About 40 professionally led CFS were established in 40 townships in 21 counties of 8 prefectures (UNICEF, 2010).

These CFS, located at community-based child protection service centers, provided earthquake-affected children and their families access to psychosocial support, including day care for pre-schoolaged children, nonformal education for schoolaged children, life-skills training for adolescents, and parenting support for parents and caretakers. The CFS were stocked with toys, library books, bikes, and sports equipment for play. Activities were conducted, including singing and dancing, creative expression (e.g., drawing pictures), recreation games, and education, to establish "normalization" of their lives.

Outreach services were also provided to parents and communities for health services, immunization, injury prevention, and child protection. In all, 100,816 children and over 5,000 parents were reported to have benefited from CFS, with almost 90% of children and women found to be able to recover with the psychosocial services provided (UNICEF, 2010).

Written and video reports by UNICEF staff further documented the helpfulness of the services, supported by reports from parents about positive changes in themselves and their children, including descriptions of reduction of fears and anxiety; demonstrations of activities; actions taken such as training volunteers from local university to help; and recommendations such as working with the Chinese government (Rutstein, Li, & Donovan, 2008). For example, the subject of children's drawings changed from capsized boats and falling buildings to colorful balloons and smiling faces, with the result that the CFS were called "a space for songs and smiles but also a haven for healing" (Nettleton, 2009). Given its success, the CFS model was included in the new National Plan for Child Development 2010–2020, China's development framework for children (UNICEF, 2011).

Oxfam Hong Kong (OHK)

After the earthquake, Oxfam Hong Kong (OHK), the Chinese arm of the international organization that offers humanitarian assistance after natural disasters, launched a wide-scale humanitarian relief effort of capacity-building and reconstruction projects supporting schools, water systems, new roads, and other rehabilitation work in the affected areas of Sichuan, Gansu, and Shaanxi, assisting more than 750,000 people in about 200 communities (Oxfam Hong Kong, 2010). Collaborating with local government units and partner organizations, OHK projects addressed needs of women, children, orphans, elderly people, and ethnic minorities, and also focused on promoting gender equity by requiring that women representatives were members of project management groups. Regarding psychological support, OHK worked with local societies to provide psychological services (e.g., to address reactions like shock, trauma, and grief) in different areas; e.g., with the Guizhou Qifeng Red Cross Society in Pengzhou County; with Gansu Yixin Psychological Consulting Center in Longnan; and with Donghua Women's Health Education Center in Huating and Pingliang Counties. Educational leaflets were distributed in the community, and individual and group services were conducted for women and children. In one assessment, 79% of women who were assisted reported they "felt better after talking with people" and 64% of children who received assistance reported improvement, e.g., in sleeping (Oxfam Hong Kong, 2010). In addition, training in social services was offered to volunteers, project personnel, and medical personnel of two township hospitals.

The reconstruction project is a five-year plan (Oxfam Hong Kong, 2011). In December 2008, this project won the 2008 China Charity Award from the Ministry of Civil Affairs.

Mercy Corps

Mercy Corps responded to the Sichuan earthquake immediately, sending staff to the affected region within hours and delivering truckloads of crucial supplies to survivors. However, an important target of the intervention was to provide psychosocial support to assist young survivors to process the tragedy and shock of loss (Burks, 2009; Mercy Corps, 2008, 2009), given that youth were considered both physically and psychologically more vulnerable than adults and that large numbers of children and adolescents in Sichuan were affected, with their home and school destroyed or damaged, friends and family members killed or injured, and basic sense of security and stability lost (Gutoff, 2009). Psychosocial support provided to children after a disaster is crucial because it has been shown to help prevent more severe psychological disorders in their lifetime (M. Streng, personal communication, January 10, 2013). Two youth psychosocial programs were initiated in cooperation with two local counterparts, namely, the Sichuan Youth Federation (a subsidiary of the All China Youth Federation) and the China Foundation for Poverty Alleviation. The play-based program to provide support and counseling aimed at improving resiliency and mental well-being has two components, called "Comfort for Kids" and "Moving Forward." The overall plan addresses three levels: the individual level, aimed at strengthening the child's inner locus of control, self-esteem, and coping skills; the micro level, aimed at building mentor relationships with an adult outside the home; and the ecosystem level aimed at reestablishing social cohesion among displaced schools and communities. The outcome of an evaluation of over 4,000 children and adolescent participants showed the value of the program and the powerful role of social support in recovery (Silberg, 2012).

The program included a "train the trainers" model, training mental health professionals as well as local caregivers and teachers to assist affected children and build local capacity by teaching caregivers to train peers. Training was offered to more than 1,600 caregivers, including teachers and psychologists. The "Comfort for Kids" program offers caregivers basic training to identify normal reactions to psychological stress, and to lead workshops (following a custom-made workbook) to help children to express feelings in a safe environment. One activity, for example, called "My Earthquake Story," involves narratives of the child's experience. Collaborating with senior-level psychologists in the Chinese American Psychoanalytic Alliance, as well as numerous volunteers, Mercy Corps translated, adapted, and printed up to 60,000 copies of the workbook (Gutoff, 2009).

The "Moving Forward" component involves training caregivers to provide organized recreational activities for children and adolescents in a safe and structured environment, which establishes a sense of normalcy, alleviates stress, and builds resiliency. The activities are targeted to help children and adolescents rebuild self-esteem, practice teamwork, regain trust, develop problem-solving skills, communicate constructively, experience greater control, and rebuild relationships with peers and adults—all considered crucial to recovery. Each youth participant is matched with an adult caregiver from the community in group activities and games. To facilitate capacity-building, the program toolkit includes detailed instructions, an activity guide, and various play tools. More than 500 caregivers were trained. By August 2012, Mercy Corps' Youth Psychosocial Program supported the resilience and well-being of over 50,000 children. The Sichuan-based program applied the same sports-and-game based methodology to build self-confidence and resilience among children of migrant workers, considered an at-risk group.

Mercy Malaysia

Mercy Malaysia is a nonprofit, nongovernmental, voluntary relief organization based in Southeast Asia that provides support to communities in crisis (Mercy Malaysia, 2009a). Their Total Disaster Risk Management (TDRM) model is divided into two phases: the pre-disaster phase (prevention/mitigation and preparedness) and the post-disaster phase (response and recovery). Emphasis is put on total stakeholder engagement, with all members of the community actively involved in the recovery effort. The organization recognizes that survivors from disaster often suffer from severe psychological scars such as anxiety, depression, and being haunted by dark memories. Given local culture, whereby communities are often suspicious of psychotherapy and other Western techniques for alleviating psychological distress, helpers are encouraged to tailor efforts with deep understanding and sensitivity to local customs and folkways (Mercy Malaysia, 2009a).

The organization's Child-Led Disaster Risk Reduction is a program aimed to reduce disaster risks facing children, conducted by Mercy Malaysia in partnership with Save the Children UK. The project was only possible when this partnership provided necessary funding (Umar, n.d.). The program is based on the model of "peer education" (Mercy Malaysia, 2009b). Children are trained to lead their peers in disaster preparedness sessions, following a Risk and Resource map, and in awareness-raising campaigns utilizing fire prevention posters and an earthquake safety booklet. There is also a train-the-trainers' workshop for teachers.

The organization has partners from government, nongovernment organizations, and private corporate and business sectors (Mercy Malaysia, 2009b; Umar, n.d.).

The China Earthquake Relief Project

The China Earthquake Relief Project (CHERP), a seven-phase training project, was spearheaded in China by psychologist Rob Blinn, PhD, department chair of the Family Counseling Center at Beijing United Family Hospitals and Clinics (Beijing UFH). In response to the Sichuan earthquake, Blinn contacted colleagues at the U.S.-based Somatic Experiencing Trauma Institute (SETI) to implement psychosocial support. SETI participated in this effort in Phases 1 and 2, and four subsequent phases were implemented by collaboration with the U.S.-based Trauma Resource Institute (TRI).

The goal of CHERP was to bring biologically based trauma intervention training and treatment to local areas suffering from the earthquake. Based on a "train the practitioner" model, the program offered trainings for volunteer mental health providers, medical professionals, and paraprofessionals (e.g., physicians, medical students, nurses, rescue workers, community leaders, teachers, and parents). The training consisted of three days of classroom-based practicum (instruction, demonstrations, exercises, and coaching) followed by two days of direct interventions with adult and child earthquake survivors, and supervision and consultation with trainees in the field. Follow-up consultations were offered in subsequent phases to reinforce the training skills and to troubleshoot potential challenges in implementing the training programs (R. Blinn, personal communication, July 15, 2009; Leitch & Miller-Karas, 2009)

The American teams were co-coordinated by trainers with extensive experience in disaster intervention program design and implementation (i.e., Lisa LaDue of SETI in Phase 2 and TRI cofounders Elaine Miller-Karas and Laurie Leitch in Phases 1 and 3–7), who collaborated with the China-based project staff. The trainings were based on TRI's brief biological model, called the Trauma Resiliency Model (TRM), which has been field-tested in natural disasters and international settings of complex trauma. Training materials and pocket guides were tailored for the cultural setting and distributed to trainees to allow for sustainability of the program. Translators were psychology students from universities in Beijing and Wuhan.

The TRM is a manual-based training program that explains the biology of fear and threat as automatic, natural defensive responses that occur when an individual is faced with life-threatening and/or dangerous situations. Symptoms are viewed as the body's attempt to reestablish balance to the nervous system and considered normal biological responses to extraordinary events, rather than as pathological or mental weakness. When traumatic stress symptoms are normalized in this way, feelings of shame and self-blame are reduced or eliminated. Given its biological base, the approach can be introduced to diverse cultures and learned simply and easily by individuals of varied educational backgrounds, including those limited in literacy (Miller-Karas, 2012).

Individuals trained in TRM learn to distinguish between sensations of distress and resiliency through various skills, including tracking the autonomic nervous system and resourcing and grounding, to bring awareness respectively to sensations in the present moment connected to images of well-being or comforting physical sensations. As attention is brought to these sensations connected to resiliency, traumatic symptoms dissipate or are reduced. The skills not only help survivors, but also reduce burnout and vicarious traumatization for the team and responders (Miller-Karas, 2012).

TRM skills taught to children were coupled with art, physical activities, and games to facilitate awareness of sensations of well-being. Parents, caregivers, and teachers were taught about the biological basis of trauma and how it affects children's behavior, as well as about the importance of learning skills for self-care, since a more stabilized caregiver can better help a child deal with trauma.

Team meetings were held to facilitate group support and team-building. These included exercises involving sharing (e.g., revealing the origins of one's name, expressing challenges, and exchanging stories of courage and resilience witnessed by the team) as well as case discussions, debriefing, and planning (e.g., making necessary changes in the program). Ongoing support was offered to the translators to reduce secondary traumatization, since they bore witness to survival stories more than once (i.e., listening in Chinese and then translating into English).

The project had seven phases. Phase 1 involved the design of the program and assessments of survivors before and after the intervention. In Phase 2, the Chinese-based hosts and American team traveled to the earthquake area for further training and supervision of trainees. Recognizing that survivors may need more intensive interventions that require additional skills by trainees, Phase 3, consisting of a three-day classroom training and two days of fieldwork, was held in September 2008 with survivors and first responders at the same sites as Phase 2. These sites included the Third People's Hospital in Mianyang, Jiangyou Psychiatric Hospital, Beichuan Leigu Relocation Camp Hospital, and the Wudu Elementary School near the epicenter.

A half-day workshop for invited physicians was conducted in Chengdu in September 2008, at the Third Provincial Hospital of Sichuan. Return visits were made to the earthquake zone for case consultation with both former and new trainees at several follow-up periods of time, specifically, in Phase 4, held in January 2009, in Phase 5 held in March 2009, and in Phase 6 held in May on the anniversary of the earthquake. A further training of 18 members of the Psychological Association, Phase 7, was held in Chengdu at the Peoples' Provincial Hospital of Sichuan.

Evaluations were conducted with 350 trainees who participated in the TRM trainings in Phases 3–7. Results indicated that 97% of trainees believed that biologically oriented TRM training will be "very to moderately" relevant or useful for their work with the Chinese earthquake survivors, and about 88% of trainees reported that they will use the skills "very to moderately" frequently during the two weeks following the training. Over 60% of the trainees reported they will use TRM skills for self-care (Leitch & Miller-Karas, 2009).

Members of the China Ministry of Health present at a training expressed appreciation, and the CHERP program was endorsed by the Mianyang Health Bureau. Funding for the program was provided by the American Chamber of Commerce in Beijing through the World Health Organization (WHO), which also provided project guidance and oversight. In a subsequent phase of the CHERP project, the training team conducted an orientation to disaster work for the WHO Collaboration Centers in Beijing and Shanghai.

Katherine A. Kendall Institute for International Social Work Education, the Council on Social Work Education (CSWE)

A year after the Sichuan earthquake, on May 8–9, 2009, the Katherine A. Kendall Institute held the 2009 Social Work Response to Disaster Relief and Management Conference in Beijing, China, in recognition of the one-year anniversary. Co-organized with several groups, namely, the Department of Applied Social Sciences at Hong Kong Polytechnic University, the Joint PolyU–Peking University China Social Work Research Centre, the China Association of Social Work Education, the *China Journal of Social Work*, and the International Association of Schools of Social Work (IASSW), the conference brought together social work researchers and practitioners from all over the world to exchange experiences and analyze a variety of topics about disaster management and response.

The first day of the conference focused on the broad issues of coping with the aftermath of natural disasters, with an emphasis on the tsunami in Thailand and Sri Lanka and the Sichuan earthquake in China. Among the topics covered were the role of different actors and institutions involved, international frameworks for addressing disaster issues, the diverse roles of social workers in disaster response, posttraumatic stress in children, mental health issues, and understanding the culture of disaster survivors (Katherine A. Kendall Institute, 2009). Discussions on the second day of the conference primarily focused on the recovery efforts after the earthquake in China, including the burgeoning role of social work in China; technical assistance collaborations among social workers, government, and universities; and the importance of integrating other disciplines such as geology and engineering to reestablish safer communities.

In conjunction with this conference, on May 11, 2009, a post-disaster reconstruction symposium was held in Sichuan Province, China, by Hong Kong Polytechnic University and Sichuan University. This symposium provided a multidisciplinary analysis of the reconstruction work after the 512 earthquake through examining various aspects. These aspects included health and social services, architectural and engineering analysis, and community economy and tourism. On May 12, the one-year anniversary of the 512 earthquake, a visit was made to one of the earthquake-hit areas.

International Federation of Red Cross and Red Crescent Societies Supporting the Red Cross Society of China

The International Federation of Red Cross (IFRC) and Red Crescent Societies is the world's largest humanitarian network, consisting of 187 national societies—including the Red Cross Society of China (RCSC)—dedicated to protect human life and health, to respect human beings, and to prevent and alleviate human suffering. Like other humanitarian organizations, Red Cross and Red Crescent member organizations understand the need to treat the severe psychological wounds caused by trauma and the fact that emotional wounds may not be visibly apparent like other injuries, but often are long-lasting and hard to heal (International Federation of Red Cross and Red Crescent Societies, 2012b). To foster active survivors rather than passive victims, the IFRC's Reference Centre for Psychosocial Support promotes psychosocial capacity in Red Cross and Red Crescent societies in all parts of the world.

The RCSC's psychosocial program, "Sunshine in Your Heart," played a frontline role, implementing psychosocial support for survivors and providing psychosocial trainings for helpers in cooperation with the IFRC (F. Markus, personal communication, January 18, 2013). Teams were deployed to care for survivors in camps for the displaced. Stages of the teams' approach included assessments through a questionnaire asking about the family situation, and emotional responses to the disaster. Help included offering practical advice, such as how to obtain grants from the government when people could not withdraw money from the bank because they had no ID to prove their identity. Basic counseling techniques used by the teams included allowing people to vent their grief. Volunteers were also trained in simple techniques to help survivors, e.g., to give people permission to cry (Markus, 2008).

Under the IFRC's Psychosocial Support Program (PSP), psychosocial support teams were deployed to Sichuan and Yunnan Provinces after the earthquake not only to provide psychosocial services, but to recruit, train, and support master trainers as well as volunteers, given that the latter can be accepted as helpful under the emergency circumstances. Master trainers were given skills and tools to support volunteers assigned to reach out to teachers and students in schools, and to provide psychosocial support to the elderly and ethnic minorities as well as to residents in an urban community and local rescue teams. Materials were translated and adapted from the IFRC's Psychosocial Toolkit, to fit the Chinese context (International Federation of Red Cross and Red Crescent Societies, 2012a).

The program consists of three parts: "Psychological Support in Emergency and Disaster Settings"; "Disaster Mental Health"; and "Psychosocial Support for Children and Teenagers." A toolkit helps aid workers, social workers, volunteers, and teachers to provide psychosocial support to people at the different phases of disaster preparedness, response, and reconstruction. The activities include active listening skills, role play, storytelling, and art therapy, e.g., using puppets to demonstrate coping.

One particularly useful technique in the IFRC psychosocial toolkit to help children involves creating narratives whereby the beginning of a story is told and the child fills in the rest. Adapted for the local context, the children were given a furry toy panda to hold, given that this animal is indigenous to the Chinese community, and that pandas were themselves survivors of the disaster (Markus, 2009). The story begins, "After his parents died in the earthquake, Qiuqiu (the panda's name) wandered around for a while, before deciding to rebuild the family's house with his own two hands." The story line told by the child, and the way the child holds the panda, reveals different psychological states.

Similar techniques were used in working with first responders, e.g., rescuers experiencing trauma from pulling people out the rubble. These included group work, mixing Western approaches of interpersonal communication with more traditional Chinese techniques, like deep meditative breathing (e.g., Tai Qi) and pressing acupressure points on the arm to help calm feelings.

As the emergency phase evolved into stages of recovery and reconstruction, the psychosocial projects targeted help for Ankang children (i.e., earthquake orphans) and children of migrant workers. In one particular school, it was estimated that between 20 and 30 of the school's roughly 1,200 children required individual psychosocial attention (Markus, 2008).

Trainings were an important part of the program. The IFRC worked with the Crisis Intervention Centre in Sichuan to hold a three-day psychosocial training program for teachers in the earthquake-affected area (Markus, 2009). The techniques involved processing their experience and keeping children busy, including through games, to distract them from focusing on their fears. Since fewer than 200 professionals before the quake had been trained to provide post-disaster psychological intervention work in China, trainings were held in 2011 in Kunming and in Beijing to teach volunteers about psychological first aid for survivors and how to organize such services in disaster situations. Also, a reference center was established at a Red Cross branch in Yunnan for psychosocial support materials, with books, a reading corner, and project files. These efforts were expanded to four other provinces (i.e., Inner Mongolia, Fujian, Jiangxi, and Hubei) staffed by volunteers and psychologists as consultants.

Media tools were produced at various stages of the recovery to document the process and achievements, and to facilitate further recovery. These tools included a flash video game for teens; a publication; a documentary, *Looking into the Future*; and advocacy films focused on psychosocial support used for training and information.

The Psychosocial Support Program in Sichuan was completed in November 2011, after servicing about 20,000 students and teachers in 10 schools. The community activities for the project in Yunnan ended in March 2012, with a summary meeting in May 2012. While many of the psychosocial problems of survivors were noted to have eased over the years since the disaster, challenges remained to support youngsters who were severely affected (F. Markus, personal communication, January 18, 2013). These include an estimated tens of millions of "left-behind" children of some of China's migrant workers left in the care of grandparents, who often face problems relating to peers and finding their place in school life (Tai, 2012).

A five-day meeting was held in 2012 of East Asian Red Cross Societies (i.e., China, Japan, Mongolia, the Democratic People's Republic of Korea, and the Republic of Korea), where psychosocial programming after disaster was a prominent theme and the need for more advocacy and sensitization about psychosocial work was highlighted. As a result, the societies agreed to take steps towards forming a regional Psychosocial Support Network (Markus, 2013). The cofacilitator of the meeting, Nana Wiedemann, who is also director of the Red Cross/Red Crescent Psychosocial Centre in Copenhagen, noted that the formation of this network recognizes how invaluable psychosocial support is, that it represents a major step forward for psychosocial support work in the region, and that it promises to help foster knowledge-sharing and encourage advocacy in the area (Markus, 2013).

International Association of Chinese Medical Specialists and Psychologists (IACMSP)

After the 512 Sichuan earthquake, the International Association of Chinese Medical Specialists and Psychologists (IACMSP) immediately mobilized to provide post-disaster psychological assistance (Deng, 2008a, 2008b, 2008c, 2008d, 2008e, 2009; Lao, 2008a, 2008b, 2009a, 2009b, 2009c, 2009d). IACMSP was founded by Chinese expert in psychosomatic medicine Dr. Ming-Yu (Miller) Deng, who has published widely and conducted innumerable trainings on many psychological topics throughout China. The organization has a headquarters in New York City.

Workshops in the field by Chinese professionals included psycho-education about normal reactions to such trauma, and also sand therapy, and play therapy techniques for children such as singing and drawing pictures. At youth gatherings at schools, students were invited to perform songs for the assembly. Teachers were trained to help students feel less fearful. Visits were made to families who had lost loved ones to show support and caring (Deng, 2008a, 2008b).

On October 12, 2008, IACMSP held the First International Forum of Post-disaster Psychological and Mental Health Aid in Sichuan 512 in Mianyang City, Sichuan (Deng, 2008c). Over 200 psychological scholars and related professionals from the United States, Canada, France, Australia, Taiwan, Malaysia, Hong Kong, Macao, and mainland China came together to exchange knowledge and experience about post-disaster psychosocial aid. At the forum, IACMSP also granted the First International Monica Humanitarian Award to outstanding volunteers in 512 psychological relief support. On August 3, 2009, the Second International Forum of Psychological and Mental Health Aid after Sichuan 512 Earthquake was held by IACMSP in Dandong City, Liaoning (Lao, 2009d). Ninety-two professionals and volunteers from mainland China, Hong Kong, Taiwan, Canada, and the United States participated in the forum. On August 8, 2009, when the Morakot typhoon struck Taiwan, IACMSP combined assistance for "Taiwan 88" and "Sichuan 512" disasters together (Lao, 2009a).

Subsequent conferences built on these issues in response to other earthquakes that occurred in China. On September 20, 2009, the IACMSP Psychological and Mental Health Aid Coordination Center for Sichuan "512" and Taiwan "88" was established in New York City (Lao, 2009c). In 2010, the Third International Forum of Post-Disaster Psychological and Mental Health Aid & Second Scientific Conference of International Society of Chinese Psycho-counselors was held in Xining City, Qinghai Province, from July 23 to 27, in response to the earthquake that occurred in Yushu, China. The main theme of the conference was "Post-disaster Psycho and Mental Health Aid," with eight main content areas (International Association of Chinese Medical Specialists and Psychologists, 2010; Deng, 2010). The first author of this chapter made several presentations for this conference about psychological first aid programs and techniques in disaster recovery (Kuriansky 2010b, 2010e, 2010f, 2012c) and traveled with the Chinese team led by Dr. Deng to the earthquake zone to do workshops and trainings for students and teachers, which was captured on video (Kuriansky, 2010g). She was also the recipient of an IACMSP Monica Award. Presentations were subsequently made about this intervention in China with this group.

The conferences and interventions for psychological first aide after Sichuan "512," as well as Taiwan "88," Haiti "112," and Yushu "414," included: the exchange of psychological counseling theories and practice used in China and other communities worldwide; recognizing volunteers who made contributions in psychological aid in disasters by the International Monica Humanitarian Award; and holding meetings of the IACMSP Council and Working Conference of IACMSP Post-Disaster Psycho and Mental Health Aid Coordination Center with local professionals as well as government leaders to evaluate the needs for psychological first aid efforts and to coordinate the efforts of IACMSP volunteer groups of psychological assistance experts. The first author participated in all these activities.

Participants of the conferences included directors of IACMSP and International Society of Chinese Psycho-counselors; directors and members of other societies related to the IACMSP; licensed and registered psychologists, counselors, psychotherapists, mental health practitioners, and social workers; psychiatrists in general hospitals and mental health centers; physicians and health care practitioners in various departments (e.g., mental health, internal medicine, emergency medicine, community medicine); psychology professors and students; teachers and other school personnel; administrators of health programs; professors and students in varied fields (e.g., psychology, education, medicine, social work); and volunteers involved in recovery efforts.

Topics of presentations included: psychological first aid for disaster and crisis intervention; identification and treatment for acute stress disorder; post-disaster psychological intervention short-term and long-term effects; identification and treatment for post-traumatic stress disorder (PTSD) and other mental disorders; disaster psychology and mental health services for children, adolescents, and people with disabilities; grief counseling; training and supervision for medical and mental health staff, and counselors in disaster areas; and international exchange and cooperation of post-disaster psychological aid and mental health services (Kuriansky, 2010d).

The World Council of Psychotherapy (WCP)

The World Council of Psychotherapy (WCP) is a nongovernmental organization (NGO) of members around the world who are psychotherapists, aimed at promoting and networking about all aspects of psychotherapy training and practice. Accredited at the United Nations Economic and Social Council, the organization also seeks to raise awareness about the need to include psychotherapy in policies and programs worldwide. At the WCP 5th World Congress of Psychotherapy held in Beijing China, in 2008, a training was conducted of a model for psychological first aid applied in other disaster situations (e.g., Hurricane Katrina in the United States), adapted to be culturally appropriate for the Chinese context (Nemeth & Kuriansky, 2008). The training was conducted by American disaster relief experts—neuropsychologist Darlyne Nemeth from Baton Rouge, Louisiana, and the first author of this chapter, a clinical psychologist from New York City who also serves on the board of WCP, as secretary general and the main United Nations NGO representative, respectively. The daylong course was offered to counselors and conference registrants with varied health and mental health backgrounds, intended to prepare them to help survivors deal with anniversary reactions from the earthquake in China. The workshop included a didactic session explaining emotional issues involved with disaster, anniversary reactions and stages in the healing process, and experiential sessions for personal healing and training in practical techniques for use in the field. The latter included individual and group experiences to facilitate relaxation and safety, and to rebuild healthy defenses and coping mechanisms. For example, in one exercise, participants identified emotions associated with pre-disaster, post-disaster, and anniversary time periods, paired with behaviors (e.g., "When left alone, I felt scared"); in another exercise, participants practiced a self-comforting technique about feeling safe. Other exercises came from a toolbox of techniques applied in many international settings (Kuriansky, 2007d). Pre and post scores for a group of previous workshop participants showed a significant decrease in anxiety (Nemeth et al., 2012).

The training was held in conjunction with another symposium at the conference, about the WCP Disaster Trauma Training/Certification Program. This program is aimed at identifying, and then training, "gatekeepers" as part of disaster risk reduction planning. These gatekeepers are identified as persons qualified to determine who locally "on the ground" can guide organizations as to how they can best provide meaningful assistance to those in need. A database of these gatekeepers makes them widely and internationally accessible so they can be easily contacted and mobilized as a resource.

The 512 Earthquake Mental Rescue Action

After the earthquake, two psychotherapists, who were foreign-born but living in China, traveled to Chengdu on May 25, 2008, with two translators and a technician, to conduct a training program. Dr. Bijan Ghaznavi was a noted Swiss psychotherapist, international lecturer, and leader in the positive psychology movement, with advanced expertise in Adlerian psychotherapy and a diploma in neuro-linguistic programming (deceased as of 2009). His wife, Dr. Agnes Ghaznavi, an American-born psychiatrist with a specialty in marriage counseling, received a certificate for trainers of trainers in 2008 from Weisbaden Academy in Germany. They lived in Switzerland and also for many years in China, where they provided extensive trainings in positive psychology across the country. Their therapeutic approach integrates bio-systemic and Adlerian techniques from a positive psychology perspective.

Using a train-the-trainers model, a two-day training course was offered to 300 trainees, including medical students, psychologists, teachers, principals and others (A. Ghaznavi, personal communication, September 4, 2012). The training used tools of positive psychology and covered education about grieving, emotional reactions as sadness and anger, and new coping and problem-solving strategies. The aim was to help survivors regain balance and gain hope and meaning in life despite extreme losses and suffering. The training included four 2-hour supervision sessions.

Following a "help the helpers" model, the therapists offered encouragement to helpers suffering from burnout, including one female psychiatrist who was feeling inadequate and a school counselor who was feeling overwhelmed. Another helper was experiencing trauma from near-death experiences, similar to other survivors who had been buried in rubble for days. The sessions were videotaped, so that others who could not be present could take advantage of the lessons.

The Ghaznavis conducted a training session about recovery for attendees of the World Congress of Psychotherapy in Beijing, China, in October 2008, and traveled to the earthquake region for 10 days in November. Their set of 10 DVDs about their training courses were distributed by the government throughout the earthquake region.

Yale Psychiatrists Independent Psycho-Education Mission

Two psychiatrists from Yale University, Ke Xu, MD, PhD, and Heather Goff, MD, were sponsored by the National Key Laboratory on Cognitive Science in the Chinese Academy of Science to conduct a psycho-educational training course for school teachers in Sichuan Province. Dr. Ke Xu, a resident in psychiatry at that time and later assistant professor in the Department of Psychiatry at the Yale School of Medicine, took vacation time to travel to Sichuan Province in the summer of 2008 (Xu, n.d.). Her cotrainer Goff was then an assistant professor at the Child Study Center at Yale University.

Given that the earthquake occurred during the afternoon when children were in schools impacted by the quake, and many experienced trauma while escaping from falling debris and seeking safety in their faraway home villages, the training focused on helping teachers understand the needs of these students. The three-week course involved lectures, discussion and role-playing about coping skills, and understanding survivors' feelings, including fears and survivor guilt. Lectures focused on (1) education for the teachers about normal and abnormal responses to trauma, (2) training in brief cognitive behavioral therapy techniques, and (3) establishing a support network. Addressing cultural factors, e.g., self-criticism, was deemed particularly important. The children's issues included school phobia (i.e., fear of going back to school), fear of being alone, and sleeping disturbances. In one case, a child was particularly sensitive to preparing for another traumatic event, by insisting on carrying supplies (e.g., food, water). Xu anecdotally reported the value of the training for the teachers.

Yeshiva University Independent Student Project

An innovative intervention was initiated by a school psychology graduate student, Emily Zeng, who was enrolled at Yeshiva University in the United States (Zeng, 2011; Zeng & Silverstein, 2011). A Chinese national who spoke the local dialect, Zeng was motivated to volunteer in the disaster zone to help children recover. Initially she intended to volunteer with an organization but found that the Chengdu City Youth League (CYL) in charge of volunteer relief efforts no longer accepted volunteers from overseas and that Mercy Corps' project involved only adult-directed activities. Thus, she traveled to Beichuan on her own via informal channels. She eventually settled in a mountainous village called West Mountain, teaching in a tent school of 30 students aged from 7 to 15 years old, predominantly of Qiang ethnic minority descent. Several other volunteers from a church community in Beijing, with no formal teaching or mental health training, were helping out in the tents.

While Zeng had no prior experience in disaster support services, she designed and implemented a community-focused participatory action project with the help of her professor, Dr. Louise Silverstein, who was teaching a course on participatory approaches. They adapted the model of the "ladder of children's participation" (Hart, 2008) as a guiding principle to promote children's resilience and recovery and to enhance their participation in community-rebuilding efforts. Zeng received supervision from Silverstein via intermittent Internet access and lengthy e-mails with the American Group Psychotherapy Association (AGPA) disaster team.

The program consisted of four phases. Phase I involved restoring structure and routine, starting with adult-initiated activities, asking the children to discuss and clarify classroom rules. For example, the rules to "respect your teacher and peers" meant "not throwing bricks," and the rule to "take care of the environment" meant "taking garbage to the garbage bin" or "sweeping the floor." The morning routine consisted of chanting ancient poetry, reading, writing, and lessons in science and English. The afternoons consisted of more academics, exercise routines, and group activities. After school and in the evenings, Zeng conducted home visits to learn the culture and to build alliances with families and village elders.

Phase II involved developing group cohesion, i.e., providing opportunities for the children to interact with one other and to process feelings about the earthquake. Many games were utilized to create opportunities for physical activities and group engagement, including common Chinese games (e.g., play-dough, handcrafts, bubble blowing, rope jumping, Chinese checkers), as well as American games (e.g., Tricky Triangle, Tumbling Tower). The children also created their own games. Their favorite game was Noah's Ark, which was associated with survival and dealt with building up and falling down. Other activities, like singing and dancing, further encouraged ethnic self-identification, honoring the Qiang minority as an ancient Chinese culture closely related to the Tibetans.

Phase III involved action-oriented activities (e.g., mapping, photography). The children were asked to describe where they lived in the village, leading to the first map in the history of this small village where all houses and buildings had been reduced to rubble. The map guided Zeng's home visits and stimulated discussions about earthquakes around the world, about their former schools, and about the school they wished to be rebuilt, which promoted feelings of hope and interconnectedness. Another activity was student journalism, with children divided into small groups taking turns being an interviewer, a journalist, and a photographer (e.g., "If you had three wishes that could come true, what would they be?"). Students shared donated mini-digital cameras among themselves to produce visual journals about familiar subjects (e.g., school, family, friends), nature (e.g., animals, plants, sky), and the debris. Eventually, these activities led to trauma-related themes and narratives (e.g., "Grandpa was buried underneath. Now it's covered with tall, green grass.").

Phase IV involved child-initiated community action, e.g., organizing movies for the entire village, thus transforming a traumatic site into a pleasurable community event, and sharing the equipment with another village, thus promoting self-efficacy. The project concluded with a memorial ritual initiated by the children to observe the three-month anniversary of the earthquake. The following year, Beichuan County was relocated 15 miles away, and the government built a national earthquake museum upon the ruins.

The project highlighted the important role of school psychologists and the usefulness of community-centered psychosocial support. Zeng argues that despite limitations (e.g., the small sample of participants, no control group, no formal data analysis procedure, and no structured outcome measures), the activities allowed valuable informal empirical observations of positive change in terms of (1) decreased negative behaviors (e.g., hypervigilance and physical acting-out); (2) increased positive behaviors (e.g., keeping their classrooms clean, group engagement, and initiating self-reflections through photography and keeping journals); and (3) connecting with the community (e.g., map-making, holding an outdoor movie night). All of these, says Zeng, indicate improvement in the children's intrapsychic states—for example, an increase in self-efficacy and self-esteem—and in their ability to contribute to the community at large (E. Zeng, personal communication, November 20, 2014).

Zeng maintained an ongoing relationship with the village through phone contact and summer visits for the next five years. In 2013, their phone lines were not connecting, and she eventually lost contact. Zeng is now a licensed psychologist in New York, serving children with various developmental disabilities.

RECOVERY EFFORTS BY PREDOMINANTLY CHINESE ORGANIZATIONS

Interventions after the earthquake were also carried out at the initiative and leadership of local Chinese organizations. The following are examples of these projects.

The International Association for Analytical Psychology (IAAP) and the Chinese Association of Analytical Psychology (CAAP)

On May 12, 2008, the first day of the Sichuan earthquake, Lei Da, a member of the Chinese Association of Analytical Psychology (CAAP) and leader of the Chengdu Jung Group (referring to famous Swiss psychoanalyst Carl Jung), initiated psychosocial support to survivors in the affected region with two other members of CAAP. The next day, Dr. Heyong Shen, the president of CAAP and a Jungian analyst with the International Association of Analytical Psychology (IAAP), and his wife, Gao Lan, formed an "Analytical Psychology Group" and traveled to Sichuan to provide psychological support in the disaster areas. In May 2009, a book authored by Shen (2009), called *San Chuan Xing Si: The Work of the Garden of the Heart and Soul*, was published, describing the logistics and techniques of the psychosocial aid provided by volunteers to survivors in the disaster areas of Sichuan, and Shen's intellectual observations and personal emotional reactions to the disaster (Chenghou & Heyong, 2010).

Together with 10 PhD and master's degree students, the project leaders started their work in one of the most affected areas in Sichuan Province (i.e., Hanwang). Later, CAAP established seven Jungian-style psychological support work stations, called "Garden of the Heart and Soul," in the affected region (i.e., in Wenchuan, Beichuan, Qingchuan, Hanwang, Dujianyan, and Deyang). Following a three-year work plan for the affected region, up to 280 volunteers participated in relief work, including 30 psychology professionals. Trainings for the volunteers were also provided. In addition, IAAP sent Italian psychoanalyst Luigi Zoja and Jungian analyst Eva Pattis Zoja, author of *Sandplay Therapy in Vulnerable Communities*, to Sichuan to do trainings. Other Jungian analysts conducted trainings over the Internet.

The interventions, based on analytical psychology and Chinese culture's psychology of heart, embody the spirit of two Chinese characters: "Ci-Bei (慈悲)." These signify loving and grief, "whose symbolic meanings convey heart-associated grief and the emerging heart that brings healing to those who suffer a lost heart or dissociated mind" (Shen, 2009).

There are three main stages of the work. The first stage aims to establish a therapeutic relationship between the helper and the survivor, and a safe and protected space to reestablish and increase survivors' sense of reality. Since most people in the Sichuan area are ethnically Qiang people who have their own music and dance form, one technique in this initial stage involved decorating the work station with Qiang totems, and playing Qiang music. In the second stage, the therapeutic relationship is enhanced by the helpers "being present with" the survivors and listening to their accounts of their experience. The team used sand play whereby individuals made constructions in beds of sand, and described what they had made. These were then discussed and the pattern interpreted as an expression of internal experiences. The sand play, considered the most important part of the therapeutic technique, gave the survivors an outlet for expressing their trauma. Several sand play constructions can be made, with interpretations then made of the changing patterns and the narratives provided by the survivors. The therapists discovered that most subsequent narratives became more consistent, organized, and positive. For example, a little boy created a construction and associated story of how the earthquake happened, but then also about how a "sister angel" saved his life, thereby suggesting the possibility for change and recovery. Other narratives about homes and schools being rebuilt reflected positive coping. Apart from individual sand play, group sand play was also used as part of the therapy offered. Interaction with each other built comradeship that furthered a sense of healing. As Shen notes, the sand play revealed the essence and basic philosophy of the "Garden of the Heart-Soul" workstation because when it "activates the potential for healing, there is the possibility of transformation" (Shen, 2009; see also Rutstein et al., 2008).

In the third stage, psychological support is offered using the "psychology of heart," guided by principles of "loving-grief" and "crisis and transformation" (Shen, 2009) In this stage, the psychologists tried to integrate the survivors' body experience with their heart feelings, guiding the survivors to experience the traditional Chinese ideology of "Ci-Bei" (loving grief). According to the theory, grief destroys the heart, which is reconstructed by love. Based on this concept of loving-grief, the team focused on helping survivors allow their heart to experience the grief; once this grief is accepted, it can be transformed and reignite love and hope for life.

The CAAP project was considered by the founders as an indispensable force in helping survivors heal their psychological problems.

Critical Incident Team of the Division of Clinical Psychology of the Hong Kong Psychological Society (HKPS)

The Critical Incident Team (CIT) of the Division of Clinical Psychology (DCP) of the Hong Kong Psychological Society (HKPS) intervened during 2008–2009 after the Sichuan earthquake. This team of eight members, convened by clinical psychologist and fellow of the HKPS Dr. Kitty K. Wu, conducted several relief activities over the period 2008–2009. On May 12, 2008, an e-mail account (dcpsichuan@gmail.com) was set up to recruit volunteers and communicate about the work involved, with the result that 48 members of the DCP signed up. Requests from organizations inviting these clinical psychologists to join their earthquake relief work were relayed to the volunteers. These organizations included Médecins Sans Frontières, CSDCU Education Fund, and the Department of Applied Social Sciences of the Hong Kong Polytechnic University. Information sheets were written and uploaded on DCP's website, including suggestions to the DCP members about psychological support work after the earthquake, and guidelines on psychological self-care for survivors, rescuers, and reporters. Treatment manuals were translated from English to Chinese by the American-Chinese Academy for Psychotherapy on cognitive processing therapy for PTSD and on complicated grief.

Team members participated in a forum, the Sixth Chinese Psychological Seminar, held on June 12, 2008. A presentation about disaster was made by two members of the DCP team (Drs. Kitty Wu and Eddie Li), and a two-hour workshop on psychological first aid was conducted by Dr. C. W. Wong.

In July 2008, a center was set up to address needs of amputees injured after the earthquake. The DeYang Disabled Person's Federation, Hong Kong Red Cross Rehabilitation, Prosthetic and Orthotic Centre was jointly organized and operated by the Hong Kong Red Cross (HKRC) and the DeYang Disabled Persons' Federation. Dr. Kitty Wu and two others (Mrs. Rachel Poon and Ms. Rose Wong) visited the center from July 5 to 7, 2008, to help launch its services and assess the psychological needs of clients. The CIT continues to offer ongoing support to provide training about psychological health at the center for local professionals (K. Wu, personal communication, January 7, 2013). A number of experienced clinical psychologists and psychiatrists agreed to volunteer their service for the project. A half-day seminar was held on September 27, 2008, titled "The Aftermath of Sichuan Earthquake: Psychological Relief Work," co-organized with the Asian Society for Traumatic Stress Studies.

Several media activities were carried out in 2008 for public information and education. These involved three press releases: (1) about psychological self-care for the Hong Kong public after the Sichuan Earthquake (on May 17); (2) about the psychological impact on earthquake survivors and considerations for volunteer helpers (on May 27); and (3) about psychological self-care for rescuers and reporters (on May 29).

The HKPS continued through to mid-2013 to co-organize a training series for health workers in the DeYang Disabled Person's Federation, Hong Kong Red Cross Rehabilitation, Prosthetic and Orthotic Centre in Sichuan.

Post Crisis Counseling Network Limited (PCCN)

The Post Crisis Counseling Network Limited (PCCN) is a nonreligious, cross-cultural charitable organization registered in Hong Kong and dedicated to provide psychological assistance to victims impacted by natural or human disasters. Its mission is to provide a platform in Hong Kong for nonmaterialistic relief effort, including post-crisis counseling and psychological support, to survivors of human or natural disaster at various places in the world, as well as to conduct public lectures and garner media attention to raise awareness and understanding of post-crisis counseling support (http://www.pccnhk.org/pages/index.asp).

The organization was founded by Timothy Wing Ching To, PCCN chairman, and managed by Mr. To and PCCN vice chairman Cheung Siu Ling. PCCN developed out of visits shortly after the 512 Sichuan Earthquake (from May 30 to June 5) by a team of 13 members led by the NLP Association, Asia Region. The team visited over a dozen towns and villages in the earthquake zone (specifically in the counties of Xiang E, Xiao Yu Tong, Jin Hua, Gong Xing, Dujiangyan City, and Qing Cheng Shan city), bringing school supplies, meeting with principals, and playing games with the students. One of the members, Mr. To, a concerned Hong Kong citizen and professional orchestral conductor married to a social worker, subsequently established the PCCN in order to continue to provide free counseling to survivors, and to train crisis counselors (T. To, personal communication, August 19, 2012).

PCCN recruited volunteer citizens from various fields (not just those with psychology careers or background). Initially, the group began letter writing, e-mail correspondences, and online messenger services (i.e., QQ, instant messenger in China) to survivors in the earthquake areas. Volunteers worked with Hong Kong schools and community centers to produce gifts (e.g., knitted scarves, cards) brought during subsequent PCCN field visits to student survivors, who then wrote messages that were returned to students in Hong Kong. Field visits were made to several towns and schools in the disaster area by PCCN volunteers, during the period July to September 2008. The team met with principals, delivered school supplies, played games with students, and assessed problems and provided emotional support. Visits on Chinese New Year included the "Wishing Tree Activity," referring to a well-known banyan tree in Hong Kong, whereby people attach their wishes written on colorful red paper, tied to oranges, and thrown up onto the tree; those that stick are said to come true. In another PCCN project, children from the earthquake zone were brought to Hong Kong for a visit during August 1–9, 2009, that was supported by companies such as McDonald's and Disney.

Volunteers were trained in the organizations' helping techniques, identified after consultation with professional counselors from Hong Kong to determine psychological therapy techniques and services for disaster recovery. Trainings were conducted both in Hong Kong and in the disaster areas where local survivors were recruited as volunteers, and taught about recovery and disaster preparedness, in order to help fellow citizens. The first author conducted one such training in Hong Kong with the PCCN volunteers. As of December 2010, there were 166 trained volunteers, including from Hong Kong, Sichuan, Yushu (Qinghai), Zhouqu (Gansu), and Taiwan.

The techniques used are derived from neuro-linguistic programming (NLP) and other psychological disciplines (e.g., gestalt therapy). Volunteers engaged in over 30 hours of lessons (for a fee), after which they were eligible to provide volunteer disaster relief. Volunteers traveled to the disaster zone, led by

Mr. To, several times in the post-earthquake period, to work with survivors. One-on-one sessions, totaling one hour, consisted of 15 minutes of discussion about the experience and a half-hour of techniques, concluding with 15 minutes of "gift-giving" and taking a picture given immediately to the survivor. Three techniques used included the NLP eye accessing cues (to assess survivors' thoughts or feelings about the event); the NLP timeline process (to manage grief and change the meaning and associations of past traumatic experiences), and an "empty chair" technique (a gestalt therapy technique to facilitate processing and completion of unresolved feelings). Survivors are also led in T'ai Chi exercises, practices to achieve peacefulness that are familiar and appealing to many Chinese people (T. To, personal communication, August 19, 2012). Media was mobilized to communicate blessings and positive messages to millions of survivors, by having guest speakers booked to speak on the radio show called *The Mind Inn* on the Mianzhu, Sichuan People's Broadcasting Station, which aired four times a week.

In another project for aiding recovery, using music, art, and narration, PCCN collected 1,200 personal stories from survivors (mostly children from schools but also some families and volunteers) in various cities hardest hit by the earthquake (i.e., Yingxiu Town, Wenchuan, Dujiangyan, and Mianzhu). The expression of personal experience follows the model of "narrative therapy," whereby people tell their own story to share personal healing and inspire others. Excerpts from 31 handwritten stories were chosen to be printed in a book, published by PCCN, called *Grateful Heart—Reflections on Life after the Disaster in Sichuan Children*. An accompanying video was produced (over the period November 20–23, 2008, with a final recording made in April 2009) with children from the disaster areas singing a popular song, which was rearranged to relate to the earthquake recovery, and produced by the PCCN team led by Mr. To (To, 2009). The book and video were circulated in the affected areas for survivors, rescue workers, and volunteers, to bring comfort and strength.

Ongoing fund-raising efforts for the PCCN activities were conducted, including an annual event called "The Survivors," held in Hong Kong. In February–March, 2010, over 18,000 RMB (i.e., not quite US$3,000) was raised to support the assistance services. Proceeds from book promotions and sales, including at the Hong Kong Book Fair, were donated to the recovery effort.

The 2008 "Grateful Heart" Earthquake Relief Charity Joint Action

Shortly after the earthquake struck, the Grateful Heart Earthquake Relief Charity Joint Action was jointly launched by a conglomerate of collaborators of Chinese organizations representing the private sector, businesses, media, and Buddhism, coordinated by the Beijing Ren Ai Charity Foundation. Partners included Hainan YM Pharmaceutical Co. Ltd., China Kejian Group, Beijing

Longshine Information System Co., Ltd., Chengdu Wenshu Monastery, Shanxi Famen Monastery, Putian Guanghua Monastery in Fujian, Beijing Longquan Monastery, Lay Buddhist Association of Beijing, Dunhuang Culture Promotion Foundation, Dadu Network, Western Returned Scholars Association (WRSA), Eastern Buddhist Network, China Overseas-Educated Scholars Development Foundation (COSDF), Buddhism FJDH Network, Zhengxintang Beijing Cultural Media Centre, Sanwei Books and Community Health News, Kunshan Life-caring Union, Yuanju Shiyin Culture Communication (Beijing) Co., Ltd., Chengdu Roots & Shoots Environmental Culture Centre, Sichuan Yimeilin, Chengdu Ren Cong Zhong Culture, Nanjingese Voluntary Service Team, Huien College, and other organizations.

Their relief work included providing emergency relief supplies, cash donations, distributing materials, and building schools. With regard to psychological help, based on the Joint Action's belief that the prime time for post-disaster psychological intervention is within 21 days of an incident, the emphasis of relief work was gradually shifted to psychological assistance for children and other victims (Voice of Longquan, 2009). Within 10 days, over 10 temporary teaching stands (called "Ren Ai Schools") were set up in settlements in Mianzhu Stadium, to provide education and psychological help to children. Psychological assistance, supervised by psychological consultants from COSDF, was incorporated into teaching at the Ren Ai schools in various towns and villages as well as to orphans at Qingchuan Menghushi "Hope Village," through interactive games, teaching English (by foreign teachers), painting, songs, stories, creative writing and other edutainment (i.e., educational and entertaining) teaching methods. This approach provides a model of how to provide psychological service to the children in the earthquake-stricken area.

Peking University Children's Psychology Intervention Program and the One Foundation

In response to the earthquake, Peking University psychology professor Dr. Qian Ming-Yi organized partnerships to launch psychosocial recovery projects in the affected province. These started in July 2008 and continued into 2009. The Psychology Department at Peking University in Beijing (PKU) is a well-respected program at the highly prestigious Chinese university. The core project team, consisting of two supervisors, two assistants, a project consultant and financial adviser, framed the project, prepared training lesson plans and designed the interventions services, research projects, and promotion activities (e.g., marketing, press releases, photography, and other information) (Qian et al., 2011).

Graduate students at PKU assisted in the field and in conducting the research. Selected clinical and counseling professionals from the Chinese Psychological Society provided training and supervision. Some German psychologists also participated, to supervise the training and review the project-related documents. The project service groups communicated with the local Bureau of Education to carry out the program and gain their support.

The main donor of the project was the One Foundation, founded by international kung fu movie star and philanthropist Jet Li, in partnership with the Red Cross Society of China. The project in the field had two goals: (1) to provide direct help to young survivors, and (2) to train local professionals, teachers, doctors, and others to provide help. Several components included a public mental health education campaign, a training of helpers in the field, and school-based interventions to help the young students.

The public mental health education campaign involved public lectures and the distribution in project sites of psycho-educational mental health brochures. The material for these brochures and lectures were developed by the Department of Psychology at Peking University. The brochures were in two editions: one was targeted for children in primary, junior high, and high school students, and another was targeted to parents.

In the professional training component, more than 70 people in the earthquake areas were trained. These trainees then conducted 2,054 individual consultations, group counseling involving 2,207 people, and group lectures for 29,511 people. The trainers were from Peking University as well as PhD candidates and local psychologists. These trainers were chosen to be well versed in theoretical knowledge of psychology and practical skills (e.g., cognitive behavioral therapy, psycho-dynamic therapy, and family therapy); trauma knowledge; developmental psychology; family systems; and ethics. The training consisted of a monthly two-day course with daily supervision, based on a social support and psychosocial rehabilitation model (Skills for Psychological Recovery) from the U.S. National PTSD Center. In addition to teaching cognitive-behavioral techniques and art therapy, core skills of problem-solving, rational emotive thinking, social support, and time management were taught.

The school-based intervention, covering 398 schools, was aimed at teaching students how to process emotions and to foster resilience. Lessons, once a month, were integrated as much as possible into the school curriculum, though certain sessions were held after school. The target group for the school intervention was elementary to high school students from 7 to 18 years old. The intervention was held only during the school year; during the summer, trainings were provided to teachers. The group intervention program was based on Skills for Psychological Recovery (SPR), a model designed by the U.S. National PTSD Center. The sessions, held in small groups, focused on problem-solving, rational emotive therapeutic techniques, social support, and time management. Four key modules were: (1) self-introductions, and discussion about the meaning of social support and the importance of psychological education; (2) getting to know each other, involving teaching about differences in strengths and weaknesses, with homework to write a small poem; (3) team building around a task (called "take the tower") and homework to write an essay about the experience; and (4) solving a group problem (e.g., to draw "the willing tree"). Four structured group sessions were given for 50–90 minutes, to groups of students on a voluntary basis, with three-month follow-up sessions, with further group sessions for students identified with psychological distress or problems. Individual sessions of 60 minutes were also offered to those students with identified needs.

The program was considered a success by the team. Students and teachers at the various schools participated in the open classes; parents seemed to welcome the talks; teachers reported value and growth by participating in the program to help themselves and their students; and press materials about the program were reported in the media. Some initial resistance from school officials dissipated, and various teachers were recognized by the Bureau of Education for their new skills in psychological counseling.

Several research projects were carried out. Assessments were done of the trainings, using scales to measure the knowledge of the intervention group versus comparison groups. Assessments of the children were made on criteria including depression and anxiety, a symptom checklist, measurement of PTSD, self-esteem and social support, using scales that were American-devised assessment instruments. Drawings used in art therapy were also reviewed. Results of the school-based interventions revealed positive outcomes and reduced symptom levels. Several papers about the project have been published in Chinese. Results of one study showed that students with higher exposure to the earthquake revealed higher levels of PTSD (Li, Yu, Qian, & Gao, 2011). Another study revealed that short-term group intervention can effectively alleviate depression and post-trauma stress symptoms in junior middle school students over the long term, e.g., in preventing relapse of post-traumatic stress symptoms (Y. Wang, Yang, Wang, Gao, & Qian, 2011).

Lessons learned included the importance of systematic training of local mental health personnel and those in treatment centers (i.e., rescue stations) in order to take advantage of the language and culture of local staff and to ensure ongoing support of local stakeholders at all levels as well as to build capacity and a sustainable psychotherapeutic network. Other lessons learned were the value of a scientific management system and an organizational framework. This includes developing workbooks; implementing a training process with quality controls and assurance of professional standards (assured in the current study by the Chinese Psychological Society); case consultations; a supervision system; and a process to ensure sustainability (e.g., by requiring participants to sign long-term project and service contracts).

The experience further revealed the value of formulating and implementing a long-term (e.g., three-year) training course to train local staff in professional competence, with built-in reviews to adapt to the increasing abilities of the trainees, trainers, and supervisors. In addition, it was determined that training is important, and also possible, for primary and secondary schoolteachers, who gain competence and skills to help students as well as derive benefit from personal growth. As in many projects, long-term research about program outcome is necessary, though often not feasible logistically or financially.

Several limitations were noted, including difficulties in the design of the professional training courses; heavy workload and time constraints of the PKU project participants; restructuring of the school settings (e.g., mergers); and psychological problems of some trainees and teachers who were disaster survivors and thus needed personal healing themselves. While local government newspapers covered the program, and researchers deemed that the program could have paid more attention to garnering more media coverage.

The project was suspended after the first two years, as internal restructuring of the One Foundation prevented donation of the second 3-year financial support.

National Psychological Aid Association (SOS 512)

Psychosocial support after the Sichuan earthquake provided by the National Psychological Aid Association (SOS 512) focused on three main areas. One effort paid special attention to mothers who lost their children during the disaster. A "Mothers' Home" was set up to offer group therapy to the traumatized mothers. In addition, professional helpers in SOS 512 did home visits to talk to these mothers and to check how they were doing. According to a staff member (X. Y. Huang, personal communication, July 5, 2010), many mothers they served were pregnant or had given birth to newborn babies after the disaster. In a second effort, SOS 512 collected donations from people to provide 100 poor children with financial aid, group therapy, and family visitations. Thirdly, SOS 512 established a Mental Health Center in Shiju School where students in need of professional mental health help received psychological counseling.

Amity Foundation

The Amity Foundation is an independent Chinese voluntary organization, and one of the main partners in China of the United Methodist Board of Global Ministries with the objective to help poor areas of the country. Created in 1985, it is headquartered in Nanjing, with offices in Hong Kong. Within hours after the Sichuan Wenchuan earthquake, the organization responded to provide relief (Amity Foundation, 2011) in reconstruction efforts called the "Love Chinese Movement" among Chinese churches, which inspires believers to demonstrate their love in general and for disaster survivors specifically, by service to communities (Sun, 2012). Financially supported in part by the international tax and consulting company, Deloitte, Touche, Tomatsu, these efforts were considered to go beyond just the physical needs of the affected people, showing "Love in Action" by holistically responding also to the emotional, mental and spiritual needs of the people.

The projects are divided into two parts. The first part involves direct psychosocial support provided by experts and volunteers. As part of the intervention, a volunteer team of social work professors and psychologists was sent in May 2008 to provide direct psychosocial support to survivors. They interviewed 1,300 people, conducted psychological assessment and counseling, and provided group counseling to vulnerable groups such as widows, children, the injured, and the disabled in the tent settlements (Amity Foundation, 2008; Carino, personal communication, August 12, 2008). Assessments revealed the need for psychosocial help complicated by the fact that many well-intended but poorly trained volunteers were trying to provide support and counseling in disaster areas, resulting in confusion among survivors. In addition, more than 5,000 children perished in the disaster, causing strong feelings of guilt and grief to surviving parents, which were expected to require a long time for recovery. A series of psychological and social issues were deemed to continue to challenge the earthquake survivors in the ensuing two or three years, and more trained mental health professionals were deemed to be desperately needed to support the traumatized survivors (Amity Foundation, 2008).

The volunteer team also lobbied for shower rooms for the survivors, especially for women, to ensure their safety and hygiene. Noticing that volunteers were disorganized, the team also helped to register and organize volunteer resources to bring about a more effective intervention. In May 2009, cooperating with a professional psychological agency, Amity collected over 11,000 books, which were distributed to survivors (Y. Xie, personal communication, August 17, 2012).

The second part of the support involved community-based projects, which did not provide direct psychological counseling but achieved psychological benefit by working through a community model (T. Carino, personal communication, August 15, 2012). This effort focused on rebuilding a village in the quake zone (Woyun Village in Mainzhu County), which had been received less attention than other affected areas, with the strategy to bring back community spirit and restore a healthy life in the village.

This model relates to a famous Chinese saying that maintains that it is no use to just treat the head when you have a headache, or to just treat the foot when your foot hurts, since the symptom is just a sign that something is wrong, but not that your head or foot specifically is wrong. This means that the root of the problem has to be found and treated; otherwise, any efforts are useless. According to this precept, since the community is an organic system, when a problem occurs with one sector in a system, it is not the problem of the single sector but of the whole system. This systemic perspective also applies to psychosocial support (Y. Xie, personal communication, August 17, 2012).

During the intervention, certain community dynamics were noticed that required addressing in order for the collective group and individuals to heal. The process appeared to progress in stages. Shortly after the event, people were in a state of emergency, feeling afraid, shocked about the heavy damage, and worried about safety, which led some people to focus on themselves to achieve self-healing. Then, they began to work together in what can be considered "community union," to meet their collective urgent survival needs. Once the emergency needs were satisfied, they reverted to self-focus, including worrying about their individual future, which manifested, for example, in caring about equity during the relief process—in other words, comparing what they had been given, received, and gained from the process, to that of the benefits of others.

Another change noted was that before the earthquake, community members helped each other without reward or payment, but after the event, some people asked for reward from their neighbors. Additionally, when Amity suggested choosing the most vulnerable families in the community to help, almost all people were against this suggestion.

To remedy this situation, Amity designed community-based activities, to reset community cooperation, so that people could trust and care about each other again and also could return to their normal life. Six community-based cultural activities were held in Amity's main target community of Woyun Village, namely, the Mid-autumn Evening in September 2008, the couplet contest, the family game contest, the group singing contest, the Lantern Festival in February 2009, and the celebration party for National Day in October 2009. These cultural activities had different objectives. The couplet contest, designed for individuals, helped people individually develop positive feelings and motivation and then to extend these positive feelings to the community; the family game contest and group singing contest, designed for families and village groups, helped increase communication, mutual understanding, and cooperation; the party, designed for the whole community, encouraged more connection and integration at the community level while also providing individuals an opportunity to present themselves as individuals. All these activities fostered individual confidence and creative abilities as well as built community friendship, trust, and cooperation.

The positive results noted by the organizers in comparison to the expenditure required were impressive (T. Carino, personal communication, August 15, 2012). The approach of focusing on the communities to organize these activities, whereby each community member become became a "target" for help and also an implementer to help others, maximized the expenditure of the activities and the projects as a whole. As local communities were facilitated to instigate several cultural activities, the cost of each activity was rather low. Thus, within a reasonable budget, the collective impact of the activities had a considerable effect on boosting individual people's mood as well as the spirit of the community as a whole.

Hong Kong Polytechnic University

Hong Kong Polytechnic University partnered with various other organizations in disaster relief after the earthquake, and maintained an ongoing Sichuan disaster project by establishing a Post-disaster Management and Reconstruction Institute in Chengdu, China, that engaged in many disaster related activities (A. Yuen, personal communication, January 8, 2013). PolyU and Sichuan University made a committed effort to sustain the research, curriculum and service development in disaster preparedness and reconstruction over the long term (S-L. Fok, personal communication, January 18, 2013).

California School of Professional Psychology (CSPP) at Alliant International University Hong Kong Campus

In response to the Sichuan disaster, PsyD graduate students from the Hong Kong–based clinical psychology doctoral program of the California School of Professional Psychology (CSPP) at Alliant International University initiated an effort to provide services and education. Called the 512 Psychological Care Action (512 PCA), the group partnered with Chinese mental health professionals to provide education and services in the affected earthquake region. The Action group was established a month after the earthquake, with support of the CSPP faculty and financial support for traveling expenses from Alliant International University and donors from Hong Kong.

Initial efforts involved visiting the disaster areas to conduct an assessment of needs (M. Chiu, personal communication, January 16, 2013). Direct intervention for survivors that was originally planned, however, posed several challenges, including a language barrier, since most survivors speak the Sichuan dialect not understood by the Mandarin-speaking team; the long-distance travel from Hong Kong to Sichuan was time consuming and costly; and busy graduate study schedules made regular visits for direct services such as traditional psychotherapy impractical.

As a result, the team provided support to local volunteer teams working with the West China Hospital, who were overstretched and suffering burnout, sacrificing their self-care. This was a useful approach, since many of the hundreds of volunteers who had appeared immediately after the earthquake to help had now ceased volunteering and returned to their everyday lives. The remaining volunteers needed psychological support and care, not dissimilar to that of survivors, although the remedies were somewhat different.

The intervention provided weekend retreats for volunteers with the goal to provide quality time for reflection, rest, and fun, and to establish internal connections among volunteers. Examples of exercises included mindful walking to slow down their normal steps; a "raisin exercise," which makes use of the five senses to calm the inner selves; art exercises; and role play for reflection of inner feelings and re-experiencing relationships with their clients (i.e., the survivors).

The retreat resulted in building trust between and among local volunteers and the intervention team that ended up feeling like "a big Chinese family" (M. Chiu, personal communication, January 16, 2013). Volunteers reported feeling refreshed and energetic after the retreat, and they invited the intervention team back for another retreat. Just before the anniversary of the earthquake in early May, the intervention team invited students and faculties of the Hong Kong PsyD program to write supportive cards to all the local volunteers to offer acknowledgement and support of their efforts with the survivors.

Through these interventions, the team's aims were achieved. Lessons were also learned by the organizer, including patience, and observing and being sensitive to the needs of whoever one is trying to support or help, rather than acting from one's own agenda and risking being insensitive or even intrusive. Graduate student participants of the team felt that their efforts were in fact limited, but that they could nonetheless work together as a group to initiate community intervention and change. The fundamental lessons for the team as clinical psychology students were: to focus on using one's heart over one's head in such disasters; to apply what they learned through this valuable experience of participation; to be creative in order to maximize resources; and to be culturally sensitive to the needs of those being served.

The students, along with some professionals, presented a symposium on August 6, 2009, at the 117th Annual Convention of the American Psychological Association in Toronto, Canada, about their work, entitled, "Culturally Relevant Community Disaster Relief: Post-Earthquake Interventions in Sichuan, China" ("Symposium on Post-Earthquake Interventions in Sichuan, China, at the American Psychological Association Convention," 2009). At this symposium, Marie Chiu of Alliant International University described the 512 PCA project, and the success, rewards, and challenges of this community psychoeducation model. She emphasized the need for culturally relevant psychological services at the community level, and the value of partnerships among local and foreign grassroots projects and mental health workers. Dr. Morgan Sammons, dean of the California School of Professional Psychology at Alliant International University, discussed the responsibility of psychologists to provide culturally relevant services in international settings. Panelist Dr. Yanchun Yang from the Department of Psychiatry at West China Hospital in Sichuan Province presented an overview of the psychological impact of the disaster and described the status of interdisciplinary interventions, and Dr. Alvin Dueck from the Fuller Theological Seminary discussed successful models of community reorganization after natural and man-made traumas.

The Methodist Church in Hong Kong

The Methodist Church center of Hong Kong collaborated with East China University of Science and Technology to set up a "community workstation" in November 2008 in the affected earthquake area in November 2008, where social workers could help survivors. Local social work supervisors were sent to coordinate the overall project, supervise local social workers, and provide training for church members, social workers, and students to serve as volunteers at the service site. The services, supported by the local government starting in February 2009, included: home visits to the elderly, disabled, and disadvantaged and single-parent families; individual case management for psychological, emotional, and medical needs; elderly services with activities and groups including exercises, making dumplings together, and free medical services; services for the disabled's special needs, improving their living environment, and helping them to establish social support; services for children and teenagers with academic support and creative activities such as "Little Designer," story drawing, sports competition, group games, and teenage volunteer workshops; and services for women. The convener of the project mentioned above of the California School of Professional Psychology (CSPP) at Alliant International University Hong Kong campus, Marie Chiu, subsequently joined the staff of the Methodist Church in Hong Kong as a clinical psychologist. As part of the church's commitment to continue psychosocial recovery years after the disaster, she planned further needs assessments and trainings in the earthquake affected area, including training local workers and volunteers on how to handle traumatic cases (M. Chiu, personal communication, January 19, 2013).

Psycho-Art Therapy Association

The Psycho-Art Therapy Association is comprised of a group of people from varied disciplines, including social workers, therapists, counselors, psychologists, registered nurses, coaches, and university lecturers dedicated to the use of art to improve mental health and well-being. Their mission is to serve society locally as well as internationally by offering therapy, counseling, and adventure-based training to promote positive psychology and to transform lives. The association is supported by noted art therapists Dr. Cathy Malchiodi and Cornelia Elbrecht, Australian clinical psychologist Dr. Janet Leigh Hayes, and artist Gaylord Chan, as well as professors from the Faculty of Medicine of Chinese University of Hong Kong and professional members of the Hong Kong Clinical Psychology Association.

In response to the earthquake, the association collaborated with Caring for Next Generation Foundation Association (a Chinese charitable organization), Sichuan University, and local psychiatric hospitals to present psychological workshops and trauma-informed training courses to groups of therapists and counselors in Sichuan, in efforts to extend professional counseling services to those in need and for these trained personnel to carry out more in-depth and regular psychological intervention. Art therapist and trauma counselor Monica Wong led a group of therapists to regularly visit families located in the core affected earthquake areas. In addition, the association was invited by the psychiatric hospital in Sichuan to set up a temporary clinic to carry out therapeutic sessions with patients as well as trainings for therapists recruited in Sichuan to continue the work of the association. The project was planned for a five-year period; however, as another earthquake occurred in April 2013 in Ya'an Sichuan, the five-year plan was prolonged. Until the time of this writing, the association has still been providing services in Sichuan, since 2008 (Wong, personal communication, April 3, 2015). Others from local areas and overseas were welcomed to participate, and to e-mail monicahhwong@yahoo.com.hk.

DISCUSSION AND LESSONS LEARNED

This report supports the value, and challenges, of collating varied interventions after a major natural disaster. Overall, it highlights the importance for organizations to maintain, and make public, detailed records about their psychosocial interventions in the aftermath of such events. Such reporting can help organizations review their activities as well as benefit the field at large.

Given the scope of the devastation like that of the Sichuan earthquake, many interventions can be accommodated. However, this report reveals some overlap in the nature and intent of services provided and thus the value of coordinated and centralized efforts. Such a lack of comprehensive recovery efforts has been pointed out to potentially lead to confusion for survivors, organizations, local as well as national governments, and all stakeholders. Communication and exchange about recovery efforts are also valuable, though not realized widely enough; while such sharing takes place at various large conferences, like those outlined above for the IACMSP, WCP, or the American Psychological Association, the content of presentations at other lesser-known or smaller gatherings is not easily accessible to broader interested audiences.

Assembling such a meta-report as the present one required considerable effort and encountered many challenges in tracking down organizations' and individuals' e-mails and phone numbers, making contacts, and collecting and fact-checking details multiple times, even to the last minute of submitting this chapter. In several cases, translations were necessary of original papers or websites needed for research that were in the Chinese language, facilitated by coauthors of this chapter. Much of the present reports evolved from the first author's personal contacts, referrals, and personal experiences collaborating with individuals and organizations in the trauma recovery field. Fortunately, connections were facilitated by the fact that the first author had spent many years in China doing trainings and workshops and making presentations at conferences on various topics related to counseling, including trauma recovery, as well as participating in an earthquake recovery mission with Chinese colleagues. Undoubtedly, more projects than those reported here were launched but not known at the time of this writing.

This report also suggests the value of standardization of logistics, interventions, and research techniques and methodologies, while still allowing for individual creative efforts and cultural specificity.

Local and International Contributions

The reports in this review suggest that despite the stigma and lack of sufficient professional psychological resources in China, advances are being made, both in the field of psychology in general, and in disaster recovery in particular (Chang, Cao, Shi, Wang, & Qian, 2012). Bolstering this progress, international cooperation, as shown in the above examples, has added value and scope to local projects. Given the number of international organizations presented here, the interest and commitment of the global community is evident, in responding to needs of a particular country suffering from a natural disaster. While assistance from international NGOs, charitable groups and humanitarian agencies has sometimes been critiqued (Wickramage, 2006), the value of, and appreciation for, such international cooperation is becoming increasingly recognized in this contemporary world when such events on a large scale are threatening many countries worldwide and especially when resources of a country are limited. Such cooperation also implements the goal of global, multi-stakeholder partnerships called for in the Sustainable Development Goals. In fact, more partners can valuably be brought together, in order to maximize the impact of these projects, and certainly to provide needed funding that is required for such programs to be sustainable. In this regard, it is noted that several projects described above did not achieve their intended reach, or failed to continue on a sustainable basis, due to lack of needed funding.

Much emphasis has rightfully been placed on cultural sensitivity in disaster relief, with caution about intervention from foreign actors. Certainly any intervention should be culturally sensitive and appropriate. Psychosocial support and psychotherapy are still very new concepts in countries like China, so people in disaster areas might be suspicious of the effectiveness of psychotherapy in general, and Western approaches in particular, for recovery; thus, consideration is required of cultural and contextual factors while providing psychosocial support work in disaster-affected regions (Médecins Sans Frontières Australia, 2009). Programs outlined above have been cultural-sensitive, while some also integrate techniques from Eastern and Western practice. For example, the Peking University intervention used a model developed in the United States, and

IAAP-CAAP combined Jungian analytical psychology with the more traditional approach of the Chinese culture psychology of the heart and incorporating the music of "Qiang," an ethnical minority in Sichuan (Shen, 2009). Mercy Malaysia asks its staff to enhance their understanding and sensitivity to local customs and folkways (Mercy Malaysia, 2009a), and the International Red Cross and Red Crescent Societies adapted and translated materials from English to fit the Chinese context (International Federation of Red Cross and Red Crescent Societies, 2012b). Reports in this chapter support that foreign-based organizations, especially in partnership with local organizations, can make major contributions that might otherwise not be possible (Save the Children, n.d.). East and West stakeholders can valuably collaborate in recovery efforts benefiting survivors. In cases, translators have functioned effectively, even to communicate complex or delicate psychological techniques and training processes.

The extent and nature of the intervention programs in this chapter suggests that such assistance was well received in China despite some lingering unfamiliarity with psychology and stigmatization of mental health services. Efforts still reasonably and appropriately center on education and simple supportive interventions for the public and volunteer trainees, but are expanding to an increasing number of volunteers learning increasingly sophisticated techniques in train-the-trainer models, with ongoing supervision.

Variety of Specific Intervention Programs

The range of programs in this report reveals wide differences in many aspects of interventions, including features like the size of the mission (e.g., from a sole person or two members to large teams), the specific program techniques, targeted population, length and extent of services provided, and sources of funding. Notably, some indigenous Chinese programs emphasize the importance of "heart" (e.g., the "Garden of Heart and Soul"), consistent with the view that caring and rapport between helper and client is more predictive of positive outcome than specific techniques or discipline. Nevertheless, the variety of techniques represented in this report suggests that the field of psychological first aid and psychosocial support would benefit from comprehensive manuals of interventions and research methods, from which projects can draw in the course of planning programs and outcome research.

Training

The organizations discussed in this chapter also underscore the importance of training programs for all workers, professionals, and volunteers who can help survivors. Many programs reported here employ the train-the-trainers model, an approach that represents best practices in the aftermath of disaster and is a gold standard in psychological first aid, psychosocial support, and humanitarian interventions, to build local capacity and enable sustainability. In many cases, including in China, trained professionals are in short supply (Zhiling, 2008). Yet, both professionals and nonprofessionals are necessary for any comprehensive provision of mental health services, given the considerable immediate and ongoing psychosocial needs of survivors, and that the number of available trained health professionals, caregivers and volunteers are usually insufficient to provide such support.

To fulfill this need, many international NGOs provide special training not only to mental health professionals and medical staff, but also to caregivers and nondegree volunteers. Organizations cited here, such as MSF, AAMH, IAAP-CAAP, Mercy Corps, Beijing UFH, and the Katherine A. Kendall Institute, all address the need of providing such training. Such training and delivery of services need to follow standardized guidelines to be monitored and effective. An important manual for such use is the *Guidelines for Interventions on Mental Health and Psychosocial Support in Emergency Settings* (Interagency Standing Committee, 2008) based on distinct levels. These guidelines outline that while many survivors may initially suffer cognitive, emotional, behavioral, and spiritual symptoms, many are resilient and can recover with only minimal intervention, and that only a percentage of survivors suffer from posttraumatic stress conditions that require specialized treatment.

Importance of Volunteers

Many projects in this report harness the help of volunteers. In the absence of trained professionals after natural disasters, either due to a paucity of professionals in general or to many professionals having died in the tragedy, volunteers can be trained to deliver support using simple techniques that can be taught by skilled counselors. These volunteers (e.g., students, sports coaches, and teachers) can then train others in the community, allowing for capacity-building and sustainability of healing efforts. Communities often have a pool of such people willing to help others, and who have the necessary personality characteristics such as caring and listening skills. These community volunteers, who have been called "comforters" in a training intervention (Kuriansky & Jean-Charles, 2012), can be trained to offer comfort and support, ranging from simple acts like offering water, to facilitating elementary psychosocial techniques to help survivors feel safe, reduce stress, accept feelings, recapture self-confidence, and reconnect to others. The importance of such volunteers in a post-disaster psychosocial recovery has been shown in the author's experience in Sri Lanka after the 2004 tsunami there, and in Haiti after the 2010 earthquake, where a study of volunteers in a train-the-trainers project also revealed the positive impact of helping on the helpers as well as on the recipients of their help (for more on this study, see Chapter 9 in this volume [Kuriansky et al., 2015]). Many organizations are showing the value of engaging volunteers to increase access to health services in emergencies and in all aspects of development (Forum, 2014, n.d.; International Federation of Red Cross and Red Crescent Societies, 2011; United Nations Volunteers, 2014; VSO International and The Institute of Development Studies, 2014).

Populations Served

Since children have been found to be particularly affected by disasters both in the immediate and long term, many aid projects pay special attention to this age group. This is evidenced by UNICEF's "Child Friendly Spaces," Oxfam's "community-based participatory projects," and Mercy Corps' "Comfort for Kids" and "Moving Forward," all aimed at helping children cope.

Some programs also "help the helpers" by providing volunteers who are trained to help survivors to also help themselves. For example, the CHERP program paid specific attention to teaching trainees about self-care and providing volunteer trainees, as well as team members themselves, with the same opportunities as offered to survivors to have personal attention and treatment by skilled clinical trainers.

The Importance of Psychological Intervention in China

This review of post-disaster interventions in China in response to a particular tragic event offers a unique perspective on the status of psychology and specific practices of post-disaster psychosocial aid in China. Psychological counseling in general has been developing as a profession in China, although up until 2008, at the time of the Sichuan earthquake, there were still only 10,000 psychological counselors in the country with a population of millions (Wickramage, 2006; Yue, 2000). Well-founded psychological principles and ideas about disaster recovery and resilience are also developing (Qian, Smith, Chen, & Xia, 2002; Satapathy & Bhadra, 2009). However, some stigmatization of mental health services persists. Pressing needs of mental health distress after such disasters can facilitate the acceptance of counseling, and the development of appropriate approaches, especially in the rural and less educated regions affected by natural disasters (for example, in Sichuan and subsequently in Yushu).

The government of China is apparently also recognizing the importance of psychological care post disaster. Even as far back as 2002, the Ministry of Health began mandating that local governments should provide mental health care for survivors of large-scale disasters, suggesting that 50 percent of survivors should be able to access psychological first aid (Hu & Cui, 2008; Zhang & Wang, 2008). Since research notes the unmet needs of survivors, it is recommended that such mandates be monitored, with full participation by local governments.

Local governments should then pool knowledge and resources to collaborate and cooperate in large-scale mental health programs designed for risk reduction as well as recovery. This action would be consistent with, and supported by, the Sendai Framework for Disaster Risk Reduction.

Relevance to International Agreements

The importance of psychosocial support, and of mental health and well-being, concepts highly relevant to the interventions in this chapter, is supported in two major international agreements that define the period of time from 2015 to 2030, and that are referred to in the beginning of this chapter. The first is the Sendai Framework for Disaster Risk Reduction, agreed to by governments of the world at the World Conference on Disaster Risk Reduction held in Sendai, Japan during March 14–18, 2015. Included among the action priorities is to "enhance recovery schemes to provide psychosocial support and mental health services for all people in need" (UNISDR, 2015a, para 30[o]). This priority provides an important foundation for projects targeting psychological resilience in the aftermath of disasters.

The second is the Sustainable Development Goals (SDGs) that sets the global agenda, agreed to by member states (governments) of the United Nations in September 2015, to achieve over the period of the years 2015–2030. Goal 3 states to "ensure healthy lives and promote well-being for all at all ages" and Target 3.4 specifies, to "promote mental health and well-being." This provides further underpinning for programs described above, to be supported by policy and even potential funding. Importantly, another goal (#17) is to create multi-stakeholder partnerships, meaning cooperation of various parties who have common interest in achieving an outcome that is deemed essential to achieve the other goals. Literature about the psychological sequelae of natural disasters notes the need for such coordination of recovery efforts.

Resilience and Well-Being

Issues of disaster recovery and risk reduction need to be considered inextricably in the context of resilience and well-being. Ultimately, the extent and value of the projects reported here reveal the importance of considering psychosocial resilience-building in the SDGs and the Sendai Framework. It is important that "resilience" be considered to extend beyond rebuilding infrastructure and basic structures, as it is currently defined in the Sendai Framework (UNISDR, 2015a, p. 2, footnote 2), and that the definition be expanded to include the psychosocial dimension. This point is central to the advocacy of the first author, in her role as chair of the Psychology Coalition of Non-governmental Organizations accredited with the Economic and Social Council of the United Nations, in collaboration with the Ambassador of Palau to the UN, Dr. Caleb Otto, a public health physician

(Kuriansky & Okorodudu, 2014; Otto, Kuriansky, & Okorodudu, 2014). Intensive advocacy resulting from this partnership led to the successful inclusion of mental health and well-being in the SDGs (Forman, 2014). This inclusion, coupled with the Sendai Framework priority, bodes well for the future of national and international efforts such as those described in this chapter.

Encouraging citizens to take an active part in their recovery, instead of just receiving help from others, is important for their resilience and achieving the sense of well-being, self-esteem, self-efficacy, and personal empowerment that is essential for recovery, healing, and growth. This is important for children, as shown in a project described above whereby children took increasing responsibility in healing activities (Zeng & Silverstein, 2011), and has also been shown in the case of involving young citizens in community development (Hart, 2008).

Community-Rebuilding and Community Resilience

The importance of community capacity-building and resilience in disaster recovery and risk reduction is gaining increasing prominence (Kuriansky, 2012d; see also Chapter 8 [Davis & Dumpson, 2015], Chapter 9 [Kuriansky et al., 2015], and Chapter 20 [Nemeth, Hamilton, & Kuriansky, 2015] in this volume). Interventions that facilitate community-rebuilding are essential in the wake of natural disasters that fracture familial and social systems. Community-building is an effective way to help citizens help each other cope with loss and grief, especially when counseling is needed but experts are not available. Group rituals and traditional practices are particularly helpful, as were incorporated in some programs described above. The Amity Foundation project described above is an example of the healing effect of community programs that bring people together to share challenges but also to celebrate in enlivening activities (T. Carino, personal communication, August 15, 2012). Such approaches strengthen survivors' relationships, reestablish trust in each other and hopefully in their leaders and government, and build "community resilience," which make recovery more likely to be sustainable.

Sustainability

The Sustainable Development Goals agreed upon by nations of the world to reach by 2030, by their very name, require achievement of its three pillars—social development, economic growth, and environmental protection—and that these achievements be sustainable (Thwink.org, 2014). Sustainability requires a healthy ecosystem in the present as well as over time. Indisputably, disaster recovery on all levels, including psychosocial, is a long-term process. To be truly sustainable, intervention and support must follow a long-term plan.

As many of the above projects have discovered, despite the best of intentions and efforts, achieving sustainability faces major challenges. Many programs are active only for a certain period of time; for example, the CHERP American trainers came to the region five times over a one-year period until the program ended due to lack of funding and availability of trainers. Understandably, few professionals can suspend their work responsibilities to spend extended periods of time in an affected area. A valuable solution involves training community volunteers, who can then train others, with intermittent supervision, an approach the first author of this chapter has found viable and effective in Haiti (see Chapter 9 [Kuriansky et al., 2015]). A system to readily and easily identify and connect helpers, and all actors, in cases of emergency, would facilitate the launch and sustainability of initiatives.

Sustainability of interventions is particularly important given research about the long-term emotional effects of disaster, as documented above. This is especially relevant given anniversary reactions when feelings are triggered on dates associated with the trauma for many subsequent years, for children as well as adults (Kuriansky, 2012f, 2012g, 2012h, 2013e, 2013f; Kuriansky & Nemeth, 2013).

Funding

Programs reported here have been funded on varying scales, but lack of financial backing remains a serious limitation, especially when it comes to providing psychosocial support. Certainly NGOs can benefit from improved fund-raising skills (Phoofolo, Kokoris, & Kuriansky, 2011). While the immediacy of a disaster often necessitates action without waiting for funding, smaller, lesser-known groups may not be able to mobilize donations quickly enough, in comparison to larger, already-funded organizations that can reallocate resources. An impediment to obtaining funding is that donors are more prone to support projects that yield obvious "hard" outcomes, like the numbers of homes built, in comparison to projects that target emotions and have "softer" measures, like the number of counseling sessions provided. Solutions can include partnerships of smaller grassroots groups or with larger well-funded organizations, as mentioned above, or building emergency funding into already existing projects whereby monies can be diverted when needed.

Some fund-raisers for the Sichuan earthquake have proved successful, as evidenced by large sums of money raised by the Jet Li One Foundation, including sources like Northwest Airlines and a Swedish food company. These have been done immediately after the disaster and on one-year anniversaries but need to be ongoing, especially when public interest and news about the event wanes.

Need for Research

Few interventions reported here were subjected to scientific evaluation of their effectiveness. This is understandable, given lack of staff, opportunity, funding for research, and priority placed on provision of basic needs. Admittedly, carrying out scientific research designs are often not practical, possible, or advisable when survivors need services and not being subjected to data collection.

However, such assessments are necessary to establish best practices, and should include periodic follow-up evaluations. Research methodologies should be part of disaster preparedness planning

Harnessing the Media

While the media has often been criticized in post-disaster situations for being intrusive or exploitative, there are positive ways media can be harnessed (Kuriansky, 2005, 2009; Miles & Morse, 2007). In her role as a journalist as well as a psychologist and traumatologist providing psychological first aid in post-disaster situations worldwide, the first author has many personal experiences of the value of the media as a partner in communicating with the public about disaster and in the healing process (*Dr.Judy on CCTV*, 2011; Kuriansky, 1990; 2007d, 2008d, 2009, 2012b, 2013a, 2013f; Masangkay, 2015).

Presentations on traditional media (television and radio) are highly valuable for public education, awareness-raising and advice. Yet mass media was used in only a few of the above psychosocial programs, or was planned but did not have the desired wide impact. For example, the Peking University Psychology Department intervention (described above) included promotion activities (e.g., marketing, press releases, photography, and pamphlet distribution), and was reported in local government newspapers, but researchers noted that the program sustainability would have benefited from wider media coverage.

The PCCN project described above is an example of using multimedia platforms to reach a broad public to create awareness about mental health needs, to offer messages of support, and to alert volunteers about how to help. Methods included broadcasting on radio programs, producing a specially targeted video and accompanying book about healing, and holding public events.

After the Sichuan earthquake, the first author and Dr. Rob Blinn from the CHERP project described above were interviewed on television in China (CCTV-9) on the popular hourlong, English-speaking *Dialogue* show, originally aired live on October 14, 2008, to discuss emotional reactions to a disaster, describe programs for psychosocial aid, and demonstrate simple techniques that can help survivors and the general public. Given the station's decision that the information was valuable, the program was reaired several times. The first author further appeared on CCTV several times thereafter about healing from other disasters, including the 2011 tsunami-earthquake in Japan. She has also written opinion articles posted on mainstream websites about healing from natural disasters.

Use of Technology

Technology offers a solution to the problem of lack of locally available professional help. The Internet provides a valuable tool for networking about disasters. Several attempts were made by various groups to use Internet technology to create a consortium of experts on disaster recovery after the Sichuan earthquake. Some were successful in connecting interested and/or experienced trainers and volunteers; while others were not able to obtain a wide enough distribution or sustain connectivity, as described in greater detail below. Some sites offered information, while others were more active in soliciting volunteers willing to actively intervene. A centralized clearinghouse for both education and intervention would be useful, so all interested individuals and groups can interact from one reliable and credible source.

Listservs and websites are valuable modes to connect disaster recovery personnel. One example is the website PreventionWeb.net, managed by the UN International Strategy for Disaster Risk Reduction (UNISDR) in Geneva. On August 14, 2012, an e-mail was sent through various professional channels announcing the Post-2015 Framework for Disaster Risk Reduction: Online Dialogues, as part of the consultations on a post-2015 framework for disaster risk reduction. The first round of online dialogues, from August 27 to November 30, 2012, was part of a series of online consultations that UNISDR arranged to take place before the World Conference on Disaster Reduction in March 2015 in Japan, whereby people were invited to contribute their views on the new post-2015 framework for disaster risk reduction (UNISDR, n.d.) Organizations posted information and tip sheets about disaster interventions. The first author continues to be involved in these efforts at the United Nations. Several international summits about climate change were held around the world including in Lima, Peru, in December 2014, and in Sendai, Japan, in March 2015, with an Ignite Stage forum and concurrent Children and Youth Forum at which the first author presented on panels and in workshops (Masangkay, 2015; UNISDR, 2015b) and delivered a statement (Kuriansky, 2015). This conference led to a summit in Paris, France, in December 2015, for governments to reach agreements about action to combat the impact of climate change and to insure environmental protection (see Chapter 17 of this volume [Kuriansky, LeMay & Kumar, 2015]).

Other efforts are individual initiatives, on specialty websites or listservs, making them more difficult to locate even through searches on Google. As a result, central sites and sources are helpful, as the preventionweb.net, to network for the exchange of information and efforts about disasters and opportunities to serve.

Postings of videos on YouTube about environmental disasters serve to visually evoke awareness and emotional reactions about the needs and suffering of survivors. For example, a video by the One Foundation, which partnered with Peking University psychology department described above, shows images set to music, of devastation and people working together collectively and helping each other in reconstruction, emphasizing community bonding that is healing (Official Jet Li Website, 2009). The videos document the foundation's visits to the earthquake region and efforts to bring people together to help those in need under the theme of "One Foundation, One Family." The foundation raised $17.5 million toward the earthquake relief efforts.

Future efforts should take advantage of all forms of media, more of which are now available, through social media, which allows for wide and instant distribution of messages (e.g., through Twitter), connectivity (e.g., through sites like Facebook) and visual displays (e.g., through YouTube video postings, and photo album postings on sites like Tumblr and Picasa). Additionally, cell phones, apps, and other devices, can be harnessed to provide education, training and supervision, as described in Chapter 8 in this volume (Davis & Dumpson, 2015).

Internet-based psychological treatments (e-therapy) have been developed to target a range of psychological conditions, including trauma. In Australia, the National e-Therapy Centre has developed effective therapist-assisted programs for anxiety disorders, inclusive of post-traumatic stress disorder, which have used postgraduate psychology students as therapists in order to train them in evidence-based approaches to psychological treatment. Such programs have been found to be effective (Klein, Meyer, Austin, & Kyrios, 2011; Klein et al., 2009; Klein et al., 2010).

With the provision of necessary equipment, trainings can be done by platforms such as Skype or Google Groups, allowing interchange, side chats, and posting information on common boards or "basecamps." Free conference-calling services can also be used for distant connections among a large number of agents.

Celebrity Power

Star power has long been harnessed in the United States to raise finds and awareness after tragedies. Celebrities from all entertainment fields (e.g., movies and music) took to the airwaves in telethons and music concert extravaganzas after events like the 2004 Asian tsunami, and the 2012 Superstorm Sandy in the New York City tristate area (Kuriansky, 2013c). Survivors of disaster appreciate when famous names (especially those locally born) come to town to offer support. Japanese superstar rock musician Shinji Harada participated in the mission the first author implemented in Sendai, Japan, after the tsunami/earthquake there, performing songs integrated into the program of simple psychosocial techniques, much to the delight of both children and adult survivors (Kuriansky, 2012d, 2013b); Harada continued to do charity concerts in the affected area. After the Sichuan earthquake, Jet Li headlined many fund-raising efforts and events, drawing attention to the needs of survivors. Given the popularity of such efforts, and the wide media coverage they attract, such efforts can usefully be harnessed to support psychosocial needs and programs. One such effort was by fashion designer icon Donatella Versace, who partnered her fashion show with Li's One Foundation, featuring an exclusive tour to Sichuan to visit their jointly financed children's center in the Shuimo Elementary School in Wenchuan, Sanjiang County, called the Versace One Children's Centre, dedicated to providing post-trauma psychological therapy for children and families. The fund-raising fashion gala, a first in China, was attended by over 800 top Chinese and Asian celebrities, socialites, officials, and business leaders; a related press conference in Beijing drew impressive media coverage by over 150 journalists. The evening raised 960,000 RMB (over US$150,000) for Sichuan earthquake victims, which was used to open a second Versace One Children's Centre. This model shows how celebrity spokespeople can be valuable used in psychosocial recovery efforts.

Jet Li said of the project, "The greatest joy in life is being able to help others find happiness . . . Now with the opening of the second children's centre, we will be able to give even more children the caring attention they deserve" (Edipresse Media, 2009). "When you take care of the soul," said Versace, "that's something the child keeps forever" (Pesta, 2009). An art therapy project was launched as follow-up and further fund-raising, with Versace collaborating with New York's Whitney Museum of Art for 900 Chinese children and 500 American children drawing on canvas tote bags carried by runway models in Milan's Fashion Week and then being sold.

LIMITATIONS

Given the challenges in assembling details about the projects described above, much more could probably be known about specific techniques and logistics of the various programs. Undoubtedly, many other initiatives were launched, which would have added to this report's comprehensiveness. A centralized place for such documentation would be useful. Several such efforts were tried. For example, a group of students and staff at Yale Medical School gathered informally and sent out an e-mail to invite interested people to contribute to a website that would be a central repository for information about recovery efforts. Unfortunately, this promising effort was neither successful nor continued. In another effort, a training in the IASC guidelines was held in New York by staff from Geneva WHO, with participants invited to register on a database, which unfortunately did not lead to ongoing contact. Further, an effort by students attending a major university in New York to create a network for other students wanting to participate in recovery efforts after the Haiti earthquake also dissipated, in part due to lack of support by the university. The students had met and initiated the project after a conference with distinguished disaster experts from various disciplines, held at the university. Other initiatives to create a coalition of mental health professionals after the Haiti earthquake also dissolved when participants got involved in individual efforts and collaborated with other organizations.

This report also is time-limited. It represents efforts through the beginning of 2013, with some selected updating until the final submission of this volume for publication. Much can be done to follow up these projects and to identify others. Formal reports were available only for some projects, in particular those from multinational aid organizations; but even those were not always intensive regarding specifics about the psychosocial programming, or documentation about outcomes. Factors limiting comparisons of projects include that agencies use different procedures, frameworks and follow-up periods for both their interventions and their reporting (Alexander, 2005).

RECOMMENDATIONS

The contributions made by these efforts in psychosocial disaster relief work are considerable, but improvements can be made to better fulfill the psychosocial needs of these and other survivors of disaster (Liu, Wu, & Zhang, 2011). Increased collaboration is advisable, among humanitarian aid groups, local government, and other stakeholders, such as has been accomplished in some projects described above. Such collaboration can help groups providing aid to achieve a better assessment about the overall conditions and psychosocial needs in the disaster areas. In addition, while each aid organization can have a unique focus and expertise, pooling resources, learning from one another, and creating partnerships can improve the quality of work, better address the needs of those served, and maximize financial support. Collaboration has been shown to increase intercultural understanding among diverse groups (Kuriansky, 2011b), which can further facilitate community cohesion that ameliorates the experience of trauma.

Interventions reported here involved partnerships among concerned individuals and groups; in some cases, multiple organizations and actors came together. The fact that such partnerships are crucial to ensure the effectiveness of programs, and that some arrangements are made in the midst of the emergency, suggests the value of organizing such connections during nonemergency times, for effective disaster preparedness. This is particularly important when it comes to funding, as some interventions reported above were prematurely terminated due to lack of funding. Psychosocial services are too commonly underfinanced, suggesting the need for identifying more sources for such support. Expanded multi-stakeholder partnerships, including significant participation of the private sector, would enhance the effectiveness and sustainability of these interventions.

Given the value of multi-stakeholder partnerships, and given that foreign interveners must have partner organizations "on the ground" to be effective, a database of local and international groups and a system to match interests and resources would be valuable. School systems and local community and religious organizations are good entryways into identifying partnerships as they are usually accessible and in need. Smaller groups can usefully merge together, or with larger multinational organizations, to maximize their individual human and financial capital; and in doing so, negotiate needs for credit or control.

Of course, the larger the aid organization, the more the resources that can be provided, and thus, the more that can be accomplished. However, this report includes some interventions initiated and implemented by individuals, which, in the case of such a large-scale disaster, can be helpful. For example, the two-woman psychiatrist team from Yale and the one-woman efforts of the Yeshiva graduate student highlight the valuable contributions of individuals taking initiative. Further, while critics have charged that international actors should not intervene in disasters, the projects reported above reveal that foreigners can be valuable in providing assistance, mobilizing local resources, and implementing important interventions in the case of such large-scale disasters.

Aid organizations are advised to take a proactive approach, focusing on disaster preparedness, guiding citizens and communities as well as governments, in reducing risk, preparing for disasters, and preventing serious consequences. For example, Mercy Malaysia's Total Disaster Risk Management model is divided into two phases: the pre-disaster phase (prevention/mitigation and preparedness) and the post-disaster phase (response and recovery) (Mercy Malaysia, 2009a). A useful approach, such as that of the International Red Cross and Red Crescent Societies, encourages all community members to play an active role in disaster preparedness as well as in recovery efforts (International Federation of Red Cross and Red Crescent Societies, 2012b).

CONCLUSIONS

This report underscores the importance and value of providing comprehensive psychosocial support after a disaster, both immediately and over a long term, to adequately address needs of survivors and the general public, and to prepare for any future tragic events. With this principle in mind, this review of psychosocial interventions after the Sichuan earthquake in China reveals the value of such a comprehensive documentation and serves as a model for similar efforts. A report of this nature serves several important purposes, by increasing professional and public awareness and understanding of disaster management, and motivating more stakeholders to contribute to psychosocial support in disaster circumstances worldwide. Such an examination also has considerable public health implications, since psychosocial interventions are being increasingly integrated into international humanitarian aid programs and primary medical care (Morris, Van Ommeren, Belfer, Saxena, & Saraceno, 2007).

The interventions in this one event—the Sichuan earthquake—even without being inclusive of all projects that might have taken place, reveals the extent and variations of efforts, with many similarities but also some differences in theory, techniques, and focus. This raises awareness about the potential value of standardized methodology and charts to compare approaches and outcomes on uniform dimensions, based on consistent record-keeping and measurements.

Cooperation, communication, and collaboration among project managers, while idealistic and perhaps complicated, would be useful, to plan and coordinate recovery efforts and to maximize the opportunities for sustainability. Also useful would be a centralized source for information about projects and resources (e.g., people available for deployment, funding sources, best practices, intervention models, and guidelines). Such cooperation would require putting aside competitiveness for resources. Coordination also needs to allow for cultural specificity and creativity. Research about interventions, such as that initiated by Peking University described above, would provide a valuable complement to already-existing extensive research about symptomotology.

The range of interventions—by indigenous Chinese professionals as well as by international agents, and by professionals as well as concerned lay individuals—indicates the extent of resources that can be mobilized for disaster recovery, resilience-building, and preparedness.

The psychosocial interventions reported here regarding China show that despite some stigma about mental illness that still exists in this country, as well as inadequate resources to serve the vast population, advances have been made in the field of counseling, psychology, and psychological first aid. These efforts have contributed to the science and practice of psychology, to mental health and well-being, and to disaster recovery and risk reduction, from which the global community can benefit.

This report can serve as the basis for a more comprehensive review of organizations involved in the earthquake recovery efforts in China as well as in other countries impacted by environmental traumas. Such reports would include details of intervention periods, locations and number of survivors served, funding sources, logistics, techniques applied, and research findings. A meta-analysis of such projects would be a valuable extension of this present type of review, which provides valuable information and perspectives upon which to develop psychosocial resilience and disaster preparedness planning and policies crucial in the process of achieving citizen and community well-being, environmental protection, and sustainable development.

ACKNOWLEDGMENTS

The authors thank all the participating organizations and individuals who gave their time and talent to help in this crisis, and all the survivors for their courage and resiliency.

REFERENCES

Alexander, D. (2005). Early mental health intervention after disasters. *Advances in Psychiatric Treatment, 11*(1), 12–18.

Amity Foundation. (2008). China: Report on Amity's Relief Work in Sichuan Earth-quake. *ReliefWeb*. Retrieved April 22, 2015, from http://css.static.reliefweb.int/report/china/china-report-amitys-relief-work-sichuan-earthquake

Amity Foundation. (2011). Remembering the Sichuan earthquake 2008. *ReliefWeb*. Retrieved April 22, 2015, from http://reliefweb.int/report/china/remembering-sichuan-earthquake-2008

Asia Australia Mental Health. (n.d.). *Protecting children in disasters (China)*. Retrieved April 22, 2015, from http://aamh.edu.au/protecting-children-in-disasters-china/

Burks, R. (2009). Healing the future. *Mercy Corps*. Retrieved August 24, 2014, from http://www.mercycorps.org/articles/china/healing-future

Chan, C. L. W., Wang, C-W., Ho, A. H., Qu, Z. Y., Wang, X. Y., Ran, M. S., . . . Zhang, X. L. (2012). Symptoms of posttraumatic stress disorder and depression among bereaved and non-bereaved survivors following the 2008 Sichuan earthquake. *Journal of Anxiety Disorders, 26*(6), 673–679.

Chan, L., Wang, C-W., Qu, Z., Lu, B. Q., Ran, M-S., Ho, A. H. Y., . . . Zhang, X. (2011). Posttraumatic stress disorder symptoms among adult survivors of the 2008 Sichuan earthquake in China. *Trauma Stress, 24*(3), 295–302.

Chang, D. F., Cao, Y-P., Shi, Q., Wang, C., & Qian, M. (2012). Serving 1.3 billion Chinese. The professionalization of counseling and psychotherapy in China. In R. Moodley, U. P. Gielen, & R. Wu (Eds.), *Handbook of counseling and psychotherapy in an international context* (pp. 182–192). New York: Routledge.

Chenghou, C., & Heyong, S. (2010). "Garden of the Heart-Soul" in the Earthquake Area of China. *Jung Journal: Culture & Psyche, 4*(2), 5–15.

Davis, D., & Dumpson, D. (2015). Empowerment in African Americans' responses to global climate change and environmental racism through an integrative bio-interpersonal/music-based approach. In D. G. Nemeth & J. Kuriansky (Eds.), *Ecopsychology: Advances from the intersection of psychology and environmental protection*, Volume 2 (pp. 105–133). Santa Barbara, CA: ABC-CLIO.

Deng, M-Y. (2008a). Collected works of psychological assistance in Sichuan Great Earth-quake. *Chinese Psychology and Health Times (CPHT-5), 1*(5): 1–62 (in Chinese). Retrieved April 6, 2015, from http://blog.sina.com.cn/s/blog_5168ec1b0100c5mv.html

Deng, M-Y. (2008b). Collected works of psychological assistance in Sichuan Great Earth-quake II. *Chinese Psychology and Health Times (CPHT-6), 1*(6): 1–48 (in Chinese). Retrieved April 6, 2015, from http://blog.sina.com.cn/s/blog_5168ec1b0100c5mw.html

Deng, M-Y. (2008c). First International Forum for Psycho Aid of "5.12" Post-disaster in Sichuan. *Chinese Psychology and Health Times (CPHT-10), 1*(10): 1–46 (in Chinese). Retrieved April 6, 2015, from http://blog.sina.com.cn/s/blog_5168ec1b0100c5pl.html

Deng, M-Y. (2008d). A report of psychological assistance of IACMSP after Sichuan Great Earthquake (4). *Chinese Psychology and Health Times (CPHT-9), 1*(9): 7–10 (in Chinese). Retrieved April 6, 2015, from http://blog.sina.com.cn/s/blog_5168ec1b0100c5pg.html

Deng, M-Y. (2008e). Where is heaven's way? Suicide's revelation after Sichuan earthquake in Sichuan. *Chinese Psychology and Health Times (CPHT-11), 1*(11): 2–9 (in Chinese). Retrieved April 6, 2015, from http://blog.sina.com.cn/s/blog_5168ec1b0100c5tu.html

Deng, M-Y. (2009). Anniversary of "5.12" earthquake in Sichuan—Psychological Assistance Album. *Chinese Psychology and Health Times (CPHT-17)*, 2(5), 1–60 (in Chinese). Retrieved April 6, 2015, from http://blog.sina.com.cn/s/blog_5168ec1 b0100dmlb.html, http://blog.sina.com.cn/s/blog_5168ec1b0100dmlj.html, and http://blog.sina.com.cn/s/blog_5168ec1b0100dmln.html

Deng, M-Y. (2010). International Forum of Third Post-Disaster Psychological and Mental Health Aid. *Chinese Psychology and Health Times*. Retrieved April 22, 2015, fromhttps://groups.google.com/forum/?fromgroups=#!msg/alt.psychology. psychoanalysis/fRv62-A_DEM/P_LGLAIGMAsJ, http://blog.sina.com.cn/s/blog _5168ec1b0100laal.html, http://blog.sina.com.cn/s/blog_5168ec1b0100lbpd.html, and http://blog.sina.com.cn/s/blog_5168ec1b0100lb7c.html

Dr.Judy on CCTV: Regarding Japan 2011 earthquake/tsunami [Video file]. (2011, April 11). Retrieved March 30, 2015, from, https://www.youtube.com/watch?v=vdB9aryYgKU

Edipresse Media. (2009). Versace and Jet Li opens second children's centre in Sichuan. *Eluxury News*. Retrieved November 17, 2014, from http://www.edipressemedia.com/ luxury-news/index.php?id=39&region=china

Everly, S., Jr., Phillips, B., Kane, D., & Feldman, D. (2006). Introduction to and overview of group psychological first aid. *Brief Treatment and Crisis Intervention*, 6(2), 130–136.

Forman, A. (2014, October 9). Five words that can change the world. *Jewish Journal*. Retrieved April 6, 2015, from http://boston.forward.com/articles/185615/five-words-that-can-change-the-world/

Forum, International Forum for Volunteering in Development. (2014, April 5). *Key messages on the Role of Volunteerism in shaping and implementing an inclusive and sustainable development agenda for the future 2014*. Retrieved April 23, 2015, from http://forum -ids.org/2014/04/key-messages-on-the-role-of-volunteerism/

Forum, International Forum for Volunteering in Development. (n.d.). *The Lima Declaration*. Retrieved April 23, 2015, from http://forum-ids.org/conferences/ivco/ivco -2014/lima-declaration/

Gutoff, B. (2009). Helping children recover. *Mercy Corps*. Retrieved April 22, 2015, from http://www.mercycorps.org/countries/china/14899

Hart, R. (2008). *Children's participation: The theory and practice of involving young citizens in community development and environmental care*. London, UK: Earthscan.

Hu, Y., & Cui, J. (2010). Survivors suffer from mental trauma. *China Daily*. Retrieved November 17, 2014, from http://www.chinadaily.com.cn/china/2010-08/12/content _11141837.htm

Interagency Standing Committee. (2008). IASC guidelines on mental health and psychosocial support in emergency settings: Checklist for field use. Geneva: IASC. Retrieved November 17, 2014, from http://www.who.int/hac/network/interagency/news/iasc _guidelines_mental_health_checklist.pdf

International Association of Chinese Medical Specialists and Psychologists. (2010). *Third International Forum of Post-Disaster Psychological and Mental Health Aid & Second Scientific Conference of International Society of Chinese Psycho-counselors* [in Chinese].

International Federation of Red Cross and Red Crescent Societies. (2011). *The value of volunteers*. Retrieved April 23, 2015, from https://www.ifrc.org/Global/Publications/ volunteers/IFRC-Value%20of%20Volunteers%20Report-EN-LR.pdf

International Federation of Red Cross and Red Crescent Societies. (2012a). Caring for volunteers: A psychosocial support toolkit. *ReliefWeb*. Retrieved November 17,

2014, from http://reliefweb.int/report/world/caring-volunteers-psychosocial-support-toolkit

International Federation of Red Cross and Red Crescent Societies. (2012b). *Emergency appeal final report: China Sichuan earthquake.* Retrieved November 17, 2014, from http://www.ifrc.org/docs/appeals/08/mdrcn003fr.pdf

Kalayjian, A., Moore, N., Kuriansky, J., & Aberson, L. (2010). A disaster outreach program for tsunami survivors in Sri Lanka: The bio-psychosocial, education, and spiritual approach. In A. Kalayjian & D. Eugene (Eds.), *Mass trauma and emotional healing around the world: Rituals and practices for resilience and meaning-making.* Westport, CT: Greenwood Publishing.

Katherine A. Kendall Institute. (2009). *Social Work Response to Disaster Relief and Management Conference.* Retrieved July 26, 2013, from http://www.cswe.org/CentersInitiatives/KAKI/16771/16776.aspx

Klein, B., Meyer, D., Austin, D. W., & Kyrios, M. (2011). Anxiety online: A virtual clinic: preliminary outcomes following completion of five fully automated treatment programs for anxiety disorders and symptoms. *Journal of Medical Internet Research, 13*(4), e89.

Klein, B., Mitchell, J., Abbott, J., Shandley, K., Austin, D., Gilson, K., . . . Redman, T. (2010). A therapist-assisted cognitive behavior therapy internet intervention for posttraumatic stress disorder: pre-, post- and 3-month follow-up results from an open trial. *Journal of Anxiety Disorders, 24*(6), 635–644.

Klein, B., Mitchell, J., Gilson, K., Shandley, K., Austin, D., Kiropoulos, L., . . . Cannard, G. (2009). A therapist-assisted internet-based CBT intervention for posttraumatic stress disorder: Preliminary results. *Cognitive Behaviour Therapy, 38*(2), 121–131.

Kun, P., Chen, X., Han, S., Gong, X., Chen, M., Zhang, W., & Yao, L. (2009). Prevalence of post-traumatic stress disorder in Sichuan Province, China after the 2008 Wenchuan earthquake. *Public Health, 123*(11), 703–707. doi:10.1016/j.puhe.2009.09.017

Kuriansky, J. (1990, January 1). Talk away your fears: Help also needed for victims of shock. *Daily Telegraph* (Sydney, Australia).

Kuriansky, J. (2002). Emotional response and recovery. In E. Hand (Ed.), *Emergency survival handbook.* White River Junction, VT: Nomad Press.

Kuriansky, J. (2003a, December 13–18). *Psychology for sustainable development and peace: Peace and healing in troubled regions and times of terrorism: Impact on relationships, what East and West can learn from each other about treating trauma and a new integrated therapy mode.* Middle East/North Africa Regional Conference of Psychology, Dubai, United Arab Emirates.

Kuriansky, J. (2003b). The 9/11 terrorist attack on the World Trade Center: A New York psychologist's personal experiences and professional perspective. *Psychotherapie-Forum [Special Edition on Terrorism and Psychology], 11*(1), 36–47.

Kuriansky, J. (2005, September 7). Healing in troubled regions and times of terrorism and trauma: Theory, techniques, and psychotherapy models. Convention of the World Council of Psychotherapy, Buenos Aires, Argentina.

Kuriansky, J. (2007a). Eros in the Red Dragon: The open door to sex in China. In M. S. Tepper & A. F. Owens (Eds.), *Sexual health: Moral and cultural foundations.* Westport, CT: Praeger.

Kuriansky, J. (2007b). Healing after a terror event on campus in Israel: Unique workshops and allied techniques for international Jewish and Arab students, staff and extended community. In J. Kuriansky (Ed.). *Beyond bullets and bombs: Grassroots peacebuilding between Israelis and Palestinians.* Westport, CT: Praeger.

Kuriansky, J. (2007c, June 5–7). Integration of mental health and psychosocial issues into disaster risk reduction and the Hyogo Framework for Action. International Conference about Disaster Risk Reduction, UN headquarters, Geneva, Switzerland.

Kuriansky, J. (2007d, June 5–7). *Media and climate change.* International Conference about Disaster Risk Reduction, UN headquarters, Geneva, Switzerland.

Kuriansky, J. (2007e, September 5–7). *Partnerships to mobilize community health and mental health resources for recovery, resilience and risk reduction of climate-related disasters: What multi-stakeholders and NGOs can do.* Annual DPI/NGO conference at the United Nations. New York, NY.

Kuriansky, J. (2007f). Peace Psychology Division supports Katrina recovery effort: Auction raises money for wellness workshops. *PEACE Psychology, Newsletter of the Society for the Study of Peace, Conflict and Violence: Peace Psychology Division of the American Psychological Association.*

Kuriansky J. (2008a). A clinical toolbox for cross-cultural counseling and training. In U. P. Gielen, J. G. Draguns, & J. M. Fish (Eds.), *Principles of multicultural counseling and therapy* (pp. 295–330). New York, NY: Taylor and Francis/Routledge.

Kuriansky, J. (2008b). Americans and Japanese commemorate 9/11 together. *Society for the Study of Peace, Conflict and Violence: Peace Psychology Division of the American Psychological Association, 17*(2), 13.

Kuriansky, J. (2008c, December 7–11). *Helping children cope with the Sichuan earthquake.* International Asia-oceanic Congress on Sexuality, Nanning, China. December 7–11.

Kuriansky, J. (2008d, November 22). *Media and psychotherapy: How do psychotherapists get their message across? Psychotherapies and a Traumatized world: Problems and Possibilities.* The 8th Latin American Congress on Psychotherapy, Anhembi Morumbi University, Sao Paolo, Brazil.

Kuriansky, J. (2008e, October). *Overview of techniques for recovery and resilience in disaster situations.* Presentation at the World Congress of Psychotherapy, Beijing, China.

Kuriansky, J. (2009). Communication and media in mass trauma: How mental health professionals can help. In J. T. Thome, M. Benyakar, & I. H. Taralli (Eds.), *Intervention in destabilizing situations: Crises and trauma* (pp. 195–232). Rio de Janeiro, Brazil: Associação Brasileira de Psiquiatria.

Kuriansky, J. (2010a). Bringing emotional first aid and hope to Haiti. *Beliefnet.* Retrieved November 20, 2014, from http://www.beliefnet.com/Inspiration/2010/02/Bringing -Emotional-First-Aid-and-Hope-to-Haiti.aspx?p=5

Kuriansky, J. (2010b, July 22). *Family health: Teaching and demonstration of skills to help children after traumatic events.* Presentation at the International Forum for Post-disaster Health Aid, Qinghai, China.

Kuriansky, J. (2010c, Spring). Haiti pre and post earthquake: Tracing professional and personal commitment past, present and future. *International Psychology Bulletin, 14*(2), 29–37.

Kuriansky, J. (2010d, August 30–September 1). *Post-earthquake psychosocial disaster relief and recovery: Overview of mission to Xinhai Province, China.* Exhibit at the United Nations Department of Public Information NGO Conference: Advancing Global Health, Achieve the MDGs.

Kuriansky, J. (2010e, July 24). *Recovery and resilience after trauma.* Presentation at the International Forum for Post-disaster Psycho and Mental Health Aid, Qinghai, China.

Kuriansky, J. (2010f, July 28). *Techniques for helping students recover from natural disaster and other stress.* Presentation at the International Forum for Post-disaster Health Aid, Qinghai, China.

Kuriansky, J. (2010g). *Watch as Dr. Judy visits Qinghai and offers several unique healing strategies* [Video file]. Retrieved November 20, 2014, from http://drjudy.com/qinghai/

Kuriansky, J. (2011a). Aftermath of the Japanese earthquake and tsunami: Immediate response and impact of events as healing efforts. *International Psychology Bulletin, 15*(2), 67–70. Retrieved July 26, 2013, from http://www.internationalpsychology.net/ newsletter

Kuriansky, J. (2011b). Civil society cooperative projects for peace. In D. J. Christie (Ed.), *Encyclopedia of Peace Psychology.* Hoboken, NJ: Wiley-Blackwell.

Kuriansky, J. (2011c, January). Guidelines for mental health and psychosocial support in response to emergencies: Experience and encouragement for advocacy. *The IAAP Bulletin of the International Association of Applied Psychology, 23*(1–2), 31–33.

Kuriansky, J. (2012a, February 13). Christmas curse or celebration: From Superstorm Sandy to Sandy Hook to the Financial Cliff, seven questions in crisis. *Huffington Post.* Retrieved April 22, 2015, from http://www.huffingtonpost.com/judy-kuriansky-phd/ sandy-hook-elementary-shooting_b_2357207.html

Kuriansky, J. (2012b, October 30). Coping after Sandy: Seven psychological tips (plus a bonus). *FoxNews.com.* Retrieved March 30, 2015, from http://www.foxnews.com/ opinion/2012/10/30/coping-after-sandy-seven-psychological-tips-plus-bonus/

Kuriansky, J. (2012c, October 20). Helping children recover from natural disasters: *Principles and practice from professional and personal experiences in the field in China, Sri Lanka, Haiti and Japan, skills building and psycho-educational techniques.* Presentation at the International Conference for Chinese Psychology and Health in Global & Fourth Congress of the IACMSP.

Kuriansky, J. (2012d, April 12–14). *International interventions: Psychosocial theory, techniques, and tools.* Presentation at the Institute for International and Cross-Cultural Psychology Conference, St. Francis College, Brooklyn, NY.

Kuriansky, J. (2012e). Our communities: Healing after environmental disasters. In D. G. Nemeth, R. B. Hamilton, & J. Kuriansky (Eds.), *Living in an environmentally traumatized world: Healing ourselves and our planet.* Santa Barbara, CA: ABC-CLIO/Praeger

Kuriansky, J. (2012f). Psychologist laments lackluster 9/11 memorials. Retrieved April 3, 2015, from, http://abcnews.go.com/Health/psychologist-laments-lackluster-911 -memorials/story?id=17207164

Kuriansky, J. (2012g, July–October). Recovery efforts for Japan after the 3/11 devastating tsunami/earthquake. *Bulletin of the International Association of Applied Psychology, 24* (2–3), Part 22. Retrieved March 30, 2015, from http://www.iaapsy.org/Portals/1/ Archive/Publications/newsletters/July2012.pdf

Kuriansky, J. (2012h). Soothing Sendai (report). *Humnews.* Retrieved March 30, 2015, from http://www.humnews.com/the-view-from-here/2012/3/22/soothing-sendai -report.html

Kuriansky, J. (2013a, May 23). Helping kids cope with the Oklahoma tornado and other traumas: 7 techniques. *Huffington Post.* Retrieved April 22, 2015, from http://www

.huffingtonpost.com/judy-kuriansky-phd/helping-kids-cope-with-the-oklahoma -tornado_b_3322238.html

Kuriansky, J. (2013b, August 7). *Japan Mission: Healing workshops by Dr. Judy Kuriansky and team on tsunami/earthquake anniversary* [Video file]. Retrieved November 21, 2014, from http://www.youtube.com/watch?v=_Q9QQK-SqWs

Kuriansky, J. (2013c, October 21) *Sandy video* [Video file]. Retrieved November 21, 2014, from http://www.youtube.com/watch?v=2W1OUHH8IPA

Kuriansky, J. (2013d). Superstorm Sandy 2012: A psychologist first responder's personal account and lessons learned about the impact on emotions and ecology. *Ecopsychology, 5*(Suppl. 1): S30–S37. doi:10.1089/eco.2013.0010.

Kuriansky, J. (2013e, October 26). Superstorm Sandy: Coping with the one-year anniversary. *Citizens Magazine*. Retrieved March 30, 2015, from https://statenislandpolitics. wordpress.com/2013/10/26/drjudy/

Kuriansky, J. (2013f). Talking to kids about the anniversary of Superstorm Sandy. *Huffington Post*. Retrieved March 30, 2015, from http://www.huffingtonpost.com/ judy-kuriansky-phd/talking-to-kids-about-the-anniversary-of-superstorm-sandy_b_416 7294.html

Kuriansky, J. (2013g). Thoughts on Katrina vs. Sandy: Judy Kuriansky. *Ecopsychology, 5* (Suppl. 1): S20–S26. doi:10.1089/eco.2013.0039

Kuriansky, J. (2014a, June 12). *Building resilience in children coping after disaster and living in crisis: Applied models in Haiti, Japan and Africa*. Presentation at the Louisiana Psychological Association, on "Resiliency, Mindfulness and Resolve: Coping with the Hand You're Dealt," New Orleans, LA.

Kuriansky, J. (2014b, June 12). *Intimacy and sex after disaster: Coping styles that make or break a relationship*, Presentation at the Louisiana Psychological Association, on "Resiliency, Mindfulness and Resolve: Coping with the Hand you're Dealt," New Orleans, LA.

Kuriansky, J. (2015, March 16–18). Statement at the Interactive Dialogue at the World Conference on Disaster Risk Reduction, Sendai, Japan [Video]. Retrieved April 7, 2015, from https://youtu.be/R72sDJ1xVZg

Kuriansky, J., & Jean-Charles, W. (2012). Haiti Rebati: Update on activities rebuilding Haiti through the Global Kids Connect Project. Part 21. *IAAP Bulletin, 24*(2–3).

Kuriansky, J., LeMay, M. & Kumar, A. (2015). Paradigm shifts in nature and well-being: Principles, programs, and policies about the environment and climate change with actions by the United Nations for a sustainable future. In D. G. Nemeth & J. Kuriansky (Eds.), *Ecopsychology: Advances from the intersection of psychology and environmental protection*, Volume 2 (pp. 307–358). Santa Barbara, CA: ABC-CLIO.

Kuriansky, J., & Nemeth, D. G. (2013). A model for post-environmental disaster wellness workshops: Preparing individuals and communities for hurricane anniversary reactions. *Ecopsychology, 5* (Suppl. 1): S38–S45. doi:10.1089/eco.2013.0006

Kuriansky, J. & Okorodudu, C. (2014). *Psychological contributions to the post-2015 development agenda* (Unpublished document), prepared for the Open Working Group sessions on the SDGs, United Nations Headquarters, New York, NY.

Kuriansky, J., Zinsou, J., Arunagiri, V., Douyon, C., Chiu, A., Jean-Charles, W., . . . Midy, T. (2015). The effects of helping in a train-the-trainers program for youth in the Global Kids Connect Project providing psychosocial support after the 2010 Haiti earthquake: A paradigm shift to sustainable development. In D. G. Nemeth &

J. Kuriansky (Eds.), *Ecopsychology: Advances from the intersection of psychology and environmental protection*, Volume 2 (pp. 135–169). Santa Barbara, CA: ABC-CLIO.

Lao, M. (2008a). Dr. Mingyu Deng leads his colleagues and subordinates go again to Sichuan earthquake disaster area. *Chinese Psychology and Health Times (CPHT-10)*, *1*(10): 16–19 (in Chinese). Retrieved April 6, 2015, from http://blog.sina.com.cn/s/blog_5168ec1b0100c5pq.html

Lao, M. (2008b). A work report from second group experts of IACMSP in Sichuan earthquake disaster area. *Chinese Psychology and Health Times (CPHT-7)*, *1*(7), 2–5 (in Chinese). Retrieved April 6, 2015, from http://blog.sina.com.cn/s/blog_5168ec1b0100c5nx.html

Lao, M. (2009a). Dr. Mingyu Deng and his group go again to Sichuan earthquake disaster area. *Chinese Psychology and Health Times (CPHT-13)*, *2*(1), 1–10 (in Chinese). Retrieved April 6, 2015, from http://blog.sina.com.cn/s/blog_5168ec1b0100c5yl.html

Lao, M. (2009b). Second International Forum of Psychological and Mental Health Aid after Sichuan 512 Earthquake was held by IACMSP in Dandong City. *Chinese Psychology and Health Times (CPHT-20)*, *2*(8), 7–8 (in Chinese). Retrieved April 6, 2015, from http://blog.sina.com.cn/s/blog_5168ec1b0100f8sa.html

Lao, M. (2009c). Chinese-American scholar assistance Taiwan's "8.8" disaster area. *Chinese Psychology and Health Times (CPHT-20)*, *2*(8), 1–2 (in Chinese). Retrieved April 6, 2015, from http://blog.sina.com.cn/s/blog_5168ec1b0100f8sc.html

Lao, M. (2009d). IACMSP Psychological and Mental Health Aid Coordination Center for Sichuan "512" and Taiwan "88" establish in New York City. *Chinese Psychology and Health Times (CPHT-21)*, *2*(9), 1–2 (in Chinese). Retrieved April 6, 2015, from http://blog.sina.com.cn/s/blog_5168ec1b0100ffyx.html

Leitch, L., & Miller-Karas, A. (2009). Case for using biologically-based mental health intervention in post earthquake China: Evaluation of training in the Trauma Resiliency Model. *International Journal of Emergency Mental Health*, *11*(4), 221–223.

Li, W., Yu, Y., Qian, Y., & Gao, J. (2011). A comparative study on level of depression and PTSD severity between the earthquake severely-exposed and mildly-exposed middle school students. *Chinese Journal of Clinical Psychology*, *19*(1). (In Chinese with English abstract)

Liu, M., Wang, L., Shi, Z., Zhang, Z., Zhang, K., & Shen, J. (2011). Mental health problems among children one-year after Sichuan earthquake in China: A follow-up study. *PLOS One*, *6*(2), doi:10.1371/journal.pone.0014706

Liu, Z., Wu, K., & Zhang, K. (2011). The current practice and challenges in psychological intervention after major natural disasters in China. *China Soft Science* (05). (In Chinese with English abstract). Accessible at http://en.cnki.com.cn/Article_en/CJFDTotal-ZGRK201105008.htm

Luce, J. (2010). Dr. Judy on the trauma of disasters—like Haitian earthquake. *Huffington Post*. Retrieved March 30, 2015, from http://www.huffingtonpost.com/jim-luce/dr-judy-on-the-trauma-of_b_461779.html

Markus, F. (2008). China: A healing touch for children. *International Federation of Red Cross and Red Crescent Societies*. Retrieved April 22, 2015, from http://www.ifrc.org/en/news-and-media/news-stories/asia-pacific/china/china-a-healing-touch-for-children/

Markus, F. (2009). Qiuqiu the panda lends to psychosocial support. *International Federation of Red Cross and Red Crescent Societies*. Retrieved July 27, 2013, from http://

www.ifrc.org/en/news-and-media/news-stories/asia-pacific/china/china-qiuqiu-the
-panda-lends-to-psychosocial-support/

Markus, F. (2013). East Asian Red Cross Societies take steps towards psychosocial network. *International Federation of Red Cross and Red Crescent Societies Psychosocial Centre*. Retrieved April 22, 2015, from http://pscentre.org/east-asian-red-cross-societies-take-steps-towards-psychosocial-network-2/

Masangkay, M. (2015), Psychologist connects disaster-affected children around the world. *Japan Times*. Retrieved March 30, 2015, from http://www.japantimes.co.jp/news/2015/03/23/national/psychologist-connects-disaster-affected-children-around-the-world/#.VR4uT0tlQRw

Médecins Sans Frontières. (2008). *China: MSF focuses on mental health and shelter.* Retrieved March 30, 2015, from http://www.doctorswithoutborders.org/news-stories/field-news/china-msf-focuses-mental-health-and-shelter

Médecins Sans Frontières Australia. (2008). *One month after the Sichuan earthquake.* Retrieved April 22, 2015, from http://www.msf.org.au/from-the-field/field-news/field-news/article/one-month-after-the-sichuan-earthquake.html

Médecins Sans Frontières Australia. (2009). *One year after the earthquake: Médecins Sans Frontières continuously offers psychological care in Sichuan.* Retrieved March 30, 2015, from http://www.msf.org.au/from-the-field/field-news/field-news/article/one-year-after-the-earthquake-medecins-sans-frontieres-continuously-offers-psychological-care-in.html

Mercy Corps. (2008, June 13). *One month after China quake, Mercy Corps helps children deal with trauma.* Retrieved March 30, 2015, from http://reliefweb.int/report/china/one-month-after-china-quake-mercy-corps-helps-children-deal-trauma

Mercy Corps. (2009, March 4). *Helping children recover.* Retrieved March 30, 2015, from http://www.mercycorps.org/articles/china/helping-children-recover

Mercy Malaysia. (2009a). *Annual report 2009.* Retrieved April 22, 2015, from http://www.mercy.org.my/upload/MERCY_AR_2009_FULL.pdf

Mercy Malaysia. (2009b). *MERCY Malaysia Conducts Child-Led DRR Workshop in Sichuan, China.* Retrieved April 22, 2015, from http://www.mercy.org.my/0909111130%C2%BBMERCY_Malaysia_Conducts_Child-Led_DRR_Workshop_In_Sichuan,_China.aspx

Miles, B., & Morse, S. (2007). The role of news media in natural disaster risk and recovery. *Ecological Economics, 63*(2–3), 365–373.

Miller-Karas, E. (2012). *Trauma resource workbook revision.* Self-published.

Morris, J., Van Ommeren, M., Belfer, M., Saxena, S., & Saraceno, B. (2007). Children and the Sphere standard on mental and social aspects of health. *Disasters, 31*(1), 71–90.

Nemeth, D. G., Hamilton, R. B., & Kuriansky, J. (2015). Reflections and recommendations: The need for leadership, holistic thinking, and community involvement. In D. G. Nemeth & J. Kuriansky (Eds.), *Ecopsychology: Advances from the intersection of psychology and environmental protection*, Volume 2 (pp. 413–428). Santa Barbara, CA: ABC-CLIO.

Nemeth, D. G., & Kuriansky, J. (2008, October 15). *Psychosocial recovery after disaster: Post-Katrina wellness applications to the Sichuan earthquake.* World Congress of Psychotherapy, Beijing, China.

Nemeth, D. G., Kuriansky, J., Reeder, P., Lewis, A., Marceaux, K., Whittington, T., ... Safier, J. A. (2012). Addressing anniversary reactions of trauma through group process: The Hurricane Katrina Anniversary Wellness Workshops. *International Journal of Group Psychotherapy, 62*(1), 129–141.

Nettleton, S. (2009). Child-friendly spaces in earthquake affected Sichuan Province. UNICEF. Retrieved April 22, 2015, from http://www.unicef.org/infobycountry/china_49701.html

Ng, C., Ma, H., Raphael, B., Yu, X., Fraser, J., & Tang, D. (2009). China-Australia training on psychosocial crisis intervention: Response to the earthquake disaster in Sichuan. *Australasian Psychiatry, 17*(1), 51–55.

Official Jet Li Website. (2009). Discussing the One Foundation with Daniele Wu. Retrieved July 26, 2013, from http://www.alivenotdead.com/jetli/blog.html?label_39_page_6

Otto, C., Kuriansky, J., & Okorodudu, C. (2014). *Mental health and wellbeing for the OWG document regarding the post-2015 development* (Unpublished advocacy document).

Oxfam Hong Kong. (2010). *5.12 Wenchuan earthquake.* Retrieved April 22, 2015, from http://www.oxfam.org.hk/en/512earthquake.aspx

Oxfam Hong Kong. (2011). *Sichuan earthquake three years on.* Retrieved April 3, 2015, from http://www.oxfam.org.hk/en/news_1542.aspx

Parker, R., Ng, C., Coghlan, A., Fraser, J., & Raphael, B. (2009). The China-Australia training on psychological crisis intervention for medical aid leaders and volunteers after the Sichuan earthquake. *The Medical Journal of Australia, 190*(9), 508–509.

Pesta, A. (2009). Donatella Versace Has Blonde Ambition: Fashion's glam survivor Donatella Versace turns heads and reboots lives in rural China. Marie Claire. Retrieved July 27, 2013, from http://www.marieclaire.com/world-reports/inspirational-women/donatella-versace

Phoofolo, R., Kokoris, C., & Kuriansky, J. (2011). Finding funding for NGOs in today's challenging global economy: A United Nations DPI/NGO Communications Workshop. *IAAP Bulletin, 23*(3), 26–28.

Qian, Y., Gao, J., Wu, H., Zhong, J., Wang, Y., Li, W., . . . Huang, L. (2011). Exploration of post-earthquake long-term psychological aid model: A one-year review of One Foundation–Peking University Children's Psychological Wellbeing Recovery Program. *Chinese Mental Health Journal, 25*(8). (In Chinese with English abstract)

Qian, Y., Smith, C., Chen, Z., & Xia, G. (2002). Psychotherapy in China. *International Journal of Mental Health, 30*(4), 49–68.

Rutstein, D., Li, L., & Donovan, K. (2008). UNICEF assists post-earthquake child support mission. *UNICEF.* Retrieved April 22, 2015, from http://www.unicef.org/media/media_44040.html

Satapathy, S., & Bhadra, S. (2009). Disaster psychosocial and mental health support in South and South-East Asian countries: A synthesis. *Journal of South Asian Disaster Studies, 2*(1), 21–45.

Save the Children. (n.d.). *Aid effectiveness.* Retrieved April 22, 2015, from http://www.savethechildren.org/site/c.8rKLIXMGIpI4E/b.6151901/k.A29A/Aid_Effectiveness.htm

Shen, Y. (2009). *San Chuan Xing Si: The work of the garden of the heart and soul.* Guangdong, China. Science & Technology Press. (In Chinese)

Silberg, N. (2012). *The utilization of movement and dance to support children in the aftermath of community disaster* (Unpublished doctoral dissertation). Drexel University, Philadelphia, PA.

Sun, P. (2012). Four Years of Sichuan Earthquake Disaster Relief Awakes China House Church to Social Services. *The Gospel Herald Church*. Retrieved April 22, 2015, from http://www.gospelherald.com/article/church/47761/four-years-of-sichuan-earthquake -disaster-relief-awakes-china-house-church-to-social-services.htm

Symposium on post-earthquake interventions in Sichuan, China at the American Psychological Association Convention. (2009, August 3). Retrieved April 22, 2015, from http://www .newswise.com/articles/symposium-on-post-earthquake-interventions-in-sichuan -china-at-the-american-psychological-association-convention

Tai, B. (2012). Psychosocial needs bear fruit in Sichuan. *International Federation of Red Cross and Red Crescent Societies*. Retrieved April 22, 2015, from http://www.ifrc.org/ en/news-and-media/news-stories/asia-pacific/china/psychosocial-seeds-bear-fruit-in -sichuan/

Than, K. (2005). Scientists: Natural disasters becoming more common. *Livescience*. Retrieved April 22, 2015, from http://www.livescience.com/414-scientists-natural -disasters-common.html

To, T. (2009, May 7). *Grateful heart—reflections on life after the disaster in Sichuan Children* [Video file]. Retrieved November 17, 2014, from http://www.youtube.com/watch? v=onE1lhrISYc

Thwink.org. (2014). *The three pillars of sustainability*. Retrieved April 3, 2015, from http:// www.thwink.org/sustain/glossary/ThreePillarsOfSustainability.htm

Umar, A. (n.d.). Child-led DRR in China. *Mercy Malaysia*. Retrieved April 22, 2015, from http://www.mercy.org.my/1006030503%C2%BBChild-led_DRR_in_China _.aspx

UNICEF. (2009). Sichuan earthquake one year report. Retrieved April 22, 2015, from http://www.unicef.org/media/files/China_Earthquake_Report_2009ENG_Part_2.pdf

UNICEF. (2010). "Build Back Better" Sichuan 2-years Report UNICEF's Recovery Work on Progress. Retrieved July 26, 2013, from http://www.unicef.org.hk/news-media/ unicef-news;news/112/-Build-Back-Better-Sichuan-Earthquake-2-Year-Report-UNICEF -s-Recovery-Work-on-Progresssection-press.

UNICEF. (2011). *Sichuan earthquake: Three year report*. Beijing, China: UNICEF Office for China. 2011. Retrieved April 22, 2015, from http://www.unicefchina.org/en/ uploadfile/2012/0201/20120201040221399.pdf

UNISDR. (n.d.). *Towards a post-2015 framework on disaster risk reduction*. Retrieved April 22, 2015, from http://www.preventionweb.net/posthfa

UNISDR. (2015a, March 18). Sendai Framework for Disaster Risk Reduction 2015–2030. Retrieved April 3, 2015, from http://www.wcdrr.org/uploads/Sendai_Framework_for _Disaster_Risk_Reduction_2015-2030.pdf

UNISDR. (2015b). WCDRR: The Global Kids Connect Project: A model programme to promote resilience, Judy Kuriansky. Retrieved April 3, 2015, from, https://www .youtube.com/watch?v=NM2DYaB4OYM&index=73&list=PLBDwPnveHho_fXUfF QaVkUGb1v4EcAcyO

United Nations Department of Economic and Social Affairs. (n.d.). *Sustainable development knowledge platform*. Retrieved April 3, 2015, from https://sustainabledevelopment .un.org/sdgsproposal

United Nations Volunteers (2014). *Volunteering for the world we want: Annual Report 2013*. Retrieved April 23, 2015, from http://www.unv.org/fileadmin/docdb/pdf/2014/ corporate/UNV-RA2013-web.pdf

U.S. Department of Education. (2008). Psychological first aid for students and teachers: Listen, protect, connect—model and teach. *Helpful Hints for School Emergency Management*, 3(3). Retrieved April 22, 2015, from http://www.ready.gov/sites/default/files/documents/files/HH_Vol3Issue3.pdf

Voice of Longquan. (2009). *2008 "Grateful Heart" Earthquake Relief Charity Joint Action Progress Bulletin*. Retrieved November 21, 2014, from http://old.longquanzs.org/eng/articlecontent.php?id=274

VSO International and The Institute of Development Studies (IDS). (2014). *Valuing Volunteering: The Role of Volunteering in Sustainable Development*. Retrieved April 23, 2015, from http://www.vsointernational.org/sites/vso_international/files/the_role_of_volunteering_in_sustainable_development_2015_vso_ids.pdf

Wang, L., Zhang, Y., Wang, W., Shi, Z., Shen, J., Li, M., & Xin, Y. (2009). Symptoms of posttraumatic stress disorder among adult survivors three months after the Sichuan earthquake in China. *Journal of Traumatic Stress*, 22, 444–450. doi:10.1002/jts.20439

Wang, Y., Yang, F., Wang, Y., Gao, J., & Qian, Y. (2011). Effects of group intervention on depression and post-traumatic stress symptoms among junior middle school students in earthquake area. *Chinese Mental Health Journal*, 25(4), 284–288. (In Chinese with English abstract)

Wang, Z. (2008). A preliminary report on the Great Wenchuan Earthquake. *Earthquake Engineering and Engineering Vibration*, 7(2), 225–234.

Wickramage, K. (2006). Sri Lanka's post-tsunami psychosocial playground: Lessons for future psychosocial programming and interventions following disasters. *Intervention*, 4(2), 163–168.

Wong, C. (2012). Humanitarian coordination and response: International partnerships in face of natural disasters. *CUREJ—College Undergraduate Research Electronic Journal*. University of Pennsylvania. Retrieved April 22, 2015, from http://repository.upenn.edu/cgi/viewcontent.cgi?article=1178&context=curej

Xu, J., & Liao, Q. (2011). Prevalence and predictors of posttraumatic growth among adult survivors one-year following 2008 Sichuan earthquake. *Journal of Affective Disorders*, 27(4), 80–133.

Xu, K. (n.d.). *Yale China Association*. Retrieved April 22, 2015, from http://www.yalechina.org/dynamicpage.php?Id=18&SubId=193

Yue, D. (2000). Practicing counseling in Chinese communities: Some reflections on cultural competence and indigenization. *Asian Journal of Counselling*, 7(1), 43–52.

Zeng, E. (2011). The earth as a classroom: Children's groups in the aftermath of mass trauma. In J. L. Kleinberg (Ed.), *The Wiley-Blackwell handbook of group psychotherapy*. Chichester, UK: John Wiley & Sons. doi:10.1002/9781119950882.ch31.

Zeng, E. J., & Silverstein, L. B. (2011). China earthquake relief: Participatory action work with children. *School Psychology International*, 32(5), 498–511. doi:10.1177/0143034311402921

Zhang, K., Shi, Z., & Wang, R. (2011, May). One year later: Mental health problems among survivors in hard-hit areas of the Wenchuan earthquake. *Public Health*, 125(5), 293–300.

Zhang, K., & Wang, R. (2008). Psychological assistance and mental reconstruction after disasters. *Bulletin of the Chinese Academy of Sciences, 4* (in Chinese with English abstract). Accessible at http://en.cnki.com.cn/Article_en/CJFDTOTAL-KYYX 200804006.htm

Zhang, Y., Kong, F., Wang, L., Chen, H., Gao, X., Tan X., ... Liu, Y. (2010). Mental health and coping styles of children and adolescent survivors one year after the 2008 Chinese earthquake. *Children and Youth Services Review, 32*(10), 1403–1409.

Zhiling, H. (2008). Survivors face legacy of stress. *China Daily.* Retrieved April 22, 2015, from http://www.chinadaily.com.cn/china/2008-10/20/content_7119761.htm

11

The Pachamama Alliance: Linking Environmental Sustainability, Social Justice, and Spiritual Fulfillment through Changing the Dream

Mia Murrietta

As a species, humankind is facing unprecedented ecological challenges, which have made it impossible to ignore the interrelated psychological, social, economic, ecological, and spiritual toll of our "modern" way of life. Statistics collected by the United Nations paint a grim picture: 75% of the world's original forests have been eliminated; 30% of the world's arable land has eroded in the last 40 years; more than 405 oceanic "dead zones" exist worldwide, up from 49 in 1960; 90% of all large fish are gone from the oceans; lung and breast cancer rates have doubled in the past 30 years; one in four mammals is threatened by extinction; and global climate change continues to result in increasingly catastrophic weather events (Cultural Design Group, 2011).

In light of these statistics, how did an intelligent, well-meaning species that for the most part only wanted to make the world better and more secure for their children, end up in such a perilous situation? Poet and activist Drew Dellinger summarizes one answer for this question by referencing the work of cultural historian and cosmologist Thomas Berry:

> The primary problem with Western civilization is that it creates and perpetuates a radical separation between the human world and the natural world—that we've given all rights to the human and no rights to the natural world. We think we're behaving very rationally, that we're on this kind of a logical economic course, but actually we're heading toward our destruction. And the only way to explain this is that we've been locked into a kind of mythic trance, a worldview that's become dysfunctional and therefore destructive. (TPA, 2011)

The indigenous Achuar people of the Amazon rain forest refer to this trance as the "dream" of the modern world. They saw, and continue to see, that dream as the underlying factor behind many of the global crises we are facing today—crises that have extended their reach deep into even remote territories such as theirs.

This chapter describes the efforts of these indigenous people, and of a non-profit organization inspired by them, to blend indigenous wisdom with modern knowledge, to foster a worldview that can guide humanity through present economic, social, and environmental challenges as well as provide a model for environmental sustainability, well-being, and spiritual growth.

ABOUT ECUADOR

The borders of modern-day Ecuador span environments among the most distinct and unique in the world, including the Amazon rain forest, the Andes Mountains, and the Galápagos Islands. Climate ranges from temperate to tropical, depending on location and time of year. With its wealth of natural resources, including minerals, metals, lumber, and oil, Ecuador has been a highly coveted colony since at least the mid-sixteenth century. Like many parts of the world, Ecuador is urgently wrestling with the economic and political pressures of resource extraction as well as the unjust social structures that grew out of colonialism.

The various human communities of Ecuador are engaging with new ideas for organizing their society, innovating models all of us can learn from as we work for a just, thriving, and sustainable future. For the indigenous peoples whose territories fall within Ecuador's borders, innovating new social and political models must include respect and recognition for indigenous communities, ancestral lands, and ways of life.

FOUNDING OF THE PACHAMAMA ALLIANCE

The Pachamama Alliance (http://www.pachamama.org) is an alliance between indigenous peoples of the Amazon rain forest and people in the industrialized world. It was born out of an invitation from the Achuar people to allies in the industrialized or so-called "modern" world to work in partnership with them to preserve their land and culture on behalf of all life, while bringing forth a new "dream" for the human family that honors and sustains our interdependence with the earth.

In 1995, a group of 12 people from the United States traveled deep into Ecuador's Amazon rain forest at the invitation of the Achuar people, among the world's most intact indigenous societies. The Achuar shared with the group the urgent threat to their lands and culture from oil extraction and exploration, their vision for self-determination, and a request for allies from the north who would "change the dream of the modern world"—work to shift the culture of exploitation that drives destruction of the rain forest to a culture that honors and sustains life.

Included in the group, who shared a connection through the Social Venture Network, were author John Perkins and his friends Lynne and Bill Twist, who committed to a partnership with the Achuar. At the time, Bill Twist had

developed an extensive career in the management consulting, equipment leas-
ing, and financial services industries. Lynne Twist had an esteemed career as a
philanthropic leader and activist. Prior to the trip, Lynne had already connected
with the Achuar while she and her husband Bill were on a trip to Guatemala
with Perkins in 1994 (Twist, 2003). At that time, she experienced a shamanic
dream ceremony for the first time, during which she had the first of a series
of recurring visions of what turned out to be the Achuar people of Ecuador's
Amazon rain forest. Together with Perkins, who had long-standing relationships
with the Shuar and Achuar people, and Daniel Koupermann, a rain forest guide
trusted by the Achuar to cocreate an eco-lodge in their territory, Lynne and Bill
organized the trip to meet with Achuar leaders deep in the Amazon rain forest.

Originally, Lynne thought that she had no time or space to consider the problems facing this region of South America, yet she and Bill felt a strong call from
the Achuar that they could not deny. On that first journey into Achuar territory,
they quickly saw that Ecuador is a microcosm of the ecological and social challenges and opportunities humankind is facing globally. Upon their return to
the United States, the Twists, together with Perkins, cofounded a nonprofit
organization, the Pachamama Alliance, based in San Francisco, California, and
dedicated to carrying out their commitment to stand with the Achuar and other
indigenous peoples for a just, sustainable, and fulfilling world.

"Pachamama" is a word in the Quechua language of the Andes that some
translate as "Mother Earth," but that more accurately includes the sacred presence of the earth, the sky, the universe, and all time. By choosing this name,
the cofounders implied a holistic approach, grounded in indigenous wisdom that
would shape the mission and vision.

A "NEW DREAM" FOR HUMANITY

The Pachamama Alliance mission is twofold: to empower indigenous people
of the Amazon rain forest to preserve their lands and culture; and, using insights
gained from that work, to educate and inspire individuals everywhere to bring
forth a thriving, just, and sustainable world—a "new dream" for humanity.

Dreams are an important part of people's lives, not just as thoughts and images
that occur during sleep, but also as inspirations for achievement, that cause individuals to reflect on their meaning and role in defining the creativity and purpose
of their past, present, and future (Greene, 2010; Waggoner, 2009). In Achuar
culture, dreams are a guiding principle of life, shared each morning before sun-
rise. Shamans maintain and pass on cultural knowledge and traditions and play
an important role in the life of Achuar communities, including the interpretation of dreams and the conducting of ceremonies for accessing dreams. For the
Achuar, dreams can often require facing and transforming that which you most
fear. They believe that retreating in fear from a powerful vision represents a lost

opportunity to transform it from a potential source of domination into a connection with ancient wisdom and individual purpose.

Indigenous cultures such as that of the Achuar people are still deeply connected with the human capacity to dream, and believe there is a relationship between dreams and a collective worldview and reality. The Pachamama Alliance works to blend the best of indigenous wisdom and modern knowledge, fostering a new worldview that can guide humanity through the economic, social, and environmental crises of our time. This synthesis can be seen in all aspects of their work, including Pachamama Journeys to Ecuador, transformational education workshops, and the Awakening the Dreamer Symposium.

THE PURPOSE OF THE PACHAMAMA ALLIANCE

The purpose of the Pachamama Alliance is to generate and engage people everywhere in transformational conversations and experiences that examine the assumptions that hold our current worldview in place and envision other possibilities. Consistent across all those conversations and experiences is the idea that environmental sustainability, social justice, and spiritual fulfillment are inextricably linked, and we cannot achieve one without the other two.

All of the work of the Pachamama Alliance is grounded in an understanding that if present trends continue, our social, environmental, and economic wellbeing—perhaps even the future of life on earth—are in jeopardy. This moment in human history is our opportunity as a species to make significant changes.

Spiritual Fulfillment

Defining "spiritual fulfillment" is a personal question for many. However, Pachamama Alliance programs have sought common ground by defining spiritual fulfillment as the experience that our lives as human beings have unique meaning and purpose, and that we are fulfilled when we devote our lives to fully realizing that meaning and purpose.

One way the dream of the modern world robs us of a sense of fulfillment is that it reduces us to consumers who have very little ability to create the world we truly want. This modern dream provides very few sources of connection with other people or with the earth, and very little sense that our lives have meaning beyond consuming and acquiring things. For many, this acquisition of more and more things ignores consequences for the earth (environmental impact) as well as consequences of the way we live on other people (social justice impact). Meanwhile, at some level we know what is happening to the earth and to the human community, and that awareness can lead to profound alienation, despair, and disconnection.

Environmental Sustainability

In this context, "environmental sustainability" is defined as "the ability of the current generation to meet its needs, without compromising the ability of future generations to meet theirs" (United Nations World Commission on Environment and Development, 1987). This definition, while proposed over a quarter of a century ago, is still applicable today and corresponds to the views and practices of many indigenous cultures.

Social Justice

The vision of a "socially just" world is captured by environmental justice activist and former White House staff member Van Jones as "a world in which, if you had to draw a lot, and it would put you anywhere in that society, you would feel perfectly confident; you wouldn't be worried, because you knew whatever lot you drew would be a good lot. It doesn't mean everything's equal. It just means that every single person in that society has a decent shot at living the fullest life that they can" (TPA, 2011).

TIPPING POINTS

The Pachamama Alliance also postulates that humanity already possesses sufficient resources, technology, and know-how to reverse these trends. What is needed are a sense of urgency and the popular and political will to act and avoid key environmental tipping points.

Humanity has been continuously increasing its resource demand to the extent of using more than what Nature can regenerate since the mid-1980s, according to Mathis Wackernagel and Susan Burns, cofounders of the Global Footprint Network. By 2007, humanity used about 30% more than what Nature can renew, putting us in "global overshoot"—essentially, living off of our ecological credit card. By using more than Nature can keep up with, we actually start to erode the natural capital on which life depends (TPA, 2011). Climate change accelerated by the burning of fossil fuels, as documented by scientists around the world and reflected in recent reports from the European Union (European Environment Agency, 2012) and the World Bank (The World Bank, 2012), is just one result of the much larger underlying issue of a modern worldview that promotes overconsumption and domination of Nature.

Whether you look at tipping points with regard to climate change, peak oil, population, or other indicators, it all comes back to the earth and its natural capital. Currently, if everyone on earth lived as North Americans do, we'd need three earths. People in other regions are also living beyond the capacity of one earth (Wackernagel & Rees, 1996).

TRAJECTORY SHIFT

The Pachamama Alliance is working to shift humanity's current trajectory, guided by some fundamental principles and values:

- The universe is friendly and the evolutionary Spirit that put the stars in motion is still moving through all of us. It is a dynamic, self-organizing process whose grace and guidance we can trust.
- Human beings are by nature collaborative and cooperative, and innately desire the success of our species and all life. When barriers to our natural expression are eliminated (i.e., resignation, myths of separation and scarcity), we cooperate for the common, long-term good.
- Human beings are not separate from each other or Nature. We are totally interrelated, and our actions have consequences to all. What we do to others, we do to ourselves. What we do to the earth, we do to ourselves.
- Indigenous people are the source of a worldview and cosmology that can provide powerful guidance and teaching for achieving our vision—a thriving, just, and sustainable world.
- One of the most effective ways to produce results is to empower other organizations through skillful alliances. A principle of skillful alliances is that amazing things can be accomplished when people are not worrying about who is getting credit.
- People's actions are correlated with how they see the world—the story they tell themselves about the world. Transforming how people see and relate to the world and the possibilities they see for the future is a powerful way to effect social change.
- Consciously and unconsciously created systems of ongoing oppression and inequality exist in the world, and the outcomes generated by those systems are directly in opposition to our vision of a thriving, just, and sustainable world.
- We are accountable to, and stand in solidarity with, those whose access to material resources and to free and full self-expression is limited by unjust systems of power and privilege.

PARTNERSHIP WITH THE ACHUAR

Deep in the Amazon rain forest, spanning the borders of modern-day Ecuador and Peru, the Achuar people have lived and thrived for centuries. Traditionally warriors with a fierce devotion to their land, they kept their sophisticated culture and worldview remarkably intact as late as the mid-twentieth century. Thanks to their interdependent approach to life, the rain forest where they make their home is also among the world's most pristine primary forests.

Since the early twentieth century, individuals and corporations from the so-called "modern" world have sought to exploit Achuar land for its oil, disregarding its irreplaceable ecological and cultural wealth. By the early 1990s, Achuar shamans and elders were having dreams of an imminent threat to their land and traditional way of life. From contact with neighboring tribes, the Achuar knew that oil exploration and extractive industries were destroying the rain forest and everything alive in it, while steadily moving closer and closer to their home. They made the courageous decision to reach out to the modern world that was threatening their very existence, which led to the 1995 visit of John Perkins and Bill and Lynne Twist. Masters of building strategic alliances for survival during wartime, the Achuar redeployed their skills to find allies in the industrialized world who would partner with them to strengthen the sovereignty of their ancient culture and their collaboration with other indigenous peoples.

The Achuar are still warriors, only now they defend their ancestral lands, wisdom, and traditions on behalf of all life. In their view, true warriors have the wisdom to stop destruction before it starts, the strength to sustain life where and when they can, and the courage to choose life every time. Of all the insight that indigenous peoples of Ecuador's Amazon rain forest have to share with the world, this dedication to warriorship can fill a crucial need at this time of increasing global challenges. Everyone can be a warrior, wherever we are. As allies of the Achuar, the Pachamama Alliance draws on this powerful new vision of warriorship in their work.

FUNDACIÓN PACHAMAMA

Through Fundación Pachamama, the Pachamama Alliance's sister organization in Ecuador launched in 1997, the Pachamama Alliance facilitated legal and technical support for the Achuar and other indigenous groups to strengthen their self-governance and preserve their lands and cultures. This included working in partnership with the Achuar people to gain collective title for nearly 1.8 million acres of their ancestral rain forest.

Thanks to advocacy by Fundación Pachamama and other allied groups, Ecuador's government has enacted visionary policies, including being the first nation in the world to recognize Rights of Nature in its constitution. But in late 2012, Ecuador moved away from that vision and back toward oil development in the Amazon rain forest. The latest plans for oil exploitation could destroy seven of the indigenous cultures Fundación Pachamama works with, including the Achuar, and millions of acres of the world's most biodiverse and pristine rain forest, a key component of regulating global climate.

In 2014, the government of Ecuador dissolved Fundación Pachamama, without prior notice, on the heels of indigenous protests against its plans to open some 2.6 million hectares of rain forest to new oil drilling, through an auction called the XIth Oil Round. Yet despite this loss of a legal entity on the ground, the work the team was doing continues, ranging from creating innovative models for sustainable economic development and community health, to mapping and land titling.

The current oil threat demonstrates that merely halting individual instances of oil extraction is a never-ending battle. Since its founding, the Pachamama

Alliance has known the necessity of getting to the root of the problem and "changing the dream of the modern world," as the Achuar have requested, by awakening others to what is at stake in the Amazon and what can be learned from indigenous peoples.

INVITING NEW ALLIES

At the invitation of the Achuar, in 1996 the Pachamama Alliance began to bring other people from the modern world to the rain forest on Pachamama Journeys. These trips support indigenous-owned ecotourism projects and other economic alternatives to oil, while also offering travelers a direct experience of indigenous wisdom and the Pachamama Alliance vision.

Amid the rush of the modern world, people can lose sight of the mysterious and essential interconnectedness shared with the earth and all of life. It is often hard to remember that humanity did not always live this way. Thankfully, the Achuar people and other indigenous people have maintained their reality, affirming on a daily basis that humans, as a species, are still hardwired for connection with each other and our environment.

The Pachamama Journey is about accessing and remembering the indigenous part of ourselves. This can fulfill a deep longing for many and is also a useful, perhaps necessary, undertaking for effectively and creatively dealing with the challenges faced in daily life by all. Based on 15 years of experience in the region, the Pachamama Journey is designed as an opportunity for participants to explore their own hearts, minds, bodies, souls, humanity, and unique contributions to the world through experiential learning. Participants are invited by the Achuar to directly experience their lands, knowledge, and wisdom, and to stand with them as allies for the protection of their ancient culture and homeland, a particularly pristine part of the Amazon rain forest that plays such a large role in regulating global climate (Avissar & Werth, 2005).

Because the size of Pachamama Journeys is necessarily small, other projects emerged in efforts to make a widespread impact to "change the dream." In 2005, the Pachamama Alliance launched a suite of transformative learning workshops with the "Awakening the Dreamer Symposium." This multimedia workshop explores the interconnection between environmental sustainability, social justice, and spiritual fulfillment, as well as each participant's personal role as an agent of change. Videos and guided personal reflection and group interaction exercises draw on knowledge from respected social and scientific experts of our time, interwoven with wisdom and inspiration from our indigenous partners, and give participants the tools to move past anxiety or anguish to a place of empowerment.

WHAT'S NEXT: SCALING UP THE APPROACH TO CONNECT WITH BIGGER MOVEMENTS

Now, the Pachamama Alliance is taking accountability for a new strategy and structure to move people from inspiration to sustained action and transformation. In 2014, the Pachamama Alliance rolled out the first of a new set of programs, the Game Changer Intensive, an online course. This course picks up where the Awakening the Dreamer Symposium leaves off, designed to catalyze the inner work of transformation and aiming to inspire and equip people to engage in effective collective action in the world.

As with the current symposium, Game Changer Intensive, and other Pachamama Alliance workshops and Journeys, new programmatic elements being designed will interconnect environmental sustainability, social justice, and spiritual fulfillment toward the goal of catalyzing a healthier and happier way of life for all while respecting the traditions and resources of the earth and all its peoples.

REFERENCES

Avissar, R., & Werth, D. (2005). Global hydroclimatological teleconnections resulting from tropical deforestation. *Journal of Hydrometeorology*, 6, 134–145. doi: http://dx .doi.org/10.1175/JHM406.1

Cultural Design Group. (2011). *Facilitating conscious capitalism*. Retrieved April 15, 2015, from http://culturaldesigngroup.com/facilitation/conscious-capitalism

European Environment Agency. (2012). *Climate change, impacts and vulnerability in Europe 2012*. Retrieved April 15, 2015, from http://www.eea.europa.eu/publications/climate-impacts-and-vulnerability-2012

Greene, G. (2010, February 15). The power and purpose of dreams. *Psychology Today*. Retrieved April 15, 2015, from http://www.psychologytoday.com/blog/insomniac/ 201002/the-power-and-purpose-dreams

The Pachamama Alliance (TPA). (2011). *Awakening the Dreamer, Changing the Dream Symposium, version 2.5*. San Francisco, CA: Author.

Twist, L. (2003). *The soul of money: Reclaiming the wealth of our inner resources*. New York, NY: W. W. Norton & Company.

United Nations World Commission on Environment and Development. (1987). *Our common future*. New York, NY: United Nations. Retrieved April 15, 2015, from http://www.un-documents.net/our-common-future.pdf

Wackernagel, M., & Rees, W. (1996). *Our ecological footprint: Reducing human impact on the earth*. Gabriola Island, BC: New Society Publishers.

Waggoner, R. (2009). *Lucid dreaming: Gateway to the inner self*. Needham, MA: Moment Point Press.

The World Bank. (2012). *Turn down the heat: Why a 4°C warmer world must be avoided*. Retrieved April 15, 2015, from http://www.worldbank.org/en/news/feature/2012/11/ 18/Climate-change-report-warns-dramatically-warmer-world-this-century

12

Merging External Biodiversity with Internal Transformation: A Model of Ecosystem and Ecopsychology in Belize

David Wood, Michael Schmidt, and Judy Kuriansky

The earth has music for those that listen.

—*George Santayana*

Belize is a country that has been challenged by natural disasters but also offers an opportunity for a unique experience of nature and biodiversity. This chapter describes a unique project in the setting of an eco-sensitive retreat that respects the ecology and indigenous nature of the environment and its people while offering an opportunity to experience personal transformation.

BACKGROUND

Centuries ago, the earth's crust shifted and caused the land mass off the coast of Belize to sink into the sea. When these three large mountain peaks sank, coral began to grow toward the surface of the water. In a process that began thousands of years ago and continues today, new coral grew upon older coral, and as a result, the three atolls and hundreds of cayes (pronounced "key") in the waters of Belize were formed. These are three of only four atolls that exist in the Caribbean.

One of the cayes inspired the first author to dedicate years of his life to design, develop, and build an island paradise known today as Thatch Caye Private Island Resort. The purpose of the project—ongoing in its development—is to provide a setting consistent with sustainable living and respect for nature and indigenous culture, in which to present trainings and workshops about personal growth and transformation. Due to its biodiversity, which is explained below, Belize attracts ecotourism; this chapter describes efforts to take this ecological aspect to an even higher level, using it to inspire people toward sustainable living and transformation in their lives.

AN OVERVIEW OF BELIZE

Belize is bordered by Mexico to the north, Guatemala to the south and west, and the Caribbean Sea to the east. It is currently an attractive tourist destination drawing over one million tourists annually, made easier given that English is the official language. On the mainland are Mayan ruins, jungles, waterfalls, isolated caves, wildlife sanctuaries, and lush countryside. A member of the British Commonwealth, Belize became a British colony in 1884 and was formerly known as British Honduras. The name was changed to Belize in 1971, and independence was granted in 1981.

Belize is ecologically diverse in that it is made up of Central American jungles and the Caribbean Sea. The biodiversity is evident in the contrast between the kaleidoscope of coral, fish, dolphins and sea turtles, and some 570 species of birds. Between its resources of land, sea, and sky—national parks, wildlife sanctuaries, and marine reserves—Belize is a leader in environmental protection, with more than 40% of the land mass designated as protected areas.

SUSCEPTIBILITY TO NATURAL DISASTER

At the same time as it is a paradise, in the context of its ecological diversity, Belize, like many of its neighbors, is also susceptible to natural disasters, such as hurricanes, tropical storms, flooding, and droughts. Resulting damages have affected natural resources like sugarcane, papaya, corn, and vegetable industries. As such, Belize has become a center of research and study regarding disaster risk reduction. Many projects have been developed for enhanced disaster preparedness to support farmers and fisheries. Some projects have focused on the issue of climate change in the context of Belize and its impact on mental health and psychosocial well-being (Weissbecker, 2008). As such, Belize has become a center for combining the perspective of well-being with ecological awareness.

ECO-SENSITIVITY OF THATCH CAYE

The island of Thatch Caye was developed to be an alternative to a typical tourist destination that drains resources. Located 30 minutes off Belize's lush tropical central coastline, the island represents a natural ecosystem designated as a UNESCO World Heritage Site. It has been developed and built over seven years without the use of any heavy machinery; in fact, for many years, a small team of dedicated men lived in tents and helped to handcraft and reclaim the island from the sea. The location is within the Southwater Marine reserve, an area dedicated to marine preservation. The warm, clear turquoise water and reef diversity create an environment for sea fly-fishing and sea kayaking. Divers and snorkelers greatly appreciate the diversity of the reef, which is a significant habitat for threatened species and exotic sea creatures, including marine turtles. Thatch Caye has deeply eco-conscious roots, harnessing the rainfall, breezes, and sunshine for the majority of the power and water used on the island. The authors of this chapter maintain that protection of this world for generations is essential, and only possible when people work together with nature and commit to a philosophy of conscious living using clean, quiet, and renewable energy.

The resort harnesses both solar and wind power to replace traditional off-grid methods of energy production and thus shows a forward-thinking effort to increase sustainability in the region. Commitment to, and respect for, the indigenous culture of Belize at the resort is also evident in hiring as staff only locals and residents who represent the local beliefs, cultures, and traditions.

THE CHALLENGE OF ECO-SENSITIVITY

Maintaining the delicate balance between preserving natural resources and business opportunity is difficult. Tourism is the country's top source of employment and investment; yet ironically, it is also the country's biggest environmental threat. Fortunately, most Belizeans are proud of their natural heritage and recognize that the goals of environmental conservation and economic prosperity are not mutually exclusive, giving the country a reputation as a paradigm of ecotourism. Many beach resorts are powered by solar energy, and jungle lodges are built from reclaimed hardwoods. Licensed guides educate visitors, for example, about the fragility of the reef, the medicinal uses of flora, and the threats to the jaguar's habitat.

The motto on the Belize flag reads "Sub Umbra Florero," referring to the mighty mahogany tree; it means "Under the shade, I flourish." Sadly, mahogany is not prevalent in present times, but with its loss has come an understanding of its value. Belizeans recognize that their country's greatest asset must be respected and protected, and that tourists have an important role to play as long as they, too, respect the environment.

THE ECODIVERSITY

The varied habitats of Belize make it home to a wide variety of organisms, inhabiting land, sea, and air. Marine life includes blue parrot fish, neon blowfish, harmless nurse sharks, and six-foot eagle rays. Varied species of birds are in 12 bird sanctuaries. A national park is more than 800 acres in size, with trails, caves, and pools surrounded by dense forest overhung with moss, vines, and ferns. There are over two miles of underground rivers with waterfalls and crystal cathedrals. Many caves are in a mountain nature preserve with carvings and calcified remains of Mayan people, including broken pottery thought to release spirits and artifacts thought to be used in ancient rituals. The ancient Maya ruins are thought to date back to 1200–1000 BC. Original inhabitants are believed to have migrated into the Belize River valley from the west in Highland Guatemala. Inside the ruins are a king's chamber, priest quarters, and meditation sweathouse.

PERSONAL STORY OF THE FIRST AUTHOR

I first read about the island of Thatch Caye in a magazine, and immediately knew that this would be the perfect location for personal growth seminars, spiritual retreats, and advanced adventure programs. When I spoke with the owner, I heard the story of how he had purchased a mangrove-infested sand spit and spent over a decade realizing his dream of owning a fully operational and stunning private island resort. This matched my previous inspiration from reading Sir Richard Branson's autobiography of how he purchased "Neckar," his own Island paradise, and how still today it is his favorite place on earth to spend time with clients, friends, family, and loved ones. When I learned of Thatch Caye, I knew this was the beginning of realizing my own dream of owning an island where people can pursue change and growth in harmony with seekers and trainers, teachers, and facilitators to design an ecologically responsible natural environment. In such a setting, they can learn to preserve the planet while transforming themselves.

WORKSHOPS THAT ADAPT AND ADVANTAGE THE BIODIVERSE ENVIRONMENT

To date, seven workshops have been held. Since the ecological setting provides an ideal backdrop for all types of personal development programs, these experiences provide an opportunity for transformation for people, and allow the facilitators to observe the impact of the workshop material and the effect of the environment.

Some workshops are for a general group of people interested in personal growth. Others are targeted as an advanced training for trainers of personal growth experiences, entitled "Good 2 Great." This program is designed in the TTT "train the trainers" model (Research Center for Leadership in Action, n.d.). The target audience is trainers, teachers, and motivational speakers who are already working with audiences in some professional capacity and were already competent, passionate, and committed to excellence in this area.

The workshops include the following activities and techniques: storytelling; improvisation; commanding presence; silent mornings and meditation; exercise; journaling (recording about your day); modeling; accelerated Whole Brain learning; practice in making a powerful presentation; and identification of various learning styles, called VAKS—Visual-Authority-Kinesthetic Learning

Styles. Other activities include yoga, laughter yoga, blindfolded trust walks, and drum circles led by local drummers. There are also sporting events, since of course the island lends itself to such activities, like snorkeling, scuba diving, zip lining, kayaking and stand-up paddle boarding.

Some activities focus on cultivating happiness, like documenting gratitudes and performing random acts of kindness. As a random act of kindness one year, the group went to a local community center and hurricane shelter to help. The walls had been daubed in graffiti and looked disheveled and forlorn, so the group painted both the inside and out. The news of this spread throughout the village and brought the whole village together, inspired by the act of kindness and collaboration. The next year, the workshop attendees returned to see that the original center was still looking as beautifully intact as the day it was painted, teeming now with vitality and pride. The group painted another community center a few miles away. Locals business and our participants all contributed funds to pay for the paint and brushes, and local youth turned up, helped out, and went home completely mint green (from being covered in the paint)!

Attendees come from diverse parts of the world, including from both the east and west coasts of Canada and the United States, and traveling long distances— e.g., as far away as Sydney, Perth, and Melbourne, Australia.

The setting itself adds greatly to the experience, given both its natural beauty and its climate unpredictability. The fact that some workshops were run the last week of November and the first week of December in 2012 meant that big storms and heavy rain occurred during both events. These climate events challenged the participants to persevere during difficult climate conditions, but similarly challenged them to stretch their possibilities. The relevancy of the techniques to personal growth, the physical activities, intimate size class, and the beauty and remoteness of the setting, as well as a deep integration with the local culture, appear to be factors that facilitated success of the workshops, both in the estimation of the facilitator (the first author) and supported by considerable satisfaction and appreciation expressed by the participants.

The workshop models continue to be refined, particularly to take advantage of the beauty of the people and the unique ecological setting of the island resort and of the country. As a result, more such trainings and experiences will be offered in the future.

CONCLUSION

A model for the future in the era of sustainable development is to respect the environment and its unique biodiversity while also harnessing natural and human resources for social progress. The present project in Belize, an ecodiverse country, represents an example of this approach that can valuably be adapted in other countries.

REFERENCES

Research Center for Leadership in Action (n.d.). *Training for trainers: A guide to designing interactive trainings using popular education techniques.* Retrieved January 13, 2013, from http://www.wagner.nyu.edu/leadership/reports/files/Trainers.pdf

Weissbecker, I. (2008, November 18). *The impact of climate change on mental health and psychosocial well being.* Presentation at Psychology Day at the United Nations, UN Headquarters, New York, NY.

13

Youth Self-Efficacy and Climate Change: Innovative Educational Approaches in the New Sustainable Development Era

Helen Courtney White

In 2002, the United Nations General Assembly proclaimed the UN Decade of Education for Sustainable Development for the years 2005–2014. The purpose was to reframe education, training, and public awareness at national levels to focus on sustainability. While many countries' education systems swiftly developed national action plans, curricula, and standards, others were slow to respond. As this dedicated decade came to a close, the sustainable development era was still in its infancy, and the work required to transform civil society at all levels continues to be more urgent than ever.

While every generation faces an uncertain future, it is evident that millions of youth in the twenty-first century and beyond will inherit rapid and unpredictable changes due to climate change. These climate-related changes are in large part the consequences of human activity and production-consumption-intensive ways of life that were triggered by the industrial era. Unlike weather, which can be observed on a day-to-day basis, climate change is analyzed by looking at scientific models over longer time scales, making it difficult to perceive risks within short time frames. In addition, some greenhouse gases, like carbon, can take several hundred years to cycle out of the atmosphere; thus, the probable impact on future generations will extend over centuries.

This chapter addresses attitudes about climate change and unique approaches to education about this crucial issue impacting our planet. It focuses on youth and therefore presents techniques that are especially appealing to this generation. The work emerges from the author's commitment to concern about the new era of sustainability, through her environmental studies graduate work and experience regarding education approaches about climate change, especially regarding the preparation of youth to assume more civic responsibilities for a more peaceful and prosperous planet. The importance of youth education and engagement is evident to the author in her role as director of partnerships for World Savvy (an organization that educates youth about world affairs, in collaboration with Columbia University Teachers College and the Asia Society); through the efforts of the United Nations' Decade of Education of Sustainable Development (2005–2014); and through the author's support of the U.S. Partnership for Education for Sustainable Development and her participation in a 2010 congressionally mandated working meeting for the "Sustainability Education Summit: Citizenship and Pathways for a Green Economy."

BACKGROUND

Climate change is frequently misunderstood, in part, due to prevailing social norms, limited formal and informal related education, and the lack of adequate media coverage. Climate change communication research studies highlight the diverse beliefs and understandings of global warming by adults and teens. In reports entitled "Global Warming's Six Americas," for March 2012 and November 2011, the results from 2011 indicated that the U.S. adult population's beliefs regarding global warming were: 9% dismissive; 16% doubtful; 10% disengaged; 24% cautious; 28% concerned; and 13% alarmed (Leiserowitz, Maibach, Roser-Renouf, & Hmielowski, 2012). This research showed only minor changes in these beliefs between 2008 and 2012. In another study, *American Teens' Knowledge of Climate Change*, conducted by the Yale Project on Climate Change Communication, 54% of teens said that global warming is happening, compared to 63% of adults (Leiserowitz, Smith, & Marlon, 2011). It is important to stress research results vary widely depending on the participants being studied, country, geography, and other variables.

Climate scientist Thomas Lovejoy explains that to stop global emissions at 2 degrees, significant changes are needed to peak by 2016, but that a 2-degree change is already unimaginable (Lovejoy, 2013). As UNESCO (n.d.) notes in its *Decade of Education for Sustainable Development* under Policy Dialogue 4, "Simply introducing new content about climate change science, causes, consequences and solutions will not be an adequate response to climate change." The longer societies wait to address greenhouse gas emissions, and the longer they continue contributing to increases in the atmosphere, the longer and more significant the global environmental impacts will be on future generations for centuries to come. This leaves a future on the edge of chaos for today's students and future generations, which is why youth self-efficacy and innovative models for transformative change are critical.

Self-efficacy is a powerful determinant for responses, especially in the face of uncertainty, fear, stress, or adversity (Sherer et al., 1982). Albert Bandura (1994) defines self-efficacy as "the beliefs people hold about their capabilities, which determine how they feel, think, motivate themselves and behave in given contexts." As individuals make decisions, there is the constant summing up of what perceived effort is needed, how much, for how long, and the anticipated outcomes. This internal processing draws upon awareness, beliefs, and knowledge, which leads to an assessment of ability, options, the likelihood of effectiveness, and the initial response (APA Task Force, 2009). Self-efficacy links beliefs, cognition, and behavior, resulting in the degree of action or inaction.

The frightening imagery of extreme weather reported by mass media is known to be effective for awareness. Unfortunately, it also can evoke hopelessness, fear, denial, and stress, which can limit the perceived effectiveness of individual and collective climate change actions. Instead, linking everyday emotions and concerns is far more useful for encouraging self-efficacy and constructive action.

Sterling (2010) notes "At personal levels, the maintenance of deep-seated worldviews tends to prevail despite evidence that they may no longer be appropriate to changed conditions." Regardless of one's climate change beliefs, the precautionary principle appears to be a wise approach for adult leaders, who are working with youth, and youth alike. The precautionary principle suggests immediate action in situations of uncertainty in order to minimize any probable harm. This principle helps move adults and youth beyond relying solely on scientific findings, stressing moral and ethical concerns to aid behavior change and action.

INNOVATIVE APPROACHES FOR YOUTH SELF-EFFICACY: TWO MODELS

Education programs have been shown to have a positive effect on both younger and older children, and on boys as well as girls, in heightening their awareness about the environment (Lindemann-Matties, 2002). In spite of the complex challenges related to climate change, there are many emerging and innovative approaches that can improve youth self-efficacy and aid social change in civil society. Two different education models for youth are presented below that illustrate the use of interdisciplinary research bridging theories and practices. Here, youth are divided into two groups: (1) children, 7 to 12 years old; and (2) adolescents, 13 to 18 years old. One model is an informal education project that is an interactive, mobile game app, called Habitat the Game. This app encourages climate-friendly behavior change for children, their caregivers, and a broader social network. The other model is an education program for adolescents, in the form of a school-based assembly that leads to action by the Alliance for Climate Education. These two models increase awareness and knowledge and also offer immediate opportunities for individual and collective behavior change aimed at protecting and improving our shared biosphere.

The Unique Approach of Habitat the Game (http://www.habitatthegame.com)

Habitat the Game is a free app for Apple and Android phones and tablets. Created by Australian interactive media company Elevator Entertainment, the concept design was initiated in 2010, followed by game development in 2013 and a public release in 2014. The primary goal of the interactive game is to inspire children 7 to 12 years old, their caregivers, and a broader social network of youth to partake in making a measurable impact on reducing greenhouse gas emissions and improving the environment upon which we depend. The two core objectives are: (1) to empower youth with intriguing information and achievable actions; and (2) to increase a sense of responsibility in making a meaningful difference in addressing climate change.

Players adopt a virtual polar bear that gets named and needs regular care in a virtual world, similar to the wildly popular interactive game of the late 1990s, Tamagotchi. As the game is played, points are earned from in-game tasks, like quizzes, and from taking real-world actions through mini missions and weekly missions that are self-reported. There are visible consequences to the virtual bear and virtual environment when there is low or no in-game care of the bear or limited self-reporting of real-world actions. This enables incremental learning with rewards, along with converting environmentally friendly behaviors into positive habits for life. The aim is for every player to contribute to a 25% reduction in carbon, water, and land use.

There are over 50 real-world actions described in fun, simple, and easy-to-understand language for youth. The following are a few examples. To accomplish energy conservation, players are prompted to turn off lights not needed at night and to unplug televisions and computers. In the case of water, players are asked to report the length of their shower and then to decrease it over time to under four minutes. With regard to transportation, players are encouraged to carpool, cycle, or walk. Buying locally grown food and composting is recommended with regard to food. Avoiding excessive packaging, recycling paper, eliminating the use of plastic bags, and making better consumer choices are recommended. Some activities are one-time actions, and others are ongoing. These actions are eco-indicators related to reducing greenhouse gas emissions, water consumption, and waste, thereby reducing ecological footprints (Skamp, Boyes, & Stanisstreet, 2009). In the case of quizzes, if an answer is incorrect, the player is required to keep trying until the correct answer is identified.

Elevator Entertainment conducted a survey with youth to determine what animals children liked most, what behaviors children felt in control of, and what kind of outcomes were expected. The results informed the design and development of the game. The Integrated Sustainability Analysis (ISA) team in the School of Physics at Sydney University developed algorithms to measure players' ecological footprint as baselines in players' profiles, in comparison to others, and as progress is calculated—showcasing behavior change improvements over time. The Centre for Research on Computer Supported Learning and Cognition (CoCo) team at Sydney University helped to identify learning objectives and contributed expertise on how children learn with digital media. Game testing was conducted to assess the ways in which learners were using the game and areas that needed further development.

The Unique Approach of the Alliance for Climate Education (http://www.acespace.org)

The Alliance for Climate Education (ACE), a U.S.-based nonprofit organization, has created award-winning ACE Assembly programs for secondary schools. These assembly programs are intended to improve students' knowledge, values, attitudes, and behaviors related to climate change. They run for approximately 40 minutes total in length, are tailored for the needs for the school, and planned to be high-energy to be appealing to youth.

Research from the American Teens' Knowledge of Climate Change showed that 48% of teens and 38% of adults are "not very well informed" or "not at all informed" about how the earth's climate system works (Leiserowitz, Smith, & Marlon, 2011). It was also noted that this lack of knowledge by U.S. teens was not surprising "as few teens have ever taken a formal course on the topic" (Leiserowitz, Smith, & Marlon, 2011). According to the ACE website, a Loyola University study indicates the ACE Assembly program in schools is making a difference, contributing to a 58% improvement of climate science knowledge.

ACE educators venture into secondary schools and present compelling videos with popular music, animation, and strong narratives. The video provides an overview of the latest climate science, stories of youth affected by climate change, and a call for action. This sets the stage at school to foster dialogue about problem-solving and the development of solutions. Students relate to the issue, bringing the grand global challenge of climate change home to what they can do alone, on a personal level, and as part of a school group or in their community.

The program has been designed with its audience of 13- to 18-year-olds explicitly in mind. Core messages are correlated with the needs and interests of today's adolescents (Winerman, 2014). Making choices is highlighted. Showcasing actions is a norm. Tweeting is encouraged. A sense of responsibility and commitment is created by calling upon students to take a pledge on the ACE website as part of the "Do One Thing" (DOT) campaign to personally reduce energy usage. Students can determine their own action or make a choice from a few options. Those who are ready to go a step further can join an ACE Action Team. Each ACE Action Team develops its own project to reduce greenhouse gas emissions.

After the presentation, students can remain engaged and join the online ACE Action Network for youth. Loeppky, Robins, Tanga, and Walsh (2012) indicate that "There are two types of social norms: injunctive norms and descriptive norms. Injunctive norms provide information on which behaviors are approved or disapproved of by a group of people. Descriptive norms indicate which behaviors are normally practiced in a group." The ACE Assembly and continued engagement online and at school powerfully foster both injunctive and descriptive norms. On the ACE website, there is a counter with the number of commitments made related to personal actions. High schools with the highest ACE Action Team points are on leaderboards. This encourages healthy competition to take efforts to another level and fosters social norming.

As Lenzen and Murray (2001) have noted, "Partnerships made up of those who are concerned about the issue of climate change and optimistic about translating awareness and concern into action that can make a difference need to seek out long-term, mainstream avenues for embedding the necessary skills and strategies in the education of school students." ACE has worked with Tufts University on concept development as the program evolved, and with Loyola University on a study regarding the program's effectiveness. In addition, expertise and research from different disciplines, including climate science and climate change communication, are instrumental in the planning and production of this media-based program.

CONCLUSION

To address climate change, youth must find sustainability to be a natural way of life, innately recognizing how each nation's ecological relationships directly correlate with well-being, the livelihood of other species, and the health of earth systems, which we directly depend on for survival. Two unique approaches to educating youth about climate change are Habitat the Game and ACE Assembly. Both approaches use experts and research from different disciplines to inform their design. They understand their audiences' needs, interests, and developmental stages, enabling the framing for effective climate change education. The two techniques empower youth through the innovative use of new media. Both programs evoke positive emotions, demonstrating that participation matters and every individual's actions count. These education innovations use applied psychology principles to create novel ways to capture and hold the attention of today's youth, stimulating self-efficacy related to positive action and environmental protection. These programs demonstrate the importance, and viability, of creative projects in education targeted at youth, as well as other age groups, regarding the crucial issue of climate change.

ACKNOWLEDGMENTS

Thank you for the generous support and encouragement of Dr. Judy Kuriansky, Dr. Martin Butler, and the NGO Committee on Education. This chapter resulted from a presentation entitled "Youth Self-Efficacy and Climate Change" at the workshop panel entitled *Promoting Mental Health and Wellbeing for Youth in the New Post-2015 Sustainable Development Agenda: Psychological Principles, Science and Practices*, held at the 65th Annual DPI/NGO Conference, 2015 and Beyond-Our Action Agenda at the UN Headquarters in New York City. The workshop was sponsored by International Association of Applied Psychology and cosponsored by Manhattan Multicultural Counselling Center, International Council of Psychologists, World Council for Psychotherapy, and Psychology Coalition of NGOS accredited at the United Nations.

RESOURCES

Alliance for Climate Education—acespace.org
Habitat the Game—habitatthegame.com

REFERENCES

American Psychological Association (APA) Task Force on the Interface between Psychology and Global Climate Change. (2009).*Psychology and global climate change: Addressing a multi-faceted phenomenon and set of challenges.* Washington, DC: Author. Retrieved April 18, 2015, from http://www.apa.org/science/about/publications/climate-change-booklet.pdf

Bandura, A. (1994). Self-efficacy. In V. S. Ramachaudran (Ed.), *Encyclopedia of human behavior* (Vol. 4, pp. 71–81). New York, NY: Academic Press.

Leiserowitz, A., Maibach, E., Roser-Renouf, C., & Hmielowski, J. (2012). *Global warming's six Americas, March 2012 and November 2011.* Yale University and George Mason University. New Haven, CT: Yale Project on Climate Change Communication.

Leiserowitz, A., Smith, N., & Marlon, J. R. (2011). *American teens' knowledge of climate change.* Yale University. New Haven, CT: Yale Project on Climate Change Communication.

Lenzen, M., & Murray, J. (2001, Spring). The role of equity and lifestyles in education about climate change: Experiences from a large-scale teacher development program. *Canadian Journal of Environmental Education, 6.*

Lindemann-Matties, P. (2002). The influence of an educational program on children's perception of biodiversity. *The Journal of Environmental Education, 33*(2), 22–31.

Loeppky, N., Robins, N., Tanga, S., & Walsh, K. (2012). *Final report: Saving energy through creative competition.* The Alliance for Climate Education and Tufts University Department of Urban and Environmental Policy and Planning.

Lovejoy, T. E. (2013, April 20). The climate change endgame. *The New York Times.*

Sherer, M., Maddux, J. E., Mercandante, B., Prentice-Dunn, S., Jacobs, B., & Rogers, R. W. (1982). The self-efficacy scale: Construction and validation. *Psychological Reports, 51*(2), 663–671.

Skamp, K. R., Boyes, E., & Stanisstreet, M. (2009). Global warming responses at the primary secondary interface: 1. Students' beliefs and willingness to act. *Australian Journal of Environmental Education, 25,* 15–30.

Sterling, S. (2010). Learning for resilience, or the resilient learner? Towards a necessary reconciliation in a paradigm of sustainable education. *Environmental Education Research*, 16(5–6), 511–528.

UNESCO. (n.d.). *Education for Sustainable Development and Climate Change*. Policy Dialogue 4. Retrieved April 18, 2015, from http://www.unesco.org/education/tlsf/mods/theme_c/img/unescopolicydialogue.pdf

Winerman, L. (2014, June). Climate change communication heats up: Environmental scientists, teachers, advocates and others are turning to psychologists' research to help them educate the public about climate change. *Monitor on Psychology*, 45(6).

14

Black Gold to Human Gold: Natural and Human Resources Interface, the Case of Azerbaijan

John E. S. Lawrence

At the crossroads of Asia and Europe, Azerbaijan is a standout oil-producing, relatively young nation in the Caucasus region, recently independent from the Soviet Union, and a member of the Commonwealth of Independent States (CIS). The country has experienced significant new wealth from its extractive industries and is fashioning broad development policies to avoid the "Dutch" disease common to single-sector economies. A small team of specialists, including the author, worked with the UN Development Programme (UNDP) and other multi- and bilateral agencies over several years to help design and implement the "Black Gold to Human Gold" initiative. This chapter describes that project and presents its value as a model of development and progress from the perspective of both human and environmental capital. In essence, it provides a model of how the extraction of oil can be converted into benefits for the people and society. Given my familiarity and involvement with the project, my personal reflections and perspective are also presented. Focus has been on priorities such as economic diversification, national employment and education strategies, and accelerated skills development, structured around a general framework for developing human resourcefulness. Such exploratory adventures into new policy territory function significantly in the interface between humans and their capacities for improved management of our planet and may have lessons beyond just the CIS region.

BACKGROUND

The name Azerbaijan is known to many today—resulting from a brilliant advertising campaign involving, for example, airport posters as far afield as Puerto Rico, and football jerseys in World Cup games throughout Europe—as "the land of fire." Few know why, and even fewer can place this country on a map. With a population of around nine million, bordered by the Caspian Sea to the east, Russia to the north, and Iran to the south, Azerbaijan's unique and relatively consistent cultural history goes back at least to the third millennium BC (Ibrahimov, 2010). Rock paintings, petroglyphs, and excavated ceramics testify to ancient high levels of culture. Underlying this historic line of continuity are the huge natural resources of oil and gas that have permitted the amazing, perpetual flames surrounding their national sites (e.g., Yanardag—"blazing mountain" in Azerbaijani—on the Absheron Peninsula, just a few miles northeast of the capital city) and giving rise to the name "Azer," meaning in Turkic roughly "brave man" or "fire-keeper." The highest mountain, Mount Bazarduzu, rises up to 4,466 meters in the Greater Caucasus range to the north, and the fertile valleys below produce highly reputable cash crops, vegetables, fruit, and cotton and tobacco. The variety in microclimates, and the vastly different ecosystems from high mountain plateaus, the marine coastal environment, and relatively arid southern plains, make for an attractive, sometimes fierce, physical landscape.

Azerbaijan's recent history is notable for several geopolitical events that are recorded in many books on the region (Swietochowski, 1995). Among the most significant historical happenings in recent times, of course, was its declaration of independence from the Soviet Union in 1991. This reflected an early restlessness to move in this new direction toward autonomy, for the second time in the twentieth century—since in April–May 1918, it became for a short time part of the Transcaucasian Democratic Federative Republic. Contrary to accounts of the comparative bloodlessness of this process, many lives were lost in the confrontation with Russian soldiers in January 1990, and also in subsequent and still ongoing conflicts with Armenia over the Nagorno-Karabakh enclave. Sensitivities understandably still run high among even the younger generation on both these issues.

Dominating national progress since independence is an immense advance in technological transfer of crude oil now to global commercial access. In 2005–2006, opening of the almost 2,000 km pipeline from Baku, through Georgia and Erzerum to the Ceyhan deepwater port on the Turkish southeastern Mediterranean coast, established a totally new stamp on the energy map. Now, Caspian oil, a crucial and much sought-after lodestone among the grasping classes worldwide, became open to the world (note, for example, that if Hitler had succeeded in his thrust northward toward Azerbaijani oilfields as planned in 1942, the outcome of the war could have been very different [Agayev, Akhundov, Aliyev, & Agarunov, 1995]). Despite supplying only a very small fraction (around 1%) of the global supply, the Heydar Aliyev Baku-Tbilisi-Ceyhan (BTC) project propelled Azerbaijan into a new geopolitical role, and both economic and political consequences were immediately significant. As noted by S. Frederick Starr, an American expert on Russian and Eurasian affairs, and Svante E. Cornell, a Swedish scholar specializing on politics and security issues in Eurasia, in their book analyzing the Baku-Tbilisi-Ceyhan Pipeline as an oil window to the West:

> What sets the BTC pipeline apart is not its technology, impressive though it is, but two sets of relationships that endured from the germination of the idea to its final completion. First, one must speak of the close correspondence that existed at all stages of the pipeline's development between the politicians, businessmen, and economists who defined the project's ends and the engineers and builders who devised the means by which those ends could be achieved. Second, and no less important, one must stress the intimate working relationship that was established between the international experts in business and technology and the three countries traversed by the pipeline and the myriad communities and millions of citizens affected by it. These relationships turned an ambitious undertaking in the hermetic worlds of business, politics and engineering into an innovative initiative in the sphere of economic, social, and civic development. (Starr & Cornell, 2005, pp. 7–8)

While many aspects of the construction, operation, and maintenance of the BTC pipeline were, and even remain, controversial (e.g., landowner agreements, environmental concerns), the impacts on the Azerbaijan economy were sudden and spectacular. According to the State Oil Fund, the pipeline is designed to last 40 years, while the capacity is one billion barrels (50 million tons) of oil per annum (State Oil Fund of the Republic of Azerbaijan, n.d.). Known reserves are projected to last into the 2020s, although estimates vary considerably, depending partly on advances in extractive technologies.

The first direct revenues from BTC were paid to the government in 2006. Oil profits for the next few years increased by about 30%, raising both huge opportunities as well as serious challenges for national development. As the IMF has pointed out (IMF, 2013), several fundamental threats faced strategic planning measures during this period: the crucial short-term need for rapid transformation of new oil revenues into productive assets that would stand the test of time (i.e., be sustainable and widely shared throughout not only the entire country, but with future generations); potential for overdependency on single-sector revenues to fund all public services; and the tendency to put off sound fiscal and monetary management policy in face of massive GDP per capita growth due to the new wealth. In short, while leading the world in GDP growth per capita, Azerbaijan faced the "Dutch disease," the classic textbook case of single-source (mostly oil-based) economies that through mismanagement experienced negative growth and exacerbated inequalities.

This term was first introduced by the *Economist* in 1977 to describe the impact of a North Sea gas bonanza on the economy of the Netherlands ("It's Only Natural," 2010). Solutions had to be found to avoid the economic pitfalls of rapid price inflation and exchange rate appreciation while acceding to the social necessities of equity and balanced growth.

Thus, a small team of development specialists (including this author) was invited under the sponsorship of the UNDP, to work with the government of Azerbaijan on achieving sustainable, long-term growth and, most specifically, on skills development necessary for economic diversification. After more than a decade of engagement with various ministries at all levels from national to local, and with welcome support from UNDP as well as the World Bank and several bilaterals (e.g., Germany, Switzerland), the team made recommendations that have become quite formative in national socioeconomic policy (Hopkins, Lawrence, Stephens, & Webster, 2007).

The catchphrase title *Black Gold to Human Gold* (BGHG) was originally coined by our team leader Michael Hopkins after informal encounters with rural farmers struggling with dual impacts of technology and fast-changing markets. As earlier research had found, "In most developing countries, agricultural colleges, universities and polytechnics train researchers, government, bank employees and extension officers, but not farmers. Producing more food with less water, less chemicals and less soil erosion requires high levels of skill" (International Commission on Peace and Food, 1994). Farmers in the Azerbaijani provinces had the need for skills but limited opportunities for accessing such skills, and thus the BGHG phrase became a catchword for national human resources development (HRD) often referred to by Azerbaijan president Ilham Aliyev and others, for example, on the UNDP Azerbaijan website, or at the Baku Humanitarian Forum in 2013.

The principles and practice, engendered by the BGHG approach and laid out in our report, are the subjects of this chapter. These are still being formulated and adapted, with implications not just for Azerbaijan, but for the region and beyond. Building on several decades of research and policy implementation in many countries (Lawrence, 2013), a blueprint is suggested for fostering human resourcefulness from the perspective of national and intersectoral strategies, with emphasis on young people.

The BGHG framework has implications for countries at all points on the development spectrum. Startled by the endurance of fiscal crises starting in 2008, and the daily, more evident effects of climate change, governments (and private-sector interests) worldwide are now waking up to the swiftly changing face of socioeconomic development. Energy is essential to human survival, but how we manage, distribute, and conserve it will require new skills and great change. We do not have long to adjust before the consequences of inaction overtake our societies. Because this is so important, forgive me if I change my tone somewhat here, and get a bit less "policy-wonkish" and a bit more personal.

FOSTERING HUMAN *RESOURCEFULNESS*

Everyone needs resources of one kind or another. Water, energy, and most basically, perhaps, oxygen. When our roof leaks in a storm, we need buckets (or receptacles of any kind) to stop the overly plentiful flow of unwanted and intrusive signals about our mismanagement from what some call "nature," or what many call "God." If, however, rain is at a premium and drought is the norm, we may indeed welcome, cherish, and store each drop, as do Yemenis, Australians, or, increasingly, Californians.

If Prometheus at least mythically brought fire into our northern lives and, consequently, energy and warmth into our communities, he must have brought with it awesome lightning, even volcanic destruction of habitat. I remember as a bushfire-fighting team member in Australia going to the very front of the line with flames bursting overhead, and rolling blazes of green shrubbery careening down slopes to start new outbreaks below. At the harsh forward edges of the fire was always a small wall of organic desperation, clambering over everything including my boots as I attempted to spray from a pathetically depleted canister on my back. Snakes, assorted critters, and insects flooded ahead, ahead, ahead— an elemental scrambling scrum seeking escape from lethal heat in a cascade of livingness and terror. Hopefully, this is no prescient metaphor for human survival.

As a formerly devoted mountain-climber and paramedic, having been many times without oxygen supplementation over the altitude limit at which human habitation is sustainable, I learned to appreciate very much the dependency we all share on clean, breathable air. I have seen struggle and death overcome a young, strong colleague on a high mountain ridge simply for want of enough oxygen. Yet now, even the entire atmospheric envelope in which we exist today is poisonously clouded. The intercontinental flights I took last week added to many other jet trails visible from my window seat, and to the distorted, oily dim view of the land below.

My argument in this chapter is that humans need a new, more adaptive kind of *resourcefulness* to best manage all resources on our planet that have sustained us yet so far. Human ingenuity has led us to the miraculous multi-millennial progress of our species. The forebrain ballooning in our evolutionary skulls has drawn us front and center, for our moment on this tiny celestial stage we call earth. We have no idea how long this moment will last. We should make the most of it, and not permit limbic, hindbrain regressive impulse to restrain us.

I have found Azerbaijan an amazing example, in many ways, of a new kind of progress, open to exploration of new HRD ideas. As evidence shows (Lawrence 2013; Stiglitz, 2013) and as our BGHG report proposes in practical terms for Azerbaijan, we must surely focus on the economics of resource management. But to do this more effectively, we must also address the way we help people prepare for all our emerging global "realities"—economic, social, cultural, and, of course, environmental. While understanding clear priorities, e.g., of youth engagement and especially women's rights (Baskakova, 2013), we cannot focus on just the few, as so many of our innovations have in the past, but explicitly on the *large* numbers of young people coming into a global labor force with high expectations but what appears to be continually, so far at least, shrinking occupational opportunity. Questions arise. How do we deal with the "livelihood" issue—i.e., the increasingly difficult relationships between the constraints of our work and the rest of our daily lives (e.g., family, social networks, leisure as personal livelihood expression)? And finally, how do we manage our institutions, corporations, communities, and societies so as to increase the probability that requisite energy for modern living becomes widely accessible to all, and wealth from any and all production processes is distributed equally enough to sustain social fabrics in reasonable stability?

In the BGHG report (Hopkins et al., 2007, p. 51), we reintroduce the term human *resourcefulness* as a goal for national HRD strategy. What is this quality? How can we define it? How can we measure, assess, and then perhaps even teach it, or at least pass it on with intergenerational improvements both institutionally and parentally? Answers to these questions are surely likely to be time-dependent and socioculturally situational, but the kinds of skills categories that seem relevant are resilience, creativity, adaptability, and various forms of intellectual and emotional courage. Although work is still proceeding on defining this concept for policy purposes, it is at the heart of the BGHG approach to HRD.

The "systems"-strategic approach to national HRD was promoted by Harbison (1968) but became associated with relatively short-lived "economistic" attempts at manpower planning, which appeared northern-driven and top-down to politicians and practitioners in younger economies. Formulated into broader and more socio-psychologically sensitive application in the Asian-Pacific region (e.g., UNESCAP Jakarta Plan of Action [UNESCAP, 1988]), it became the foundation for spurts in South Asian development during the 1990s. Subsequently, the concept became more globally visible through several HRD reports by the UN Secretary-General to the UN General Assembly. This conceptual emergence is evident in United Nations' Reports on HRD (A/50/330; A/52/540; and A/56/162 through A/66/206), three of which this author was responsible for compiling.

Since then, many countries have been and are experimenting with the idea of national HRD in all world regions, with various degrees of success (Lynham, Paprock, & Cunningham, 2006; McLean, Lynham, Azevedo, Lawrence, & Nafukho, 2008). The BGHG framework for HRD is constructed on the idea of a coordinated, intersectoral public policy platform of rights-based legislative and regulatory support with four key components, each of which is designed with the goal of enhancing capacities of Azerbaijani citizens, in terms explicitly of increasing peoples' options and choices. These are:

1. *Access to assets* (at the most basic levels, shelter, sustenance, nutrition, and health care; and at more developed levels, credit and social services).

2. Opportunities to *acquire across a lifetime* the necessary education and training to provide skills and competencies to work, sustain a livelihood, and contribute to self, community, and larger society.
3. Opportunities to *apply* skills and competencies in chosen occupational (e.g., employment) or other livelihood settings.
4. Sophistication, adaptation, and updating of the overall HRD policy framework so as to *conserve and strengthen* the nation's human resources.

Several requisites are essential to make this kind of strategy work. Links between the occupational "supply" and "demand" sides of the economy (in the middle two elements) must be explicitly acknowledged and HRD policies must be directed toward their successful articulation. All relevant ministries must avoid the traditional tendency to "silo" themselves and their operations and instead seek better coordinative policy and operational mechanisms. Sufficient data systems such as labor force surveys (of households as well as business establishments) must be routinely conducted to provide timely information on jobs, employer expectations, education and training, and competitive skills profiles for all parties. In this way —and if effective—the resultant human resources "radar" scanning can be instrumental in (a) keeping education and training well-tuned to labor market needs, (b) assisting in informing personal occupational choice, and (c) engaging employers in the crucial balancing of labor market supply and demand.

Moreover, the necessary flexibility in wage structures, place and hours of work (e.g., options for telecommuting), and contractual occupational arrangements must be considered in accommodating a variety of workers' situations (e.g., first-time labor force entrants, women with young children, people living and working with disabilities, part-time employees) and those with other constraints (e.g., displaced persons, elderly still working, ex-prisoners), all with the aim of motivating and increasing productivity throughout all segments of national citizenry. This implies different skill sets, particularly among managers, around the employee interface between work and livelihood.

Perhaps, above all must be fostering new aspects of human resourcefulness in response to the stress and pace of change. There is an extensive, if primarily Western, psychological literature on the concept of resilience; but this limits itself somewhat to reactivity and "hardiness" (Luthans, Vogelgesang & Lester, 2006). There is much less on the qualities of resourcefulness that constitute proactive sharpness, intellectual athleticism, emotional stability, and reliable problem-solving aptitudes that are directly useful across many situations and applications. Most employers seem to want these kinds of meta-capacities, and many will say they know them when they see them, but education and training systems are mostly anchored to more traditional knowledge and skill sets. So there is much room for innovation here, and Azerbaijan is moving ahead in most interesting ways, especially through its openness to new ideas.

THE WAY FORWARD

The BGHG framework, in suggesting a systems approach to both sides of the human resources supply and demand policy space, made a number of recommendations for action. Key among these were inter-ministerial and public-private-sector coordination, educational reform, HRD data and occupational information, employment services, and accelerated skills development. Most of these recommendations have been either partially or fully implemented and, while besides hopefully advantaging Azerbaijani progress, are offering a sort of clinical field-test of these elements of a broader national HRD strategy for future human development.

Government commitment is clear. As President Aliyev's spokesman said in a recent interview with the *New Times*:

> You may know that one of the major priorities of our state policy is to transform "black gold into human gold". The government is implementing consistent efforts toward bolstering information and knowledge centered human resources. New educational institutions are being inaugurated, and [the] science and education system is being enhanced. In the meantime, state scholarships on education abroad are being realized. (*New Times*, 2014)

During the BGHG project, coordinating committees were set up such as a BGHG Advisory Board, and coordination among key constituencies has been acknowledged as central to all mandates since. A new Workforce Development Agency has been planned, and integration of new legislative decrees in employment, general education, and technical and vocational education and training has been a national priority. Not only has it been important to establish stronger relationships between key public sector ministries (e.g., labor, education, planning, information/communication, and health), but business, government, and the employer community are coming together also in new ways. One example is in the provision of data at the strategically most practical intervention points in the HRD system's routine "radar" scanning.

Realizing from the outset that information and communication are fundamental neural pathways in the political anatomy of progress, the government has pushed them to the front of the line. As a result, technological advances have been rapid, and the ICT sector is one of the most profitable in the national economy (Lawrence & Alakbarov, 2004). Furthermore, its contribution to all other sectors has been extensive, most notably to education, in ICT curriculum development, teacher training in ICT, and infrastructural support to pedagogy at all levels (Republic of Azerbaijan, 2014).

An ambitious vision for bringing students into the environmental debate has been effected by the introduction of textbooks on *Sustainable Human Development and Basic Ecological Civilization*. These cover socioeconomic aspects of development within the Azeri culture but break entirely new ground in opening young minds to *ekotsivila*, the recognition of the need for broader civil society planning and resource management in working toward a greener economy (Alakbarov, 2013).

Job analysis is another new avenue currently being paved by the government. Aligning its procedures as far as possible with the European Qualifications Framework, Azerbaijan has begun a national research effort to define and disseminate occupational and training/competency-based standards, along with assessments and accreditation procedures. Illustrative of the cooperative nature of this effort among key stakeholders, the DIOS project has set up sector commissions for the selection of priority occupations across several industries (Nazarov & Charkazov, 2014). Two hundred occupations have so far been analyzed, training manuals prepared, and the website completed to permit widespread access to the information. As a result, Azerbaijan has established a promising structure, process, and initial results for the future in promoting skills development. This information is of course valuable for employers, and employees either entering or reentering the labor force, as well as for students, educators, and trainers. Maintaining the quality, timeliness, and relevance of this database in response to technological change is indispensable in national HRD planning.

Major improvements have also been achieved in Azerbaijan's employment services (ES). After a review (Lawrence & Bakhshaliyev, 2011) of international "good practice" in what are called "active labor-market programs" (ALMPs) in several countries, and official study tour visits to Austria and Lithuania, the Ministry of Labor has embarked on extensive revisions to ES infrastructure. In addition to bringing occupational information out to the local level, ALMPs include employment assistance strategies such as job-search skills training, job clubs, specially targeted programs for vulnerable groups (new entrants into the labor force, internally displaced persons [IDPs] and refugees, persons living with disabilities, released prisoners), job fairs, employer outreach programs, and small business advisory services. The challenge is to upgrade not only the physical facilities of deteriorated offices outside the capital city region (Baku and environs) but also to even the quality of ES outreach into the rest of the country, especially in rural areas. Two new centers (Ismayilli and Gabala) have been built in the north of the country, and plans are to extend this center construction project further into other districts.

Most notably, the BGHG concept of accelerated skills development was picked up almost immediately. The Presidential Decree Number 2090 (April 16, 2007) in its second paragraph authorized an eight-year State Program on Education of Azerbaijani Citizens Abroad. Financed by the State Oil Fund (SOFAZ), this initiative was managed within the Ministry of Education. As of April 2014, since 2008, SOFAZ has supported more than 2,300 students at the college level overseas in mostly UK institutions, in fields varying from medicine to economics and business at a cost of more than 90 million manats (over US$100 million) (Government of Azerbaijan, 2014).

CONCLUSIONS

The BGHG approach has been a bellwether for the country of Azerbaijan and also serves as a useful example of how strategic HRD can be practically incorporated into national development planning and practice. In spite of all the progress, of course, many challenges remain, particularly in ensuring that the four foundational elements mentioned above are more widely accessible for all Azerbaijanis. But follow-up information from the central statistical office has indicated positive trends in numbers of students graduating from vocational schools and getting jobs, as well as the encouraging numbers qualifying for, and supported by SOFAZ for study abroad. To the extent this model represents opening of gateways for the larger numbers needing opportunity, it is a welcome step forward. So, it seems clear that with enough political will and strong leadership, negative consequences of extraction of oil (black gold), can be mitigated through commitment to accelerated and advanced skills enhancement among the citizenry (human gold). Azerbaijan is a key country case study in this regard. It remains to be seen how sustainable the BGHG approach will become, how well it is managed across time, and what the rest of the region, and other countries beyond the region, can learn from the results.

REFERENCES

Agayev, V., Akhundov, F., Aliyev, F. T., & Agarunov, M. (1995). *World War II and Azerbaijan*. Baku, Azerbaijan: Azerbaijan International.

Alakbarov, U. (2013). Transition to ecological civilization: Experience of Azerbaijan. In *Materials of Baku International Humanitarian Forum* (pp. 239–244). Baku, Azerbaijan.

Baskakova, M. (2012). *Young people in Azerbaijan: The gender aspect of transition from education to decent work*. ILO Working Paper #5. Moscow, Russia: ILO.

Government of Azerbaijan. (2014, April 1). *Information on implementation of the state program on education of Azerbaijani youth abroad for the years of 2007–2015*. Baku, Azerbaijan: Author.

Harbison, F. H. (1968). A systems analysis approach to human resource development planning. In P. H. Coombs (Ed.), *Manpower aspects of educational planning* (pp. 7–9). Paris, France: UNESCO, IIEP.

Hopkins, M., Lawrence, J. E. S., Stephens, T., & Webster A. (2007). Converting black gold into human gold. Baku, Azerbaijan: UNDP. Retrieved July 30, 2014, from http://www.az.undp.org/content/azerbaijan/en/home/library/human_development/blackgold_humangold/

Ibrahimov, E. (2010). *When we say Azerbaijan*. Baku, Azerbaijan: Abseron Resm Qalereyasi.

International Commission on Peace and Food. (1994). Strategies for developing human resourcefulness. In *Uncommon opportunities* (Chap. 7). Report of International Commission on Peace and Food. London, UK: Zed Books.

It's only natural. (2010, September 9). *The Economist*. Retrieved March 30, 2015, from http://www.economist.com/node/16964094

International Monetary Fund (IMF), Middle East and Central Asia Department. (2013, June). *Republic of Azerbaijan: Selected issues.* Retrieved March 30, 2015, from http://www.elibrary.imf.org/abstract/IMF002/20604-9781484338124/20604-9781484338124/20604-9781484338124_A002.xml?rskey=r1kZU3&result=3

Lawrence, J. E. S. (2013, October–November). *Human resources and sustainable development: Silo or synthesis?* Presentation to Baku Humanitarian Forum.

Lawrence, J. E. S., & Alakbarov, U. (2004). Rapid progress of ICT in Azerbaijan: Information technologies in the public service. In M. Gurstein & V. Tischenko (Eds.), *Community informatics and community networking in the CIS: Practical and policy implications.* Moscow, Russia: Editorial URSS.

Lawrence, J. E. S., & Bakhshaliyev, R. (2011, January). *International review of employment service policy and practice. Technical report to Government of Azerbaijan and World Bank.* Baku, Azerbaijan.

Luthans, F., Vogelgesang, G. R., & Lester, P. B. (2006). Developing the psychological capital of resiliency. *Human Resource Development Review, 5,* 25.

Lynham, S. A., Paprock, K. E., & Cunningham, P. W. (Eds.). (2006). HRD in transitioning societies in the developing world. *Advances in Developing Human Resources, 8*(1), 435–448.

McLean, G. N., Lynham, S. A., Azevedo, R. E., Lawrence, J. E. S., & Nafukho, F. M. (2008, June). A response to Wang and Swanson's article on national HRD and theory development. *Human Resource Development Review, 7,* 241–258.

Nazarov, I., & Charkazov, A. (2014, February 19). *Forecasting and optimization of skill needs.* DIOS Project Seminar International Labor Organization and European Training Foundation.

New Times. (2014, March 5). Novruz Mammadov: Deputy head of the presidential administration of the Republic of Azerbaijan and head of Foreign Relations Department. Baku, Azerbaijan.

Republic of Azerbaijan. (2014, December). A sector assessment: Accelerating growth of high-speed Internet services in Azerbaijan. Washington, DC: World Bank.

Starr, S. F., & Cornell, S. E. (Eds.). (2005). *The Baku-Tbilisi-Ceyhan Pipeline: Oil window to the West.* Washington, DC: Central Asia–Caucasus Institute & Silk Road Studies Program; Baltimore, MD: Johns Hopkins University Press.

State Oil Fund of the Republic of Azerbaijan. (n.d.). Heydar Aliyev Baku-Tbilisi-Ceyhan Main Export Pipeline. Retrieved March 30, 2015, from http://www.oilfund.az/index.php?page=baki-tbilisi-ceyhan-esas-ixrac-boru-kemeri&hl=en_US#sthash.q7vl7fB6.dpuf

Stiglitz, J. (2013, January 7). The post-crisis crises. *Project Syndicate.* Retrieved July 30, 2014, from http://www.project-syndicate.org/commentary/global-warming—inequality—and-structural-change-by-joseph-e—stiglitz

Swietochowski, T. (1995). *Russia and Azerbaijan: A borderland in transition.* New York, NY: Columbia University Press.

United Nations, Economic and Social Commission for Asia and the Pacific (UNESCAP). (1988). *Jakarta Plan of Action.* Bangkok, Thailand: UNESCAP.

15

Can the Private Sector Help Heal the Planet? Contributions of the Private Sector to Sustainable Development through Consumer Education, Awareness, and Mobilizing Positive Psychological and Prosocial Behavior

Daniel W. Bena and Judy Kuriansky

As the international community moves into a new era focused on sustainable development to achieve global goals, including ending poverty, ensuring healthy lives and well-being, access to energy, quality education, and promoting economic growth and peaceful societies, a major means of implementation is through global partnerships. Such partnerships involve collaborations between, and contributions of, many stakeholders, including governments and the public and private sectors. This chapter addresses the important role the private sector can play as well as the varied and often complex stressors placed upon the private sector, looking through an environmental lens. It also offers examples of where the private sector, in collaboration with other actors, can help heal the planet—and are having a positive impact on relieving societal stress over environmental trends and crises. Many of the underlying principles of these processes are psychological in nature, as they tap into influences on consumer confidence and behavior, company integrity, and principles of communication.

The title of this chapter, "Can the Private Sector Help Heal the Planet?" is a challenging question that immediately elicits a cascade of psychological and psychosocial considerations. "Healing the planet" is surely a magnanimous goal, but what role does the private sector play? Doesn't the ecologic domain to heal the planet belong to governments and environmental nonprofit organizations—with the former's obligation to fulfill myriad human rights (including among them the right to water and sanitation, as a result of the most recent UN General Assembly vote on the subject), and the latter's purist passion and mission? Hasn't the private sector received criticism for many instances of, in fact, doing the opposite, through oil spills and contaminations and other controversial acts that pollute the environment?

The answer to all these questions, of course, is yes. But as this chapter presents, the private sector actually *does*—and *can*—play an important and critical role in healing the planet. This is demonstrated by several factors, named in the title of this chapter: consumer education, awareness, and mobilizing positive psychological and psychosocial behavior. Indeed, a remarkable global trend is emerging over the last five years of innovative collaboration toward collective impact, which involves the creative engagement of the private sector as a partner in the mission to help heal the planet and the people on it who share its resources (Hanleybrown, Kania, & Kramer, 2012).

Until 2015, this trend coincided with the Eighth Millennium Development Goal set by the United Nations for member states to achieve over the years 2000–2015. The goal was to "develop a global partnership for development," which includes cooperating with the private sector, for example, in making available new technologies, for achieving the other goals including goal #7, to ensure environmental sustainability. It now coincides with the new Sustainable Development Goals (SDGs), which reinforce the importance of partnerships for development, and which highlight the importance of environmental sustainability in development. These goals were agreed to by the member states of the United Nations in 2015 for countries to achieve by the year 2030 (UNDESA, n.d.). The 17 SDGs outline global goals, including to end poverty, to ensure quality education and gender equality, to provide access to energy, and to promote economic growth and peaceful societies. Goal #17 refers specifically to "[s]trengthen the means of implementation and revitalize the global partnership for sustainable development," which includes the important involvement of the private sector. Many sessions and events have been held at the UN to address how to involve the private sector in partnerships to achieve these SDGs. In fact, a major means of implementation of the SDGs is through such global multi-stakeholder partnerships.

Multi-stakeholder partnerships are defined as collaborations between, and contributions of, individuals, groups, organizations, or systems who become involved in a common mission and bring their idiosyncratic goals together for a common exploration, and who affect or are affected by an action or event. Such partnerships can be in any area of social concern; for example, the second author has documented examples of these in the case of community-based programs for teen sexuality education as well as for a girls' empowerment program in Africa (Kuriansky & Berry, 2011a, 2011b; Kuriansky & Corsini Munt, 2009). Stakeholders, including academia, civil society, media, and religion, play an important role in the dialogue about nature, well-being, consumption, and environmental protection, bringing expertise that contributes significantly to expanding knowledge of these issues (see Chapter 17 of this volume [Kuriansky, LeMay, & Kumar, 2015]).

The value of partnership in the case of government working with civil society was evident in the inclusion of Goal #3 in the SDGs, to "Ensure healthy lives and promote well-being for all at all ages," with its target specifically to "promote mental health and well-being." This outcome was due largely to the advocacy partnership of the second author of this chapter in her role as chair of the Psychology Coalition of NGOs accredited at the United Nations, with the Ambassador of the Mission of Palau to the UN Dr. Caleb Otto (Forman, 2014). Well-being of the people is certainly critical in achieving the healing of the planet, and a noble goal in which big business is increasingly becoming involved despite criticisms and cases to the contrary that can be pointed to. Given the SDGs, partnerships among multi-stakeholders—bringing together private sector, e.g., corporations and big business, with government and the public sector—will become more common in coming decades, for the benefit of the 3 P's being pointed to in the new Post-2015 Agenda: the people, the planet, and prosperity. This evolution builds on corporate social responsibility programs that became popular in recent past.

The SDGs address what is considered the "big three" challenges of the world—water scarcity, climate change, and food insecurity—which are also addressed in this chapter and which certainly affect the well-being of the planet and the people. This is consistent with the SDGs being built on three pillars: economic, social, and environmental.

WHAT IS ENVIRONMENTAL SUSTAINABILITY?

The pillar to ensure environmental sustainability includes many goals and targets that address sustainably making safe water accessible to people, reversing the loss of environmental resources, protecting the forests, and conserving use of the oceans. These aspects of sustainable development must then be integrated into country policies and programs.

In the UN document, "Our Common Future, Chapter Two: Towards Sustainable Development," sustainable development is defined as follows:

[S]ustainable development is a process of change in which the exploitation of resources, the direction of investments, the orientation of technological development; and institutional change are all in harmony and enhance both current and future potential to meet human needs and aspirations. (United Nations, 1985)

As the first author is a sustainable development practitioner within the private sector, it is clear how these tenets are critical to both the short- and long-term success of any business. No longer is it enough to merely provide financial returns to shareholders of the company; the proverbial bar has been raised—and raised significantly. Multiple, diverse parties who have a stake in a business have expanded their expectations for companies in the private sector. For the consumer goods industry, this means that products must not only meet expectations of quality, but they must also be sourced, produced, and transported in socially and environmentally sound ways. For producers of foods and beverages, the relationship with the consumer is an intimate one—either consciously or subconsciously—because the products being manufactured are, after all, ingested. Taking a substance into one's body—as personal a relationship as you can get—brings with it expectations of safety, consistency, and now corporate conscience. In a major trend in these recent times, an increasing number of companies are demonstrating this corporate conscience (Goodpaster, 2007).

This chapter addresses the varied and often complex stressors placed upon the private sector, looking through an environmental lens. It also offers examples of where the private sector, in collaboration with other actors, can help—and are having—a positive impact on relieving societal stress over environmental trends and crises. Many of the underlying principles of these processes are psychological in nature, as they tap into consumer confidence and behavior influences, company integrity, and communication.

In the context of the SDG document and this chapter, the "private sector" refers to business in all of its facets. It includes the spectrum of for-profit enterprises from small, entrepreneurial businesses to large, multinational corporations, and everything in between. It does not include government bodies, nongovernmental organizations (NGOs), nonprofits, or academia, although every single one of these entities plays a critical role in collaborative partnership with the private sector if lasting sustainable development is to be achieved.

The private sector has understood the environmental dimension of sustainable development for decades—long before the term was formalized in the previously mentioned UN report. The main reason for this is due to the inherently positive benefits that the private sector can reap. For example, being eco-efficient users of water and energy can save millions of dollars each year from operational costs. For one, by not polluting water or other resources at the start, less money would be needed for remediation. And secondly, legitimate examples of corporate conscience strengthen a company's ability to operate and grow in the eyes of the communities they serve.

Increasingly, companies understand these benefits, quantifying them, and transparently disclose them into the public domain. In today's society, it is important for the survival of any business to heed the expectations of stakeholders for social, economic, and environmental stewardship.

THE SCOPE OF THE GOAL OF HEALING

The reality is, however, that short of an anthropogenically induced nuclear cataclysm, the planet proper will persist. It will, over time, equilibrate and adapt to changing conditions, which constitutes, in essence, healing itself. In fact, the lens of "healing" applies to people in society, more than to the planet itself. Despite this semantic specificity, the future of the planet's resources is integrally tied to the future and healing of the people on the planet. This is, perhaps, a provocative premise, but intentionally so. The intent is to make a clear distinction between "planet" and "life on it." The planet—the physical aggregation of soil, magma, water, air, etc.—has always equilibrated in the past when faced with stressors, like the ice age, giant meteor strikes, earthquakes, extinctions, and so much more. Life died, species became extinct, but the planet recovered. The point here is that even if carbon emissions continue unchecked, or water scarcity runs rampant, and billion-dollar weather events increase, humans may cease along with other life forms, but the planet itself will evolve, as it has over billions of years.

Water is a good example. Certainly, water resources are shifting in their availability. Water scarcity already affects every continent. Businesses, like people, need water to survive and flourish. Around 1.2 billion people, or almost one-fifth of the world's population, live in areas of physical scarcity of water resources, and 500 million people are approaching this dire situation. Another 1.6 billion people, or almost one-quarter of the world's population, face economic water shortage, where countries lack the necessary infrastructure to take water from rivers and aquifers. The important point is that water scarcity is both a natural and a human-made phenomenon. There is enough water on the planet for six billion people, but it is distributed unevenly, and too much of it is wasted, polluted, and unsustainably managed (UNDESA, 2011). The idea of water being polluted has no real bearing on the long-term health of the planet—only on the health of those organisms living on it, and their being able to use this water as a life's blood. We should explicitly note that resources such as water are critical for all living things, not for the planet itself. Nature has provided remarkably effective and efficient means to help the planet purify itself of troublesome contaminants—from the oxidative ability of solar radiation in air, to the ion-exchange and other chemical attenuative mechanisms of the soil, to the simple settling of contaminants in water.

People are an amazing and diverse group of living beings on the planet in every way—physically, spiritually, intellectually, emotionally, and culturally. Every single being on the planet consumes something. And every single being on the planet has practices in which they engage on a daily basis that involves consumption. Why is this worth emphasizing? In early 2012, the population of the planet surpassed seven billion people. Between now and 2050, the global population is expected to increase to more than nine billion, with 98% of this growth happening in the developing and emerging world, according to UN estimates. The global urban population will double. Meanwhile, populations are aging and stabilizing in many developed countries. Local demographic patterns will become increasingly diverse (UNDESA Population Division, 2008).

These changes intuitively will mean more mouths to feed, more water to drink, and more resources used. To assure that the people on the planet live well and thrive within the environmental boundaries of the earth, both production and consumption behaviors must change.

THE ROLE OF THE PRIVATE SECTOR: APPLYING PSYCHOLOGICAL PRINCIPLES ABOUT BEHAVIOR

In light of this problem, how can an organization, private sector or not, even begin to hope to change its behavior? One common way by which to increase motivation for necessary change is awareness-building. Another, sometimes more controversial way, depending on the methods, is through making a visceral emotional appeal. This might involve making people momentarily emotionally distressed—through high-impact photographs, or startling statistics—to help them see the results of their consumption. Once that connection is made, you have essentially drawn people's attention to the dangers of what will result from unchecked consumption, and they are more receptive to raising awareness.

Given these potential valuable solutions, an important question arises: Why would the private sector care about changing people's behavior toward the planet and environment? In other words, why would a consumer products company expend financial and other resources to engage in this activity? After all, if you want to change the behavior of an elected official, you need only advise them of what the majority of their constituents want. Similarly, for a consumer products company to change behavior, they need only to understand what consumers want. But, this relationship with the consumer is a two-way street and requires an understanding of balance and tradeoffs. Oftentimes, it is clear through data about what is called "consumer insights" (literally scientifically based insight by a company into the preferences of their consumer base) what consumers want around the world with great precision and granularity. But, in many cases, the application of these data can be complex and ambiguous.

For example, in 2009, the Grocery Manufacturer's Association in association with Deloitte (a large global consulting firm) conducted a survey of over 6,000 shopper experiences at 11 major retailers to understand the characteristics of the "green shopper." Of the consumers surveyed, 95% said they would buy green products (e.g., products perceived as being better for the environment than others). Yet, in the same study, only 75% of the consumers admitted to knowing what a green product is; only 63% were actively looking for green products; and only 22% actually purchased green products! Clearly, the results showed a gap between the intent of consumers to do what they perceived as good, and their actual behavior (GMA, 2009).

The study above offered insight into consumer purchase intent and their perception. Perception is a fascinating and crucial psychosocial phenomenon (Rookes & Wilson, 2000). Many have heard the phrase, particularly in the field of marketing, that "perception is reality." Perception may be experienced or thought of as reality, but it is often not founded upon sound science. This is proven by another example involving water, since aside from air, there is nothing more acutely important to life as we know it. Consumer products companies, particularly those who produce beverages to drink, are all too aware of the dichotomy between the desire of a consumer to take an active part in solutions to the water crisis, and their understanding of the fundamental science justifying those very solutions. Specifically, consider the fact that water treatment technology, safety monitoring protocols, and management approaches are readily available to effectively treat human sewage and make it safe for consumption as drinking water. "Not from my tap," would likely be most people's reply to drink this water, reflecting an emotional response. But in the United States alone, more than 2.1 trillion gallons of water are flushed down toilets every year (Barone, 2008). If the psychological barrier responsible for the reluctance to use toilet water for drinking can be removed, and replaced with an understanding of sound science, imagine the positive impact on the ecosystem that can result. The public officials in Orange County, California, have been doing just this—using treated wastewater for drinking—since 2008 and are being lauded for their leadership in innovative water reuse.

In fact, a project transforming waste into usable water is being tested in Haiti, as presented in a special session at the Clinton Global Initiative, an annual summit of stakeholders to form partnerships to solve global problems, founded by former U.S. president Bill Clinton. The point made in that presentation, similar to the one made above, is that psychological perceptions must be confronted and changed in order to create a more efficient and sustainable environment and an ecologically sound system of survival and use of resources.

THE ROLE OF TRUST IN PERCEPTION

Ultimately, perception comes down to relationships—relationships with yourself, your family, friends, governments, the media, and other stakeholders. Based on these relationships people have, their perceptions are often created and developed. A behavioral element that often drives perception—and, indeed, drives all relationships—is trust. Just as people have (or do not have) trust in individuals, they also have (or do not have) trust in organizations—and in companies. A critical way in which consumer behavior can be changed by a company is through developing trust.

For more than 10 years, the international public relations firm Edelman has been conducting yearly surveys of people around the world, and synthesizing the findings in what is called the "Edelman Trust Barometer." These studies provide invaluable insights to companies (and other stakeholders) about the factors that comprise trust in consumers' minds. In their 2015 survey (Edelman Trust Barometer, 2015), they saw an evaporation of trust across all institutions. For the first time, two-thirds of the 27 nations surveyed (general population data) fell into the "distruster" category. According to Edelman, the horrific spread of Ebola

in western Africa, the disappearance of Malaysia Airlines Flight 370 plus two subsequent major air disasters, the arrests of top Chinese government officials on corruption charges, the foreign exchange rate rigging by six of the world's largest
banks, and the constant drumbeat of data breaches, most recently from Sony Pictures, have shaken confidence in all institutions. In addition, there is a new factor
depressing trust: the rapid implementation of new technologies that are changing
everyday life, from food to fuel to finance. The 2015 Trust Barometer has uncov-
ered a profound concern about the pace of change. By a two-to-one margin,
respondents in all nations feel the new developments in business are going too fast
and there is not adequate testing. Even worse, 54% say business growth or greed/
money are the real impetuses behind innovation—that is two times more than
those who say business innovates because of a desire to make the world a better
place or improve people's lives. The greatest concerns are about genetically modified foods and hydraulic fracturing (trust levels in the 30–40% range), with somewhat more confidence in personal health trackers (69%), electronic payments
and cloud computing (trust levels in the 50% range). The industries charged with
implementing these new technologies have a clear vote of no confidence.
The energy industry is trusted by only 48% to implement fracking. There is a desire
for more government regulation of these developments by a four-to-one margin,
but less than half have confidence in government to do it effectively.

The majority of people need to hear information three to five times to believe
it; skepticism requires repetition. Thus, if the private sector hopes to engage consumers in a movement to collectively heal our planet, or to use resources more
efficiently, or to volunteer to help others in need, it is most effective for these
consumers to be provided with information in multiple ways so they can develop
the necessary trust. This is consistent with psychological theory and research
about learning, including the importance of repetition.

It is understood that consumers largely have the best of intentions, but that
their behavior does not necessarily reflect this intent (Arts, Frambach, &
Bijmolt, 2011). Individuals know, intuitively as well as from their experiences,
that perception is often reality and might even be true in some sense; but it is
also often not based in science, but rather on emotional and visceral responses
to stimuli or other information. We know that trust is the ultimate prerequisite
for receptive and engaged audiences to change their behavior permanently.

THE LINK BETWEEN TRUST AND THE ENVIRONMENT

Several factors come into play in the link between trust and preservation of
the environment, and ultimately the healing of the planet. One factor is that
consumers around the globe, by and large, say they want to buy products that
are produced in environmentally and socially responsible ways from companies

that give back to society (Nielsen, 2012). Also relevant, however, are the visceral or emotional reactions that arise between awareness and taking action when consumers express concern as to the urgency of environmental and social crises. We also know from myriad public relations and corporate communications firms that consumers listen to the portion of the population known as "thought leaders" or "opinion elites" (those individuals or sources perceived to have an inside track on important issues). But even in that situation, the link may take some time to be perceived. For example, anecdotal information from global survey companies, like that of Coulter (2011), suggest a roughly three-year time lag from when recognized experts express a particular opinion to when the general populace adopts it.

What are these experts or thought leaders saying that the general population will eventually accept? In a partnership between GlobeScan and SustainAbility, yearly opinion surveys of recognized sustainability experts representing 17 different sectors are conducted around the world. The 17 sectors studied are: Forest Products, Information Technology, Life Sciences/Biotechnology, Telecommunications, Agriculture/Food/Beverage, Packaging, Electric Utilities, Public Sector Institutions/Government Agencies, Consumer Goods, Banking/Finance, Chemical, Automotive, Pharmaceutical, Electronics, Alcoholic Beverage, Oil/Gas, and Mining.

In their 2011 report, based on 512 qualified sustainability experts representing 64 countries, key findings (GlobeScan/SustainAbility Survey, 2011) concluded that:

- Climate change, water scarcity, and food security are perceived to be the world's most urgent challenges; this highlights the concern for what's being called "the energy-water-food nexus."
- The degree of urgency to attend to the problems with these top three issues (climate change, water security, and food security) has declined since 2009.
- Energy and climate change are predicted to pose the most urgent sustainable development challenge in the expert respondents' respective countries in 2012.
- Europeans and North Americans are most concerned with energy and climate, while those from emerging countries (like India and China) focus on climate and water issues.
- No sector is managing the transition from traditional "business as usual" to sustainable development effectively; all 17 sectors are perceived as net negative (net numeric survey responses between ratings of "good" and "poor").
- Leading sectors—including forest products, information technology, life sciences/biotechnology, telecommunications, and agriculture/food/beverage—have shown marginal improvement in their ability to manage the transition to sustainability in recent years.
- The electronics and chemical sectors' ability to manage the transition to sustainability has deteriorated most among the 17 sectors studied since 2000.

Based on these results, given the voices of the global experts, the "big three" challenges of water scarcity, climate change, and food insecurity continue to be of urgent concern. The bottom line conclusion is that for a company to be trusted, to manage how they are perceived, and to address scientific global realities, they must engage in legitimate and demonstrated impact in areas of concern to society.

THE IMPORTANCE OF CORPORATE CONSCIENCE

The Merriam-Webster dictionary defines the word "conscience" as follows: "The sense or consciousness of the moral goodness or blameworthiness of one's own conduct, intentions, or character together with a feeling of obligation to do right or be good." A conscience can be manifested by an individual, or it can be collectively owned and expressed by a group of people, including a corporation.

Former U.S. president Abraham Lincoln is often credited with the quote, "When I do good, I feel good; when I do bad, I feel bad. That's my religion." While Lincoln's motto might be seen as a gross oversimplification of what has become a highly complex area, there remains a lot of truth to his simple approach. The vast majority of people, barring any psychological or emotional anomaly, know innately what is right and what is wrong. This is also true of governments, businesses, and NGOs—all of which are merely a collection of people. Make no mistake, companies have a collective "corporate conscience"—preferably founded upon their values, which are actively and aggressively manifested every single day.

This attention to conscience, arguably, could be the single most impactful enabler of behavioral change that companies can offer to consumers. People know, viscerally, when a message is legitimate and pure, and driven by the right motivations. Companies need to heed this. Governments need to heed this. NGOs and academics need to heed this. It is only through the legitimacy of tangible actions that trust can be built, perceptions can be managed, and companies' "license to grow" can be secured, so that they can proceed to allocate resources to insure ecologically safe and sustainable processes that benefit the community and other parties.

CONCLUSION AND RECOMMENDATIONS

The private sector, as one partner in a collaboration of partners, can help enable positive impact on the health of the planet and on the society that inhabits it. Such multi-stakeholder partnerships are mandated by the new Sustainable Development Goals agreed by countries who are members of the United Nations, to achieve in the years 2015–2030. This collaboration, however, requires innovative approaches and perhaps less traditional partnerships. All stakeholders must have a seat at the proverbial table, focusing on the task where companies, governments, NGOs, academia, individuals, media, and other interested parties and stakeholders must find the common ground for collective progress. Each must leverage its own strengths and competencies, yet also commit to weave together a fabric that is resilient and supportive. No single entity can solve the crises of the magnitude of those we face in achieving a sustainable and ecologically sound society today. Psychological principles must be applied, to build trust and awareness, encourage corporate and collective social conscience, and facilitate cooperation for the common good. The costs for lasting, sustainable solutions will be challenging—but the cost of inaction will be far greater. After all, the gains for all stakeholders—from the individual to the governmental to the corporate—will be great, and certainly worth the effort. The outcome is essentially healing for the planet.

Note: The views expressed in this work are solely those of the author, and do not necessarily reflect the views of the publisher or PepsiCo, and the publisher and PepsiCo hereby disclaim any responsibility for them.

REFERENCES

Arts, J. W. C., Frambach, R. T., & Bijmolt, T. H. A. (2011, June). Generalizations on consumer innovation adoption: A meta-analysis on drivers of intention and behavior. *International Journal of Research in Marketing, 28*(2), 134–144. Retrieved April 19, 2015, from http://www.sciencedirect.com/science/article/pii/S016781161100022X

Barone, J. (2008, May). From toilet to tap. *Discover* magazine (digital online edition). Retrieved April 19, 2015, from http://discovermagazine.com/2008/may/23-from-toilet-to-tap

Coulter, C. (2011, March). Personal communication between president of GlobeScan and Daniel W. Bena.

Edelman Trust Barometer. (2015). Retrieved April 7, 2015, from http://www.edelman.com/insights/intellectual-property/2015-edelman-trust-barometer/trust-and-innovation-edelman-trust-barometer/executive-summary/

Forman, A. (2014, October 9). Five words that can change the world. *Jewish Journal.* Retrieved April 19, 2015, from http://boston.forward.com/articles/185615/five-words-that-can-change-the-world/

GlobeScan/SustainAbility Survey (2011). Retrieved April 19, 2015, from http://www.globescan.com/expertise/trends/globescan-sustainability-survey.html

Goodpaster, K. E. (2007). *Conscience and corporate culture.* Hoboken, NJ: Wiley-Blackwell Publishing.

Grocery Manufacturers Association (GMA). (2009). Green Market Survey Report, 2009. *Finding the green in today's shoppers: Sustainability trends and new shopper insights.* Retrieved April 19, 2015, from http://www.deloitte.com/assets/Dcom-lebanon/Local%20Assets/Documents/Consumer%20Business/DeloitteGreenShopperStudy_2009.pdf

Hanleybrown, F., Kania, J., & Kramer, M. (2012, January 26). Channeling change: Making collective impact work. *Stanford Social Innovation Review*. Retrieved April 19, 2015, from http://www.ssireview.org/blog/entry/channeling_change_making _collective_impact_work?cpgn=WP%20DL%20-%20Channeling%20Change

Kuriansky, J., & Berry. M. O. (2011a). Advancing the UN MDGs by a Model Program for girls empowerment, HIV/AIDS prevention and entrepreneurship: IAAP Project in Lesotho Africa (pp. 36–39). Retrieved June 9, 2012, from http://www.new.iaapsy .org/uploads/newsletters/April2011.pdf

Kuriansky, J., & Berry, M. O. (2011b). The Girls Empowerment Programme: A multistakeholder camp model in Africa addressing the United Nations Millennium Development Goals. *Centerpoint Now*. New York, NY: The World Council for Peoples of the United Nations.

Kuriansky, J., & Corsini Munt, S. (2009). Engaging multiple stakeholders for healthy teens sexuality: model partnerships for education and HIV prevention. In E. Schroeder and J. Kuriansky (Eds.), *Sexuality education: Past, present and future*, Vol. 3 (Chapter 14). Westport, CT: Praeger.

Kuriansky, J., LeMay, M. & Kumar, A. (2015). Paradigm shifts in nature and well-being: Principles, programs, and policies about the environment and climate change with actions by the United Nations for a sustainable future. In D. G. Nemeth & J. Kuriansky (Eds.), *Ecopsychology: Advances from the intersection of psychology and environmental protection*, Volume 2 (pp. 307–358). Santa Barbara, CA: ABC-CLIO.

Nielsen. (2012, March). *The global, socially conscious consumer*. Retrieved April 19, 2015, from http://www.nielsen.com/us/en/insights/reports/2012/the-global—socially -conscious-consumer.html

Rookes, P., & Wilson. J. (2000). *Perception: Theory, development and organisation*. New York: Taylor & Francis.

United Nations. (1985). Our common future, chapter 2: Towards sustainable development. In Report A42/427, *Report of the World Commission: Our Common Future*. Retrieved April 19, 2015, at http://www.un-documents.net/ocf-02.htm

United Nations Department of Economic and Social Affairs (UNDESA). (2011). *International Decade for Action "Water for Life" 2005–2015*. Retrieved April 19, 2015, from http://www.un.org/waterforlifedecade/scarcity.shtml

United Nations Department of Economic and Social Affairs (UNDESA). (n.d.). Sustainable Development Knowledge Platform. Retrieved March 30, 2015, from https:// sustainabledevelopment.un.org/sdgsproposal

United Nations Department of Economic and Social Affairs (UNDESA) Population Division. (2008). *World population prospects: The 2008 revision*. Retrieved April 19, 2015, from http://www.un.org/esa/population/publications/wpp2008/wpp2008 _highlights.pdf

16

Transforming an Academic Climate from Political Correctness to Truth Seeking: The Rocky Road Faced by Whistleblowers

Ivor Ll. van Heerden

Science has played a major role in the development of the sophistication of present humankind since humans first realized how to strike two stones together and make fire. Scientists, certainly until the 1990s, were held in high esteem by most of society. Now, however, a tenth of the way into the twenty-first century, *mainstream* science is getting a bad rap. The emergence and growth of the ultra-conservative media heralded by Fox News, well-funded political lobbying by the fossil fuel industry amongst many other American corporations, and the funding of institutes that can be considered as distorting science (i.e., deliberately misrepresenting facts), have been responsible for a lot of doubt cast on science today, especially that which pits special interests such as big oil companies against groups calling for action with respect to issues such as global warming. Unfortunately, policy makers are often the targets, and ordinary citizens the victims, of *faux* science (i.e., science that is biased or based on subjectivity rather than objectivity).

Whistleblowers, because of their inside knowledge, have become crucial to ensuring that science is a source of reliable, repeatable, and precise information, rather than the unrepeatable, imprecise concepts of the naysayers and distortion advocates. Theirs has become a critical role in today's distortion-riddled world.

Academics have to comprehend that their research culture and ideals are under attack and are going to have to find better ways to articulate their science, especially as it relates to public policy decisions. Additionally, faculty at academic institutions need to realize that there is a trend to exclude them from the selection process of upper administration, reflecting the growing influence of big-money donors and, hence, the increasing probability that upper administrators will not be supportive of scientific data that opposes the agendas of the big-money donors. This, then, precipitates further the need for "whistleblowers." The latter, therefore, need much better protection.

This chapter discusses the need for whistleblowers in the present political landscape; presents four examples of concerns that distort scientific truth to serve their own interests; and, describes the role of whistleblowers. It is presented in the context of the author's own experience and ends with recommendations for a more open, truthful society in academia, politics, and the public.

BACKGROUND: WHY THE NEED FOR "TRUTH"

I am writing this chapter as someone who was terminated by an academic institution for articulating the truth about governments' failures, and who fought to get my position back. I lost, but I received a sort of settlement. Even so, I suffered many consequences, both emotionally and also practically, including being divorced from an academic position. Perhaps what befell me reflected that throughout my education and subsequent academic career, I have always felt that science was the search for the physical truth whatever the discipline. So, why is it so important that the truth be told, especially in science, and even more crucially as the science may impact or effect public policy?

In my view, the characteristics of good science include:

- Science needs to explain the natural world.
- Its findings are testable, reproducible, and predictive in contrast with biased policy positions.
- Science generates knowledge that is useful; for example, scientific knowledge can provide the basis for political action.
- Science is a source of reliable information.
- There is utility for this dependable information.
- Oftentimes, the catalyst to compromise in policy decisions is a thorough understanding of the science.

As will be discussed further below, the actions of well-funded special interest groups and some willing media outlets have led to a situation in which the public and policy makers are not always receiving reliable information that can be used to solve or ease problems. One could well ask, why the need for reliable, repeatable science?

EXAMPLES OF THE NEED FOR SCIENCE IN TODAY'S WORLD

Presently, there is much discussion about the need for sustainable development—in other words, trying to live within environmentally sustainable means. This is a very tough task especially given the problems caused by a booming world population.

In 1950, the world's population was estimated at 2,556,000,053, with a 10-year growth rate of about 20%. By 2010, there had been about a threefold increase, with an estimated world population of 6,848,932,929, but a reduced 10-year growth rate of 10.7%. By 2050, there are expected to be about 9.5 billion persons on this planet, about a fivefold increase from 1950—with the 10-year growth rate perhaps less than 5% (U.S. Census Bureau, 2014). Troubling questions arise. Just how are we going to feed all these people? Will there be any edible fish left in the great water bodies of this planet? Will there be any forests left? Will there be any wild lands for recreation or species protection and the like? Will there be sufficient potable water for future generations? And, what about energy? Much of the world's population growth has being fueled by cheap, but finite, fossil energy (Zabel, 2009).

Since 1950, the share of world energy production provided by fossil fuels has varied between 85 and 93 percent. Moreover, the period from 2000 to 2005 marked the largest absolute five-year increase ever in world energy production, with fossil fuels accounting for nearly 92 percent of that increase. While the reserves are not limitless—fossil fuels are a nonrenewable resource—they still provide nearly all of world energy production and increases to that production.

However, world fossil fuel production per capita will begin an irreversible decline between 2020 and 2030 (Nehring, 2009). Although their recoverable amounts are vast and are being gradually augmented by advances in technology and improvements in their economics of discovery and development, they are not limitless. They cannot grow indefinitely, particularly when their production has already reached high absolute levels (Nehring, 2009). The byproducts of the burning of this heretofore relatively cheap resource have had a marked global impact. Dramatic increases in carbon dioxide (CO_2) levels in the earth's atmosphere are forcing global warming (IPCC, 1990).

Atmospheric carbon dioxide levels are predicted to become *double* preindustrial levels by 2050 ("Atmospheric Carbon Dioxide Levels Double," 2010). The increase now appears to be following an exponential upward trajectory. Consequently, the resultant rise in global temperature is expected to be about 2.5 degrees Centigrade (4.5 degrees Fahrenheit) by 2050 from the CO_2 increase alone. This may not seem like much, until you realize that the warmest our earth has been in the last 100 million years was only about 5 degrees Centigrade higher than present!

Accompanying this temperature rise are a host of other disquieting responses. The melting of the polar ice caps and glaciers, the exponential thermal expansion–induced rise in sea level, and the increases in global land and sea temperatures are expected to cause huge variations in local weather and climate, and hence vegetation distribution patterns. Overall, by 2050, sea level rise due to thermal expansion alone is predicted to be about a half meter (19 inches), not insignificant in terms of coastal wetlands damage and coastline alteration and erosion. Change in rainfall patterns both spatially and temporally will force a host of environmental outcomes from fluvial/river discharge and sediment transport variances; agricultural, flora, and fauna disruptions; migrations; and survivability.

The next 40 years are going to witness dramatic changes on our earth, our only habitable piece of our universe. How many of these truths are really being communicated to public policy makers and the public? Perhaps the question to ask is, how much of this crucial data and information is being filtered out by politicians and other special interests, as well as certain elements of the "media"; and how much is being demonized, along with the truth tellers? We are facing potential catastrophe after catastrophe—untold human suffering, some would say, of biblical proportions—but just how much of this truth is really registering with policy makers? In my opinion, right now, not much. Why?

FILTERING AND DEMONIZING THE TRUTH: SCIENCE DISTORTERS

There are a number of organizations and end users—call them "special interests"—who substantially benefit from an ill-informed public and policy makers. These groups and individuals relish expounding *faux* science—information reflecting bias and subjectivity rather than objectivity and open-mindedness. Such information emphasizes uncertainties but never answers the question about how to improve the answers to the uncertainties they inspire. Some concepts become sanctified, while the real science or scientist is marginalized and demonized. The example of global warming discussed below is a prime example of sowing distrust and maligning mainstream science. For a full discussion of the "Climate Change Denial Machine," the reader is referred to Dunlap and McCright (2011).

Suffice it to say, the fingerprints of special interests in distorting the truth, or trying to put their spin on it, is not hard to discern. I will discuss four examples, each involving a separate entity but, hopefully, giving a scope and scale of the distortion process; but there are many more.

Example 1: ExxonMobil Attempts at Defining Scientific Truth

Exxon Mobil Corp., or ExxonMobil, is an American multinational oil and gas corporation headquartered in Irving, Texas, in the United States. The world's third-largest company by revenue, ExxonMobil is also the second-largest publicly traded company by market capitalization (Associated Press, 2013) and is the largest fossil fuel refiner in the world with daily production of 3.921 million BOE (Hoyos, 2008). ExxonMobil has drawn criticism for funding organizations that are skeptical of the scientific opinion that global warming is caused by the burning of fossil fuels. A report by the Union of Concerned Scientists (2007) stated:

In an effort to deceive the public about the reality of global warming, ExxonMobil has underwritten the most sophisticated and most successful disinformation campaign since the tobacco industry misled the public about the scientific evidence linking smoking to lung cancer and heart disease. As this report documents, the two disinformation campaigns are strikingly similar. ExxonMobil has drawn upon the tactics and even some of the organizations and actors involved in the callous disinformation campaign the tobacco industry waged for 40 years. Like the tobacco industry, ExxonMobil has:

- Manufactured uncertainty by raising doubts about even the most indisputable scientific evidence.
- Adopted a strategy of information laundering by using seemingly independent front organizations to publicly further its desired message and thereby confuse the public.
- Promoted scientific spokespeople who misrepresent peer-reviewed scientific findings or cherry-pick facts in their attempts to persuade the media and the public that there is still serious debate among scientists that burning fossil fuels has contributed to global warming and that human-caused warming will have serious consequences.
- Attempted to shift the focus away from meaningful action on global warming with misleading charges about the need for "sound science."
- Used its extraordinary access to the (last) Bush administration to block federal policies and shape government communications on global warming.

As discussed below, one of the "media" outlets ExxonMobil and their like have benefitted from is Fox News under the leadership of Roger Ailes (Sherman, 2014).

Example 2: Fox News

Fox News Channel (FNC), also known as Fox News, is an American basic cable and satellite news entertainment television channel that is owned by the Fox Entertainment Group subsidiary of 21st Century Fox. The channel was created by Australian-American media mogul Rupert Murdoch, who hired former NBC executive Roger Ailes as its founding CEO. It was launched on October 7, 1996. Many observers have stated that Fox News Channel promotes ultraconservative (right-wing) political positions and biased reporting (Memmott, 2004; Sherman, 2014). Gabriel Sherman's excellent book (2014), *The Loudest Voice in the Room*, is a must-read for anyone concerned about how "news" is being distorted to reflect a singular ultraconservative doctrine.

Murdoch has faced allegations since 2011 that his companies, including the *News of the World* owned by News Corporation, had been regularly hacking the phones of celebrities, royalty, and public citizens. He faces police and government investigations into bribery and corruption by the British government and the U.S. Federal Bureau of Investigation (FBI). However, the driving force behind Fox News is Ailes, who in setting up the network was much influenced by the methods used by the Nazi propagation machine. In 2010, he told Fox executives that he wanted to elect the next president (Sherman, 2014). Ailes, in my opinion, chooses to ignore the democratic process and rather engages in distorting the truth and playing the propaganda machine! As Sherman (2014, p. xix) concludes, "That a news executive was essentially running the Republican Party was a remarkable development in American Politics." According to Sherman (2014, p. xii), Ailes "helped polarize the American electorate, drawing sharp, with-us-or-against-us lines, demonizing foes, preaching against compromise." He "remade American politics."

When it came to the global warming debate, Ailes used Fox News to try to muddle the science, to get the general population to question and then doubt the science. For years, he was successful. After the 2012 election, he stated that climate change was a "worldwide conspiracy" spun by "foreign nationals" to gain control of America's resources (Sherman, 2014, p. xiv) while criticizing President Obama.

In January 2014, Fox News reporter John Stossel (2014), under the byline "Let's chill out about global warming," went out of his way to discredit the concerns of scientists and many of their fellow citizens. More recently Fox gave much coverage to a Heartland Institute report that really tried to mock the current research on global warming (Taylor, 2014).

Example 3: The Heartland Institute—Paid to Distort Mainstream Science?

The Heartland Institute was founded in 1984. Headquartered in Chicago, it is a conservative public policy think tank and claims it promotes free market policies (Mohr, 1995). It is one of many such conservative think tanks (Dunlap & McCright, 2011). A full-time staff of 29, including senior fellows and editors, is supported by 200-plus unpaid policy advisers. Based on its 2011 990 Tax Form, revenues are in the order of $4.7 million (http://heartland.org/media-library/pdfs/2011-IRS-Form-990.pdf). Tobacco company Philip Morris used the group in the 1990s to question serious cancer risks to secondhand smoke. Additionally, the institute lobbied against government public-health reforms (Tesler & Malone, 2010). Recently, the institute has concentrated its efforts on questioning the science of climate change, as resulting from human practices and has been labeled as "the primary American organization pushing climate change skepticism" by the *New York Times* (Gillis, 2012). One of its activities has been to sponsor meetings of climate change skeptics, and it has apparently sponsored public school literature decrying the scientific consensus on human-caused climate change.

This institute has—through publications mentioned above—distorted and disrupted the scientific truths coming out of mainstream academic research organizations. One of its more bizarre acts was to put up a digital billboard in Chicago in May 2012, which linked belief in global warming to madness and terrorism. It depicted the "Unabomber," a mass-murderer called Ted Kaczynski, with the slogan, "I still believe in Global Warming. Do you?" The offending sign lasted only for a day! ("Toxic Shock: A Climate-Change Sceptic Is Melting," 2012).

While this institution will not supply the names of those who donate to its cause, there is information available. Backers have included foundations with politically conservative agendas such as the Sarah Scaife Foundation, the Castle Rock Foundation, the Lynde and Harry Bradley Foundation, the John M. Olin Foundation, and the Charles G. Koch Foundation. Additionally, fossil fuel companies have contributed to the Heartland Institute, including ExxonMobil (between 1998 and 2005). As mentioned previously, the Heartland Institute received funding from tobacco giant Philip Morris, but others such as Altria and Reynolds American have done the same. Pharmaceutical giants such as GlaxoSmithKline, Pfizer, and Eli Lilly have also been financial supporters. State Farm Insurance, USAA, and Diageo were also once backers. The *Independent*, a British national morning newspaper published in London, stated that Heartland's financial support by ExxonMobil and Philip Morris indicates a "direct link … between anti-global warming skeptics funded by the oil industry and the opponents of the scientific evidence showing that passive smoking can damage people's health" (Connor, 2008).

The Walton Family Foundation (managed by the family of the founder of Wal-Mart) had contributed approximately $300,000 to Heartland as of 2006. Not surprisingly, perhaps, this institute opined an op-ed in the *Louisville Courier-Journal* in order to protect Wal-Mart from criticism over its treatment of workers. The donations, of course, were not disclosed in the op-ed. Subsequently, the *Courier-Journal* editor revealed that he was unaware of the connection and, had he known, would probably not have published the op-ed (Adair, 2006). Others such as the *St. Petersburg Times* defined the Heartland Institute as being "particularly energetic defending Wal-Mart." Heartland responded that it was not "paid to defend Wal-Mart" and had not received funding from the corporation; rather, it chose not to reveal the $300,000 from the Walton Family Foundation (Adair, 2006). Full disclosure? Not apparently. However, this very well-funded institute has a front seat in the downplay, distortion, and manipulation of mainstream academic science with its culture of a relatively healthy peer-review process, a strong contrast.

In February 2012, Peter Gleick, an environmental scientist and president of the Pacific Institute, acquired internal Heartland Institute documents and disclosed them to public websites (Gleick, 2012). The documents included the 2012 Heartland budget, board materials, and a fundraising plan (UPI, 2012). Revealed were the names of donors to the institute—including all those mentioned above, but in addition were Microsoft, liquor companies, and an anonymous donor who over the previous five years had given $13 million (Goldenberg, 2012a; UPI, 2012). Also revealed by the documents were disbursements to climate skeptics and their research programs, including the founder of the Center for the Study of Carbon Dioxide and Global Change, Craig Idso ($11,600 per month), physicist Fred Singer ($5,000 plus expenses per month), geologist Robert M. Carter ($1,667 per month), and a pledge of $90,000 to Anthony Watts, a meteorologist. Two of these, Carter and Watts, confirmed the payments (UPI, 2012). The documents also revealed the institute's plans to provide literature, undermining the teaching of global warming, to school teachers in the United States (Gillis & Kaufman, 2012; UPI 2012).

As a consequence of the above document leak and an associated controversial advertising campaign, corporate donors started to dissociate themselves from the institute, and it lost a significant portion of its annual funding. The advocacy group, Forecast the Facts, stated that Heartland lost more than a third of its corporate fund-raising in that year, a total of $825,000. However, the financial loss apparently led to the Illinois coal lobby subsidizing the Institute's May 2012 climate conference—the "first publicly acknowledged donations from the coal industry" (Goldenberg, 2012b). Additional outcomes of the disclosures were that the Institute lost "a couple of directors and almost its entire branch in Washington, DC" ("Toxic Shock: A Climate-Change Sceptic Is Melting," 2012).

Very telling, perhaps, is that the institute's "Tea Party Toolbox" web page, which includes *The Patriot's Toolbox* (subtitled *Eighty Principles for Restoring Our Freedom and Prosperity*), seeks to promote the Tea Party movement. If an academic institution or research center took such a political stance, it would, at the very least, be severely chastised!

One question academics need to ask themselves is, what role can they and other mainstream scientists play in discrediting groups like the Heartland Institute, who in my opinion are more interested in propaganda than in scientific truth?

Example 4: U.S. Army Corps of Engineers after Hurricane Katrina

I, and others, from shortly after the levees failed during Hurricane Katrina, started to suspect that either U.S. Army Corps of Engineers (Corps) employees or their paid contractors were deliberately attacking those who tried to question the shoddy construction of the New Orleans levee system through media report comment columns, at public talks, and through offensive blogs; to name a few. According to a letter dated June 23, 2009, sent by St. Julien, Rosenthal, Bosworth, and Pasquantonio to Senator Mary Landrieu, the following information was offered: "On June 17, 2009, WWL-TV in New Orleans exposed an apparent campaign of disinformation by employees of the U.S. Army Corps of Engineers regarding the failure of the flood walls and levees during Hurricane

Katrina and in response to any subsequent public discussion of the Corps' failure" (St. Julien et al. to Landrieu, 2009, p. 1). Jon Donley, the founder and editor-in-chief of the *New Orleans Times-Picayune*'s online affiliate, NOLA.com, provided an affidavit in which he detailed evidence of user comment activity emanating from Corps Internet Protocol (IP) addresses (St. Julien et al. to Landrieu, 2009).

In his affidavit, Donley states that beginning about a year after Katrina, he became aware of a group of registered users whose comments led him to believe they were employees, colleagues, or friends of the Corps. The group became very active as news stories evolved that questioned and or criticized the design of the levees especially by outside groups. (I headed up the official state of Louisiana levee failure forensic team known as "Team Louisiana" [http://thebiguneasy.com/resources.html] and the role that a major navigation channel, the Mississippi River Gulf Outlet [van Heerden et al., 2014] played in the flooding of New Orleans.) Newspaper employees, using a backend tool available to any blogger to check IP addresses of those posting to the NOLA.com website, realized very quickly that a cadre of about a dozen Corps stakeholders were very active; that the wording of many comments were often very similar to Corps talking points—sometimes verbatim—while others rose to verbal abuse of Corps critics; and others had strong racial tones. In his affidavit, Donley concludes that the pattern of response to any article that did not represent the Corps' own rhetoric, involved individuals at the Corps, using taxpayer-funded time and resources, to be overly abusive to critics of the Corps. Over a six-week period, he determined that comments coming from the Corps IP address numbered at least 15 per day—that this was a systematic attack on critics of the Corps of Engineers via NOLA.com's user-engagement features.

One of the groups being attacked in these blog comments was Levees.org, a nonprofit founded by Sandy Rosenthal (a homemaker and mother who was transformed by the Katrina catastrophe) in October 2005 (Levees.org, n.d.). In June 2009, this nonprofit wrote Louisiana U.S. Senator Mary Landrieu to request a Department of Justice investigation into these Corps activities. Landrieu, in essence, punted the ball and wrote the inspector general of the U.S. Department of Defense requesting a report concerning the allegations coming from Levees.org and Donley. Not surprising, the Corps claimed that they had taken action and informed employees about the "policy on the use of government communications resources and stating that this type of interaction is unprofessional and subject to disciplinary action" (http://levees.org/wp-content/uploads/2009/09/2009_us_IG-Response-to-Landrieu2.pdf). In my opinion, not even a wrap over the knuckles. As someone who was constantly being interviewed by the media (I had a lot of pertinent science at hand and was also the head of "Team Louisiana"), I can attest that these blog comments went a long way in clouding the truth, as evidenced by some reporters' questions. Nevertheless, the truth did get out.

I, for one, undertook thousands of interviews; our research was featured in tens of documentaries; and I wrote a book to make sure the truth was in black and white (see van Heerden & Bryan, 2007). The disinformation by a very well-funded Corps public relations machine is, in my belief, hiding the truth even right now, that New Orleans is still not safe. Most recently, the Corps has started to claim that it is in the "risk reduction" business. Well, I ask, what happened to flood protection as defined in the original 1965 mandate the Corps was given (van Heerden & Bryan, 2007)?

THE CRITICAL ROLE OF WHISTLEBLOWERS

If the public and policy makers are the targets of *faux* science, then how can they make informed decisions? Try to picture a world based on science distortions. In many cases today, as outlined above, we are facing problems of global proportions. If for some reason the truth is not being told and it could seriously impact people's lives and/or property, what happens next? Could this lead to one or more catastrophes? In some cases, the real facts are buried, those in the know go into denial, and only after the negative consequences of not acting on the truth are known does the fact surface that some individual or group knew the truth but did not make it known to the relevant authorities or the public. On occasions, however, an individual or group that knows the truth or has the supportive data decides to "get it out." This often predicates the birth of a "whistleblower." Whistleblowers are on the inside of an issue; they have reliable, repeatable data and information. They are often embattled.

There are various definitions in the literature of a whistleblower, but the following best captures the essence of the act of whistleblowing: "The disclosure by a person, usually an employee in a government agency or private enterprise, to the public or to those in authority, of mismanagement, corruption, illegality, or some other wrongdoing" (Whistleblower, n.d.).

Whistleblowers are crucial in today's world. Their role is often to counter what the distorters have done through filtering, distortion, doubt casting, abuse of motivated reasoning, reinforcing confirmation bias, and defaming opponents. Whistleblowing is becoming more and more prevalent in our society, and more and more crucial. Since the early 1960s, various state and federal laws have been passed to protect whistleblowers. As many can attest, this seeming protection does not always prove a deterrent to whistleblowers being penalized for their courage to speak out and go public with what they know. Almost weekly, one hears of cases of whistleblowers being fired from, or having their freedoms restricted by, the entities where they are employed; many other cases, I am sure, are unreported in the media.

SOME EXAMPLES OF ACADEMICS "BLOWING THE WHISTLE"

In my view, it is always right—and it is one's duty—to tell the truth, especially if you have the data that indicates that a certain action by government (in all forms thereof), industry in its multiple practices, or resource harvesting and agriculture, is going to cause irreparable harm to our earth and its inhabitants. It is the humane and compassionate thing to do. This section briefly describes whistleblowing by a few academics.

The Case of William O. Pruitt and Leslie Viereck, University of Alaska: Preventing a Catastrophe

One of the most significant cases of academics exposing government follies is captured in Dan O'Neill's book *The Firecracker Boys*. Here, academics William O. Pruitt and Leslie Viereck, as part of a team, forced a stop to the Atomic Energy Commission's (AEC) plan to use atomic bombs to blow a hole in the coastline of Alaska to create a harbor in the 1960s. This was known as "Project Chariot." After the end of World War II, the AEC was looking for "peaceful" uses for nuclear weapons. Physicists and engineers from AEC spoke of "a new and important" discipline: geographical engineering. "We will change the earth's surface to suit us" (O'Neill, 2007, p. 28). From its very conception, Project Chariot had its detractors, and as fieldwork progressed on the impact study, doubts and second thoughts burgeoned in the minds of Pruitt and Viereck, among others. These scientists realized that they had to speak out, choices forced when they realized that the AEC and its research contractor, the University of Alaska, were misrepresenting environmental research findings from the locale of the proposed test site. These actions were meant to bolster the AEC's public statements that creating a crater and harbor in northwestern Alaska by detonating a series of buried nuclear bombs presented no significant environmental or health risks.

Thus, Viereck and Pruitt had to make career-altering choices of conscience. Eventually, these scientists charged the AEC with duplicity and outright censorship in the way they were handling the environmental impact study and in the progress reports that were disseminated to the press and to the public. For their trouble, they were dismissed from the grant-conscious university, which was attempting to put up a facade of progressive attitudes—which included taking the atomic advocates seriously. If the federal government would have gone ahead with its plan, much of Alaska would have been devastated and still radioactive today. These two courageous researchers were forced out by the University of Alaska, whose upper administration supported the projected nuclear-engineering project. The university then also sought to tarnish their names. However, as courageous scientists, they succeeded in putting a halt to Project Chariot and thus, in my opinion, richly deserve a nation's gratitude.

The Case of Ivor Ll. van Heerden, Louisiana State University and Hurricane Katrina: How Dare You Tell the Truth!

In 1992, Hurricane Andrew devastated Homestead, Florida, which was close to the Atlantic landfall site, and damaged parts of coastal Louisiana after its Gulf of Mexico landfall. The major storm could well have hit both Miami and New Orleans with just a small change in course. Observing the devastation and realizing that a New Orleans landfall would have been shattering—essentially an early form of Hurricane Katrina—I embarked on trying to secure research funding to better understand hurricane impacts on coastal Louisiana. Many observers, including Louisiana scientists, spoke about the vulnerability to the "Magic Bullet" storm that I was often told "would track up the Mississippi River and sink New Orleans." While there were efforts at modeling storm surges, there was no real-world applicability. No one was trying to quantify the outcomes of widespread surge-induced flooding, and certainly no one was reviewing the levee designs or questioning the incompleteness of the protection. Additionally, the loss of wetlands and their hurricane wind, waves, and surge protection roles were not being quantified, and were often ignored.

I thus embarked on a pathway to either generate the research myself, or help others to do it; to really understand environmentally, economically, and socially what would happen to southeastern Louisiana the next time a major hurricane hit. To enable funding for my hurricane research, I took a political appointee position to head up the state's coastal restoration program in the mid-1990s; encouraged working relationships with some key legislators and environmental groups; and subsequently gained the confidence of several governors by supplying good science related to hurricane preparedness and response. I worked with one of my colleagues, Dr. Marc Levitan (a wind engineer), to convince Louisiana State University (LSU) to allow us to set up a Hurricane Center, achieved in 1999, and then used that as a platform to be the recipient of a multimillion-dollar, multiyear grant from the Louisiana Board of Regents in 2001. In this way, I achieved my dream; I set up a multidisciplinary team of scientists ranging from medical doctors to veterinarians and engineers to fully understand New Orleans and its residents' vulnerability to major hurricane strikes. Along the way, I did get many letters of support from influential politicians on both side of the aisle, from the sitting governor, Mike Foster, to a host of environmental and disaster relief organizations. Some critics would charge that I played the political game to achieve my goals, but I do know that the actions of the LSU Hurricane Center saved tens of thousands of lives during Hurricanes Katrina and Rita, and many of the heartwarming rescues from attics, for instance, was because of our mapping and Geographical Information System (GIS) preparation.

I also spent hundreds of hours giving public talks to senior citizens groups and science conferences and worked closely with the media to inform the public. It is not by chance that several New Orleans TV stations used interviews done previously when earlier storms threatened, to try to convince residents to leave before Katrina struck, and the local newspapers and cable TV used some surge computer-model runs that we posted on an open web page to help inform their viewership.

So, why was I fired from LSU? In my case, I blew the whistle, along with others, on the failed federal government response immediately after the storm (NBC News, 2005). But more importantly, I exposed the shoddy engineering design that included ignoring up-to-date mainstream science that resulted in the catastrophic failure of the New Orleans levee system during the passage of Hurricane Katrina (van Heerden & Bryan, 2007). The U.S. Army Corps of Engineers wanted the world to believe that the failures were an "Act of God!" Within a week of Katrina's landfall, I started to sense, and then feel, the ire of upper administration and the Corps at my articulating the science we had carefully researched. This rage only got worse once I was appointed by the governor, six weeks after the storm's landfall, to head up the state of Louisiana's official levee failure forensic team known as "Team Louisiana."

Intimidation of me included:

- I was told not to talk to media, then threatened if I did.
- Senior Corps officials visited the campus and complained.
- Corps contractors directly tried to pressure the university to shut me up.
- Attempts were made to remove me from Team Louisiana.
- Actions were aimed at firing me early in the levee study, efforts that failed.
- Upper administration used the *New York Times* to try to trash my qualifications.
- The LSU chancellor stopped me from testifying in federal court.
- My duties were severely curtailed—I was not allowed to teach, restrictions were placed on the scope of my research, and I was denied access to the university's super computer to run surge models.
- I was removed from projects I had helped developed that were a lot of my ideas, including funding from the National Science Foundation.
- Harassment of my coworkers.
- I was fired and, when I asked for an explanation, was told, "We don't have to tell you why, it was not for performance reasons. Your performance was very good."

Perhaps the best indication of my qualifications is the quality of the work generated by the team in which I was privileged to participate. The conclusions of Team Louisiana have been borne out by both the National Science Foundation team and the Corps of Engineers' IPET team. Indeed, the NSF-sponsored

Independent Levee Investigation Team in their final report (2006), thanks the "State of Louisiana's independent investigation team, Team Louisiana, for their tremendous efforts and dogged persistence under very difficult circumstances, and for their generous sharing of data and insights throughout this investigation. . . . The people of Louisiana, and the nation, owe these gentlemen a great debt as their persistent efforts have, time and again, produced critical data and insights that would not otherwise have been available" (p. xxvii).

In my case, the American Association of University Professors (AAUP) really stepped up to the plate and undertook their own investigations (Kurland, 2011); but their efforts were just scorned by the university (Basu, 2012). I eventually filed a lawsuit and reached an out-of-court settlement after the state, under Governor Bobby Jindal's leadership, had spent about $1 million trying to defend itself (Business Report Staff, 2013). Sadly, the centers we created that played such a crucial role in Louisiana hurricane disasters from 2000 to 2009 no longer exist; all the staff have left LSU, and none have returned to academia.

All in all, LSU was the big loser from alumni withdrawing support, potential graduate students deciding to study elsewhere, and the stigma of attacking a person considered by many in Louisiana as a "hero" in such a mean way. Unfortunately, the whole issue has a put a big damper on Louisiana academics' willingness to speak out or even be willing to be expert witnesses on any controversial issue that may potentially offend the Jindal administration, big oil industry, or the large civil engineering companies that profit from Corps construction projects in Louisiana. The latter are very effective lobbyists for the Corps— which, as a federal agency, cannot, or is not supposed to, lobby Congress at all.

The Case of Richard Steiner, University of Alaska: Big Oil Disapproved!

Over a 30-year career, Rick Steiner became recognized as one of the most accomplished, high-profile professors in the history of the University of Alaska's (UA) Marine Advisory Program (MAP) (Andrews & Creed, 2010). In 2009, Steiner resigned from UA after pressure to stop articulating the negative environmental impacts related to big oil and their exploration and mining activities (Andrews & Creed, 2010).

In Steiner's case, pressure from upper administration started early in his career, immediately after his high-profile work on the *Exxon Valdez* oil spill began in 1989. From 1991 through 1994, university administrators pressured Steiner concerning his public statements, objecting to his "advocacy" regarding oil spill prevention, restoration, response, and oil and environmental issues in general. Despite support from his peers, the university administration denied him promotion, citing his "advocacy" as the reason (ESWR, 2010). Importantly, the denial was overturned the next year. In response to Steiner's media comments concerning the 2004

Selendang Ayu oil spill in the Aleutian Islands—a disaster Steiner had warned about and tried to prevent for years—the new dean of the School of Fisheries and Ocean Sciences (SFOS) wrote Steiner that he should not publicly criticize state government, "as that is where we get our money," and sent all faculty members in the school an e-mail requiring them to clear all press contact and inquiries through the Public Relations staff of SFOS. The dean also ordered Steiner's news coverage removed from the SFOS website (ESWR, 2010). In my view, this is a good example of one dean who seemingly did not believe in academic freedom!

Between December 2007 and June 2008, then-governor Sarah Palin publicly stated that the State of Alaska (Alaska Department of Fish and Game, or ADFG) marine mammal biologists disagreed with the federal proposed rule to list polar bears under the Endangered Species Act, and invoked this claim to back the state's opposition to listing (ESWR, 2010). The ADFG refused to release the documents to Steiner when he made a request under the Alaska Public Records Act. After a few months, he eventually obtained the state review through a Freedom of Information Act (FOIA) request from the federal government. The state science review showed unequivocally that, contrary to the governor's public assertion, state marine mammal scientists agreed that polar bears are at considerable risk due to climate change and agreed with the federal science behind the listing. Obviously, a considerable amount of media attention resulted, given the lack of transparency and the dishonesty of the Palin administration related to this issue, as Palin was at that time, in 2008, running for vice president of the United States on the Republican ticket with John McCain running for the presidency (ESWR, 2010).

Steiner then criticized the risks of a proposed offshore oil drilling project in Alaska's Bristol Bay (the largest red salmon run in the world), due to concerns of a blowout and large oil spill. It is important to note that the federal government eventually agreed with Steiner's concerns and the oil lease was canceled. Nevertheless, oil company officials met with University of Alaska officials and told them that the university "would not get a dime" from their company "as long as Rick Steiner continues saying the things he is saying about oil."

Subsequently, Jim Murray, the deputy director of the National Sea Grant Program, which paid one month of Steiner's salary, suggested that his salary support should be eliminated as they have an "issue with Rick Steiner." They felt he was acting as an advocate (ESWR, 2010). Murray expressed concern and stated that "one agent can cause problems nationally." Early in 2009, the MAP director used a public teleconference to criticize Steiner's activities and work performance and scientific credentials, and to deny media reports that Steiner's federal funding was in jeopardy. In April 2009, the University of Alaska Fairbanks provost officially informed Steiner that indeed his federal (Sea Grant) funding had been terminated. This is the first time in Alaska—and, as far as can be determined, in the nation—where federal grant-funding for a university faculty member was eliminated due to the faculty member's public comments. As such, this is a nationally historic event (ESWR, 2010).

Steiner subsequently filed an internal grievance seeking to have the university reverse its adverse administrative decision toward him, as it had been based solely on his public statements that should have been protected by academic freedom; but the university did not reverse its decision. Shortly thereafter, Steiner resigned on principle from the university. Two months later, in April 2010, the BP Deepwater Horizon suffered a catastrophic blowout in the Gulf of Mexico, killing 11 rig workers and spilling over 4 million barrels of oil into the Gulf. This catastrophe served to confirm the concerns Steiner had expressed about offshore drilling in Alaska.

The University of Alaska, and NOAA, received considerable public condemnation and embarrassment due to their mishandling of Steiner's case, and their valuing oil industry interests over academic freedom. Upon his resignation, Steiner was nominated for professor emeritus status at the university, but he was denied, making him the only such faculty member to be denied emeritus status in university history.

There are many more examples of retaliation against academics for telling the truth that I could list. By only including these examples of academia stepping up to the plate, I am not saying that any others are of less value in their importance to society. Rather, I am trying to indicate the scope of the problem.

A GENERAL WHISTLEBLOWER PATHWAY FROM AWAKENING TO TERMINATION

In many cases, whistleblowing follows a predictable course. First, the whistleblower realizes that there are those who have high stakes in the success of their project or commercial endeavor and who are actively falsifying the truth, relying instead on distortions and motivated reasoning. This person feels a moral obligation that the truth needs to be told and needs to be publicly out, and decides to do so, knowing that there would be difficulties and consequences for oneself from management that could well further impact their family's well-being.

Second, there is a lot of "ducking and diving" to try to stay off upper administration's radar screen as much as possible in order to try to "gain" some time. Why? This is because of the "rush" or the "need" to get all the research out, and all the report writing complete, before the hammer falls.

Then one is forced to retire or is fired, terminated, or let go—the term used does not really matter; the outcome is the same. Even though one has known it was coming, there is almost disbelief. One thinks, "Surely upper administration comprehends they are committing suicide by doing this to me and my family; don't they realize how this will impact the university?" Slowly, thereafter, comes the realization that one's academic career is over—no other institution (at least in your state) is going to hire you or even give you an adjunct position. Tied to your release is often the spreading of false rumors and innuendos to diminish or blunt your message and/or discredit you. And, of course, there is the realization that they have cut you off from your body of work—access to computers, students, and all your academic activities and involvement. You may also become so frazzled, or desperate, to come to the conclusion that the only real chance you have at an academic future is to try to get your old job back!

UPPER ADMINISTRATION'S BEHAVIOR: ONE CASE OF SUPPORT IN CONTRAST TO MY CASE

How a whistleblower is treated very much depends on the ethical stature of upper administration at their institution. During the Hurricane Katrina levee investigations, researchers from the University of California, Berkeley, appreciated that upper administration officials were being pressured by groups or influential persons to stop the "advocacy practices of certain faculty." The university's response was to give an award to a researcher, Dr. Robert Bea, known as the "Chancellor's Public Service Award for Research in the Public Interest"—the first award ever of this type at Berkeley. However, the chancellor did call two of the levee investigators into his office because of the complaints concerning "advocacy." The researchers' response was; "How could we help lead this investigation without being advocates?" The two parties (investigators and researchers) agreed to disagree. Dr. Bea, in an e-mail (personal communication, October 18, 2013) stated that "It was a good experience because the Chancellor did not take any obvious steps to stop our work." This is in stark contrast to my case, in which LSU behaved very differently.

In my case, once we started to make known our concerns about the "catastrophic structural failure" of the levees, upper administration's heavy-handed response was to try to put a stop to our research moving forward, even though they had accepted the research dollars from the state (van Heerden & Bryan, 2007). In April 2007—soon after Team Louisiana's release of its final report—attorneys for the plaintiffs in litigation against the United States and the Corps relating to the Mississippi River Gulf Outlet ("MR-GO") asked me to serve as an expert witness. In addition to the Corps' engineering errors regarding the breached levees, I had spoken and written critically of the Corps' design of MR-GO, which produced a "funnel" with the Intracoastal Waterway that comes to a point just east of New Orleans, exposing the city to the brunt of a storm surge from Lake Borgne to the east (van Heerden & Bryan, 2007, pp. 79–83). I thus submitted a request for permission to testify pursuant to the established LSU procedure but received no response notwithstanding follow-up over a period of months.

One of the attorneys for the plaintiffs, Jerry McKernan, raised the issue directly with Chancellor Sean O'Keefe (former NASA administrator) and reported back that O'Keefe had told him that I would be fired if I testified against the Corps. McKernan advised his cocounsel in an e-mail that O'Keefe told him that LSU "does not want Ivor or anyone else associated with LSU to testify against the Corps." "They just don't want their people front and center in such politically charged conflicts, especially in a capacity that opposes the current Republican regime" (AAUP, 2011). In the end, I did not serve as an expert witness but did aid the plaintiffs in the capacity of a nontestifying expert in which I became highly visible to Corps representatives at depositions that began early in 2008.

SUCCESSES AND FAILURES WITH ADMINISTRATION TO TELL THE TRUTH

As stated earlier, the ethical character of upper management is so important. My career at LSU lasted 18 years, during which I was fired twice, and there was an additional attempt to get me fired by lawyers (who were LSU alumni) representing a large industrial waste landfill. After the first firing in 1996 by middle management, some powerful politicians who wanted to weaken the Clean Water Act and specifically wetland regulations, "ended up with egg on their faces," according to the university's Washington, DC, lobbyist. As a result, the then-chancellor of LSU reinstated me and moved me to a new department. The attack by the landfill lawyers in 2001, as a consequence of being part of a citizens' group that exposed illegal permits and public corruption, ended when that chancellor appointed a review committee, which concluded that the complaints had no validity and were an attempt to harass me. In both of these instances, the chancellor in office at the time was not going to bow to outside pressure, even if middle management was. Unfortunately, the third and last time related to the levee failures during Hurricane Katrina, the then-new chancellor took a hands-off approach, and the faculty senate committee that reviewed my termination was ineffective. It is possible that this lack of the faculty review committee to address the issues at hand reflected that the university faced severe budget cuts at the hands of a very conservative Governor Jindal, who was a very big "stick."

Comparing my situation with that of Professor Steiner's case, the cultural values were different, but the outcome was similar. Mark R. Hamilton was president of UA from 1998 until his retirement in 2010. *Progressive Alaska* (Andrews & Creed, 2010), which reviewed Steiner's "removal" from UA, concluded that after 31 years in the military, it is not difficult to understand the awkward mismatch of Hamilton, who was a former army general, with academia. Soldiers are trained to follow orders, keep their mouths shut, and listen. Universities, on the other hand, are supposed to encourage free and vigorous debate, including on some of society's most controversial issues. As society's free marketplace of ideas, colleges and universities work best when public policy can be freely and vigorously argued in the search for truth. Hamilton never seemed to grasp how to uphold such bedrock university principles (Andrews & Creed, 2010). Hamilton is now retired from the university and is a public spokesperson for oil interests in Alaska.

University of Alaska Professor Emeritus Rudy Krejci stated in 2010 that UA has changed little in the past 50 years. He compared Steiner to William O. Pruitt and Leslie Viereck, the two professors fired by the administration of the late William R. Wood, a former UA president, also over conservation issues. The Steiner case has left a distinctive cloud over academic freedom at UA, whereby faculty no longer feel protected in criticizing the oil industry or government.

HOW TO PROTECT WHISTLEBLOWERS

History has shown time and time again the importance of whistleblowers in exposing corruption, greed, and the ills associated with these character traits. Unfortunately, many potential whistleblowers are silenced by threats of personal or family injury or retaliation. Many whistleblowers will at some time discuss the costs of their actions with family members and friends, and their dismissal or removal is often not a surprise to many close to the person.

A major dilemma that emerges is, how is retaliation against academic whistle-blowers to be prevented? Since the 1960s, the public value of whistleblowing has been increasingly acknowledged. Federal and state statutes and regulations have been enacted to protect whistleblowers from various forms of retaliation. Even without a statute, numerous legal decisions encourage and protect whistle-blowing on grounds of public policy. The Federal False Claims Act (31 U.S.C.A. § 3729) will reward a whistleblower who brings a lawsuit against a company that makes a false claim or commits fraud against the government. However, despite these steps, the system is obviously not working. Yes, one can always file a lawsuit in federal or state court, and maybe there will be a cash set-tlement, but very rarely is there any reinstatement. When reinstatement occurs, those reinstated have often felt pressure from administration and eventually move to another academic institution. As trying as that may be, at least they could stay in academia. However, academia in general needs to rethink some of its culture and practice. From consideration of this dilemma, I offer the follow-ing recommendations:

Ethics Training for Graduate Students

All new graduate students should be required to take a course in the ethics of science and the need for reliable, repeatable, testable conclusions. A course in logic may also be a benefit.

Appoint Ethically Minded Upper Administrators

From my short review of academic whistleblowers' experiences, it is obvious that the ethical stature of upper administration and their commitment to seeking truth are crucial. Unfortunately, it appears that the standard is not uniform across the country. So, what needs to be done? Increasingly, faculty are being removed from the opportunity to comment on, or be involved in, upper administration appointments. In March 2013, the LSU Faculty Senate unanimously passed a resolution of "no confidence" in the LSU Board of Supervisors, casting criticism on the group that decided to accept the candidacy of F. King Alexander as the president and chancellor of the LSU system. The Faculty Senate listed 12 reasons, including the Board not appointing faculty members to the Presidential Search Committee, as to why it had no confidence in the Board. "We want to make it clear that the faculty has its standards and principles as well," LSU Faculty Senate president Kevin Cope said. "We want to signal to the Board that they have behaved atrociously" (Newell, 2013). Similar complaints have been voiced in other university systems.

Review by a Committee of Campus Peers

After many discussions with other whistleblowers and academics, the conclusion in today's world has to be that if an internal university committee does not have the authority to reinstate a whistleblower, then the only pathway open to a researcher is to file a lawsuit. Unfortunately, while the opinion of national faculty associations or societies may be highly regarded by some upper administrators; it is not always the case. Maybe, if groups such as AAUP had much larger memberships, or maybe if all universities were unionized, then they could yield a bigger "stick." There is definitely strength in numbers, but academics in their fiercely competitive world, where often egos get in the way, have not fully appreciated this fact. Perhaps, some benefactor will inject a large sum of money in one or more national faculty associations so that they can do large-scale campus drives and thus increase their numbers, thereby increasing their power. Certainly, unionizing could be a very effective tool in more ways than one.

State and/or Federal Legislation Changes

If the laws of the land do not stop upper management at academic institutions from bending to outside pressures to discard the principles of academic freedom, then an independent review board is needed that has the legal power to have a whistleblower reinstated. These could be at the federal level, or state boards. For instance, state legislatures could pass a law that institutes a "Whistleblower Review Board," with subpoena power, that could appoint a review committee made up of out-of-state academics, representatives of groups such as the AAUP, and then conduct a hearing. If correctly instituted, that Review Board could then assess each case without interference from any outside groups. Many states have "Ethics Boards" that could take on the role of administrating the review board, but the latter's effectiveness must not be compromised by any political leader being given the right to appoint review board members.

A Possible Award System

Some have suggested that universities need to institute an award system for whistleblowers. However, as mentioned earlier, academics who speak truth to power do so not for awards and recognition, but out of a deep-seated and strong sense for truth and justice. Hence, awards or other such anointments are completely irrelevant to such persons. Additionally, others will not be more courageous and able to withstand the immense intimidation and public humiliation connected to standing up just because there are possible awards to be had.

Greater National Recognition for Scientists

Many children growing up today in America only see, or are only shown, modern-day heroes in the form of football, baseball, and such sport athletes. The military and veterans are also often cast in this mold. While not decrying these practices, since admittedly our military is important in this day and age and sport can be entertaining, why are not scientists being portrayed as heroes? Where are the scientists of today acclaimed as heroes for youth, like Louis Pasteur, Alexander Fleming, Isaac Newton, Albert Einstein, John Harrison, and a host more? Why not bestow national recognition on some scientists of today who are shaping our future?

CONCLUSIONS

Whistleblowers are insiders, and there is a critical need for them today especially to counter the well-funded and positioned science distorters and their special interests (Dunlap & McCright, 2011). Les Viereck (one of the Firecracker Boys) in his letter of resignation from the University of Alaska, stated, "A scientist's allegiance is first to truth and personal integrity and only secondarily to an organized group such as a university, a company or a government" (O'Neill, 2007, p. 321). As a result, in reality, philosophical values must trump corporate and scientific intentions. O'Neill (2007, p. 322), had the following observation:

> The Western University is built on a concept of academic freedom—the opportunity to pursue any avenue of inquiry in an atmosphere of pure scholarship and freedom from political pressure. This special latitude allows a researcher to follow obstinately his or her own idea until its truth might ultimately be established.

But throughout history; one ideology or another has infected the university: religious ideology in the Middle Ages, racist ideology in Germany, social ideology in communist Russia, and a mercantile ideology in America. During the 1950s and 1960s, the cold war came onto American campuses. It is not surprising that the University of Alaska lost sight of its mission and yielded to the cold war political ambience by dismissing Pruitt and Viereck. What is surprising—and the lesson here—is that some scholars were able to hold strong to the principal of academic freedom and were willing to pay the highest professional cost in defense of that ideal.

Mainstream science is getting a bad rap, mostly orchestrated by ultraconservative right-wing special interest corporations, and/or their board members; so-called research institutes; and right-wing special interests, supported by media giant Fox News. As a consequence, the needs of the public, who fund a lot of mainstream science through their taxes, are often not being met.

Academics need to find new pathways to get their science out in the public domain, especially into popular (social) media. Unfortunately, very few in the general public read scientific journals, where most of mainstream science is presently published. Perhaps there is now a need for truth-seeking philanthropists to band together and help fund science TV shows, for example, a nonprofit science-based equivalent to the Public Broadcasting System. At present, we are not succeeding in articulating all the science, and we are not supplying scientific data in a form that public interest advocates can use. This raises the stakes for academics with data that can save lives, property and the environment. Not everyone wants to be a whistleblower. However, those presently thinking of it—including those who read this chapter—intrinsically know it will be worthwhile.

The question that whistleblowers are often asked is, "Was it worth it?" All those whistleblowers to whom I have spoken, answer in the affirmative. I, too, would give that answer. As I have told many high school and college students, "When I shave in the morning, I can look the person reflected back at me straight in the eye and feel proud of his achievements. There are no regrets. As a human being I did my duty!"

We all inhabit this wonderful planet, our earth. If it is destroyed, or irreversibly harmed, we all suffer. It is my view, as a human being, that no one's greed should harm or destroy my children, or their children, or generations to come, from living full and healthy lives. To destroy our earth for short-term gain and greed is a *sin*, no matter your religious beliefs or persuasion.

ACKNOWLEDGMENTS

I wish to thank Professor Frank Fletcher, Professor Emeritus of Susquehanna University in Pennsylvania, and fellow Northern Neck resident, for his valuable discussion and providing reviews of earlier versions of this manuscript. His help and support is much appreciated. Lastly, many thanks to all those who supported my family and me during the dark LSU days.

REFERENCES

Adair, B. (2006). Corporate spin can come in disguise. *Tampa Bay Times*. Retrieved April 18, 2015, from http://www.sptimes.com/2006/09/10/Worldandnation/Corporate_spin_can_co.shtml

American Association of University Professors (AAUP). (2011, July). Academic freedom and tenure: Louisiana State University, Baton Rouge. Retrieved April 18, 2015, from http://www.aaup.org/NR/rdonlyres/28F1CE64-5ABE-4FB0-829C-3D9C9807A44D/0/LSUJuly2011Report.pdf

Andrews, S. B., & Creed, J. (2010, December 3). Former UA professor receives Cook Inletkeeper's highest award. *Progressive Alaska*. Retrieved April 18, 2015, from http://progressivealaska.blogspot.com/2010/12/former-ua-professor-receives-cook.html

Associated Press. (2013). Apple loses title of world's most valuable company to Exxon. *Fox News*. Retrieved April 18, 2015, from http://www.foxnews.com/tech/2013/04/17/apple-loses-title-world-most-valuable-company-to-exxon/

Atmospheric carbon dioxide levels double. (2010). *Our Earth in 2050*. Retrieved April 18, 2015, from http://greenphysicist2.blogspot.com/2010/02/atmospheric-carbon-dioxide-levels.html

Basu, K. (2012, June 18). AAUP censures three universities. *Inside Higher Ed*. Retrieved April 18, 2015, from http://www.insidehighered.com/news/2012/06/18/aaup-censures-three-louisiana-universities

Business Report Staff (2013, April 2). LSU, state spent nearly $1M defending van Heerden case. *Greater Baton Rouge Business Report*. Retrieved April 18, 2015, from http://www.businessreport.com/article/lsu-state-spent-nearly-1m-defending-van-heerden-case

Connor, S. (2008, March 3). Tobacco and oil pay for climate conference. *The Independent*. Retrieved April 18, 2015, from http://www.independent.co.uk/environment/climate-change/tobacco-and-oil-pay-for-climate-conference-790474.html

Dunlap, R. E., & McCright, A. M. (2010). Climate change denial: Sources, actors, and strategies. In C. Lever-Tracy (Ed.),*The Routledge international handbook of climate change and society* (pp. 240–259). New York, NY: Routledge Press.

Endangered Species & Wetlands Report (ESWR). (2010). Chronology of Professor Richard Steiner academic freedom case—University of Alaska. Retrieved April 18, 2015, from http://www.eswr.com/docs/031710/09_20_10_Chronology_of_Steiner_case.pdf

Gillis, J. (2012, April 30). Clouds' effect on climate change is last bastion for dissenters. *The New York Times*. Retrieved April 18, 2015, from http://www.nytimes.com/2012/05/01/science/earth/clouds-effect-on-climate-change-is-last-bastion-for-dissenters.html?_r=0

Gillis, J., & Kaufman, L. (2012, February 16). Leak offers glimpse of campaign against climate science. *NYTimes.com*. (Also published in *The New York Times*, p. A23, with the title "In documents, a plan to discredit climate teaching.") Retrieved April 18, 2015,

from http://www.nytimes.com/2012/02/16/science/earth/in-heartland-institute-leak
-a-plan-to-discredit-climate-teaching.html?ref=science&pagewanted=all&_r=0#h

Gleick, P. (2012). The origin of the Heartland documents. *Huffington Post*. Retrieved
April 18, 2015, from http://www.huffingtonpost.com/peter-h-gleick/-the-origin-of
-the-heartl_b_1289669.html

Goldenberg, S. (2012a, February 17). Heartland Institute faces fresh scrutiny over tax status. *The Guardian*. Retrieved April 18, 2015, from http://www.theguardian.com/
environment/2012/feb/17/heartland-institute-fresh-scrutiny-tax?INTCMP=SRCH

Goldenberg, S. (2012b, May 20). Heartland Institute facing uncertain future as staff
depart and cash dries up. The Guardian. Retrieved April 18, 2015, from http://www.
theguardian.com/environment/2012/may/20/heartland-institute-future-staff-cash

Hoyos, C. (2008). FT's profile of ExxonMobil. *Financial Times*. Retrieved April 18, 2015,
from http://www.ft.com/cms/s/0/0b2f7b36-cda0-11db-839d-000b5df10621,dwp
_uuid=0bda728c-ccd0-11db-a938-000b5df10621.html

Independent Levee Investigation Team. (2006, July 31). *Investigation of the performance of
New Orleans flood protection systems*. Retrieved April 18, 2015, from http://www.ce
.berkeley.edu/~new_orleans

Intergovernmental Panel on Climate Change (IPCC). (1990). *First assessment report* (J. T.
Houghton, G. J. Jenkins, & J. J. Ephrams, Eds., p. xi). Cambridge, UK: Cambridge
University Press.

Kurland, J. E. (2011, September–October). Report finds violations of academic freedom.
Academe. Retrieved April 18, 2015, from http://www.aaup.org/article/report-finds
-violations-academic-freedom#.UoKtHOKQPe4

Levees.org. (n.d.). *Mission and goals of Levees.org*. Retrieved April 18, 2015, from http://
levees.org/mission-and-goals-of-levees-org/

Memmott, M. (2004). Film accuses Fox of slanting the news. *USA Today*. Retrieved
April 18, 2015, from http://usatoday30.usatoday.com/news/politicselections/2004
-07-11-outfoxed_x.htm

Mohr, M. (1995, January 8). Back-yard think tanks. *Chicago Tribune*. Retrieved April 18,
2015, from http://articles.chicagotribune.com/1995-01-08/features/9501080156_1
_tanks-policies-chicago-public-schools

NBC News. (2005). Transcript for September 11. *Meet the Press*. Retrieved April 18,
2015, from http://www.nbcnews.com/id/9240461/ns/meet_the_press/t/transcript
-september/#.U-o0kWOK2M0

Nehring, R. (2009, October 27). Traversing the mountaintop: World fossil fuel production to 2050. *Philosophical Transactions of the Royal Society of London: Series B, Biological Sciences*, 364(1532): 3067–3079. doi:10.1098/rstb.2009.0170

Newell, S. (2013, March 24). LSU faculty criticize Board of Supervisors, Alexander's credentials. *Daily 49er*. Retrieved from http://www.daily49er.com/news/2013/03/24/
lsu-faculty-criticize-board-of-supervisors-alexanders-credentials/#sthash.pUiCGS5c
.dpuf

O'Neill, D. (2007). *The firecracker boys: H-bombs, Inupiat Eskimos, and the roots of the
environmental movement*. New York, NY: Basic Books. (Originally published 1994 by
St. Martin's Press)

Sherman, G. (2014). *The loudest voice in the room: How Roger Ailes and Fox News remade
American politics*. New York, NY: Random House.

St. Julien, M., Rosenthal, S., Bosworth, H. J., Jr., & Pasquantonio, V. (2009, June 23). Letter to Senator Mary Landrieu. Retrieved April 18, 2015, from http://levees.org/wp-content/uploads/2009/09/Landrieu-Letter-to-DOD_IG-August-4.pdf

Stossel, J. (2014, January 22). Let's chill out about global warming. *Fox News*. Retrieved from http://www.foxnews.com/opinion/2014/01/22/let-chill-out-about-global-warming/

Taylor, J. M. (2014, April 8). *Comprehensive report documents beneficial impacts of global warming*. Retrieved April 18, 2015, from http://news.heartland.org/newspaper-article/2014/04/08/comprehensive-report-documents-beneficial-impacts-global-warming

Tesler, L. E., & Malone, R. E. (2010, July). "Our reach is wide by any corporate standard": How the tobacco industry helped defeat the Clinton health plan and why it matters now. *American Journal of Public Health, 100*(7), 1174–1188. PMID 20466958. doi:10.2105/AJPH.2009.179150

Toxic shock: A climate-change sceptic is melting. (2012, May 26). *The Economist*. Retrieved April 18, 2015, from http://www.economist.com/node/21555894

Union of Concerned Scientists. (2007). *ExxonMobil report: Smoke, mirrors and hot air*. Retrieved April 18, 2015, from http://www.ucsusa.org/global_warming/solutions/fight-misinformation/exxonmobil-report-smoke.html

UPI. (2012, February 18). Heartland Institute documents published. *UPI.com*.

U.S. Census Bureau. (2014). *Total Population of the World by Decade, 1950–2000*. Retrieved April 18, 2015, from http://www.infoplease.com/ipa/A0762181.html

van Heerden, I. Ll., & Bryan, M. (2007). *The storm: What went wrong and why during Hurricane Katrina—the inside story from one Louisiana scientist*. New York, NY: Penguin/Viking.

van Heerden, I. Ll., Kemp, G. P., Bea, B., Shaffer, G., Day, J., Morris, C., . . . Milanes, A. (2014). How a navigation channel contributed to most of the flooding of New Orleans during Hurricane Katrina. In A. Farazmand (Ed.), *Crisis and emergency management: Theory and practice* (2nd ed., pp. 413–442). Boca Raton, FL: CRC Press.

Whistleblower. (n.d.). *The Free Dictionary*. Retrieved April 18, 2015, from http://legalictionary.thefreedictionary.com/Whistleblowing

Zabel, G. (2009, April 20). Peak people: The interrelationship between population growth and energy resources. London School of Economics, MSc Demography/Energy Economics. Originally published by *Energy Bulletin*. Retrieved April 18, 2015, from http://www.resilience.org/stories/2009-04-20/peak-people-interrelationship-between-population-growth-and-energy-resources

17

Paradigm Shifts in Nature and Well-Being: Principles, Programs, and Policies about the Environment and Climate Change with Actions by the United Nations for a Sustainable Future

Judy Kuriansky, Meaghan LeMay, and Anjali Kumar

The link between nature and the well-being of people and all beings and elements on the planet has long been known, but is garnering increased attention in present times (Buzzell & Chalquist, 2009; Doherty & Chen, in press; Howell & Passmore, 2013; Jordan, 2015; Kaplan, 1995). This interest is evident in the plethora of conferences, research centers, associations, journals, books, and professional and public websites addressing the topic (University of Illinois at Urbana-Champaign, 2012).

This chapter presents an overview of this relationship from the perspective of the emerging field of ecopsychology and focuses on the importance of nature in sustainable development and environmental protection, as reflected in research and conferences in the professional field as well as recent actions and agreements at the United Nations. The first author has been involved in the latter, as chair of the Psychology Coalition of nongovernmental organizations accredited at the United Nations, leading the campaign to include mental health and well-being in the new UN global agenda, referred to as the Sustainable Development Goals (Forman, 2014).

This chapter further synthesizes academic findings and global policies to protect natural resources and peoples' well-being in these current times of prevalent environmental disasters, crises from climate change, and the diminishing supply of natural resources. These issues are top priorities at the United Nations, and the subject of many international summits aimed at reaching intergovernmental agreements about action and forming alliances and multi-stakeholder partnerships—among governments and the private and public sectors—to achieve the goals set for a healthy planet in the "Future We Want" (United Nations, 2012, General Assembly Resolution 66/288). A holistic view is presented, as nature and well-being are intricately tied to many of the global goals agreed upon by the member states of the United Nations.

DEFINITION OF WELL-BEING

Increased attention to the topic of well-being requires an understanding of the concept. Dictionary definitions refer to well-being as the state of being happy, healthy, or successful (Merriam-Webster, n.d.), or prosperous (Oxford English Dictionary, n.d.). In the psychology field, well-being is often similarly referred to as a state of being happy and healthy, with added constructs contributed by positive psychology such as hardiness, resilience, and quality of life. One recent exploration of the multifaceted nature of the term proposes that well-being is "a type of equilibrium state where an individual's resources are in balance with faced challenges" (Dodge, Daly, Huyton, & Sanders, 2012). Generally, well-being is seen as a subjective measure, including emotional and cognitive aspects; as an outcome measure of emotional state (the presence of positive emotions and the absence of negative emotion); and as reports of perceived life satisfaction, happiness, and fulfillment (Centers for Disease Control and Prevention, n.d.; Diener, Oishi, & Lucas, 2003; Diener, Suh, Lucas, & Smith, 1999; Kahneman, Diener, & Schwarz, 1999; Keyes, Schmotkin, & Ryff, 2002; Seligman, 2011). Interest has also focused on well-being in children (Stratham & Chase, 2010). Much attention has recently highlighted the debate about whether well-being requires financial assets, a distinction highly relevant to the discussion about including alternate measures of development other than just GDP, popularly known as "Beyond GDP" (Diener, 2009; Helliwell, Layard, & Sachs, 2013). In a review of definitions of well-being, the United Kingdom's Department of Children, Schools and Families offered a holistic approach, including the component of sustainability (Ereaut & Whiting, 2008). This view is certainly consistent with this chapter and with the global agenda. Efforts on a grassroots level to define happiness include a walk across the United States by two women, asking people along the way to describe what happiness means to them; most people refer to being with their family and loved ones (Kuriansky, 2012b).

THE LINK BETWEEN NATURE AND WELL-BEING

While "well-being" usually describes human traits and/or experiences, considerable research is focusing on the interaction between well-being of humans and connection to nature (Howell, Dopko, Passmore, & Buro, 2011; Howell & Passmore, 2013; Kahn, 2014). Some research has focused on theories attempting to explain this interaction. The biophilia hypothesis suggests that humans have an innate and subconscious drive to interact not only with other living things, but also with nature, plants, and animals (Wilson, 1984). The Gaia theory, formulated by scientist and environmentalist James Lovelock in the mid-1960s— whereby "Gaia" refers to "Mother Earth"—proposes the interconnectedness of all beings with no separation between nature and self, other, and object (Lovelock, 2006). Other orientations that support this connection include phenomenology, which maintains that we become more human when our senses are fully open to an abundant physical natural world; and a transpersonal view that interaction with nature facilitates optimal mental health, inner peace, compassion, trust, selfless service, fully realized aliveness, and even mystical and spiritual experiences (Kahn, 2014).

The overall strong influence of the environment on emotions, thoughts, and actions has been pointed out by *New York Times* journalist Winifred Gallagher in her book, *The Power of Place* (1994). In recent years, personal experiences of this interaction have been supported by an ever-increasing number of scientific studies. Research has shown that immersion in nature, or proximity to "green space," can increase an individual's positive affect (Mayer, Frantz, Bruehlman-Senecal, & Dolliver, 2009); aid in mental restoration and recovery from tiredness (Furnass, 1979; Hartig, Mang, & Evans, 1991; Kaplan & Kaplan, 1989, 1990; Maller, Townsend, Pryor, Brown, & St. Leger, 2006); reduce psychological and physiological stress (Maller et al., 2006; Parsons, 1991; Ulrich, 1984; Ulrich et al., 1991; van den Berg, Maas, Verheij, & Groenewegen, 2010); lead to a healthier immune system and minimize pain (Diette, Lechtzin, Haponik, Devrotes, & Rubin, 2003; Tse, Ng, Chung, & Wong, 2002); increase resiliency after disasters (Masten & Obradović, 2008); create greater connectivity with others, resulting in less conflict and more cohesive communities (Coley, Kuo, & Sullivan, 1997; Kuo & Sullivan, 2001; Kuo, Sullivan, Coley, & Brunson, 1998); and lead to longer life (Mitchell & Popham, 2008; Takano, Nakamura, & Watanabe, 2002).

A study at the University of Washington showed that the more time people spent looking through a window at a nature scene of a large fountain and trees, the more their heart rate tended to decrease (Kahn et al., 2008). Given these extensive benefits, contact with nature has been suggested as a public health strategy to promote well-being (Maller et al., 2006).

MEASUREMENTS OF WELL-BEING

In order for countries to define policy and assess their progress related to healthy natural environment and citizen wellbeing, these conditions must be measurable and specific indicators must be identified (OECD, 2014). While assessment in this field has yet to be fully developed, some measures are available. For example, the Happy Planet Index (HPI) ranks countries along three dimensions: (1) experienced well-being, based on scoring on a scale from "0" to "10" where "0" represents the worst possible life and "10" the best possible life; (2) life expectancy, based on data from the Human Development Report of the United Nations Development Programme; and (3) ecological footprint, a measure promoted by the environmental charity World Wildlife Federation to gauge resource consumption as the amount of land required to sustain a country's consumption patterns reflected in terms of global hectares of land with average productive biocapacity (Happy Planet Index, 2014). Costa Rica won the HPI in 2014, with Vietnam, Colombia, Belize, and El Salvador in the top 5; Denmark rated highest in 2013.

The Better Life Index measures well-being in 34 countries based on the environment as well as 10 other dimensions of material living conditions and quality of life, including housing, income, jobs, community, education, governance, health, life satisfaction, safety, and work-life balance (OECD, 2014). The Index is part of the Better Life Initiative of the Organisation for Economic Co-operation and Development (OECD) to promote "Better Policies for Better Lives." The index is based on a set of "green growth" indicators that measure economic growth and development and track the improvement in citizens' environmental quality of life. A wide variety of countries participate, given the OECD's membership of 34 countries, including "advanced countries, emerging countries like Mexico, Chile and Turkey, emerging giants like China, India and Brazil, and developing economies in Africa, Asia, Latin America and the Caribbean" (OECD, 2014).

The Social Progress Index measures three dimensions of social progress: (1) basic human needs, assessed in questions like "Does a country provide for its people's most essential needs?"; (2) foundations of well-being, referring to "ecosystem sustainability" evident in questions like, "Are the building blocks in place for individuals and communities to enhance and sustain well-being?"; and (3) opportunity, qualified by questions like "Is there opportunity for all individuals to reach their full potential?" (The Social Progress Imperative, 2014). Launched in April 2013, the index ranked 50 countries, with Sweden taking first place and Ethiopia rated as last.

The 2010 Human Development Report from the United Nations Development Programme (UNDP) included indexes of "Perceptions of individual well-being and happiness" and "Civic and community well-being," measuring the percentage of satisfaction with aspects of well-being in various areas, such as affordable housing, community, education system, and quality of health care, air, and water (United Nations Development Programme, 2010). The 11 dimensions of satisfaction in the Report were derived from the Gallup World Poll, including measurement of satisfaction with personal dimensions (job, personal health, and standard of living); saying "yes" to elements of happiness (e.g., having a purposeful life, being treated with respect, and having a social support network); and an overall life satisfaction rating (on a scale of 0 to 10, with 10 being the most satisfied). The 10 countries ranking highest on the scale were Norway, Australia, New Zealand, the United States, Ireland, Lichtenstein, Netherlands, Canada, Sweden, and Germany, and the 10 countries ranking lowest on the scale were Zimbabwe, the Democratic Republic of the Congo, Niger, Burundi, Mozambique, Guinea-Bissau, Chad, Liberia, Burkino Faso, and Mali.

The "Gross National Happiness" (GNH) Index developed by the Royal Government of Bhutan includes ecological diversity and resilience among the domains in the assessment of the concept of well-being (Centre for Bhutan Studies & GNH Research, 2014; Kuriansky, 2012e). This domain includes the measure of responsibility toward the environment, as well as pollution of air and rivers, absence of or inadequate green spaces, and lack of friendly streets. The index postulates that "beneficial development of human society takes place when material and spiritual development occur side by side to complement and reinforce one another."

That well-being and happiness can be measured has been extensively documented in the World Happiness Report (Helliwell, Layard, & Sachs, 2013). This comprehensive report further supports that well-being is crucial to measure development besides the monetary assessment of gross national product. This report was commissioned for the April 2012 United Nations High-level Meeting on Wellbeing and Happiness: Defining a New Economic Paradigm that was mandated by the UN General Assembly (and to which the first author of this chapter was invited). The report reflects a new worldwide demand for more attention to happiness and well-being as criteria for government policy.

The state of Maryland in the United States has been a pioneer in devising a measurement of sustainable development. Its "Genuine Progress Indicator" measures well-being based on dimensions such as what people buy, as well as the downsides to well-being of environmental hazards such as water and air pollution (S. McGuire, personal communication, May 7, 2013). The motto of the state's initiative is appropriately called "smart, green and growing" (State of Maryland, n.d.). Other states are exploring this approach.

Measures have also been developed by individual researchers. For example, in his "Doherty Sustainability Inventory," psychologist Thomas Doherty includes a section on "Nature and Sustainability" with ratings on scales of "comfort with your level of consumption and ecological footprint," "being a naturalist: knowledge of local ecosystems, weather patterns and natural history," and "connection with nature: contact with the outdoors, green spaces and other species." These are included along with the importance of promoting social and environmental justice, and more traditional measures such as having trusting relationships, work satisfaction, and fun (Doherty, 2009).

EXPANSION OF THE FIELD OF ECOPSYCHOLOGY AND ENVIRONMENTAL PSYCHOLOGY

The discussion about nature and psychology falls under various subdisciplines, including ecopsychology, environmental psychology, and conservation psychology (Teaching Psychology for Sustainability, n.d.). Increasing interest in the subject is evidenced by the number of articles and books written on the topic (Clayton & Myers, 2009; Doherty & Clayton, 2011; Fisher & Abram, 2013; Kahn & Hasbach, 2012; Jordan, 2015; Steg, van den Berg, & de Groot, 2012). In addition, there are an increasing number of professional publications specifically targeting environmental psychology, including *Ecopsychology* (http://www .liebertpub.com/overview/ecopsychology/300/) that addresses the relationship between environmental issues and mental health and well-being, and that published its first issue in 2010; the *European Journal of Ecopsychology* (http://eje .wyrdwise.com); the *Journal of Environmental Psychology* (http://www.journals .elsevier.com/journal-of-environmental-psychology/); and *The Sustainable Psychologist* newsletters and bulletins (Australian Psychological Society Member Groups, n.d.). A journal appropriately titled *Health and Well-Being* was launched by the International Association of Applied Psychology (http://onlinelibrary .wiley.com/journal/10.1111/(ISSN)1758-0854). Increasing interest in establishing a scientific base for the interface of humans and nature has further led to efforts to identify specific methodologies for such research (Abrahamse, Schultz, & Steg, 2014; Gifford, in press).

Furthermore, societies on the topic have been formed within psychological associations. The Division of Ecopsychology of the American Psychological Association (the Society for Environmental, Population and Conservation Psychology), formed in 1973, has become increasingly popular in recent years. Areas of research and exchange among members include the relationship between humans and with nature and resulting implications for identity, health, and well-being, as well as the impacts of environmental disasters and global climate change. In addition, the Division of Environmental Psychology of the International Association of Applied Psychology brings together professionals from all over the world to share research and ideas about ways to stimulate eco-friendly behavior, innovative approaches to environmental education, and solutions to environmental problems (reported later in this chapter). The overlap of such studies in various fields is seen as extremely valuable given the importance of an interdisciplinary approach (Ernst & Wenzel, 2014). The crucial integration of science and psychology in today's world replete with environmental traumas has been pointed out by the coeditors of this volume in a previous book (Nemeth, Hamilton, & Kuriansky, 2012). Leading experts from varied disciplines have come together to share their varied perspectives in publications such as the *Handbook of Research on Sustainable Consumption* (Reisch & Thørgersen, 2015).

Many academic programs at established universities and independent institutes now offer interdisciplinary courses and degrees in environmental studies (Society for Environmental Population and Conservation Psychology, n.d.). A particular field of interest is education about the environment. Environmental psychologists versed in developmental psychology are planning and assessing approaches, curricula, and teaching models for environmental education (EE) for children, particularly to encourage their healthy relationships with the environment. One such 4-day education program in Germany, called "Water in Life—Life in Water," was effective in increasing the knowledge, utilization, and preservation behaviors of young children ages 9–13, using a scale measuring "the inclusion of nature in self" (Liefländer, 2014). In another study, adults working in a hospital in Australia changed their conservation behavior after being exposed to visual prompts set around the workplace (Whitmarsh & O'Neil, 2010).

A clinical intervention to improve mental and physical health and well-being—called ecotherapy—is also being developed by psychologists with interests in the environment and clinical interventions (Buzzell & Chalquist, 2009; Doherty & Chen, in press). This approach supports people to be active outdoors, e.g., in activities like gardening, growing food, and conserving the environment (Buzzell & Chalquist, 2009; Mind, 2013).

RESEARCH ABOUT THE ENVIRONMENT AT AN INTERNATIONAL APPLIED PSYCHOLOGY CONFERENCE

Given the value of interdisciplinary exchange and collaboration emphasized in this chapter as well as by other experts and by the United Nations, an increasing number of conferences, forums, and summits have been held to foster this exchange in various venues (Kuriansky, 2012e), discussed in subsections below of this chapter.

At the International Congress of Applied Psychology in Paris, France, in July 2014, the Division of Environmental Psychology of the International Association of Applied Psychology, the convenor of the Congress, presented an extensive program with over 100 presentations of research about various aspects of the topic (ICAP 2014 Updates, 2014). Presentations explored theories of environmental psychology, for example, "Campbell's Paradigm" about how attitudes affect behavior (Kibbe, Arnold, Otto, & Kaiser, 2014); a newly developed General Model of Threat and Defense, to heighten awareness of the dangers of climate change (Uhl, Jonas, & Klackl, 2014); the Social Influence Model, purporting that people are influenced by others' pro-environment behavior (Estrada, Schultz, Silva-Send, & Boudrias, 2014); the Hue-Heat Hypothesis, which states that changing the color of office light can save energy by using more reddish hues in the cold-weather heating season and more bluish hues in warm-weather air-conditioning conditions (Huebner, Gauthier, Witzel, Chan, & Shipworth, 2014); and Function Theory of Values, reflecting how concern for others is linked to concern for the natural environment resulting in pro-environment actions like water conservation and support for solar power (Taciano, Milfont,

Coelho, Pessoa, & Gouveia, 2014) as well as how collectivist cultures and older generations are more inclined to behave in a ecofriendly way than societies and younger generations that value individualism (Gao & Hansen, 2014).

Many presentations addressed effective ways to increase knowledge about biodiversity and to encourage pro-environment behavior (PEB), especially in the face of climate change. These include using technology to teach children (Crawford & Holder, 2014), and using graphics more than text to raise awareness in the public (Pahl, Stahl-Timmins, White, & Depledge, 2014); encouraging zoo visits (Clayton, Prevot-Julliard, & Germain, 2014); giving food vouchers as incentives to reduce energy use (Cloherty, Jansson-Boyd, & Jiminez-Bescos, 2014); activating spirituality and community feelings (Lee, Frederick, & Grouzet, 2014); and heightening awareness of climate change risk in order to encourage recycling behavior (Dorofeeva, Ceschi, & Sartori, 2014).

To improve scientific methodology, study results were reported about the usefulness of various assessment measures. These include the Environmental Motives Scale (EMS) used to motivate use of wood polymer products over plastic (Osburg, Strack, & Toporowski, 2014); the scale of Perceived Residential Environmental Quality Indicators (Bonaiuto & Fornara, 2014); the Neighborhood Environment Walkability Scale (Takacs, Kristjansson, & Pearce, 2014); the Revised Residential Environment Assessment Tool (Poortinga, 2014); and the Consideration of Future Consequences scale, used to predict environmentally responsible behavior like switching off lights and lowering thermostats (Enzler, 2014).

Emerging environmental constructs were reported, for example, enhancing "place attachment" as people's connection to an environment (Turton, Murtagh, Uzzell, & Gatersleben, 2014); identifying "interpretive communities" that share similar views and understandings about climate change (Hine, Phillips, & Reser, 2014); and measuring the "cosmopolitan identity"—qualities of global altruism, openness to foreign cultures, and support for open economies—that predicts the likelihood to engage in pro-environmental behaviors for environmental protection, like supporting an environmentalist organization, purchasing biodegradable products and looking for ways to reuse and repurpose things (Leung, Koh, Ong, & Tam, 2014).

Well-known constructs were expanded upon, like linking resilience to community involvement with ecology after a disaster (Ross, 2014) and connecting environmental resilience with posttraumatic growth after an earthquake in Turkey (Ikizer, Dogulu, & Nuray Karanci, 2014). Semantics of different concepts were also compared; for example, respondents in a Mexican survey viewed the word "well-being" as more related to health than the word "happiness," while "happiness" implied relationships when compared to the word "satisfaction" that evoked thoughts of achievement (Urbina-Soria & Flores-Cano, 2014).

Presentations reflected the trend that educators and practitioners around the globe are appreciating the importance of environmental education (EE), proven effective for preschoolers in Japan (Isobe, 2014) and for workers in Germany using a web-based program for changing energy-relevant behaviors (Kastner & Matthies, 2014). Several projects were reported that were launched at the UN headquarters in Geneva. These included trainings to promote social responsibility and dedication to hard work in young people in three ecobiological centers in the Russian Federation (Odintsova, 2014), and a project in Brazil teaching youth to value their cultural identify and their homeland (Capasso, Lacerda e Silva, Garcia, & Rockenbach, 2014). Another project, related to the UN Millennium Development Goals, involved the restoration of a medieval village in central Italy, with its beautiful natural environment, as a heritage landmark and the heart of a worldly humanistic culture. Its recovery was described as (1) an educational eco-biological model of using cultural, artistic, and touristic tools to contribute to local sustainable development; (2) an example of applying an ontopsychological approach (meaning a reciprocal causality, in this case between humans and nature) that fosters interdisciplinary leadership skills; and (3) a demonstration of the convergence of science, technology, and innovation to promote sustainable development and achieving global goals set by the United Nations (Palumbo, Bernabei, De Santis, & Cecconi, 2014).

MODELS OF ENVIRONMENTAL SUSTAINABILITY

Several model programs represent a positive interaction of psychology with environmental protection, incorporating principles of ecopsychology with honoring the natural environment. For example, the project by the Pachamama Alliance in the remote village of the Achuar peoples in the Amazon rain forest of Ecuador (one of the most remote cultures on earth) is focused on healing through indigenous knowledge of the environment (see Chapter 11 in this volume [Murrietta, 2015]). Another model is the retreat for personal and professional growth workshops in Belize with techniques and activities like storytelling and trust walks that are consistent with the vast diversity of cultures of the people and ecosystems of the country with its rainforest, wildlife sanctuaries, and barrier reef (described in Chapter 12 in this volume by Wood, Schmidt, and Kuriansky [2015]). Additionally, the Women's Earth Alliance is a grassroots program in both India and Africa that trains women to be community leaders, with education in ecological topics like climate, water, food, and sanitation as well as about their rights, for example, obtaining land rights, given that women do 80% of the farming in rural countries but cannot own the land (Kirkman & Kuriansky, 2012).

Another example is the Girls Empowerment Programme in Lesotho, Africa, where village girls were taught income-generating activities, life skills, and HIV/AIDS education, a model of which was codeveloped by the first author (Berry et al., 2013; Blind, 2010; Kuriansky, 2010a; Kuriansky & Berry, 2011).

In one activity that particularly exemplifies the use of elements in the indigenous environment, girls in teams competed to build a structure resembling a "home" out of sticks and earth that would resist falling apart when water was poured upon it, thus teaching lessons about survival and sustainability as well as competence, resourcefulness, and resilience.

PROGRESS ON NATURE AND WELL-BEING AT THE UNITED NATIONS

Efforts have been made over the past few decades by the international community at the United Nations to foster dialogue surrounding nature and living harmoniously with the environment and to create inclusive policies about nature for sustainable development and a sustainable future. These efforts, described below, are based on the principle that it is critical to "build governance structures in which nature is treated in partnership with humankind" (United Nations, 2014).

Actions by the United Nations (UN) are usually reflected in resolutions, a text issued by any UN body but primarily by the Security Council or by the General Assembly (GA). The GA is made up of the governments of the world who are members of the UN, referred to as "member states." These resolutions are reviewed at high-level meetings, which are attended by heads of state of governments and delegates of the UN missions, as well as other invited stakeholders and observers that can include members of UN agencies, civil society, experts, nongovernmental organizations, and others who can be called upon for expert input.

Early UN Conferences, and Actions about Nature

Actions about the topic of nature at the United Nations can be traced back to 1972, when the UN Conference on Human Environment convened in Stockholm where member states created the *Report of the United Nations Conference on the Human Environment* (A/CONF.48/14/Rev.1) (United Nations, General Assembly, 1972), acknowledging that man shapes the environment and that environmental protection is central to the wellness and economic development of all people. The report notes that millions of people are prevented from having a quality human experience both in developing countries, due to underdevelopment, and in developed countries, caused in part by technology and industrialization (United Nations, General Assembly, 1972). The document concludes that a "point has been reached in history where we must shape our actions throughout the world with a more prudent care for their environmental consequences"—a situation that remains true over 40 years later, into present times. Further developments described below reveal that this need for environmental protection requires both group and individual responsibility.

Years later, UN action for environmental protection continued with two resolutions passed by the GA. Resolution 35/7 in 1980 called for international and domestic efforts to prevent environmental destruction and exploitation of resources, and Resolution 36/6 in 1981 called for global cooperation for environmental protection. The next year, in 1982, the GA adopted the World Charter for Nature (A/RES/37/7), which stated that mankind and civilization are imbedded in nature; that harmonious existence with nature provides the best opportunity to develop and prosper; and that maintaining this harmony is urgent. The charter further warned that overconsumption and misuse of resources by man would lead to exploitation and degradation of habitats. Conservation of resources was noted as essential for peace, given that conflict is deepened by competition for scarce resources. Recommendations were made that all people should participate in environmental decision-making, and that scientific research and information on nature should be made available to all people through means such as ecological education.

A groundbreaking conference to discuss increasing global economic change and the protection of nature was convened in 1992, called the "United Nations Conference on Environment and Development," which became popularly known as the "Earth Summit" or the "Rio Summit" since it was held in Rio de Janeiro, Brazil (Meakin, 1992; United Nations Department of Public Information, 1997). This conference resulted in the Rio Declaration on Environment and Development that outlined 27 key principles pertaining to international partnership for protecting the integrity of the environment. These included principles that: "environmental protection shall constitute an integral part of the development process and cannot be considered in isolation from it" (Principle 4); "[to] achieve sustainable development and a higher quality of life for all people, States should reduce and eliminate unsustainable patterns of production and consumption and promote appropriate demographic policies" (Principle 8); and "States should cooperate to strengthen endogenous capacity-building for sustainable development by improving scientific understanding through exchanges of scientific and technological knowledge, and by enhancing the development, adaptation, diffusion and transfer of technologies, including new and innovative technologies" (Principle 9). This Rio Declaration confirmed the interlinkage of peace, development, and conservation of nature and highlighted the importance of participation of all citizens, particularly women, youth and indigenous peoples (United Nations Environment Programme, n.d.).

Environmental progress was slow until 10 years later, when the World Summit on Sustainable Development was convened in 2002 in Johannesburg, South Africa (World Summit on Sustainable Development, 2002). The resulting Johannesburg Declaration on Sustainable Development acknowledged continuing global disparities in wealth and resources, despite the fact that global society "has the means and is endowed with the resources to address the challenges of poverty eradication and sustainable development confronting all humanity" (United Nations, General Assembly, 2002). The declaration supported the leadership role of the United Nations to promote sustainable development, while also underscoring the previously noted importance of participation by all people—an approach that continues in present times.

Twenty years after this landmark Rio Summit in 1992, and 10 years after the 2002 World Summit in Johannesburg, global leaders reconvened in a significant follow-up conference, the United Nations Conference on Sustainable Development, popularly referred to—not surprisingly—as "Rio + 20," since it was purposefully held again in Rio de Janeiro, Brazil. The goal was to focus on two major themes: poverty eradication and sustainable development (United Nations Conference on Sustainable Development, 2012). The outcome document—entitled *The Future We Want*—reaffirmed commitment of the 193 UN member states (i.e., governments) to sustainable development goals, which included poverty eradication as well as environmental safeguards. These goals, to eradicate poverty and to achieve environmental sustainability, were among the eight goals outlined in the Millennium Development Goals (MDGs), which governments agreed to accomplish by the year 2015, with Goal #7 to "ensure environmental sustainability," requiring the reversal of the loss of environmental resources and reduction by half the proportion of people without access to safe drinking water. The document specifically noted the need to address the rights of Mother Earth and living harmoniously with nature (paragraph 39) and offered means of implementation and recommendations for a wide range of environmental concerns, including climate change, chemical waste, land degradation, and disaster risk reduction. This document was continuously referred to in the formation of the post-2015 agenda, outlined in the Sustainable Development Goals (SDGs) for the years 2015–2030, which replaced the MDGs that were in effect from the years 2000–2015.

The Year of Planet Earth

Acknowledging the Rio (1992) and Johannesburg (2005) meetings, the UN General Assembly named 2008 as the "Year of Planet Earth" (A/RES/60/192) and in 2009 adopted a resolution declaring April 22 as International Mother Earth Day (A/RES/63/278). This document recognized that "Mother Earth is a common expression for the planet earth in a number of countries and regions, which reflects the interdependence that exists among human beings, other living species and the planet we all inhabit."

The UN Resolutions on Harmony with Nature

To date, there have been four UN resolutions on Harmony with Nature, adopted from 2009 to 2013. Each resolution builds on the previous resolution regarding the importance of considering harmony with nature, and calls for a report from the Secretary-General and for an interactive dialogue on the subject. During the actions outlined below, the UN Secretary-General (SG) has been His Excellency Ban ki-Moon, South Korean diplomat and politician, who took office on January 1, 2007, and continued to serve until December 31, 2016.

The first Resolution on Harmony with Nature in 2009 stated that man can and should live harmoniously with nature. In response to the resolution's request, the SG issued an inaugural *Report on Harmony with Nature* that discussed the evolution of human health in relation to nature and proposed the holistic nature of sustainable development. Important recommendations focused on providing education on sustainable production and consumption in schools, as well as resources (including virtual platforms) for nonformal learning.

The Second Resolution on Harmony with Nature, in 2010, adopted at the 65th session of the UN General Assembly, recognized that gross domestic product (GDP) was an inadequate measure of development—an important issue that would be later explored by the president of France, Nicolas Sarkozy, and in subsequent UN high-level meetings and recommendations leading to the view that well-being is critical as an adjunctive measure of development. As in the previous resolution, this resolution recognized the important contributions of other stakeholders, for example, scientists, academia, and civil society, in furthering sustainable production and consumption models and patterns. The resolution requested that in observance of International Mother Earth Day, the UN host the first Interactive Dialogue of the General Assembly; that the SG issue a second *Report*; and that an official Harmony with Nature website be developed.

Significantly, the two new actions requested were enacted. The first interactive dialogue of the UN General Assembly on Harmony with Nature was held in 2011, and the website of the UN Harmony with Nature was launched, which presented rights of nature law, country policies, and links to UN reports on Harmony with Nature and interactive dialogues, resolution documents and the UN Conference on Sustainable Development outcome document. In addition, the SG issued his second report on Harmony with Nature (A/66/302, 2011), which, like the first report, recognized the contributions of scientists, scholars, and others and focused on the dynamic relationship between mankind and nature; but also included lessons from ancient civilizations and historical trends (such as the integration of nature, men, and deities in many Eastern religions). It also recommended that consumerism does not increase happiness.

The third resolution on Harmony with Nature (A/RES/66/204) in 2011, adopted at the end of the 66th session of the GA, recognized the importance of improving statistical data related to the three pillars of sustainability—social inclusion, environmental protection, and economic growth—and the need for societies to rethink production and consumption patterns. The resolution requested convening the next Interactive Dialogue on Harmony with Nature; produced the third *Report of the Secretary-General* on the relationship of humankind with nature, which this time focused more intensely on the relationship between science and economics with sustainable development (A/67/317, 2012) and recommended ensuring that policy making on sustainable development is based on scientific findings; and prepared the website with information about the upcoming Rio + 20 Conference.

At the 67th GA in 2012, the fourth resolution on Harmony with Nature (A/68/325) was adopted, requesting another Interactive Dialogue, another report from the SG, and continued efforts on the Harmony with Nature website. That year's report called for considering nature as a social and human construct; country development through environmental transformation; the harmonious interaction with the environment; further exploring statistical indicators of social, economic and environmental progress in policy; and including "Harmony with Nature" in the post-2015 agenda.

The Fifth Resolution on Harmony with Nature, in 2013, adopted at the 68th GA, requested further discussion on harmony with nature, called for the next Interactive Dialogue and encouraged member states to review existing studies and reports and to continue research on Harmony with Nature, particularly with the approaching development agenda.

The Interactive Dialogues of the General Assembly on Harmony with Nature

As mentioned above, each resolution on harmony with nature led to an interactive dialogue at the UN on the topic, celebrated annually at UN headquarters in New York City to coincide with Mother Earth Day, and focusing on human's relationship with the planet.

The first Interactive Dialogue of the General Assembly on Harmony with Nature in 2011 focused on how countries could move toward sustainable development, and how they celebrate International Mother Earth Day with their national practices and experiences. Chinese delegate Mr. Wang Qun described discussions about the earth held in schools as well as an online Earth Day–themed cartoon contest for children. Brazilian Minister Maria Teresa Mesquita Pessôa noted that her country updated its national indicators on sustainable development every four years.

The Second Interactive dialogue, in 2012, on the theme of "Scientific findings on the impacts of human activities on the functioning of the Earth System," focused on how human activity has negatively impacted the regeneration of the earth and on how science and economics can contribute to sustainable development. The Permanent Representative of Chile to the UN, Ambassador Octavio Errázuriz Guilisasti, speaking on behalf of the Community of Latin-American and Caribbean States (CELAC), stated that while people have the right to development as a way to overcome poverty and inequality, respect for the rights of Mother Earth is necessary. Ambassador Jorge Valero, Permanent Representative of the Mission of the Bolivarian Republic of Venezuela to the UN, noted that the pursuit of global capitalism irresponsibly misuses resources, particularly in wealthy societies, while poverty remains rampant, particularly in countries considered as the "south," in UN-speak.

The third interactive dialogue, in 2013, centered on the ethical interaction of nature and man through various economic approaches. The Permanent Observer from the Inter-Parliamentary Union, Miguel Bermeo, stated that growth is often not an answer to economic and social challenges that people face, but may be part of the problem, since strong growth does not imply more happiness. Robin Milam, on behalf of the Global Alliance for the Rights of Nature, remarked on the need to move away from the idea of nature as property, and to embrace being a part of a unified global community.

On April 22, 2014, the UN hosted the 4th Interactive Dialogue, focused on moving from a human-centered to an earth-centered view of the world, thus making Nature a partner with humanity rather than being a commodity or resource to be used. This dialogue occurred at a particularly important time when the UN was outlining the post-2015 agenda and Sustainable Development Goals. The first two authors of this chapter were in attendance and the first author was one of two civil society representatives invited to make a formal statement.

The SG's message, delivered by Thomas Gass, Assistant Secretary-General for Policy Coordination and Inter-Agency Affairs, UN Department of Economic and Social Affairs (DESA), said:

> The air we breathe, the water we drink and the soil that grows our food are part of a delicate global ecosystem that is increasingly under pressure from human activities. From tropical deforestation to depleted ocean fisheries, from growing freshwater shortages to the rapid decline of biodiversity and increasingly polluted skies and seas in many parts of the world, we see the heavy hand of humankind.
>
> As our population grows, we have to recognize that our consumption of the planet's resources is unsustainable. We need a global transformation of attitude and practice. It is especially urgent to address how we generate the energy that drives our progress. Burning fossil fuels is the principal cause of climate change, which increasingly threatens prosperity and stability in all regions. That is why world leaders have pledged to reach a global legal climate agreement in 2015.
>
> Action on climate change presents multiple opportunities to reset our relationship with Mother Earth and improve human well-being, especially for the poorest and most vulnerable. Sustainable energy for all can increase health, wealth and opportunity for billions of people, as can climate-smart agriculture, more efficient cities and better-managed and protected forests. . . .
>
> I appeal to all people everywhere to raise their voices. Speak out on behalf of this planet, our only home. Let us care for Mother Earth so she can continue to care for us as she has done for millennia.

In the dialogue, Ambassador John W. Ashe, the Permanent Representative of Antigua and Barbuda to the UN who was President of the GA that year, noted the complex connection between humankind and the earth "home," which is essential to reflect in the upcoming post-2015 global agenda. He further noted that modern patterns of consumption and production are leading to exploitation of resources and disruption of ecosystems, with the result that nature has been negatively—and possibly irrevocably—impacted by man's actions, technologies, and practices. Since infinite growth cannot be expected from a finite planet, he called for moving toward a more balanced, earth-centered relationship, reconciling needs of people with needs and capacity of the planet, with special attention to living harmoniously with nature and one another in order to ensure the sustainability of future generations.

Ambassador Mr. Sacha Llorentty Solíz, Permanent Representative of the Mission of the Plurinational State of Bolivia to the UN, emphasized the rights of Mother Nature (consistent with the country's pioneering nature-friendly laws) and called attention to important issues including agriculture and food security, sustainable consumption patterns, nonpolluting production patterns, and adaptation to climate change. Ms. Tonya Gonella Frichner, a civil society representative of the American Indian Law Alliance of New York and New Jersey, posed Mother Earth as a relative, not a resource. She emphasized the cultural and spiritual dimensions of humans' relationship to the land and the responsibilities to repair the integrity of the environment and to consider the impact of actions and decisions on future generations. As a member of the Iroquois nation, she noted that harmony with nature has long been the basis of indigenous existence, and that the protection of nature requires the full and effective participation of indigenous peoples.

Panelist Professor Frank Biermann, chair of the Earth System Governance project and VU University in Amsterdam, the Netherlands, emphasized the need to strengthen international environmental treaties and reforms in voting since the practice of "one country, one vote" underrepresents countries with large populations. He further called for novel accountability of global institutions that take into account financial disparities.

Panelist Professor Barbara Baudot, chair of the Department of Politics at Saint Anselm College in New Hampshire, highlighted the importance of differentiating the definition of the words "environment" and "nature," asserting that nature should be perceived in broader terms as the source and cradle of life and not just material progress measured by GDP. She called for a holistic and interdisciplinary view of harmony with nature, to be explored by scientific inquiry, philosophic reflection, artistic expression, and spirituality.

Panelist Mr. Jim Gerritsen, an organic potato seed farmer who co-owns Wood Prairie Farms in Maine and is president of the Organic Seed Growers and Trade Association, presented the extreme predicaments faced in organic farming, including the need for healthy soil, the fight against genetically modified crops, and complaints that political actions amount to theft of farmers' production by patenting crops as life forms. In a lawsuit in which he was involved, a partial victory was won so a large agricultural biotechnology corporation could not sue farmers if their fields became contaminated with trace amounts of genetically engineered material like the company's patented seeds.

Panelist Mr. Fander Falconi Benitez, research professor at the Latin America Social Sciences Institute in Ecuador, discussed the economics of sustainable development in the face of finite resources, noting that everyone is responsible for the state of the planet, and highlighting the positive examples of the constitutions of Bolivia and Ecuador that recognize the rights of nature and refer to the concept of "living well."

Various member states' representatives made interventions. The Deputy Permanent Representative of Algeria to the UN, Ambassador Djamel Moktefi, stated that nature could not be considered a commodity and called for a paradigm shift that production and consumption is essential for sustainable development—a sentiment echoed by many representatives. The Permanent Representative of Ecuador to the UN, Ambassador Xavier Lasso, noted that recognizing the rights of nature does not mean we cannot use resources, but rather requires respect and responsible use. Counsellor Amit Narang of India underlined the principle of taking only what is needed and leaving no waste. Minister-Counsellor of Malaysia to the UN Mr. Loh Seck Tiong stated that many small yet concrete lifestyle changes, like shutting off lights when leaving a room, can be done to benefit the environment. Some steps, like installing systems for catching rainwater, may seem to be somewhat pricey investments in the short term but will pay off over the long term. The Deputy Permanent Representative of Kenya to the UN, Ambassador Ms. Koki Muli Grignon, discussed ways that simultaneously help people and the environment, evident in the example of tree nurseries, which allow women to support themselves and also combat deforestation. Ambassador Jean-Francis R. Zinsou, Permanent Representative of the Mission of the Republic of Benin to the UN, spoke about the need for balance and setting rules to regulate the relationship between man and nature.

As a selected civil society discussant at this dialogue, the main author of this chapter stated that the field of ecopsychology offers much research linking nature to benefits of physical and psychological health, including an improved immune system and healthier emotional state; longer life; resiliency after disaster; cohesive communities; and peaceful societies—all important for sustainable development (Kuriansky, 2014c). Her presentation further offered examples of programs in different parts of the world that address sustainable development (see Chapter 9 [Kuriansky, Zinsou, et al., 2015] and Chapter 20 [Nemeth, Hamilton, & Kuriansky, 2015] in this volume); the importance of multi-stakeholder participation; and references that well-being and ecological footprint can indeed be measured, as in the examples of measurements given above—an important factor for the indicators and means of implementation essential for the SDGs.

THE POST-2015 AGENDA: GOALS ABOUT NATURE

The SDGs, which replace the Millennium Development Goals (n.d.) for the years 2015–2030, were defined and agreed upon by the governments of the world who are members of the UN, with input from expert groups in many disciplines (Sustainable Development Goals, n.d.). These SDGs enumerate goals and targets, built on the three pillars noted above, namely, social inclusion, economic growth, and environmental protection, where the latter extensively recognizes the importance of nature in global development. The framework includes nature in several goals and targets, which holds much promise for the world and also for the future development of the field of ecopsychology. Actions are called for on: climate change (to take urgent action to combat climate change and its impact, and strengthen resilience and adaptive capacity to climate related hazards and natural disasters); harmony with nature (ensure that people everywhere have relevant information and awareness for lifestyles in harmony with nature, provide access to safe, green, and public spaces, and protect the world's cultural and natural heritage); preservation of coastal and terrestrial ecosystems (conserve the oceans, seas, and marine resources; protect the forests; and halt biodiversity loss); and make cities and human settlements inclusive, safe, and resilient.

These advances are consistent with a trend toward what can be called "earth-centered governance." This means that government bodies institute and implement laws, policies, and programs that promote and protect a healthy environment.

The United Nations Environment Programme's "Green Economy Initiative"

An approach to policy and actions about managing natural resources in the interests of public well-being—as well as growth and prosperity—is evident in the "Green Economy Initiative" launched in 2009 by the United Nations Environment Programme (UNEP), an agency of the UN. The "green economy" is based on a cleaner, more efficient energy system especially regarding use of agricultural lands and forests for overall well-being, in comparison to a "brown economy" that relies heavily on fossil fuels and does not consider the negative side-effects that economic production and consumption have on the environment. Steps include building national capital in natural resources like the forests, water, soil, and fish stock, and by promoting "green jobs." "Green jobs" does not mean that everyone becomes gardeners, but that people engage in job activities that promote sustainability, meaning that jobs are healthier, contribute to society, and build on sustainable use of natural resources like land and water.

The Post-2015 Agenda Addressing Well-Being

Psychologists have had increasing impact on global policy through advocacy efforts at the UN (Kuriansky, 2012a). This has been in areas related to disaster recovery as well as health, education and human rights, and more recently about the inclusion of mental health and well-being in the new global agenda. In the SDGs, the title of the goal (#3) that refers to health includes the phrase "the promotion of wellbeing" and the target under that goal (#3.4) includes the reference "to promote mental health and wellbeing." The importance of civil society advocacy in this process was evident by the success of the major advocacy campaign to achieve these inclusions, led by the first author on behalf of the Psychology Coalition of NGOs accredited by the UN (PCUN), as its chair, with assistance of team members and interns for PCUN and the International Association of Applied Psychology (an NGO accredited at the UN), in partnership with the Ambassador of Palau to the United Nations, Dr. Caleb Otto, who is a physician and long-time public health advocate (Forman, 2014; Otto, Kuriansky, & Okorodudu, 2014). Discussions were held with nearly half the member states of the UN and a "Friends of Mental Health and Wellbeing" of delegates was formed and met to strategize (Kuriansky, 2014a). Concept papers were developed for this advocacy campaign, including reports of documents, actions, and agreements by the UN and UN agencies supporting the importance of including mental health and well-being in the framework (Kuriansky & Okorodudu, 2014), as well as sections on global statistics about economic and social costs and benefits, the reciprocal relationship between physical and mental health, and cross-cutting issues.

The UN Secretary-General's Statements about Well-Being

The UN Secretary-General mentions "well-being" three times in his report *Poverty Eradication* (United Nations Economic and Social Council, 2012). The report says: "Not only do the idle young suffer deterioration in their skills set and motivation, and physical *and mental well-being*, but the loss of human and productive potential undermines social cohesion and stability"; "Social protection measures shield individuals and families from economic shocks as well as social and economic changes, and enhance their capacity to manage and overcome situations that affect their *well-being*"; and "The right to social security calls for a progressive move towards universal social protection to ensure the basic *well-being* of all individuals, regardless of where they work or love, or the state of the economy."

THE INTERRELATIONSHIP BETWEEN WELL-BEING, NATURE, SUSTAINABLE DEVELOPMENT, AND CLIMATE CHANGE

The preservation of nature and achievement of sustainable development is inextricable with the issue of climate change, which then impacts well-being (Doherty, in press). The well-being of vast numbers of peoples in many countries throughout the world has been gravely affected by devastation of the environment caused by natural disasters. Much research has shown the emotional trauma experienced both immediately and over the long term after such tragedies as fires, floods, earthquakes, and tsunamis, consistent with vast experience by the first author (Kuriansky, 2010b, 2012c, 2012d; see also Chapter 10 in this volume [Kuriansky, Wu, et al., 2015]). Recovery from disaster is a crucial aspect of environmental protection that is particularly important in present times given the number of these natural disasters that have affected many countries worldwide. Consistent with the fact that recovery and resilience after such disasters is not just related to physical structure but also psychosocial well-being, many programs addressing the importance of a psychosocial perspective have shown this importance in helping individuals and communities emotionally recover, rebuild, and become more resilient, as demonstrated in the first author's projects in Haiti, Japan, China, and Africa (Kuriansky, 2010b, 2012c, 2012d, 2014b; Kuriansky & Jean-Charles, 2012) and as shown in an extensive review of over two dozen projects by local and international organizations that provided psychosocial aid in China after the devastating 2008 earthquake (see Chapter 10 of this volume [Kuriansky, Wu, et al., 2015]). One unique approach, developed by the first author, integrates psychosocial techniques with indigenous cultural arts (see Chapter 9 in this volume [Kuriansky, Zinsou, et al., 2015]). Another unique proposal being developed for an African American community setting provides emotional support in a community setting as well as music-based website and apps providing information regarding the impact of global climate change (see Chapter 8 in this volume [Davis & Dumpson, 2015]). That approach is intended to mitigate against what has been described as "environmental racism" against African Americans.

Combatting climate change and facilitating resilience is a critical part of the global agenda at the United Nations, since achieving sustainable development demands awareness about the dangers of climate change and assurances of disaster risk reduction.

THE UNITED NATIONS CLIMATE SUMMIT

The UN Secretary-General convened a climate summit on September 23, 2014, at UN headquarters in New York City, which was attended by 100 heads of state and governments as well as leaders in business and civil society. The goals were to elicit new ideas and commitments addressing the challenges

of climate change—specifically, to strengthen resilience and reduce emissions—
and to mobilize political will for an ambitious global agreement about action in
the areas of climate finance, energy, transport, industry, agriculture, cities, forests, and building resilience. A specific goal is to limit the world to a less-than-
2-degree Celsius rise in global temperature. Major climate change summits were
held in Lima, Peru, in December 2014, and Paris, France, at the end of 2015,
where governments would agree to definitive actions about climate change and
achieve progress where the much-touted climate summit in Copenhagen in
2009 had failed. All such agreements work under the United Nations Framework
Convention on Climate Change, referred to as UNFCCC (United Nations
Framework Convention on Climate Change, n.d.), that provides guidelines for
governments to negotiate international treaties (called "protocols") to set bind-
ing limits on greenhouse gases.

Some success was achieved in Lima in that government leaders announced
contributions to the Green Climate Fund and several countries committed to
the summit's outlined goals. For example, several European countries said that
they would pursue the target of 40% greenhouse gas reductions over 1990 levels.
The United States announced an initiative to bolster resilience efforts. China
committed to reducing carbon intensity and raising forest stock. India said it
would double wind and solar power production by 2020. Costa Rica said it would
use 100% clean energy by 2016, and Chile aims to green 45% of its energy by
2025. Partnerships were promised among coalitions of governments, civil society, and businesses. Insurance companies committed to set up a climate risk
investment framework and pension funds promised to shift assets to clean-
energy portfolios.

As in other meetings, the emphasis was on less talk and more action. The UN
Secretary-General was pleased, saying, "This Summit was not about talk. History
is made by action. And now we have seen that the world is ready to act" (United
Nations Climate Change Summit, 2014).

THE CLIMATE MARCH IN NEW YORK

Leading up to the United Nations Climate Change Summit described above
was "The People's Climate March" that mobilized over 2,500 events in over
160 countries. The march in New York City reportedly drew 400,000 people
(including the UN Secretary-General, former U.S. Vice President Al Gore,
and actor Leonardo DiCaprio) from over 1,500 organizations demanding climate
change action. Attending the march, the first author of this chapter noted creative messaging demonstrated by novel papier-mâché, parade-like, oversized
constructions depicting Mother Earth or cattle (protesting meat consumption)
and pithy sayings on banners and signs carried by marchers, such as: "There is
no Planet B" (referring to the usual practice of a "Plan B"); "Ask a dodo [bird],

extinction is forever"; "Climate Changes, Can We?"; "2° [degrees reduction in global warming] is 2 little 2 live"; "If you can't breathe, you can't be"; "Don't be fossil fools"; with critiques of business and of the UN, e.g., "UN Stop Fiddling"; and even an allusion to President Barack Obama's campaign slogan, "Yes, we can"; and using brash words, e.g., "Stop Screwing Mother Earth" and "Stop fracking, you fracking gassholes" (with spelling of "gassholes" purposeful, to allude to the word without the "g").

THE CASE OF THE SMALL ISLAND STATES

Countries throughout the world are vulnerable to climate change, and many international conferences have been held on the topic, including in Copenhagen in 2009 (noted above) and the Bahamas in 2014. Climate change was also a major focus of the UN Conference on Small Island Developing States (SIDS) held in Samoa in early September 2014, the motto of which was, "Island voices, global choices" (SIDS Action Platform, n.d.). Representatives of 115 countries formed partnerships with business and civil society—amounting to about 1,200 groups mobilizing US\$1.9 billion—and adopted the Samoa Pathway, a roadmap to help the small island developing states with projects about climate change, disaster resilience, environmental protection, access to energy and social development, and transfer of technology. They also affirmed the need for a legal agreement on climate change, to be reached at the climate conference in Paris in 2015.

CIVIL SOCIETY ADDRESSES NATURE AND ECOSYSTEMS AT THE UNITED NATIONS: THE UNITED NATIONS DEPARTMENT OF PUBLIC INFORMATION/NON-GOVERNMENTAL ORGANIZATIONS (DPI/NGO) CONFERENCE

Issues about climate change and also ecosystems were topics of roundtables at the 65th Annual United Nations Department of Public Information/ Non-Governmental Organizations (DPI/NGO) Conference, held at UN headquarters in New York on August 27–29, 2014. The DPI/NGO conference, typically convened annually, is hosted by civil society to come together with representatives of governments, business, and other groups to discuss issues of major global importance. Previous years' conference topics have addressed global health, sustainable cities, and disarmament. This year, the title—"Beyond 2015: Our Action Agenda"—was purposefully selected to coincide with the new agenda of the Sustainable Development Goals, to input the voice of civil society. The first author has been involved in these conferences over many years.

At the roundtable on ecosystems, the issue of climate change took center stage, since an ecosystem—the balance of elements such as air, water, and earth—is gravely affected by the climate that affects all these elements.

Surprisingly to many, the question of whether climate change should be a specific goal of the SDGs had been in debate. As outlined in one panel on Climate Change, "Post 2015 and the UNFCCC Processes: Can They Be Friends?" the Ambassador and Permanent Representative of the Mission of Peru to the UN, Gustavo Meza-Cuadra Velásquez, reported that Peru strongly supports climate change as a goal since development in his country, as well as in surrounding nations, is gravely affected. Warm and wet weather caused by El Niño affects crops; impends construction, especially along rivers where soil is already too weak to build structures; and imperils fisheries and other activities of the seas (Meza-Cuadra, 2014). Others prefer that the issue be addressed in other initiatives, explained another panelist, with positions affected by shifting political priorities (Gave, 2014).

The UN Ambassador of Peru further emphasized that climate change, ecosystems, and environmental unsustainability are inextricably related to poverty, notably with the eradication of poverty as the top priority of the UN SG and listed as the first Sustainable Development Goal. Peru, as a middle-income country, has sustained growth and halved poverty from 50% to 25%, but climate change can still pose threats to this success.

At the roundtable about "Climate Justice in Practice," Ambassador and Permanent Representative of Palau to the UN, Dr. Caleb Otto, emphasized—to considerable audience applause—that climate change is of course about science and politics, but it is mainly about people. "Climate change has to be people-centered, putting the face, voice and will of the people first," said Ambassador Otto (2014), a view echoed by panelist Uwem Robert Otu, president of the African Youth Movement from Abuja Nigeria, who is the Nigerian country representative of the Global Network for Disaster Reduction, a platform of a large network of stakeholders active on climate change and disaster risk reduction to advocate about policy, stimulate dialogue, and ensure social services to the poor and marginalized populations.

Climate justice has to start with a human face, said Otto, especially as it is the poor, weak, and children in rich nations who are the most affected. This connection is evident in events like Hurricane Katrina in the United States, Typhoon Haiyan in the Philippines, and the earthquake in Haiti, where the environmental disasters further gravely threatened food security as well as the health of those already suffering. For Pacific islands and small island states, even sovereignty is at stake in the face of climate change, as three islands—Tuvalu, the Marshall Islands, and the Solomon Islands—being low and flat, are at risk of losing their territory and being totally submerged, with nowhere to go when tides rise (Otto, 2014). While people say residents of these imperiled islands can move to Australia and New Zealand (in fact, New Zealand had agreed to grant permanent residency to a family based on climate change), Ambassador Otto pointed out that this is not a good solution, as they would suffer from being uprooted from their homes, being refugees, and having no rights.

Another panelist described how climate change in rural China, with its already intense smog and pollution, is impacting tea plantations, as abnormal weather results in health problems and bankruptcy of the farmers who then abandon their farms and move to the cities to survive. This situation proves the cyclical nature of the environment and development. A private-sector company, the Asia Now Consulting Group, is trying to stem this tide by bringing technology to help farmers and small businesses to keep producing tea and food (Littlewood, 2014).

Several solutions to combat climate change—including sharing technology and global commitment to carbon neutral growth—are possible, said the Counsellor for Development and Sustainable Development for the Permanent Mission of France to the UN, Mr. François Gave (Gave, 2014). But the problem, he said, lies in three issues, that are actually psychological in nature. They are: (1) perceptions, whereby governments have to convince ordinary citizens that climate action is important; (2) building confidence, which requires having rules and transparency; and (3) creating incentives—for example, as long as fossil fuels are cheap, they will be used, leaving no incentive to develop new cleaner technologies. These points underscore the contributions of psychology to critical issues about climate change, and to the global agenda.

People also have to be educated, to rethink how they look at climate change. For example, Gave explained, climate is usually thought of as primarily a green policy, but this is only part of what it is about; it is actually about transforming economies, about growth and jobs, and about rethinking how we do business and reinvesting. In short, it is a tremendous opportunity to move forward. The overall conclusion of the roundtable discussion was that action about climate change will lead to a better outcome for everybody in the world.

THE VOICE OF THE PEOPLE MATTERS: THE IMPORTANCE OF PARTNERSHIP BETWEEN GOVERNMENTS AND CIVIL SOCIETY

The importance of partnership for a thriving country is reflected in a proverb that reveals the philosophy of Vietnam, as recounted by Minister and Deputy Permanent Representative (DPR) of the Socialist Republic of Vietnam to the UN, Mr. Do Hung Viet. It outlines how people care about each other: "If you are a whole leaf, you can help cover a torn leaf" (Do, 2014). It means that those who are healthier help those who are less able, and those who are rich help the poor, and those who are poor help those who are poorer (Ambassador Do Hung Viet, personal communication, April 22, 2015).

While governments set policy, they are increasingly taking the voice of the people into account, especially when it comes to issues of nature. The UN has held several meetings about the importance of what is called multi-stakeholder partnerships—partnerships between governments who are member states at the

UN who set policy, with other "actors" including the private sector (businesses and corporations) and civil society, which includes NGOs (nongovernmental organizations). This was evident in the positive reception the first author received in the advocacy described above, in approaching governments about the importance of mental health and well-being in the new agenda. Expertise was also welcome from public interest groups on issues such as gender, aging, refugees, and children's rights. Such dialogue bodes well for citizens and advocacy groups, to know that governments respect, welcome, and hear their voice.

It is valuable to know which governments are most receptive to the voice of the people and engaging with civil society. One indication is those missions who participated on the roundtables at the 2014 DPI/NGO conference since it was organized by civil society. These included Palau (Ambassador Otto); Peru (Ambassador Meza-Cuadra); Hungary (Deputy Permanent Representative, Ambassador Zsolt Hetesy); Nigeria (Deputy Permanent Representative, Ambassador Usman Sarki); Vietnam (Deputy Permanent Representative, Minister-Counselor Do Hung Viet); Spain (Minister Mr. Fernando Fernandez Arias); France (Minister Mr. François Gave); Indonesia (First Secretary Mr. Guruh Samudera); and the Netherlands (Second Secretary Mr. Anne Poorta).

Several of those participating government representatives, including from Peru, Palau, and Vietnam, particularly expressed great appreciation at the DPI/NGO Conference for all the information and proposals they received from civil society over the year-and-a-half process of governments' negotiating the SDGs. DPR Do Hung Viet pointed out that there are 1,000 international NGOs operating in Vietnam, who bring resources and valuable expertise, expressing appreciation that it is the NGOs working at the very grassroots level who impact the daily lives of the people and will do the groundwork to implement the SDGs (Do, 2014). Ambassador Meza-Cuadra of Peru mentioned how his mission works closely with several NGOs with expertise related to gender, children issues, and environmental issues, and in some cases, adopted several points from these experts into their government statements proposed at the Open Working Group, proving a dynamic partnership and key participation of civil society even though the OWG was an intergovernmental process (Meza-Cuadra, 2014).

"Leaders have agreed that they need to understand what citizens care about," said Daniel Thomas, senior communications officer for the UN Secretary-General's Climate Change Support Team, in his presentation on the panel about climate change at the DPI/NGO Conference. This is evidenced by the "My World" survey, hosted by the platform The World We Want (2015) that was launched in 2012 to gauge citizens' opinions and inform leaders about 16 issues that would make the most difference in people's lives. By 2014, five million people had taken the web-based survey about what matters to them. The results show that a good education, better health care, and better job opportunities were voted as the three top priorities, while "action taken on climate change" was last on the list (http://data.myworld2015.org). Yet experts maintain that many of the priorities ranked are actually affected or undermined by climate change, including health; access to clean water; reliable energy at home; better transport; protecting the forests, rovers and oceans; and even phone and Internet access.

Another project to learn what real people want for their world involves a web-based survey, in different languages, called "My Green World: The United Nations Global Survey on Climate Change." This website allows people at all levels of society to show their level of concern and to choose which measures they want their governments to address and what actions they want their governments to take about climate change.

CIVIL SOCIETY ADVANCES IN RECOGNIZING WELL-BEING

Besides advances in government recognition about well-being, described above in this chapter, advocacy efforts by psychologists have also resulted in recognition of mental health and well-being by other sectors of civil society. This was evident in the outcome declaration of the DPI/NGO Conference, entitled "Beyond 2015: Our Action Agenda" to be consistent with the topic of the conference and the new global agenda. A declaration is a statement made in a public way that officially recognizes an important position by a specific constituency. The declaration from the DPI/NGO Conference welcomed the inclusion of goals that will ensure the SDGs deliver a truly transformative agenda for poverty eradication, the reduction of inequalities and the emphasis on sustainability, including goals on climate change, sustainable cities and human settlements, sustainable consumption and production, oceans, and ecosystems and biodiversity. Significantly, the declaration also supported mental health and well-being, using language that was specifically suggested by the first author of this chapter as part of the advocacy campaign of the Psychology Coalition:

> We affirm that physical and mental health and psychosocial well-being are essential for all peoples at all ages in order to achieve the three dimensions of sustainable development;
>
> We further assert mental health and psychosocial well-being is cross-cutting, and interlinked across several goals, e.g., ensure quality education; ending poverty; achieving gender equality and empowerment of all women and girls; promoting economic growth and decent work for all; making cities and human settlements safe; taking urgent action to combat climate change and promote disaster recovery and risk reduction; global partnerships and promoting peaceful and inclusive societies;
>
> We call on governments to ensure that all people of all ages have access to affordable, essential, and quality physical and mental health care services, without discrimination and without suffering financial hardship. (65th Annual DPI/NGO Conference Outcome Document Declaration, 2014)

Declaration by Psychologists about Well-Being

In addition to the declaration of civil society mentioned above, a declaration about the importance of well-being in sustainable development was drafted and read at the closing ceremony of the July 2014 International Congress of Applied Psychology (ICAP) in Paris, France, on the topic of "From Crisis to Sustainable Well-Being" (http://www.icap2014.com). The text, for which the drafting team was led by the main author of this chapter, with input from Norwegian and British psychologists and members of the International Association of Applied Psychology and other conference participants, read as follows: that the thousands of ICAP attendees:

> affirm our support for the United Nations' Sustainable Development Goals for 2015–2030 and support the contribution of psychology to these SDGs: to end poverty everywhere; to promote economic growth and decent work for all; to reduce inequality; to tackle climate change; to promote sustainable ecosystems; and to attain gender equality, quality education, and peaceful and inclusive societies and justice for all.
>
> We also affirm that mental health and well-being is fundamental to the achievement of the proposed Sustainable Development Goals.
>
> Therefore, we urge the United Nations to specify in the document that where appropriate, the word "health" refers to "physical and mental health and well-being," consistent with the World Health Organization (WHO) definition of health as "a state of complete physical, mental and social well-being, and not merely the absence of disease or infirmity."
>
> We further urge the United Nations to include in the chapeau of the final document, among the rights listed, including the rights to food and the rule of law, to affirm the "right to the highest standard of physical and mental health and well-being." In the way forward—towards identifying the indicators and means of implementation of these Sustainable Development Goals—we affirm that psychological science and practice has much to contribute to achieve in "*the future we want.*" (ICAP 2014 Declaration for the United Nations' Sustainable Development Goals for 2015–2030, 2014)

This position was endorsed by other major groups of psychologists representing worldwide constituencies, including the Order of Portuguese Psychologists (OPP), the Norwegian Psychological Association (NPA), the European Federation of Psychology Associations (EFPA), and the Federation of Iberoamerican Associations of Psychologists (FIAP).

ADVOCACY ABOUT DISASTER RISK REDUCTION

Psychologists at the United Nations have been involved with advocating about climate change issues with specific reference to disaster recovery and risk reduction, with the goals to highlight psychological contributions to the issue and to create multi-stakeholder partnerships. As an example, the first author of this chapter and a colleague, Inka Weissbecker, drafted a statement on behalf of the UN NGO Committee on Mental Health about the importance of, and ways to, include mental health and well-being in disaster risk reduction within the Hyogo Framework, and presented this as well as delivered an oral statement at the International Disaster Risk Reduction (ISDRR) conference in Geneva in 2007 (Kuriansky, 2012a). A major goal is to focus government attention on resilience, including psychosocial dimensions as well as physical infrastructure; since resilience in the face of climate change all too often refers only to structural rebuilding, even though much research has shown that resilience is also about the psychosocial adjustment of people (Inter-Agency Standing Committee Working Group, 2007; Kuriansky, 2012c, 2015). A side event was also held, "Integration of Mental Health and Psychosocial Issues into Disaster Risk Reduction and the Hyogo Framework for Action," addressing how psychosocial/mental health interventions are an integral part of any comprehensive program of disaster preparedness and risk reduction, and presented supporting research. Moderated by the first author of this chapter, the panelists purposefully represented multi-stakeholders, including a high-level UN official, Margareta Wahlström, then Assistant Secretary-General for Humanitarian Affairs and Deputy Emergency Relief Coordinator of the Office for the Coordination of Humanitarian Affairs; Mark van Ommeren from the World Health Organization, Department of Mental Health and Substance Abuse, who announced the newly released guidelines by the UN Inter-Agency Standing Committee, *IASC Guidelines on Mental Health and Psychosocial Support in Emergency Settings* (Inter-Agency Standing Committee Working Group, 2007); and two psychologists representing UN-accredited psychological organizations—Mary Weed, who discussed applications from a perspective of organizational and social psychology, and Inka Weissbecker, who presented a multi-stakeholder model for disaster preparedness and response in developing countries, like Belize and Tanzania. The first author of this chapter was also a panelist in the Media Workshop to alert journalists to the role psychologists can play in addressing the issue and impact of climate change, and joined the discussions of the Global Network of NGOs concerned about disaster risk reduction. Follow-up after the meeting included submission of a detailed report to Chair John Holmes and Secretariat Sálvano Briceño, and suggestions for incorporating mental health and psychosocial issues were submitted for inclusion in that body's working document, called *Global Network of NGOs for Community Resilience to Disasters*.

The theme was reprised at a midday workshop related to the topic of psychological issues in disaster risk reduction and climate change, held during the annual meeting of the Department of Public Information/NGO Conference in 2007 on the topic of "Climate Change: How it Impacts Us All." The workshop, addressing the topic "Partnerships to Mobilize Community Health Resources for

Recovery, Resilience and Risk Reduction of Climate Related Disasters: What Multi-stakeholders Can Do," was moderated again by Judy Kuriansky, the first author of this chapter, and once again included UN official Margareta Wahlström as a panelist, given her commitment to psychological issues. Other panelists were psychologists, including the lead editor of this volume, who spoke about post-Katrina wellness workshops as a collaboration of religious and community groups, the state psychological society, and local and state government.

THE IMPACT ON YOUTH

The importance of policy regarding nature is especially relevant for youth and future generations, as they will inherit a lack of resources, an unsustainable planet, and climate-change-related debt (Alhendawi, 2014). As a result, decision-making in policy has to take a long-term view, when resources will be fewer (McKibben, 2014), and take into account the rights and needs of future generations, as well as ensure commitment by government and the private sector (Sarki, 2014).

The youth population is growing, with countries experiencing a "youth bulge" whereby the large majority of their population are under 30 years of age, facing a myriad of social problems (Hart, Atkins, Markey, & Youniss, 2004), including unemployment and lack of education. Yet, youth are not participating in government, where they could have the opportunity to change the very conditions that pose problems for their future. As pointed out by the Secretary-General's Special Envoy on Youth, Ahmad Alhendawi, at the International Day of Youth Conference at the UN in 2014, young people have low civic knowledge, and their lifestyle of being absorbed in digital and social media is not conducive to the platforms or practices of government participation, since they can vote instantaneously via social media for favorites on the *American Idol* TV show but must wait for hours to vote in a political election (Alhendawi, 2014). Less than 1% of parliamentarians worldwide are under the age of 35, complicated by the fact that participation in policy often requires being over 30 years of age. As a result, young people need to be encouraged, and welcomed, to participate in policy-setting. A recent positive example of youth engagement in policy is evident by the participation of the Major Group of Children and Youth in making recommendations for the post-2015 framework of SDGs and for the Global Youth Call that includes suggestions resulting from hundreds of youth meetings around the world.

Youth commitment to learn about government is evident in Model UN conferences, where young people come together from around the world, and where they role-play being delegates in debates, committees, and negotiations that happen at the United Nations. Learning about climate change through this process was one major focus at the "Conferencia Internacional de Las Américas" (CILA)

(Asociación Dominicana de las Naciones Unidas, 2009), sponsored by the United Nations Association of the Dominican Republic (UN-ADR), where youth at the Model UN program in the Dominican Republic made agreements about commitment to action about climate change as they advocated to "Seal the Deal" (about a global agreement on climate change) in anticipation of the United Nations Copenhagen Climate Change Conference in December 2009. At the CILA conference, the first author of this chapter led an international student journalism program, during which students produced a newsletter about the issues (UN Student Journalism Program, 2009) and a video, appropriately called "Seal the Deal" (Bateson, Chireno & Kuriansky, 2009) in anticipation of the climate change conference in Copenhagen in 2009. While the outcome of the actual Copenhagen summit was disappointing to many because governments did not reach firm agreements about actions, the participation of the youth in the Model UN mobilized their awareness, knowledge, enthusiasm, and activism concerning this topic.

Youth also need to be educated for the kind of jobs that are sustainable and also relevant. This includes subject matter of what is called STEM (science, technology, engineering, and mathematics), incorporating technology with web-based access, and important reforms in education, e.g., producing "job inventors" (entrepreneurs) and not only "job seekers," and teaching youth "*how* to think not *what* to think" (LeMay & Aldhuwaihi, 2014).

Given the proven interlinkage between nature and ecofriendly behavior and well-being, paying attention to the mental health of youth is fundamental. The recent International Day of Youth at the United Nations focused on "Mental Health Matters," with youth on the panels talking about their recovery from clinical depression and suicidal impulses. A report about the mental health issues of youth was also issued about overcoming stigma and prevention approaches in the family, school, community, and workplace (United Nations Department of Economic and Social Affairs, 2014). The first author of this chapter also produced a video about mental health and youth, with youth voices and actions at the United Nations, including comments by many ambassadors about the importance of governmental attention to youth mental health, optimism offered through the inclusion of mental health and well-being in the SDGs, and their advice to youth. The participating UN missions included Kenya, Palau, Spain, Benin, Costa Rica, New Zealand, Romania, Belize, and the Philippines (Kuriansky & Zinsou, 2014).

An increasing number of organizations and movements are aimed at awareness-raising, education, and activism of youth, specifically with regard to climate change. Involving youth has been a major focus at the United Nations. The important role young people play as agents of change in climate change is affirmed by the UN Office for the Special Envoy on Youth as well as in the UN World Youth Report that offers ways to become actively involved

(Department of Economic and Social Affairs, 2010). Many projects, initiatives and campaigns are outlined in the publication "Youth in Action on Climate Change: Inspirations from Around the World" (United Nations Joint Framework Initiative on Children, Youth and Climate Change, 2013).

Innovative approaches are also being developed and applied. In a workshop presentation about "Youth Efficacy and Climate Change" at the 65th Annual UN DPI/NGO Conference, a member of the UN NGO Committee on Education discussed unique approaches for youth attention to climate change and self-efficacy for pro-conservation action through use of a mobile app called Habitat the Game, school-based assembly presentations as used by Alliance for Climate Education, and collaborative learning through teleconferencing classrooms as implemented by Global Nomads, a nonprofit that fosters dialogue and understanding among youth (White, 2014).

THE RIGHTS OF NATURE RECOGNIZED IN COUNTRIES: THE CASES OF ECUADOR, BOLIVIA, COSTA RICA, AUSTRALIA, AND THE GLOBAL ALLIANCE FOR THE RIGHTS OF NATURE

Several countries in South and Central America are exemplary in their consideration of natural resources, by enacting laws about the rights of nature. A "wild law" grants equal rights to nature based on the concept that humans do not have the right to destroy the natural environment, and that the rights of natural ecosystems overrule the interests of other species, including humans. Ecuador is the first country to recognize rights of nature in its constitution, reflecting a significant paradigm shift in government policy. Rewritten in 2007–2008 and ratified by the people in 2008, the constitution includes a chapter and articles on "Rights for Nature" that does not treat nature as property under the law, but acknowledges that nature in all its life forms has the "right to exist, persist, maintain and regenerate its vital cycles" and that the people have the legal authority to enforce these rights on behalf of ecosystems. From a legal perspective, the ecosystem itself can be named as the defendant.

Bolivia also amended its constitution to give equal rights to nature as to people. The "Mother Earth Law" resulted from pressure from the large indigenous community that considers the environment and the Andean goddess of Mother Earth, Pachamama, as the center of life, that treats nature as a sacred home, and that honors teachings from the elders that plants, animals, humans, and all things on the planet belong to one family. These perspectives and values guide the country's solutions to the climate, energy, food, and financial crises. The law gives nature legal rights, for example, to life, water, clean air, balance, and restoration. Despite limitations—for example, caused by mining for raw materials—the law significantly provides a basis for public policy guided by the indigenous concept of people and nature living in harmony and "living well," in stark comparison to a focus of most societies on producing more goods and consumption. This perspective represents a major foundation for the inclusion of targets about sustainable consumption, urgent action about climate change, and preservation of nature included in the United Nations Sustainable Development Goals (Orellana Halkyer, 2014). The law requires the government to develop new economic indicators that include the impact on ecology (like the Happy Planet Index noted above); to transition from nonrenewable to renewable energy; to invest resources in organic agriculture; and to monitor and make accountable the ecology-friendly or environment-damaging activity of all private and state companies.

A number of forward-thinking laws have also been enacted in Costa Rica, a country considered exemplary in ecotourism because of its biodiversity and protection of the environment. The National Law of Archaeological Heritage protects all sites of native heritage, and the Law of Wildlife Conservation protects the diverse wildlife and rare flowers and plants, so that these natural resources must not be disturbed or displaced.

Other countries have taken an earth-centered approach to law and governance, including Australia, in its Australian Earth Laws Alliance (http://www .earthlaws.org.au). The movement, called "Earth Jurisprudence," proposes the redefinition of legal, political, economic, and social systems to support the health of the earth instead of its sabotage. Australia and Ecuador have further joined other countries as members of the Global Alliance for the Rights of Nature, including the United States, the United Kingdom, India, and New Zealand. This Alliance is founded on the principle that all life and all of the earth's ecosystems have a right to exist, thrive, and evolve. Launched in 2010 at the International Gathering for Rights of Nature held in Ecuador, the Alliance was inspired by Ecuador's adoption of the Rights of Nature in its constitution, by the Universal Declaration of Rights of Mother Earth from the People's Conference held in Cochabamba, Bolivia, and by growing community developments in the United States. This movement bodes well for the future preservation of the planet, respecting indigenous culture, honoring ecosystems' rights, and grounding these in firm public policy. Further optimism is evidenced by the fact that countries have come together in an alliance with these principles and toward these goals.

THE MULTI-STAKEHOLDER APPROACH

While some governments, and the United Nations, are taking a lead in the international rule and policy on nature, as outlined above, the influence and contribution of other sectors is invaluable. Since 1972, the UN has underlined the importance of the active participation of all people in decision-making regarding the environment, as noted above in the *Report of the United Nations*

Conference on the Human Environment (1972), the World Charter for Nature (1982), and subsequent UN documents. Stakeholders, including academia, civil society, media, and religion, play an important role in the dialogue about nature, well-being, consumption, and environmental protection, bringing expertise that contributes significantly to expanding knowledge of these issues. Over many years, for example, the convening of Psychology Day at the United Nations has highlighted the contributions of psychological research and practice to issues on the global agenda (Kuriansky, 2013), with the 2014 conference specifically addressing psychology's contributions to sustainable development (American Psychological Association, 2014). The annual UN Dialogues on Nature will continue to offer civil society, academia, and other institutions an opportunity to contribute their views. Synthesis of contributions from all these stakeholders will allow for the most comprehensive and effective plans, programs, and policies to protect the well-being of humans and nature.

Forming Partnerships to Reduce Disaster Risk and Build Resilient Communities: "Wake Up, Shake Up"

Many global conferences mentioned above are intended to forge strategic and innovative partnerships to reduce the risk of natural disasters and build resilient communities and economies. One such notable effort, the "High-Level Symposium on Coastal Resilience: The Road to Sendai," brought together international experts, policy makers, environmentalists, and other stakeholders to discuss coastal protection in vulnerable areas such as New York, the Netherlands, Southeast Asia, and the Pacific islands. Held at the Ford Foundation in New York City and cohosted by the Global Partnerships Forum and its founder Amir Dossal, R3ADY Asia-Pacific (launched by U.S. Secretary of State Hillary Clinton in 2011), and the US-Japan Council, the dialogue presented a prelude to the World Conference on Disaster Risk Reduction (WCDRR) in Sendai, Japan, in March 2015 (just after the fourth anniversary of the tragic tsunami-earthquake on March 11). The theme of resilience was evident in the campaign presented by New York City's Office of Recovery and Resilience Post-Superstorm Sandy, on implementing "A Stronger, More Resilient New York."

The honored guest, the First Lady of Japan, Her Excellency Madam Akie Abe, described the debate about the building of the seawall to protect Japan's shores, between those who point to the positive effect of the seawall protecting the land and those who argue that a 5-story-building-high wall interferes with the natural coastline and views and could therefore deter tourism, and also would have to be rebuilt within time due to deterioration. Yet, the First Lady pointed out the ultimate goal to restore harmony between man and nature, saying poetically, "The forest longs for the sea and the sea longs for the forest." Other panelists pointed out alternatives to seawalls in the form of green infrastructure, like oyster reefs, which can serve as natural breakwaters and coastal buffers. Similarly, mangrove tree fields saved many lives when the devastating tsunami struck several nations around the Bay of Bengal and the Indian Ocean on the December 26, 2004, as people got trapped in them instead of being drowned or washed away.

The problem is serious given that the state of the oceans is related to food security, as 100 million people rely on fish, yet 90% of the fish stock are gone from our planet and will dwindle unless action is taken. In a major move, President of Palau Tommy Remengesau Jr. closed his country's waters to commercial fishing and exports until the stock regenerates, creating the world's first nationwide marine sanctuary, a move that earned him the UN's top environmental accolade, the Champions of the Earth award. Local fishing zones are allocated for domestic use. In bestowing the award, UN Under-Secretary-General and United Nations Environment Programme Executive Director Achim Steiner said, "Palau is an inspiring example of a small island nation courageously addressing the global challenges of climate change and biodiversity loss" (UNEP, 2014). In another lauded conservation initiative, President Remengesau established a shark sanctuary. At the World Conference on Disaster Risk Reduction in Sendai Japan, the Palau Ambassador to Japan, Francis M. Matsutaro, delivered a statement drafted by Palau UN Ambassador Caleb Otto, about the relevance to disaster risk reduction and combatting climate change, of this marine sanctuary, along with the importance of breastfeeding as a crucial source of child health, and a focus on psychosocial resilience in addition to structural resilience (Matsutaro, 2015).

Fortunately, while loss of life is severe due to water hazards, the crisis is being stemmed in East Asia, because of early warning systems, training citizens to evacuate, and building better infrastructure, explained Margareta Wahlström, special representative of the UN Secretary-General for Disaster Risk Reduction. She stressed the importance of implementation and partnerships between public and private, government and civil society, north and south (which refers to government regions). Technology can play a crucial role, increasing information dissemination to save lives, said Gary Fowlie, director of the International Telecommunication Union New York Office.

"We are in a life jacket, as the risks from climate are real, whether island or not," warned Mr. Nikhil Chandavarkar, Chief of Communication and Outreach for the Division of Sustainable Development at the United Nations. He offered three takeaways from the Climate Change conference of the Small Island States held in Samoa (described above): (1) climate change is linked to sustainable development; (2) the risks from climate change are real, whether we live on an island or not, and (3) all nations and peoples are in global solidarity—since we are all islanders, and the oceans are shared.

The psychological aspects of this situation were poignantly noted by Georg Kell, executive director of the United Nations Global Compact, when he explained, "Like human behavior, we need to think and prepare, but as the situation has reached crisis proportions, it is time for 'No more thinking, time to act'," adding that we have to change from short-term to long-term thinking and "Plan today for the disaster tomorrow." In closing, he declared dramatically, "We must 'Wake up, shake up.'"

Another Vehicle for Partnerships: The Clinton Global Initiative (CGI)

The Clinton Global Initiative (CGI) is another forum to encourage partnerships. The annual summit is convened by former U.S. president Bill Clinton to bring together leaders of governments, business, and the public sector to discuss global issues and form partnerships for global wellness and improvement on issues of global concern like poverty, women and girls' rights, peace, and education (Clinton Global Initiative, n.d.). Climate change was addressed at the 2014 meeting, with a panel addressing the importance for governments and business. "Climate change is not only a risk to the environment but it is the single biggest risk that exists to the economy today," said Henry Paulson of the Paulson Institute, former treasury secretary under President George W. Bush. He added that government does not focus on controversial issues, especially if they are longer term, but we are going to have future "natural disasters, floods and the Hurricane Sandys. . . . [and] If you don't take action there is a huge fiscal risk." The prime minister of Denmark, Thorning-Schmidt, pointed out the importance of reducing the cost of alternative energies, but also of a psychological issue: changing consumer behavior.

A HOLISTIC VIEW: HARMONY WITH MOTHER EARTH, POVERTY, AND CLIMATE CHANGE

Harmony with Mother Nature is inextricably connected with all global issues, including poverty and climate change. This holistic view is promoted in Chapter 18 of this volume by Dr. René Orellana Halkyer (2015), professor and coordinator of environment, water, and climate change of the University of la Cordillera in Bolivia, and honorary UN Ambassador on Issues of Environment and Development, who was chair of the G77 + China on behalf of Bolivia to the Open Working Group of the UN for the proposal of the SDGs. As he outlines also in his book on "Development and Harmony with Mother Earth: An Assessment of the Issue of Poverty, Capitalism, and Climate Change" published in Spanish as well as in Chapter 18 of this volume:

> Disasters caused by extreme events impact on the economy, sources of food, sources of employment, infrastructure, transport and production, as well as on ecosystems, progressively destroying the natural, environmental, economic, and social basis of life of the people and affecting factors and resources necessary for sustained development and... aggravating health conditions ... In a situation of an increase of

more than 2 degrees C., we will face loss of glaciers in the Andes and Himalayas, sea rise of more than 1 meter in this century, threatening more than 60 million people ... Between 100 and 400 million people are at risk of hunger and between 1,000 and 2,000 million people will suffer from insufficient water to satisfy their basic needs. (Orellana Halkyer, 2014)

He further warns developing countries against following a capitalistic model that promotes "excessive consumption with addictive patterns and life styles" (Orellana Halkyer, personal communication, May 7, 2014). A fundamental task is to create conditions for living well, including food security, education, health, jobs, provision of water and sanitation, job creation, and provision of housing. All countries must cooperate to combat the climate crisis, he advises, with developed countries taking the lead and reducing their emissions.

The holistic approach Orellana Halkyer supports is consistent with the declaration of the Rio + 20 Conference on Sustainable Development, "The Future We Want," that states: "We call for holistic and integrated approaches to sustainable development that will guide humanity to live in harmony with nature and lead to efforts to restore the health and integrity of the Earth's ecosystem." In his view—which I and many others share—"development, is not a matter of growing to meet a robust GDP, but to grow in happiness, in joy, in complementarity between human beings and nature. The growth of a virtuous relationship involves the harmonization, balance, restoration and regeneration of vitalities of the ecosystems and their natural energies. We aim to grow economically, yes, but also to grow spiritually and culturally, using natural resources sustainably" (see Chapter 18 of this volume [Orellana Halkyer, 2015]).

FUTURE DIRECTIONS AT THE UNITED NATIONS

Since creating and protecting a sustainable environment has been established as one of the three key pillars and specific targets of the UN Sustainable Development Goals, efforts to achieve this will be supported and monitored through the period 2015–2030. UN bodies such as the United Nations Environment Programme (UNEP) and United Nations Environment Assembly (UNEA) will continue to focus on sustainable environmental practice issues throughout the post-2015 agenda. The UNEA had its first inaugural meeting in Nairobi in June 2014 where representatives from all the UN member states discussed the post-2015 agenda with particular emphasis on environmentally relevant issues (UN News Centre, 2014). Plans are to meet every two years. The major responsibility of monitoring the achievement of the SDGs' framework is in the hands of the UN Statistical Commission and an assigned team of experts, many from the relevant departments of the member states. To encourage the input and participation of civil society in this important process of evaluation and monitoring of the implementation of the SDGs, as the chair of the Psychology Coalition of

NGOs at the UN, I convened a task force of psychologist experts in measurement and evaluation and in the field of industrial/organizational psychology.

DISCUSSION AND RECOMMENDATIONS

Since the amount of resources left on the planet is limited, those that exist must be used efficiently, and other renewable resources need to be developed. Programs and policy need to pay serious attention to the preservation of the environment. Stakeholders at all levels are already taking note of the urgency of action toward this end. Public groups have mobilized for pro-environment activities and advocacy. Individual countries have recognized the rights of nature. On the international stage, the United Nations holds major summits, dialogues, and conferences on the topic and has launched public websites. The Sustainable Development Goals offer hope, with governments' agreement to focus on natural resources and environmental protection as one of the three pillars of development, i.e., with economic growth and social development.

Communities play a key role, as pointed out in the first author's previous work (Kuriansky, 2012c) and in her section in the "Reflections and Recommendations" chapter in this volume (Nemeth, Hamilton, & Kuriansky, 2015). Community projects addressing prosocial and climate change issues need to be supported. Since the problems related to preserving nature are multidimensional and involve many actors, including governments and the private and public sectors, solutions must involve all stakeholders in devising programs and policy. Corporations, business, and all agents in the private sector must be engaged in collective efforts. As the saying goes, all involved in the problem must take part in the solution. Policy has to balance the needs of all parties, including governments, business, and the people, to maintain or enhance the quality of life and standard of living of individuals, communities, and countries, while not exploiting people or nature. The voice of the people has to be taken into account, and for their part, the public has to reach out to government, confident that their voice matters. While talk is important, all parties must recognize the need for urgent action. A long-term view is necessary, especially to protect future generations, as "The price of today should consider the price of tomorrow" (Harris, 2014).

People have also to examine their psychological approach to nature, develop greater appreciation of their environment, and revise their overuse of resources. A useful warning about overconsumption, attributed to actor Will Smith, is evident in this saying: "Too many people buy things they don't need with money they don't have to impress people they don't like."

The subspecialties of environmental, conservation, and ecological psychology have catalyzed in-depth explorations of environmental behavior, change, and policy. These fields are leading to the understanding of the psychological reasons people are reluctant to adopt environmentally friendly attitudes and behaviors, and to the development of interventions and educational programs that contribute to positive change.

Understanding human behavior is crucial to understanding conservation. The study of personality types can help shape pro-environment behavior, including changing attitudes and behavior from being egocentric in their approach to energy use—that is, motivated by whatever saves time and money and therefore using technologies regardless of their environmental impacts—to foregoing personal benefit and convenience. A cost-benefit analysis is a helpful guide in such a change in perspective and behavior (Visschers & Siegrist, 2014). One study showed that high levels of aesthetic appreciation, creativity, and inquisitiveness, more than altruism, can motivate pro-environmental actions (Markowitz, Goldberg, Ashton, & Lee, 2012). Researchers have pointed out that people with "individualistic and fatalistic" cultural thinking justify their lack of environmental conservation on the fact that the environment is elastic in its health, while those who are "hierarchical and egalitarian" defend conservation on the basis that the environment is vulnerable (Price, Walker, & Boschettib, 2014). Another study found that people with the personality characteristic of "belief superiority"—perceiving their own viewpoint as more correct than others—disagreed more with articles that argued a viewpoint about hydraulic fracturing in oil drilling that differed from their own (Raimi & Leary, 2014). Another study, using an environmental sustainability index, found that individuals with characteristics associated with agreeableness and openness to experience displayed more conservation behaviors; likewise, countries with more individuals of this personality type were more likely to act in a more environmentally friendly way (Hirsh, 2010). Increased exposure to the value of nature also helps, as proven in one study, where researchers found that individuals who had more access and exposure to nature had a greater appreciation for nature (Roczen, Duvier, Bogner, & Kaiser, 2012).

Besides such studies of personality and exposure to nature, experts are developing theories to explain pro-environmental behavior and guide observations of people toward the environment. Some point back to early concepts, such as the "field theory" of social psychologist Kurt Lewin (1939) that people and their surroundings depend on one another; and "ecological systems theory" that proposes individuals have roles within four spheres, expanding from close interpersonal relationships and immediate surroundings to their social and cultural context that affect their beliefs and behavior; all of which influence and feedback one another (Bronfenbrenner, 1979). The increasingly popular field of "transpersonal psychology" maintains that identity extends beyond the personal self to wider aspects of life and humankind (Friedman & Hartelius, 2013). The growth of fields of environmental studies, exploring theories and applications related to the environment, holds great promise for the future of the planet. These include the disciplines of psychology as well as economics, architecture, city planning, the law, and global studies. Collaboration among all these experts is necessary. Such an interdisciplinary approach is reflected in the diverse chapter contributions in this volume. Advances in these interrelated fields, as well as recent events at the United Nations, provide further encouragement that psychological science and practice can contribute to the global agenda related to the environment, and help direct productive programs and policy. The inclusion of mental health and well-being in the Sustainable Development Goals holds particular promise that psychologists and expert stakeholders—individually and collectively, on national, regional, and international levels—can get support both in principle and in concrete financial terms, for projects and programs that can make a difference in the future of the people and the planet. Since the community plays such a key role, the field of community psychology will become increasingly important in coming decades.

While many advances have been outlined in this chapter, there is more to be done in programming and policy to protect the environment. Raising awareness in the public and mobilizing partnerships and action are crucial. Also important is the development of sophisticated measurement techniques and methodologies to assess programs and policies. One such effort on methodology is by Gifford (in press). While there are many international conferences being convened on these topics, other venues, platforms, and opportunities for collaborations among disciplines can be created, given the significant value of such interdisciplinary exchange.

This chapter has highlighted the importance of sustainability and consumption patterns and preservation of the environment. Hopefully, increased responsibility will be assumed by all parties, including governments, corporations, and individuals. People can take simple actions to reduce their "carbon footprint," like separating plastic and paper for recycling, turning off lights, water, televisions, and computers when not in use, and buying energy-efficient cars—steps mentioned by the youth participating in video at the Model UN CILA conference mentioned earlier in this chapter. A consumer product company can use less plastic. A government can follow other countries' lead and pass a law about the "rights of nature" or commit to reduce its carbon footprint.

The review in this chapter, and all the work being done in diverse fields by a confluence of stakeholders, affirms and confirms a paradigm shift from exhausting the planet's resources to the preservation of nature and the environment. This move is critical to the survival and well-being of individuals and all beings and elements on the planet, and the importance of taking action in this process for the world we want, and need.

REFERENCES

Abrahamse, W., Schultz, P. W., & Steg, L. (in press). Research designs: Conducting research on environmental issues In R. Gifford (Ed.), *Research methods for environmental psychology*. Hoboken, NJ: John Wiley & Sons.

Alhendawi, A. (2014, August 28). Presentation on panel, "Sustainable development: Urgent! Sustainable management of natural resources and ecosystems." Roundtable at the 65th Annual Conference of the Department of Public Information/ Non-Governmental Organizations, UN Headquarters, New York, NY.

American Psychological Association. (2014, April 24). *Psychology Day at the UN: 7th annual Psychology Day at the United Nations: Psychology's contributions to sustainable development: Challenges and solutions for the global agenda.* Retrieved October 24, 2014, from http://www.apa.org/international/united-nations/psych-day.aspx

Asociación Dominicana de las Naciones Unidas. (2009). Conferencia Internacional de las Américas. http://unadr.org.do/index.php?option=com_content&view=front page&Itemid=89&lang=es

Australian Psychological Society Member Groups (n.d.). *Psychology and the environment.* Retrieved April 20, 2015, from https://groups.psychology.org.au/GroupContent .aspx?ID=4552.

Bateson, T., Chireno, E., & Kuriansky, J. (Co-Executive Producers). (2009, November 6). *Seal the deal at CILA 2009* [Video]. Retrieved April 6, 2015, from https://www .youtube.com/watch?v=vP-yjpdXO8M

Berry, M. O., Kuriansky, J., Lytle, M., Vistman, B., Mosisili, M. S., Hlothoane, L., ... Pebane, J. (2013, December). Entrepreneurial training for girls empowerment in Lesotho: A process evaluation of a model programme. *South African Journal of Psychology, 43*(4), 446–458. Retrieved October 2014 from http://sap.sagepub.com/ content/early/2013/10/03/0081246313504685.abstract

Blind, E. (Producer). (2010). *Girls Empowerment Camp in Lesotho, Africa, camp experience* [Video]. Retrieved April 20, 2015, from http://youtu.be/Yg9znQvAmcI

Bonaiuto, M., & Fornara, F. (2014). *PREQIs' structure and reliability in cross-cultural surveys.* Presentation at the 28th International Congress of Applied Psychology (ICAP), Paris, France.

Bronfenbrenner, U. (1979). *The ecology of human development.* Cambridge, MA: Harvard University Press.

Buzzell, L., & Chalquist, C. (Eds.). (2009). *Ecotherapy: Healing with nature in mind.* San Francisco, CA: Sierra Club Books.

Capasso, M., Lacerda e Silva, W., Garcia, P. & Rockenbach. G. (2014, July 8–13). Identidade Jovem: The project involving young people in promoting the MDGs. Presentation at the 28th International Congress of Applied Psychology (ICAP), Paris, France. Retrieved April 8, 2015, from http://www.icap2014.com

Centers for Disease Control and Prevention. (n.d.). *Well-being concepts.* Retrieved October 2014 from http://www.cdc.gov/hrqol/wellbeing.htm

Centre for Bhutan Studies & GNH Research. (2014). *Gross national happiness.* Retrieved August 14, 2014, from http://www.grossnationalhappiness.com/articles/

Clayton, S., & Myers, G. (2009). *Conservation psychology: Understanding and promoting human care for nature.* Hoboken, NJ: Wiley-Blackwell.

Clayton, S., Prevot-Julliard, A-C., & Germain, L. (2014, July 8–13) *Promoting positive attitudes toward protection of biodiversity: The role of personal experience.* Presentation at the 28th International Congress of Applied Psychology (ICAP), Paris, France.

Climate change: Post 2015 and the UNFCCC processes: Can they be friends? Roundtable of the 65th Annual Conference of the Department of Public Information/ Non-governmental Organizations. UN Headquarters, New York, NY.

Clinton Global Initiative. (n.d.). Retrieved April 24, 2015, from http://www
.clintonfoundation.org/clinton-global-initiative

Cloherty, R., Jansson-Boyd, C. V., & Jiminez-Bescos, C. (2014, July 8–13). *Helping
people to help themselves: Encouraging people to reduce their energy consumption.* Presentation at the 28th International Congress of Applied Psychology (ICAP), Paris,
France.

Coley, R. L., Kuo, F. E., & Sullivan, W. C. (1997). Where does community grow? The
social context created by nature in urban public housing. *Environment & Behavior,
29*(4), 468–494.

Crawford, M. R., & Holder, M. D. (2014, July 8–13). *Technology and nature: Unlikely allies.*
Presentation at the 28th International Congress of Applied Psychology (ICAP).
Paris, France.

Davis, D., & Dumpson, D. (2015). Empowerment in African Americans' responses
to global climate change and environmental racism through an integrative
bio-interpersonal/music-based approach. In D. G. Nemeth & J. Kuriansky (Eds.),
Ecopsychology: Advances from the intersection of psychology and environmental protection,
Volume 2 (pp. 105–133). Santa Barbara, CA: ABC-CLIO.

Department of Economic and Social Affairs (2010). *The United Nations World Youth
Report: Youth and Climate Change.* Retrieved October 12, 2014, from http://www.un
.org/esa/socdev/unyin/documents/wyr10/YouthReport-FINAL-web-single.pdf

Diener, E. (Ed.). (2009). *The science of well-being: The collected works of Ed Diener.*
New York, NY: Springer Science and Business Media.

Diener, E., Oishi. S., & Lucas, R. E. (2003). Personality, culture, and subjective well-
being: Emotional and cognitive evaluations of life. *Annual Review of Psychology, 54,*
403–425. doi:10.1146/annurev.psych.54.101601.145056

Diener, E., Suh, M., Lucas, E., & Smith, H. (1999). Subjective well-being: Three decades
of progress. *Psychological Bulletin, 125*(2), 276–302. Retrieved October 2014 from
http://dx.doi.org/10.1037/0033-2909.125.2.276

Diette, G. B., Lechtzin, N., Haponik, E., Devrotes, A., & Rubin, H. R. (2003). Distraction
therapy with nature sights and sounds reduces pain during flexible bronchoscopy:
A complementary approach to routine analgesia. *Chest, 123,* 941–948.

Do, V. D. (2014, August 27). Presentation on panel, "Poverty eradication: Fighting inequal-
ities – economic, social, political and environmental." Roundtable at the 65th Annual
Conference of the Department of Public Information/Non-governmental Organizations,
UN Headquarters, New York, NY.

Dodge, R., Daly, A., Huyton, J., & Sanders, L. (2012). The challenge of defining well-
being. *International Journal of Wellbeing, 2*(3), 222–235. doi:10.5502/ijw.v2i3.4

Doherty, T. J. (2009). Doherty Sustainability Inventory. Retrieved August 22, 2014, from
http://www.selfsustain.com/images/stories/dsi_sustainability_inventory_version_1
.2__3-24-09.pdf

Doherty, T. J. (in press). Mental health impacts. In J. Patz & B. S. Levy (Eds.), *Climate
change and public health.* Oxford, UK: Oxford University Press.

Doherty, T. J., & Chen, A. (in press). Improving human functioning: Ecotherapy and
environmental health approaches. In R. Gifford (Ed.). *Research Methods for Environmental Psychology.* Hoboken, NJ: John Wiley & Sons.

Doherty, T. J., & Clayton. S. (2011). The psychological impacts of global climate
change. *American Psychologist, 66,* 265–276.

Dorofeeva, K., Ceschi, A., & Sartori, R. (2014, July 8–13). *Household climate change risk perception and recycling behavior.* Presentation at the 28th International Congress of Applied Psychology (ICAP), Paris, France.

Enzler, H. B. (2014, July 8–13). Consideration of future consequences as a predictor of environmentally responsible behavior: Evidence from a general population study. Presentation at the 28th International Congress of Applied Psychology (ICAP), Paris, France.

Ereaut, G., & Whiting, R. (2008). *What do we mean by "wellbeing"? And why might it matter?* (Research report No DCSF-RW073, Lighting Landscapes). London, UK: Department for Children, Schools and Families. Retrieved October 2014 from http://dera.ioe.ac.uk/8572/1/dcsf-rw073%20v2.pdf

Ernst, A., & Wenzel, U. (2014). Bringing environmental psychology into action: Four steps from science to policy. *European Psychologist, 19*(2), 118–126. doi:10.1027/1016-9040/a000174

Estrada, M., Schultz, P. W., Silva-Send, N., & Boudrias, M. (2014, July 8–13). Infusing climate change education with a social influence model. Presentation at the 28th International Congress of Applied Psychology (ICAP), Paris, France.

Fisher, A., & Abram, D. (2013). *Radical ecopsychology: Psychology in the service of life* (2nd ed.). Albany, NY: State University of New York Press.

Forman, A. (2014, October 9). Five words that can change the world. *Jewish Journal.* Retrieved April 19, 2015, from http://boston.forward.com/articles/185615/five-words-that-can-change-the-world/

Friedman, H. L., & Hartelius, G. (Eds.). (2013). *The Wiley-Blackwell handbook of transpersonal psychology.* Hoboken, NJ: John Wiley & Sons.

Furnass, B. (1979). Health values. In J. Messer & J. G. Mosley (Eds.), *The value of national parks to the community: Values and ways of improving the contribution of Australian national parks to the community* (pp. 60–69). Sydney, Australia: University of Sydney, Australian Conservation Foundation.

Gallagher, W. (1994). *The Power of place: How our surroundings shape our thoughts, emotions, and actions.* New York, NY: HarperPerennial.

Gao, X., & Hansen, N. (2014, July 8–13). *Modernisation decreases pro-environmental action: Generational differences in value endorsement and pro-environmental action in China.* Presentation at the 28th International Congress of Applied Psychology (ICAP), Paris, France.

Gave, F. (2014). Presentation on panel, "Climate change: Post-2015 and the UNFCCC Processes: Can They Be Friends?" Roundtable at the 65th Annual Conference of the Department of Public Information/Non-governmental Organizations, UN Headquarters, New York, NY.

Gifford, R. (2007). *Environmental psychology: Principles and practice.* Colville, WA: Optimal Books.

Gifford, R. (Ed.). (in press). *Research methods for environmental psychology.* Cambridge, MA: John Wiley & Sons.

Happy Planet Index. (2014). Retrieved August 22, 2014, from http://www.happyplanetindex.org/

Harris, E. (2014). Presentation on panel, "Sustainable Development: Urgent! Sustainable management of Natural Resources and Ecosystems." Roundtable at the 65th Annual

Conference of the Department of Public Information/Non-governmental Organizations, UN Headquarters, New York, NY.

Hart, D., Atkins, R., Markey, P., & Youniss, J. (2004). Youth bulges in communities: The effects of age structure on adolescent civic knowledge and civic participation. *Psychological Science, 15*(9), 591–597.

Hartig, T., Mang, M. & Evans, G. W. (1991). Restorative effects of natural environment experiences. *Environment and Behavior, 23,* 3–26.

Helliwell, J., Layard, R., & Sachs, J. (Eds.). (2013). *World happiness report* (1st & 2nd eds.). New York, NY: Earth Institute. Retrieved October 2014, from http://unsdsn. org/happiness/

Hine, D., Phillips, W., & Reser, J. (2014, July 8–13). *Preaching to different choirs: How to engage audiences that are alarmed, uncommitted, and skeptical about climate change?* Presentation at the 28th International Congress of Applied Psychology (ICAP), Paris, France.

Hirsh, J. B. (2010). Personality and environmental concern. *Journal of Environmental Psychology, 30*(2), 245–248.

Howell, A. J., Dopko, R. L., Passmore, H. A., & Buro, K. (2011). Nature connectedness: Associations with well-being and mindfulness. *Personality and Individual Differences, 51,* 166–171.

Howell, A. J., & Passmore, H-A. (2013). The nature of happiness: Nature affiliation and mental well-being. In C. L. M. Keyes (Ed.), *Mental well-being: International contributions to the study of positive mental health* (pp. 231–257). New York, NY: Springer Publishing.

Huebner, G., Gauthier, S., Witzel, C, Chan, W-S., & Shipworth, D. (2014, July 8–13). *Seeing red, feeling hot? Research shows you could save energy by changing the colour of your office light.* Presentation at the 28th International Congress of Applied Psychology (ICAP). Paris, France.

ICAP 2014 Declaration for the United Nations' Sustainable Development Goals for 2015–2030. (2014, July 13). Presented at the 28th International Congress of Applied Psychology: From Crisis to Sustainable Well-being, Paris, France.

ICAP 2014 Updates. (2014). *Division 4: Environmental Psychology.* Retrieved April 20, 2015, from http://www.icap2014.com/divisional-programs/div-4-environmental -psychology/46

Ikizer, G., Dogulu, C., & Nuray Karanci, A. (2014, July 8–13). *Psychological impacts of earthquakes and psychological resilience.* Presentation at the 28th International Congress of Applied Psychology (ICAP), Paris, France.

Inter-Agency Standing Committee Working Group. (2007). *IASC guidelines on mental health and psychosocial support in emergency settings.* Geneva: IASC. Retrieved October 2014 from http://www.who.int/mental_health/emergencies/guidelines_iasc _mental_health_psychosocial_june_2007.pdf

Isobe, M. (2014, July 8–13). *A pilot study of S-HTP method to evaluate the effectiveness of environmental education for preschool children.* Presentation at the 28th International Congress of Applied Psychology (ICAP), Paris, France.

Jordan, M. (2015). *Therapy and nature.* London: Routledge.

Kahn, P. H., Jr. (2014). *The next phase for* Ecopsychology: *Ideas and directions from the incoming editor.* Retrieved August 22, 2014, from http://www.liebertpub.com/lpages/ ecopsychology-next-phase/35/

Kahn, P. H., Jr., Friedman, B., Gill, B., Hagman, J., Severson, R. L., Freier, N. G., & Stolyar, A. (2008). A plasma display window? The shifting baseline problem in a technologically mediated natural world. *Journal of Environmental Psychology, 28*(2), 192–199.

Kahn, P. H., Jr., & Hasbach, P. H. (Eds.) (2012). *Ecopsychology: Science, totems, and the technological species.* Cambridge, MA: MIT Press.

Kahneman, D., Diener, E., & Schwarz, N. (Eds.) (1999). *Well-being: Foundations of hedonic psychology.* New York, NY: Russell Sage Foundation Press.

Kaplan, R., & Kaplan, S. (1989). *The experience of nature: A psychological perspective.* Cambridge, UK: Cambridge University Press.

Kaplan, R., & Kaplan, S. (1990). Restorative experience the healing power of nearby nature. In M. Francis & R. T. Hester Jr. (Eds.), *The meaning of gardens: Idea, place and action* (pp. 238–243). Cambridge, MA: MIT Press.

Kaplan, S. (1995). The restorative benefits of nature: Toward an integrative framework. *Journal of Environmental Psychology, 15*, 169–182.

Kastner, I., & Matthies, E. (2014, July 8–13). *Changing energy related behavior using a web-based program.* Presentation at the 28th International Congress of Applied Psychology (ICAP), Paris, France.

Keyes, C. L. M., Shmotkin, D., & Ryff, C. D. (2002). Optimizing well-being: The empirical encounter of two traditions. *Journal of Personality and Social Psychology, 82*, 1007–1022. doi:10.1037/0022-3514.82.6.100

Kibbe, A., Arnold, O., Otto, S., & Kaiser, F. (2014, July 8–13). *Electricity consumption—money or attitude?* Presentation at the 28th International Congress of Applied Psychology (ICAP), Paris, France.

Kirkman, C., & Kuriansky, J. (2012, July–October). Transforming communities through psychosocial empowerment of poor rural women and girls: Parallel event of the psychology NGOs accredited at the United Nations at the 56th session of the Commission on the Status of Women. *Bulletin of the International Association of Applied Psychology, 24*(2–3), Part 13.

Kuo, F. E., & Sullivan, W. C. (2001). Environment and crime in the inner city: Does vegetation reduce crime? *Environment & Behavior, 33*(3), 343–367.

Kuo, F. E., Sullivan, W. C., Coley, R. L., & Brunson, L. (1998). Fertile ground for community: Inner-city neighborhood common spaces. *American Journal of Community Psychology, 26*(6), 823–851.

Kuriansky, J. (Producer). (2010a). *Girls Empowerment Programme in Lesotho Africa, 2010 News Report* [Video]. Retrieved April 20, 2015, from https://www.youtube.com/watch?v=sr0EQeqOGtY

Kuriansky, J. (2010b, Spring). Haiti pre and post earthquake: Tracing professional and personal commitment past, present and future. *International Psychology Bulletin, 14*(2), 29–37. Retrieved April 24, 2015, from http://internationalpsychology.files.wordpress.com/2013/01/ipb_spring_2010_4_27_10.pdf

Kuriansky, J. (2012a, Summer). Advocacy about psychological contributions to the global agenda at the United Nations: Preliminary experiences, case studies and lessons learned about principles, procedures and process. *International Psychology Bulletin, 16*(3), 46–60. Retrieved October 2014 from http://internationalpsychology.files.wordpress.com/2013/01/ipb_summer_2012-07-14-8_final.pdf

Kuriansky, J. (2012b, November 2). Happiness, GDP, and the presidential race: Opinion. *ABC News*. Retrieved April 5, 2015, from http://abcnews.go.com/Health/Wellness/happiness-gdp-presidential-race/story?id=17619613

Kuriansky, J. (2012c). Our communities: Healing after environmental disasters. In D. G. Nemeth, R. B. Hamilton, & J. Kuriansky (Eds.), *Living in an environmentally traumatized world: Healing ourselves and our planet* (pp. 141–167). Santa Barbara, CA: ABC-CLIO/Praeger.

Kuriansky, J. (2012d, July–October). Recovery efforts for Japan after the 3/11 devastating tsunami/earthquake. *Bulletin of the International Association of Applied Psychology, 24*(2–3), Part 22.

Kuriansky, J. (2012e, July–October). Well being: An important issue at the United Nations and for the International Association of Applied Psychology. *Bulletin of the International Association of Applied Psychology, 24*(2–3), Part 10, 64–70.

Kuriansky, J. (2013, March 14). *Psychology Day at the UN, overview* [Video]. *YouTube*. Retrieved October 24, 2014, from https://www.youtube.com/watch?v=FrfcoWq7OfE

Kuriansky, J. (2014a). *Advocacy about mental health and wellbeing for the intergovernmental negotiations of the Sustainable Development Goals*. Unpublished manuscript.

Kuriansky, J. (2014b). *Building resilience in children coping after disaster and living in crisis: Applied models in Haiti, Japan and Africa*. Presentation at the Louisiana Psychological Association on "Resiliency, Mindfulness and Resolve: Coping with the Hand You're Dealt." New Orleans, LA.

Kuriansky, J. (2014c). Invited civil society discussant remarks at the United Nations General Assembly Dialogue on Harmony with Nature. Retrieved August 22, 2014, from http://webtv.un.org/watch/panel-presentations-interactive-dialogue-of-the-general-assembly-on-harmony-with-nature/3496394095001/ at 2:08 into the video.

Kuriansky, J. (2015, March 16). *Resilience in disaster recovery and risk reduction: Statement presented at the High-level Multi-Stakeholder Partnership Dialogue, World Conference on Disaster Risk Reduction, Sendai, Japan, 2015* [Video]. Retrieved April 20, 2015, from https://youtu.be/R72sDJ1xVZg

Kuriansky, J., & Berry. M. O. (2011, April). Advancing the UN MDGs by a model program for girls empowerment, HIV/AIDS prevention and entrepreneurship: IAAP Project in Lesotho Africa. *IAAP Bulletin*, April, 2012, 36–39.

Kuriansky, J., & Jean-Charles, W. (2012). Haiti Rebati: Update on activities rebuilding Haiti through the Global Kids Connect Project. Part 21. *IAAP Bulletin, 24*(2–3), 116–124.

Kuriansky, J. & Okorodudu, C. (2014). *Concept papers on psychological contributions to the post-2015 development agenda* (various editions). Unpublished manuscript.

Kuriansky, J., Wu, L-Y., Bao, C., Chand, D., Kong, S., Spooner, N. & Mao, S. (2015). Interventions by national and international organizations for psychosocial support after the Sichuan Earthquake in China: A review and implications for sustainable development. In D. G. Nemeth & J. Kuriansky (Eds.), *Ecopsychology: Advances from the intersection of psychology and environmental protection*, Volume 2 (pp. 171–231). Santa Barbara, CA: ABC-CLIO.

Kuriansky, J., & Zinsou, J. C. (2014). *Youth and mental health: Youth and UN ambassadors speak out* [Video]. Retrieved April 20, 2015, from https://www.youtube.com/watch?v=rtkvLSMlLmE

Kuriansky, J., Zinsou, J., Arunagiri, V., Douyon, C., Chiu, A. Jean-Charles, W., Daisey, R. & Midy, T. (2015). Effects of helping in a train-the-trainers program for youth in the global kids connect project providing psychosocial support after the 2010 Haiti earthquake: A paradigm shift to sustainable development. In D. G. Nemeth & J. Kuriansky (Eds.), *Ecopsychology: Advances from the intersection of psychology and environmental protection*, Volume 2 (pp. 135–169). Santa Barbara, CA: ABC-CLIO.

Lee, E., Frederick M. E., & Grouzet, F. M. E. (2014, July 8–13). *Activating nature relatedness through spirituality: Toward a more person-centered approach to sustainability*. Presentation at the 28th International Congress of Applied Psychology (ICAP), Paris, France.

LeMay, M., & Aldhuwaihi, N. (2014). DPI/NGO youth led briefing: Educating and employing youth: The influence of the public-private partnerships in a technological era. *IAAP Bulletin, 26*(2), 54.

Leung, A. K-Y., Koh, K., Ong, L. S., & Tam, K. K-P. (2014, July 8–13). *Being a socially responsible cosmopolitan: The endorsement of a cosmopolitan identity predicts higher environmental protection tendencies*. Presentation at the 28th International Congress of Applied Psychology (ICAP), Paris, France.

Lewin, K. (1939, May). Field theory and experiment in social psychology: Concepts and methods. *American Journal of Sociology, 44*(6), 868–896. Retrieved October 2014 from http://www.jstor.org/stable/2769418

Liefländer, A. K. (2014). Effectiveness of environmental education on water: Connectedness to nature, environmental attitudes and environmental behavior. *Environmental Education Research*. doi:10.1080/13504622.2014.927831. Retrieved April 24, 2015, from http://www.researchgate.net/publication/264242942_Effectiveness_of _environmental_education_on_water_connectedness_to_nature_environmental _attitudes_and_environmental_knowledge

Littlewood, S. (2014, August 29). Presentation on panel, "Climate Change: Climate Justice in Practice." Roundtable at the 65th Annual Conference of the Department of Public Information/Non-governmental Organizations, UN Headquarters, New York, NY.

Lovelock, J. (2006). *The revenge of Gaia: Earth's climate in crisis and the fate of humanity*. New York, NY: Basic Books.

Maller, C., Townsend, M., Pryor, A., Brown, P., & St. Leger, L. (2006). Healthy nature healthy people: "Contact with nature" as an upstream health promotion intervention for populations. *Health Promotion International, 21*(1), 45–54.

Marina, C., Lacerda e Silva, W., Garcia M. Leonardi, P., & Rockenbach, G. (2014, July 8–13). *Identidade Jovem: The project involving young people in promoting the MDGs*. Presentation at the 28th International Congress of Applied Psychology (ICAP), Paris, France.

Markowitz, E. M., Goldberg, L. R., Ashton, M. C. and Lee, K. (2012), Profiling the "pro-environmental individual": A personality perspective. *Journal of Personality, 80*, 81–111. doi:10.1111/j.1467-6494.2011.00721

Masten, A. S., & Obradović, J. (2008). Disaster preparation and recovery: Lessons from research on resilience in human development. *Ecology and Society, 13*(1), 9. Retrieved October 2014 from http://www.ecologyandsociety.org/vol13/iss1/art9/

Matsutaro, F. M. (2015, March 17). Statement at the World Conference on Disaster Risk Reduction, Sendai, Japan. Retrieved April 10, 2015, from http://webtv.un.org/ meetings-events/conferencessummits/3rd-un-world-conference-on-disaster-risk

-reduction-14-18-march-2015-sendai-japan/official-statements/watch/
representative-from-palau-8th-plenary-meeting/4116317505001

Mayer, F. S., Frantz, C. M., Bruehlman-Senecal, E., & Dolliver, K. (2009). Why is nature
beneficial? The role of connectedness to nature. *Environment and Behavior*, *41*,
607–643.

McKibben. T. (2014, August 28). Presentation on panel, "Sustainable Development.
Urgent! Sustainable Management of Natural Resources and Ecosystems." Roundtable
at the 65th Annual Conference of the Department of Public Information/
Non-governmental Organizations, UN Headquarters, New York, NY.

Meakin, S. (1992). *The Rio Earth Summit: Summary of the United Nations conference on
environment and development*. Retrieved September 4, 2014, from http://publications.
gc.ca/Collection-R/LoPBdP/BP/bp317-e.htm

Merriam-Webster. (2014). Well-being. *Merriam-Webster.com*. Retrieved August 28, 2014,
from http://www.merriam-webster.com/dictionary/wellbeing

Meza-Cuadra, G. (2014, August 28). Presentation on panel, "Climate Change: Post-2015
and the UNFCCC Processes: Can They Be Friends?" Roundtable at the 65th Annual
Conference of the Department of Public Information/Non-governmental Organizations, UN Headquarters, New York, NY.

Millennium Development Goals. (n.d.). Retrieved April 24, 2015, from http://www.un
.org/millenniumgoals

Mind. (2013). *Feel better outside, feel better inside: Ecotherapy for mental wellbeing, resilience
and recovery*. Retrieved August 22, 2014, from http://www.mind.org.uk/media/
336359/Feel-better-outside-feel-better-inside-report.pdf

Mitchell, R., & Popham, F. (2008). Effect of exposure to natural environment on health
inequalities: An observational population study. *The Lancet*, *372*(9650), 1655–1660.
doi:10.1016/S0140-6736(08)61689-X

Murrietta, M. (2015). The Pachamama Alliance: Linking environmental sustainability,
social justice, and spiritual fulfillment through changing the dream. In D. G. Nemeth
& J. Kuriansky (Eds.), *Ecopsychology: Advances from the intersection of psychology and
environmental protection*, Volume 2 (pp. 233–241). Santa Barbara, CA: ABC-CLIO.

Nemeth, D. G., Hamilton, R. B., & Kuriansky, J. (Eds.). (2012). *Living in an environmentally traumatized world: Healing ourselves and our planet*. Santa Barbara, CA: ABC-
CLIO/Praeger.

Nemeth, D. G., Hamilton, R. B., & Kuriansky, J. (2015). Reflections and recommendations: The need for leadership, holistic thinking, and community involvement.
In D. G. Nemeth & J. Kuriansky (Eds.), *Ecopsychology: Advances from the intersection
of psychology and environmental protection*, Volume 2 (pp. 413–428). Santa Barbara,
CA: ABC-CLIO

Odintsova, V. (2014, July 8–13). *Out of laboratory: Ecobiological projects in Bernia, Niotan,
Diostan*. Presentation at the 28th International Congress of Applied Psychology
(ICAP), Paris, France.

OECD. (2014). *Green Growth Indicators, 2014*. OECD Green Growth Studies. Paris,
France: OECD Publishing. http://dx.doi.org/10.1787/9789264202030-en. Retrieved
August 22, 2014, at http://www.keepeek.com/Digital-Asset-Management/oecd/
environment/green-growth-indicators-2013_9789264202030-en#page3

Orellana Halkyer, R. (2014, May 7). Personal communication to Judy Kuriansky.
New York, NY: United Nations Headquarters.

Orellana Halkyer, R. (2015). Development and harmony with Mother Earth: An assessment of the issue of poverty, capitalism, and climate change. In D. G. Nemeth & J. Kuriansky (Eds.), *Ecopsychology: Advances from the intersection of psychology and environmental protection*, Volume 2 (pp. 359–383). Santa Barbara, CA: ABC-CLIO.

Osburg, V.-S., Strack, M., & Toporowski, W. (2014, July 8–13). *Consumers' acceptance of innovative, eco-friendly materials: A conjoint analytical approach.* Presentation at the 28th International Congress of Applied Psychology (ICAP), Paris, France.

Otto, C. (2014, August 29). Presentation on panel, "Climate change: Climate justice in practice." Roundtable at the 65th Annual Conference of the Department of Public Information/Non-governmental Organizations, UN Headquarters, New York, NY.

Otto, C., Kuriansky, J., & Okoroduru, C. (2014). *Advocacy about mental health and well-being for the sustainable development goals.* Unpublished manuscript.

Oxford English Dictionary. (2014). Well-being. *OED.com.* Retrieved August 28, 2014, from http://www.oed.com/view/Entry/227050?redirectedFrom=wellbeing#eid

Pahl, S., Stahl-Timmins, W., White, M. P., & Depledge, M (2014, July 8–13). *Improving public understanding of the health impacts of climate change using information graphics.* Presentation at the 28th International Congress of Applied Psychology (ICAP). Paris, France.

Palumbo, G., Bernabei, B., De Santis, E., & Cecconi, C. (2014). *Lizori: Civilizations in progress through cultural diversity and MDGs achievement.* Presentation at the 28th International Congress of Applied Psychology (ICAP), Paris, France.

Parsons, R. (1991). The potential influences of environmental perception on human health. *Journal of Environmental Psychology, 11,* 1–23.

Poortinga, W. (2014, July 8–13). *Neighbourhood quality and attachment: A validation of the revised Residential Environment Assessment Tool.* Presentation at the 28th International Congress of Applied Psychology (ICAP), Paris, France.

Price, J. C., Walker, I., & Boschettib, F. (2014). Measuring cultural values and beliefs about environment to identify their role in climate change responses. *Journal of Environmental Psychology, 37,* 8–20. Retrieved August 21, 2014, from http://dx.doi.org/10.1016/j.jenvp.2013.10.001

Raimi, K. T., & Leary, M. R. (2014). Belief superiority in the environmental domain: Attitude extremity and reactions to fracking. *Journal of Environmental Psychology, 40,* 76–85.

Reisch, L. A., & Thørgersen, J. (Eds.). (2015). *Handbook of research on sustainable consumption.* UK: Edward Elgar Publishing.

Roczen, N., Duvier, C., Bogner, F. X., & Kaiser, F. G. (2012). The search for potential origins of a favorable attitude toward nature. *Psychology, 3,* 341–335

Ross, H. (2014, July 8–13). *Resilience: An environmental psychology interpretation.* Presentation at the 28th International Congress of Applied Psychology (ICAP), Paris, France.

Sarki, U. (2014, August 28). Presentation on panel, "Sustainable Development: Urgent! Sustainable management of Natural Resources and Ecosystems." Roundtable at the 65th Annual Conference of the Department of Public Information/Non-governmental Organizations, UN Headquarters, New York, NY.

Seligman, M. E. P. (2011). *Flourish—a new understanding of happiness and well-being—and how to achieve them.* London, UK: Nicholas Brealey Publishing.

SIDS Action Platform. (n.d.). Retrieved October 2014 from http://www.sids2014.org

65th Annual DPI/NGO Conference Outcome Document Declaration. (2014). Retrieved April 20, 2015, from http://outreach.un.org/ngorelations/files/2014/08/DPINGO OutcomeDoc-DeclarationFinal.pdf

The Social Progress Imperative. (2014). Accessed August 14, 2014, from http://www .socialprogressimperative.org/data/spi

Society for Environmental Population and Conservation Psychology (n.d.). Graduate programs in environmental and conservation psychology. Retrieved April 20, 2015, from http://www.apadivisions.org/division-34/about/resources/graduate-programs.aspx

State of Maryland. (n.d.). *Maryland's Genuine Progress Indicator.* Retrieved October 2014 from http://www.dnr.maryland.gov/mdgpi/index.asp

Steg, L., van den Berg, A. E., & de Groot, J. I. M. (Eds.). (2012). *Environmental psychology: An introduction.* Malden, MA: Wiley-Blackwell.

Stratham, J., & Chase, E. (2010). *Childhood wellbeing: A brief overview.* Loughborough, UK: Childhood Wellbeing Research Centre.

Sustainable Development Goals. (n.d.). Retrieved April 24, 2015, from https://sustainable development.un.org/sdgsproposal

Taciano, L., Milfont, J., Coelho, A. P. M., Pessoa, V. S., & Gouveia, V. V. (2014, July 8–13). *Encouraging pro-environmental behavior in Brazil: A review of research using the functional theory of values.* Presentation at the 28th International Congress of Applied Psychology (ICAP), Paris, France.

Takacs, T. A., Kristjansson, E. A., & Pearce, S. (2014, July 8–13). *A preliminary report on adapting a walkability questionnaire for northern climates: The NEWS-North.* Presentation at the 28th International Congress of Applied Psychology (ICAP), Paris, France.

Takano, T., Nakamura, K., & Watanabe, M. (2002). Urban residential environments and senior citizens' longevity in megacity areas: the importance of walkable green spaces. *Journal of Epidemiology and Community Health.* 56, 913–918. doi:10.1136/jech.56.12.913

Teaching Psychology for Sustainability. (n.d.). *Establishment of APA Division 34 (Population & Environment).* Retrieved October 2014 from http://www.teachgreenpsych .com/history-and-systems.php#APA

Tse, M. M. Y., Ng, J. K. F., Chung, J. W. Y., Wong, T. K. S. (2002). The effect of visual stimuli on pain threshold and tolerance. *Journal of Clinical Nursing, 11,* 264–269.

Turton, C., Murtagh, N., Uzzell, D., & Gatersleben, B. (2014, July 8–13). *Identifying which factors are pertinent to the occurrence of place attachment to the neighbourhood and the relationship between place attachment and sustainable behavior.* Presentation at the 28th International Congress of Applied Psychology (ICAP), Paris, France.

Uhl, I., Jonas, E., & Klackl, J. (2014, July 8–13). *The power of worries—an effective-use perspective on climate change threat.* Presentation at the 28th International Congress of Applied Psychology (ICAP), Paris, France.

Ulrich, R. S. (1984). View through a window may influence recovery from surgery. *Science, 224,* 420–421.

Ulrich, R. S., Simons, R. F., Losito, B. D., Fiorito, E., Miles, M. A., & Zelson, M. (1991). Stress recovery during exposure to natural and urban environments. *Journal of Environmental Psychology, 11,* 231–248.

UNEP. (2014). *Small island developing states spotlighted in top global environmental awards.* Retrieved April 6, 2015, from http://www.unep.org/champions/news/champions-of -the-earth-2014-tommy-remengesau-announced.asp#sthash.NTZfbz9M.dpuf

United Nations. (2014). *Harmony with nature*. Retrieved October 2014 from http://www
.harmonywithnatureun.org/

United Nations Climate Change Summit. (2014). Catalyzing action. Retrieved April 24,
2015, http://www.un.org/climatechange/summit/

United Nations Conference on Sustainable Development. (2012). *Rio + 20*. Retrieved
April 24, 2015, from http://www.uncsd2012.org/index.html

United Nations Department of Economic and Social Affairs (2014). Mental Health
Matters: Social inclusion of youth with mental health conditions. Accessed September 30, 2014 at: http://www.un.org/esa/socdev/documents/youth/IYD2014/reportsocial
inclusionofyouthwithmentalhealth.pdf

United Nations Department of Public Information. (1997). *Earth summit: UN Conference
on Environment and Development*. Retrieved April 20, 2015, from http://www.un.org/
geninfo/bp/enviro.html

United Nations Development Programme. (2010). *Human development report 2010: The
real wealth of nations: Pathways to human development*. Retrieved October 2014 from
http://www.ph.undp.org/content/philippines/en/home/library/human_development/
2010-human-development-report/

United Nations Economic and Social Council. (2012). *Poverty Eradication*. E/CN.5/2012/
3. Retrieved October 2014 from http://daccess-dds-ny.un.org/doc/UNDOC/GEN/
N11/590/98/PDF/N1159098.pdf?OpenElement

United Nations Environment Programme. (n.d.). Rio Declaration on Environment and
Development. Retrieved April 20, 2015, from http://www.unep.org/Documents.
Multilingual/Default.asp?documentid=78&articleid=1163

United Nations Framework Convention on Climate Change. (n.d.). Retrieved April 24,
2015, from http://unfccc.int/2860.php

United Nations, General Assembly. (1972). *Report of the United Nations Conference on the
Human Environment*. A/CONF.48/14/Rev.1. Retrieved October 2014 from http://
undocs.org/A/CONF.48/14/Rev.1

United Nations, General Assembly. (1980). *Draft World Charter for Nature*. A/Res/35/7.
Retrieved October 2014 from http://undocs.org/A/Res/35/7

United Nations, General Assembly. (1981). *Draft World Charter for Nature*. A/Res/36/6.
Retrieved October 2014 from http://undocs.org/A/Res/36/6

United Nations, General Assembly. (1982). *World Charter for Nature*. A/Res/37/7.
Retrieved October 2014 from http://undocs.org/A/Res/37/7

United Nations, General Assembly. (1992). *Report of the United Nations Conference on
Environment and Development*. A/CONF.151/26 (Vol. I).

United Nations, General Assembly. (2002). *Report of the World Summit on Sustainable
Development*. A/CONF.199/20. Retrieved October 2014 from http://undocs.org/A/
Conf.199/20

United Nations, General Assembly. (2010). *Harmony with nature: Report of the secretary-
general*. A/65/314. Retrieved October 2014 from http://undocs.org/A/65/314

United Nations, General Assembly. (2011). *Harmony with nature: Report of the secretary-
general*, A/66/302. Retrieved October 2014 from undocs.org/A/66/302.

United Nations, General Assembly. (2012). *Harmony with nature: Report of the secretary-
general*, A/67/317. Retrieved October 2014 from http://undocs.org/A/67/317.

United Nations, General Assembly. (2013). *Harmony with nature: Report of the secretary-
general*. A/68/325. Retrieved October 2014 from http://undocs.org/A/68/325

United Nations, General Assembly Resolution 60/192. (2005). *Year of Planet Earth, 2008.* A/RES/60/192 (2005). Retrieved October 2014 from http://undocs.org/A/RES/60/192

United Nations, General Assembly Resolution 63/278. (2009). *International Mother Earth Day.* A/RES/63/278. Retrieved October 2014 from http://undocs.org/A/RES/63/278

United Nations, General Assembly Resolution 64/196. (2009). *Harmony with Nature.* A/RES/64/196. Retrieved October 2014 from http://undocs.org/A/RES/64/196

United Nations, General Assembly Resolution 65/164. (2011). *Harmony with Nature.* A/RES/65/164. Retrieved October 2014 from http://undocs.org/A/RES/65/164

United Nations, General Assembly Resolution 66/204. (2012). *Harmony with Nature.* A/RES/66/204. Retrieved October 2014 from http://undocs.org/A/RES/66/204

United Nations, General Assembly Resolution 66/288. (2012). *The future we want.* A/RES/66/288. Retrieved October 2014 from http://undocs.org/A/RES/66/288

United Nations, General Assembly Resolution 68/216. (2013). *Harmony with Nature.* A/RES/68/216. Retrieved October 2014 from http://undocs.org/A/RES/68/216

United Nations, Joint Framework Initiative on Children, Youth and Climate Change. (2013). *Youth in action on climate change: Inspirations from around the world.* Retrieved September 30, 2014, from http://unfccc.int/cc_inet/files/cc_inet/information_pool/application/pdf/youth_in_action_on_climate_change_en.pdf

UN News Centre. (2014, June 23). New UN high-level body on environment opens inaugural session in Nairobi. Retrieved April 20, 2015, from http://www.un.org/apps/news/story.asp?NewsID=48104#.VT8yi0vYwRw

UN Student Journalism Program. (2009). *Newsletters about CILA 2009.* Retrieved April 6, 2015, from http://drjudy.com/un-student-journalism-program/

University of Illinois at Urbana-Champaign. (2012). *Environmental psychology organizations.* Retrieved October 2014 from http://www.library.illinois.edu/arx/envorg.html

Urbina-Soria, J., & Flores-Cano, O. (2014, July 8–13). *Meaning of well-being through semantic networks.* Presentation at the 28th International Congress of Applied Psychology (ICAP), Paris, France.

Van den Berg, A. E., Maas, J., Verheij, R. A., & Groenewegen, P. P. (2010). Green space as a buffer between stressful life events and health. *Social Science and Medicine, 70,* 1203–1210.

Visschers, V. H. M., & Siegrist, M. (2014). Find the differences and the similarities: Relating perceived benefits, perceived costs and protected values to acceptance of five energy technologies. *Journal of Environmental Psychology, 40,* 117–130.

White, H. C. (2014, August 29). Youth efficacy and climate change. Panel presentation, *Promoting Mental Health and Wellbeing for Youth in the New Post-2015 Sustainable Development Agenda: Psychological Principles, Science and Practices. Workshop at the 65th Annual DPI/NGO Conference, 2015 & Beyond—Our Action Agenda,* UN Headquarters, New York, NY.

Whitmarsh, L., & O'Neil, S. (2010). Green identity, green living? The role of pro-environmental self-identity in determining consistency across diverse pro-environmental behaviours. *Journal of Environmental Psychology, 30*(3), 305–315. Retrieved August 21, 2014, from http://dx.doi.org/10.1016/j.jenvp.2010.01.003

Wilson, E. O. (1984). *Biophilia: The human bond with other species.* Cambridge, MA: Harvard University Press.

Wood, D., Schmidt, M., & Kuriansky, J. (2015). Merging external biodiversity with internal transformation: A model of ecosystem and ecopsychology in Belize.

In D. G. Nemeth & J. Kuriansky (Eds.), *Ecopsychology: Advances from the intersection of psychology and environmental protection*, Volume 2 (pp. 243–248). Santa Barbara, CA: ABC-CLIO.

World Health Organization. (2013). *Mental health: A state of well-being*. Retrieved April 24, 2015, from http://www.who.int/features/factfiles/mental_health/en/

World Summit on Sustainable Development. (2002). Retrieved April 24, 2015, from http://www.un.org/jsummit/

The World We Want. (2015). Retrieved April 24, 2015, from http://www.world wewant2015.org

18

Development and Harmony with Mother Earth: An Assessment of the Issue of Poverty, Capitalism, and Climate Change[1]

René Orellana Halkyer

The global agenda is shifting at this time, as the governments of the world have the responsibility to adopt a set of Sustainable Development Goals (SDGs). These SDGs outline the advances in development that the states that are members of the United Nations will have to achieve during the period 2015–2030, which replace the eight Millennium Development Goals that were targeted until the year 2015. This author has been a member of the government delegates that participated in the Open Working Group of member states that negotiated the document outlining the proposed SDGs held at UN headquarters in New York City over a period of almost a year and a half, and ending in July 2014. The subsequent steps in adopting the SDGs included a synthesis report of the UN secretary general, further input from stakeholders, and then a final vote by the UN member states during the General Assembly in September 2015.

This author also participated in earlier discussions about these goals during major international meetings, e.g., in Rio de Janeiro (the Rio + 20 UN Conference on Sustainable Development), and additionally in major summits related to climate change. The observations in this chapter are based on these participations, leading up to the directions that the governments of the world are committing to, regarding major social, economic and environmental issues.

In moving ahead for achievement of the SDGs, in what is referred to as the post-2015 agenda, a major evaluation has been necessary of how much nations have achieved the MDGs. This progress underlies the launch and progress of the SDGs, and thus, this analysis below has been undertaken. After all, as the popular saying goes, you cannot know where you are going unless you know where you have been. An issue that has occupied much of the international debate regarding the post-2015 agenda and its SDGs is the accomplishments of the Millennium Development Goals (MDGs) and the evaluation of their scope and compliance. This analysis below is important, because countries, in trying to implement the SDGs, will inherit the degree of progress they have made in the MDGs, and will have to build on the amount of what they have, or have not, achieved. Some countries, for example, will have to greatly escalate their progress. In this context, we need to redefine our approach to development, with a greater emphasis on the environment and Mother Earth. Intrinsic to this view is to understand the drastic impact of climate change and the need for urgent action to curb its negative effects.

Throughout this chapter, and to understand this issue, it is important to note that there are differences between the developed and the developing countries— also known as the "north" and the "south," respectively. There are also what is called the "emerging countries," which essentially are "emerging economies," countries that are not fully developed but that have made advances in their economic status, in other words, countries with social or economic activities in the process of rapid growth and industrialization. Each of these groups have different responsibilities to the global development into the necessary path of harmony with Mother Earth.

AN OVERVIEW OF THE SUSTAINABLE DEVELOPMENT GOALS

A look at the SDGs shows that some goals reiterate the MDGs, but have been greatly expanded and elaborated. The SDGs are built on three pillars, namely social inclusion, economic growth, and environmental protection. The latter was also one of the MDGs, although greater emphasis is now being placed on the value, importance, and preservation of the environment. Protection of the environment is intricately tied to the attainment of the other goals, including the priority goal of eradicating poverty, as will be addressed in this chapter. As such, a holistic view to development is being adopted, which is consistent with this author's perspective.

As an honorary ambassador on issues of environment and development to the United Nations, and professor of environment, water, and climate change issues, as well as former vice minister of basic services and former minister of the environment and water of Bolivia, I assert that countries' development demands respect for the environment and for Mother Earth, and that conditions of the environment with regard to climate change greatly impact the level of poverty, food insecurity, health, and living well of the population.

AN OVERVIEW OF THE MILLENNIUM DEVELOPMENT GOALS

The MDGs consisted of eight goals the governments of the world agreed to achieve by the year 2015. They included:

1. To eradicate extreme poverty and hunger
2. To achieve universal primary education
3. To promote gender equality and empower women
4. To reduce child mortality

5. To improve maternal health
6. To combat HIV/AIDS, malaria, and other diseases
7. To ensure environmental sustainability
8. To develop a global partnership for development

The MDGs are linked to problems that are symptoms of deeper causes within the structure of the economy and society not only of the individual country, but also at the global level. This is particularly evident in the case of poverty and hunger. It is important to point out that the MDGs placed a priority on eradicating extreme poverty and hunger, as do the SDGs. The conditions of poverty and hunger, as well as the gradual deterioration of ecosystems and the planet, are undoubtedly causes, but also effects, of a configuration of the global economy and its models of development. An economic and social order based on private accumulation, economic growth, consumerism, pollutant production patterns, and the concentration of wealth in few hands, with the assumption that nature is a capital and a provider of services, without rights, has helped to trigger cycles of impoverishment and hunger—an increasingly predatory path to eroding the foundation and sustenance of life.

LIGHTS AND SHADOWS OF THE MILLENNIUM DEVELOPMENT GOALS

A first look at the progress of the Millennium Development Goals gives a seemingly encouraging picture. The following are some of the significant progress evident in the MDGs (United Nations, 2012a, p. 4):

- The proportion of people living on US$1.25 a day fell from 47% in 1990 to 24% in 2008.
- Water coverage has increased from 76% in 1990 to 89% in 2010; the proportion of people living in slums decreased from 39% of the total world population in 2000 to 33% in 2012.
- In terms of education, one of the poorest regions of the world, sub-Saharan Africa, has increased the enrollment of children in primary education from 58% in 1999 to 76% in 2010.
- The unpaid family and self-employed workers have fallen from 67% in 1990 to 58% in 2011.
- The number of people with access to safe water rose from 4.1 billion people in 1990 to 6.1 billion people by 2010.

In Latin America and the Caribbean, the situation also shows remarkable results, as shown by the following data (Naciones Unidas, 2012, p. 20):

- The proportion of poor in the total population has fallen from 48% in 1990 to 31% in 2010.

- The proportion of the population living in slums of the total has dropped from 33.7% in 1990 to 23.5% in 2010.
- The population without access to energy has also dropped from 17% to 6.4% in the same period.
- The population with sanitation services has increased from 69% in 1990 to 79% in 2009, and the population with access to safe drinking water has increased from 85% in 1990 to 93% in 2008.
- The percentage of protected areas has increased from 9.7% in 1990 to 20.3% in 2010.

THE CRISIS OF POVERTY IN THE WORLD

Despite this optimism, the data shows that poverty and hunger prevail in the world and tend to worsen. The two main causes for this—the crisis of capitalism and the climate crisis—will be addressed later in this chapter. It is estimated that 1.3 billion people in the world still live on less than US$1.25 a day. This is equivalent to four times the population of the United States and two and a half times the population of the European Union.

In 2008, 15.5% of the world population were suffering from hunger, more than 850 million people were undernourished; and 788 million people were hungry in Asia and sub-Saharan Africa (United Nations, 2012a, pp. 11–12). The proportion of undernourished people in the world has declined in very little percentage, and has even grown in absolute terms (United Nations, 2012a, p. 12). This sends an urgent call to the world. The global financial crisis and the impacts of climate change have only served to exacerbate the hunger crisis.

If we compare the total population living in poverty in China with the total population of the United States, poor people of China represent the equivalent of 66% of the total population of the United States in 2012 and India's population of poor is equivalent to 126% of the total population of the United States. In comparison to the countries of the European Union, China in 2010 had an equivalent of almost 35% of the population of EU living in poverty, while India had the equivalent of 78% of the EU population living in poverty. This comparison is useful in order to understand the remaining effort that has to be done by these emerging countries in the years of the SDGs, in order to improve their social situation while decarbonizing their economies—efforts that took decades for developed countries to accomplish.

CASES OF COUNTRY EFFORTS TO ERADICATE POVERTY: CHINA, INDIA AND SOUTH AMERICA

Given the priority given to poverty eradication in both the MDGs and the SDGs, it is important to assess progress in national efforts for poverty eradication and also the enormous challenges still pending.

With regard to poverty eradication, there are certainly admirable efforts in the world. Brazil stands out as one of the countries with significant poverty reduction, from 17.2% in 1990 to 6.1% in 2009 (PNUD, 2013, p. 13). Also notable is the case of Bolivia, where moderate poverty has decreased from 63.5% to 45% and extreme poverty from 40.7% to 20.9% between 1999 and 2011 (Morales Ayma, 2012). More than a million people (in a country of 10.3 million) have joined the middle class in the last seven years, i.e., the equivalent of almost 10% of the population has risen to the middle social stratum.

China is a remarkable case, where poverty fell from 60% in 1990 to 13% in 2008. More than 510 million people have risen out of poverty in 18 years (PNUD, 2013, p. 26), which is an impressive feat; but unfortunately, the development model in China linked to poverty eradication implies higher emissions and an economic growth that comes at a price to the environment.

The good news is that China is making significant efforts to change a highly consumer model based on fossil fuel sources of energy, particularly coal, and is showing remarkable progress in the implementation of renewable energy, with the challenge and obligation to achieve a decreasing curve over the short term. The pressure of a large population, and consistent and consequent obligations of the state, has certainly conditioned its model of development to emphasize the social and the economic dimensions as central to its development approach (UNICEF, 2013, p. 62).[2] China still has the challenge of eradicating poverty in about 174.6 million people. Yet, progress has been impressive, given improvement from 1981, when China had far more people—namely, 972 million— living on less than US$2 a day, and 835 million people living on less than US$1.25 a day (UNICEF, 2013, p. 32).

Poverty and hunger are inextricably tied. India, with a population of 1.241 billion people by the end of 2011 (UNICEF, 2013, p. 72) has a dramatic scenario of hunger, affecting two-thirds of the population (JARE, IPFRI, & Concern Worldwide, 2012, p. 14),[3] leading to the country having a rating in the Global Hunger Index (GHI) category as "highly alarming." Despite significant efforts made between 1990 and 2005 to solve this problem, the number of hungry people in India increased by 65 million people. One in four people suffering from hunger in the world is in India (Chilosi, n.d., p. 471).

Both India and China are in similar situations. Both countries are making progress in poverty reduction, but large numbers of the population still suffer extreme hunger, mainly in rural areas. In a related important issue, both countries are feeling pressured, particularly by developed countries, to reduce emissions while trying to achieve poverty eradication.

Latin America and the Caribbean had an estimated 177 million poor people in the year 2010, which was lower than in 1990, but more than in 1980 (United Nations, 2012a, p. 27). In fact, 22% of the population of Latin America and the Caribbean do not have household water connections; while 45% of the rural population and 14% of urban population did not have improved sanitation services by 2008 (Naciones Unidas, 2012, p. 34). In Latin America and the Caribbean, the number of undernourished people in 2010 totaled 52 million, an increase from 2007. The curve of hunger in this region follows the same pattern as the global curve and is motivated by the same causes. For example, malnutrition in countries like Guatemala, Honduras, Peru, and Haiti in children under 5 years in the region is alarming (Naciones Unidas, 2012, p. 49).

POVERTY AS A MULTIDIMENSIONAL PROBLEM

Poverty is actually multidimensional, which means there are overlapping deprivations suffered by people at the same time. This means that indicators of poverty include aspects like provision of electricity (High-Level Panel of Eminent Persons on the Post-2015 Development Agenda, 2013, p. 44),[4] housing, drinking water, and sanitation, as well as education and health.

It is estimated that 1.57 billion people live in conditions of multidimensional poverty (PNUD, 2013, p. 13). These are not only in less developed countries (or low-income countries), as would be expected, but also in in middle-income countries. In fact, 72% of the people of the world living in multidimensional poverty of the world live in middle-income countries (Alkire, Roche, & Seth, 2013, p. 5).

China has made some progress in reducing multidimensional poverty. With regard to agriculture and food production, China has invested significantly in irrigation. In the past five years, China increased irrigated areas by 7.7 million hectares, by applying technologies of water-saving systems and implementing a system of subsidies to agricultural production grains—which in 2012 amounted to 192.3 billion yuan, equivalent to US$31.3 billion[5]—in addition to financial services and credit to farms—which in 2012 amounted to 6.12 trillion yuan, or US$29 trillion (State Council of China, 2013). Advances were also made in housing, whereby China has remarkably invested 1.26 trillion yuan (about US$205 billion) to build subsidized homes over a period of two years. Between 2008 and 2012, 18 million subsidized housing units were built, 12 million households were improved, and 10.33 million rural homes were built (State Council of China, 2013).

India has also made significant progress, albeit slowly, in eradicating multidimensional poverty, which fell by 16% between 1999 and 2006. Some studies suggest that the eradication of multidimensional poverty in countries such as Bolivia or Colombia could take 10 years, while India, in comparison, could take 41 years (Alkire et al., 2013, p. 5)[6] at the current pace. But, of course, the governments have to make significant efforts to accelerate the process of sustainable development and poverty eradication. Bolivia has shown that a clear agenda with a strong leadership of the state as well as the redistribution of wealth contributes to advance significantly toward living well. The challenge facing India in eradicating poverty involves distributing wealth, providing services, creating jobs, and improving the living conditions of the people.

China, for its part, has made significant achievements in education and created conditions for developing basic education and also education in innovation and technology. In the last five years, by 2012, China's total expenditure dedicated to education was US$1.7 trillion (or 4% of the GDP by 2012); and US$1.6 billion was invested to financially support students from poor families, with the result that 80 million students benefited from state support. Moreover, China promoted a system of improving teaching by linking the payment to teachers to their performance (State Council of China, 2013).

The links between training, capacity building, ability, skills, and knowledge to productivity have been strengthened in China. In the last five years, 28 million college graduates and 8.3 million urban residents having difficulties in finding employment could find work. To do so, the state invested US$32 billion and created 58.7 million urban jobs in the last five years (State Council of China, 2013).

In efforts to eradicate multidimensional poverty, India has made a large financial investment in development, evident in the increased budget in social services and rural development from 13.4% in 2006–2007 to 18.5% in 2011–2012, and the increase in budget allocated to social services from 21.6% of total expenditure in 2006–2007 to 25% in 2011–2012 (PNUD, 2013, p. 69).

India's ambitious efforts to combat massive poverty has led to innovative efforts to generate programs for social development and particularly for employment, but even these have not been enough to stem the tide of poverty significantly. To India's credit, 11.3 million jobs per year were generated in the period 2000–2005 (Embajada de la India, n.d.). As another effort to combat widespread hunger, India implemented a subsidy program for food, fuel, and other essential goods for the poor. An example of these programs is the National Rural Employment Guarantee Scheme, implemented since 2005, which pays 100 days of unemployment per year to one adult member of each rural residential unit living below the poverty line. Other noteworthy programs include the National Social Assistance Program, the National Food-for-Work Program, the Accelerated Rural Water Supply Program, and other programs that build social housing and roads for access to villages and that offer fertilizer subsidies (Embajada de la India, n.d.).

Unlike China, which has made balanced investments between rural and urban areas, India seems to have concentrated its efforts on urban development and still has a big task to solve social inequalities and inequality gaps between urban and rural areas. In comparison to China, India's efforts face a big challenge due to the rate of population growth. This rate is 1.4% per year—three times more than China—with a predominance of young people, given that half the population is under age 25. It is expected that, by the year 2030, India will have a higher population than China (La Tercera, 2011).

Brazil has combined sustained and accelerated economic growth with reducing hunger by half between 1992 and 2007 using a multisectoral strategy called "Zero Hunger," which includes 50 measures including transferring money to poor mothers and services of technical assistance to small farmers (OXFAM, 2011, p. 4).

My own country, Bolivia, is in second place of multidimensional poverty reduction among 22 developing countries with the highest indicator of poverty. Huge efforts have been made, particularly in the past seven years, to invest in water services, electricity, sanitation, nutrition, and education, among others, achieving a decrease of almost 10 percentage points. Remarkably, multidimensional poverty reduction in Bolivia has been made in poor and rural regions characterized by a significant presence of extreme poverty, such as Potosí, Chuquisaca, and Beni. Sustained, accelerated, and increased investment in the social sector in rural and urban communities has undoubtedly had a positive effect (PNUD, 2013, p. 3). Adding to the advances was a permanent and substantial mobilization of economic resources and services in these rural areas, beginning in 2006, that built an educational and health infrastructure as well as generated production projects, housing, communication, and water services. Other social achievements have been made—for example, the school dropout rate fell from 6.1% in 2000 to 4.2% in 2012; the rate of chronic malnutrition in children under 2 years dropped from 32% to 15.8%; the rate of maternal mortality decreased from 229 in 2003 to 90 in 2012; a system of social bonus improved school attendance, that benefitted 1.7 million children[7] and led to the reduction of school dropouts; the coverage of electricity rose from 64% to 77% between 2001 and 2010; and the urban unemployment rate fell from 8.7% in 2003 to 3.84% by 2011 (Morales Ayma, 2012).

THE CASE OF OTHER COUNTRIES IN SOUTHEAST ASIA

In Southeast Asia, emerging countries are building strong economies linked to the electronics industry—with the provision of components, manufacturing, and services—that have entered vigorously into the international market. This is due to several factors, including: applying a model of industrial development with strong ties in Asia, with the remarkable leadership of China, strong leadership in their own states, and significant central planning with business flexibility that has allowed for building alliances between companies in manufacturing that has led to considerable job creation. The Asian model, and its ability to create jobs, has undoubtedly contributed to the eradication of poverty in the region.

Thailand is an important case because of its creative and consistent attention to production networks consisting of components and parts in the automotive and electronics industries. Between 2009 and 2010, exports of parts and components were US$48 billion. In the case of Southern Asia—which is one of the most populated regions of the world, even more than Eastern Asia and much more than Western Asia, mainly because of the demographic weight of India—there is a similar process. India is becoming a powerful engine of development. Bangladesh still holds a special role in innovation and growth of its economy and is joining industrial and manufacturing economies (PNUD, 2013). Vietnam is another interesting case in Southeast Asia, as it has achieved the goal of more than halving the rate of hunger and poverty, which reduced from 58% in 1993 to 19% in 2006. Vietnam has followed an industrial and manufacturing model similar to that of several countries in the region, and also significantly strengthened its agricultural production. Notably, in just a few years, Vietnam went from being a rice importer to be the world's second-largest exporter (OXFAM 2011, p. 50).

THE CRISIS OF WATER IN ENVIRONMENTAL PROTECTION

Water is inextricably tied to poverty and hunger. China took a giant leap in providing safe water to its people, increasing by 457 million the number of people with access to safe water. Similarly, India increased by 522 million the number of its people with access to safe water in the same period (United Nations, 2012a, p. 52). Between 2008 and 2012, China has provided drinking water to 300 million rural residents and electricity services to 4.5 million people. In order to improve the provision of water sources, China has reinforced and improved 18,000 water reservoirs (e.g., dams) and has created infrastructural conditions for better utilization of 24,500 km of rivers (State Council of China, 2013).

Water should be a human right, yet millions of people suffer from lack of clean drinking water. This constitutes an environmental disaster. In fact, 2.5 billion people still lack access to improved sanitation and 783 million people lack access to safe drinking water or water supply services.

The challenge for the effective realization of the human right to water is even greater in the context of climate change. Today, three billion people live in areas where demand exceeds supply. By 2030, demand will have increased by 30% (OXFAM, 2011, p. 17). This scenario requires strengthening integrated water management in the context of sustainable access to adequate quantity and quality, prioritizing human consumption and irrigation. Experiments of privatization promoted by international financial institutions—particularly the World Bank and the International Monetary Fund (IMF)—cannot be repeated because they ended up generating exclusion, putting profits in the hands of a few transnational corporations, and resulting in private appropriation of community water sources and increased water prices, affecting the economy of the poor. The same criticisms can be leveled at the approach of privatizing water, which promoted water markets and water rights markets.

THE RELATIONSHIP BETWEEN POVERTY ERADICATION AND CLIMATE CHANGE NEGOTIATIONS

It is clear to me that the dangers of climate change are real in our world today. When I exerted the role of chair, on behalf of my country, Bolivia, of the group of countries G77 + China in the context of the United Nations Framework Convention on Climate Change (UNFCCC) in 2014, I strongly supported the need for agreements for combatting the problem of climate change. It is also clear that climate change is intricately tied to the other major global problems.

Ending poverty is tied to the challenge of climate change. The situation in India demonstrates this relationship. In other words, the problem in India with regard to poverty eradication sheds some light on the position India has taken in the international debate on climate change, in requesting to be given differential treatment concerning the agreements about reductions in emissions. On the multilateral stage of climate change negotiations, India has maintained a position demanding the principles of Equity and Right to Development (which also involves the right to the eradication of poverty), and the construction of a legal instrument on climate change and climate mitigation programs. As of this writing, these were being discussed in the UN framework.

THE RELATIONSHIP BETWEEN POVERTY AND THE GLOBAL FINANCIAL CRISIS

Poverty and hunger are also linked to the global financial crisis. For example, the financial crisis had a significant impact on food prices, generating speculation and thus worsening hunger in the world. Food prices shot up in 2010 and 2011, following a pattern similar to that of oils and raw oils. A study by OXFAM found that if there had not been a financial crisis and the concomitant rise in food prices, the world today would have 413 million fewer hungry people (OXFAM, 2011, p. 30).

THE NEED FOR A HOLISTIC APPROACH

To eradicate poverty in developing countries in a short time requires a huge effort on many fronts, including with regard to resources, employment generation, transformation of economic structures, and investments. Fundamentally, what is required is a paradigm shift from traditional models of development based on growth—no matter how "green" or ecological it is shaped or labeled—to a comprehensive and integral development, with a holistic approach, where humanity and nature, together with Mother Earth, are at the center of a vision of development that allows balance, harmony, and equality. Eradicating poverty while maintaining a pace of growth that respects the limits of regeneration of nature but at the same time grows in providing material, cultural, and spiritual conditions to live well, solving the central problems of hunger, unemployment, and lack of health services, requires a different approach from that of simple economic growth. This change in approach to solve the social ills of humanity must happen urgently, but also with the constraints and limitations required by the context of environmental and climate crisis, which in turn requires the reduction of emissions mainly in those countries with capacities to accelerate this march.

Traditional approaches to measure poverty based on income or GDP per capita do not give us the complete picture of the reality. We cannot understand poverty based on the classification used by the World Bank regarding income categories. An approach of this type leads to the wrong conclusion that poverty is primarily in low-income countries.

By the same token, some assume wrongly that measuring GDP per capita affirms that certain developing countries are already in the medium- or medium-high-income category. This automatically implies their full capacity to eradicate poverty and to assume international obligations equal to those of developed countries. This is not true. Indeed, we should differentiate countries according to their capacity—technological, economic, institutional—but also according to their conditions and social characteristics, as well as their challenges in the eradication of poverty. This approach brings the concepts of equity and common but differentiated responsibilities into the post-2015 agenda.

India is a case where this observation applies. Countries like India cannot be expected to perform to the standards of developed countries in terms of obligations such as climate mitigation commitments, since, for example, conditions of dramatic poverty drastically challenge their development. But it is also true that the climate crisis requires that developing countries, mainly the emerging ones, also have the duty to make significant efforts to transform their development models in the short term. The path to do that implies that developing countries do not follow the same lifestyles and the same patterns of consumption and production of developed countries. Such a profound change of development model should also imply building equity and equality within the countries.

There is a growing potential for developing countries, particularly emerging ones, to contribute to climate change solutions. Their present conditions are, however, different from those which developed countries had in the past. For example, they do not have the advantage of the same extended time that benefited developed countries to begin lowering their curves of emissions of greenhouse gases, after achieving economic, social, and technological advances over a long historical period since the Industrial Revolution. (Of course, it is this evolution that made these very countries historically responsible for the climate crisis.)

WHERE PROGRESS IN THE MDGS IS POOR

The MDGs have sorely not been achieved in some areas and by some countries. For example:

- Sub-Saharan Africa has not met the goal of halving the number of poor people.
- The lowered mortality rate of children has not been achieved in sub-Saharan Africa, South Asia, Oceania, Caucasus, and Central Asia.
- The MDG related to halving of infant deaths per thousand live births has not been fulfilled. In 1990, the rate of infant deaths was 97 per thousand live births and in 2011 it was 63 (United Nations, 2012a, pp. 26–27). Globally, the number of deaths of children under 5 years in 1990 was 32 per thousand, while in 2010, it was 23; however, in sub-Saharan Africa, this rate had increased to 35.
- The goal of mortality per 100,000 live births has not been achieved in the Caribbean and Oceania (United Nations, 2012a, p. 44).
- The number of cases of tuberculosis has increased in sub-Saharan Africa, Caucasus, and Central Asia.
- Regions that did not reach the MDGs on drinking water supply coverage include Oceania, sub-Saharan Africa, Caucasus, Central Asia, and West Asia.
- The proportion of people living in slums fell very little in sub-Saharan Africa, Latin America, and the Caribbean, and remained constant in Oceania. The number of people living in slums in Latin America and the Caribbean rose from 105 million in 1990 to 110.8 million in 2010 (Naciones Unidas, 2012, p. 20).

It should be noted, however, that over the past 20 years, several countries have reduced the proportion of people living in slums, including Nicaragua, Colombia, and Peru, where the rate decreased by 25%, and Brazil, where the rate of people living in slums decreased from 37% in 1990 to 28% in 2007 (Naciones Unidas, 2012, p. 34).

DEFORESTATION, EXPANSION OF THE AGRICULTURAL FRONTIER AND "AGRO-FORESTRY PREDATION"

Regarding progress in environment sustainability, the overall results are worrying. While MDG#7 called for reducing deforestation, the regions of South America and Africa had the largest forest loss between 2000 and 2010 (United Nations, 2012a, p. 46). Latin America and the Caribbean, with 24% of the world's forests (Naciones Unidas, 2012, pp. 113–128) experienced a loss in the area of forest cover from 49.1% in 1990 to 45.6% in 2005, with a cumulative loss of 68.6 million hectares in the period (United Nations, 2012a, pp. 89, 90). Deforestation in the region accounts for a third of global deforestation (Naciones Unidas, 2012, p. 119).

This process has been driven among other things by an extension of crop and livestock frontier. Extensive and related generation of agro-export crops greatly increased the agricultural area encroaching upon the woods. Soybeans are a crop that has led to the deforestation of large areas. In the period 1990–2005, 22.3 million hectares in Latin America were extended, equivalent to almost a third of the deforested area. Between 1990 and 2007, cattle stock increased from 326 million to 392 million heads, additionally pressing on forest area.

The agro-livestock models focused on large markets and mono-production, without regulation or land use planning that can lead to illegal deforestation, lead to biofuels in some countries, based on soybeans, corn, and sugar cane. This model in some regions further leads to land degradation, desertification, and displacement of small farmers and indigenous communities. The impact of such a model, if exported to regions like sub-Saharan Africa, would undoubtedly affect 33 million small producers with farms averaging 1.6 hectares (OXFAM, 2011, p. 53).

Some countries of Latin America and the Caribbean, Africa, and Asia, are being motivated by a food system that is turning developing countries into mass producers of certain food products in order to satisfy the consumerism of developed countries. A perverse and dangerous link is developing between unsustainable consumption patterns of developed countries and an agro-export model based on monocultures in developing countries. This scenario—comprised of an expanding agricultural frontier that causes deforestation and promotes forest plantations with high production performance based on technological packages —is a system that we can call "*agro-forestry governance of predation*." This unsustainable model facilitates regulations to elites and gradually leads to the elimination of agro-biodiversity that is a valuable source of nutrients.

Certainly the solution is not to eliminate large agriculture, but to propose balance and sustainable agro-forestry with complementarity between small, medium, and large plots, oriented to food security and food sovereignty, all within harmony with nature. The adequate and sustainable management of the expanding agricultural frontier is desirable where the ecosystem's capacity allows it, and if relationships exist among different scales of agriculture while maintaining biodiversity, agro-biodiversity and forest conservation and can contribute to complementary practices between scales that increase production/productivity and conservation. But this requires planning, institutional mechanisms, and regulatory and food production policies oriented by an approach that respects and insures environmental sustainability and food security.

Such a challenge must be defined with operational detail in national public policies and trans-boundary arrangements. However, in a world where 500 million small farms generate 1.5 billion jobs, it is clear that agricultural policies, employment, and hunger reduction should aim to strengthen indigenous smallholders and peasants. A prodigious investment in small-scale production will generate more jobs, reduce hunger, and eradicate poverty.

Admittedly, the expansion of the agricultural frontier, if well planned— respecting and strengthening environmental functions of ecosystems accompanied by integral actions of forestation, afforestation, and sustainable agroforestry as well as preservation—can benefit allocation of land to small farmers and create food security conditions, integral management of ecosystems, and jobs, while reducing poverty and ensuring access to food and income. However, there is no possibility of sustaining economic growth while following an approach that encourages the destruction of forests.

THE CRISIS CAUSED BY CAPITALISM

In a world interconnected through trade and finance, with processes of decentralized and chain production whose links are located in different countries and regions, the crisis of the world's most powerful economies can severely affect the economies of developing countries and their progress in eliminating poverty.

Efforts and progress in development and poverty eradication are vulnerable to crises of capitalism. This is evident in the impact of the financial crisis from 2007 onward, in the increase in food prices and the effect this had on the increase in the number of hungry people in the world and also in the loss of jobs. In China alone, 20 million people lost their jobs (Stiglitz, 2010, p. 9). The vulnerability to crisis and to the volatility of capitalist global markets is particularly high in countries whose economies are oriented to international markets and integrated into global networks of production processes.

China responded quickly to the crisis, with policies that redirected much of its economy to the domestic market: taking monetary and fiscal measures, increasing investment, reducing interest rates, and guaranteeing provision of financial resources for business and productive enterprises with high capacity for employment generation. These policies were accompanied by social measures that undoubtedly strengthened efforts to safeguard their path to eradicating poverty. The presence of a strong state and central planning also played a role in controlling vulnerability to the menaces of markets. India did not seem to have overcome this crisis as successfully, but its orientation to southern markets has played a crucial role in creating better conditions to manage the crisis.

In my view, the United States—one of the strongest economies and consumers in the world (Stiglitz, 2010, p. 42) and even bigger than several emerging countries combined—has dragged the world into crisis with a significant impact on the emerging and developed countries. The American development model based on consumerism certainly has served as an example for other countries. Yet in present days, there are chains of interdependent development models and sensitive interdependencies between economies and societies. The American growth model is based on the accumulation of public and private debt to generate a consumer dynamism that increases geometrically the aggregate demand; this dynamic dragged the world into collapse of employment, poverty, and hunger. In this crisis, the gap of financial public governance, facilitated by the absence of regulation, empowered the banks and gave them the freedom to finance without limits. The short cycle of what Nobel Prize–winning economist Joseph Stiglitz calls "consumption binge financed with debt" mobilized mortgage loans amounting to US$975 billion (equivalent to 7% of U.S. GDP) and additional consumer loans, creating an economy in which about three-quarters of GDP was tied to the property market. At the time of this hallucinogenic boom cycle, a quarter of the toxic mortgages were converted into titles or in debt securities issues that were sold outside the United States, bought by banks, pension funds companies, and private and public entities (Stiglitz, 2010, pp. 16, 26, 42, 72). When the bubble burst, as a result of the mismatch between debt and inability to pay, the economies floundered of both the developed countries and the developing countries, with the latter suffering aggravated hunger, unemployment, and poverty.

The power of banks and funds in the judiciary, arbitral, political, and economic systems is impressive. These continue to exercise a decisive power in international financial markets. They undermine national financial systems, where states are weak, and give the illusion of economic boom led by the banks' financial freedom and the free market. Banks took advantage of this cycle of crisis, by exercising perverse financial governance, speculation and fraud, and bankrupted citizens. As savers and debtors struggled for survival in the volatile situation, capitals and citizens alike attempted to take money out of countries menaced by bankruptcy. Spanish journalist and researcher Ignacio Ramonet notes that in the early months of 2012, 220 billion Euros escaped from Spain; this was an amount equivalent to twice the credit requested by Spain to save the Spanish banking system (Ramonet, 2013, p. 3). In addition, banks exercised speculative practices with bank interest rates. An example is the manipulation of the Libor rate, calculated globally through a survey of 16 international banks, of which 10 provided false information about interests on their own loans. This affected 350 billion Euros in loans in the world (Ramonet, 2013).

As Stiglitz points out, capitalism operates similarly across countries, which can lead to financial crisis. For example, the bubble burst in the global financial crisis of 2007–2008, despite the system of financial governance and despite the fact that senior political operators of the powerful countries in 2007 felt "déjà vu" before the initial symptoms of the debacle—even though they disregarded warnings about the upcoming fall and did not take the necessary measures.

Ironically, unlike many developed countries, some emerging countries and developing countries were able to skillfully manage the crisis by relying on a strong role by the state and a process of strengthening the potential of the South.

This brief look at the financial crisis indicates that progress in the MDGs was extremely vulnerable to systemic crisis. This can continue into the SDGs, unless we change patterns of consumption and production, and even more if we do not change a capitalist system that generates greed and consumer addiction to promote consumerism and private accumulation.

Developing countries, and emerging countries in particular, need to take heed, because, as Stiglitz says, moments of crisis must lead to changes in policies and ideas toward building a new society. In my view, this translates into radically transforming our worldview and our view of development and nature, aiming not to the mercantilist fetish but to building societies of living well.

Emerging countries have a great responsibility in that transformation of worldview. They cannot copy the consumerism models of some developed countries; that would drive us toward a worsening crisis and, of course, the climate crisis. They cannot follow the models of unsustainable urbanization with ostentatious architecture and excessive energy consumption. They must not promote consumption with addictive patterns and lifestyles dependent on markets of the superfluous, with the pretext of increasing aggregate demand so as to create an obese middle class, liable to accumulation and individualism, without respect for their community or the environment. I regret that some developing countries, and among them some emerging countries, have unfortunately decided to follow this route, despite the historic examples of the developed countries' responsibility for the climate, environment, and financial crises. How could emerging or developing countries criticize developed countries if they themselves decide to copy the American model?

VULNERABILITY OF THE SDGS TO THE CLIMATE CRISIS

Undoubtedly, one of the most complex situations of this historical moment is climate change and implies challenges of adaptation and mitigation. The climate crisis requires that developing countries, and the most vulnerable, implement urgent measures to adapt their economies and production activities, their health and education systems, planning instruments, and institutions as well as their development paths to climate change in a complicated scenario with increase temperature prospects even more than 3°C. In addition to this, there is an urgent need to implement mitigation actions, with developed countries taking the lead and with significant efforts of emerging economies to reduce their emissions.

Adaptation and mitigation actions have a cost in terms of development and poverty eradication (i.e., they may limit or condition development). They may brake acceleration and radically transform technology and energy processes, affect budgets, social programs, and employment dependent on economic structures with high emissions. Consequently adaptation and mitigation actions, particularly structural mitigation measures involving changes in the energy mix and consumption patterns, for example, implies major changes in models of development because they go beyond the introduction of renewable energy technologies.

The impact of climate change on the quality and quantity of water and its availability for human consumption and production is certainly affecting extreme poverty and hunger. This goal is undoubtedly affected in the context of a critical temperature increase scenario like the one provided, generating backsliding on the progress made to date. Climate-induced migration due to extreme events and gradual processes of erosion and land degradation, the deterioration of basic services, the impact on the quality of natural resources, and the destruction of ecosystems that are sources of food, water, and life make vulnerable displaced populations and become more sensitive to the situation of the poor. Urban areas will see increased needs and social demands associated with education and health services, among others, while pressing on resources and ecosystems that provide those resources necessary for the survival of urban areas and to support production processes and supply services.

Disasters caused by extreme events also impact the economy, sources of food, sources of employment, infrastructure, transportation, and production as well as ecosystems, progressively destroying the natural, environmental, economic, and social basis of life of the people. They affect factors and resources necessary for sustained development and sustained employment generation. These environmental disasters also generate diseases, cause mortality, and aggravate health conditions. The pressure for rebuilding infrastructure and economies as well as the restoration of ecosystems and life zones and systems will have a significant burden on public and social economies at national and subnational levels. If we add to this situation the necessary, gradual but sustained investment in means, financial services and infrastructure, institutionality, planning, regulation, provision of factors, and means to support processes and local economic enterprises, family, business, community, public, budgets will systematically see their investment capabilities eroded.

Water is seriously affected by climate change. Between 12 million and 81 million people will suffer shortages of drinking water in Latin America and the Caribbean by 2025 and between 79 million and 178 million people by 2055 (Naciones Unidas, 2012, p. 75). The shortage of water for drinking and irrigation, increased resource demand, and deterioration of water quality as a result of decreased flow, in addition to pollution of water sources, will generate supply problems in cities and seriously deteriorate health conditions. A health crisis will arise. Furthermore, energy sources based on water resources will be equally affected, with decreasing volumes and loss of sources reducing the capacity of power generation. This will lead to energy cuts and rationing, with consequent negative effects in the industry and the economy in general.

Water stress and temperature rise, and high evapotranspiration will affect populations and generate strong pressure on health systems. This will certainly impact agricultural processes, investment demand, and productive efficiency. It will also disable lands, decrease production and productivity, and reduce food availability, and thus generate malnutrition and hunger.

Increasing deforestation with an associated deterioration of biodiversity, and the natural of environmental functions of forests and biodiversity areas, will destroy living systems and generate population loss and increase their vulnerability. This will cause production losses, malnutrition, and hunger and will affect the food supply.

The impacts of increased temperature at 4 degrees are multiple: stronger heat waves, more frequent cyclones, decreased precipitation (in boreal forests, mountainous regions, and dry tropics), reduced availability of water in agricultural regions, millions of people exposed to water shortages, decreased grain productivity, loss of species and productivity, increased malnutrition, and diarrheal and respiratory diseases. If the temperature exceeds 3 degrees, between 40% and 70% of the species of biodiversity will be lost (IPCC, 2007, p. 7).

In warmer ecosystems, crops will be affected by pests and will decrease. In the vulnerable regions, the impact of rain, floods, and droughts will decrease the food supply, and crops will be lost. Droughts and extreme events increase the risks of desertification and erosion. They will impact the productivity of the soil and therefore agricultural production and productivity. This leads to a food crisis, with raised prices and shortages, transferring the direct impacts on production infrastructure and on the agricultural economy to the purchasing capacity of the population, exacerbating food availability and affecting nutrition and quality of life of the people. As a result, poverty, hunger, and malnutrition increase (Orellana Halkyer, 2012). Furthermore, governance problems emerge, particularly in developing countries.

Developing countries will be the most affected by climate change. Of the total estimated cost, between 75% and 80% of the burden will be borne by developing countries. If the increase in temperature persists, to more than 2°C compared to preindustrial temperature, Africa and Asia could see its GDP reduced by more than 4% (Banco Mundial, 2010b, p. xvii).

In a situation of an increase of more than 2°C, we will face loss of glaciers in the Andes and Himalayas, and sea rise of more than 1 meter in this century, threatening more than 60 million people and generating losses of over US$200 billion in assets in developing countries, especially leading to declining agricultural productivity in the tropics. Between 100 million and 400 million people are at risk of hunger and between 1 billion and 2 billion people will suffer from insufficient water to satisfy their basic needs (Banco Mundial, 2010b, p. xvii).

Agricultural yields in developing countries would fall drastically, mainly of wheat, corn, soybeans, and rice. Agriculture yields will suffer a drop of up to 6% in Latin America, 11% in northeastern Africa, up to 15% in sub-Saharan Africa and South Africa, and 18% in Asia. Excluding South Africa, the loss of agricultural GDP in sub-Saharan Africa would be 23% (Banco Mundial, 2010b, p. 5).

Between 2006 and 2007, low global crop production related to climatic factors aggravated the volatility of food prices and contributed to the financial crisis. In 2010, a heat wave reduced wheat production in Russia by 40%

(OXFAM, 2011, p. 38). Floods in Pakistan and Australia, and drought in Brazil, aggravate the crisis by motivating price increase (OXFAM, 2011, p. 37).

Climate change will generate inflation in food prices, a process further exacerbated by low productivity. By 2030, corn prices are estimated to increase by 86%, and prices of wheat and rice will rise by over 70%, while wheat yields will fall by 22%. In Central Africa, maize prices will be increased by 20% in 2020. In the Andean region, prices of wheat and maize will increase by 25% by 2020, and 65% in the case of corn prices by 2030. Maize productivity will fall by over 32% in sub-Saharan Africa and more than 12% in Latin America and the Caribbean (OXFAM, 2011, pp. 23, 28). All this adversely affects child nutrition. In sub-Saharan Africa, child malnutrition will increase to 8 million in 2030, and 30 million by 2050.

In Brazil, the climate crisis will cause an 18% reduction in agricultural productivity and a correlated rural poverty increase of 3.2% (Naciones Unidas, 2012, p. 110). My own country of Bolivia will suffer greater agricultural GDP losses than its neighbors Chile, Peru, and Paraguay. By 2020, the impact will be decreased to 17.8%, and in 2050 it will be 18.5% (Naciones Unidas, 2012, p. 128).

The financial resources required to cope with climate impacts through adaptation and mitigation processes are significant. The World Bank has estimated that adaptation requires between US$28 billion and US$100 billion annually if the temperature exceed 2°C. In developing countries, the costs of mitigation would be between US$145 billion and 175 billion (Banco Mundial, 2010b, pp. 23–24). Extreme events could require even higher amounts.

The impacts of climate change in Central America will cause increased vulnerability to hurricanes, storms, and extreme events in general, including the risk of extinction by 2050 of mammals, reptiles, and several species, and the disappearance of mangroves in shallow coasts due to increased sea level. The Amazon could lose 43% of species by the end of the century. Serious degradation and desertification, and increasing aridity of the soil, will affect crop areas of southern Amazonia and the Great Chaco Region, which has the second-largest biomass in South America of importance in biodiversity.[8]

Significant impacts of climate change have been observed in Latin America. Studies conducted by ECLAC and GTZ (Samaniego et al., 2009), for example, warn that in South America and the Caribbean, rainfall has decreased, particularly in southern Chile, southeastern Argentina, and southern Peru.

The expected impacts of temperature increase in the Andean region, if the temperature exceeds 2°C, would be: drastic reduction of crops (particularly affecting cereals, rice, potatoes, and soybeans); loss of approximately 1.3% of GDP, mainly due to impacts in agriculture; loss of grassland, with impacts on both livestock and meat production, which have an impact on food security; reduced rainfall from up to 50% in regions of Colombia, to 20% in Ecuador; annual loss of 30% of runoff (which will bring competition for water); drastic reduction of glaciers (affecting regions of Bolivia); loss of up to 30% of plant and animal species; and 49% of tree species. Increases superior to 3°C would lose up to 40% of the Amazon, with the risk of a process of losses of the forests, increased fire, and impact on health with vectors such as dengue and malaria (Samaniego et al., 2009). If global warming worsens, the impacts of climate change in the Andean region could result in substantial economic losses. The Andean Community of Nations (CAN) has estimated that by 2025, the Andean region could lose more than US$29.8 billion (CAN, 2008).

All of these projected impacts of climate change have certainly affected the MDGs, and will continue to negatively impact the SDGs that are part of the post-2015 agenda. Hunger, poverty, and lack of employment will be aggravated. Progress in universal primary education will have significant setbacks, with migration and displacement due to extreme climate events leading to school dropouts; disease and mortality[9] will increase; maternal health will worsen; vector-borne diseases will increase; ecosystems, water supply, basic sanitation, and the environment will be severely affected (ONU, 2010: 71).

CHALLENGES IN DEVELOPMENT COUNTRIES FOR EMISSION REDUCTION

The construction of a low-carbon economy, resulting from the implementation of current and future significant reductions in emissions, involves at least six major challenges to developing countries:

1. Continue promoting overall development and maintaining economic growth rates that are not significantly lower than those usually given in the context of high-carbon economies. This involves decoupling the carbon emissions from GDP growth. In order to achieve the decoupling of economic growth from emissions, there is a need to have adequate funding and technology development and transfer to replace fossil-based energy with renewable sources.
2. Eradicate poverty by overcoming problems emerging from decoupling emissions from economic growth, and achieve the latter in a sustainable way. Hunger and poverty must be overcome,[10] despite the drastic reduction of emissions over a short period of time.
3. Create material conditions to improve the quality of life of the population. This requires making substantial investments in the provision of livelihoods, adequate infrastructure, and services and providing for material, spiritual, cultural, human, and social needs, which are essential conditions for well-being and for living well.
4. Adapt to climate change, taking necessary and urgent actions in different sectors, including the economy, health, education, food production, and water. The costs of adaptation may represent an investment of US$28 billion to US$100 billion annually over the short term, and between US$75 billion and US$100 billion annually by 2030 (Banco Mundial, 2010b, pp. xi, 23–24).

5. Reconstruct and restore infrastructure and services affected by the impacts from extreme weather events. Losses and disasters resulting from droughts, floods, hurricanes, typhoons, landslides, and other events resulting from the impact of climate change cause significant economic costs. Some studies estimate that these costs could represent 3.2% of annual global GDP.

6. Reduce and limit emissions, which means investing in substitution of energy sources and conversion of technology, which also has a significant economic cost. The United Nations Environment Programme (UNEP) report, called "Emissions Gap," estimates that the cost of mitigation would be on average US$38 per tonne of carbon equivalent (UNEP, 2011, p. 10). This also means investing in these seven sectors: electricity, industry, transport, buildings, forests, agriculture, and waste management. These seven sectors have a potential reduction of 16 GtCO2e. Achieving substantial reductions would necessitate a significant investment— which would also be a significant burden to developing countries—as some studies estimate that 420 billion Euros annually would be required by 2020, which would increase to 864 billion Euros a year in 2030. Specific annual investments by 2030 for developing countries would constitute a heavy burden—e.g., 49 billion Euros for Latin America, 72 billion Euros for India, and 34 billion Euros for Africa (McKinsey & Company, 2010, p. 10).

MITIGATION ACTIONS: HIGH COSTS AND SIGNIFICANT EFFORTS

The holistic, interrelated approach is evident in developing mitigation actions. Developing mitigation actions in developing countries entails creating conditions of food security, education, health, universal energy access, provision of water and sanitation, provision of services and infrastructure communication, job creation, provision of housing, reconstruction resulting from loss and damage caused by extreme weather events, and adaptation actions, among others. We cannot detach mitigation, adaptation, integral development, and poverty eradication. These four elements are mutually related, and therefore require rigorous and careful planning on all those fronts, as well as sufficient and adequate provision of finance and technology.

Financing all these aspects—mitigation, adaptation, integral development, and poverty eradication—cannot be left solely, or primarily, to private investment. Additionally, financial solutions alone will not solve the climate crisis. The needs of developing countries facing the challenge of development, poverty eradication, and climate change are not going to be covered by foreign direct investment (FDI)—an approach some developed countries are proposing. Historical trends of FDI give a clear indication that its interests do not often coincide with the needs of countries it is attempting to help. FDI flows between 2005 and 2011 in South America have been focused 35% on natural resources and 36% on services; in Central America and the Caribbean, including Mexico, 54% of FDI has been concentrated in services. FDI in research and development between 2008 and 2011 in Africa—one of the continents most affected by climate change—represents 0.7% of global investment, in contrast to Latin America, which only represents 4% of the overall investment (CEPAL, 2012, pp. 135, 138).

THE WAY FORWARD: STRUCTURAL CHANGE AND A VIRTUOUS RELATIONSHIP BETWEEN HUMANS AND NATURE

The vision in which economic and social dimensions have been the focus of development has resulted in severe environmental impacts, contamination of nature, a growing ecological footprint, and a planet that is rapidly warming and can no longer sustain consumption levels escalated by ever-increasing consumerism and depletion of natural resources.

This vision must undergo a structural change. Such a transformation cannot repeat the tenets of development based primarily on promoting inclusion in global growth markets, strengthening aggregate demand, expanding production, or connecting production to high technology. Instead, there is an urgent need to build a development paradigm where social and natural conditions are in balance. This is not a matter of simply promoting a pragmatic and functional economy that measures success by accelerated and sustained economic growth; but instead, by measuring growth whereby the social/cultural and natural dimensions are integrated, and oriented toward the promotion of happiness and of living well in harmony with nature. The declaration of the Conference on Sustainable Development (Rio + 20)—called "The Future We Want"—supports this goal, in paragraph 40: "We call for holistic and integrated approaches to sustainable development that will guide humanity to live in harmony with nature and lead to efforts to restore the health and integrity of the Earth's ecosystem."

A vision of structural change based primarily on economic growth runs the risk of ignoring, or minimizing, the environmental dimension, which instead is a resource that must be managed efficiently—hence leading to the concept of "environmental efficiency." This concept is in contrast to the unsustainable view—one we must abandon—that nature is an endless, infinite source of resources that we need to use, a "natural capital" that is an instrument or input for development and growth.

This structural change involves the achievement of equality, and the strengthening of social rights. Such quality requires the distribution of wealth, and the economic and political empowerment of the poor, the excluded, and the marginalized actors. It further requires the allocation and provision of means to develop skills, full enjoyment, health and education, knowledge, and tools for strengthening communities and building cohesive and inclusive societies.

We must strive for a virtuous relationship between humans and nature, meaning a relationship that is complementary and interdependent. Growth per se does not create this virtuous relationship. In this virtuous relationship, economy is a means, and not an end in itself. Various factors, including appreciation for culture, can enhance this virtuous relationship, making it a powerful vehicle for the sustainable provision of material and spiritual means to live well.

In summary, it is not a matter of growing to meet a robust GDP, but growing in happiness, joy, and complementarity between human beings and nature. The growth of a virtuous relationship involves the harmonization, balance, restoration, and regeneration of vitalities of ecosystems and their natural energies. There is a need to take a leap beyond, so that a new vision of development guides our construction of the economic dimension, and not vice versa. Certainly we aim to grow economically, but we must also grow spiritually and culturally, using natural resources sustainably.

NOTES

1. This chapter is an abstract of an original summary of my book, reprinted with permission from my publisher. Edits, translation, and transliterations from the original Spanish, with the assistance of Dr. Judy Kuriansky, have been made to accommodate this chapter for this current volume. The original citation is: Orellana Halkyer, R. (2013). *Desarrollo con Pobreza o la Pobreza del Desarrollo.* La Paz, Bolivia: Universidad de la Cordillera-Fundación de la Cordillera (http://ucordillera.edu.bo/index.php/2013-05-14 -22-20-09/madre-tierra-y-desarrollo/finish/24-madre-tierra-y-desarrollo/117-desarrollo-con -pobreza-o-la-pobreza-del-desarrollo/0).

2. China had a population of 1.347 billion in 2011; which represents more than four times the population of the United States and two times the population of Europe in that year (UNICEF, 2013, p. 62).

3. International Hunger Index is constructed with the following variables: (1) malnutrition (ratio to the total population); (2) proportion of children who are underweight; and (3) infant mortality (death rate of children under 5 years) (JARE et al, 2013, p. 7).

4. Access to electricity is a major indicator of poverty; 1.3 billion people of the world do not have access to this service (High-Level Panel of Eminent Persons on the Post-2015 Development Agenda, 2013, p. 44).

5. These agricultural subsidies are less than those granted by developed countries to their agriculture. The total annual agricultural subsidies in developed countries since 2004 totaled US$350 billion. Since 2009, agricultural subsidies represent three times the total amount of development assistance, 0.9% of GDP in that year (United Nations, 2012b, p. 214). Agricultural subsidies in the European Union can also be understood as indirect subsidies to fossil fuels. This of course is inconsistent with its speech and global proposal to eliminate fossil fuel subsidies in developing countries.

6. The Multidimensional Poverty Index is determined based on three dimensions: health, education, and standards and lifestyles. For this purpose, 10 indicators, which include nutrition, infant mortality, years of schooling, and school attendance are used. These include health and education dimensions, which carry significant weight in the index construction. Regarding "living standards," there are considered the following indicators: fuel used for cooking, sanitation, water, electricity, and features floor housing and property (Alkire et al., 2013, p. 5).

7. Note that Bolivia is a country of 10.3 million inhabitants.

8. About the vulnerability of the Great Chaco Region, see http://ucordillera.edu.bo/index.php/2013-05-14-22-20-09/debate-mundial-sobre-desarrollo/finish/25-gran-chaco-americano-cambio-climatico/124-via-gran-chaco-americano-version-larga/0

9. The World Health Organization (WHO) has identified that climate change is responsible for 3% of deaths due to diarrhea, 3% to malaria, and 3.8% to dengue (Naciones Unidas, 2012, p. 111). Each year, 760,000 children under age 5 die from diarrhea (High-Level Panel of Eminent Persons on the Post-2015 Development Agenda, 2013, p. 43).

10. There are 121 children per 1,000 still dying in sub-Saharan Africa and 66 in South Asia. Maternal mortality is 500 per 100,000 births in sub-Saharan Africa and 190 in the Caribbean, far from the Millennium Development Goals. There are 783 million people who still lack access to drinking water by 2010, and by 2015, about 605 million will be in the same situation (see United Nations, 2012a, pp. 6, 7, 30, 52). It is also important to notice that more than 170 million people lived in poverty in Latin America and the Caribbean in 2010—i.e., 32.1% of the total population (see "La Sostenibilidad del Desarrollo en 20 años," in Naciones Unidas [2012, p. 20]). It can also be noted that 1.6 billion people lack access to electricity and about 3 billion people lack sanitation (see Banco Mundial, 2010a, p. viii).

REFERENCES

Alkire, S., Roche, J. M., & Seth, S. (2013). Multidimensional Poverty Index 2013. Oxford, UK: Oxford Poverty and Human Development Initiative, University of Oxford. Retrieved April 18, 2015, from http://www.ophi.org.uk/wp-content/uploads/Multidimensional-Poverty-Index-2013-Alkire-Roche-and-Seth.pdf

Banco Mundial. (2010a). *Desarrollo y cambio climático*. Retrieved April 18, 2015, from http://siteresources.worldbank.org/INTWDR2010/Resources/5287678-12260145279 53/Overview-Spanish.pdf

Banco Mundial. (2010b). *Informe sobre el desarrollo mundial. Panorama general. Desarrollo y cambio climático*. Washington, DC: Author.

CEPAL (2012). *Cambio estructural para la Igualdad: Una visión integrada del desarrollo*. Retrieved April 18, 2015, from http://www.eclac.org/pses34/noticias/documentos detrabajo/4/47424/2012-SES-34-Cambio_estructural.pdf

Chilosi, A. (n.d.). Poverty, population, inequality, and development: The historical perspective. *The European Journal of Comparative Economics, 7*(2), 469–501.

Comunidad Andina de Naciones (CAN). (2008). *El cambio climático no tiene fronteras: Impacto del cambio climático en la comunidad Andina*. Lima, Perú: Author.

Embajada de la India ante Colombia y Ecuador. (n.d.). Retrieved April 18, 2015, from http://www.google.com.bo/url?sa=t&rct=j&q=&esrc=s&source=web&cd=25&ved =0CHUQFjAOOAo&url=http%3A%2F%2Fwww.embajadaindia.org%2Fdocs%2F Presentacion.ppt&ei=UESQUbXXLcf64AO21YFo&usg=AFQjCNFbPL2sb1-akj9Bb 6o6xgtvh3zReA&bvm=bv.46340616,d.dmg

High-Level Panel of Eminent Persons on the Post-2015 Development Agenda. (2013). *A new global partnership: Eradicate poverty and transform economies through sustainable development*. New York, NY: United Nations Publications. Retrieved April 18, 2015, from http://www.un.org/sg/management/pdf/HLP_P2015_Report.pdf

IPCC. (2007). *Informe del grupo internacional de expertos sobre cambio climático*. Cambio Climático 2007. Informe Síntesis. (Ed. OMM-PNUMA)

JARE, IPFRI, & Concern Worldwide. (2012). *Global Hunger Index 2012*.

La Tercera, Chile. (2011, January 4). *Población en India llega a los 1.200 millones y superará a China en 2030*. Retrieved April 18, 2015, from http://diario.latercera.com/2011/04/01/01/contenido/mundo/8-64269-9-poblacion-en-india-llega-a-los-1200-millones-y-superara-a-china-en-2030.shtml

McKinsey & Company. (2010). *Impact of the financial crisis on carbon economics*. Retrieved April 18, 2015, from https://www.mckinsey.com/~/media/McKinsey/dotcom/client_service/Sustainability/cost%20curve%20PDFs/ImpactFinancialCrisisCarbonEconomics GHGcostcurveV21.ashx

Morales Ayma, E. (2012). *Informe de Gestión 2012* (Ed. Ministerio de Comunicación del Estado Plurinacional de Bolivia). Retrieved April 18, 2015, from http://comunicacion.presidencia.gob.bo/docprensa/pdf/20130124-15-33-48.pdf

Naciones Unidas. (2012). *La sostenibilidad del desarrollo a 20 años de la cumbre para la tierra: Avances, brechas y lineamientos estratégicos para América latina y el Caribe*. Summary retrieved April 18, 2015, from http://www.iadb.org/intal/intalcdi/PE/2012/11004.pdf

Orellana Halkyer, R. (2012). *Cambio climático y agenda de adaptación y mitigación*. Retrieved April 18, 2015, from https://docs.google.com/file/d/0B7_0_E1m4hKV N2I2ZDM2NTMtZDIwMi00ODBlLThkNzUtMDllZjY5MzVlNWRm/edit?pli=1

OXFAM. (2011). *Cultivar un mundo mejor: Justicia alimentaria en un mundo de recursos limitados*. Retrieved April 18, 2015, from http://www.oxfam.org/sites/www.oxfam.org/files/growing-a-better-future-010611-es_0.pdf

PNUD (Ed.). (2013). *Informe sobre desarrollo humano 2013: El ascenso del sur: Progreso humano en un mundo diverso*. Retrieved April 18, 2015, from http://www.undp.org/content/dam/undp/library/corporate/HDR/2013GlobalHDR/Spanish/HDR2013% 20Report%20Spanish.pdf

Ramonet, I. (2013). No es una crisis, es una estafa. In *Le Monde Diplomatique*, Edición.

Samaniego, J. L. (Coord.). (2009). *Cambio climático y desarrollo en América Latina y el Caribe: Una Reseña*. Santiago de Chile: ECLAC-GTZ.

State Council of China. (2013). *Quinquennial report of the Prime Minister of the State Council of China to the 12th National People's Congress of China on March 5, 2013*. Retrieved April 18, 2015, from http://m.blog.sina.com.cn/s/blog_6f3e7c200101a8j2.html

Stiglitz, J. (2010). *Caída libre: El libre mercado y el hundimiento de la economía mundial*. Bogotá, Colombia: Taurus.

United Nations. (2012a). *The Millennium Development Goals report 2012*. United Nations. Retrieved April 18, 2015, from http://www.un.org/millenniumgoals/pdf/MDG% 20Report%202012.pdf

United Nations (Ed.). (2012b). *Sustainable development 20 years on from the Earth Summit: Progress, gaps and strategic guidelines for Latin American and the Caribbean*.

UNEP (2010). *Bridging the emissions gap: A UNEP synthesis report*. Retrieved April 18, 2015, from http://www.unep.org/pdf/UNEP_bridging_gap.pdf

UNICEF. (2013). *Improving child nutrition: The achievable imperative for global progress*. Retrieved April 18, 2015, from http://www.unicef.org/media/files/nutrition_report _2013.pdf

19

Psychological Distress from Environmental Damages: An Overview and Personal Story about Getting Your Rights through Environmental Law and Claiming Damages

Andrew A. Lemmon

When the environment is endangered and people's physical and mental health are compromised by industrial or commercial activities, one way to approach the problem is through legal action. Environmental claims are becoming increasingly familiar in the legal profession, as disputes related to the environmental crises and mental health consequences increase. The field of environmental law addresses these disputes, which involve a wide range of "green" issues, including water and air quality, waste management, biodiversity, agriculture, species protection, and hazardous waste, as well as working with clients' complaints against companies whose products or operations have led to physical or mental health complaints. Recovery of financial damages for environmentally caused injuries, particularly with regard to emotional or mental health, is challenging, given environmental regulations and tolerance for the deleterious consequences of development. As with other damage claims, the process is imperfect and always looking for new reasonable criteria and rulings as more information becomes available or as injuries become more prevalent.

This chapter reviews how this interaction has developed through specific cases as well as through examples through history. The outcome of such cases is exceptionally important in present times because the likelihood of additional disputes and disagreements relating to greenhouse gases, climate change, and global warming signals that the need for environmental legal expertise especially as it relates to mental health sequelae could increase in coming years. Taking legal action of course involves factual assessment of the situation. But, peoples' emotions are invariably triggered and must be recognized and handled throughout the legal process. Therefore, this chapter further also highlights the importance of the psychological dimension regarding suits related to the environment. I am familiar with the need for this holistic approach, as I have professionally served as legal counsel in such cases. But, I have also been personally involved in such a case myself, which I present in this chapter as an example for readers of the importance of this holistic approach.

BACKGROUND

The crossroads between the environment and mental health comes in many shapes and sizes. In law, the original commonly discussed interface between these two often involves traditional questions of what constitutes "nuisance"— which refers to inconvenience that goes beyond acceptable norms—and what amount of nuisance should be tolerated or would be expected to cause injuries that need protection through the law. These cases are considered under the specialty called "tort" law. Tort law refers to a wrongful act or an infringement of a right (other than under contract) against a person or property that leads to civil legal liability. Whether or not legal action is appropriate is related to two criteria: (1) the reasonableness of the action that created the nuisance or injury and (2) the reasonableness of the alleged response. It may surprise people to know that this legal determination is as imprecise as people are different.

Many people are also surprised to find out how few foreign products, including imported food, are subject to any inspection whatsoever. It is a mammoth undertaking to perform the required inspections and, with shrinking budgets and a "starve the beast" mentality, the numbers of these inspections, and corresponding protections, are becoming fewer and fewer. Agencies have been put in a bind, owing to the strategy of the American political right that involved limiting the budgets of various agencies and then criticizing the agency for not being able to accomplish its directive and using that fact to reduce its budget even further, which ends up meaning fewer protections.

In addition, those filing complaints against companies face many hurdles. For example, when a lawsuit is filed against a company, irrespective of the merits, the frequent and almost automatic retort from industry and from its supporters— many of whom are parroting the antibusiness rhetoric from the U.S. Chamber of Commerce claim (called "lawsuit abuse") that virtually every claim against a business is made up and unfairly "bad for business"—is that industry is already regulated sufficiently.

One recent example of how this misdirection attempted to prevent a case against a company, regardless of the merit of the actual case, is the litigation surrounding the settlement of the damage claims that arose from the BP oil spill, when millions of gallons of BP's oil spilled into the Gulf of Mexico, in part because BP failed to comply with basic safety rules and regulations. The U.S. Chamber of Commerce filed a written statement in the U.S. Supreme Court on behalf of BP in the litigation (called an "amicus brief," Latin for "friend of the court," whereby a nonparty to a lawsuit can participate in the argument in which they have an interest by filing a brief with the court), claiming that the settlement that BP freely entered into was somehow unfair, illegal, and an insult to every company's ability to do business. In protest, disagreeing with this move by the U.S. Chamber of Commerce, many local Chambers of Commerce filed a response brief, in which they stated that the U.S. Chamber was not speaking for them. The final story has not been told until the Supreme Court makes a final decision and the settlement is either confirmed, amended, or destroyed, but the response filed by the local Chambers is interesting and may signal a break in the dam toward reasoned thinking, rather than automatic response.

A related issue about the interaction between environmental regulation and mental health is the false "crisis" created by overblown statements of the effect of regulation on the economy. Economist and Nobel Prize–winning op-ed columnist Paul Krugman recently wrote an article printed in the *New Orleans Times-Picayune* newspaper that cogently discussed the misnomer regarding the economic impact of environmental regulation of carbon emissions (Krugman, 2014). Krugman makes the point well that fear-mongering has created obstacles to reasonable changes in the way we manage our resources that are ideologically, rather than factually, driven to the point of an anti-intellectual bias against real science. He proposes that such propaganda has been very effective in limiting regulation, but at a cost of leaving consumers without protection on the front end and without a remedy on the back end. The problem is compounded by the lack of meaningful regulation in the manufacture and import of products—from China and other countries—or in the regulation of many local products.

Another dilemma arises in striking the balance between social, economic, and health interests. Following the commonly used phrase that "every action causes a reaction," one would expect that mental health consequences would result, which affect both the regulated and the injured from such contact. Yet, tort law asks whether these consequences are severe enough to merit compensation, thus requiring that some criteria of severity would have to be proven.

The laws of many states, including that of Louisiana where I practice, perform these balancing acts. I will focus on Louisiana law in this chapter, though the principles and points are of broad interest because the analysis is often the same. The cases below address important issues concerning the interface of mental health and the environment in this state.

CHINESE DRYWALL AFTER HURRICANE KATRINA: A VERY PERSONAL STORY OF DISTRESS AND DAMAGES

Consumer products often raise both environmental and mental health concerns. Most consumers make purchases thinking they are doing what they can to protect themselves and their families. Unfortunately, environmental and health concerns are often unknown at the time of purchase, even to a savvy consumer, and the commonly known phrases apply: "Buyer beware" and "What you don't know can't hurt you."

The media exposes many stories that products bought from certain sources or countries often contain toxins. Examples include the dangerous presence of lead paint in toys or melamine in dog food. People generally do what they can to avoid these products, but often are hamstrung by several factors, including that companies do not fully reveal dangerous components of their products and consumers are powerless to determine the origin of the component parts of every product. The problem is escalated by the fact that many sellers and resellers of products buy them because they are cheaper or more readily available. A reduced cost passed on to consumers in the public can make such a product appealing to some customers. Without the knowledge of others, manufacturers or sellers can end up cornering the market, sometimes leading to serious and deleterious outcomes.

I discovered that Chinese Manufactured Drywall is one such product. The history and other parts of the following discussion come from an opinion by Judge Fallon in the litigation called *In Re: Chinese Manufactured Drywall* (E.D. La. 2010). During approximately 2005 to 2008, hundreds of millions of square feet of gypsum wallboard manufactured in China were exported to the United States, primarily along the East Coast and Gulf South, as a result of an exceptionally high demand for building supplies in the aftermaths of Hurricanes Rita and Katrina, as well as a general new-housing boom. The Chinese drywall was then installed in newly constructed and reconstructed properties. After installation of this drywall, owners and occupants of the properties began noticing unusual odors, blackening of silver and copper items and components, and the failure of appliances, including microwaves, refrigerators, and air-conditioning units. Some people also experienced health problems, such as skin and eye irritation, respiratory issues, nosebleeds, and headaches. As a result, these property owners began filing lawsuits in both state and federal courts against those involved with Chinese drywall, including the installers, homebuilders, suppliers, importers, exporters, and manufacturers, as well as their insurers and sureties.

My own story is the crescendo of many stories from the impact of Hurricane Katrina, since nearly everyone in New Orleans has such a story, and since the mental health consequences of surviving such environmental disasters are well documented, including in chapters in this anthology. Ten feet of water inundated my home and my car, ruining my valued photos and furniture, my five-year-old son's toys, his first haircut hair and baby rattle, and the treasured great oak table given to me by my recently deceased Aunt Zoe. The flooding experience was traumatic based on three major strikes. Strike one: surely what many describe as our overly intrusive government should have protected us from the flood waters. Strike two: surely that same government is protecting us from the predators in the insurance and construction industry and making them do what they contracted to pay or do. And, Strike 3: surely that same government is protecting us from toxic building products that were shipped into the United States to fill the shortage of domestic materials.

Like many others, I was forced out of my flooded home, neighborhood, and beloved city of New Orleans. I was not only out of luck, but I was out of a substantial investment in rebuilding my home, my future, and my plan to return to the only home my son knew, in the city my family loves. For two years, we had been exiled to live out of town in a rental or with whoever would take us in. Lack of electric power to our neighborhood, and the failure of our insurance company to pay what it owed under the clear language of our policy, meant that we could not even begin to rebuild our home. And so it seemed like there was a light at the end of this dark tunnel, when, through perseverance and sweat, we were able to finally find a contractor to rebuild our flooded home—this, however, after another trauma of having one contractor steal about $25,000. As with everyone else whose home was flooded or who was impacted in other ways—as is shared by other contributors in chapters in this book—these trials and tribulations extracted a substantial emotional toll on us.

We finally moved back into our old, now repaired, home, almost two years to the day after it had been flooded when the levees broke and led to the flood. It seemed we finally realized our dream to return to our home and build our new life. Little did we know that lurking behind the walls of our home was the steady flow of various sulfur compounds, eating steadily away at our copper wires and plumbing, as well as the copper and silver components of virtually every appliance and knickknack we owned.

Fast forward three years from then, to the fact that we undertook a renovation to add new space onto what was to be this now-perfect home for our new family. Granted, as a family, we were already going through stress, which is recognized by much psychological research about the impact of life events—of planning a wedding (no matter how happy an occasion), reconstituting our family, and saving money. In the midst of this transition, both of our boys developed asthma-like symptoms whenever they were in the house. Funny, too, that our less-than-three-year-old microwave and our less-than-three-year-old dryer suddenly stopped working at about the same time as our light bulbs kept going out.

Frustration set in, as there was now no time for our perfect wedding planned for Saturday, our perfect honeymoon planned for a few days, and then returning to that perfect home we planned with the new family (i.e., my new wife, my son, and my new stepson). Instead, our dream was crushed by the fact that construction workers had to be called in. When they opened up the kitchen wall, that was the end of our dream and our dream home. As the wall opened, I swallowed my heart, as I read the phrase on the back of the drywall just removed that said, "Made in China" to "ASTM Standards."

This phrase explained everything. I knew the devastation these words meant, because for the prior three years, I had been litigating cases about Chinese drywall. The cases did not discriminate as to who was affected: laborers, doctors, lawyers, football coaches, firefighters, business people, industry leaders, psychologists, Habitat for Humanity, a U.S. congressman, and now me, who is ironically one of the members of the litigation team. The whole litigation team came for dinner at our home and doubted the irony, until we pulled back the walls and checked the wiring in the outlets. Until then, we had no idea of the invisible damage being done. With no other choice, I joined in the litigation, adding my name to all the others who filed suit against the mysterious company. This filing also led to all of the stress that comes with litigation. We had to gut our dream home, and move into an apartment, and wait.

We were emotionally devastated. As parents, we had to learn to accept our inability to protect our children, as well as to cope with our own grief over the situation, on top of the flood loss itself, stress brought on by our new marriage and two moves in six months, and now the litigation. It felt like the trifecta of life's most stressful events.

More irony and stress were in store. Looking at the labels on the drywall, we saw that our drywall was manufactured by a company called "Crescent City" Gypsum, which we at first thought was great because we live in the "Crescent City," named for New Orleans' location at the crescent in the Mississippi River. But, much to our own chagrin, it turns out that the "Crescent City" on the drywall is an Americanized name for "Taishan T'ian Tashe Dongshen" Drywall. The renaming using an English name was an obvious marketing ploy by a Chinese company to sell products in the United States.

The company turned out to be even more clever—or actually devious— because when sued in the U.S. District Court for the Eastern District of Louisiana—the same jurisdiction to which it named and arranged for the delivery of its drywall—it claimed that the U.S. courts have no jurisdiction over it, since it is a Chinese company that has no offices in or contact with the United States that would allow jurisdiction by the U.S. courts. So far, its arguments have failed, but it has now appealed to the U.S. Supreme Court, and no decision has been rendered to the date of this writing.[1]

FEAR AND FRIGHT: CASES DETERMINING EMOTIONAL DAMAGES

Louisiana law permits recovery of what is called "fear and fright" damages (not limited to environmental injuries), irrespective of physical injury, harm, or even contact, in cases where there is "the especial likelihood of genuine and serious mental distress, arising from the special circumstances, which serves as a guarantee that the claim is not spurious" (*Moresi v. State Ex Rel. Wildlife and Fisheries*, 1990). One category of cases that provides this "especial likelihood of genuine and serious mental distress" includes those cases "allowing damages for fright or nervous shock, where the petitioner was actually in great fear for his personal safety" (*Moresi v. State Ex Rel. Wildlife and Fisheries*, 1990). The "fear and fright" injuries themselves are compensable, even without a concurrent physical impact. (This principle is discussed in the case of *Beis v. Bowers* [1995], citing *Bordelon v. St. Francis Cabrini Hospital* [1994].)

Louisiana law also permits recovery for injuries sustained by individuals who are exposed to toxic substances and who develop physical or emotional symptoms. This principle is discussed in the cases of *Adams v. Marathon Oil Co.*, 1997; and *Rivera v. United Gas Pipeline Co.*, 1997. Thus, chemical exposure, without knowing the amount or duration of exposure when it begins, should be expected to evoke genuine and serious "fear and fright."

The "special circumstances" surrounding any given person's claim is inherently individual. These circumstances include: individual issues that would make a particular person susceptible of injury; the location of each individual at the time of the event; what that person heard or saw; whether they were caring for children or sick or elderly people; whether they had somewhere to go in the event of an evacuation; what information they received about the events in progress; when they received an all-clear notice; and literally hundreds of other individual inquires that might be required to determine whether a particular person's fear was reasonable under the circumstances.

In some cases, the law has developed to make more predictable claims brought in environmental suits for emotional injuries. At some points in the past, this type of recovery was limited to damages suffered during an "ordeal in progress," like the case of *Butler v. Pardue* (1982), which allowed recovery for emotional trauma suffered without physical injury by the occupant of a vehicle that was involved in an accident; and the case of *Carroll v. State Farm Insurance Co.* (1983), which allowed for mental anguish suffered during an ordeal in progress when a boat became airborne and passed directly over the person who brought the complaint. In the case of *Harper v. Illinois Central Gulf R.R.* (1987), the mental distress occurred during an ordeal in progress when people were evacuated from their homes and businesses after a train transporting chemicals overturned nearby. The U.S. Fifth Circuit Court of Appeals emphasized that in order to recover money damages for fear and mental anguish sustained in an ordeal in progress, a person must prove that "he was involved in a hazardous situation, that is, within the zone of danger—and that his fear was reasonable given the circumstances." The good news is that such a rigid formula is no longer required because those exposed are by definition in the zone of danger and expert medical testimony is used more effectively to assure that the emotional reaction is reasonable under the circumstances.

More recently, the Louisiana Fifth Circuit Court of Appeal affirmed an award of damages to the family of a woman who died a month after a mandatory evacuation due to a chemical spill. The decision in the case of *Simmons v. CTL*

Distribution (2004) was that the physical symptoms that came from her fear caused her injuries and death. The woman became anxious and nervous during the evacuation, which caused her breathing problems and trembling, which led to her being taken to the hospital, and she ultimately died. The court found that respiratory problems, such as those she suffered, would be a reasonable result from the release of molten sulfur into the neighborhood, whether the harm was actual or potential. The court applied traditional duty/risk tort principles and had no problem finding an association between the evacuation (stressor) and the plaintiff's purely emotional-based injury. The decision emphasized that regardless of what the basis for recovery is called, the injuries were the predictable result of the release, or threatened release, of toxic substances. This was an important change—in favor of those bringing cases—because until fairly recently, the primary methodology for predicting symptoms or damages was symptom-based and extrapolated from the general population, and there was little consideration given to the background experiences of the particular individuals in the exposed population.

THE ROLE OF EXPERT PSYCHIATRIC TESTIMONY

Scientific findings and expert testimony are important in these decisions and are now essential to prove emotional damages. The late Tulane Medical School professor of psychiatry neurology, Dr. Chester B. Scrignar, explained that the release of chemicals from refineries, chemical plants, or allied industries that utilize hazardous substances often pose real and understood threats to those people who live in or are present in the communities near a facility. He identified several psychiatric or emotional disorders that may develop, or be exacerbated, in individuals subjected to the exposure. He believed that beyond substance abuse disorder, the most common trauma-induced disorders are depression, acute stress disorder, post-traumatic stress disorder, specific (traumatic) phobia, generalized anxiety disorder, adjustment disorder, and various degrees of major depressive disorders. Also, according to more recent research, depression may be re-associated with the death of a loved one in the context of the trauma. Thus, grief reactions are often caused by triggers such as subsequent traumatic events, including an industrial accident endangering those living near or working in the plant. Each of these disorders can result from exposure that is acute or dramatic, periodic and expectant, or gradual and insidious.

Psychological reactions to "fear and fright" affect the mind of individuals. Exposure constitutes a trauma and is measured by applying what Scrignar referred to as the "Traumatic Principle," which in part states:

> Any environmental stimulus, which poses a realistic threat to life or limb, if perceived by one, or more likely a combination of the five sensory pathways to the

brain, and cognitively interpreted as dangerous (a serious threat to life or physical integrity to self or others), whether it produces physical injury or not, can be regarded as a traumatic event which can precipitate a mental disorder in a vulnerable individual who is in the zone of danger.[2]

Some individuals may meet the criteria that they suffer from one of several mental disorders after exposure to toxic substances, according to the *Diagnostic and Statistical Manual of Mental Disorders*, 5th edition.[3] These injuries would be expected from a certain trauma and are therefore eligible for compensation under Louisiana law. Further, they are distinguished from what is called "fear of future disease," which may certainly feel real, but that falls under a different standard in Louisiana law (as stated in the case of *Bonnette, et al. v. Conoco, Inc., et al.*, 2003).

The Value of Psychological Testimony

Besides the above example, expert psychological testimony assists the court by explaining the process by which a person may be evaluated clinically for a psychological injury and what that person might be expected to have experienced. Regardless of whether the expert (or the court) contemporaneously evaluated any particular person, the methodology would be the same and the conclusions would be scientifically and legally based. The reasonable expectation of injury would usually be proven with expert testimony from a mental health professional. While mental health professionals are well equipped to diagnose a particular complaint, and relate it to a particular event, it is much more difficult to take an event and project the expected mental anguish reaction, particularly in light of the different backgrounds of the people in an exposed population. As information becomes more easily manipulated, however, it is much easier to particularize a damage award for individuals, even when resolving a large number of claims.

Dr. Scrignar testified frequently in Louisiana cases on the "fear and fright" issues relevant to the injuries sustained by people who either did or did not experience physical symptoms.[4] In court proceedings, he was allowed to give his opinion regarding expected and reported psychological responses to exposure to chemicals as proof of general causation, even if he did not treat a particular patient. It was often important that at the onset of the exposure, the person did not know to which chemical they were exposed, or the amount of the chemical to which they were exposed. Dr. Scrignar would then consider the person's report about his or her suffered physical and emotional response and determine its reliability based on whether, given the facts presented, people in general can experience the complained of mental disorders with or without suffering physical injury. Then, while recognizing that some individuals are more prone to these psychiatric reactions depending on their predispositions, anatomical makeup, proximity to chemical plants, and physical sensibilities, he would also give his opinion on whether the particular complaint and stimulus can be generally connected to this case in consideration.

Dr. Scrignar's professional psychiatric testimony assisted the courts to determine the credibility of the claim. The first step was to establish that there were recognizable injuries as described above, in order to assure that the claims are not spurious. Then, this general causation is combined with the testimony of the injured party to determine if that specific person's complaints fit within the realm of reasonable injuries or symptoms and to determine whether that plaintiff is being truthful. The testimony of each individual is then evaluated by the court for its credibility and then to decide on the damages, if appropriate.

A Technique to Decide on Credibility and Damages in Claims: Contributions of a Famous Psychologist

One methodology to decide on a plaintiff's credibility and then decide on damages was developed and used by a well-respected psychologist, Dr. Charles Figley, who is an expert in trauma and who often provides court testimony. Figley, a resident of New Orleans since 2008, is the Distinguished Chair in Disaster Mental Health and Graduate School of Social Work professor at Tulane University in Louisiana. Also the founder of the Green Cross Academy of Traumatology that provides trauma services after disasters, he was awarded the National Organization for Victim's Assistance's (NOVA) highest honor to a researcher. The technique, called "victim profiling," is guided by the theory of human development. In a book, which was reviewed by the Editorial Board of the Psychosocial Stress Book Series, Figley identified a profile of behavioral symptoms associated with combat stress injury that would predict operational (combat) stress injuries. He used that research to develop a profile of behavioral symptoms associated with exposure to the events at the facility involved in a case I worked with him on.

The model of human development Figley used accounted for the victim's resilience, self-care, level of thriving, and orientation to learning, an approach that has been used as part of the assessment of victims of traumatic events for more than 30 years. Indeed, this approach is the basis for the diagnosis of post-traumatic stress disorder (PTSD) that Figley helped define, in the process of developing the diagnostic criteria of disorders outlined in the third edition of the American Psychiatric Association's *Diagnostic and Statistical Manual* (DSM-III), an edition published in 1980 and peer-reviewed. Thus, what emerged over the years is a profile of victims who are at risk of mental illness. Figley then used the profile to predict what might happen in that particular situation. Another confirmatory application is demonstrated in a study published in *The Journal of Nervous and Mental Disease* (Boscarino & Figley, 2009), which utilized a large data set of military veterans suffering from PTSD to make determinations of the impact of traits on mortality.

Figley was engaged to help me in a case evaluating whether a particular plaintiff suffered a particular injury. The behavioral symptoms profile he developed was helpful to the court. As mentioned above, those behavioral traits had to be accompanied by credible testimony from the individual bringing the case, in order for that individual to recover damages. Using this methodology, Figley was able to predict what the stimulus "may cause," when referring to the particular injuries alleged. If he concluded that a particular plaintiff was injured, without hearing the testimony or interviewing that person while the symptoms existed, Figley might rightly be accused of overreaching.

Figley's opinion allowed the court to anticipate several exposure scenarios that would have been expected to arise during the trial testimony, because not every situation would apply to every person. For example, not every person exposed to a trauma would suffer from reawakened feelings associated to the earlier traumatic events—a symptom that is part of post-traumatic stress syndrome. To the extent that a given situation did not apply to a particular person, it was not part of the opinion, or the calculation of the damage to that person. But, it would have been in error to discount a particular confounding factor that might be expected to apply to a certain percentage of the population, since each person's testimony involved specific circumstances and history.

THE TRAGEDY OF THE BP OIL SPILL

The BP Oil Spill litigation that began with the largest oil spill in human history on April 20, 2010, illustrates several angles to the regulation conundrum. The company Transocean was in the process of completing a drilling well for BP from its Deepwater Horizon MODU (Mobile Offshore Drilling Unit) vessel, when the well blew out and spilled 4.9 million barrels of crude oil into the Gulf of Mexico. This resulted in an environmental catastrophe of epic proportions, the effects of which will not be known for many years, if ever, due to a multiplication of the butterfly effect.

Because BP was totally unprepared for an event of this magnitude, everyone with an idea leapt into action. BP even opened up a hotline to the public to offer ideas. The actor Kevin Costner proposed a suction barge; the Netherlands offered the use of ships to extract the oil; and people proposed giant sponges. Thousands of engineers from various companies and specialties were deployed to Houston to come up with a solution to a problem that had never before been contemplated—an oil spill from a deep-water well. Eventually, four attempts were made to "kill" the well (i.e., to plug it up, to stem the spillage) and a relief well was in the process of being drilled in case all other ideas failed. In simple terms, efforts were made to try to kill the well in several ways: with a junk shot by shooting golf balls and other debris into the opening to clog it up; with a top hat to cover the opening of the well and close off its pressure; and by a cofferdam that would create a temporary enclosure to allow the enclosed areas to be pumped out. Eventually the release was stopped, after 87 days of near-free flow of oil into the Gulf.

The Case of the BP Spill: A Possible Step Backward for Emotional Damages

As a result of the oil spill, thousands of people lost their jobs and ways of life, many of whom were just recovering from the devastation of Hurricanes Katrina and Rita in the region. Even before the well was killed, or before the damage to the ecosystem, the economy, and peoples' physical and mental health were assessed, the question of blame was being considered by the government and by citizens, and the question of avoiding liability was being considered by BP. Several BP employees have been investigated or charged with misdirecting the investigation, deleting important information, and outright lying to the authorities and the public. The mental process that led to these distortions will be studied for many years. The mental health of the exposed population will also be valuable fodder for study, particularly when the damage model memorialized in the settlements includes personal injuries without adequate consideration of mental anguish.

Eventually, the case against BP for the oil spill was settled—at least that is what BP told the federal court presiding over the case. Perhaps this statement was made to stop the litigation from proceeding to trial; perhaps they thought it was truly settled; perhaps BP tried to manipulate the system. But, BP is now challenging its own settlement. The part of the settlement that BP does not challenge, however, is the fact that it does not compensate emotional damages. Although mental anguish as an item of damage in environmental litigation is well established and limited to that which would be reasonably expected from a particular insult or exposure, the BP case represents a departure from complete compensation. In fact, noted Washington-based attorney Kenneth Feinberg, who specializes in mediation and alternative dispute resolution and who famously handled the victim assistance funds established in the wake of the 9/11 terrorist attacks and the 2013 Boston Marathon bombings, was hired by BP to administer a $20 billion fund for oil spill claimants. Feinberg testified to Congress that: "If you start compensating purely mental anguish without a physical injury—anxiety, stress—we'll be getting millions of claims from people watching television." He continued, "You have to draw the line somewhere. I think it would be highly unlikely that we would compensate mental damage, alleged damage, without a signature physical injury as well" (Chavkin, 2010). That thinking carried forth into the actual final settlement of the medical claims. Thus, the medical settlement does not include mental harm or anguish as a "specified physical condition" for which a claimant can receive financial compensation. In order to receive compensation for mental anguish, a claimant would have to file suit against BP and prove causation.

Still, although the Medical Benefits Class Action Settlement Agreement excludes recovery for emotional or mental harm or anguish, it does include several provisions that attempt to address the issue in the form of grant money. The grants, which are intended to cover a minimum of five years of services, include $36 million to address behavioral and mental health needs, expertise, capacity, and literacy in the Gulf Coast communities of Louisiana, Mississippi, Alabama, and the Florida Panhandle. The settlement recognizes that "there are significant mental and behavioral health needs directly attributable to the Deepwater Horizon oil spill" and sets out to build mental and behavioral health treatment capacity and literacy to help the communities prepare for future man-made and natural disasters. Therefore, in addition to the $36 million, $4 million will be used to train community health workers, and another $15 million will be used to expand environmental health and literacy. The mental health problems in the aftermath of this environmental crisis persist, and are discussed in several articles (Juhasz, 2012; National Alliance on Mental Illness, 2010; Schleifstein, 2012; Shern, 2010).

Increased Public Inclination to Legal Action

Despite valiant efforts by the U.S. Congress, as well as by state legislatures to protect the citizenry, toxic exposure and injury has not been adequately controlled or interdicted by statute, regulation, the common law, or industry self-regulation.[5] As a result, citizens have been forced to rely on the tort system to supplement other statutes to help protect their health and safety.[6] With increasing education and affluence, society has become more aware, and less tolerant, of the diminishing quality of our mental and physical health and of the environment—and therefore, more willing to take legal action. Additionally, news reports of chemical waste disposal indelibly imprint the cost of industrialization to society in the minds of citizens. Society has begun to understand that monitoring consumption and industrial development is an important prophylactic in the prevention of potentially severe consequences (Shapo, 1984, at 5-45–5-57; see also Bowler, 1993; Gore, 1992).[7] Many people also now believe that courts are at least as qualified as regulatory agencies to determine appropriate levels of risk to which citizens may be exposed (Shapo, 1984, at 10-189). Similarly, they recognize that traditional common law remedies alone are inadequate to completely address and remedy the problems generated by hazardous waste and industrial activity (Senate Committee on Environment and Public Works, 1980; see also Holtzinger, 1982).

Determination of Who Is Responsible for Injury

Legal responsibility for damages or injuries that are caused by activities of others, like in the cases discussed above, are rooted in traditional notions of fault that the person who is in the best position to control the activity or its consequences, or the person who most benefits from the activity, should bear responsibility. This favors victims, as it dictates that the costs or consequences should not be externalized to the victim. Across civil and common law jurisdictions, responsibility for damages can either be based on negligence or fault-based (establishing who did something wrong), or based on the principle of "strict liability," which is more activity-based. Of the tort remedies available for toxic waste personal injuries, only strict liability serves the tort system's functions of compensation and deterrence (Weiner, 1986).

The celebrated case of *Rylands v. Fletcher* (1865) is often credited as the origin of determining strict liability (i.e., who is responsible) for dangerous activities that injure the person, or the property of someone. However, this concept has been around for many centuries. Even before the law distinguished between injuries caused as a tort and those that are now considered criminal, strict liability for injuries to persons and property was often the rule (see Harris, 1932). The doer of an act was required to reimburse an injured party for any damage he caused, in the interest of peace and proper justice, regardless of whether he acted innocently or inadvertently (Harris, 1932; see also Salmond, 1928).[8] In this way, strict liability helped to preserve the peace and compensate the parties who were injured as a result of the conduct of others.

The law of torts developed out of criminal law into and through two theories: (1) the defendant is liable only if he intended the harm or failed to take reasonable steps to avoid causing the harm, commonly thought of as negligence; or (2) the defendant is prima facie liable for harm caused, regardless of intent or precautions he takes, commonly thought of as strict liability (Epstein, 1980).

Strict liability has been the dominant and preferred method for apportioning liability throughout most of history (Wigmore, 1894). As far back as the fourteenth and fifteenth centuries, there has been some recognition of the idea that an individual who injures another, especially his property, should be liable for the harm caused (Wigmore, 1894). Such liability was usually justified to "preserve the peace" (Burdick, 1926). Liability was imposed as a vengeance on the doer of an activity that caused harm with the intention of "buying off" a feud (Burdick, 1926, p. 10). Justice of this sort was based on the moral principle of "oughtness" (Harper, James, & Gray, 1926) (what ought to happen) and responsibility or fault is found in the unreasonable interference with a person's use and enjoyment of his property (Keeton, 1959b).[9]

Strict liability did not enjoy complete and immediate acceptance (in name) in the courts because of a reluctance to impose liability on someone who could not be found "at fault" (Prosser, 1959).[10] In many early cases, the courts discussed the terms "fault" and "negligence", but those terms were used in the strict liability context, not as they are understood today (Prosser et al., 1984, Sec. 78, p. 181).[11] Fault and negligence were merely part of the simple analysis performed by the courts of the time to achieve corrective justice by imputing fault to the visible source that set the harm in motion (see Harris, 1932, p. 345).[12]

MORALITY REQUIRES FAULT AS A PREREQUISITE TO LIABILITY

In the later part of the nineteenth and the beginning of the twentieth centuries, common notions of fairness began to change, and negligence became the preferred method to allocate liability among actors.[13] The shift to negligence from strict liability was associated with the rapid industrialization and growth during that period and the perceived necessity to externalize the costs of industrialization commensurate with the benefits of industrialization shared by society (Posner, 1986, pp. 235–236).[14] The shift was also a moral or business preference that no one should be subject to liability without some degree of specific "fault" or mistake on his part (Posner, 1986). The desire to protect burgeoning industries, and to maintain their growth, undoubtedly influenced the morals of the day,[15] much like the U.S. Chamber of Commerce today has successfully interjected itself into discussions of liability and regulation, to protect business interests and to prevent reasonable regulation, responsibility, and liability. Strict liability was deemed by some at the time to be an interference with expanding civilization. Nevertheless, even during that period, cases of strict liability were being decided in favor of some injured parties (Harris, 1932, p. 330; Isaacs, 1917).

Use of the concept of "fault" as a requirement for imposing liability has equitable appeal, particularly in an unstable economic environment. Stemming from industry's argument that strict liability inhibits expansion of business and results in job loss—especially for novel industries and in relation to the drive for industrial expansion in the late nineteenth and early twentieth centuries (and today)—it is easy to understand how negligence based on specific fault could supplant strict liability in the law of torts. Business and industry groups bargained to maintain the correlation between accountability and compensation favorable to their interests, rather than according to the risk created by their activities (Gaskins, 1989).

Since strict liability was often referred to as "liability without fault," it was an easy target. The phrase "liability without fault" probably originated in an article by noted U.S. Supreme Court justice Oliver Wendell Holmes (Gaskins, 1989, referring to Holmes, 1873).[16] But, Holmes also believed that American law had always required some showing of fault before liability would attach (Holmes, 1881). American legal scholar and law professor William L. Prosser, often called the "father of tort law," also opined that some form of fault has always been required, at least to the same extent that fault is required in negligence.[17] However, the articulation of a specific fault requirement did not mature until required by the exigencies of industrialization. Negligence thus became the preferred method to compensate victims and distribute harm.

The preference for a fault requirement before imposing liability was first expressed in the case of *Brown v. Kendall* (1850).[18] *Brown* and its progeny began to demonstrate the new social order that whether the defendant was culpable or blameworthy in causing the injury was a product of the religious concept that no man should be forced to make good for harm that he innocently caused (see Harris, 1932, p. 352).[19]

The issue in using fault to determine liability may really relate to how "fault" is defined. Fault is not the same as blame-worthiness; rather, it is a societal judgment of compliance with the appropriate standards of conduct. The meaning of the term "fault" often becomes lost in the circular reasoning that "if a person is not liable without fault, if he is liable, then there is fault" (Prosser et al., 1984, Sec. 75, p. 536). This fault concept is also often rationalized and explained through the concept of "conditional fault" (Keeton, 1959a). An actor "is not regarded as at fault unless or until his conduct causes some harm to others, but he is then at fault, and to be held responsible" (Prosser et al., 1984, Sec. 75, p. 535).

Such an interpretation assures that conduct is considered legitimate for purposes of injunctive relief, but the actor is, nevertheless, liable for damages should they arise. Fortunately, strict liability does not concern itself with such semantic acrobatics. It has progressed beyond repugnance of the maxim of "no liability without fault" to specifically define certain instances where an actor may be liable regardless of moral wrongdoing, deviation from social norms, or reasonable standards of care. Liability is imposed by placing a value on the activity and recognizing that the enterprise, while it will be tolerated, must pay its own way for the damage it may cause (Prosser et al., 1984, Sec. 75, p. 536).

PAY FOR THE HARM YOU CREATE!

Society has come to relate industrial risks as "inseparable accompaniments and expenses of industrial enterprises" (Prosser et al, 1984 '75, p. 342)[20] and has imposed liability because it has determined that "the social consequences of uncompensated loss are far greater than the amount of the loss itself" (Harper et al., 1986, pp. 195–196; see also James, 1946). Following the determination by society that the injury should be compensated, the courts will begin to extend strict liability to new activities through the common law (White, 1980, p. 109). The person is then required to pay all damages reasonably resulting from his activity, even if the harm is unavoidable. To say otherwise would make innocent victims bear the cost of all nonnegligent consequences of the activity.

Current morals hold that "the basis of liability . . . is the intentional behavior in exposing the community to the abnormal risk."[21]

The principles that pass costs onto a party who caused the harm evolved from a sense of justice that requires parties who create very great risks to compensate those who are injured within the community as a result of those activities (Shapo, 1984, pp. 5–52). The courts that extend the principle of strict liability based on the relative positions of the parties have taken a pragmatic approach in determining when private freedom to conduct an activity must yield to an individual's right not to be placed in abnormal jeopardy (Huber, 1988, pp. 64–65).

The first principle involves imposing strict liability on nonnegligent actors who injure others to force internalization of all costs of the activity. The proper functioning of the free market demands that an injuring party pay all costs of its activity. Secondly, policies of social engineering and social expediency allocate the probable or inevitable loss to the party best able to shoulder the loss in pursuit of the least hardship to any individual. It further attempts to reduce the overall risk of harm to the community.[22]

When the loss is deemed worth compensating, the industry or individual who caused harm should incorporate and distribute the risk into its balance sheet as a cost of doing business regardless of the precautions it took to prevent the injury. Compassion and the desire that an innocently injured party not go uncompensated also play a role in the push toward strict liability (Galligan, 1992, p. 362). The decision maker and society would generally be sympathetic to an unwittingly injured person and hold the person liable who is best identified as causing the injury.

The case for a sympathetic decision-maker is strongest when the injured person is essentially innocent of any fault (see Jones, 1992). As is often the case, that person has not done anything besides being in the wrong place at the wrong time. Between two "innocent" parties, the person who controls the instrumental of harm should bear its risks.[23] Even when the activity that causes the harm is socially desirable, the entity that controls the activity should pay its own way (see City Services Co. v. State, 1975). Economic fairness would place the burden on the party who creates and profits from the activity.

The law recognizes that when it comes to two "innocent" parties, the risk should fall on the one who created the harm (see McLane v. Northwest Natural Gas Co., 1970). Once it is proved that one party caused the harm, it is presumed that this party is liable for the harm "because proof of the non-reciprocal source of the harm is sufficient to upset the balance where one person must win and the other must lose" (Epstein, 1980, p. 28). The harm creates a moral or ethical obligation against the injuring party to compensate the injured party for the harm, a situation that is sometimes called "ethical compensation" (Epstein, 1980; see also Williams, 1951).

With any system of compensation based completely on fault, some injured parties remain uncompensated, regardless of who can best bear the loss

(Committee for Economic Development, 1989; see also Harper et al., 1986, p. 195). To prevent this unjust result, legal rules have evolved through statutory enactments and judicial decisions to expand compensation, spread the risk, and force internalization of the full costs of an activity by the individual best able to shoulder its costs or prevent the injury (see *Bridgeton v. British Petroleum Oil, Inc.*, 1976; Huber, 1988; *Kenny v. Scientific, Inc.*, 1985).

SPREADING THE RISK TO SOCIETY

As has been pointed out in this chapter so far, in environmental law and assignment of liability, the best interests of individuals is balanced against the best interests of society and the interests of business. All are taken into account according to different procedures and principles. For example, the party who controls the activity is also in the best position to spread the risk of its miscarriage, since its liability is tempered by the understanding that the price of its goods or services will reflect its liability to society (Prosser et al., 1984, Sec. 75, p. 537). The business can distribute the costs of the hazards of production or operation to the broadest segment of society through increased prices.[24] This system of distribution accomplishes two socially desirable benefits: "(1) the adverse impact of any particular misfortune is lessened by spreading its cost over a greater population and over a longer time period, and (2) social and economic resources can be more efficiently allocated when the actual costs of goods and services (including the losses they entail) are reflected in the price to the consumer" (*Chavez v. Southern Pacific Transportation Co.*, 1976). Since all of society benefits from the loss producing conduct due to the utility of the conduct, the spread of the risk to all of society is also appropriate and efficient.

Spreading the risk through strict liability is efficient because "it is less costly for many people to contribute small amounts to offset the loss than for the individual victim to bear it all: (and) . . . it reduces the costs in human suffering and decreased productivity following an accident" (Weiner, 1986, p. 1613). Otherwise, innocent and often defenseless victims rather than the instigator of the harm producing conduct would be forced to internalize the entire cost of the injury and the defendant would neither internalize the real cost of its conduct nor spread the loss (Weiner, 1986, p. 1614).

INCENTIVES FOR SAFETY AND PROTECTION

Another important goal of any liability scheme is to provide an incentive to make the activity as safe as reasonably possible. The potential for strict liability encourages potential defendants to minimize costs by avoiding or deterring the accident in the first place (Calabrisi, 1970). Casting the party who injures another in judgment for the injury encourages that party to avoid injury to the full extent it is practicable.

A stringent liability scheme is used to encourage prudent companies to conduct their activities in as safe a manner as possible, but it should be recognized that even liability may not be enough to prevent injuries. This policy requires more sophisticated defendant-operator of the activity to determine how best to prevent damages over which it maintains complete control (see Galligan, 1992, p. 344). Strict liability gives the defendant incentive "to experiment with methods of preventing accidents ... (by) relocating, changing, or reducing (perhaps to the vanishing point) the activity giving rise to the accident" (*Indiana Harbor Belt Railroad Co. v. American Cyanamid Co.*, 1990). The attention paid by potential defendants to the imposition of strict liability demonstrates that the policy of strict liability is successful in forcing companies to careful evaluate their safety policies (cf. Cunningham, 1992). "The main goal of the tort system, then, is future control to discourage accident-producing conduct" (Gaskins, 1989, p. 37)[25]

The appeal of strict liability to protect people from dangerous activities controlled by others is heightened for new or untested enterprises and for those where the risk of harm is present regardless of the precautions taken to prevent injury (Morris, 1952). Often, these same new industries contend that strict liability (or any liability) prevents them from succeeding (Posner, 1986).[26] However, in contrast to this argument posed by industry, liability is not intended to prevent activities of new industries from succeeding, but only to encourage them to be conducted safely and to compensate innocent victims who are injured by their activities. In other words, the unknowing public should not be used as guinea pigs in the defendant's lab.[27] Under the present Restatement formulation of strict liability, the benefits and deterrents to the industry and to the public are specifically allowed to be considered.[28] Although the fears of unreasonable regulation is often a created crisis to prevent regulation, to the extent that the concern is real (rather than spurious), it can cause stress, anxiety, or other mental health consequences to the owners, operators, or employees of these industries. Unfortunately, there is no required analysis to determine whether the concerns are real or created to avoid reasonable regulation.

THE CHALLENGES OF ENFORCEMENT

The application of state tort principles to environmental injuries inevitably overlaps with enforcement of regulatory environmental statutes. Some courts have even borrowed principles from legislation intended for remedial purposes to raise presumptions or draw conclusions pertinent to tort liability (see Harris, 1932, p. 338). In the case of *T & E Industries v. Safety Light Corporation* (1991), the New Jersey court fashioned a tort remedy using the principles and language of the regulatory law created to address toxic waste sites called the Comprehensive Environmental Response, Compensation, and Liability Act (commonly referred to as "CERCLA"). The court ruled in favor of the defendant, based on the placement of the company's site on the National Priorities List and the risk of cancer associated with the company's former activities at the site.[29] Essentially, it was decided that the dangers created by the company's site subjected the defendant to both statutory regulations and common law strict tort liability to assure protection of the people.

Many jurisdictions have struck their own balance and determined that the risks of personal and emotional injuries associated with hazardous materials are best distributed through strict liability.[30] The intellectually similar policies served by remedial statutes and by common law tort recovery for toxic personal injuries allocate the externalities caused by toxic release to the party creating the danger. The actor creating the danger is thereby required to more fully internalize the costs of conducting its business.[31] The addition of a strict tort liability remedy helps to assure proper compensation for plaintiffs, despite procedural and damage limitations that might have otherwise limited their recovery of damages.[32]

THREATS IN SOCIETY TODAY OF EXPOSURE TO HAZARDOUS WASTE

Modern science continually provides us with new products and new chemicals. From the already existing mass of organic and inorganic substances, there are approximately 10,000 new substances synthesized in chemical laboratories each year (Lee & Lindahl, Sec. 28.01, 1991; Nothstein, 1984, 1.01).[33] Approximately 1,000 of this group enter commerce each year (Carlin, 1992) and many other substances will be disposed into the environment. One hazardous waste remediation company has identified over 100,000 different hazardous wastes that have been discharged into our environment (Hazardous Waste Action Coalition, 1991). In addition to the impression created by the sheer number of substances entering the environment, the general public is now becoming aware of, and concerned with, how the existence and combination of these chemicals affects their health and environment.

Fears of the public in the face of an increasing amount of environmental hazards were fueled by a 1980 congressional study that estimated the existence of approximately 30,000 to 50,000 hazardous waste sites in the United States, many of which were improperly managed (Fred C. Hart Assoc., 1979).[34] The study further showed that merely 10% of the then-current annual waste of 77.1 billion pounds of hazardous waste was being safely disposed (Fred C. Hart Assoc., 1979). The proliferation of chemical production and the urbanization and expansion of the population has also increased the number of individuals who are exposed to chemicals. The dangers from a particular exposure are further complicated by synergistic reactions among these chemicals and reactions with other available substances (Huber, 1988).[35] In our concentrated and complex society, the interaction and exposure among peoples and products multiply, and protection from hazardous activities and production becomes that much more imperative (Harris, 1932, p. 343).

Modern technology has complemented this proliferation of chemical substances with a corresponding sophistication of mechanisms and instruments to measure even the most minute levels of exposure. Forensic experts can use the information generated by these instruments to extrapolate to the number of deaths per exposed population. The conclusions drawn from these figures and statistics help to prove causation of injuries by an increasing number of substances and activities. The resulting information provides real but frightening clues into formerly mysterious diseases and blurs previous distinctions between what were considered minor annoyances and grave risks (Huber, 1988, p. 65).

The net result of these technological developments and the expansion of the awareness of environmental issues has been an expansion of tort liability against those who control hazardous substances, particularly in the form of strict liability (Huber, 1988, p. 65). Success of toxic personal injury suits is also related to the average citizen's expectation that hazardous substances will be kept under tight control (Gaskins, 1989, p. 35). With more hazardous substances and greater danger from their escape, manufacturers and those who control hazardous substances are held to a higher standard of care for the general public.

CONCLUSION

The cases involving environmental issues that are discussed in this chapter, and the historical background of the legal issues, show that even after many years of painful development to recognize mental health injuries as legitimate and even under careful scrutiny, courts—and society—continue to struggle with how to recognize and compensate such injuries. We are left with several dilemmas. One dilemma involves the temptation for people to make claims about "television"-type injuries—that imply frivolous or spurious complaints—that open the floodgates to all comers. Another dilemma is whether the courts are capable of conducting an analysis of claims involving the environment, making awards when claims are legitimate and insuring appropriate safeguards to prevent spurious legal suits. The development of the law would suggest that, indeed, the legal field is increasingly capable of making that determination and insuring the protection of both the environment and the public. Despite the naysayers, emotional injuries to people from environmental crises must be expected, and protected, in this increasingly complex, industrialized, and globalized society.

NOTES

1. The last word spoken to date was by the U.S. Fifth Circuit Court of Appeals, which found jurisdiction in the U.S. courts. In Re: Chinese Manufactured Drywall Products Liability Litigation, No. 12-31213 (5th Cir. 5/20/2014).

2. R., V.7, 1606 lines 21–32.

3. R., V.7, 1608 lines 3–9.

4. R. V. 7, 5, line 20–page 11, line 19.

5. Congress considered and rejected a strict liability cause of action for personal injuries during the initial passage of CERCLA, but the cause of action was removed from the final version of the bill. See S. 1480, 96th Cong., 2d sess., Sec. 4(a) (1980).

6. Private remedies for toxic personal injuries are not generally provided under federal laws, nor can private remedies be implied from federal environmental laws (*Middlesex County Sewerage Authority v. National Sea Clammers Association*, 1981). See also Shapo (1984).

7. The National Cancer Institute now estimates that between 60% and 90% of cancers in the United States are caused by environmental contaminants (Shapo, 1984, Toxic Torts)

8. Nevertheless, early tort theorists wrote of "mens rea" in tort law, but with a narrower application than in criminal law.

9. This terminology sounds very similar to nuisance requirements. Indeed, there are many scholars who believe that there is substantial overlap between strict liability and nuisance, and that those jurisdictions that refuse to apply strict liability by name often apply the principle covertly through the concept of nuisance (Prosser et al., 1984, Sec. 78).

10. Strict liability is sometimes regarded as a primitive and amoral system of liability used primarily today as vestiges with no place in modern jurisprudence. See Ames (1908).

11. The use of these concepts was likely based on a "naive approach to juristic problem solving rather than a profound attempt at social engineering."

12. Likewise, when the common sense of justice and fairness began to perceive that strict liability was unfair or unreasonably impeded progress, liability schemes evolved to negligence.

13. The phenomena of the evolution of law is often a product of changing social conditions and corresponding changes in community morals (Pound, 1923). "Legislative enactments (and often courts) make articulate the social pressures which necessitate changes in the scope and direction of these standards" (Harris, 1932, p. 342; see also Epstein, 1980). "Until the last quarter of the 19th Century, there was a strong current of opinion (that) one was liable for injury done to the person of another by his lawful acts, though tainted with no negligence" (Harris, 1932, p. 346).

14. The use of negligence rather than the old system of strict liability was seen as a well-spent "subsidy" to encourage the activity. Essentially, an injured party was forced to subsidize the growth of the industry on his own to facilitate entrepreneurial activity. See also Horwitz (1977).

15. Indeed, there were many cases in which the landowners were held to a different standard of liability under the auspices of promoting economic growth. See Prosser et al. (1984, 549, fn. 55).

16. Holmes even believed that vengeance required fault or blameworthiness by citing to the law of trespass which refused to impose liability for those harms which were foreseen but not an intentional consequence of the defendant's act. See Burdick (1926, p. 10).

17. He believed that the issue of whether fault was required was a matter of how "fault" is defined. Even negligence did not mean "fault" in the sense of culpability or moral blame. Negligence is a "failure to live up to an ideal standard of conduct beyond the knowledge or capacity of an individual, in an honest error of judgment, and in acts which

are normal and usual in the community and without moral reproach in its eyes." Even legal fault, as defined today is a "deviation from social standards of conduct which will not be permitted with immunity; and in this sense it seems clear that the activity of the defendant who creates an abnormal, excessive, and inappropriate risk to his neighbor, if it is not to be called fault, is at least the same thing by another name. It is for such reasons that . . . have jettisoned the word 'fault,' and speak instead of 'strict' or 'absolute' liability" (Prosser, 1959). Additionally, the meaning of fault has been obfuscated through the concept of "reasonable person." Is a superior actor any less at fault if he acted in accord with what a reasonable person would do, but fell short of his own personal ability of care and judgment and injured an innocent party? See Laflar, 1952.

18. The court stated that, "the plaintiff must come prepared with evidence to show either that the intention was unlawful, or that the defendant was in fault." Id. See Harris (1932, at footnote 42) for the "sizeable line of cases" during that period of realignment to adopt that same position from both the United States and Great Britain. For a discussion of the various views of the actual historical development of fault, see Isaacs (1917).

19. The Church was very influential in bringing about this moral transformation and requiring intention and fault for an actionable wrong (Burdick, 1926). The realities and practicalities of specific cases led to deviations from the basic considerations of fault requirements. Additionally, the law lagged behind public morals to some extent, blurring the actual developmental periods of fault law. See Winfield (1926).

20. By 1941, Prosser was questioning whether fault was of any value whatsoever in such risk allocation. Once liability was divorced from moral blameworthiness, the question of fault seemed superfluous See White (1980).

21. 74 Am. Jur. 2d Torts Sec. 14 (1974).

22. "Strict liability theory proposed to conduct the interest balancing altogether unburdened by notions of fault." See White (1980, p. 109).

23. Restatement (2d) of Torts Sec. 519, comment d (1977).

24. Strict liability distributes the risk to the party best able to "administer the loss so that it will ultimately be borne by the public" (*Smith v. Lockheed Propulsion Co.*, 1967).

25. "The traditional and foremost policy of the tort law is to deter harmful conduct and to ensure that innocent victims of that conduct will have redress" (*Elam v. Alcolac, Inc.*, 1988).

26. See also Galligan (1992), wherein the author argues that fears such as this are based on a misunderstanding of what strict liability actually means.

27. This argument has a renewed emotional appeal in light of recent discoveries that the U.S. government used its citizens as guinea pigs and the statement of former Atomic Energy Commission official Charles Edington approving the tests (Edington, 1963).

28. Restatement (2d) of Torts, Sec. 520 (1977).

29. 42 U.S.C. Sec. 9605 (a)(8)(B) (1983). The National Priority List is a compilation of the most polluted sites in the country as determined by a scoring system established by Congress when CERCLA was originally enacted.

30. A graph of state "mini-CERCLA" statutes is appended to Ryan and Wright (1990).

31. 5 U.S.C.C.A.N. 6119, 6137 (1980). See also Chen & McSlarrow, 1992.

32. *See County Line v. Tinney*, 1991, where CERCLA action for contribution was limited based on the claimant's failure to provide for public comment. Under a scheme of strict liability, plaintiff's claim would not be so limited. Other advantages of strict liability

as a complement to CERCLA liability include access to state court, cleanup beyond that required or consistent with the NCP, the circumvention of CERCLA's petroleum exclusion, additional damages unavailable under CERCLA for medical monitoring (*Werlein v. United States*, 1990), and consequential damages (*T & E Industries v. Safety Light Corp.*, 1991), and limiting the defendant's ability to contribution unless it brings a separate CERCLA action (Chen & McSlarrow, 1992, pp. 1045–1047).

33. Presently, there are more than 65,000 chemical substances that are licensed for manufacture or processing for commercial use in the United States. When the byproducts and intermediates of chemical and other processes are added to that number, the number of chemical substances added to the environment is staggering (Carlin, 1992).

34. See 5 U.S.C.C.A.N. 6119, 6119–20 (1980).

35. Of course, to the extent that these reactions are either unseen or unpredictable, the danger is extremely enhanced (Baurer, 1980). On the other hand, the reactions may also counteract the effects of the individual elements. Such reactions are called "antagonistic reactions." See *United States v. Conservation Chemical Co.* (1985).

REFERENCES

Adams v. Marathon Oil Co., 96-693 (La. App. 5th Cir. 1/15/97), 688 So.2d 75.

Ames, J. (1908). Law and morals. *Harvard Law Review, 22*, 97.

Baurer, T. (1980). Love Canal: Common law approaches to a modern tragedy. *Environmental Law (NWU), 11*, 133.

Beis v. Bowers, 649 So.2d 1094 (La. App. 4th Cir. 1995).

Bonnette, et al. v. Conoco, Inc., et al., 837 So2d. 1219 (2003).

Bordelon v. St. Francis Cabrini Hospital, 640 So.2d 476 (La. App. 3rd Cir.1994).

Boscarino, J. A., & Figley, C. R. (2009). The impact of repression, hostility, and PTSD on all-cause mortality: A prospective 16-year follow-up study. *The Journal of Nervous and Mental Disease, 197*(6), 461–466.

Bowler, P. (1993). *The Norton History of the Environmental Sciences* (1993). New York, NY: W. W. Norton & Company.

Bridgeton v. British Petroleum Oil, Inc., 146 N.J. Super. 169, 369 A.2d 49 (Law Div. 1976).

Brown v. Kendall, 6 Cush. 292 (Mass. 1850).

Burdick, F. (1926). *Burdick's law of torts*. Albany, NY: Banks & Co.

Butler v. Pardue, 415 So.2d 249 (La. App. 2d Cir. 1982)

Calabrisi, G. (1970). *The cost of accidents*. New Haven, CT: Yale University Press.

Carlin, A., Scodari, P. F., & Garner, D. H. (1992, March). Environmental investments: The cost of cleaning up. *Environment, 34*(2), 12.

Carroll v. State Farm Insurance Co., 427 So.2d 24 (La. App. 3d Cir. 1983).

Chavez v. Southern Pacific Transportation Co., 413 F.Supp. 1203, 1209 (E.D. Cal. 1976).

Chavkin, S. (2010, July 27). Mental health claims from oil spill probably won't be paid. *ProPublica*. Retrieved April 2, 2015, from http://www.propublica.org/article/mental-health-claims-from-oil-spill-probably-wont-be-paid

Chen, J. & McSlarrow, K. (1992). Application of the abnormally dangerous activities doctrine to environmental cleanups. *The Business Lawyer, 47*, 1031, 1032.

City Services Co. v. State (1975), 312 So.2d 799 (Fla. App. 1975).

Committee for Economic Development. (1989). *Who Should Be Liable?* Washington, DC: Author.

County Line v. Tinney, 933 F.2d 1508 (10th Cir. 1991),

Cunningham, F., Jr. (1992). *Liability of municipal owners for environmental damage on construction sites*. In *Hazardous waste on the construction site—who is liable* (p. 73). Chicago, IL: American Bar Association.

Edington, C. W. (1963). Review of recent proposal, Division of Biology and Medicine, U.S. Atomic Energy Commission, April 14, 1963, at the Institute for Energy and Environmental Research.

Elam v. Alcolac, Inc., 765 S.W. 2d 42, 176 (Mo. App. W.D. 1988).

Epstein, R. (1980). A theory of strict liability. *Journal of Legal Studies, 2*(1), 151–204.

Fred C. Hart Assoc. (1979). *Preliminary assessment of cleanup costs for national hazardous waste problems*. EPA Contract # 68-01-5063.

Galligan, T. (1992). *Strict liability in action: The truncated learned hand formula. Louisiana Law Review, 52,* 323.

Gaskins, R. (1989) *Environmental accident*. Philadelphia, PA: Temple University Press.

Gore, A. (1992). *Earth in the Balance*. Boston, MA: Houghton Mifflin.

Harper, F., James, F., Jr., & Gray, O. (1986). *The law of torts* (2nd ed.). Boston, MA: Little, Brown & Co.

Harper v. Illinois Central Gulf R.R., 808 F.2d 1139 (5th Cir. 1987).

Harris, R. (1932). Liability without fault. *Tulane Law Review, 6,* 337.

Hazardous Waste Action Coalition (1991). *The Hazardous Waste Practice—para. 3: Technical and Legal Environment 1991*. Washington, DC: Author.

Holmes, O. W. (1873). The theory of torts. *American Law Review, 7,* 652.

Holmes, O. W. (1881). *The Common Law*. Boston, MA: Little, Brown & Co.

Holtzinger, K. (1982). Common law and the toxic tort: Where does Superfund leave the private victim of toxic tort? *Dickinson Law Review, 86,* 725, 726–727.

Horwitz, M. (1977). *The transformation of American law, 1780–1860*. Cambridge, MA: Harvard University Press.

Huber, P. (1988). *Liability: The legal revolution and its consequences*. New York, NY: Basic Books.

Indiana Harbor Belt Railroad Co. v. American Cyanamid Co., 916 F.2d 1174 (7th Cir. 1990).

Isaacs, N. (1917). *Fault and Liability: Two Views of Legal Development*. Cambridge, MA: Harvard University Press.

James, F., Jr. (1946). Accident liability: Some wartime developments. *Yale Law Journal, 55,* 365.

Jones, W. (1992). Strict liability for hazardous enterprises. *Columbia Law Review, 92,* 1705, 1751.

Juhasz, A. (2012, May 7). Two years after the BP spill, a hidden health crisis festers. *The Nation*. Retrieved April 2, 2015, from http://www.thenation.com/article/167461/investigation-two-years-after-bp-spill-hidden-health-crisis-festers

Keeton, P. (1959a). Conditional fault in the law of torts. *Harvard Law Review, 72,* 401–444.

Keeton, P. (1959b). Trespass, nuisance and strict liability. *Columbia Law Review, 59,* 458.

Kenny v. Scientific, Inc., 204 N.J. Super. 228, 497 A.2d 1310 (Law Div. 1985).

Krugman, P. (2014, June 11). Economic impact isn't the biggest obstacle to reducing carbon emissions. *The New Orleans Times-Picayune*, p. B-9.

Laflar, R. (1952). Negligence in name only. *NYU Law Review, 27*, 564, 566.

Lee, J. D., & Lindahl, B. (1991). *Modern tort law, liability and litigation*. St. Paul, MN: Thomson Reuters.

McLane v. Northwest Natural Gas Co., 255 Or. 324, 467 P.2d 635 (1970).

Middlesex County Sewerage Authority v. National Sea Clammers Association, 453 U.S. 1 (1981).

Moresi v. State Ex Rel. Wildlife and Fisheries, 567 So.2d 1081, 1096 (La. 1990).

Morris, C. (1952). Hazardous enterprises and risk bearing capacity. *Yale Law Journal, 61*, 1172.

National Alliance on Mental Illness. (2010, August 11). BP oil spill fund should cover mental health claims; NAMI warns Administrator Kenneth Feinberg that exclusion would be "neither fair nor equitable." *National Alliance on Mental Illness*. Retrieved April 2, 2015, from http://www.nami.org/Template.cfm?Section=Top_Story&template=/ContentManagement/ContentDisplay.cfm&ContentID=104670

Nothstein, G. (1984). *Toxic torts: Litigation of hazardous substance cases*. New York, NY: McGraw-Hill.

Posner, R. (1986) *Economic analysis of law* (3rd ed., Sec. 8.2). Boston, MA: Little, Brown & Co.

Pound, R. (1923). *Interpretations of Legal History*. New York, NY: Macmillan.

Prosser, W. (1959). The principle of *Rylands v. Fletcher*. In *Selected Topics on the Law of Torts*, 180-81 University of Michigan Law School, at 179.

Prosser, W. L., Keeton, W. P., Dobbs, D. B., Keeton, R. E., & Owen, D. G. (1984). *Prosser and Keeton on torts*. Eagen, MN: West Group Publishers.

Rivera v. United Gas Pipeline Co., 96-502 (La. App. 5th Cir. 6/30/97), 697 So.2d 327.

Ryan, W., Jr., & Wright, R. (1990). Hazardous waste liability and the surety. *Tort and Insurance Law Journal, 25*, 663.

Rylands v. Fletcher (1865), 3 H.C. 774, 159 Eng. Rep. 737 (1865), rev'd. 1 Exch. 265 (1866), modified 3 H.L. 330 (1868).

Salmond, J. (1928). *The law of torts*, 11 (7th ed.).

Schleifstein, M. (2012, May 6). BP oil spill settlement grants will pay for health, mental health services on Gulf coast. *The New Orleans Times-Picayune*. Retrieved April 2, 2015, from http://www.nola.com/news/gulf-oil-spill/index.ssf/2012/05/bp_oil_spill_settlement_grants.html

Senate Committee on Environment and Public Works. (1980). *Six case studies of compensation for toxic substances pollution: Alabama, California, Michigan, Missouri, New Jersey, and Texas*, S. Doc. No. 13, 96th Cong., 2d Sess.

Shapo, M. (1984). *Report to the American Bar Association: Towards a jurisprudence of injury: The continuing creation of a system of substantive justice in American tort law*. Chicago, IL: American Bar Association.

Shern, D. (2010, August 25). Mental health and the spill: Let's stop discriminating. *Psychology Today*. Retrieved April 2, 2015, from http://www.psychologytoday.com/blog/minding-the-nations-health/201008/mental-health-and-the-spill-lets-stop-discriminating

Simmons v. CTL Distribution, 03-1301 (La. App. 5th Cir. 2/23/04), 868 So.2d 918.

Smith v. Lockheed Propulsion Co., 247 Cal. App. 2d 774, 785, 56 Cal. Rptr. 128, 137 (1967).

T & E Industries v. Safety Light Corporation, 123 N.J. 371, 587 A.2d 1249 (N.J. 1991).

United States v. Conservation Chemical Co., 628 F. Supp. 391 (W.D. Mo. 1985).

Weiner, J. B. (1986). Developments in the law—toxic waste litigation. *Harvard Law Review, 99*, 1458, 1610.

Werlein v. United States, 746 F. Supp. 887 (D. Minn. 1990).

White, G. E. (1980). *Tort law in America* (p. 109). New York, NY: Oxford University Press.

Wigmore, J. (1894). Responsibility for tortuous acts: Its history. *Harvard Law Review, 7,* 42.

Williams, G. (1951). The aims of the law of tort. *Current Legal Problems, 4,* 137, 142.

Winfield, P. (1926). The myth of absolute liability. *Law Quarterly Review, 42,* 37.

20

Reflections and Recommendations: The Need for Leadership, Holistic Thinking, and Community Involvement

Darlyne G. Nemeth, Robert B. Hamilton, and Judy Kuriansky

This chapter focuses on three important components of ecopsychology and environmental protection. They are as follows: Leadership, Holistic Planning, and Community Involvement. Recommendations for future behavior regarding the ecokinetics and ecodynamics of ecopsychology are also offered. Specifically, how nature affects people and all living things (i.e., ecokinetics) and how people and all living things affect nature (i.e., ecodynamics) are integral components of the challenges we face today. We begin with discussion of three salient styles of leadership. The discussion of holistic planning is offered by Bob Hamilton, editor of Volume 1, and then, Judy Kuriansky, editor of Volume 2, highlights the importance of community involvement.

LEADERSHIP STYLES

Three styles of leadership are examined in the following section of this chapter. They are as follows: psychoid leadership, robust leadership, and altruistic leadership.

Psychoid Leadership

Psychoid leaders are the most dangerous of all. Their effects on people and the environment are usually disastrous. That is why this type of leadership is emphasized herein. A psychoid leader bullies himself into a position of power and authority by espousing half-truths and manipulating perceptions. Remember, perceptions are based on beliefs, not facts. People's perceptions can be easily molded by clever individuals seeking power at all costs. Basically, if people hear something long enough and over and over again, they will begin to believe the orator. Psychoid leaders are typically brilliant, though partially insane, individuals who are skilled at political manipulation. They quickly find scapegoats to blame. Dependent followers eventually fall for such chicanery and become mesmerized by the rhetoric. Consider Hitler in pre–World War II Germany. He managed to turn neighbor against neighbor and to order unspeakable atrocities in the name of the "Arian Race." Yet, Hitler was not Arian. Even today, the legacy of Nazism lives on in some minorities (e.g., the skinheads).

Although innately insane, psychoid leaders, who *demand authority*, can ravage the world of its decency and humanity. They are not at all concerned about the environment. They act to promote their own aggrandizement.

Robust Leadership

This second form of leadership is offered by an individual who exhibits a robustness that can withstand the test of time, circumstances, and politics. These leaders are supportive of the theme of this anthology. They function for the benefit of the people and of the environment. They make decisions that are protective of both. These robust individuals *command authority* by their very presence. They respect what is right and decry what is wrong. Lieutenant General Russel Honoré, the hero of Hurricane Katrina, is one such individual (as described in Chapter 2 [Nemeth, 2015] and Chapter 7 [Nemeth & Songy, 2015] of this volume). By doing what was right in post-Katrina New Orleans, Honoré quickly restored order and facilitated recovery.

Several years later, Honoré established the grassroots Green Army to mobilize ordinary citizens to fight for and protect their home environments. For the love of home, the oikophilia, Honoré took stands against corporations that were telling half-truths and ignoring the needs of those affected by their profit-driven motives and decisions. At times of environmental trauma, affected citizens are often unable to think clearly. They typically turn to their elected officials for help, as was the case in Bayou Corne and Lake Peigneur. No help was forthcoming (as described in Chapter 4 of this volume [Crowley & Pastrana, 2015]). When they turned to the companies involved, they were ignored. Grassroots citizens needed a champion—one with name recognition, courage, and unflappable ethics. Honoré rose to the occasion. With his leadership and with considerable citizen-based grassroots efforts, the tide changed. Resolution was possible.

Robust leaders are not perfect people. But they do have the gifts of being in the right place at the right time and of knowing how to lead. This form of active leadership during both acute (i.e., Hurricane Katrina) and chronic (i.e., Bayou Corne) environmental trauma is crucial to resolution. Most grassroots organizers are very good at gathering the facts and at putting in long hours over time to keep those facts before the public. They, however, often lack the charisma that is needed to mobilize an army (e.g., the Green Army) in order to force resolution. Government and company officials, who are often in collusion, either intentionally or unintentionally, lack the desire to protect the environment, let alone the people. Without a robust leader, with a strong following, shaming these entities into public awareness, nothing would change. Profit would prevail. Those who attempt to tell the truth (e.g., Professor van Heerden) would be vanquished.

Oftentimes, the truth is inconvenient. It takes a robust leader to rise to the forefront in order to make sure that truth prevails. University professors are usually not robust leaders. They typically report scientific truths and findings with an academic demeanor, but they usually lack the political charisma needed to foster their acceptance. At times, academic freedom does not prevail. This is to the detriment of all. Short-term solutions based on fear and intimidation usually end up being disastrous. Robust leadership is required to keep things on track.

Altruistic Leadership

And then there is a third, very special type of leadership. These leaders are typically caretakers of the people and their environment. These are altruistic leaders. These people are rare. They may come along once in a century. They do what is right each and every day because it is the right thing to do. They are often motivated by a calling or a higher power. One such quiet leader was Mother Teresa. She never sought power or authority, and she was always respectful. Mother Teresa became a revered individual. By her very grace, Mother Teresa *begot authority*. She led through example. With love and good deeds, with humility and grace, Mother Teresa, an altruistic leader, was able to effect change (see Figure 20.1).

On December 11, 1979, in her acceptance speech for the Nobel Prize, Mother Teresa pointed out that, "Calcutta was everywhere, that poverty was material, social, and spiritual" (Carville, 2014). To use her words, Hitler was a *material* leader. He wanted to own the world. Honoré was and is a *social* leader. He wanted to right the world, to bring order to chaos. Mother Teresa was a *spiritual* leader. She wanted to love the world by rekindling the innate value of every form of life and to live in harmony with every form of nature.

EFFECTIVE LEADERSHIP FOR THE FUTURE

When we move away from valuing life and nature, we hasten our own demise. Our indigenous people know this. Perhaps our Westernized people have forgotten this. Our indigenous people live in harmony with the land. They value and care for Mother Earth. They are very spiritual. Our Westernizing world often perceives people who are different as inferior and their lands as theirs for the taking. They conquer. They destroy. They deplete. All without conscience. They are very secular. Many, but not all, corporations function with this mentality. There are those corporations that are trying to work toward more harmonious goals. Yes, it is possible to have a profitable business and to be a good corporate stakeholder as well. One such corporation, as described in Chapter 15 (Bena &

Figure 20.1.
Official photograph used for Mother Teresa's beatitude ceremony at the Vatican.
(Photo by Marie Constantine)

Kuriansky, 2015), is striving to do so. We must support those people and those corporations that are striving to make a difference.

Change is here. It is all around us. Our planet is alive and ever-changing. We must change as well. If we do not work together to make sure that all amongst us, as Mother Teresa pointed out, thrive and that Mother Earth flourishes, we will not be able to manage this change. Altruistic (i.e., prosocial) behavior will be necessary to manage change. This will require collaboration on all levels and with all entities. People, corporations, and governments must work together. Whether we like it or not, we have become a globalized society. Therefore, we must contain and eliminate psychoid leaders, seek out and promote robust leaders, and recognize and appreciate the altruistic leaders in our midst.

HOLISTIC PLANNING

This section reflects the perspective of the second author of this chapter, who is the editor of Volume 1. He focuses on change and the importance of a holistic view of ecopsychology and environmental protection.

Our Past from a Holistic Perspective

How did humans get from our humble ancestry in southern Africa to where we are today, a world with more than 7.28 billion people and still growing—a world that is constantly changing from what it was when we began to what it is today? It was a heterogeneous world of great diversity and bounty. We had bountiful resources and vast resources of energy, both internal and external. It is with the management of these resources and our own unique human capabilities that our species has gotten us to the "here and now" with less diversity and much of our bounty being utilized in one way or the other to benefit only humans and an increasing utilization of a constant external-energy supply at the expense of other earth residents.

Different Approaches

But there is a dichotomy of approaches, as demonstrated now in the rain forests of Brazil and other places. The residents there have accepted the environment as it is and have flourished in it until now. Their numbers are low because the carrying capacity for humans is low, but the total carrying capacity for all species combined is extremely high. The diversity of the environment is high as the component species have interacted with each other continuously in evolutionary time and have developed a variety of chemical and behavioral solutions to survive in the never-ending struggle for survival. Humans here are happy and oppose the changes being forced on them by the outsiders who are invading their ancestral land.

The invaders are following the other path. They are seeking resources available in this barely disturbed land. They respect neither the rights of the indigenous people nor the environment that is their home. Their numbers must continue to grow. That is their path.

The indigenous people's future is predictable if the environment persists and they do not change. It would continue like it is now. Their approach is altruistic. Altruism saves them. It is basically the Golden Rule—"Do unto others as you would have them do unto you." But altruism is not universal, and they will be usurped by selfish interlopers.

I do not know the future of the interlopers. They will probably eventually destroy or manage the rain forests, and the indigenous people will need to adapt to whatever concessions are given. But undisturbed environments are disappearing. Thus, they are destroying their environment. They must find another way. Resources cannot continue forever. This approach is selfish and not sustainable. This future is uncertain. We cannot anticipate the future of those with this selfish approach.

Management of Change

Management is done to accomplish a goal. Management itself must be holistic to avoid unintended consequences. These occur because the effects of the management action at all temporal and spatial scales are not analyzed. We will not know what will happen at other places than where the action occurs or at other times than those considered in the management actions. If the scope of management was not holistic, we could not anticipate actions on unconsidered groups. If the action was taken to benefit birds, for example, what is its effect on mammals? There may even be unanticipated interactions in time and space among unconsidered elements. We do not really know what is going to happen. How can we propose an action with so many unknowns? This narrow focus is often made because the managers do not have holistic responsibilities. If they are refuge managers, for example, effects outside of the refuge may not seem relevant to them. Because of the complexity of our environments and the prevalence of unintended consequences (many of which are not known), an approach that allows the projected action to occur in small steps and be reversed if unintended consequences appear, seems reasonable.

All of us should be involved in setting the goals. Leaders should help us determine them. In democracies, goals are often important issues in elections. We all must understand the current conditions and problems and have a vision for the future. It is here that we must be altruistic. The goals should be to benefit all as much as possible. Those making the decisions should not benefit more than anyone else. In these days of crony capitalism, bribes, and influence pedaling, altruism is a necessity.

Leadership occurs at all levels, and decisions are made at these levels, whether they be family, clan, city, state, nation, and/or groups of nations like the United Nations. We are concerned with our biosphere; unfortunately, no group truly represents it. We must find a way to consider this level more, because it affects us all.

Present Conditions and Unanticipated Consequences

Today, we worry about many problems; most of them are due to our nonholistic decisions in the past. As we write this chapter, climate change and an Ebola threat are of great concern. Both of these problems are complex, but are due somewhat to our approach to expanding our economy. They will need objective, holistic decision-making to solve without creating additional problems. Perhaps this could be expected with a prevailing altruistic approach, but paths that enrich our decision makers and further modify our environments are likely. Unfortunately, we seem to have a separate leadership class in most of the world. Oftentimes, our leaders are not one of us; however, Mother Teresa was a citizen of the world. She led by example. Our leaders often benefit from their decisions. Mother Teresa did not seek material gain. Good decisions cannot be made if the leaders do not suffer the same consequences as their followers.

Many of our problems are due to our enormous population and its continuous growth. That, obviously, cannot be sustained. Because we tend to ignore this problem, the obvious result will likely be more damage to our ancestral environments and a more unpredictable future. Will we change the climate unintentionally to cause our demise? Will we be destroyed by some unanticipated danger that corrupts or destroys the electronic devices we have become so dependent upon? Will some pathogen, like Ebola, evolve and kill us all? There are so many frightening possibilities.

We must not continue down our present path. Altruistic leaders with holistic approaches can lead by example locally, as did Mother Teresa. Let her example show us the way.

THE ROLE OF COMMUNITY IN THE INTERSECTION OF PSYCHOLOGY AND ENVIRONMENTAL PROTECTION

The third important component reviewed in this chapter in the intersection of ecopsychology and environmental protection is community involvement. The role of the community is crucial in achieving the pillars of social development and environmental protection that are at the foundation of the Sustainable Development Goals (SDGs). This section, contributed by the third author of this chapter, reviews the interaction between the community and environmental protection as manifested through pro-environment behavior (PEB). This relationship is important for the health and well-being of individuals as well as of the collective, and also can inform policy makers, which is important for the attainment of the new SDGs set forth by the United Nations for the years 2015–2030. These goals call for promoting the very topics addressed in these volumes, namely, ensuring well-being, protecting the environment, and combatting the deleterious impacts of climate change.

A community is often referred to as a whole unto itself, a collective entity, made up of individual parts (Merriam-Webster Dictionary, 2014). Dictionary definitions identify a community as a group of people considered collectively who live in the same place, district, or country and who have a particular characteristic and/or share ownership, fellowship, common attitudes, interests, goals, social values, or responsibilities. Besides referring to people, "community" can also refer to a particular area or place considered together with its inhabitants, or even to a body of states or nations unified by common interests. Synonyms for the word "community" include: group, body, set, circle, clique, faction, society, public, populace, people, citizenry, population, collective, residents, inhabitants, citizens, brotherhood, sisterhood, fraternity, sorority, congregation, district, region, zone, area, locality, locale, and neighborhood.

Much research is currently focusing on various aspects of community behavior related to climate change, disaster recovery, and PEB. The latter is also referred to as pro-ecological behavior. Particular interest is on how to heighten citizen awareness of, and commitment to, PEB.

Theories have been proposed that underlie this relationship between community and PEB. Social influence theory—that behavior is affected by what others do and think—has been applied to pro-environment behavior. This theory suggests that people would be more willing to engage in PEB if they knew that their friends would do so. One meta-analysis of 29 studies revealed that social influence approaches were effective in encouraging behavior to save energy, especially when compared to other interventions such as information provision or goal setting (Abrahamse & Steg, 2014). The fact that behaviors of community members can affect the behavior of neighbors was also shown in a study in Austria, applying a social diffusion method that is considered a promising way to reduce the carbon-intensive transport system in Western industrialized countries (Seebauer, 2014). The results showed that targeted recipients who were offered subsidies to buy an electric vehicle were persuasive with others to follow this behavior.

Pro-environment behavior has been linked not only to the bonds among community members and bonds of people to their surroundings, but also to bonds within families. Researchers in Germany found that parents influenced their children's travel mode choice, and purchase of organic products and food (Matthies & Wallis, 2014). Also, researchers in Italy found that positive early attachment styles developed in childhood between mother and child not only have the well-known effects on adult relationships and behavior, but also affect choices in pro-environment situations (Carrus, Gambioli, Maricchiolo, & Pirchio, 2014). Transfer of PEB from parent to child makes personal sense to the coauthor of this chapter, Kuriansky, as she recalls the sources of her own environmental prosocial behavior:

> I remember fondly how my father taught me, as a ten-year old, to take great care in trimming the hedges of our home and upkeep of the borders of our flower garden; many years later on a trip to Bali, I was sickened by the refuse of shampoo packets strewn carelessly in beautiful streams. Respect for the environment now makes me an avid recycler. I was further greatly influenced by my experience producing a video with a group of youth about responsible energy conservation and advocacy about climate change, when leading an International Student Journalism Program for the model UN in the Dominican Republic as part of the Conferencia Internacional de la Americas in October 2009. The video covered their negotiating about a climate change agreement in anticipation of the Climate Change Conference in Copenhagen that December. I still remember the commitment the teens made on the video that they would pay attention to turning off lights and their computer, and even influence their parents to buy an energy-efficient car (http://www.youtube.com/watch?v=hInGbuOyaxg). Emblazoned in my mind is the scene of the dancing and cheering of the team advocating for a strong agreement about climate change who "won" the mock negotiations. (J. Kuriansky, personal communication, November 12, 2014)

Another area of community concern is how to appeal to, and engage, the public in pro-environment behavior. For example, a campaign using graphic depictions of health outcomes of storms, floods, and changes in air quality was more effective in increasing public knowledge than text information (Pahl, Stahl-Timmins, White, & Depledge, 2014). Also, economic appeals that emphasize financial benefits of behavior have been found to be less persuasive than biospheric appeals that emphasize environmental benefits of behavior, in encouraging PEB (Van Den Broek, Bolderdijk, & Steg, 2014).

The physical context of the community, or the quality of the environment or space is another factor that has been shown to affect PEB (Poortinga, 2014). Attachment to the neighborhood, called "place attachment"—to refer to the person's affective link to a specific place—has been gaining attention in human-environment research and also in how it affects sustainable behavior. For example, walkability has been shown to be an important component of community livability and related to better health outcome for residents. Residents of walkable neighborhoods reported greater physical and mental health compared to low walkable residents (Takacs, Kristjansson, & Pearce, 2014). Other studies have shown that the quality of a housing development (e.g., crowding, noise, poor air quality) has a direct effect on residents' mental health and well-being, and sense of belonging, with the results having implications for how low-cost housing settlements are built. This finding is important not only to residents but also to city planners and policy makers, as an increasing number of people move from rural to urban environments (Leary, 2014). Research is also exploring the quality of the environment in a health setting. One study, using the model of well-being from the New Economics Foundation (a British think tank examining indicators of sustainability), explored staff well-being in terms of components such as emotions, vitality, competence, and supportive relationships, in relation to aspects of the physical environment, including access to natural light, gardens, exposed sound levels, walking distances, and community spaces (Payne, Potter, & Cain, 2014).

Attachment to place is relevant to the field of disaster psychology, in determining how the destruction of their home affects people. For example, after the Asian tsunami and the Japan tsunami earthquake, some people could not, and did not, move back to their neighborhoods, which can be linked to emotional reactions about displacement and community dissolution (Turton, Murtagh, Uzzel, & Gatersleben, 2014). Architects have an important role to play in how communities are rebuilt, taking people's emotions and needs into consideration when creating communal space.

Resilience—personal strengths and ability to bounce back from a crisis—has been an important concept in disaster recovery, which usually refers to individual responses. However, a collective perspective is also relevant, in what is referred to as "community resilience" (Ross, 2014). Experts from various disciplines are interested in this concept. Ecologists, for example, have explored the concept of ecological resilience, including within social-ecological systems. Experts in the disaster management field have emphasized several factors related to resilience, including physical infrastructure as well as psychosocial recovery. Other experts focus on the relationship between risk reduction and participation and sharing of responsibility between various stakeholders, including between the public and governments.

The editors of Volume 2 have been particularly involved in projects that build community resilience after disasters, including after Hurricane Katrina in a community wellness workshop (Kuriansky & Nemeth, 2013) and after the Haiti earthquake and Superstorm Sandy in New York (Kuriansky, 2013a, 2013b). Other work has shown how youth volunteers in particular contribute to rebuild stronger societies (Kuriansky, 2012a, 2012d, see also Chapter 9 in this volume [Kuriansky, Zinsou, et al., 2015]), and how community programs empower women and girls (Kirkman & Kuriansky, 2012).

Community action after a crisis is of importance, as communities can either pull together or be fractured by an environmental crisis. Rebuilding together can allow residents to bond. One study in New Zealand that examined citizen motivations to volunteer after an oil spill in 2011 proved the value of citizen volunteers to bring a community together. An impressive 8,000 people signed up to help in the cleanup effort. The researchers found that the oil spill had a significant emotional, physical, cultural, and spiritual impact on both individuals and communities. People had various motivations to volunteer. These included a sense of duty; a desire to contribute to their community; a sense of responsibility to ensure the health of the environment for future generations; the desire to connect with others; and efforts to cope with their negative emotions. After volunteering, most participants reported a sense of satisfaction, renewed social ties, and renewed optimism (Sargisson, Smith, Hunt, & Hamerton, 2014). Another study confirmed that volunteering in a community cleanup—a coastal environ-mental activity of beach cleaning—was beneficial for the volunteers themselves (Wyles, Pahl, & Thompson, 2014). Chapter 9 in this volume (Kuriansky, Zinsou, et al., 2015), about a program implemented by the coauthor of this chapter, Kuriansky, and colleagues after the Haiti earthquake in 2010, further supports the positive outcome of bonding among helpers with each other and also with recipients of their help.

Trainings of community members to aid in post-disaster situations are possible with teaching simple techniques to increase the capacity of support, especially in conditions where human resources are limited. The coauthor's (Kuriansky) experiences as outlined in Chapter 9 (Kuriansky, Zinsou, et al., 2015) have proven the viability and value of such an approach, conducting train-the-trainer programs both in Haiti and China after the earthquakes in those countries.

A unique model of community resilience is presented in Chapter 8 in this volume (Davis & Dumpson, 2015) about empowering African Americans' responses to climate change through an integrative bio-interpersonal/music-based approach. The model involves both bricks-and-mortar community center and virtual communities making connections through smart phones and mobile apps, providing citizens with information on the effects of climate change, descriptions of stress reduction exercises and strategies, and resource lists.

Community resilience is particularly evident at anniversary dates of trauma, when people have opportunities to gather together for further healing. Of course, honoring people's style of dealing with trauma is important, as not all people prefer such group experiences. Anniversary dates, however, as has been pointed out in this volume and other sources, do trigger re-experiencing of emotions, and as such, communities may benefit from processing (Kuriansky, 2012a, 2012b, 2012c, 2013b; Kuriansky & Jean-Charles, 2012; Kuriansky & Nemeth, 2013; see also Chapter 9 [Kuriansky, Zinsou, et al., 2015] and Chapter 10 [Kuriansky, Wu, et al., 2015] of this volume). Those who have been through disaster may also appeal to the broader community to not forget, when time, and the news cycle of the event, has passed (Jean-Charles, 2011; Kuriansky & Jean-Charles, 2012). Talking to children at these times requires particular sensitivity (Kuriansky, 2013c).

Globalization has led to the emergence of a new construct of "cosmopolitan identity" and exploring how this identity cultivates socially responsible values and behavior. Researchers in Singapore identified four dimensions of cosmopolitan identity: global altruism, openness to foreign cultures, support for open economies, and support for equal human rights. Survey results showed that cosmopolitans who scored high on the first three dimensions were more likely to engage in environmental protection (supporting an environmentalist organization) and specific pro-environmental behaviors (looking for ways to reuse things, purchasing biodegradable products) as well as to advise the government to incorporate environmental impact and life satisfaction as indicators to assess a nation's development (Leung, Koh, Ong, & Tam, 2014).

As the Sustainable Development Goals encourage greater participation from multiple stakeholders, including businesses, research is focusing on how to engage corporations in pro-environment activity. Increasing pressure is being put on business and industry to implement policies and practices that address climate change, including encouraging greater employee pro-environmental behavior. This poses a challenge in that the values and goals of the organization are not always congruent with environmental goals (Fielding, Russell, & Evans, 2014). Multinational corporations can have a positive impact on communities and prosocial behavior by applying psychological principles of trust-building and cooperation, as pointed out in Chapter 15 in this volume (Bena & Kuriansky, 2015).

According to ecological systems theory, individuals operate within spheres, expanding from close interpersonal relationships and immediate surroundings to their social and cultural context that affect their beliefs and behavior; all of which influence and feedback one another (Bronfenbrenner, 1979). Cooperation among individuals within a community, between communities within a nation, and then among nations is essential for the global achievement of the Sustainable Development Goals. Through united action, individuals can have an impact on the preservation of natural resources in their environment and the collective well-being of all (see Chapter 10 in this volume [Kuriansky, Wu, et al., 2015]).

Studies like those reported above hold great promise for the future of encouraging pro-environmental behavior. Fortunately, research and resulting programs and policy are now more likely, given the success of the campaign led by the third author of this chapter (Kuriansky) to include "promote mental health and well-being" in the Sustainable Development Goals (Forman, 2014). When advocating about this issue with member states of the United Nations, this author was questioned by a delegate about what psychology can contribute to the SDG of sustainable consumption. The studies presented above answer that question, supporting that the field of ecopsychology has much to contribute to sustainable consumption. After all, it is people and their motivation and emotions that influence their behavior to preserve the environment (e.g., to not throw shampoo packets in the beautiful Bali rivers), to conserve resources, and to take action against the impact of climate change. The contributions of ecopsychology to these sustainable development goals can be applied by researchers, program planners, policy makers, community activists, and other stakeholders in order to make for a better "Future We Want" (United Nations, 2012) that includes healthy communities and a healthy environment.

RECOMMENDATIONS AND CONCLUSIONS

Given the above three areas of reflection—leadership, holistic thinking, and community involvement—the following recommendations and conclusions are offered for a more sustainable future, taking into account psychological and scientific principles and practices as presented in these volumes. Change is inevitable; therefore, we have to be holistic in making decisions about managing our environment. Lack of holistic thinking and planning has led to many unfortunate unintended consequences—for example, acid rain and the effect of DDT on eagles and falcons. As the world becomes increasingly globalized, we must move beyond provincial interests. Our various cultures must find ways of blending their unique ideas and interests in order to share the planet and preserve our resources.

Ever since our ancestors discovered tools and how to use fire, they have been modifying their environment to the detriment of most of the other species occupying it. To facilitate the 7.28 billion people on earth now, we have had to make more drastic modifications, and most places where we live today are quite different than our ancestral environments. We have cleared out most of our forests and converted them to agriculture and other uses. We have hunted many species to extinction, even the passenger pigeon, whose population numbers were almost unimaginable. Environmental modifications, such as levee building and crop fertilization, result in the ability to support more people. As more and more resources are being used to support more and more people, environmental changes are accelerating. We have undergone the Industrial Revolution. We have harvested and used energy to increase agricultural production. We have modified agriculture during the green revolution, and we have developed the atomic bomb and nuclear energy. Our numbers are still increasing, and energy demands are increasing even further. In the long run, this approach should not prevail. Such exponential changes in our environment lead us further away from our historic roots. For example, now children think milk comes from grocery stores, not cows. Do we really want this? Is cutting down the rain forest in order to harvest more resources the answer?

We must reexamine our priorities. Responsible sustainability, rather than unattainable sustainability, is key to caring for our earth environment. If we are going to change our environment to grow more crops or produce more fuel, responsibility must follow. There is a price to be paid for every environmental modification. Individuals, special interest groups, private sectors, and governments must not be allowed to alter the environment without conducting appropriate restoration. Any cost involved should be borne by those profiting from the change.

Regarding environmental protection, governments sought to adopt policies that seemed appropriate at the time. But those policies were static. They applied to the past, but perhaps not to the present and the future. Some, if not all, of our efforts have had negative impacts because decisions were not holistic. For example, building hydroelectric dams along coastal rivers to produce electricity almost doomed the salmon. Environmental policies must keep pace with environmental changes. They must be unencumbered by political and special interests. Inertia or lack of action regarding environmental protection must not prevail.

Psychological research, programs, and principles must be used to promote truth, rather than mere accommodation. Perception of the earth environment is an important component of change. Assisting individuals in developing a greater understanding of the inevitability of change and implementing pro-environmental programs and policies will lead to increased environmental awareness and protection, the underlying goal of this anthology.

REFERENCES

Abrahamse, W., & Steg, L. (2014, July 8–13). *Social influence approaches to encourage resource conservation: A meta-analysis.* Presentation at the 28th International Congress of Applied Psychology (ICAP), Paris, France.

Bena, D., & Kuriansky, J. (2015). Can the private sector help heal the planet? Contributions of the private sector to sustainable development through consumer education, awareness, and mobilizing positive psychological and prosocial behavior. In D. G. Nemeth & J. Kuriansky (Eds.), *Ecopsychology: Advances from the intersection of psychology and environmental protection*, Volume 2 (pp. 269–280). Santa Barbara, CA: ABC-CLIO.

Bronfenbrenner, A. (1979). *The ecology of human development.* Cambridge, MA: Harvard University Press.

Carrus, G., Gambioli, C., Maricchiolo, F., & Pirchio, S. (2014, July 8–13). *Adult attachment styles and pro-environmental behavior.* Presentation at the 28th International Congress of Applied Psychology (ICAP). Paris, France.

Carville, F. (2014, August 8). Memories of saints past: Mother Teresa part 3. *The Catholic Commentator*, p. 16.

Crowley, N., & Pastrana, F., Jr. (2015). Grassroots leadership and involvement: Experiences and guidelines. In D. G. Nemeth & J. Kuriansky (Eds.), *Ecopsychology: Advances from the intersection of psychology and environmental protection*, Volume 2 (pp. 35–51). Santa Barbara, CA: ABC-CLIO.

Davis, D., & Dumpson, D. (2015). Empowerment in African Americans' responses to global climate change and environmental racism through an integrative bio-interpersonal/music-based approach. In D. G. Nemeth & J. Kuriansky (Eds.), *Ecopsychology: Advances from the intersection of psychology and environmental protection*, Volume 2 (pp. 105–133). Santa Barbara, CA: ABC-CLIO.

Fielding, K. S., Russell, S., & Evans, A. (2014, July 8–13). *Greening the workplace: Goal congruence as a barrier to encouraging pro-environmental behavior in organizations.* Presentation at the 28th International Congress of Applied Psychology (ICAP), Paris, France.

Forman, A. (2014, October 9). Five words that can change the world. *Jewish Journal.* Retrieved April 3, 2015 from, http://boston.forward.com/articles/185615/five-words-that-can- change-the-world/

Jean-Charles, W. (2011, January/March). Rebati: After the earthquake, the IAAP UN team continues to remember Haiti. *IAAP Bulletin of the International Association of Applied Psychology, 23*(1–2), 33–35.

Kirkman, C., & Kuriansky, J. (2012, July–October). Transforming communities through psychosocial empowerment of poor rural women and girls: Parallel event of the Psychology NGOs accredited at the United Nations at the 56th Session of the Commission on the Status of Women. *Bulletin of the International Association of Applied Psychology, 24*(2–3), Part 13. Retrieved September 20, 2014, from http://www.iaapsy.org/Portals/1/Archive/Publications/newsletters/July2012.pdf

Kuriansky, J. (2012a). Our communities: Healing after environmental disasters. In D. G. Nemeth, R. B. Hamilton, & J. Kuriansky (Eds.), *Living in an environmentally traumatized world: Healing ourselves and our planet.* Santa Barbara, CA: ABC-CLIO/Praeger.

Kuriansky, J. (2012b). Psychologist laments lackluster 9/11 memorials. Retrieved April 3, 2015, from, http://abcnews.go.com/Health/psychologist-laments-lackluster-911 -memorials/story?id=17207164

Kuriansky, J. (2012c). Report: Soothing Sendai. Retrieved March 30, 2015, from http://www.humnews.com/the-view-from-here/2012/3/22/soothing-sendai-report.html

Kuriansky, J. (2012d). Train, retain, gain: Workshop on youth volunteer leadership for intercultural cooperation to build stronger societies at the DPI/NGO conference in Bonn Germany. *Bulletin of the International Association of Applied Psychology*, *24*(2–3), 23–26. Retrieved September 30, 2014, from http://www.iaapsy.org/Portals/1/Archive/Publications/newsletters/July2012.pdf

Kuriansky, J. (2013a). Superstorm Sandy 2012: A psychologist first responder's personal account and lessons learned about the impact on emotions and ecology. *Ecopsychology*, *5*(Suppl. 1): S30–S37. doi:10.1089/eco.2013.0010.

Kuriansky, J. (2013b). Superstorm Sandy: Coping with the one-year anniversary. *Citizens Magazine*. Retrieved March 30, 2015, from https://statenislandpolitics.wordpress.com/2013/10/26/drjudy/

Kuriansky, J. (2013c). Talking to kids about the anniversary of Superstorm Sandy. *Huffington Post*. Retrieved March 30, 2015, from http://www.huffingtonpost.com/judy-kuriansky-phd/talking-to-kids-about-the-anniversary-of-superstorm-sandy_b_4167294.html

Kuriansky, J., & Jean-Charles, W. (2012, July–October). Haiti Rebati: Update on activities rebuilding Haiti through the Global Kids Connect Project. *Bulletin of the International Association of Applied Psychology*, *24*(2–3), Part 21, 116–124.

Kuriansky, J., & Nemeth, D. G. (2013, September). A model for post-environmental disaster wellness workshops: Preparing individuals and communities for hurricane anniversary reactions. *Ecopsychology*, *5*(Suppl. 1): S38–S45. doi:10.1089/eco.2013.0006.

Kuriansky, J., Wu, L-Y., Bao, C., Chand, D., Kong, S., Spooner, N., & Mao, S. (2015). Interventions by national and international organizations for psychosocial support after the Sichuan Earthquake in China: A review and implications for sustainable development. In D. G. Nemeth & J. Kuriansky (Eds.), *Ecopsychology: Advances from the intersection of psychology and environmental protection*, Volume 2 (pp. 171–231). Santa Barbara, CA: ABC-CLIO.

Kuriansky, J., Zinsou, J., Arunagiri, V., Douyon, C., Chiu, A., Jean-Charles, W., . . . Midy, T. (2015). Effects of helping in a train-the-trainers program for youth in the Global Kids Connect Project providing psychosocial support after the 2010 Haiti earthquake: A paradigm shift to sustainable development. In D. G. Nemeth & J. Kuriansky (Eds.), *Ecopsychology: Advances from the intersection of psychology and environmental protection*, Volume 2 (pp. 135–169). Santa Barbara, CA: ABC-CLIO.

Leary, M. B. (2014, July 8–13). *The effect of build environments on the well-being and mental health of inhabitants in South Africa—a study undertaken in an informal housing settlement*. Presentation at the 28th International Congress of Applied Psychology (ICAP), Paris, France.

Leung, A. K-Y., Koh, K., Ong, L. S., & Tam, K. K-P. (2014, July 8–13). *Being a socially responsible cosmopolitan: The endorsement of a cosmopolitan identity predicts higher environmental protection tendencies*. Presentation at the 28th International Congress of Applied Psychology (ICAP), Paris, France.

Matthies, E., & Wallis, H. (2014, July 8–13). *Family socialization and sustainable consumption*. Presentation at the 28th International Congress of Applied Psychology (ICAP), Paris, France.

Merriam-Webster Dictionary. (2014).

Nemeth, D. G. (2015). From chaos to community: The federal response—an account of Lieutenant General Russel Honoré's leadership during Hurricane Katrina. In D. G. Nemeth & J. Kuriansky (Eds.), *Ecopsychology: Advances from the intersection of psychology and environmental protection*, Volume 2 (pp. 5–13). Santa Barbara, CA: ABC-CLIO.

Nemeth, D. G., & Kuriansky, J. (2008, October 15). *A train-the-trainers program for community health workers to help survivors of the earthquake in China.* Workshop at the World Congress of Psychotherapy, Beijing, China.

Nemeth, D. G., & Songy, C. (2015). Robust leadership and problem-solving in the face of environmental trauma. In D. G. Nemeth & J. Kuriansky (Eds.), *Ecopsychology: Advances from the intersection of psychology and environmental protection*, Volume 2 (pp. 89–104). Santa Barbara, CA: ABC-CLIO.

Pahl, S., Stahl-Timmins, W., White, M. P., & Depledge, M. (2014, July 8–13). *Improving public understanding of the health impacts of climate change using information graphics.* Presentation at the 28th International Congress of Applied Psychology (ICAP), Paris, France.

Payne, S. R., Potter, R., & Cain, R. (2014, July 8–13). *Staff well-being and the physical design of healthcare environments.* Presentation at the 28th International Congress of Applied Psychology (ICAP), Paris, France.

Poortinga, W. (2014, July 8–13). *Neighbourhood quality and attachment: A validation of the revised residential environment assessment tool.* Presentation at the 28th International Congress of Applied Psychology (ICAP), Paris, France.

Ross, H. (2014, July 8–13). *Resilience: An environmental psychology interpretation.* Presentation at the 28th International Congress of Applied Psychology (ICAP), Paris, France.

Sargisson, R., Smith, K., Hunt, S., & Hamerton, H. (2014, July 8–13). *Motivations to volunteer and effects of volunteering for oil-spill clean-up on citizen volunteers.* Presentation at the 28th International Congress of Applied Psychology (ICAP), Paris, France.

Seebauer, S. (2014, July 8–13). *Drivers in the social diffusion of electric vehicles: A survey among early adopters.* Presentation at the 28th International Congress of Applied Psychology (ICAP), Paris, France.

Takacs, T. A., Kristjansson, E. A., & Pearce, S. (2014, July 8–13). *A preliminary report on adapting a walkability questionnaire for northern climates: The NEWS-North.* Presentation at the 28th International Congress of Applied Psychology (ICAP), Paris, France.

Turton, C., Murtagh, N., Uzzell, D., & Gatersleben, B. (2014, July 8–13). *Identifying which factors are pertinent to the occurrence of place attachment to the neighbourhood and the relationship between place attachment and sustainable behavior.* Presentation at the 28th International Congress of Applied Psychology (ICAP), Paris, France.

United Nations. (2012). *The future we want.* Retrieved September 30, 2014, from http://www.un.org/en/sustainablefuture/

Van Den Broek, K., Bolderdijk, J. W., & Steg, L. (2014, July 8–13). *Tailoring persuasive messages: Comparing biospheric, economic and combined appeals to promote pro-environmental behaviour.* Presentation at the 28th International Congress of Applied Psychology (ICAP). Paris, France.

Wyles, K., Pahl, S., & Thompson, R. C. (2014, July 8–13). *What's in it for me? The psychological benefits of engaging in beach cleans compared to other coastal activities.* Presentation at the 28th International Congress of Applied Psychology (ICAP), Paris, France.

Epilogue

Darlyne G. Nemeth

Our planet, often referred to as Mother Earth, has provided for human beings and all living things from time immemorial. She has sustained us, protected us, and nurtured us. Over the centuries, Mother Earth has been very good to us, even helping us to heal from catastrophic events. Now, with the advances of technology, things are moving faster than the natural evolutionary process can manage.

We have spoken in this anthology about the spatial and temporal conditions that occur with change. Yet, with technological advances, these conditions are often exacerbated. The natural ebb and flow has been disturbed. These disturbances, which have been outlined in these two volumes, have been caused by changes in nature itself, evident in natural disasters. We have referred to this concept of how our changing environments affect humans and all living things as *ecokinetics*. Yet, these disturbances have also been created by the earth's human inhabitants. We have conceptually referred to how humans affect nature as *ecodynamics*. Therefore, it is the responsibility of the earth's people to help Mother Earth to manage these changes and, once again, to become whole. Change is inevitable. This is a basic truth.

Truth is very simple. Lies, however, are quite complex. We know when we are lying. Deep inside our being, we know. Yet we do it anyway. Why? Lies are far more complicated and are usually uncoverable. Yet, as a culture, we are often rewarded for lies and cover-ups and punished for telling the truth and speaking out.

There are two types of lies—lies of commission (i.e., active lying) versus lies of omission (i.e., passive lying). We often actively lie when we are confronted with uncomfortable truths and are trying to avoid taking responsibility for our role in their cover-up (e.g., the Watergate scandal that caused Richard Nixon to resign the U.S. presidency). We passively lie when we know what needs to be done, but we either hesitate to or choose not to do so in a timely manner (

e.g., the BP oil spill). Very seldom do people pay the price for errors of omission. Their consequences are usually matters of conscience.

Oftentimes, individuals rise to positions of power where matters of conscience do not bother them. These individuals may be referred to as antisocial. History is replete with such individuals. They usually have their Waterloos. Yet history is also replete with prosocial individuals who choose to do the right thing—often against all odds. Their legacy (e.g., Mother Teresa) is far more profound than those who choose to abuse and/or exploit.

Consider the word "conscience." It is defined as "the part of the mind that makes you aware of your actions as being either morally right or wrong; a *feeling* that something you have done is morally wrong" ("Conscience," 2014; emphasis added). It is about knowing the truth. Science, on the other hand, is defined as "*knowledge* about or study of the natural world based on *facts* learned through experiments and observation" ("Science," 2014; emphasis added). Conscience and science are compatible. Conscience and beliefs, however, may be incompatible.

Perception may be defined as "the way you think about or understand someone or something; the ability to understand or notice something easily; the way that you *notice or understand* something using one of your senses" ("Perception," 2014; emphasis added). It is the process of becoming aware of reality, of truth. A belief may be defined as "a feeling of being sure that someone or something exists or that something is true; a feeling that something is good, right, or valuable; a feeling of *trust* in the worth or ability of someone" ("Belief," 2014; emphasis added). A belief is often accepted as true, yet it may not be true. One's conscience brings together truth and knowing. One's beliefs bring together trust and accepting. When we believe, we accept something as true; we have faith in others' teachings or experiences. For example, we used to believe that the world was flat. Beliefs are often disproven by science (e.g., the work of Galileo).

It is the responsibility of science to challenge beliefs and to seek truth. Likewise, it is the responsibility of human beings to consciously act upon their self-evident truths. Such truths require no explanation. When we violate our own conscience, we act against Mother Earth. In doing so, we set in motion a chain of events that has far-reaching consequences, not only for our planet, but also for generations to come.

Mother Earth has always provided an exquisite balance for all living things. The field of ecopsychology studies this balance and encourages its continued existence. Not all things are sustainable, however. Chaos is inevitable; yet the desires of the earth to regain balance and of all living things to return to their oikophilia, which is "the love and feeling for home" (Scruton, 2012, p. 3), are irrefutable truths. It is also true that, due to temporal and spatial conditions, this balance will change over time.

We human beings must find ways to adapt to change, to seek balance, and to protect Mother Earth. As she has sustained us, so now we must sustain her.

REFERENCES

Belief. 2014. *Merriam-Webster.com*. Retrieved July 15, 2014, from http://www.merriam-webster.com/dictionary/belief

Conscience. 2014. *Merriam-Webster.com*. Retrieved July 15, 2014, from http://www.merriam-webster.com/dictionary/conscience

Perception. 2014. *Merriam-Webster.com*. Retrieved July 15, 2014, from http://www.merriam-webster.com/dictionary/perception

Science. 2014. *Merriam-Webster.com*. Retrieved July 15, 2014, from http://www.merriam-webster.com/dictionary/science

Scruton, R. (2012). *How to think seriously about the planet*. New York: New York, Oxford University Press.

About the Editors

ROBERT B. HAMILTON (VOLUME 1 EDITOR), PhD, is a retired Associate Professor from the School of Natural Resources, formerly the School of Forestry, Wildlife, and Fisheries, at Louisiana State University, where he served until his retirement. As a teenager, he became interested in the outdoors and the environment although he has never lived in the countryside.

He graduated high school in 1954 and started college in engineering. Although interested in mathematics and science, after several years his outdoor interests prevailed, and he changed his major to zoology. After graduation, he served for three years as an officer in the U.S. Navy and "saw the world." Afterwards, he attended the University of California at Berkeley to get his PhD. While there, he had opportunities to see more of the world while participating in research in Alaska on lemmings, and going on a museum-collecting trip to the wilds of Peru. His research in San Francisco Bay was a comparison of the ecology and behavior of two closely related birds, the American Avocet and the Black-necked Stilt. His approach was much more holistic than most current research because it combined aspects of anatomy, behavior, and ecology to explain how each of these closely related species could minimize completion in relatively simple habitats. He was able to see patterns and relationships not normally discerned. The holistic nature of his research led to his dissertation being published as written by the American Ornithologists' Union as a monograph.

He started his professional life on the faculty of a small regional university in Louisiana where he taught introductory biology and most natural history courses. This further increased his holistic background. After several years, he joined the faculty at LSU in 1972. At LSU he taught wildlife courses and developed a research program that primarily was centered on breeding success of bottomland hardwood forest birds in various managed habitats. He had numerous research contracts and supervised many master's and PhD students. Venturing into wildlife management was an opportunity to see new relationships and become even-more holistic.

He had an opportunity early in his career to participate in a NSF postdoctoral workshop on using linear computer modeling to analyze biological systems. This broadened his already broad interests in birds and wildlife to include ecosystem considerations. An indication of his holistic approach is that he is the only person who has served as president of both the Louisiana Chapter of the Wildlife Society and president of the Louisiana Ornithological Society.

Dr. Hamilton has always considered himself more of a philosopher than an ornithologist or wildlife manager. He has always been a holistic thinker and has spent many years analyzing wildlife management in a broad sense. Many of its problems seemed to him to be due to a too-narrow vision. After retiring, he started paying attention to national issues and decided that special interests were narrower than desirable and sometimes pushed their narrow views to the detriment of the holistic picture and the national interests. Our leaders seem more concerned with reelection than their constituents. Public discourse is becoming almost completely propaganda, and should be viewed skeptically. His holistic views are difficult to fit into a limited space, but he hopes he has approached that in these books.

JUDY KURIANSKY (VOLUME 2 EDITOR), PhD, is a world-renowned clinical psychologist with extensive experience working with individuals, families, groups, and communities in varied settings and cultures, as well as leading trainings and workshops worldwide. On the faculty of Columbia University Teachers College and a visiting professor at Peking University Health Science Center in Beijing, China, she was a senior research scientist at the New York State Psychiatric Institute and the Maudsley Hospital in London. She is an expert in relationships and in trauma, and the range of her expertise is evident in her book topics, from international relations and the environment (*Beyond Bullets and Bombs: Grassroots Peacebuilding between Israelis and Palestinians* and *Living in an Environmentally Traumatized World: Healing Ourselves and Our Planet*) to personal relationships (*The Complete Idiot's Guide to a Healthy Relationship, 31 Things to Raise a Child's Self Esteem*, and *Sex Education: Past, Present and Future*), and in her many publications and features on disaster recovery, women's empowerment, well-being, HIV/AIDS education, human rights, cinematherapy, schizophrenia and depression, and supervision in psychotherapy. Her book series for Praeger are "Practical and Applied Psychology" and "Sex, Love, and Psychology." Her many projects include the Global Kids Connect Project in China and Japan, and the Girls Empowerment Programme and the Post-Ebola Children's Workshop in Africa. Also a musician, her Stand Up for Peace Project presents symposia and concerts with original music. She serves on the boards of U.S. Doctors for Africa, Voices of Africa Mothers, the World Psychiatric Association Disaster Psychiatry Section, and the Library of American Broadcasting, and is a member of the Women's Foreign Policy Group. A fellow of the American Psychological

Association, she cofounded the Media Division and is the Public Policy liaison for the International Division.

At the United Nations, she is chair of the Psychology Coalition of NGOs accredited at the UN and the main NGO representative of the International Association of Applied Psychology (IAAP) and the World Council of Psychotherapy. The organizer of many events at UN commissions, she was a panelist at the UN International Day of Happiness and a respondent at the UN Interactive Dialogue of the General Assembly on Harmony with Nature. In partnership with the Ambassador of Palau to the UN, Dr. Caleb Otto, she has also led the successful advocacy to include "mental health and well-being" in the Sustainable Development Goals, as well as other advocacy about psychosocial support and disaster recovery.

Dr. Kuriansky has hosted many conferences, including the U.S.-Africa Business Summit, the U.S. Doctors for Africa Health Summit, and several awards ceremonies honoring First Ladies of Africa. Her many awards include the "Lifetime Achievement in Global Peace and Tolerance" from Friends of the UN, the Award for Distinguished Professional Contributions from IAAP, the "First International Outreach Award" from American Women in Radio and TV, and several humanitarian awards. An award-winning journalist who has hosted top-rated radio call-in advice shows and *Money and Emotions* on CNBC, and who has been a television feature news reporter for WABC-TV, WCBS-TV, and others, she comments on news for media worldwide, including CNN and CCTV in China. Her many articles and columns have been published in professional journals, and mainstream media, including the *Singapore Straits Times*, *South China Morning Post*, *Chicago Tribune WomenNews*, *Newsday*, the *New York Daily News*, *Family Circle*, and *Hanako Magazine* in Japan, and her opinion editorials are posted on *ABCNews.com*, *FoxNews.com*, and the *Huffington Post*. She has produced many educational documentary films, including *Youth Mental Health: Youth and UN Ambassadors Speak Out* and *Progress of the First Ladies of African in Achieving the Millennium Development Goals*.

A graduate of Smith College, Dr. Kuriansky earned a master's degree from Boston University and her PhD in clinical psychology from New York University and studied at the University of Geneva. Her website is http://www.DrJudy.com.

DARLYNE G. NEMETH (SET EDITOR), PhD, MP, MPAP, CGP, an accomplished clinical, medical, and neuropsychologist, has a broad-spectrum practice at the Neuropsychology Center of Louisiana (NCLA) in Baton Rouge, Louisiana. She also was director of neuropsychology at Sage Rehabilitation Hospital Outpatient Services. Dr. Nemeth was among the first medical psychologists in Louisiana to obtain prescriptive authority. She is a fellow of the American Psychological Association (APA) and serves as Louisiana's delegate to the

APA Council of Representatives. Dr. Nemeth has served as the World Council of Psychotherapy's (WCP) United Nations (UN) nongovernmental organization (NGO) delegate and vice president for the U.S. chapter. She is now WCP's co-secretary general.

As an expert in group dynamics, Dr. Nemeth has been nationally and internationally recognized for her Hurricane Anniversary Wellness Workshops, which were offered to the victims/survivors of Hurricanes Katrina and Rita in the summer of 2006. Anniversary Wellness Workshop Training Programs were also conducted in China at the 2008 WCP Meeting and in Australia at the 2011 WCP Meeting. In August, 2014, Dr. Nemeth gave the Keynote Address on Psychological Leadership in the Event of Environmental Trauma at the WCP Meeting in Durban, South Africa.

Dr. Nemeth obtained a bachelor's degree from Indiana University in music and radio/television broadcasting, a master's degree from Oklahoma State University in higher education/student personnel, a second master's degree and a doctoral degree from Louisiana State University in clinical psychology, and a postdoctoral master's degree from the California School of Professional Psychology in clinical psychopharmacology. Dr. Nemeth is active in the practice of clinical, medical, and neuropsychology, and psychopharmacological management. She has written chapters on the history of psychotherapy in the United States, anger management for children, and pediatric medical psychopharmacology.

In March, 2003, she was the lead author on a book titled, *Helping Your Angry Child*. Dr. Nemeth served as the lead editor for the 2012 book, *Living in an Environmentally Traumatized World: Healing Ourselves and Our Planet*, published by ABC-CLIO/Praeger. In 2012, she was also the lead author on an anniversary wellness workshop article that was published in the *International Journal of Group Psychotherapy* (*IJGP*). Dr. Nemeth published an article in 2013 in *Ecopsychology* on preparing individuals and communities for hurricane anniversary reactions. She has developed a Hope Therapy Group Program for brain-injured adults and was the lead author on an article about this process (published in *IJGP* in January 2015).

Besides being in active clinical practice at NCLA, Dr. Nemeth also serves as an externship adviser for future psychologists on placement from their respective universities. She is currently serving in a leadership role on the Executive Committee of the Louisiana Psychological Association. She is a member of the American Group Psychotherapy Association, where she has obtained recognition as a Certified Group Psychotherapist (CGP). Dr. Nemeth has served as a member and past Vice Chair of the Louisiana State Board of Examiners of Psychologists.

Her website is http://www.louisiananeuropsych.com.

About the Contributors

VINUSHINI ARUNAGIRI, MA, her master's degree in clinical psychology from Columbia University Teachers College, where she now volunteers as a research assistant in the Global Mental Health Lab based on her international interests and experiences, having been born in Malaysia and living in Indonesia, Thailand, and Australia. She also volunteers as a research assistant at the Substance Use Research Center and Residency Training at the New York State Psychiatric Institute and for IMPACT Leadership 21 that promotes women's leadership. Inspired by studying under Dr. Judy Kuriansky, she advocates about mental illness, with a special interest in schizophrenia in Malaysia due to her sister's book, *In My Shoes*, and leading to her work with the organization Vishal Minds Creation. She presented a paper on self-fulfilling effects of stereotypes on mothers at the Black Student Network's Diversity in Research and Practice Conference at Columbia University Teachers College.

CHENLAN BAO, BA, graduated from Amherst College in 2011 with a double major in economics and English. She has worked with the Humane Worlds Center that is focused on teaching leadership and encouraging youth to participate in public service, and conducted phone interviews for a new organization called Future Search that enables people with a shared stake in their community to cocreate a shared vision. During college, she worked as a summer intern for Dr. Judy Kuriansky doing psychological research about international issues. She now works in the financial industry in Hong Kong.

DANIEL W. BENA currently heads the Sustainable Development agenda for PepsiCo Global Operations. He has served in various capacities for the Safe Water Network; World Business Council for Sustainable Development (WBCSD); Steering Board of the IFC 2030 Water Resources Group; United Nations CEO Mandate; WEF Global Agenda Council on Water Security; U.S. Water Alliance; Creative Visions Foundation; the documentary *Water Pressures*; the Environmental Leader publications group; and others. He delivered the keynote address at the Royal Swedish Gala and has spoken at over 100 diverse venues, including the *Our Food, Our Future* Summit, attended by the prime minister and agriculture minister of Ireland. Mr. Bena provided testimony to the U.S. Senate, and opening remarks at the United Nations Youth Assembly to over 1,000 youth delegates from over 100 countries.

DIVYA CHAND, BA, graduated from Smith College with a bachelor of arts in psychology. Currently she works as a counselor about domestic violence and sexual violence at Independence House in Hyannis, Massachusetts. She is particularly interested in the fields of mental health for minority populations and also in trauma, especially related to women's health and gender issues. She has worked on a variety of projects about the aftermath of trauma and the process of healing, including during an internship with Dr. Judy Kuriansky at the United Nations and on projects related to the Asian tsunami and earthquakes in China. She plans to continue combining her areas of interest with providing services to many communities. She comes from Delhi, India.

ADRIAN CHIU, PhD, obtained his doctoral degree from St. John's University, where he conducted research on developing a screener for personality disorders as well as exploring the validity of a dimensional model of personality that was initially proposed for DSM-5. Given his interest in working with college students in university counseling centers, he is currently a staff psychologist at Drexel University Counseling Center in Philadelphia, Pennsylvania, where he provides individual and group therapy and clinical supervision. Clinically, he has worked in different inpatient and outpatient settings in Singapore and the United States, reflecting his other interest in global mental health, which stems from spending formative years in Singapore and England and witnessing disparities in mental health treatment from different cultural frameworks. During graduate studies, he interned for the International Association of Applied Psychology at the United Nations.

NARA CROWLEY, MA, is a native New Yorker and second-generation Italian who has spent most of her life in both the United States and Italy. Her BA degree from the University of Massachusetts in Amherst centered on advocacy studies, and her Phi Kappa Phi MA from Louisiana State University focused on ethnic studies, particularly the Italian culture in Louisiana. Fluency in languages gave her numerous opportunities to work throughout the United States and overseas. She and her husband Bill live in New Iberia, Louisiana, and are proud grandparents of eight grandchildren. She is executive producer of the short documentary *Salt of the Earth*, about the history and future of Lake Peigneur. Former president of Save Lake Peigneur, Inc. and a devoted environmental advocate, Ms. Crowley is working on a book that is an in-depth analysis of the past 10 years in the battle to preserve our water and environment. She can be contacted at sossullivan@bellsouth.net.

RUSSELL DAISEY is a music therapist and internationally known pianist and singer-songwriter. An NGO representative at the United Nations of the International Association of Applied Psychology and member of the Psychology Coalition of NGOs at the UN, he is a founding member of the NYC Peace Museum and cofounder with Dr. Judy Kuriansky of the Stand Up for Peace and Global Kids Connect Projects. He has performed for world leaders, including Presidents Bill Clinton and George H. W. Bush, Canadian prime minister Brian Mulroney, and New York City mayor Rudy Giuliani, and produced concerts and presentations at international congresses, interfaith events and memorials world-wide with Dr. Kuriansky, including after 9/11; earthquakes in Haiti and Japan; the International Congresses of Applied Psychology in Cape Town, South Africa, and Paris, France; the European Congress of Psychology in Stockholm, Sweden; the United Nations Department of Public Information/NGO conference in Mexico City; the UN Commission on the Status of Women and the UN International Day for the Culture of Peace; the U.S. Doctors for Africa's First Ladies of Africa Health Summit in Los Angeles; and the First Hiroshima International Peace Summit in Japan with HH The Dalai Lama, Betty Williams, and Archbishop Desmond Tutu. He and Dr. Kuriansky have written original songs with humanitarian themes that have been performed worldwide.

TOMMY DAVIS III, PhD, is a psychologist whose publications and presenta-tions have focused on cultural diversity, family therapy, strengths-based inter-ventions, talent recovery, and resilience. Currently he is president of Davis Socio-Psychological Services, LLC, and clinical director for the Empowerment Resources Associates, Inc. He has served as codirector of Philadelphia Multi-systemic Therapy Project, assistant professor at Widener University's Graduate Clinical Psychology Program, and counseling director for Prep for Prep 9, a New York City–based leadership program. As a vocalist and commentator, he has produced hundreds of musical presentations and appeared on radio and TV. In 2005, he released a music-based self-help CD, *You Are Still Loved*; and in Feb-ruary 2015, he released a neo-gospel album, *The Truth about Love*. Dr. Davis received his PhD from the City University of New York and trained at NYU/ Bellevue Hospital Center. He can be contacted at tommy-davis@msn.com or through http://www.tommydavisonline.com.

CHRISTINA DOUYON, MA, received her master's degree in clinical psychol-ogy from Teachers College, Columbia University in 2014, where she was a research assistant in Dr. Lisa Miller's research lab doing work with young home-less mothers. During that time, Ms. Douyon was also a research assistant at the

New York Obesity Nutrition Research Center at St. Luke's Hospital contributing to fMRI obesity research. She is currently a doctoral student in counseling psychology at Boston College, working under Dr. Janet Helms and Dr. A. J. Franklin, where her research interest focus on the racial identity of black immigrants. Her Haitian heritage, and taking Dr. Judy Kuriansky's class about relationships and learning about her work in Haiti, led her to be involved in the chapter about healing in Haiti.

J. DONALD DUMPSON, PhD, is minister of music and arts at the Arch Street Presbyterian Church in Philadelphia, Pennsylvania and founding director of the Philadelphia Heritage Chorale. He was the founding conductor of the Westminster Choir College Jubilee Singers; assistant professor of choral music and director of the Cheyney University Center for Cultural Enrichment and Appreciation; and music educator and administrative assistant for the School District of Philadelphia. He has served as producer, artistic and music director, and chorus master for the Kimmel Center and the Philadelphia and New Jersey Symphony Orchestras, and co-producer of the *An Evening of Stars* telecast benefiting the United Negro College Fund, featuring internationally acclaimed stars like Oprah Winfrey, Quincy Jones, and Patti LaBelle. His goal is to build bridges for creative cultural exchanges through the arts, music education, and ministry. His dissertation was on *Four Scholars' Engagement of Works by Classical Composers of African Descent: A Collective Case Study*.

ROBIN K. GAY, PhD, is a neuropsychologist in a medical practice in the greater Boston, Massachusetts, area. Previously, she worked as a senior psychologist at Mount Sinai Medical Center in New York City specializing in neurorehabilitation and brain injury. While in New York City, where she lived for 15 years, she was granted an honorary faculty appointment at Columbia University, where she supervised PhD candidates and taught psychological assessment at the graduate level. She received her PhD in clinical psychology at the New School for Social Research and has received several distinctions, including the Sidney Orgel Award. Her research has been presented in conferences in the United States and Europe, and most recently she published an article in *NeuroRehabilitation* on the use of neurocognitive measures in the assessment of vestibular disturbances in patients with brain injury.

WISMICK JEAN-CHARLES, PhD, is a Haitian Catholic priest and the current vice president of the University of Notre-Dame of Haiti. He received his doctorate in psychology and a master's degree in counseling psychology and education from Fordham University in New York. He founded the Center of Spirituality and Mental Health (CESSA, according to the French name) in Haiti,

integrating spirituality with contemporary psychology. Along with Dr. Judy Kuriansky, he provided disaster relief immediately after the devastating earthquake
that struck Haiti on January 2010 and for years subsequently, and colaunched
train-the-trainer programs and the Global Kids Connect project in Haiti that is
sustainable. An NGO representative to the United Nations of the International
Association of Applied Psychology, he has published many articles and delivered
presentations at national and international conferences about post disaster and
spirituality. Now living in his native Haiti, he previously taught at Fordham
University and Montclair State University in the United States.

SHUYAO KONG, BA, is a graduate of Smith College, where she double maj-
ored in psychology and economics and was awarded the highest honors in the
Psychology Department. She subsequently worked for Dr. Judy Kuriansky as
her research assistant, teaching assistant at Columbia University Teachers
College, and intern at the United Nations for the International Association of
Applied Psychology. Currently, she manages the Diversity and Inclusion Program for IBM Africa based in Lagos, Nigeria, consistent with her research interests in clinical psychology and organizational psychology, and her passion about
the topics of gender diversity and inclusion in the workplace of people with
disabilities.

ANJALI KUMAR is a student at Smith College majoring in psychology, with a
focus on emotional perception, neuropsychology, and women and gender issues
specifically regarding sexual assault and health, including HIV/AIDS. She
interned with psychologist Dr. Judy Kuriansky at the United Nations for the
International Association of Applied Psychology, assisting and participating in
many global projects. She has been a member of multiple musical groups at
Smith College and is interested in the emotional and physiological impact of
music and art on the brain.

JOHN E. S. LAWRENCE, PhD, has been adjunct professor at the School of
International and Public Affairs at Columbia University in New York since
2002, teaching management and advising graduate students in workshops with
the United Nations Development Program (UNDP). He was formerly principal
adviser and deputy director of the Social Development Division, Policy Bureau
of UNDP. Before that, he was senior research psychologist with RTI
International in North Carolina. His work has involved professional experience
on all seven continents and is mainly devoted to the promotion of capacity
development and human resourcefulness through effective public policy. His
CV can be accessed at http://www.cambridgedata.com/johnlawrence *and his
website at http://jeslawrence.com.*

MEAGHAN LEMAY, MA, earned her master's degree from Columbia University Teachers College in clinical psychology, focusing on trauma and global mental health. During an internship at the United Nations for Dr. Judy Kuriansky with the International Association of Applied Psychology (IAAP), she was involved in many global issues, including the IAAP event for the Commission on the Status of Women, and presented a poster at the 2014 American Psychological Association Conference on the IAAP multi-stakeholder project helmed by Dr. Kuriansky and Dr. Mary O'Neill Berry about a girls' empowerment programme in Lesotho, Africa. She is interested in the critical intersection of health programming and international policy and contributing to the discussion on global health trends and strategies to improve wellbeing worldwide. She currently lives and works in Washington, D.C.

ANDREW A. LEMMON, JD, is a New Orleans–born trial attorney who has practiced law in Louisiana and many U.S. federal courts for 27 years. He has worked on many cases in the field of environmental law, torts involving toxins, and other complex litigation. He earned a master of laws degree (LLM) in environmental law from the George Washington University National Law Center, and a juris doctor degree from Loyola University. He also served as an intern for the U.S. Department of Justice in the Environmental Enforcement Section. He is on the boards of directors of a number of civic and charitable organizations, including Reach Out America, an organization formed to assist evacuees after Hurricanes Katrina and Rita; Louisiana Bayou Keeper, Inc., an affiliate of Waterkeeper Alliance, Inc.; and Public Justice Foundation.

SHIQIAN MAO, BA, earned her bachelor's degree in psychology from Smith College in 2013. She was a summer intern for Dr. Judy Kuriansky and a summer research fellow at the Clark Science Center in 2012 and published her research, "A Longitudinal Study of Personality and Life Outcomes." She has spent some time in her native China and was accepted into the master's degree program in human development and psychology at the Harvard Graduate School of Education, where she plans to pursue her education and career plans.

SUSAN MELMAN, MA, is a native New Yorker now making her home on Whidbey Island in Puget Sound in the state of Washington. She holds an MA in theater and has worked professionally in theater and with regional theater companies for the past 36 years. She is the recipient of the Outer Critic Circle Award and the Lucille Lortel Award for *Jelly Roll*, the best off-Broadway musical of 1995. She has produced and directed an original New Orleans musical, *Salty Dogs*, for the Edinburgh Jazz Festival. She is the author of two plays, *Blackwater in the Attic* and *Blooms of Orchard Street*, and her poetry was published in *The*

Louisiana Review. She currently acts as dramaturge for Whidbey Island Center for the Arts in Langley, Washington.

TARAH MIDY, MA, received her master's degree in clinical psychology from Teachers College, Columbia University in 2012. While a student in Dr. Judy Kuriansky's class, she went with her on a post-earthquake mission to Haiti. She currently attends Binghamton University, where she works in the Marriage and Family Studies Laboratory run by Dr. Matthew D. Johnson.

MIA MURRIETTA is a writer and nonprofit communications professional who is currently the communications manager for Bioneers, a nonprofit educational organization that highlights breakthrough solutions for restoring people and the planet, with programs on women's leadership, indigenous wisdom, community resilience networks, and youth leadership development. Previously, she has worked in various communications roles with the Ella Baker Center for Human Rights, Fair Trade USA, Buddhist Peace Fellowship, the Pachamama Alliance, and other San Francisco Bay Area nonprofits.

TRACI W. OLIVIER, MS, is a doctoral candidate at Nova Southeastern University in Fort Lauderdale, Florida, majoring in clinical psychology with a neuropsychology concentration. She will be completing her internship at the Kennedy Krieger Institute at Johns Hopkins University. Olivier completed an elective practicum under the supervision of Dr. Darlyne G. Nemeth at the Neuropsychology Center of Louisiana in Baton Rouge, Louisiana, where she was part of several projects about environmental trauma. Olivier has authored and coauthored several peer-reviewed journal articles, poster presentations, and symposia for state, national, and international conferences.

YASUO ONISHI, PhD, adjunct professor at Washington State University in the Department of Civil and Environmental Engineering and president of Yasuo Onishi Consulting LLC, works extensively on U.S. and international environmental and energy issues and is a pioneer in conducting environmental and risk assessments. He received two awards in 2011 from the U.S. Department of Energy, called "The Secretary's Achievement Award," for his contributions to the response to the 2011 Fukushima nuclear accident and the 2010 Gulf of Mexico oil spill accident. His computer models are the most advanced contaminant transport codes for surface waters to date. He has been the U.S. government coordinator of the Chernobyl nuclear disaster water and soil environments, an environmental adviser to the International Atomic Energy Agency, an adjunct member of the National Council of Radiation Protection and Measurements, and a member of the National Academy of Sciences' oil spill committee, as well as chief scientist of the Pacific Northwest National Laboratory.

RENÉ ORELLANA HALKYER, PhD, was an honorary ambassador of Bolivia on issues of the environment and development at the United Nations. He served in the Open Working Group of the UN member states negotiating the outcome document of the Sustainable Development Goals (SDGs), and as chair on behalf of Bolivia and the Group of G77 + China at the United Nations Framework Convention on Climate Change (UNFCCC) in 2014, as well as head of the Delegation of Bolivia during the Conference of Sustainable Development (Rio + 20) and in the 17th, 18th, and 19th Conference of the Parties (COPs) of the UNFCCC. Previously, he was vice minister of basic services, and minister of environment and water, of Bolivia. He earned his PhD degree in sociology from the University of Amsterdam and is Professor and Coordinator of Environment, Water and Climate Change of the University of la Cordillera in Bolivia.

FERNANDO PASTRANA JR., PhD, is a New Orleans area native. After graduating from Louisiana State University, he earned a doctoral degree in clinical psychology with a concentration in neuropsychology from Palo Alto University. He then completed a postdoctoral fellowship in rehabilitation psychology at the Shepherd Center in Atlanta, Georgia, and subsequently heeded the call of his home and heart to return to Louisiana, where he currently practices as a clinical psychologist at the Neuropsychology Center of Louisiana at Gretna and at the Neuropsychology Center of Louisiana in Baton Rouge, Louisiana, founded by Dr. Darlyne Nemeth. His clinical interests include providing general clinical cognitive behavior therapy and stress management to adolescents and adults, as well as psychoeducation, treatment, and emotional support to persons who have sustained acquired brain injuries, and their families.

ROSANNE PRATS, MHA, ScD, works for the Louisiana Department of Health and Hospitals (DHH) as the executive director of emergency preparedness. Dr. Prats received her doctorate at Tulane University. She came to DHH with health care work experience in the federal, state, and private sectors. Her current position involves coordinating between local, state, and federal agencies. In addition to serving as the emergency preparedness director for DHH, she serves as the grant principal investigator for the Hospital Preparedness Grant. Over the past 14 years at DHH, Dr. Prats has served as the state's ESF-8 point of contact in events such as Katrina/Rita (2005), Gustav/Ike (2008), H1N1 (2009), Mississippi River Flooding (2010), and MSC252 BP Oil Spill (2010), and most recently TS Isaac (2012).

MICHAEL SCHMIDT, BPhEd, DC, graduated from the Canadian Memorial Chiropractic College in 2001 and is a practicing chiropractor in British Columbia, Canada, who has also worked in Australia. He founded, and is the clinical director of, a large multi-disciplinary health center called Okanagan Health and Performance. He is certified and trained in several hands-on and tool-assisted manual therapies, including Active Release Techniques (ART) and the Cox Technique of Spinal Traction, Flexion-Distraction and Spinal Decompression. He believes in using a team approach to health care and has professional interest in workplace ergonomics, athletic injuries, and the treatment of conditions such as headaches, neck pain, low back pain, and repetitive strain injuries. He has worked with professional and amateur athletes, both "on the field" and in clinical settings. He is a partner with David Wood in a unique personal transformation project in Belize.

CHELSIE SONGY, BA, received her bachelor's degree in psychology from Nicholls State University in Thibodaux, Louisiana, and served a clinical externship at the Neuropsychology Center of Louisiana as well as at Sage Rehabilitation Hospital Neuro-Outpatient Services under the supervision of Dr. Darlyne G. Nemeth. Ms. Songy is a member of the American Psychology Association Divisions 40, 22, 47, and 49, as well as APAGS (the Division of Graduate Students), the Louisiana Psychological Association, the National Academy of Neuropsychology, and the International Neuropsychological Society. The editorial coordinator for the two-volume anthology, *Ecopsychology: The Interface between Psychology and Environmental Protection*, she has authored and coauthored several peer-reviewed journal articles, poster presentations, and symposia for state, national, and international conferences.

ANTHONY H. SPEIER, PhD, is a developmental psychologist and former assistant secretary for the Louisiana Office of Behavioral Health. Dr. Speier previously served as the deputy assistant secretary for the Office of Mental Health, and director of disaster mental health services for over 20 years. He was the executive director for the Louisiana Spirit Hurricane Recovery Program following Hurricane Katrina. After 33 years of state service, Dr. Speier retired in 2013 and currently holds an appointment as an associate professor of clinical psychiatry at Louisiana State University Health Sciences Center. He is currently involved with the Mental and Behavioral Health Capacity Project in response to the Deepwater Horizon oil spill in the Gulf of Mexico, part of the Gulf Region Health Outreach Program across Alabama, Florida, Louisiana, and Mississippi. Dr. Speier can be contacted at aspei1@lsuhsc.edu.

NIA DARA SPOONER, BA, earned her bachelor's degree in education and child study from Smith College. During her junior year in college, she lived in Shanghai and studied Chinese language and culture at Fudan University. While an undergraduate, she did an internship with Dr. Judy Kuriansky. In the spring of 2013, she was awarded a Fulbright scholarship to teach English to elementary students in Kinmen, Taiwan. Currently, she is an academic facilitator at InLight

Education, an education consultancy in Shanghai focused on teaching academic soft skills to Chinese high school students. Passionate about teaching, she plans to further develop her skills by pursuing a master's degree in international education.

JOSEPH TRAMONTANA, PhD, received his BA in psychology at LSU/NO and his MA and PhD in clinical psychology from the University of Mississippi, and did a clinical internship at the University of Tennessee Medical School. A former clinical director of a community mental health center, he was elected president of the Mississippi Mental Health Center Directors organization, and also served on several State of Mississippi advisory boards. He studied clinical hypnosis, culminating in two books, *Hypnotically Enhanced Treatment for Addictions: Alcohol Abuse, Drug Abuse, Gambling, Weight Loss and Smoking Cessation* (Crown House, 2009), and *Sports Hypnosis in Practice: Scripts, Strategies, and Case Examples* (Crown, 2011). Currently president of the New Orleans Society of Clinical Hypnosis and of the Louisiana Psychological Association (LPA), the LPA recognized him in 2013 with the Distinguished Psychologist Award. Currently in private practice, he shares office space with his colleague and friend, Dr. Nemeth, lead editor of this anthology.

IVOR LL. VAN HEERDEN, PhD, the former deputy director of the Louisiana State University (LSU) Hurricane Center and faculty member in the Department of Civil and Environmental Engineering, was fired in 2009 for resisting attempts to stifle academic freedom. An out-of-court settlement was reached in 2013. Dr. van Heerden holds undergraduate degrees from the University of Natal, in South Africa and graduate degrees from LSU. He led the state of Louisiana's official team that investigated the Hurricane Katrina levee failures and was responsible for the dissemination of information regarding the findings. He has given many interviews and appeared in documentaries about Hurricane Katrina, such as Harry Shearer's *The Big Uneasy*, Spike Lee's HBO documentary, and shows on NOVA (PBS), History Channel, Discovery Channel, National Geographic, and the BBC. He and coauthor Mike Bryan chronicle these events in *The Storm: What Went Wrong and Why during Hurricane Katrina—the Inside Story from One Louisiana Scientist* (2006).

HELEN COURTNEY WHITE is a PhD candidate in environmental studies at Antioch University and director of Partnerships for World Savvy, an organization that helps strengthen the capacity of teachers to educate youth about issues of global significance and ways to take action. She holds a BFA from Savannah College of Art and Design, and an MSEd in museum education from Bank Street Graduate School of Education. She has presented on panels about education at the United Nations and supported the efforts of the UN Decade of Education for Sustainable Development (2005–2014) and the U.S. Partnership for Education for Sustainable Development. Her work focuses on revolutionizing education movements for greater relevancy, preparing youth and teachers to advance global competencies, sustainable practices, climate change education, and civic responsibilities for a more peaceful and prosperous planet.

DAVID WOOD is a Canadian-born author, trainer, life coach, humanitarian and business leader who has lived, traveled, and worked in over 50 countries. He has grown several multimillion-dollar companies and is a strategic consultant for a $3.2 billion U.S. health and wellness company. Internationally recognized as "The Trainers Trainer," he leads dynamic and effective adventures, courses and workshops for teachers, educators, trainers and others committed to transformational work. These take place in many settings, including on a private island he purchased off the coast of Belize, in partnership with good friend and business partner Jack Canfield (author of the *Chicken Soup for the Soul* series) and on a recent climb up Mt. Kilimanjaro, with Dr. Judy Kuriansky and Dr. Michael Schmidt on the team. As a humanitarian, he is a spokesperson, fund-raiser, and advocate for the Make-a-Wish Foundation and helped raise millions of dollars as an International Spokesperson for Childhelp.

LI-YEN WU, EdM and MA, earned her master's degrees in psychological counseling from Teachers College, Columbia University, and volunteered as a research assistant on Dr. Lawrence Yang's research team at the Mailman School of Public Health to assist research on psychiatric stigma among Asian Americans. She also interned as a mental health counselor at the Community Consultation Center and Parent Center at Henry Street Settlement in New York City, where she provided psychotherapy and psycho-education for a large population of Chinese immigrants to promote their personal and family well-being. She is now working as a licensed mental health counselor and instructor at National Chiao Tung University in Taiwan. Her orientation of psychotherapy is psychoanalytic therapy, and she receives trainings of psychoanalytic therapy from Taiwan Center for the Development of Psychoanalysis. She feels happy to contribute to the research on the psychosocial intervention after the Sichuan earthquake because part of her family roots come from Sichuan.

JOEL C. ZINSOU is finishing his BA at the City University of New York–Hunter College, double majoring in psychology and sociology. At the United Nations, he is a youth representative for the Department of Public Information/NGO section as an intern for Dr. Judy Kuriansky, with the International Association of Applied Psychology and the Psychology Coalition of NGOs at the UN. In this role, he participated with her in the advocacy for mental health and well-being in the new Sustainable Development Goals and in presentations at the World Conference for Disaster Risk Reduction in Sendai Japan in March 2015. He has also edited and assisted in Dr. Kuriansky's videos about "Youth and Mental Health: Voices of Youth and Ambassadors at the United Nations"; challenges of young males in a burial team during the Ebola Epidemic in Sierra Leone; therapy supervision in American for a conference in Russia; and others.

Index

Note: n after page number indicates note number.